JERRY S. WIGGINS
Department of Psychology
University of Illinois
Champaign

PERSONALITY AND PREDICTION: PRINCIPLES OF PERSONALITY ASSESSMENT

ADDISON-WESLEY PUBLISHING COMPANY
Reading, Massachusetts
Menlo Park, California · London · Don Mills, Ontario

This book is in the
ADDISON-WESLEY SERIES IN PSYCHOLOGY

89514

To ORI: the people and the concept

PREFACE

This book is meant to be a relatively sophisticated introduction to the art and science of personality assessment, a field which Cronbach (1956) has defined as "the obtaining and evaluating of information regarding individual differences." An overriding emphasis on the prediction of socially relevant criteria has prompted me to adopt Donald W. Fiske's suggestion that the principal title, *Personality and Prediction*, is the most appropriate characterization of the subject matter of this text. The secondary title, *Principles of Personality Assessment*, reflects my own conviction that there are certain lessons to be drawn from the conceptualizations and research findings of workers, in this and related areas, which should be more widely heeded by those who forecast future performance from fallible data.

In exploring the diverse, technical areas that provide the basis for the practice of personality assessment, I have sought and received a great deal of help from others, for which I am deeply grateful. In particular, I am indebted to several individuals who generously devoted their time to providing me with detailed criticisms of one or more chapters. I wish to thank Lee J. Cronbach, Donald W. Fiske, Maurice Lorr, Quinn McNemar, Warren T. Norman, Gordon L. Paul, Leonard G. Rorer, and Jacob O. Sines for their kindness and for their patience. Lewis R. Goldberg read and reacted to every draft of every chapter in this book. The closeness of our collaboration over the years now makes it difficult for me to distinguish his contributions from my own. In fairness to myself, I must assert that this book *could* have been written without Goldberg's help, but not as easily or as well.

The writing of this book was greatly facilitated by an opportunity to spend several summers and a sabbatical year at Oregon Research Institute in Eugene, Oregon. I did so as a co-investigator on the Research Program in Personality Assessment, sponsored by the National Institute of Mental Health, U.S. Public Health Service (Grant No. MH 12972), whose principal investigator is Lewis R. Goldberg. I would like to acknowledge the hospitality of the Institute's Director, Paul J. Hoffman, who consistently encouraged me to take full advantage of the stimulating intellectual atmosphere which prevails at that institution. The burdens of manuscript preparation were graciously assumed by Linda Mushkatel, to whom I am very grateful. Sheila Yamagiwa provided additional assistance during certain critical periods.

Champaign, Illinois   J. S. W.
December 1972

ACKNOWLEDGMENTS

The author wishes to acknowledge permission to reprint or adapt the following materials from the sources noted.

Figure 1.1 (p. 11), after R. B. Cattell, *Personality and Motivation, Structure and Measurement*, World Book, Yonkers, N.Y. (1957).

Table 1.3 (p. 35), after S. C. Fulkerson, "An acquiescence key for the MMPI," *USAF School of Aviation Medicine, Report No. 58-71*, Randolph Air Force Base, Texas (July 1958).

Table 2.1 (p. 56), after N. Frederiksen and S. D. Melville, "Differential predictability in the use of test scores," *Educational and Psychological Measurement* **14**, 647–656 (1954); also N. Frederiksen and A. Gilbert, "Replication of a study of differential predictability," *Educational and Psychological Measurement* **20**, 759–767 (1960).

Table 2.2 (p. 63), after E. E. Ghiselli, "Differentiation of tests in terms of the accuracy with which they predict for a given individual," *Educational and Psychological Measurement* **20**, 675–684 (1960).

Figure 2.4 (p. 73), after N. M. Abrahams, "Off-quadrant comment," *Journal of Applied Psychology* **53**, 66–68 (1969).

Table 2.4 (p. 76) and Table 2.5 (p. 77), after J. H. Ward, "An application of linear and curvilinear joint functional regression in psychological prediction," *Research Bulletin 54-86*, Air Force Personnel Training Research Center, Lackland Air Force Base, Texas (1954).

Table 4.2 (p. 125), after L. J. Cronbach, "Processes affecting scores on 'understanding of others' and 'assumed similarity'," *Psychological Bulletin* **52**, 177–193 (1955).

Table 4.3 (p. 133), after L. R. Goldberg, "The effectiveness of clinicians' judgments: The diagnosis of organic brain damage from the Bender-Gestalt Test," *Journal of Consulting Psychology* **23**, 25–33 (1959).

Table 4.4 (p. 138) and Table 4.5 (p. 139), after L. K. Sines, "The relative contribution of four kinds of data to accuracy in personality assessment," *Journal of Consulting Psychology* **23**, 483–492 (1959).

Figure 4.4 (p. 156), after K. R. Hammond, C. J. Hursch, and F. J. Todd, "Analyzing the components of clinical inference," *Psychological Review* **71**, 438–456 (1964).

Figure 4.5 (p. 166), Figures 4.6 and 4.7 (p. 168), and Figure 4.8 (p. 170), after P. J. Hoffman, "The paramorphic representation of clinical judgment," *Psychological Bulletin* **57**, 116–131 (1960).

Figure 4.9 (p. 173) and Table 4.6 (p. 175), after N. Wiggins and P. J. Hoffman, "Three models of clinical judgment," *Journal of Abnormal Psychology* **73**, 70–77 (1968).

Excerpt (p. 177), from P. J. Hoffman, "Cue-consistency and configurality in human judgment," in B. Kleinmuntz (ed.), *Formal Representation of Human Judgment*, John Wiley and Sons, Inc., New York (1968), pp. 53–90.

Table 5.2 (p. 188), after L. R. Goldberg, "Diagnosticians vs. diagnostic signs: The diagnosis of psychosis vs. neurosis from the MMPI," *Psychological Monographs* **79** (1965) (9, Whole No. 602).

Table 5.3 (p. 194) and Table 5.4 (p. 197), after J. Sawyer, "Measurement *and* prediction; Clinical *and* statistical," *Psychological Bulletin* **66**, 178–200 (1966).

Table 5.5 (p. 203) and Table 5.6 (p. 205), courtesy of W. Swenson, Mayo Clinic.

Table 5.7 (p. 208), copyright, Hoffman-LaRoche Inc.

Table 5.8 (p. 210), courtesy of J. Finney, University of Kentucky.

Table 5.9 (p. 213), Table 5.10 (p. 214), and Table 5.11 (p. 215), after B. Kleinmuntz, "MMPI decision rules for the identification of college maladjustment: A digital computer approach," *Psychological Monographs* **77** (1963) (14, Whole No. 477).

Excerpt (p. 239), from R. L. Thorndike, *Personnel Selection: Test and Measurement Techniques*, Copyright 1949 John Wiley and Sons, Inc.

Figure 6.10 (p. 262), adapted from L. J. Cronbach and G. C. Gleser, *Psychological Tests and Personnel Decisions* (2nd ed.), University of Illinois Press, Urbana (1965).

Excerpts (pp. 286 and 294), from L. J. Cronbach, N. Rajaratnam, and G. C. Gleser, "Theory of generalizability: Liberalization of reliability theory," *British Journal of Statistical Psychology* **16**, 137–163 (1963).

Excerpt (pp. 307–309) and Figure 7.2 (p. 308), from G. R. Patterson, R. S. Ray, and D. A. Shaw, *Manual for Coding of Family Interactions* (5th rev.), Oregon Research Institute, Eugene (1968).

Table 7.4 (p. 310), after J. Withall, "Development of a technique for the measurement of social-emotional climate in classrooms," *Journal of Experimental Education* **17**, 347–361 (1949).

Excerpt (p. 317), from R. G. Barker, "Ecology and motivation," *Nebraska Symposium on Motivation*, Copyright 1960 The University of Nebraska Press, used by permission.

Figure 7.4 (p. 318), from R. G. Barker (ed.), *The Stream of Behavior*, Appleton-Century-Crofts, New York (1963).

Excerpts (p. 330), from W. T. Norman, "2800 Personality trait descriptors: Normative operating characteristics for a university population," Department of Psychology, University of Michigan, Ann Arbor (April 1967).

Excerpt (p. 340), from E. C. Tupes and R. E. Christal, "Recurrent personality factors based on trait ratings," *USAF ASD Technical Report*, No. 61-97 (1961).

Table 8.1 (p. 341), from W. T. Norman, "Toward an adequate taxonomy of personality attributes: Replicated factor structure in peer nomination personality ratings," *Journal of Abnormal and Social Psychology* **66,** 574–583 (1963).

Table 8.2 (p. 344), reproduced by permission of the American Anthropological Association from R. G. D'Andrade, "Trait psychology and componential analysis," *American Anthropologist* **67,** No. 5, 215–228 (1965).

Table 8.3 (p. 345), adapted from M. D. Hakel, "Significance of implicit personality theories for personality research and theory," *Proceedings*, 77th Convention of the APA (1969), pp. 403–404.

Table 8.4 (p. 347), from F. T. Passini and W. T. Norman, "A universal conception of personality structure?" *Journal of Personality and Social Psychology* **4,** 44–49 (1966).

Table 8.5 (p. 351), after H. J. Hallworth, "Dimensions of personality and meaning," *British Journal of Social and Clinical Psychology* **4,** 161–168 (1965).

Excerpts (pp. 351–354) and Table 8.6 (p. 352), from D. Peabody, "Trait inferences: Evaluative and descriptive aspects," *Journal of Personality and Social Psychology Monograph* **7** (1967) (4, Whole No. 644).

Excerpt (p. 377), from D. R. Peterson, *The Clinical Study of Social Behavior,* Appleton-Century-Crofts, New York (1968). By permission of Appleton-Century-Crofts, Educational Division, Meredith Corporation.

Excerpt (p. 383), from L. Levy, *Psychological Interpretation*, Holt, Rinehart and Winston, Inc., New York (1963).

Table 9.2 (p. 387), adapted with permission of the publishers from *Vocational Interests of Men and Women* by Edward K. Strong, Jr. (Stanford: Stanford University Press, 1943), Table 2, p. 75.

Items from the *Minnesota Multiphasic Personality Inventory* (pp. 390, 391, 394, 395, 396) and Table 9.3 (p. 390), reproduced by permission. Copyright 1943, renewed 1970 by the University of Minnesota. Published by the Psychological Corporation, New York, N.Y. All rights reserved.

Table 9.5 (p. 397), from H. G. Gough, "Some common misconceptions about neuroticism," *Journal of Consulting Psychology* **18,** 287–292 (1954).

Figure 9.1 (p. 399), after W. S. Torgerson, *Theories and Methods of Scaling,* John Wiley and Sons, Inc., New York (1958).

Excerpts (pp. 400–401, 402, 403, 425), reprinted with permission of author and publisher from J. Loevinger, "Objective tests as instruments of psychological theory," *Psychological Reports* **3,** 635-694 (1957). Monograph Supplement 9. Available separate from journal at $1.50 per copy.

Figure 9.3 (p. 407), after D. T. Campbell and D. W. Fiske, "Convergent and discriminant validation by the multitrait-multimethod matrix," *Psychological Bulletin* **56,** 81–105 (1959).

Table 9.6 (p. 414), after D. N. Jackson, *Personality Research Form Manual*, Research Psychologists Press, Goshen, N.Y. (1967).

Excerpt (p. 421), from A. L. Edwards and J. N. Walsh, "Response sets in standard and experimental personality scales," *American Educational Research Journal* **1**, 52–61 (1964). Copyright by American Educational Research Association, Washington, D.C.

Excerpt (pp. 421–422), from J. Block, *The Challenge of Response Sets: Unconfounding Meaning, Acquiescence and Social Desirability in the MMPI*, Appleton-Century-Crofts, New York (1965). By permission of Appleton-Century-Crofts, Educational Division, Meredith Corporation.

Table 9.7 (p. 432), after L. R. Goldberg, "Parameters of personality inventory construction and utilization: A comparison of prediction strategies and tactics," *Multivariate Behavioral Research Monographs* **7**, No. 2 (1972).

Figure 9.7 (p. 434), after A. L. Edwards, *The Social Desirability Variable in Personality Assessment and Research*, Holt, Rinehart and Winston, Inc., New York (1957). Copyright 1957 by the Dryden Press, Inc.

Table 10.1 (p. 448), from William K. Estes *et al.*, *Modern Learning Theory*. Copyright 1954. Reprinted by permission of Appleton-Century-Crofts, Educational Division, Meredith Corporation.

Excerpt (pp. 446–447) and Table 10.2 (p. 450), from C. S. Hall and G. Lindzey, *Theories of Personality*, John Wiley and Sons, Inc., New York (1957).

Excerpt (p. 453), from Albert Mehrabian, *An Analysis of Personality Theories.* Copyright 1968, Prentice-Hall, Inc.

Table 10.4 (p. 479), after J. L. Rinn, "Structure of phenomenal domains," *Psychological Review* **72**, 445–466 (1965).

Excerpts (pp. 483 and 484), from H. A. Murray, *Explorations in Personality*, Oxford University Press, New York (1938).

Excerpt and Figure 10.6 (p. 486), from G. G. Stern, *People in Context: Measuring Person-Environment Congruence in Education and Industry*, John Wiley and Sons, Inc., New York (1970).

Table 10.5 (p. 493), from L. H. Levy and R. D. Dugan, "A factorial study of personal constructs," *Journal of Consulting Psychology* **20**, 53–57 (1956).

Excerpt (pp. 496–497), from R. B. Cattell, *Personality and Motivation, Structure and Measurement*, World Book, Yonkers, N.Y. (1957).

Figure 10.8 (p. 504), from R. B. Cattell, *The Scientific Analysis of Personality*, Penguin, Baltimore (1965).

Excerpts (pp. 509 and 510) and Figure 10.10 (p. 511), from M. R. Goldfried and T. J. D'Zurilla, "A behavioral-analytic model for assessing competence," in C. D. Spielberger (ed.), *Current Topics in Clinical and Community Psychology*, Vol. 1, Academic Press, New York (1969), pp. 151–196.

Excerpt (pp. 517–518), from C. N. Parkinson, "The short list or principles of selection," in C. N. Parkinson, *Parkinson's Law*, Houghton Mifflin Co., New York (1957), pp. 45–58.

Excerpts (pp. 519–520, 522, 525, 527), Table 11.1 (p. 523), Table 11.3 (p. 533), and Table 11.4 (p. 534), from *Assessment of Men* by OSS Assessment Staff. Copyright 1948 by Holt, Rinehart and Winston, Inc.

Excerpts (pp. 540, 547) and Table 11.7 (pp. 544–545), from D. W. MacKinnon, R. S. Crutchfield, F. Barron, J. Block, H. G. Gough and R. E. Harris, *An Assessment Study of Air Force Officers: Part I. Design of the Study and Description of the Variables*, Wright Air Development Center Technical Report No. 91 (I), Personnel Laboratory, Lackland Air Force Base, Texas (April 1958).

Excerpts (pp. 557–558, 559, 564–565), from E. L. Kelley and D. W. Fiske, *The Prediction of Performance in Clinical Psychology*, University of Michigan Press, Ann Arbor (1951).

Table 11.12 (p. 570), Table 11.13 (p. 573), and Table 11.14 (p. 578), are respectively Tables I-4.1, I-10.1, and I-12.1 appearing on pp. 36, 155, 206 of *Personality Patterns of Psychiatrists: A Study of Methods for Selecting Residents* by Robert H. Holt and Lester Luborsky. Copyright 1958 by Basic Books, Inc., Publishers, New York.

Excerpt (p. 592), from E. B. McNeil, "The measure of man," *Trends* **2**, No. 2 (1969), University of Hawaii Peace Corps Training Program, Hilo.

Table 11.15 (p. 596), from L. R. Goldberg, "Reliability of Peace Corps Selection Boards: A study of interjudge agreement before and after board discussions," *Journal of Applied Psychology* **50**, 400–408 (1966).

CONTENTS

Part 1

THE PREDICTION OF HUMAN BEHAVIOR

CHAPTER 1

THE BASIC PREDICTION MODEL
AND ITS APPLICATIONS

CORRELATIONAL AND EXPERIMENTAL METHODS
IN SCIENTIFIC PSYCHOLOGY

Scientific psychology in the present century has been characterized by developments along two essentially parallel paths that have come to be known as experimental and correlational psychology, respectively. The roots of experimental psychology may be found in the Leipzig laboratory where Wundt and his many famous students applied the scientific methods of biology and physics to the study of consciousness. Laboratory procedures were developed with the aim of controlling aspects of the subject's environment in such a way that variations in the behavior of a subject might be attributed to operations performed by the experimenter. By holding all known sources of stimulation constant and varying one aspect of stimulation at a time, the experimenters made an attempt to discover the functional laws relating the various independent (stimulus) variables to dependent (behavioral) variables.

This quest for the general laws expressing behavior as a function of the stimulating environment was enormously facilitated by two developments in mathematical psychology. Using the method developed by Weber (1846), Fechner (1860) demonstrated that such functional relationships, $R = f(S)$, could be stated with considerable mathematical precision and generality. Later, Sir Ronald Fisher (1937) provided a schema for analyzing the contributions of many independent variables to the determination of the dependent behavior measured in the laboratory. The introduction of animals as subjects and concomitant developments in instrumentation made possible the relatively complete control of antecedent independent variables and more precise recording of dependent response variables. Considering the short past and long history of psychology, it must be conceded that monumental strides were rather rapidly achieved in implementing Wundt's dream of a laboratory-based scientific psychology that would uncover the general laws of human behavior.

Modern experimental psychology is characterized by technologies whose complexity and precision exceed, in many respects, those of the biological and physical sciences of Wundt's day. The automated and electronically complex apparatus that fills many psychological laboratories today is reminiscent of the settings in the early Frankenstein films. The mathematics employed by an ever-increasing number of experimental psychologists is such as to strike terror in the hearts of the mathematically inept. Yet, despite these visible signs of a rapidly maturing science, the achievements of modern experimental psychology are celebrated in relatively narrow segments of our society. Even within academic groups specifically designed for their celebration (introductory psychology courses), a characteristic resistance may be noted on the part of a substantial minority of otherwise intelligent students. Although conceding that psychology has established laboratories that may be favorably compared with those of other scientific disciplines, these resistant students are prone to remark that the limited behaviors that occupy the attention of experimental psychologists do not seem related in any obvious way to the everyday behaviors of people that they themselves observe. This type of subversion is usually met with patient efforts to imbue such students with the spirit of the Scientific Method. The need for operationalism and experimental control is emphasized. The dangers of introspectionism, intuitivism, and "common sense" psychology are stressed. A sense of the enormity of scientific psychology's eventual goal is conveyed, along with the necessity for deferring immediate issues in favor of longer-range considerations. Even when so chastised for his impatient, intuitive pragmatism, the astute student is likely to remark that the long-range goals of science would be better served in psychology by a more enlightened initial selection of the *relevant variables* which determine human behavior. Such students are often encouraged to embark on a career in the individual-differences sciences (clinical, personality, industrial psychology), and their "applied" interests may eventually lead them to texts such as the present one.

It is now generally recognized that laboratory control, instrument development, and mathematical techniques are themselves not sufficient to ensure the inclusion of *relevant variables* in a scientific study of human behavior. Behaviors which are most accessible to control and quantification are not necessarily those which may open up fruitful avenues of exploration. Indeed, the laws which govern the isolated fragments of behavior studied in contrived laboratory situations may be of a different order than the laws which govern behavior in more complex naturalistic settings. Correlational psychology may be defined as that branch of psychology which attempts to clarify relations already existing in nature and to point the way toward clusters of such variables which might be most representatively studied in the more controlled setting of the laboratory. In addition, whereas experimental psychology attempts to discover relationships which hold, within error, for *all* individuals, correlational psychology is most concerned with differences among individuals within such laws.

Strangely enough, it was one of Wundt's own students, James McKean Cattell, who is credited with launching the individual-differences movement in psychology. The variable of reaction time was a central measure in the Leipzig laboratory in that different reaction times to different modalities of stimulation were used as a basis for inferring the structure of consciousness. Even within the same modality (e.g., reaction time to light), however, there were noticeable individual differences among subjects. Although Wundt tended to view such individual differences as "error" which might be reduced by averaging, Cattell felt that individual differences themselves might shed considerable light on the structure of consciousness. Some individuals may be observed to have quick reaction times to stimulation in all modalities whereas others, by comparison, may be observed to have relatively slower reaction times in all modalities. The characteristic of high reactivity to a variety of stimuli may in turn be related to broader classes of individual-differences variables (intelligence?) and as such may reveal relationships which would be masked by the averaging approach of experimental psychology.

For reasons more historical than logical, the individual-differences movement progressed in relative isolation from the experimental tradition. The traditions of Galton, Cattell, Binet, and Spearman were continued in this country by such men as Terman, Thurstone, and Goddard quite independently of the experimental psychology of the times. (As we shall see later, the personality-assessment tradition, which dates roughly from the advent of World War I, had even less connection with experimental laboratory psychology.) In his presidential address to the American Psychological Association, Cronbach (1957) pleaded for a reconciliation between "the two disciplines of scientific psychology." Whereas previous writers (and even previous APA presidents) had emphasized the dangers in a bifurcating science, Cronbach demonstrated convincingly the absolute necessity of incorporating both designs ("person-treatment interactions") in arriving at realistic appraisals of psychological situations. In a similar vein, R. B. Cattell (1966a) has argued that the traditional association of bivariate (two variables) analysis with "experimental" psychology and multivariate (many variables) analysis with "individual differences" psychology is without logical foundation. Cattell pleads for a *flexibility* in design and analysis that would transcend this traditional dichotomy. That the near future may be characterized by such flexibility is evidenced by the increasing recognition that experimental and correlational psychology share a common mathematical basis (Cohen, 1968).

As we have implied, personality-assessment procedures have been based largely on some variant of the group of methods we have termed correlational. Personality assessment has the quite applied aim of generating predictions about certain aspects of behavior that will contribute to decisions concerning the disposition or treatment of individuals. Although personality-assessment procedures of the future may not, we hope, be so closely tied to traditional correlational methods, we must confine ourselves to descriptions of accomplishments today. We turn, therefore, to the description of a quite modest computational procedure, one variant of which (partial correlation) has been described as "the only 20th century discovery comparable in importance to the conditioned-response method" (Murphy, 1929).

CORRELATIONAL ANALYSIS

The correlation coefficient was suggested by Galton (1888) and developed by Pearson (1896) as a standard method of expressing the extent to which two variables are observed to co-vary in nature. We can best illustrate the properties of this very useful index by reference to actual data. Table 1.1 provides the results of two sets of observations obtained on the same 30 individuals. For purposes of illustration, we have manufactured personality test scores on dominance, X, and leadership ratings, Y, for 30 subjects. The immediate interest is the extent to which the trait of dominance is related to the circumstance of being perceived as a leader. The eventual aim might be the prediction of one variable (leadership) from the other (dominance) in a new sample of subjects.

Deviation and Standard Scores

From the distribution of raw scores on dominance, X, we can see that Parker obtained a dominance score of 50 and Rice obtained a dominance score of 40. Parker is thus more "dominant" than Rice, but with respect to what? The most appropriate frame of reference here seems to be the *group* of which Parker and Rice are members. Summing the raw scores on dominance in column 2 and dividing by the number of subjects gives us the mean (average) dominance score for this group of subjects: $M_X = \Sigma X/N = 1500/30 = 50$. Given the mean of the distribution of raw dominance scores, it is possible to express all scores as deviations from this group mean: $x = X - M_X$. The distribution of *deviation scores* is given in columns 4 and 5 for dominance, x, and leadership, y, respectively.

From the deviation scores in column 4, it is clear that Parker is the "average man" since his raw dominance score, 50, falls right at the group mean, 50, and his deviation score, $X - M_X$, is thus zero. Rice, on the other hand, achieved a dominance score that was 10 units *below* the group average

($x = -10$). Hence Rice is not only less "dominant" than Parker, but less "dominant" than the average member of his peer group. The same kinds of within-group comparisons can be made with respect to the deviation leadership scores given in column 5. Parker and Rice are both "average" with respect to their perceived leadership qualities.

Given the frame of reference provided by deviation scores, it is tempting to compare dominance and leadership scores. For example, Barber has a dominance deviation score of $+7$ and a leadership deviation score of $+7$. May we say that Barber has "equal amounts" of dominance and leadership ability? The answer is an unqualified "no." We have neglected the problem of the size of the *units* by which dominance and leadership were originally measured. If an X variable is measured in terms of pennies and a Y variable is measured in terms of dollars, we would not assert that $+7\textcent = +7\$$. Similarly, if dominance is measured by a 100-item self-report test and leadership is measured by a 7-place rating scale, we would not assert that 7 items of dominance are equivalent to a rating of 7 on a leadership scale. Dominance scores may vary from 0 to 100, but leadership scores can assume values between 1 and 7 only. What is required is an index that will transform these scores to a comparable or "standard" metric.

In the present example, we can easily calculate standard deviations by squaring the deviation scores (columns 6 and 7), summing them for each variable, and calculating $\sigma_x = \sqrt{\sum x^2/N}$ for dominance and $\sigma_y = \sqrt{\sum y^2/N}$ for leadership. From the computations of Table 1.1, we can see that the standard deviation of dominance scores is $\sigma_x = 10.73$ and that the standard deviation of leadership scores is $\sigma_y = 8.96$. Such standard deviations[1] express the degree of variability of scores in units that may be directly compared from one set of observations to another. Therefore, we can make scores from the two sets of observations comparable by expressing them as *standard scores*: $Z_x = x/\sigma_x$; $Z_y = y/\sigma_y$. Barber's standard score on dominance is

$$Z_x = \frac{+7}{10.73} = +.65.$$

His standard score on leadership is

$$Z_y = \frac{+7}{8.96} = +.78.$$

It is now clear that, relative to his position in the two distributions of scores, Barber is somewhat more a leader ($Z_y = +.78$) than he is a dominant person

---

1. Throughout the present text, the symbol σ will be used to refer to the standard deviation of a distribution of scores obtained in a given *sample* of subjects.

Table 1.1 Computation of the correlation coefficient between dominance scores and leadership ratings

Subjects	Dom- inance scores (X)	Leader- ship ratings (Y)	(X − M_X) x	(Y − M_Y) y	x²	y²	xy
Adams	42	66	− 8	+ 2	64	4	− 16
Barber	57	71	+ 7	+ 7	49	49	49
Brown	45	62	− 5	− 2	25	4	10
Chapman	37	38	− 13	− 26	169	676	338
Decker	59	62	+ 9	− 2	81	4	− 18
Fox	38	62	− 12	− 2	144	4	24
Graham	64	72	+ 14	+ 8	196	64	112
Hastings	71	70	+ 21	+ 6	441	36	126
Johnson	47	68	− 3	+ 3	9	9	− 9
Lamb	62	80	+ 12	+ 16	144	256	192
Lane	36	56	− 14	− 8	196	64	112
Martin	41	60	− 9	− 4	81	16	36
Nelson	51	62	+ 1	− 2	1	4	− 2
Norris	47	46	− 3	− 18	9	324	54
Parker	50	64	0	0	0	0	0
Pierce	42	49	− 8	− 15	64	225	120
Rice	40	64	− 10	0	100	0	0
Russell	60	76	+ 10	+ 12	100	144	120
Scott	59	72	+ 9	+ 8	81	64	72
Stone	41	72	− 9	+ 8	81	64	− 72
Swartz	39	61	− 11	− 3	121	9	33

Subjects	Dominance scores (X)	Leadership ratings (Y)	$(X - M_X)$ x	$(Y - M_Y)$ y	x^2	y^2	xy
Thompson	38	57	−12	−7	144	49	84
Townsend	30	60	−20	−4	400	16	80
Turner	51	62	+1	−2	1	4	−2
Vaughn	69	77	+19	+13	361	169	247
Wade	54	68	+4	+4	16	16	16
Walker	48	71	−2	+7	4	49	−14
Weber	60	60	+10	−4	100	16	−40
Williams	57	62	+7	−2	49	4	−14
Zimmermann	65	72	+15	+8	225	64	120
$\sum$ (sum):	1500	1922	0	0	3456	2407	1758
M (mean):	50	64	0	0	115.13	80.23	

Computations

$\sum xy = 1758$

$\sigma_x = \sqrt{\sum x^2/N} = \sqrt{3456/30} = \sqrt{115.13} = 10.73$

$\sigma_y = \sqrt{\sum y^2/N} = \sqrt{2407/30} = \sqrt{80.23} = 8.96$

$r_{xy} = -\dfrac{\sum xy}{N\sigma_x\sigma_y}$

$r_{xy} = \dfrac{1758}{(30)(10.73)(8.96)}$

$r_{xy} = .6095 = .61$

$(Z_x = +.65)$. This difference, of course, was not apparent from the deviation scores alone.

As may be apparent from the manner in which they are derived, standard scores, Z, always come from a distribution whose mean is zero. Thus an individual with a standard score of $Z_x = 0$ will be the "average man" of his group. What may not be so readily apparent is the fact that the standard deviation of a distribution of standard scores, σ_z, is always one.[2] Thus standard scores express all measures in terms of a common, meaningful metric and have a highly convenient distributional property: $M_{z_x} = 0$; $\sigma_{z_x} = 1$. In describing the statistical basis of prediction in personality assessment, we shall make frequent use of deviation scores, x. The reader is asked to bear in mind that deviation scores represent an individual's score with reference to the average score of the group of which he is a member: $x = X - M_X$. On occasion, we will wish to take advantage of the convenient property of standard scores: $\sigma_{z_x} = \sigma_{z_y} = 1$. Here it is necessary to recall that scores are being expressed with reference to both the mean and the standard deviation of the group of subjects: $Z_x = (X - M_X)/\sigma_X$.

The Correlation Coefficient

The Pearson *product-moment* correlation coefficient may now be defined as

$$r_{xy} = \frac{\sum xy}{N\sigma_x\sigma_y} .$$

A moment's reflection will reveal that this index is simply *the mean of the products of standard scores on two variables*. Were we to calculate this index the hard way, we would determine for each subject his standard score on dominance, x/σ_x, his standard score on leadership, y/σ_y, and the product of these two scores $(x/\sigma_x)(y/\sigma_y)$. To find the *average* product for the entire group, we sum all these products and divide by the number of subjects:

$$\frac{\sum \left(\frac{x}{\sigma_x} \cdot \frac{y}{\sigma_y} \right)}{N} .$$

To save time, we simply summed the products of the two deviation scores and divided by the standard deviations only once, at the end.

The correlation coefficient, r_{xy}, indicates the extent to which individuals who score high on dominance (with respect to the mean of the group) also score high on leadership (with respect to the mean of the group): If each subject has the identical standard score on dominance that he has on leadership, then $r_{xy} = +1.00$. If each subject has the same standard score but with

---

2. $\sigma_z^2 = \dfrac{\sum Z^2}{N} = \dfrac{\sum (x/\sigma_x)^2}{N} = \dfrac{\sum x^2}{N} \cdot \dfrac{1}{\sigma_x^2} = \sigma_x^2 \cdot \dfrac{1}{\sigma_x^2} = 1.$

reversed sign on the two tests (e.g., dominance $= +2$; leadership $= -2$), then the correlation is perfectly negative: $r_{xy} = -1.00$. Such a correlation could occur in the present example if the dominance scale were scored in the direction of "submission" rather than in the direction of dominance. If there is no consistent relation at all between an individual's standard score on dominance and his standard score on leadership, then $r_{xy} = .00$.

At the bottom of Table 1.1, the necessary measures are assembled for calculating the Pearson product-moment correlation coefficient between dominance and leadership in this group of 30 subjects. Having determined the standard deviation of dominance to be $\sigma_x = 10.73$, the standard deviation of leadership to be $\sigma_y = 8.96$, and the sum of the cross-products of deviation scores to be $\sum xy = 1758$, we enter these figures into the formula and the result of .6095 is rounded to an $r_{xy} = .61$. We can now state that the Pearson product-moment correlation coefficient between dominance (as measured by a personality test) and leadership (as measured by peer ratings) is .61. What can we conclude from this datum?

It is clear that, at least to some extent, individuals who score high on a dominance test are perceived as leaders, and those who score low on a dominance test are not so perceived. From a statistical point of view, variance (variation in test scores) in one measure is associated with variance in another measure for this group of individuals. As we shall see later (p. 20), we can assert that 37 percent—$r_{xy}^2 = (.61)^2 = .37$—of the variance in the leadership ratings may be reliably predicted from dominance scores. As to *why* this prediction is possible, there are three rather different interpretations, which Cattell (1957, p. 29) has represented by diagrams similar to those shown in Figure 1.1.

The diagrams in Figure 1.1 represent the three possible interpretations that might be placed on an r_{xy} of .61 between dominance and leadership

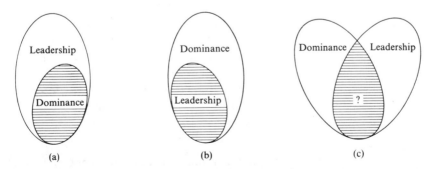

(a)   (b)   (c)

Fig. 1.1 Three possible interpretations of a correlation coefficient of .61 between dominance and leadership. (a) All elements of dominance are in leadership. (b) All elements of leadership are in dominance. (c) 61 percent of elements in leadership are in common with dominance. (After Cattell, 1957, p. 29.)

scores. In diagram (a), the trait of dominance is subsumed under the broader category of leadership and would lead to the statement "Dominance is an important component of leadership," since it constitutes 37 percent of leadership behavior. In diagram (b), however, leadership is subsumed under the trait of dominance, which might lead us to assert, "Leadership is an important component of dominance," since it constitutes 37 percent of dominance. Still another possible interpretation is represented by diagram (c), in which 61 percent ($r_{xy} \times 100$) of the elements in leadership are shown to be in common with those of dominance. Some third factor or influence is seen to be held in common by the two variables. Such a state of affairs would be compatible with the assertion "Both dominance and leadership are manifestations of the underlying *source trait* (factor) of extraversion."

From the correlation coefficient alone, it is not possible to determine whether dominance "causes" leadership, whether leadership "causes" dominance, or whether both are surface manifestations of a more basic dimension of personality. This is, at once, the weakness and strength of the correlation method, and it is a feature that has not endeared it to the experimental psychologist.[3] Nevertheless, it should also be apparent that, given the relationship indicated by an r_{xy} of .61, we should be able to make predictions from one variable to the other. That is, given an individual's dominance score, we should be able to forecast his leadership behavior.

The field of applied personality assessment has not been deeply concerned with the problem of which of two correlated personality measurements "causes" the other. Prediction, the main goal of assessment, can be accomplished in total ignorance of such theoretical niceties. As a matter of fact, that strategy of personality assessment which has come to be known as the "empirical approach" is openly intolerant of such attempts to bring theoretical enlightenment into the realm of prediction studies. The basic paradigm of personality assessment calls for the prediction of a "criterion" from tests or other procedures which yield quantifiable information about individuals. Although personality assessors are much concerned with a "criterion problem," it does not take the form of an inability to distinguish among predictor and criterion variables. The criterion is that which we (or those who bear the financial burden of our enterprises) wish to predict. Predictors are, literally, anything we can employ to increase the accuracy of forecasts. It is not assumed that predictor measures "cause" criteria or vice versa, only that one (criteria) may be predicted from the other (predictors).

---

3.   In defense of correlation, we must add that certain extensions of correlational analysis, such as factor analysis, have been developed to deal more precisely with the interpretative issues raised in Figure 1.1. The previously cited work of Cattell (1957) is an excellent introduction to that topic.

In our example, it is likely that leadership will be perceived by most as the *criterion* variable. No small amount of effort has gone into attempts to predict this behavior (Gibb, 1969). Governments, the military, industry— all have vested interests in the accuracy of forecasting this kind of behavior, as their support of this type of research indicates. Like most criteria, leadership behavior is of critical social importance. However, it is not difficult to conceive of research situations in which an investigator of more academic persuasion may be interested in the antecedents of dominant behavior in adults. Conceivably, such an investigator might wish to examine the relationship between leadership in high school and dominant behavior as an adult. Within this framework, dominance would become a criterion variable to be predicted from leadership ratings. Regardless of the direction of prediction, the r_{xy} of .61 indicates that some forecasting of one variable from the other is possible. Having defined the correlation coefficient, we may now turn to an examination of the mechanics whereby such predictions are made.

REGRESSION AND PREDICTION

Prediction becomes possible when the relationship between two variables can be specified by means of an equation of the general form $y = f(x)$, which is read, "y is a function of x." It means that for every value of x, a value of y can be generated by performing the appropriate mathematical operations on the value of x. Where x is a predictor variable, y (the criterion) can be forecasted by determining the appropriate function, f, which relates the two variables. Perhaps the most familiar of all functional relationships is that which gives the equation for a straight line: $y = bx$. Here f is interpreted to mean that for every increase in x, there is a corresponding increase in y which may be determined by multiplying x by a constant "coefficient," b. Plotting this functional relationship, $y = bx$, will result in a straight line or "linear" function.

Figure 1.2 is a scatterplot of deviation scores for dominance and leadership from Table 1.1. Referring to Table 1.1, we can see that Vaughn obtained a dominance deviation score of $+19$ and a leadership deviation score of $+13$. Vaughn is represented in Figure 1.2 by the dot whose coordinates are: $x = +19$, $y = +13$. A similar entry has been made for each of the 30 subjects given in Table 1.1. Inspection of the scatterplot in Figure 1.2 indicates that the relationship between the two variables approximates a straight line[4] and hence might be "summarized" by an equation of the form

---

4.   Space limitations prohibit the presentation of data from a sample of more representative size, e.g., $N = 200$. Were such data plotted in full, the approximation to a straight line would be much more evident.

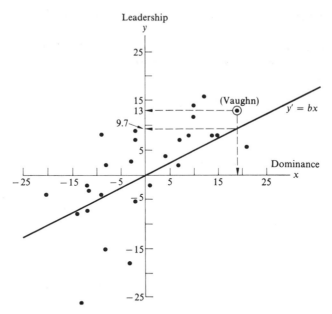

Fig. 1.2 Prediction of leadership ratings from dominance scores.

$y = bx$, which is represented by the heavy black line extending through the points of the plot. The heavy black line is referred to as a *regression line*.

The extent to which the equation $y = bx$ "summarizes" the actual relationship between these two variables can be assessed by noting the extent to which the scores actually fall on this regression line, as opposed to falling above or below it. The *predicted value*, y', for any x score may be determined by extending a projection upward (for positive values of x) from the dominance axis to the regression line and then reading off the corresponding value of y from the leadership axis. The *observed value*, y, for any x score in Table 1.1 may be determined by simply reading the y value of the point representing an individual's score. Vaughn has a dominance deviation score, x, of $+19$ and, as we can see from the figure, a leadership deviation score, y, of $+13$. Extending a projection from Vaughn's dominance score, $+19$, up to the regression line and then reading the corresponding score from the leadership axis reveals that Vaughn's predicted leadership score, y', is $+9.7$.

The difference between observed and predicted leadership scores for Vaughn ($y - y' = 13 - 9.7 = 3.3$) is the amount by which our prediction via the regression line is in error. Our prediction is off by 3.3 units of leadership deviation scores. In like manner, we could summarize the average error in prediction from the regression equation for all subjects by an index such as $\sum (y - y')/N$. However, as the student of elementary statistics will immediately recognize, underestimates of y (e.g., $y - y' = +3.3$) will be compensated for by overestimates of y (e.g., $y - y' = -3.3$). Actually, for reasons which are not quite so obvious, the expression $\sum (y - y')/N$ will always be equal to zero, a highly misleading state of affairs for an index of predictive accuracy. For that reason, predictive "misses" are squared, and the index of predictive accuracy is taken as $\sum (y - y')^2/N$.

We can now state that the goal of prediction, via linear regression equations, is to find a value for the coefficient b in the equation $y' = bx$, such that the index of predictive accuracy, $\sum (y - y')^2/N$, is a *minimum*. When we have found *the* value of b, from among all possible values, that satisfies the condition $\sum (y - y')^2/N \to$ minimum, we have achieved a *least-squares solution* of our linear regression equation, $y' = bx$. Since such a solution will yield an equation that minimizes predictive error (in the least-squares sense), it is referred to as the "best-fit" line for summarizing the data. Using some other value of b will yield a linear equation, but it will not be the best-fit line, since it will always involve a greater average error of prediction.

The expression $\sum (y - y')^2/N$ or, by substitution, $\sum (y - bx)^2/N$ will be minimized at that value of b for which the first derivative of the function is zero. We first expand the function,

$$\frac{\sum (y - bx)^2}{N} = \frac{\sum (y^2 + b^2x^2 - 2byx)}{N},$$

and obtain the first derivative with respect to b:

$$\frac{df}{db} = \frac{\sum (2bx^2 - 2yx)}{N} = \frac{-2(\sum xy - b \sum x^2)}{N}.$$

We next set the derivative equal to zero and solve for b:

$$\frac{-2(\sum xy - b \sum x^2)}{N} = 0,$$

$$\frac{\sum xy}{N} - \frac{b \sum x^2}{N} = 0.$$

Since $\sum xy/N = r_{xy}\sigma_x\sigma_y$, and since $\sum x^2/N = \sigma_x^2$,

$$r_{xy}\sigma_x\sigma_y - b\sigma_x^2 = 0,$$

$$b = r_{xy}\frac{\sigma_y}{\sigma_x}.$$

The regression coefficient, $b = r_{xy}(\sigma_y/\sigma_x)$, in the equation $y' = bx$ is the slope of the equation of the straight line which expresses the rate of change in y' as a function of changes in x. This slope is dependent on two parameters: (1) the degree of correlation that exists between the two variables, r_{xy}; and (2) the variability of criterion scores about their mean relative to the variability of predictor scores about their mean, σ_y/σ_x. We may consider the contribution of the correlation coefficient separately by first discussing prediction in situations where the standard deviation of criterion scores is *equal* to the standard deviation of predictor scores, $\sigma_y/\sigma_x = 1$. Figure 1.3 plots regression equations for several values of b, with equal standard deviations assumed for both variables. In this situation, the equation $y' = r_{xy}x$ is equivalent to $y' = (\sigma_y/\sigma_x)r_{xy}x$, and the slope is determined entirely by the size of the correlation coefficient.

In Figure 1.3, the predicted y' value is obtained by extending a projection from the intersection of x and any given regression line to the y axis. In this example, projections have been extended from the points where an x score of $+6$ intersects the regression lines. When $r_{xy} = 0$, $b = 0$ and the regression line becomes the x axis itself. In this instance, the mean of y is

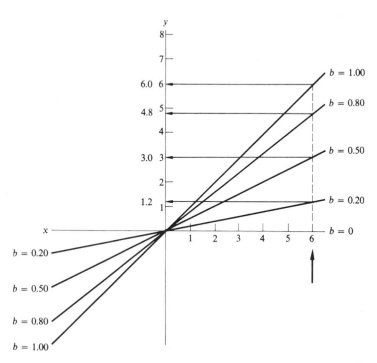

Fig. 1.3 Regression equations for several values of b (when $\sigma_x = \sigma_y$).

predicted for *every* value of x, and since the mean of distributions of deviation scores is zero, the prediction for the x score of $+6$ is zero. When $b = .20$, the y' predictions increase one-fifth of a unit for each increase of one unit in x. When $x = +6$, y' is $\frac{1}{5} \cdot 6 = +1.2$. For the other values of b given in the figure, it is clear that for every unit increase in x, there is a corresponding *fractional* increase in the predicted y' value. Since the correlation coefficient cannot exceed the value $+1.00$, the limiting case here is that of $b = 1.00$, in which y' advances exactly one unit for each unit advanced by x. The functional relationship between x and y' here could be expressed simply as $y' = x$ (since $b = 1.00$).

Inspection of Figure 1.3 leads to the generalization that when the standard deviations of predictor and criterion scores are the same, predicted criterion values, y', will be closer to the mean of criterion scores, $M_y = 0$, than the corresponding predictor scores, x, will be to their own mean, $M_x = 0$. For this reason the standard deviation of predicted scores, $\sigma_{y'}$, will always be *less* than the standard deviation of scores on which predictions are based, σ_x, except in the limiting case where $r_{xy} = 1.00$. The tendency for predicted scores, y', to converge on the mean criterion score, M_y, was described by Galton as a "reversion" or *regression* toward the mean of criterion scores (Walker, 1929). The terminology of Galton was carefully preserved by Pearson, and it is still customary to speak of "the regression of y on x," to describe the equation of prediction as a "regression equation," and to denote the correlation coefficient as r, which Galton used to refer to the slope of "reversion."

Although Galton spoke of regression in the context of the inheritance of traits, the statistical generalization holds for any two traits that have natural, or imposed, upper and lower limits in their magnitude. If an individual scores at the upper end of a dominance test, he can be rated either at the upper end of a leadership scale or anywhere *below* the upper end. Another individual, scoring at the lower end of a dominance test, can be rated at the bottom of the leadership scale or anywhere *above* the bottom. As can be seen from Figure 1.3, least-squares prediction equations take these limitations into account by "regressing" toward the mean of criterion scores in proportion to the amount by which the two variables are correlated. When the two variables are uncorrelated ($r_{xy} = 0$), a complete regression on the mean of y occurs, and $M_y = 0$ is predicted for every value of x. When the two variables are perfectly correlated ($r_{xy} = 1.00$), no regression toward the mean of y occurs, and the distance of y' from the mean of y is predicted to be the same as that of x from the mean of x.

The second parameter of the regression coefficient, b, is the ratio between criterion and predictor variability, σ_y/σ_x. It should be apparent from this ratio that when $\sigma_y > \sigma_x$, predicted criterion scores will be *increased* by the amount of this ratio times the fraction represented by r_{xy}. For example, if $\sigma_y = 10$, $\sigma_x = 5$, $r_{xy} = .50$, then for $x = +6$,

$$y' = \left(\frac{\sigma_y}{\sigma_x} r_{xy}\right) x = \left(\frac{10}{5} \times .50\right)(6) = +6.$$

In comparing this y' value for $x = +6$ with that given in Figure 1.3 for $x = +6$ when $r_{xy} = .50$ *and* $\sigma_y = \sigma_x$, we note that the predicted criterion value has doubled (from $+3$ to $+6$) as the ratio σ_y/σ_x goes from 1.00 to 2.00. When the variability of criterion scores exceeds the variability of predictor scores, we must "spread out" our predictions, y', accordingly. Similarly, when the variability of criterion scores is less than the variability of predictor scores ($\sigma_y < \sigma_x$), we must compress or "regress" our predictions, y', even more than is already accomplished by multiplying by the fraction r_{xy}.

Although in situations in which $\sigma_y > \sigma_x$ it is necessary to "spread out" our predictions, it is nevertheless true that the variability of *predicted* criterion scores will always be equal to or less than the variability of the observed criterion scores ($\sigma_{y'} \leq \sigma_y$). Although this latter fact may not be immediately obvious, it stems from the general phenomenon of "regression" mentioned earlier and may be demonstrated mathematically by recognition of the fact that $\sigma_{y'} = \sqrt{\sum (y')^2/N} = \sqrt{\sum (bx)^2/N}$, since $y' = bx$. Expansion of the terms under the radical leads to the expression $\sigma_{y'}^2 = r_{xy}^2 \sigma_y^2$, in which we can see that the variance of predicted criterion scores is equal to (when $r_{xy} = 1$) or less than the variance of the observed criterion scores.

The Standard Error of Estimate

What we have been referring to as the "index of predictive accuracy," $\sum (y - y')^2/N$, is the variance of observed criterion scores, y, around the regression line that specifies predicted criterion scores, y'. The square root of this expression is a standard deviation, symbolized as $\sigma_{y \cdot x}$ and referred to as the *standard error of estimate* in predicting y from x. Expressing the error of estimate in standard-deviation form allows us to compare the results of different studies of a criterion (with different predictor variables and differing numbers of subjects) in terms of a common index. In our example involving the prediction of leadership ratings from dominance scores, the standard error of estimate, $\sigma_{y \cdot x} = \sqrt{\sum (y - y')^2/N}$, will turn out to have the value of 7.10. Before concerning ourselves with the mechanics of calculating this value, we will illustrate the interpretation placed on this statistic.

Since the standard error of estimate is a standard deviation, we can erect confidence limits around a predicted leadership rating, within which we would expect an actual leadership rating to fall. In the prediction of leadership from dominance scores, $\sigma_{y \cdot x} = 7.10$ is to be considered the standard deviation of the actual leadership ratings about the regression line $y' = bx$. When predictions are made with this equation, we can be 68 percent confident that subjects with a given dominance score, x, will have an actual leadership rating, y, within the limits $y' \pm 7.10$. That is, if all subjects with a dominance score of 10 are predicted to have a leadership rating of 5.09, the limits 2.01 to 12.19 (5.09 ± 7.10) will contain the actual leadership ratings of the subjects 68 percent of the time. By the same characteristics of a standard deviation, the limits $y' \pm 3(7.10)$ will almost always (99 percent of the time) contain the actual criterion ratings.

To further illuminate the characteristics of the standard error of estimate, we substitute the regression equation for y' into the formula

$$\sigma_{y \cdot x} = \frac{\sqrt{\Sigma \{ y - [r_{xy}(\sigma_y / \sigma_x)x] \}^2}}{N}$$

and by appropriate manipulation obtain

$$\sigma_{y \cdot x} = \sigma_y \sqrt{1 - r_{xy}^2},$$

which is the more common formula for the standard error of estimate. In addition to providing a more convenient computational procedure, this latter formula illustrates the properties that enter into predictive error. Error in prediction via regression equations is dependent on (a) variability in the criterion, σ_y, and (b) the magnitude of the correlation between predictor and criterion, expressed as $\sqrt{1 - r_{xy}^2}$.

When the predictor-criterion relationship yields a zero correlation, we do not simply predict "at random" or by resort to coins or dice. Rather, as previously indicated, we predict the mean value of the criterion, M_y, for *every* value of the predictor by a completely horizontal regression line. Our error in prediction will be equal to the variability of the actual criterion scores around their mean, expressed as σ_y. This fact is neatly illustrated by the formula for the standard error of estimate,

$$\sigma_{y \cdot x} = \sigma_y \sqrt{1 - r_{xy}^2} = \sigma_y \sqrt{1 - (0)^2} = \sigma_y.$$

From this it should be apparent that *anyone*—a gambler, a clinician, a layman with good "common sense"—can predict with standard error equal to σ_y if he knows the M_y of the criterion scores and predicts this value for all subjects. We therefore consider the standard error of prediction, σ_y, as a *base line* of predictive error which any regression equation worth its salt must improve on (i.e., must reduce).

We have already alluded to the square of the correlation coefficient, r_{xy}^2, as the "proportion of variance explained," and we are now in a position to indicate more precisely what it is that is explained. From the formula for the standard error of estimate, we can see that the expression $\sqrt{1 - r_{xy}^2}$ provides an index of the amount by which the *base line* of predictive error, σ_y, is *reduced* by the magnitude of the correlation between predictor and criterion. The expression $\sqrt{1 - r_{xy}^2}$ has been termed the coefficient of alienation (Kelley, 1919), and it provides a useful statement of the proportion of error reduction associated with different magnitudes of r_{xy}. When $r_{xy} = .60$, the standard error of estimate is reduced by $\sqrt{1 - (.60)^2} = .80$. That is, a 20 percent reduction in error has occurred with reference to our base-line situation, where $r_{xy} = 0$ and $\sigma_{y \cdot x} = \sigma_y$. When $r_{xy} = .87$ and $\sqrt{1 - (.87)^2} = .50$, we can reduce our error by 50 percent over the base-line situation. Actually, improvement over base-line predictions is not very remarkable for correlations in the range from .30 to .50, which, as we shall see later, are typical correlations in personality assessment (McNemar, 1969b, p. 141).

The formula for the standard error of estimate, $\sigma_{y \cdot x} = \sigma_y \sqrt{1 - r_{xy}^2}$, may be solved directly for r^2 to further illuminate the meaning of the correlation coefficient, $r_{xy}^2 = 1 - \sigma_{y \cdot x}^2 / \sigma_y^2$. The square of the correlation coefficient is thus equal to one minus the ratio of unpredictable criterion variance, $\sigma_{y \cdot x}^2$, to total criterion variance, σ_y^2. The smaller the amount of unpredictable criterion variance, the larger the amount of total criterion variance that can be reliably predicted from the x variable. The index, r_{xy}^2, is frequently multiplied by 100 to yield the expression often referred to as the "percentage of criterion variance explained." In discussing the correlation of .61 between dominance and leadership scores, we indicated that several possible interpretations might be placed on that relationship. With reference to the standard error of estimate, we can now indicate, somewhat more precisely, that 37 percent of the variance in leadership ratings may be *reliably predicted* from dominance scores.

The Prediction of Leadership Ratings from Dominance Scores

With the foregoing as background, we may now consider, more concretely, the mechanics of the prediction process. Columns 2 and 3 of Table 1.2 repeat the dominance and leadership deviation scores obtained in Table 1.1. The problem is to obtain *predicted* leadership scores, y', from the regression formula, $y' = bx$. From the computations of Table 1.1, we carry over the values for the correlation coefficient ($r = .6095$), the standard deviation of the predictor scores ($\sigma_x = 10.73$), and the standard deviation of the criterion scores ($\sigma_y = 8.96$) and enter them in the formula given at the lower left of Table 1.2. The regression weight, b, for this prediction situation is .5089. Therefore, for each of the individuals in the group, we obtain a predicted leadership score, y', by multiplying his dominance score by a constant of

Table 1.2 Predicting leadership ratings from dominance scores by a regression equation

Subjects	Dominance scores x	Observed leadership ratings y	Predicted leadership ratings $y' = bx$	Predictive error $y - y'$	Squared predictive error $(y - y')^2$
Adams	−8	+2	−4.07	6.07	36.84
Barber	+7	+7	+3.56	3.44	11.83
Brown	−5	−2	−2.54	−.54	.29
Chapman	−13	−26	−6.62	−19.38	375.58
Decker	+9	−2	+4.58	−6.58	43.30
Fox	−12	−2	−6.11	4.11	16.89
Graham	+14	+8	+7.12	.88	.77
Hastings	+21	+6	+10.69	−4.69	22.00
Johnson	−3	+3	−1.53	4.53	20.52
Lamb	+12	+16	+6.11	9.89	97.81
Lane	−14	−8	−7.12	−.88	.77
Martin	−9	−4	−4.58	.58	.34
Nelson	+1	−2	+.51	−2.51	6.30
Norris	−3	−18	−1.53	−16.47	271.26
Parker	0	0	.00	.00	.00
Pierce	−8	−15	−4.07	−10.93	119.46
Rice	−10	0	−5.09	5.09	25.91
Russell	+10	+12	+5.09	6.91	47.75
Scott	+9	+8	+4.58	3.42	11.70
Stone	−9	+8	−4.58	12.58	158.26
Swartz	−11	−3	−5.60	2.60	6.76
Thompson	−12	−7	−6.11	−.89	.79
Townsend	−20	−4	−10.18	6.18	38.19
Turner	+1	−2	+.51	−2.15	4.62
Vaughn	+19	+13	+9.67	3.33	11.09
Wade	+4	+4	+2.04	1.96	3.84
Walker	−2	+7	−1.02	8.02	64.32
Weber	+10	−4	+5.09	−9.09	82.63
Williams	+7	−2	+3.56	−5.56	30.91
Zimmermann	+15	+8	+7.63	.37	.14

Computations $\sum (y - y')^2 = 1510.89$

Regression weight

$$y' = bx$$

$$b = r_{xy}\frac{\sigma_y}{\sigma_x}$$

$$b = (.6095)\frac{(8.96)}{(10.73)} = .5089$$

$$y' = (.5089)x$$

Standard error of estimate

$$\sigma_{y \cdot x} = \sqrt{\sum (y - y')^2/N}$$

$$\sigma_{y \cdot x} = \sqrt{(1510.89)/30}$$

$$\sigma_{y \cdot x} = 7.10$$

$$\sigma_{y \cdot x} = \sigma_y\sqrt{1 - r_{xy}^2}$$

$$\sigma_{y \cdot x} = (8.96)\sqrt{1 - (.6095)^2}$$

$$\sigma_{y \cdot x} = 7.10$$

.51. These predicted leadership scores are given in column 4, which shows that Adams, for example, has a predicted leadership score of $(.5089)(-8) = -4.07$.

The degree to which our regression equation makes accurate predictions varies considerably from individual to individual, as column 5 indicates. Parker, whose scores on both variables fall at the mean of their respective distributions, 0, is completely predictable from the equation. Very accurate predictions are also made for Zimmerman, Brown, and Martin. Notable predictive "misses": Chapman, whose leadership rating fell far below what would be predicted by the equation; Norris, for whom the same is true; and Stone, whose actual leadership rating was considerably above his predicted value.

Column 5 of Table 1.2 gives the error of prediction, $y - y'$, for each individual. Column 6 gives the squares necessary for calculating the standard error of estimate for the entire group. The sum of column 6 is entered directly into the first formula at the lower right of Table 1.2 to determine the standard error of estimate. Below this, the more conventional computational formula involving the standard deviation of y and the square of the correlation coefficient, $\sigma_y \sqrt{1 - r_{xy}^2}$, gives equivalent results.

We may now summarize the mechanics of predicting the criterion of leadership from personality test scores on dominance. Raw scores on the two variables were first converted to deviation scores to simplify the calculation of the correlation coefficient, which was interpreted as the mean of the products of standard scores on dominance and leadership. The correlation coefficient, in turn, was seen to be an important component of the regression coefficient, which gives the least-squares solution of the linear equation relating the criterion and predictor variables. Substituting observed predictor scores into the regression equation yielded a predicted criterion score for each individual. Error in prediction for the entire group was expressed as the standard deviation of differences between observed and predicted criterion scores, which is called the standard error of estimate. The standard error of estimate may also be expressed in terms of the standard deviation of criterion scores and the correlation between predictor and observed criterion scores. (We anticipate that some readers will experience a sense of uncertainty about some or all of the preceding recapitulation, and we strongly encourage such readers to review in detail the mechanics presented in Tables 1.1 and 1.2 and Figure 1.2.)

Multivariate Prediction

From our introductory remarks about the nature of correlational analysis, it should be apparent that prediction problems in personality assessment are not limited to the two-variable case. A more representative situation is that in which a number of prediction variables are combined to forecast a given criterion. In the prediction of leadership behavior from dominance scores, we did not assume that dominance was the only trait that might conceivably be systematically related to the criterion of leadership. Leadership is, no doubt, a many-faceted behavior, with dominance only one of its components. In addition to being ascendant, the good leader seems to be one who gets along with people. More systematically, we are asserting that a personality test of "sociability" will be systematically associated (correlated) with the leadership ratings of peers. This situation is represented in Figure 1.4.

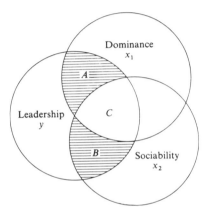

Fig. 1.4 Components of variance in multivariate prediction.

In Figure 1.4, variation in the criterion behavior of leadership is represented by the circle on the left, y. The portion of this criterion variance which is predictable from dominance scores, x_1, is represented by the overlap of the circle on top with the one on the left (shaded area A plus area C). The manner in which this common variation between dominance and leadership may be employed for prediction has been demonstrated in considerable detail. In our empirical example, we found the correlation between dominance and leadership to be .61, and we predicted leadership ratings from dominance scores via a regression equation with a standard error of estimate of 7.10.

Figure 1.4 shows that the relationship between personality test scores on sociability and leadership ratings is identical to that found between dominance test scores and leadership ratings. That is, $r_{x_2 y}$, the correlation between sociability, x_2, and leadership, y, is .61. Leadership ratings can thus be forecasted from sociability scores by use of the regression equation $y' = b_2 x_2$.

Since the standard error of estimate, $\sigma_{y \cdot x} = \sigma_y \sqrt{1 - r_{xy}^2}$, does not depend on the variability of the predictor variable, σ_x, leadership ratings can be predicted from sociability scores equally as well as from dominance scores. However, it should also be clear that leadership ratings may be more accurately forecasted from a *combination* of dominance and sociability test scores than they can be from either predictor score alone because *different components* of the criterion of leadership are predicted by dominance and sociability, respectively. Shaded area A represents that portion of the criterion variance which is uniquely predicted from test scores on dominance. Shaded area B represents that portion of the criterion variance which is uniquely predicted by sociability test scores. Since dominance scores and sociability scores predict different aspects or components of the criterion of leadership, the combination of these two scales in prediction will result in a more comprehensive prediction of variation in leadership ratings.

Figure 1.4 also illustrates the fact that while dominance and sociability test scores account for unique aspects of criterion variance (represented by shaded areas A and B, respectively) they are also associated with some of the same components of leadership variance (represented by area C). The area in which variances from all three measures are associated (area C) represents variance that is *redundant* from the standpoint of prediction. That is, although dominance test scores predict components of criterion variance uniquely (shaded area B), there is an area (area C) predicted by *both* variables which will not result in an increment in prediction over that obtained with either test separately. We can see that the extent of predictive redundancy is a function of the correlation that exists between the two predictors, $r_{x_1 x_2}$.

Figure 1.4 illustrates very nicely two principles of multivariate prediction that can be grasped intuitively in advance of understanding the details of the prediction model. First, employing additional variables which are themselves correlated with the criterion will result in more comprehensive (and hence more accurate) prediction to the extent that the additional variables are associated with *different* components of variance in the criterion. Second, additional predictors will be associated with different or unique aspects of criterion variance to the extent that the predictors themselves are uncorrelated. Multivariate prediction may thus be understood as an attempt to improve on the comprehensiveness of prediction by judicious selection of variables that are highly correlated with the criterion ($r_{x_1 y}, r_{x_2 y}, \ldots, r_{x_n y}$) but only slightly correlated among themselves ($r_{x_1 x_2} = r_{x_1 x_n} = r_{x_2 x_n} = 0$). Selection of predictor variables which are themselves uncorrelated ensures that a minimum amount of predictive redundancy will occur, so that the variance accounted for by each additional variable will add a unique increment of prediction.

In our discussion of components of criterion variance, we have assumed implicitly that variance in criterion scores can be represented by an *additive* combination of associated predictor variances.   The basic multivariate prediction model makes this assumption explicitly.   Variance in criterion scores is assumed to be most efficiently predicted by the summation of weighted predictor scores:

$$y' = b_1 x_1 + b_2 x_2 + \cdots + b_n x_n.$$

The expression above is a general expression of which our previously considered two-variable prediction problem was a special case. The regression of a number of variables on the criterion is expressed as the additive combination of each predictor multiplied by its associated b value. Prediction by multiple regression is not so easy to visualize geometrically as was the two-variable prediction problem.   An attempt is made in Figure 1.5 to give a

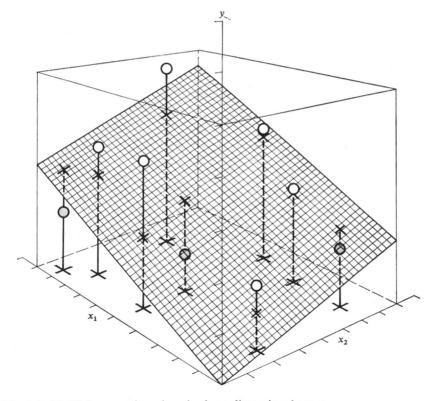

Fig. 1.5 Multiple-regression plane in three-dimensional space.

geometric representation of the prediction of a criterion from the additive combination of two predictors.

As shown in Figure 1.5, the three coordinates representing three variables, y, x_1, and x_2, may be thought of as the three lines converging at the corner of a room. In the room, canes of different heights stand at different distances from the corner. The handle or top of each cane is that point in three-dimensional space which represents the intersect of the criterion scores, y, and the scores on the two predictors, x_1 and x_2. A regression plane of the form $y' = b_1x_1 + b_2x_2$ has been extended from the bottom of the corner (origin) into the three-dimensional space. Points along this plane correspond to all possible y' values. For any values of x_1 and x_2, there is a corresponding y value of the actual criterion score represented by the top of the canes. Some of these values fall on the regression plane ($y' = b_1x_1 + b_2x_2$), some fall above it, and some fall below. The expression $\sum (y - y')^2/N$ gives the amount of predictive error involved in prediction of y values from values of x_1 and x_2.

On the basis of considerations raised by Figure 1.5, it can now be stated that the goal of multivariate prediction is the same as that of prediction from a single variable. In the two-predictor case illustrated in Figure 1.5, the goal is to find an expression, $y' = b_1x_1 + b_2x_2$, such that predictive error is at a minimum. By our least-square criterion, predictive error will be minimized when

$$\frac{\sum (y - y')^2}{N} \rightarrow \text{minimum}.$$

Note that in this two-predictor example, there are two unknown regression coefficients, b_1 and b_2, which must be determined.

The function $\sum (y - y')^2/N$ or, by substitution, $\sum (y - b_1x_1 - b_2x_2)^2/N$ will be minimized at those values of b_1 and b_2 for which the corresponding partial derivatives are zero. Thus, to find those values of b_1 and b_2 at which the function is a minimum, we obtain the partial derivatives of the function $\sum (y - b_1x_1 - b_2x_2)^2$ with respect to b_1, and then with respect to b_2:

$$\frac{df}{db_1} = \frac{-2 \sum x_1(y - b_1x_1 - b_2x_2)}{N},$$

$$\frac{df}{db_2} = \frac{-2 \sum x_2(y - b_1x_1 - b_2x_2)}{N}.$$

We next set both of these derivatives equal to zero and solve them simultaneously for b_1 and b_2 by resorting to definitions of the correlation coefficient and the variance term:[5]

$$
\begin{aligned}
\frac{-\sum x_1 y}{N} + b_1 \frac{\sum x_1^2}{N} + b_2 \frac{\sum x_1 x_2}{N} &= 0, \\[2mm]
\frac{-\sum x_2 y}{N} + b_1 \frac{\sum x_1 x_2}{N} + b_2 \frac{\sum x_2^2}{N} &= 0.
\end{aligned}
$$

$$
b_1 = \left(\frac{r_{x_1 y} - r_{x_2 y} r_{x_1 x_2}}{1 - r_{x_1 x_2}^2} \right) \frac{\sigma_y}{\sigma_{x_1}},
$$

$$
b_2 = \left(\frac{r_{x_2 y} - r_{x_1 y} r_{x_1 x_2}}{1 - r_{x_1 x_2}^2} \right) \frac{\sigma_y}{\sigma_{x_2}}.
$$

Although considerably more elaborate, the regression weights, b_1 and b_2, for the multivariate prediction equation are of the same general form as those employed in the single-predictor case.   A correlational term, in parentheses, is multiplied by the ratio of variation in the criterion, σ_y, to variation in the predictor, σ_{x_1}.   Examination of the correlation term for b_1 reveals algebraically the two principles that were expressed graphically in Figure 1.4.   In the multivariate prediction equation, the first predictor, x_1, is weighted by the expression

$$
b_1 = \left(\frac{r_{x_1 y} - r_{x_2 y} r_{x_1 x_2}}{1 - r_{x_1 x_2}^2} \right) \frac{\sigma_y}{\sigma_{x_1}}.
$$

The correlation term, in parentheses, indicates that the first predictor is to be weighted by the extent to which it correlates with the criterion, $r_{x_1 y}$, adjusted for the amount of redundant predictive variance in the second predictor, $r_{x_2 y} r_{x_1 x_2}$, expressed as a ratio to an expression indicating the degree of independence of the two predictors, $1 - r_{x_1 x_2}^2$.   The correlation term, in parentheses, thus indicates that predictor x_1 should be weighted to the extent that it contributes unique predictive variance to the regression equation.   The correlation term is, in turn, adjusted by the ratio of the criterion standard deviation to the predictor standard deviation for the reasons discussed previously under simple linear regression.   The regression weight for the second predictor, b_2, expresses the same properties, this time in terms of characteristics of the second predictor.   The unique predictive variance of

---

5.   These simultaneous equations may be solved by direct algebraic expansion and substitution, although the resultant expressions are too burdensome for inclusion here.   Readers familiar with the algebra of determinants may see an excellent application to this problem.

both predictors is combined by summation in the basic multivariate prediction model:

$$y' = \left(\frac{r_{x_1y} - r_{x_2y}r_{x_1x_2}}{1 - r_{x_1x_2}^2}\right)\frac{\sigma_y}{\sigma_{x_1}} x_1 + \left(\frac{r_{x_2y} - r_{x_1y}r_{x_1x_2}}{1 - r_{x_1x_2}^2}\right)\frac{\sigma_y}{\sigma_{x_2}} x_2.$$

Multiple Correlation

In our discussion of the Pearson product-moment correlation coefficient, we emphasized the relationship between scores on the predictor and observed criterion scores. Multiplying the predictor by a constant, b_1x_1, does not change its correlation with the criterion: $r_{yx_1} = r_{y(b_1x_1)}$. From this it follows that the correlation between predictor and criterion scores is equivalent to the correlation between observed and predicted criterion scores:

$$r_{yx_1} = r_{y(b_1x_1)} = r_{yy'}.$$

By similar reasoning, the *multiple correlation* between observed and predicted criterion scores, $R_{yy'}$, expresses the correlation between the criterion scores and an additive combination ($y' = b_1x_1 + b_2x_2$) of predictor scores: $R_{y \cdot x_1x_2}$. Note that the multiple-correlation coefficient is indicated by a capital R.

We may now define the multiple correlation, in deviation scores, as

$$R_{yy'} = R_{y \cdot x_1x_2} = \sqrt{b_1 \frac{\sigma_{x_1}}{\sigma_y} r_{x_1y} + b_2 \frac{\sigma_{x_2}}{\sigma_y} r_{x_2y}}.$$

By reference to our definitions of b_1 and b_2 (p. 27), we can see that we have, in effect, converted our variables to standard scores.[6] The formula above is obviously not a computational formula, although it does illustrate the properties of the multiple-correlation coefficient. As before, consideration of the b_1 and b_2 terms indicates the manner in which the "zero-order" correlations, r_{x_1y} and r_{x_2y}, are adjusted by the extent of correlation existing between the two predictors, $r_{x_1x_2}$, before they are summed.

We may now return to our example of leadership prediction from dominance and sociability scores. Referring again to Figure 1.4, we can now illustrate the manner in which the correlation between the two predictors affects the multiple-correlation coefficient. In Figure 1.4, we have assumed that the "predictive validity" of both dominance and sociability are the same. That is, the correlation between each predictor and the criterion of leadership

---

6. This bit of notational legerdemain is necessitated by the fact that regression weights for deviation scores are *not* equivalent to regression weights for standard scores. Here we are preserving the notation of deviation score regression weights (b_1, b_2) while capitalizing on properties of standard scores ($\sigma_{z_{x_1}} = \sigma_{z_{x_2}} = \sigma_{z_y}$).

was assumed to be .61. Using either dominance or sociability scores by themselves, we would be able to predict 37 percent of the variance of the leadership criterion: $(.61)^2 = .37 \times 100 = 37$. The practical question to be raised involves the extent to which increments in predictive validity will be attained by inclusion of the additional variable of sociability in the forecasting of leadership. The following examples indicate the size of the multiple-correlation coefficient between leadership and the composite of dominance and sociability, with different degrees of correlation existing between dominance and sociability.

$$\left.\begin{array}{l} r_{x_1 y} = .61 \\ r_{x_2 y} = .61 \\ r_{x_1 x_2} = .00 \end{array}\right\} \quad R_{y \cdot x_1 x_2} = .86$$

$$\left.\begin{array}{l} r_{x_1 y} = .61 \\ r_{x_2 y} = .61 \\ r_{x_1 x_2} = .20 \end{array}\right\} \quad R_{y \cdot x_1 x_2} = .71$$

$$\left.\begin{array}{l} r_{x_1 y} = .61 \\ r_{x_2 y} = .61 \\ r_{x_1 x_2} = .40 \end{array}\right\} \quad R_{y \cdot x_1 x_2} = .66$$

When the correlation between dominance and sociability is zero, a multiple-R of .86 is obtained by using the two variables in composite prediction. A multiple-R of .86 indicates that 74 percent of the leadership criterion is reliably predicted by the composite and this figure represents an increment in predictive validity of 37 percent (74–37) over that obtained by use of dominance scores alone. When the two predictor variables are correlated .20, the multiple-R is .71 and the increment in predictive validity is only 13 percent. When dominance and sociability scores are correlated .40, the multiple-R is only .66, which represents a net gain in predictive validity of only 7 percent. It should be apparent, from this example, that the utility of additional predictor variables falls off rather sharply to the extent that additional predictors are correlated among themselves. In general, optimal prediction of personological criteria requires predictor tests which are not only valid, r_{xy}, but which are independent as well: $r_{x_1 x_2} = r_{x_2 x_3} = 0$.

As with predictions from a single test, the goal of multivariate prediction is to minimize discrepancies between observed and predicted criterion scores: $\Sigma (y - y')^2 / N$. The standard error of estimate in multivariate prediction is therefore expressed in terms that are the same as those employed in bivariate prediction:

$$\sigma_{y \cdot x_1 x_2} = \sqrt{\Sigma (y - y')^2 / N} = \sigma_y \sqrt{1 - R^2_{y \cdot x_1 x_2}}.$$

Predictive accuracy in the multivariate case can be seen to depend on the variability of criterion scores, σ_y, and the coefficient of alienation (indicating the amount by which *base-line* predictive error is reduced by the magnitude of the multiple correlation between composite predictors and the criterion). Should the multiple-R be zero, the standard error of estimate can be seen to be equal to the standard deviation of criterion scores. Increases in magnitude of the multiple correlation will reduce this error of estimate in the manner indicated by the expression involving the radical. The prediction example illustrated in Figure 1.4 indicates that the predictive validity of dominance and sociability test scores is the same, $r_{x_1 y} = r_{x_2 y} = .61$, and that the two predictors are correlated, $r_{x_1 x_2} = .40$. As we have already indicated, this constellation of correlations yields a multiple-R of .66. From our previous computations, we know that the standard deviation of leadership scores is $\sigma_y = 8.96$. Hence the standard error of estimate for this multivariate prediction situation is

$$\sigma_{y \cdot x_1 x_2} = \sigma_y \sqrt{1 - R_{y \cdot x_1 x_2}^2} = (8.96)\sqrt{1 - (.66)^2} = 6.73.$$

When predictions are made with the two-predictor multiple-regression equation, we can be 68 percent confident that subjects with given dominance, x_1, and sociability, x_2, scores will have an actual leadership rating, y, within the limits $y' \pm 6.73$. By comparison with the previously obtained standard error of estimate for prediction from dominance scores alone, 7.10, we can see that the utilization of sociability as an additional predictor enabled us to reduce predictive error. We may also note that the absolute amount by which predictive error has been reduced is not great, primarily because the additional predictor (sociability) was itself rather highly correlated with the original predictor (dominance).

SUPPRESSOR VARIABLES

Characteristics of Suppressor Variables

The basic prediction model calls for predictor variables, $x_1, x_2, \ldots, x_n$, that are highly related to the criterion, r_{xy}, but generally unrelated to each other, $r_{x_1 x_2}$. Ideally, we might have a set of predictors of high criterion relevance whose average intercorrelations approach zero. Each predictor in this situation would be validly predicting a different component of the criterion with a minimum of predictive redundancy. In practice, however, it is often difficult to find more than one or two highly valid predictors that do not share variance in common with other valid predictors.

Horst (1941) was first to call attention to the fact that additional predictors need not always function in the manner above to contribute predictive increments to the multiple-regression equation. In fact, variables which have exactly the *opposite* properties of conventional predictors may function in such a manner as to produce surprising increments in multiple prediction. Such variables are called "suppressor variables" (Horst, 1941) and they are characterized by a lack of predictive validity, $r_{xy} = 0$, and high apparent redundancy with other predictors, $r_{x_1x_2}$. To understand this apparently paradoxical behavior of a "suppressor" variable, it is helpful to consider once again the hypothetical components of variance entering into prediction.

In Figure 1.6 hypothetical components of variance are represented by three overlapping circles which stand for the criterion behavior, y, the predictor variable, x_1, and a third variable, s, which operates as a "suppressor." The criterion behavior, y, might be thought of as the psychological trait of anxiety, a complex and multifaceted set of behaviors (Cattell and Scheier, 1961). The predictor in this case, x_1, can be thought of as a questionnaire measure of "anxiety" that enjoys a limited amount of success in predicting at least some of the variance of the trait of anxiety. This predictive success is represented by the heavily shaded area shared in common by the trait, y, and the test, x_1.

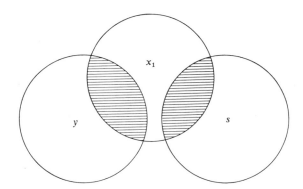

Fig. 1.6 Components of variance involved in suppressor effects.

The fact that the anxiety test is not successful in predicting all the components of the trait of anxiety is indicated by the unshaded area of y, representing components of anxiety which might, in principle, be predictable from other tests or procedures. Of equal importance here is the fact that a considerable portion of the test variance, x_1, is irrelevant to the predictive task at hand. This means that the test is carrying a heavy load of "baggage" which is of no use for the present purpose. One such irrelevant component of test variance might be the trait of "defensiveness," known to operate in questionnaire measures of this type (Meehl and Hathaway, 1946). Regardless of its importance as a contributor to test-score variance, such "defensiveness" is irrelevant to the prediction of anxious behavior.

Let us now suppose that we discover a third variable, s, that possesses the properties illustrated in Figure 1.6. The suppressor variable, s, overlaps with that portion of the test variance that is irrelevant to the prediction of the criterion (shaded area). Thus our suppressor variable will be uncorrelated with the criterion (no overlapping components) but correlated with the predictor (overlapping components). What is most important is the fact that the suppressor variable overlaps (correlates with) that portion of the test variance which is unwanted "baggage" and which might be conveniently "checked" for the purpose of this prediction. The use of a suppressor variable in multiple-regression prediction does just that.

We will now make this illustration concrete by specifying the intercorrelations that exist among the variables above. Let us assume the correlation between predictor and criterion, $r_{x_1 y}$, to be .60; the correlation between the suppressor and the criterion, r_{sy}, to be .00; and the correlation between the predictor and suppressor variable, $r_{x_1 s}$, to be .50. Computing the multiple correlation between the criterion and the two predictors, $R_{y \cdot x_1 s}$, we obtain the value of .70, a surprising predictive increment over the use of the test alone. Computing the regression equation by the method of least squares, we find that the optimal regression weight of the suppressor variable, s, is *negative* in sign: $y' = .8x_1 - .4s$. This latter equation illustrates the manner in which unwanted, irrelevant variance in a test, x_1, is literally *subtracted* out of the prediction equation by the suppressor.

The logical and mathematical bases of suppressor effects have been explicated in great detail (Chandler, 1961; Lubin, 1957; Marks, Christal and Bottenberg, 1961; McNemar, 1945; Meehl, 1945b; Wherry, 1946), and procedures for locating suppressor variables have been suggested (Levine, 1952). Although the use of suppressor variables does not require a departure from the basic multiple-regression prediction model, the decision to use such variables requires a revision of the usual criteria for "good" predictors. Traditionally, predictor variables that are uncorrelated with the criterion of interest are automatically excluded from further consideration. The class of variables which are uncorrelated with significant criteria is, unfortunately, a very large one, and some rationale must guide the identification of those variables which have suppressor properties. Further, since suppressor methodology is a somewhat costly departure from standard procedures, the use of suppressor variables should lead to a *practical* increment in predictive validity. For this reason, it is appropriate to consider the available evidence relating to the empirical effectiveness of suppressor variables in predicting socially relevant criterion measures.

Acquiescence as a Suppressor Variable

Acquiescent response tendencies constitute part of a large class of individual differences in test-taking behavior that have been designated as "response sets" (Cronbach, 1946) and, more recently, "response styles" (Jackson and Messick, 1958).   Cronbach (1950) was among the first to suggest that the tendency to answer *true* to objective test items, irrespective of their content, represented a criterion-irrelevant variable that might be effectively employed as a suppressor.   This would require an independent measure of response acquiescence that was uncorrelated with the criterion of interest but substantially correlated with scales designed to predict this criterion.   Although the idea was originally formulated with respect to aptitude and ability testing it has been adapted to personality-assessment procedures which employ true-false items in criterion prediction.

   In achievement testing, extremely difficult items may have relatively little meaning for subjects of moderate ability, and hence they may fall back on habitual response mechanisms (agreement) mainly irrelevant to the task at hand (Cronbach, 1950).   Personality-inventory items that reflect subject matter about which the respondent has no very strong or definite opinions may also provide occasion for the emergence of ingrained stylistic tendencies irrelevant to the content of the items (Wiggins, 1962; Hanley, 1962). Individuals who characteristically agree with such items introduce response variance that may lower the correlation of the predictor scale with the criterion measure.

   Fricke (1956) selected items from his Opinion Attitude and Interest Survey (Fricke, 1963) that seemed to represent subject matters about which college students, as a group, had no very strong opinions.   These items were answered *true* by about 50 percent of a sample of University of Michigan students and answered *false* by about the same percentage.   Fricke reasoned that individuals who answered many more than half of this pool of 69 items in the *true* direction were doing so on the basis of acquiescent tendencies rather than on the basis of attitudes toward the subject matter.   Therefore, he used these 69 items as a "trap" for the overacquiescent individual by combining them into a single scale in which all items were keyed *true*.   Since these items had been selected on the basis of their "neutrality" for college students, high scores on this scale were considered indicative of acquiescence.

   In previous work, Fricke had developed an empirical personality scale, x_1, that predicted the criterion, y, of grade-point average during the freshman year in college: $r_{xy} = .33$.   The rationally derived 69 item "all true" scale, s, was found to have suppressor properties in this prediction situation.   That is, the "all true" scale was uncorrelated with grade-point average ($r_{sy} = -.04$) but substantially correlated with the personality scale ($r_{sx_1} = -.57$).   The use of the "all true" scale as a suppressor variable in multiple-regression prediction of grade-point average resulted in a multiple correlation of .39 in a group of 209 male freshman students. Considering both the modest size of the initial validity coefficient, .33, and the rather meager increment gained by use of a suppressor, .06, the practical implications of this demonstration are far from dramatic. Nevertheless, Fricke's study does represent a successful application of suppressor methodology to a prediction problem involving a personality variable.

A study by Fulkerson (1958) provides a representative example of the application of suppressor methodology to a realistic prediction problem in personality assessment. Fulkerson was interested in improving the predictive validity of an empirically derived adjustment key, x_1, in forecasting carefully constructed criterion measures of adjustment, y, among Air Force personnel. In developing his acquiescence measure, Fulkerson followed a procedure designed to ensure that the resultant scale would meet the theoretical requirements of a suppressor measure that had been previously enumerated by Cronbach (1950).

Following the line of reasoning Fricke had taken, Fulkerson first selected a set of items that were answered *true* by approximately 50 percent of subjects in samples of Air Force personnel. In a group of subjects for whom criterion measures of adjustment were available, the responses of subjects with high and low scores on adjustment were contrasted in an item analysis of the previously selected "ambiguous" (50 percent endorsement) items. On the basis of this latter analysis, only those items were selected which did *not* discriminate between high- and low-adjustment groups. This second step of item selection is of considerable importance in that criterion irrelevance is thereby statistically ensured for the final suppressor measure. To ensure a degree of internal consistency in his final acquiescence measure, Fulkerson eliminated all items that were not significantly correlated with the total acquiescence score (based on all items). The 24 items constituting the final acquiescence key, s, thus met the criteria of: (a) "ambiguity" (50 percent endorsement); (b) criterion irrelevance (lack of significant differentiation between high- and low-adjustment groups); and (c) internal consistency (high inter-item correlations).

In a sample of 200 aviation cadets, the final acquiescence key was not significantly correlated with a composite adjustment criterion based on interviews, tests, records, and ratings: $r_{sy} = .11$. As required, however, the acquiescence key, s, was significantly correlated with the adjustment key: $r_{sx_1} = .61$. (This latter correlation was not ensured by item-selection procedures but was expected on the basis of theoretical formulations regarding the role of acquiescence as a suppressor variable in adjustment measures.)

The criterion prediction to be improved on was the correlation of .36 between the adjustment key, x_1, and the composite-criterion measure of adjustment, y. The addition of the acquiescence key to the predictor yielded a multiple correlation of .39. The regression equation was

$$y' = 3.6x_1 - 4.4s.$$

Since the regression weights for both predictor and suppressor were so nearly equal in weight, a simple subtraction of the acquiescence key from the adjustment key was performed in three additional samples. Correlations with the criterion measure of the adjustment key alone and the adjustment key minus the acquiescence key are presented in Table 1.3. Predictive increments due to the use of a suppressor variable are found in samples of aircraft commanders, copilots, and ROTC students. Statistically significant increases in the size of the correlation coefficients occurred in the latter two samples.

Table 1.3 Validity coefficients of adjustment key alone and corrected by an acquiescence suppressor. (After Fulkerson, 1958.)

	Aircraft commanders ($N = 191$)	Copilots ($N = 196$)	ROTC students ($N = 130$)
Adjustment scale	.25	.29	.29
Adjustment *minus* acquiescence	.28	.32*	.36*

* Significant (p < .05) increase over preceding correlation

Fulkerson's findings are similar to those reported by Fricke (1956) in that relatively small increments in prediction are obtained in a situation of initially limited predictive validity. Fulkerson's study is especially noteworthy for its ingenuity of scale-construction procedures, methodological rigor, and employment of additional validation groups.[7] The practical and representative nature of the prediction paradigm in Fulkerson's study suggests that suppressor variables may serve a useful, though limited, function in the forecasting of adjustment. Again, however, the practical increment in prediction achieved appears low in relation to the elaborateness of the method whereby the suppressor was developed.

---

7. The purpose of additional or "cross-validation" groups will be explained at the end of this chapter.

Other Response Styles

Acquiescence is but one of several "response styles" that have been identified in relation to self-report personality inventories (see Chapter 9). The response styles of "social desirability" and "good impression" have also been nominated as candidates for suppressor variables. Social desirability refers to stylistic tendencies to answer personality test items in a direction considered socially desirable (culturally approved) rather than in terms of honest self-evaluation (Edwards, 1957). Good impression refers to the tendency of subjects to attempt to make a maximally favorable impact on the administrators or possible interpreters of a personality test (Gough, 1952). Although such response styles may cloud the "logical validity" of personality tests (Cronbach, 1950), they may also be exploited as suppressors of variance irrelevant to the prediction at hand (Jackson and Messick, 1958; Meehl and Hathaway, 1946).

A thorough and systematic evaluation of the possible use of the above-mentioned response styles as suppressor variables has been made by Dicken (1963). Dicken evaluated the possible use of response styles as suppressors with the California Psychological Inventory (CPI). The choice of this instrument was especially fortunate in that both predictor and criterion scores are available (Gough, 1957) for a number of personality dimensions relevant to social adjustment. Moreover, most of these scales were empirically constructed without concern for stylistic response "contamination." In evaluating the effects of response style, Dicken employed measures that were generally representative of those utilized in this field of research (Wiggins, 1962).

Assessment samples included high school students ($N = 443$) rated by principals, applicants to medical school ($N = 70$), engineering students ($N = 66$), research scientists ($N = 45$), and female college students ($N = 51$)—all of whom were rated by professional psychologists on the basis of a variety of tests and situations during a two-day "living in" assessment (MacKinnon *et al.*, 1958). All ratings were made with respect to the personality dimensions putatively measured by the scales of the CPI, e.g., dominance, responsibility, impulsivity, etc. Validity coefficients were thus available for a variety of carefully constructed empirical scales which had been correlated against carefully selected criterion measures on personality variables of considerable social and interpersonal relevance.

The suppressor potential of three response-style measures was investigated with respect to the prediction situations noted above. The first of these measures was an empirically constructed scale of "good impression" (Gough, 1952) which had previously been established as an accurate forecaster of such tendencies (Dicken, 1960). By reference to ratings of social desirability given by high school students and normative endorsement frequencies from another group of high school students, Dicken constructed a scale of social desirability designed to trap subjects whose item responses were primarily determined by this response style. Dicken's scale of social desirability comprised relatively "neutral" items (50 percent endorsement) that were keyed in the direction of rated social desirability. Subjects answering many more than half of these items in the keyed direction were considered to be responding in terms of social desirability. This same group of items was also made to serve as an "acquiescence" scale by keying all responses in the *true* direction. Although there are several shortcomings to such a measure of acquiescence, it is representative of acquiescence measures employed by other workers in the field (Hanley, 1957). Intercorrelations among predictors, x, criterion ratings, y, and the three potential suppressors, s, were obtained for the 60 separate predictions included in the design. Dicken summarized his findings as follows:

Suppression of desirability resulted in significant predictive gain in only 4 of 24 comparisons in the high-school data. In the non-high-school data, only 2 of 36 comparisons show a significant suppression effect, a result attributable to chance. There is no instance in the grand total of 50 comparisons of a large gain in validity by suppressing desirability.... The expectation that correcting personality scores for individual differences in desirability responding will increase validity is not fulfilled. There were no instances of successful suppression of acquiescence variance. (Dicken, 1963, p. 712.)

The most frequent reason for the failure of stylistic scales to behave as suppressor variables was their generally insignificant correlations with the predictor measures, r_{xs}. For this reason, Dicken suggests that the extent of irrelevant contribution of response styles to prediction has been exaggerated, at least for instruments of the CPI variety. The second most frequent reason for failing to obtain suppression effects lay in the low, but positive, association between certain suppressors and certain criterion measures, r_{sy}. Unfortunately, the magnitude of the correlations between response styles and criterion measures was not great enough to encourage the inclusion of stylistic measures as additional predictors in the conventional multiple-regression model.

Dicken's conclusions received further support from an extensive series of analyses conducted by Goldberg, Rorer, and Greene (1970). These authors were also interested in the suppressor potential of response-style measures from the California Psychological Inventory. In addition to two of the stylistic scales employed by Dicken (1963), Goldberg *et al.* employed eleven specialized response-style scales, most of which were developed by Lovell

(1964). Thirteen diverse criterion measures of such characteristics as peer-rated personality traits, social conformity, popularity, and academic interest and achievement were available for 152 freshman college women who had also been administered the CPI.[8] The acquiescent potential of each of the 13 stylistic scales, s_i, was evaluated in the prediction of all 13 criterion measures, y_i, from CPI scales, x_i, which were known to be related to at least one of the criterion measures.

The base line of prediction in this study was taken to be the correlation between each of the 13 criterion measures, y_i, and the CPI scale, x_i, with which it was most highly correlated. Attempts were made to improve on this single variable regression equation, $y_i' = b_1 x_i$, by including each of the 13 suppressor variables one at a time: $y_i' = b_1 x_i \pm b_2 s_i$. In each comparison, the inclusion of a stylistic variable could result in: (a) an improvement over the original correlation between predictor and criterion (either as a suppressor or as an additional predictor), (b) essentially the same correlation, or (c) decreased prediction of the criterion. Since there were 13 such comparisons for each of 13 criterion measures, 169 regression analyses were performed.

Of the 169 comparisons, only 30 showed evidence of stable suppressor effects. Of these 30, only half were numerically higher than the original correlations, $r_{x_i y_i}$, and only *one* showed any substantial improvement over the original predictor alone. As was true of Dicken's (1963) study, the stylistic scales did not correlate highly enough with the CPI predictors to provide any general suppressor effects. The authors concluded: "It is hard to see how even the most enthusiastic advocate could interpret these findings as indicating support of the hypothesis that stylistic scales are potentially useful as suppressor variables" (Goldberg *et al.*, 1970).

Considered as a whole, the available evidence relating to the empirical effectiveness of suppressor variables in predicting socially relevant criterion measures is not impressive. In those instances in which suppressor variables have been developed successfully (Fricke, 1956; Fulkerson, 1958), the net predictive *gain* does not appear to be greater than that which would have been achieved by employing a more conventional variable as an additional predictor. Systematic efforts to exploit at least one class of variables (stylistic) that would logically seem to be potential suppressors (Dicken, 1963; Goldberg *et al.*, 1970) have yielded extremely discouraging results. The number of *unpublished* failures to find suppressor variables cannot be estimated. It seems reasonable to conclude that the utility of suppressor variables remains to be demonstrated.

---

8.   The original study (Hase and Goldberg, 1967), from which these data were obtained, will be described in more detail in Chapter 9.

THE PREDICTION PARADIGM IN PERSONALITY ASSESSMENT

Steps in Prediction

In our consideration of the practical problem of forecasting leadership ratings from measures of dominance and sociability, we have focused exclusively on the *statistical* procedures employed. Such statistical procedures are merely tools existing in the context of a much broader set of considerations and procedures in personality assessment. Until now, we have not mentioned the manner in which "leadership" was defined, the reasons for selecting dominance and sociability, or the method by which one actually implements the regression equation in the selection of potential leaders. These considerations belong to a class of procedures which are generally agreed to constitute the basic steps in the prediction process (Bechtoldt, 1951; Horst, 1941; Sarbin, 1944; Thorndike, 1949). The steps are: (a) criterion analysis, (b) selection of instruments, (c) development of predictor battery, (d) combination of data, (e) cross-validation, and (f) application of predictor battery. These steps are best illustrated by reference to procedures that are routinely followed in the selection of personnel for business and industrial settings. They are not limited to these settings, however, and should be considered as basic issues involved in the prediction of human behavior for any purpose.

Criterion Analysis

The criterion is, of course, that aspect of human performance which we wish to predict in a given assessment problem. Although such a concept may appear obvious on first consideration, criterion analysis has proved to be the most recondite and vexing issue confronting personality assessment today. In fact, criterion analysis is typically referred to as "the criterion problem" in much the same manner as we speak of "the racial problem" or other complex issues defying easy solution. Basically, the "problem" resides in the considerable discrepancy that typically exists between our intuitive standards of what criteria of performance should entail and the measures that are currently employed for evaluating such criteria.

Criteria are value judgments concerning standards of performance that are made by the sponsors of an assessment program. On the surface, such value judgments seem simple enough in that the stated goal is phrased as the selection of "good" salesmen, physicians, students—that is, individuals who will perform well in their chosen vocation. These value judgments represent *ultimate* criteria of performance (Thorndike, 1949) which refer to behaviors that are temporally quite distant from the time of assessment. Ultimately, the "good" physician may be expected to diagnose his patients correctly, to make them better, to contribute basic knowledge to his field, and to participate actively in the affairs of his profession and his community. But which of these several activities constitutes "the criterion" of a good physician? Perhaps they all do, but if so, we must inquire into the relations that exist among them. The physician who participates in community affairs is not necessarily the best diagnostician, nor is the most successful healer necessarily the man who will contribute to scientific knowledge. These individual components of the ultimate criteria of a good physician may be slightly, or even negatively, correlated with one another. Attempts to develop a global index of *the* criteria of a good physician by use of a weighted or unweighted composite of individual components may result in a measure with very unsatisfactory metric properties.

As thorny as the problems of ultimate criteria may be, they are, at present, mainly academic since few such criteria are actually employed in practice. Even where it is possible to define such criteria precisely enough to obtain measures, the collection of such measures is so time-consuming and expensive as to be practically prohibitive. Personality-assessment procedures are primarily based on *intermediate* criteria of performance (Thorndike, 1949) which are presumed to be related to ultimate criteria. Graduation or non-graduation from medical school is substituted for the more long-term values implicit in the notion of a "good physician." Under current standards of licensing, it is certainly necessary for a man to obtain an M.D. to become a physician, but the degree, in itself, hardly ensures that he will become a "good physician" (Kelly, 1957; Gough, 1965). The expense and professional time involved in a medical education prohibits the acceptance of all applicants to medical school and that fact, in turn, leads to an emphasis on more *immediate* criteria of performance (Thorndike, 1949), such as grade-point average (GPA) during the first year or even first semester of medical school. In this connection, it is disconcerting to note that the widely used Medical College Admissions Test correlates $+.18$ with first-year GPA in medical school and $+.07$ with fourth-year grades (Gough, Hall and Harris, 1963). The correlations of this test with the ultimate criteria of a "good physician" are not known, but there is ample reason to be pessimistic.

Although psychologists are continually berated for their present inability to cope with the almost insurmountable criterion "problem" in most areas (Roman and Prien, 1966), they must also be admired for their courage in taking this first and most difficult step in the prediction process. Positions must be filled, decisions must be made, and society must somehow go on in the absence of final solutions to the problems posed by ultimate criteria. At best, the assessment psychologist can develop an informed awareness of and sensitivity to the pitfalls of criterion analysis and supplement this by common sense. Criterion measures should be selected with respect to their *relevance* to both intermediate and ultimate criteria. Careful attention should be given to the likely *multidimensional* nature of any criterion, and global measures should be developed with extreme caution. Criterion measures should be *reliable* and should be evaluated by the same psychometric standards applied to predictor measures. Finally, criterion measures must be *practical* in the sense that they must become available in time to be used in the evaluation of an ongoing assessment program.

Selection of Instruments

Whether the criterion standard is ultimate, intermediate, or immediate, the next step in the prediction process involves the selection of assessment instruments to be employed in the forecasting of criterion scores. Ideally, such instruments would involve components of the criterion standard itself, as in the "job-sample" technique (Wernimont and Campbell, 1968). A two-hour typing assignment under conditions similar to working conditions provides a "sample" of the actual criteria to be predicted in the selection of typists. The simulated job conditions of the In-Basket Test (Frederiksen, Saunders, and Wand, 1957) provide a sample of the decisions made by executives in the course of their everyday work routine. Although there are many industrial and clerical positions for which job-sample techniques are appropriate, the majority of positions for which personality-assessment programs are developed involve criteria that are too complex or too distant to lend themselves readily to this approach. As a consequence, the second stage of the prediction process typically involves a choice of instruments believed to sample behaviors which are *related* to components of the criterion. The importance of this stage of the prediction process should not be under-estimated since the overall success of the assessment program will be determined by the extent to which such instruments are, in fact, related to the criterion of interest.

The point of view offered in the present volume holds that human judgment should play a major role in this step of the prediction process (Chapter 5) and that this judgment should be guided by explicit theoretical considerations (Chapter 10). From this viewpoint, it is necessary to take exception to current practice with respect to the selection of instruments in many areas of assessment. In some areas of industrial, clinical, and governmental selection, testing instruments have often been selected on the basis of such considerations as tradition, face validity, convenience, and economy. Although there are virtues associated with each of these considerations, there are limitations as well, and the relative emphasis placed on each consideration must be carefully evaluated for each selection program.

Once a particular type of instrument has been introduced in a selection program, its continued usage tends to be institutionalized as a "tradition."

Because "intelligence" and "personality characteristics" are thought to be important components of many job criteria and because the Wonderlic (1939) Personnel Test and the Bernreuter (1931) Personality Inventory appeared as early measures of these two components, their employment in industrial selection has tended to become traditional. Because the Rorschach (1921) Test was among the earliest measures of "total personality functioning," its usage has become traditional in global clinical assessment. Although there is no reason why tradition should be avoided, it is critically important that the *reasons* for any given tradition in personality assessment be carefully scrutinized.

There are two quite distinct reasons why traditions exist in personality assessment: (a) a given test or battery of tests has consistently been found to be highly correlated with certain kinds of criterion standards; or (b) a given test or battery of tests has become a "standard operating procedure" in the prediction of certain types of criteria, in the absence of any empirical confirmation of its usefulness in forecasting such criteria or even in the face of specific evidence suggesting that the instrument is virtually unrelated to the criterion of interest. Selecting a traditional test for the first reason is based on the sound rationale that a test of *known* validity is preferable to a test of *unknown* validity, regardless of how "promising" the unknown test may appear. There is no scientific justification for selecting traditional tests under the second rationale, and perpetrators of such practices must be condemned for their inertia.

Even when instruments are selected on the basis of their known predictive capability, it is still important to guard against the establishment of rigid traditions. It seems unlikely that there are any selection problems for which completely optimal test batteries have been discovered. Regardless of any one test's degree of success in selecting candidates for a given position, there almost certainly exist other tests or procedures that might result in improved selection. For this reason, research in test development is an essential aspect of any selection program. Continuous experimentation and evaluation of procedures benefit both institutions which practice selection and the science of personality assessment.

Face validity refers to the extent to which an applicant views the content of a given test as relevant to the position for which he is being considered. An applicant for a typing position would tend to view a 15-minute typing test as quite reasonable, i.e., *relevant* to the job for which she is applying. However, if she were given a personality questionnaire and asked to respond *true* or *false* to the statement "My sex life is satisfactory," she might become disconcerted by the apparent lack of relationship between the test item and the job for which she was applying. In addition to being puzzled by its apparent irrelevance, the applicant might consider such a question an unwarranted invasion of privacy. Because of the widespread use of personality questionnaires and projective techniques in personality assessment, it is almost inevitable that many assessment batteries will contain tests that seem "irrelevant" to the job or are "offensive" to some of the applicants. As we will see later (Chapter 9), the complexities of self-report frequently require the employment of apparently "irrelevant" items.   Resistance to such measurement can be overcome only by appropriate instructions to candidates and education of the general public with respect to the intricacies of psychological testing.

The issues of offensiveness and personal privacy are more complex. If "offensive" items are the *only* means of accurate assessment in a given selection problem, their employment can be justified on the basis of the social importance of accurate selection. Frequently, however, psychologists will defend the use of a traditional instrument (e.g., the Minnesota Multiphasic Personality Inventory) without full exploration of alternative possibilities. Invasion of privacy is a vital issue, and deviations from psychologists' official ethical standards (American Psychological Association, 1963) are not to be condoned. Face validity is primarily an issue of public relations and not one of predictive validity. The use of a given instrument for a given selection problem can never be justified solely on the grounds of face validity. Given two equally valid tests, the test possessing face validity might be chosen, although such a circumstance seldom arises in practice. Empirical validity is the primary consideration in the selection of psychological tests for an assessment battery.

From a practical point of view, considerations of convenience and economy must enter into the choice of instruments to be included in an assessment battery. Such considerations may often be at odds with the more basic concern for criterion relevance, and compromises which seriously impair the effectiveness of an assessment program must be avoided. It is paradoxical that those who are willing to concede the necessity of several hours of testing to appraise the relatively "narrow-band" dimensions of verbal and numerical aptitude will often question the necessity of devoting more than 15 minutes to the appraisal of a domain as complex as "personality."   On the continua of convenience and economy there are many steps, ranging from elaborate individual clinical and situational assessment to self-administering and self-scoring group tests. Other things being equal, it is in the best interests of the institution to employ the most convenient and economical assessment procedure. As we will show in Chapter 6, the cost of any psychological test or assessment procedure can be evaluated only in terms of the value or utility placed on accurate and inaccurate selection decisions. Where the "cost" of inaccurate decisions is especially high for individuals or institutions, the employment of expensive assessment procedures may be more than justified.

Two additional sets of characteristics of psychological tests must be considered in evaluating their appropriateness for inclusion in a prediction battery: the degree of *specificity* of the characteristics measured by the tests and the extent to which the tests employed are *independent* of one another. The greatest specificity of measurement occurs when "job-sample" techniques are employed as predictors since specific components of the criterion itself are measured under simulated circumstances. Such specificity of measurement is possible only when the criterion is concrete and narrowly defined. In selection programs in which two or more jobs are being considered simultaneously (Chapter 6), the employment of job-sample measures may be inefficient in that a large battery of specific skills may have to be administered to all applicants. Under such circumstances, it would be more appropriate to attempt to assess general traits or skills which underlie the specific behaviors involved in job samples. Factor analysis is a commonly employed statistical technique for reducing a large number of specific measures to their underlying general components.

Although individual tests may be selected on the basis of their own merits, the nature of multivariate prediction requires that "redundancy" of measurement be held to a minimum. Tests which are *independent* of one another may tap different components of the criterion and allow for a greater degree of predictive accuracy when combined in the multiple-regression model. Here again, factor analysis is commonly employed to select underlying dimensions of criterion-related performance that are independent of one another. In addition to their efficiency, measures of general traits tend to be less affected by minor changes in the nature of the criterion and by changes in the composition of subject samples. Although general measures of personality functioning may be developed by the statistical examination of many empirical studies, the discovery of such general measures may be enormously facilitated by the explicit utilization of existing psychological theories or models of personality (Chapter 10).

Development of Predictor Battery

Once decisions have been made about the instruments to be employed, it is necessary to obtain empirical information on the relationships between predictor variables and measures of criterion performance. Under ideal circumstances, the predictor measures would be administered to a typical group of applicants, all of whom would be accepted for the position, irrespective of their scores on the predictor battery. At some subsequent time, measures of criterion performance would be obtained, and the relations between predicted, y', and actual, y, criterion scores would be computed.

This ideal design is seldom realized in practice because there are few practical selection situations in which it is possible to accept all applicants. More typically, selection decisions must be made on the basis of the preliminary battery itself or of other selection procedures currently employed by the institution. When selection occurs during the preliminary tryout of a selection battery, at least two sources of bias enter the picture. Assuming that the selection procedure employed possesses some validity, it will result in a restriction of range on criterion measures, σ_y, as well as on predictor measures, σ_x, and thereby tend to give underestimates of the degree of relationship between predictors and criterion measures that would have obtained in an unselected population. More important, especially where the validity of the selection procedure is unknown, is the fact that the actual performance of unaccepted candidates will never be known. Under such conditions, it is seldom possible to determine the number of rejected candidates who might have achieved a satisfactory level of performance on the criterion task. For these reasons, it is desirable whenever possible to institute an "experimental" selection program in which all applicants are accepted, at least until criterion measures become available. The usefulness of information gained under such a procedure may well justify the costliness of such an "experimental" selection program.

When the criterion standard is of an intermediate or ultimate nature, it is often not practical to wait until such measures become available for current applicants. Under such circumstances, one course of action is to administer the selection battery to currently employed applicants on whom intermediate or ultimate criterion scores are already available—a procedure known as *concurrent validation*. Where earlier selection has already taken place, concurrent-validation designs are subject to the shortcomings already mentioned: a restriction of range of criterion and of predictor scores and an absence of criterion measures for preselected subjects. In addition, concurrent-validation designs assume a *comparability* between new applicants for a position and individuals who have been employed for some time. In addition to changes which may take place on the basis of specific training or experience in the criterion situation, the motivation and test-taking attitudes of employed workers are likely to be different from those of applicants taking the battery under conditions of actual selection.

Combination of Data

Whether criterion measures are obtained under conditions of free selection, simultaneous selection, or concurrent employment, the predictor measures must be combined in such a manner as to yield the most accurate forecast of criterion scores. Although the multiple-regression model discussed earlier in this chapter is the most common method of combining data in large-scale assessment programs, it is by no means the only method available. For example, the "multiple-cutoff" approach (Chapter 6) ensures a minimal level of acceptable performance on important attributes for all individuals selected. In addition, there exist a variety of alternative methods for combining predictor data to obtain a forecasted criterion score (Chapters 2 and 3). Together with the choice of *statistical* procedures to be followed in combining data, a decision has to be made regarding the extent to which *human judgment* will enter into the final prediction (Chapter 4). Finally, it must be decided whether selection decisions will be determined entirely by the nature of the obtained empirical relationships between predictor variables and criterion scores or whether selection decisions will be guided by a theoretical framework, involving a personality "model" (Chapter 10) which interprets such relationships.

Cross-Validation of Predictor Weights

In the typical multivariate-prediction situation in which multiple-regression equations are employed, a weighted linear combination of variables is determined in such a way as to minimize the discrepancy between actual and predicted criterion scores: $\sum (y - y')^2/N$. When the correlation is computed between predicted criterion scores generated by the multiple-regression equation and actual criterion scores earned by the subjects, $r_{yy'}$, an *estimate* is obtained of the degree of relationship between this combination of predictor scores and the criterion measures. In an example presented earlier in this chapter, we found that uncorrelated measures of dominance and sociability could be combined to forecast leadership scores to the extent of yielding a multiple correlation of .86 between predictors and the criterion of leadership. Because the multiple-regression equation provides a least-squares solution in any given *sample*, the question arises as to how accurate an estimate such a multiple correlation would be of the degree of relationship expected between predictors and a criterion measure in *similar samples* of subjects. Although the issue of generality of results is not unique to personality assessment, there is an aspect of *prediction* paradigms that requires a distinction between what we may call "shrinkage" and what will be referred to as "cross-validation."

Our example involving the prediction of leadership from dominance and sociability scores may be thought of as prediction from a *fixed set*—in this instance, $n = 2$—of predictor variables. The least squares solution yielded by the multiple-regression technique provides an optimal combination of predictor variables that "fits" the peculiarities of the sample under consideration. When these "custom-made" weights are applied to other samples that differ in any way from the original sample, the degree of predictive accuracy attained in the new samples will always be less. Consequently, it is appropriate to correct the multiple-R obtained in the original sample for the degree of shrinkage expected when the regression weights are applied to the same predictors in new samples of subjects. Several formulas have been suggested for estimating the shrinkage of multiple-R when weights are applied to new samples (Lord, 1950; McNemar, 1969b; Wherry, 1931), all of which correct for the extent to which the number of predictors is large relative to the number of subjects. Although such formulas do not yield equivalent results (e.g., Uhl and Eisenberg, 1970), each provides a means of estimating shrinkage in multiple-R that does not require the use of additional samples of subjects.

Shrinkage formulas for multiple-R are based on a number of statistical assumptions (e.g., Wherry, 1951) that are seldom realized in practice. For this reason and others, the procedure known as *cross-validation* has been advocated as an appropriate alternative to shrinkage estimation in practical selection settings (e.g., Mosier, 1951). Typically, a group of subjects, for whom both predictor and criterion measures are available, is divided at random into a *derivation sample* and a *cross-validation sample*. A set of regression weights is determined for the derivation sample, and the same weights are then employed for prediction of the criterion in the cross-validation sample. The correlation between predicted and obtained scores in the cross-validation sample is then interpreted as a realistic estimate of the predictive validity of a fixed set of predictors in practical selection situations. A common variant of this cross-validation design is that of *double cross-validation* (Mosier, 1951; Norman, 1965). Here a large sample of subjects is randomly divided into groups designated Sample A and Sample B. Regression weights derived from Sample A are employed to calculate a multiple-R in Sample B. Conversely, regression weights derived from Sample B are used to calculate a multiple-R in Sample A. The average of the two resulting multiple-R's is assumed to be a realistic estimate of the validity of the fixed set of predictors.

McNemar (1969b, p. 208) has recently argued that the cross-validation procedures above are inappropriate when multiple-R is estimated with respect to a *fixed set* of predictors. Shrinkage estimates based on the total sample of subjects should be more accurate than estimates based on the smaller sample sizes employed in cross-validation procedures (Gollob, 1967). In addition, the "random" assignment of subjects to cross-validation groups may introduce new sources of sample bias that are greater than the bias present in the total sample (Campbell, 1967). Empirical studies of prediction from a set of fixed predictors have demonstrated that, in typical selection situations, estimates of multiple-R based on the entire sample are more accurate than estimates obtained from cross-validation procedures (Campbell, 1967;

Chandler, 1964).   Similarly, Herzberg (1969) has demonstrated that, despite
the assumptions under which correction for shrinkage formulas are applied,
they tend to give satisfactory estimates of the multiple-R that exists in the
total population.   Hence, despite the fact that the use of cross-validation
procedures for fixed sets of predictors is widely advocated, there appears to
be little theoretical or empirical justification for employing such procedures
as an alternative to correction for shrinkage formulas based on the entire
sample of subjects available.

Frequently, a *selected set* of predictor variables is chosen from a larger
number of variables on the basis of the results obtained in a given sample.
Such a procedure runs the risk of capitalizing on the peculiarities of the
original sample in two distinct ways: (a) the most promising predictor
variables in the original sample may not be the most promising variables in
other samples, and (b) the multiple-R based on regression weights determined
in the original sample will be an overestimate of the degree of predictive
accuracy to be expected in different samples of subjects.   Although shrinkage
formulas correct for the second kind of bias, they do not take into account
the fact that predictor variables have been *selected* on the basis of their
predictive validities and intercorrelations in a single sample of subjects.
When predictor variables have been selected, it is essential to employ some
variant of the cross-validation procedure to obtain an estimate of the
multiple-R that would be obtained in other samples of subjects (McNemar,
1969b, p. 208).   Cross-validation is required whether the variables selected are
combinations of scales, single scales, or items.   Scales are frequently constructed by means of *item-analysis* procedures that select the most promising
items from a larger pool.   Although the "weights" assigned to these items in a
scale may be simply 1 or 0, the predictive validity of the items can be
determined only through cross-validation on other samples of subjects.

Cross-validation designs range in complexity from simple cross-validation on another sample, to double cross-validation (Mosier, 1951), to
elaborate extensions of double cross-validation (Norman, 1965), to the
prediction of *each* subject's criterion score from the regression equation
computed on the basis of data for the other N-1 subjects (Gollob, 1967).
McNemar (1969b) has suggested that *new* regression weights be calculated
for the cross-validation sample and that the *corrected* (for shrinkage) multiple-
R from that sample be taken as an estimate of the validity of the subset of
predictors in realistic selection situations.   Such a procedure circumvents the
implied need for infinite cross-validation, since regression weights derived
from Sample A will not be optimal for Sample B; weights for Sample B will
not be optimal for Sample C; etc.   Although the optimal cross-validation
procedures have not been established for the many different prediction
situations in which such procedures are applied, there is general agreement

that *some* form of cross-validation is mandatory when predictions are made from a selected set of variables.

Application of Predictor Battery

The final step of the prediction process involves the actual application of an assessment battery for purposes of selection. A testing program is instituted to provide standard conditions for the administration of tests to applicants for the position in question. The test responses are scored by clerical or mechanical means to yield the basic data for prediction. Cross-validated regression weights are applied to the test scores, which are then combined in such a manner as to yield a predicted criterion score for each applicant. Applicants may then be rank-ordered in terms of their predicted criterion scores, which represent their probable degree of success on the job. A "cutoff point" on the predicted criterion scores is then employed for making the final personnel decisions. Depending on a number of external considerations, the cutoff point will be set so that a certain proportion of applicants falling above it will be accepted for the position and the remainder will be rejected.

Although the basic form of the prediction paradigm is the same for most large-scale assessment programs, the details of implementation will vary widely with the nature of the prediction problem. The "external considerations" just referred to will be discussed in some detail in later chapters. They are such considerations as the nature of the personnel decision being made, the number of applicants to be accepted, the proportion of potentially successful applicants available, and the consequences to the individual and the institution of certain outcomes of prediction. Recognition of the critical importance of these and other external considerations leads to a shift of emphasis from the psychological testing techniques of the prediction paradigm to the broader set of issues involved in the theory of personnel decisions (Chapter 6). But the issues of decision theory must be postponed until after we have considered several important features of the basic prediction paradigm.

SUMMARY

Scientific psychology in the present century has been characterized by developments along two parallel paths that have come to be known as experimental and correlational psychology. Although the distinction is arbitrary and primarily traditional, it is nevertheless true that personality-assessment procedures have been based largely on correlational methods. The *product-moment correlation coefficient* is the mean of the products of standard scores on two variables. Although this index expresses the percentage of variance that two variables share in common, it does not lend itself to inferences regarding causality. Nevertheless, it serves the very useful function of enabling us to predict one variable (criterion) from scores on another (predictor). The correlation coefficient is an important component of the *regression coefficient*, which gives the least-squares solution of the linear equation relating predictor and criterion variables.

Prediction problems in personality assessment typically involve the linear combination of a number of predictors for the purpose of forecasting criterion scores. For optimal multivariate prediction, it is desirable to have predictors that are highly correlated with the criterion but uncorrelated with one another. An exception is the *suppressor variable* which is highly correlated with a predictor but uncorrelated with the criterion. Suppressors operate in such a manner as to subtract criterion-irrelevant variance from a predictor variable. Although suppressor variables are mathematically plausible, the available evidence relating to their empirical effectiveness as predictors of socially relevant criterion measures is not impressive.

It is generally agreed that the prediction paradigm in personality assessment consists of several distinct steps: (a) criterion analysis, (b) selection of instruments, (c) development of predictor battery, (d) combination of data, (e) cross-validation, and (f) application of predictor battery. These steps were illustrated by reference to procedures that are routinely followed in the selection of personnel for business and industrial settings. They are not limited to these settings, however, and should be considered as basic issues involved in the prediction of human behavior for any purpose.

ALTERNATIVE PREDICTION MODELS: I. MODERATOR VARIABLES AND HIGHER-ORDER FUNCTIONS

The predictive limits that seem to have been reached in applications of the basic prediction model to personality data (Chapter 1) have inspired many workers to experiment with alternative models of prediction. Although suppressor variables represent a class of *variables* not usually considered in linear multiple regression, their inclusion in prediction equations in no way departs from the mathematical assumptions underlying multiple regression. That is, although the correlational properties of potential suppressors are different from those previously held desirable for inclusion in multiple-regression equations, the utilization of such variables in prediction is accomplished by simply "plugging them in" to the familiar equation. The present chapter considers a number of instances in which the linear multiple-regression equation itself has been challenged as being inadequate for the prediction of human behavior and in which alternative mathematical procedures have been employed.

Computational complexities, which were once thought to limit the application of more elaborate methods of prediction, have been tremendously reduced since the advent of high-speed computers (Borko, 1962). However, the goal of a prediction model is, as always, efficient prediction. Therefore, the introduction of more complex models into the field of personality assessment must be justified on this basis and not in terms of mathematical elegance or the pursuit of complexity for its own sake. This premise will guide our consideration of alternative models that have been suggested as showing promise in the prediction of personological criteria.

MODERATOR VARIABLES

When the multiple-regression equation is employed in prediction, it is assumed that the criterion variable, y, can be best expressed as an additive combination of predictor variables, each of which has been weighted for its unique contribution to criterion variance: $y' = b_1 x_1 + b_2 x_2 + \cdots + b_n x_n$. Because this function is a simple additive one, it is assumed that any combination of predictor variables which yields the same weighted sum will be associated with the same value of the criterion variable. There is no provision in this model for special patterns or configurations of predictor variables that might be associated with unique values of the criterion. Should a situation be encountered in which special patterns of predictor variables are associated with unique values of the criterion, the multiple-regression model would not do justice to the situation. Let us consider one such possible situation.

Returning to an earlier example (Chapter 1, p. 31), we may once again consider the prediction of anxious behavior, y, from a questionnaire measure of anxiety, x_1, and an index of test-taking "defensiveness," x_2. It now seems more realistic to assume that both predictors are correlated with the criterion measure, and to make the example simple, we shall make both correlations positive by keying our defensiveness measure, x_2, in the direction of "openness." Experience suggests that the anxious behavior of extremely "open" subjects may be quite predictable from self-report measures of anxiety. It is not implausible that pathologically "defensive" subjects might also be highly predictable from their self-reports, if one were to ignore the *sign* of the correlation. Since it is likely that most people are somewhat reluctant to say "bad" things about themselves, subjects in the middle ranges of defensiveness might turn out to be the least predictable from test measures.

In the situation above, we would expect a high positive correlation between predictor and criterion, $r_{x_1 y}$, for subjects scoring high on "openness," x_2; a moderate and possibly not significant correlation between predictor and criterion for subjects of intermediate "openness"; and a moderate and possibly significant negative correlation for defensive subjects scoring low on the "openness" variable. This being the case, we can no longer assume that any combination of predictor variables which yields the same weighted sum will be associated with the same value of the criterion variable. In fact, certain patterns or configurations of predictor variables appear to be regularly associated with unique values of the criterion. Specifically, the relationship between self-reported anxiety and anxious behavior, $r_{x_1 y}$, varies directly as a function of degree of openness, x_2.

When $r_{x_1 y}$ varies in a non-chance fashion as some function of x_2, we speak of a significant *interaction* existing between x_1 and x_2 in the prediction of y (Lee, 1961). Since the relationship between anxious behavior and self-report is modified by concurrent status on an openness measure, the openness index belongs to the class of variables that have been termed "moderator variables" (Saunders, 1955, 1956). Because moderator variables combine in a fashion other than that expressed by the multiple-regression equation, it has been proposed that more appropriate mathematical models be employed in prediction situations involving such variables.

Differential Predictability

Saunders (1956) coined the term "moderator variable" to refer to what he alleges are "many examples of situations in which the predictive validity of some psychological measure varies systematically in accord with some other independent psychological variable" (p. 209). In point of fact, Saunders' case rests mainly on the data, provided by Frederiksen and Melville (1954), that called attention to the "differential predictability" phenomenon in an academic prediction situation. "Differential predictability" refers to a situation in which the correlation between a predictor and criterion, $r_{x_1 y}$, can be shown to vary as a function of classification on a third variable, x_2 (Frederiksen and Melville, 1954). In such a situation, the third variable, x_2, is designated a "moderator variable" (Saunders, 1956).

Compulsiveness as a Moderator Variable

Frederiksen and Melville set for themselves the rather courageous task of attempting to predict grade-point average during the freshman year in engineering school from interest scores on the Strong Vocational Interest Blank (Strong, 1959). On the basis of more general considerations regarding the expected relationship between interest and achievement measures, it is not surprising that the engineer scale of the Strong, x_1, is correlated with grade-point average, y to the extent of $r_{x_1 y} = .10$ in a group of 154 engineering freshmen at Princeton University (Frederiksen and Melville, 1954). What is novel, however, is the ingenious reasoning that led Frederiksen and Melville to suggest that this predictive relationship, $r_{x_1 y}$, would vary as a function of the degree of "compulsiveness" of the engineering students involved. That is, assuming some relationship between interest and achievement, they expected that this relationship would be stronger (more predictable) for less compulsive students than it would be for compulsive students. The relationship between interest and achievement in the compulsive student might be obscured by the fact that compulsive tendencies interfere with the expression of motivation in performance. In the noncompulsive student, who is free of such inefficient tendencies, the relationship between interest and achievement might be of greater magnitude. By indirect but insightful reasoning, Frederiksen and Melville hypothesized that the accountant scale of the Strong Vocational Interest Blank might serve as an index of compulsiveness and hence moderate the relationship between engineering interest and performance in engineering school.

Indeed, when the 154 freshmen were divided into two groups on the basis of high and low scores on the accountant scale, evidence for differential predictability was found. Within the compulsive subgroup of engineering students (those with high scores on the accountant scale) the correlation between engineer scale and grade-point average, $r_{x_1 y}$, was $-.01$. For the noncompulsive subgroup (low scores on the accountant scale) the correlation was .25. Thus, although the overall correlation between interest and performance was only .10, reclassification of subjects on the basis of their accountant scale score, x_2, led to considerable differential predictability (the difference between correlation coefficients in the two subgroups was significant at the .05 level).

An independent replication of the study was performed six years later by Frederiksen and Gilbert (1960) with a group of 107 Princeton freshmen engineering students. The correlation between engineering interest and grade-point average was .15. Division of the subjects into high- and low-compulsive (accountant scale) groups resulted in correlations of .07 for compulsives and .20 for noncompulsives. Although the latter two values are not significantly different from each other, the direction is clearly the same as that of the original study.

In the original student sample, Frederiksen and Melville (1954) employed an additional index of compulsiveness which was, perhaps, even more ingenious than that provided by the Strong accountant scale. Their reasoning was as follows: Although independent measures of *speed* of reading comprehension and of vocabulary tend to be highly correlated, there are nevertheless some individuals who read more slowly than would be expected on the basis of their vocabulary score. It might very well be that engineering students who read more slowly ("carefully") than would be considered necessary from their verbal intelligence (vocabulary) do so because of "compulsive" tendencies to read and reread material unnecessarily. A scatter plot of the positive correlation between speed of reading comprehension and vocabulary in a group of engineering students might look something like Figure 2.1.

The data presented in Figure 2.1 represent a moderate positive correlation between speed of comprehension and vocabulary score. The regression line drawn through the points represents the least-squares prediction of reading speed from vocabulary. In general, subjects falling above this regression line read well for their verbal intelligence level. Subjects below the line read more slowly than would be expected from their vocabulary scores. Using such a regression line as a dividing point, Frederiksen and Melville classified all subjects falling above the regression line as "noncompulsive" and all falling below as "compulsive." As already indicated, the relationship between engineering interest and grade-point average was found to be $r_{x_1 y} = .10$ in the total group of 154 students. However, when the students were subdivided

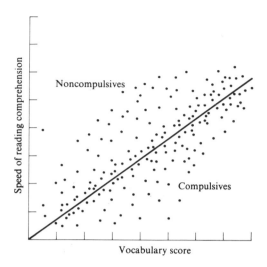

Fig. 2.1 Regression plot of speed of comprehension on vocabulary.

into high- and low-compulsive groups on the basis of falling above or below a regression line such as that in Figure 2.1, the correlation was found to be $-.04$ in the compulsive group and $.29$ in the noncompulsive group (a significant difference at the .05 level).

The 1960 replication of this study with 107 engineering students indicated that differential predictability held for this group also; the correlation between engineering interest and grade-point average was .15 for the entire group. Splitting the group into those falling above and below the regression line resulted in a correlation of $-.01$ for compulsives and $.36$ for noncompulsives, a replicated difference clearly significant at the .05 level. Similar results were obtained using the Strong mathematics–physical science teacher scale as a predictor, x_1, as Table 2.1 indicates. However, that table also suggests the probable instability of the accountant scale as a compulsiveness measure, due to the fact that a *reversal* in differential predictability occurred in the 1960 study. Some additional doubt regarding the construct validity of one or both of the compulsiveness measures employed in these studies stems from the fact that the two indices of "compulsiveness" (accountant scale and reading test scores) correlated zero in both the 1954 and 1960 studies.

Further evidence of the instability and lack of generality of "compulsiveness" as a moderator variable is provided in a more recent replication by Stricker (1966). In a group of 145 freshmen engineering students from Stanford University, no evidence for differential predictability of grade-point average was found for the engineer or math–physical science teacher scales

Table 2.1 Differential predictability of academic success (GPA) in "compulsive" and "noncompulsive" groups. (Frederiksen and Melville, 1954; Frederiksen and Gilbert, 1960.)

| | 1954 study (N = 154) | | | |
| | Accountant Scale | | Reading Comprehension | |
	Compulsive (N = 79)	Non-compulsive (N = 75)	Compulsive (N = 81)	Non-compulsive (N = 73)
Engineer scale	−.01	.25	−.04	.29
Math–physical science teacher scale	.09	.21	.07	.26

| | 1960 study (N = 107) | | | |
| | Accountant Scale | | Reading Comprehension | |
	Compulsive (N = 55)	Non-compulsive (N = 52)	Compulsive (N = 54)	Non-compulsive (N = 53)
Engineering scale	.07	.20	−.01	.36
Math–physical science teacher scale	.34	.03	.08	.17

when the group was dichotomized on the accountant scale and on the reading test. Although evidence for differential predictability was found with some of the 50 occupational-interest scales scored (e.g., "farmer"), they were different scales than had been previously reported to yield differential predictability. Moreover, virtually no evidence of differential predictability with the two compulsiveness measures was found in samples of liberal arts men ($N = 598$) or women ($N = 393$), indicating a decided lack of generality of the phenomenon. As before, the two indices of "compulsiveness" correlated zero in both engineering and liberal arts groups, a finding which, Stricker (1966) argues, cannot be attributed to the unreliability of the measures.

The latest—and possibly it will remain the final—replication of the original Frederiksen and Melville (1954) study was reported by Kellogg (1968). In a group of 212 freshmen engineering students from Alfred University, no evidence for differential predictability of grade-point average was found for the engineer scale when the group was dichotomized on the accountant scale and on the reading test. The math–physical science teacher scale predicted better for noncompulsives ($r = .22$) than for compulsives ($r = -.03$) when groups were dichotomized on the accountant scale. However, when groups were dichotomized on the reading test, there was a tendency for the math–physical science teacher scale to predict better for compulsives ($r = .16$) than for noncompulsives ($r = .03$), a reversal of direction from the original studies. The results in the three replications of the original study suggest that when the procedures of Frederiksen and Melville are repeated the findings are likely to be nonsignificant or even reversed. At best, the presumed differential-predictability effect is a very weak one.

Other Moderators

In a quite different assessment context, Steineman (1964) has demonstrated that a variable selected on logical grounds leads to modest differential predictability of a criterion measure from a predictor variable. In a sample of impressive size, 13,448 Navy enlisted men, Steineman attempted to predict reenlistment in the Navy from responses to a single biographical item relating to reenlistment plans. Responses to this item ranged from negative, through undecided, to positive career intentions. Criterion data (reenlistment versus termination) were collected approximately four years after response to the biographical item. In the total sample of subjects, the validity coefficient of the item was: $r = .13$.

Reasoning that item responses made by recruits with some knowledge about the Navy would be more valid than responses made by less-informed individuals, Steineman employed a 45-item Naval Knowledge Test as a possible moderator of the relationship between biographical item response and the criterion of reenlistment. When all subjects were trichotomized on the Naval Knowledge Test, the following evidence for differential predictability was obtained.

Group	Range of r_{xy}	Median r_{xy}
High	$-.29$ to $.31$	.20
Middle	$-.08$ to $.29$	.10
Low	$-.09$ to $.32$	.10
Total	$-.08$ to $.22$	.13

Because of the sample size involved, this result must be considered evidence of a "significant" differential-predictability effect. Further, because of the importance of career prediction in assignment and training, Steineman argues that any means of improving the prediction of reenlistment is of practical value to the Navy. However, as will be demonstrated in Chapter 6, prediction of an infrequent event (less than 20 percent of Navy men reenlist) from a predictor of low validity ($r = .20$) is unlikely to be of practical value, especially since predictions can be made only for approximately one-third of the total sample.

The widespread belief that motivational factors "moderate" the relationships between trait predictors and performance criteria has been partially substantiated by Ghiselli (1968). A forced-choice inventory, presumably measuring a variety of traits and motives, was administered to 271 individuals holding middle-management positions in a variety of business and industrial settings. Criterion ratings of managerial success were used as a basis for classifying each individual as "more" or "less" successful. On four "motivational" factors, selected from the forced-choice inventory, managers were classified as "strong" or "weak" on the motive in question. The relationship between three "trait" predictors (also from the forced-choice inventory) and criterion ratings of success were examined within the "strong" and "weak" subgroups on each motive. The most significant results were as follows:

Traits	Job security		Self-actualization	
	Strong	Weak	Strong	Weak
Supervisory ability	.24	.58	.23	.47
Self-assurance	.48	.00	.06	.37
N	134	137	121	150

In the prediction of managerial effectiveness from "supervisory ability," motives of "job security" and "self-actualization" appear to function as moderators. The success of managers low on these motives is more predictable from a measure of supervisory ability. The trait of "self-assurance" predicts managerial success, but only for those managers who have a desire for "job security." Finally, "self-assurance" predicts success for those managers who are unconcerned with "self-actualization." These findings suggest that moderator variables may indeed be useful in applied-assessment settings. Unfortunately, the extent of their usefulness cannot be evaluated from the data presented by Ghiselli. In addition to the obvious issue of replicability, there was no direct comparison of the use of motivational factors as "moderators" with the use of motivational factors as additional predictors in multiple regression.

Moderated Multiple Regression

The evidence of "differential predictability" presented by Frederiksen and Melville led Saunders (1956) to conclude that compulsivity (as measured by the Strong accountant scale) acts as a "moderator variable" by modifying the relationship between interest, x_1, and performance y. Saunders argued that if differential predictability can be obtained by *dichotomous* groupings of subjects on the basis of their scores on the moderator variable, x_2, then modifications in the mathematical model of linear multiple regression must be made for prediction in the continuous case. Clearly, some predictive increment in the prediction of grade-point average might accrue from the employment of a continuous compulsiveness variable along with the original interest predictor, x_1. The traditional multiple-regression model for inclusion of this additional variable would be as follows:

$$y' = b_1x_1 + b_2x_2,$$

where

$\quad y' =$ predicted grade-point average;

$\quad x_1 =$ Strong interest key;

$\quad x_2 =$ compulsiveness index.

The expression above assumes that the correlation between the interest measure and the criterion, r_{x_1y}, is the same for all levels of the compulsiveness index. In fact, however, we know that the relationship r_{x_1y} varies directly as a function of values on x_2. One such mathematical expression of this, suggested by Saunders, would be

$$y' = b_1x_1 + b_2x_2 + b_3x_1x_2.$$

For the usual linear multiple-regression equation we have substituted an expression known as a *linear joint function* (Ezekiel and Fox, 1959). For students of experimental psychology, it might be helpful to view the expression above as the correlational counterpart of the concept of "interaction" in analysis of variance (Saunders, 1956; Lee, 1961). In this sense, components of criterion variance, y, are broken down into an additive (linear) combination of variance due to interest test scores, x_1, "compulsiveness," x_2, and their interaction, x_1x_2. If the interaction effect is one in which high values of x_2 are "unpredictable" (as is true of compulsiveness) the regression weight, b_3, will be negative in sign. If high values of x_2 are "predictable," the regression weight will be positive in sign. If a significant moderator effect is not present, b_3 will be equal to zero and the conventional multiple-regression equation will remain.

Saunders (1956) applied the linear-joint-function model above to the 1954 data of Frederiksen and Melville summarized in Table 2.1. Applying the linear-joint-function model to prediction of grade-point average from engineer scale, x_1, and accountant scale, x_2, he obtained a "moderated multiple correlation" of .153. Such a multiple correlation is not appropriately contrasted with the original zero-order correlation, $r_{x_1y} = .102$, but rather it should be compared with the multiple correlation obtained from using both x_1 and x_2 as predictors: $y' = b_1 x_1 + b_2 x_2$. In this case, the "moderated" multiple-R of .153 did not represent a significant improvement over the conventional multiple-R of .128, nor did the conventional multiple-R of .128 represent a significant improvement over the original zero-order correlation, $r_{x_1 y} = .102$. This particular example of Saunders does not represent a very strong argument for departure from the usual method of computing multiple correlations.

In further analyses, Saunders obtained a significant moderator effect by using the accountant scale as a moderator of the relationship between the math–science teacher scale and grade-point average. Here the original zero-order correlation, $r_{x_1 y} = .153$, was not significantly improved by employment of the accountant scale as an additional variable in conventional multiple correlation: $R_{y \cdot x_1 + x_2} = .163$. However, when the linear-joint method of computing a "moderated" multiple correlation was employed, the "moderated" multiple-R was found to be equal to .227, a value significantly different ($p < .05$) from the conventional multiple-R. Although statistically significant, the absolute increment in predictive power gained through the use of "moderated" regression is not of the size that would lead many to abandon the more conventional model. In addition, it is apparent from Table 2.1 that, rather than replicating in the 1960 study, the alleged moderator effect actually reverses itself.

Saunders also presents analyses of the accountant scale as a potential moderator of eight additional Strong scales in predicting grade-point average. Although two of these interest keys (real estate salesman and chemist) show significant moderator effects, they are not so striking as those found with the math–science teacher scale. In addition, the lack of any theoretical rationale for moderator effects to exist with these particular variables seriously detracts from the demonstration. In the same vein, Saunders' incidental finding that the accountant scale acts as a *suppressor* variable in conjunction with the psychologist scale, mortician scale, and banker scale must be judged as a theoretically trivial result.

In summary, a number of writers (Frederiksen and Melville, 1954; Saunders, 1955, 1956; Lee, 1961) have called attention to the highly plausible hypothesis that the "interaction effects" routinely reported by experimental psychologists may well be operating within the realm of individual differences. To account for such interaction effects, a modification of the conventional multiple-regression equation has been proposed by Saunders (1956) in the form of a linear joint function (Ezekiel and Fox, 1959). Although the presence of such interaction effects seems likely and the model proposed for handling them appropriate, evidence for the practical utility of the linear-joint-function model in personality assessment is at best suggestive. We emphasize "at best" because of some additional evidence, to be presented in the final section of this chapter, which illustrates a principle operating in opposition to the practical application of models departing in complexity from conventional multiple regression.

THE PREDICTION OF PREDICTABILITY

An interesting and provocative alternative to the usual multiple-regression method of prediction may be found in the work of Ghiselli (1956, 1960a, 1960b, 1963, 1968; Ghiselli and Sanders, 1967). Rather than elaborating on the basic mathematical model of multiple regression, Ghiselli has chosen to attack the problem of improved prediction directly by use of empirical procedures.

Differentiation of Individuals in Terms of Their Predictability

Ghiselli emphasizes the fact that the goal of prediction is to develop a method that will forecast criterion scores, y', as little different as possible from actually obtained criterion scores, y. That is, the goal of prediction is to minimize the absolute difference $|y - y'|$. The *direction* of such differences is, in Ghiselli's view, unimportant as both over- and under-estimates count as "errors." Any procedure which minimizes $|y - y'|$ is therefore, by definition, a good prediction procedure.

Figure 2.2 illustrates a typical situation of linear regression prediction in deviation form. In attempting to forecast criterion scores, y, from the predictor, x_1, we use the least-squares regression line as the basis for predicting criterion scores, y', for each value of x_1. Although this procedure tends to minimize the expression $|y - y'|$ for the entire group of individuals, it is clear that for *some individuals* such forecasted criterion scores are more accurate than for others. From among this group of subjects, we may consider subjects A, B, and C. As an individual, Subject A was rather poorly predicted by the regression equation, which tended to underestimate his actual criterion score. The absolute distance between the regression line and Subject A's actual position, $|y - y'|$, may be taken as an index of predictive accuracy for this subject, D_A. Similarly, for Subject B, whose criterion score was overestimated, the index D_B provides a measure of the amount of predictive error. The actual criterion score of Subject C was very accurately forecasted by the regression equation, and his D value will be close to zero.

It should now be clear that the statistic D represents an index of predictive accuracy, $|y - y'|$, which varies for different individuals in any prediction situation. That is, some subjects are more "predictable" than others and this can be expressed in terms of their D values. Except for the extremely unlikely case in which $r_{x_1 y} = 1.00$, it will always be possible to order individuals in

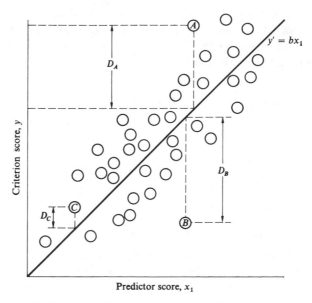

Fig. 2.2 A typical situation of linear regression prediction.

terms of this index of their absolute predictability (the *direction* of predictive error is of no importance here).

Let us suppose, as Ghiselli (1960b) does, that we knew subjects' predictability scores, *D*, in *advance* of making our predictions for them. Forgetting for a moment where this information comes from, let us consider the practical implications of such foreknowledge. If we were to restrict our predictions to those individuals whose *D* scores were close to zero ("most predictable"), we would be predicting with a great deal of accuracy in a subgroup of individuals for whom the correlation r_{x_1y} was close to unity. For the remaining individuals, whose *D* scores are very high ("least predictable"), we might suggest that predictions be made on the basis of some other test or, if predictions *are* made on this basis, that they be treated with considerable skepticism. From the standpoint of making vital decisions about the future life plans of individuals, it is clear that the *accuracy* of a prediction is as important as the nature of the prediction. When an undergraduate is told that a medical career is not his cup of tea, the question of the accuracy of such a statement arises as a more obvious issue than the question of what vocational alternatives he might consider. Certainly, no one would dispute the utility of possessing such foreknowledge of individuals' relative "predictability." Ghiselli's unique contribution lies in his specification of the conditions and procedures under which it might actually be possible to have such foreknowledge.

Returning to the D scores depicted in Figure 2.2, let us further suppose that we have discovered another test, x_2, that is *highly correlated* with the statistic D. That is, individuals who obtain high D scores also obtain high scores on Test x_2 and low-scoring subjects on D tend to score low on Test x_2. This second test, x_2, would be termed a "predictability test" by Ghiselli (1960b) since it could be used to predict subjects' "predictability" *in advance* of the administration of Test x_1. As Ghiselli (1963) indicated later, such a "predictability test" may be thought of as a "moderator variable" (Saunders, 1956) since it moderates the relationship between predictor and criterion by grouping subjects on a third variable.

Ghiselli's (1960b) first prediction study involved the forecasting of scores on a sociability questionnaire, y, from an empirically derived intelligence scale, x_1, appearing in a 64-item, forced-choice, self-description inventory (Ghiselli, 1954). A group of 232 students, who had taken the tests, was divided into a derivation group of 108 subjects and a cross-validation group of 124 subjects. The procedures followed with these two groups are outlined under "Study 1" in Table 2.2. In the derivation group of subjects, the correlation between sociability and intelligence, $r_{x_1 y}$, was used to generate

Table 2.2 Differentiation of individuals in terms of their predictability. (After Ghiselli, 1960b.)

Study 1: Intelligence, x_1, versus sociability, y

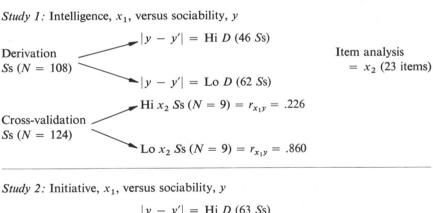

Study 2: Initiative, x_1, versus sociability, y

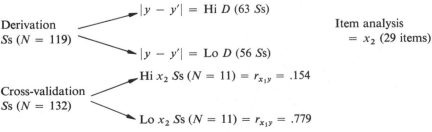

predicted criterion scores: $y' = b_1 x$. Differences between predicted and obtained standard scores, $D = |y - y'|$, were obtained for all subjects.

The 46 subjects with the highest D scores ("least predictable") and the 62 subjects with the lowest D scores ("most predictable") were selected as contrasted groups for item analysis. The responses of each of these two groups were compared for each of the 64 items in the self-description inventory. Those items were selected in which the difference in proportion of endorsement between the two groups exceeded ten percent. Twenty-three such items met this criterion and thus defined the "predictability" scale, x_2. Hence, by employing groups that were *known* to differ with respect to their predictability for this prediction situation, item-analysis procedures could be employed to select items which were *empirically* associated with this differential predictability. Although the 23-item predictability scale, x_2, thus constructed would, by definition, be effective in the population from which it was derived, its discriminating properties had to be assessed in an independent group of subjects.

The group of 124 cross-validation subjects, who had been set aside earlier, were arranged in order of their scores on the "predictability" test, x_2, and clear-cut evidence of differential predictability was found. In the group of nine subjects with the highest predictability scores ("least predictable"), the correlation between the predictor and the criterion was found to be only .226. In the group of nine subjects with the lowest scores on the predictability test ("most predictable"), the correlation was found to be .860. As subjects were eliminated from consideration on the basis of high scores on Test x_2, the validity coefficient, $r_{x_1 y}$, was found to vary as a monotonic increasing function of this elimination (Ghiselli, 1960b). In other words, as predictions are restricted to increasingly smaller proportions of the total sample on the basis of x_2 scores, the predictive validity of Test x_1 approaches unity. The practical implications of possessing this kind of *foreknowledge* with respect to individuals' predictability have already been discussed.

The second study reported by Ghiselli follows the same design as the first and differs little in detail, as Table 2.2 indicates. In this instance, the criterion of sociability, y, was predicted from an "initiative" scale derived from the same 64-item self-description inventory employed in the first study. Subjects of high and low "predictability" were differentiated on the basis of their D scores in the regression of sociability on initiative. An item analysis between high- and low-D subjects on the 64-item inventory this time yielded 29 items (11 of which overlapped with the earlier predictability scale). In applying the new predictability scale, x_2, to the cross-validation group, Ghiselli again obtained clear-cut evidence of "differential predictability." Exclusion of subjects on the basis of their "unpredictability," x_2, again led to successive increases in the validity coefficient, this time ranging from .154 to .779.

Although there was little difference in the nature of the tests employed in these two studies, it is clear that the results obtained in the first study may be replicated in other student groups.

In subsequent research, this same methodology has been successfully employed in the prediction of supervisors' ratings of factory workers, foremen, and executives (Ghiselli, 1963) and in the prediction of the psychometric characteristics of reliability of test response (Ghiselli, 1963) and of distribution of error scores (Ghiselli and Sanders, 1967). Although varying in the criterion predicted, almost all of these studies have employed predictor scales, x_1, and developed predictability indices, x_2, from the same 64-item forced-choice inventory. Thus the generality of the phenomenon has been demonstrated within a highly circumscribed set of items. The fact that the same item pool has been repeatedly investigated as a source of items for predictability scales allows for an assessment of the degree of generality of specific predictability scales. Although some overlap of items has been found in predictability scales developed for different purposes, Ghiselli (1963; Ghiselli and Sanders, 1967), like Saunders (1956), has emphasized that moderator scales are *highly specific* to a given test in a given prediction situation. This lack of generality of predictability measures has been reported elsewhere as well (Brown and Scott, 1966).

The apparent specificity of moderator scales has implications for both their theoretical status and the manner in which they are developed. One view of moderators is that they represent a *class of variables* which moderate other relationships, in the way that "motivational" variables are thought to moderate aptitude variables or in the way that the trait of "compulsivity" is thought to moderate interest variables. Another view of moderators is that they represent items which, for one reason or another, are associated with systematic error of prediction in a given prediction situation. The usual view of predictive error is that it is truly "random" and therefore not systematically associated with other variables (Chapter 7). Ghiselli's work appears to suggest that much of what is considered "random" error is, in fact, systematic although the precise nature of such error cannot be specified. Given the specificity of such error, one must develop special moderators for each situation studied. Further, it does not seem possible to specify, in advance, the kinds of items or scales that might have moderator properties.

Although much of Ghiselli's work gives the impression that predictability scales are rather easy to come by, they are not necessarily so. Brown and Scott (1966) report a series of discouraging attempts to improve on the prediction of academic achievement by use of predictability measures. In one study, high school grades and aptitude tests were combined to forecast college grade-point average (GPA) in freshman groups from several fields of study. The discrepancy between predicted and obtained GPA was then computed for each subject. This discrepancy measure failed to correlate with several measures of study habits and attitudes, which were expected to exhibit moderator properties. In another study, the discrepancy between predicted and obtained GPA was correlated with a number of personality scales thought to be related to over- and under-achievement. The few positive relationships were attributed to chance. Predictability scales constructed from an item analysis of high- and low-D groups failed to cross-validate. On the basis of these several efforts, the authors concluded: "In no case did we find a moderator variable that resulted in any significant improvement in validity. In fact, in most cases we could not even identify a moderator variable. When we did find moderators they still did not aid prediction." (Brown and Scott, 1966, p. 299.)

Granting the fact that moderators may be somewhat elusive in character, the sequence of demonstrations by Ghiselli requires that this approach to prediction be given serious consideration. One of the chief stumbling blocks to the evaluation of Ghiselli's predictability methodology is the difficulty of comparing this approach to conventional multiple regression. In Saunders' (1956) approach to moderator variables, it was possible to compare directly the "moderated multiple-R" with the multiple-R yielded by conventional multiple regression. Ghiselli (1960b, p. 6) has indicated that his predictability variables, x_2, tend to be uncorrelated with either the original predictors, $r_{x_1 x_2}$, or with the criterion measures, $r_{x_2 y}$. Therefore, he feels that predictability variables will contribute little or nothing to conventional multiple regression. Direct evidence on this point has not been presented.

Another problem encountered in Ghiselli's approach is the fact that, in practice, predictions must be *withheld* for sizeable portions of the total population of subjects ("unpredictables"). This fact contrasts with conventional multiple-regression prediction in which predictions are made for *all* individuals. However, most problems in personnel selection require the selection of some *fixed portion* of individuals who are "most likely to succeed" and the rejection of all others. In at least one selection situation, Ghiselli (1956) has demonstrated that the use of both moderator and predictor scores in selecting a fixed portion of applicants results in the selection of better applicants than would have been obtained from the use of predictor scores alone. It is difficult to estimate how general this finding might be.

In summary, Ghiselli's approach to the prediction of predictability has shown considerable promise and appears to warrant further investigation, particularly with instruments and subject groups other than those employed by Ghiselli. At the very least, it is clear that Ghiselli has developed a method for detecting moderator effects that represents an improvement over earlier procedures (e.g., French, 1961). Whether Ghiselli's approach will, in the long run, prove more fruitful than the search for additional predictor variables in conventional multiple regression cannot be answered at this time. In this connection it is noteworthy that Ghiselli himself has expressed some skepticism about the future of moderators.

It is quite possible that the time and effort required to develop moderators might be more fruitfully spent in seeking improvements in reliability and validity of the sort that follow from classic psychometric theory . . . . Furthermore, since the indications are that moderators are rather specific it might be that they, like suppressors, do not hold up well from sample to sample. (Ghiselli, 1963, p. 86.)

Differentiation of Tests in Terms of Their Predictiveness

Not only do individuals differ with respect to their predictability from a given test, but individuals differ also in terms of which *one* of a number of tests predicts best for them. It is a common observation in clinical work that the pathology of some patients is best predicted by the Rorschach Test and that the pathology of other patients is best predicted by the MMPI. Given contradictory findings from the two tests for one patient—a frequent occurrence—which test will be the more predictive for that patient? Similarly, of two equally valid vocational-interest tests administered to a student, one suggests a career of dentistry, and the other indicates that his interests would be most compatible with those of members of the legal profession. The question here is not which test is more valid for people in general, but which test is more predictive for this particular student. Having such *foreknowledge* would be an extremely valuable adjunct to any prediction situation. Are there means—other than clairvoyance—of obtaining such valuable information? The study of Ghiselli (1960a) to be presented next suggests that there are indeed such means and that they represent a simple but ingenious extension of his basic method of predicting predictability.

We have already indicated that the accuracy with which a test, x_1, will predict a criterion, y, for an individual is given by the statistic D_1, where $D_1 = |y = y'_1|$. Let us now consider the accuracy of another test, x_2, for predicting the same criterion as expressed by the statistic D_2, where $D_2 = |y - y'_2|$. The expression D_1 serves as an index of the accuracy of Test x_1 in predicting y. The index D_2 reflects the extent to which Test x_2 predicts the same criterion for the same individual. For any number of tests, $x_1, x_2, x_3, \ldots, x_n$, we may compute the predictive accuracy of each test for a given individual by the statistics $D_1, D_2, D_3, \ldots, D_n$.

Let us now consider the statistic DT as given by the expression $DT = (D_2 - D_1)$. It should be apparent that DT reflects the *relative* accuracy of prediction of Test x_1 as compared with that of Test x_2. In a group of individuals, those having high scores on DT will be better predicted by Test x_1 than they will by Test x_2. Individuals with *negative* scores on DT will be better predicted by Test x_2 than they will by Test x_1. Hence we can order all individuals in this group on the basis of their DT scores and assert that Test x_1 will be most effectively employed with individuals falling in the upper range of DT scores, whereas Test x_2 will be more appropriate for those falling in the lower or negative range of DT values. With this much of Ghiselli's (1960a) reasoning provided, the next important question should be easily anticipated. "What would happen if we were to find a test, x_3, that was itself highly correlated with the statistic DT?" The answer is that this third test should enable us to specify *in advance* which individuals will be best predicted by Test x_1 and which individuals will be best predicted by Test x_2.

Ghiselli (1960a) divided a group of 165 undergraduates into a derivation group of 120 subjects and a cross-validation group of 45 subjects. This time, the criterion, y, was a score on 25 statements measuring "self-perceived effectiveness as a person." Two predictor scales were employed: Test x_1 was an "initiative scale" and Test x_2 was a "sociability scale." Both predictors were correlated separately with the criterion in the group of 120 derivation subjects. Predictability scores were obtained, as previously, from the regression of each of the predictors on the criterion. For Test x_1, the predictability score was $D_1 = |y - y_1'|$. For Test x_2, the predictability score was $D_2 = |y - y_2'|$. On the basis of the statistic $DT = (D_2 - D_1)$, subjects were classified into two groups: those for whom Test x_1 was the better predictor and those for whom Test x_2 was the better predictor. These two groups served as contrasted groups in an item analysis performed on responses to the 64-item forced-choice inventory used in Ghiselli's earlier studies. Ten items were found that significantly differentiated subjects in the derivation group for whom Test x_1 was the better predictor from those for whom Test x_2 was the better predictor. These ten items constituted a new test, x_3, that could, in principle, forecast which of two tests (initiative or sociability) would give the more accurate predictions of the criterion (effectiveness) for a given individual.

In the group of 45 cross-validation subjects, scores were obtained on the two predictor scales, x_1 and x_2, the criterion measure, y, and the ten-item predictability scale, x_3. Because of the manner in which the predictability scale was derived, subjects scoring very high on this scale should be better predicted by Test x_1, and subjects scoring very low on this scale should be better predicted by Test x_2. The first column of Table 2.3 shows the different cutoff scores that were possible on the basis of the predictability scale, x_3. The second column shows the proportion of subjects for whom the sociability scale, x_2, was employed as a predictor at or below a given cutting score. The third column shows the remaining proportion of subjects for whom the initiative scale, x_1, was employed as a predictor at or below a given cutting

Table 2.3 Validity coefficients for self-evaluation ratings using, for various proportions of subjects, their scores on the sociability and initiative inventories. (From Ghiselli, 1960a.)

Cutoff score on the differential predictability variable (x_3)	Sociability scale (x_2)	Initiative scale (x_1)	Validity coefficient $(r_{yy'})$
–	100	0	.17
3	96	4	.28
4	93	7	.37
5	82	18	.41
6	60	40	.73
7	38	62	.70
8	20	80	.58
9	4	96	.52
–	0	100	.51

score. The final column shows the overall validity coefficient, $r_{yy'}$, obtained at each cutting score where predictions are based on varying proportions of subjects for the two scales.

At a cutting score of 2 or less, predictions are made on the basis of the sociability scale, x_2, for all subjects, and as Table 2.3 indicates, the validity of this test alone is .17. As the cutting score is increased, Test x_2 is employed for fewer and fewer subjects, and the overall validity coefficient increases to a maximum of .73. However, beyond the cutoff score of 6 on x_3 (where approximately half the cases are being predicted by x_1 and the other half by x_2), the validity coefficient decreases to the value of the validity of Test x_1 used as a predictor for all subjects, $r_{yy'} = .51$. As an *exclusive* basis for predictions, Test x_1 clearly has greater validity (.51) than does Test x_2 (.17). However, by using Test x_2 as a predictor for those subjects whose scores on the predictability variable, x_3, were 6 or less and Test x_1 for those whose scores were greater, one can achieve an overall validity coefficient of .73. The use of a predictability variable makes possible the attainment of an overall validity coefficient which greatly exceeds that which could be attained by exclusive use of either test.

Two additional demonstrations of differential predictiveness of tests were provided by Ghiselli (1960a). In one study, all scales and the criterion itself were derived from the 64-item forced-choice test. In the other study, motor and spatial tests were differentiated by age and education in the prediction of work productivity. The results of these demonstrations were essentially the same as the results of the first study; the use of a predictability variable resulted in an overall validity coefficient greater than that of either of the two predictors used separately. In none of these studies was the use of a third variable, x_3, as a predictability variable compared with the use of a linear combination of the two predictors, or the two predictors plus the third variable, in conventional multiple regression. Although Ghiselli (1960a, pp. 683–684) discusses this issue at some length, the relevant regression equations were not computed.

The utility of the differential predictiveness of tests in an academic prediction situation has been questioned by Brown and Scott (1967). A group of 254 freshman engineering students were divided into a derivation sample of 122 subjects and a cross-validation sample of 132 subjects. The predictability of subjects on each of four commonly employed predictors of academic success, D_1, D_2, D_3, D_4, was determined by Ghiselli's procedure. Measures of differential predictability were then computed for each of the six possible combinations of the four predictors (e.g., $DT = D_4 - D_2$). The six measures of differential predictability were, in turn, correlated with 18 potential moderators, which included various aptitude and ability measures plus several scales from the Strong Vocational Interest Blank. Of the 108 predictor-moderator combinations investigated, only 13 involved significant DT versus moderator correlations in the derivation sample (the highest was $r = .27$). None of the 13 correlations were significant when computed in the cross-validation sample. As was true of the differential predictability of individuals, the differential predictiveness of tests has not been widely established with instruments and subject groups other than those employed by Ghiselli.

Off-Quadrant Analysis

Moderator variables can be developed with even greater simplicity than has been described thus far. In one of his studies, Ghiselli (1963, pp. 82–83) utilized an "off-quadrant" analysis procedure that bypassed the need for computing regression equations. This procedure may be best understood with reference to Figure 2.3, in which the dotted line represents the best-fit regression equation for predicting deviation scores on a criterion from deviation scores on a predictor. Typically the absolute difference, $D = |y - y'|$, is computed for each individual, and an item analysis is performed to develop a scale which differentiates "High D" (unpredictable) from "Low D" (predictable) subjects.

The usual regression analysis may be approximated by simply dividing subjects into high and low groups on the predictor scores, x_1, and on the criterion scores, y. In Figure 2.3, the intersect of lines extended from

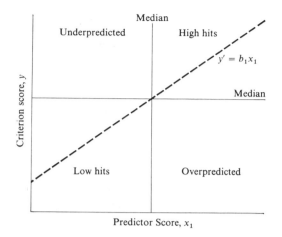

Fig. 2.3 Division of subgroups in off-quadrant analysis.

the median of each of the variables forms four quadrants. The "high hits" are subjects with high predictor scores and high criterion scores. The "low hits" are subjects with low predictor and criterion scores. Together these subjects are considered to represent "on-quadrant" (predictable) cases. The "underpredicted" and "overpredicted" subjects are "off-quadrant" and therefore unpredictable. An attempt is then made to find a third variable which will differentiate the predictable on-quadrant (high-hit plus low-hit) subjects from the off-quadrant (underpredicted plus overpredicted) subjects. Note that this procedure does not require the computation of the regression line shown in Figure 2.3.

The off-quadrant analysis just described is an approximation to the procedure of obtaining the *absolute differences* between actual and predicted criterion scores: $D = |y - y'|$. By considering both underpredicted and overpredicted cases as falling in the off-quadrant group, we ignore the *direction* of predictive error. Hobert and Dunnette (1967) have called attention to the possibility that the direction of predictive errors may be an important consideration and that *algebraic differences* between actual and predicted criterion scores may provide a more fruitful basis for the development of moderators. They argue that underpredicted subjects (those who perform better than predicted) and overpredicted subjects (those who perform worse than predicted) appear to form two distinct groups that might differ from each other on a number of characteristics important to prediction. In academic prediction, for example, it appears sensible to distinguish between "underachievers" and "overachievers" on the grounds that they may represent groups quite distinct from each other on a number of personality and background variables (Thorndike, 1963). Hobert and Dunnette (1967) maintain that the procedure of combining underpredicted and overpredicted subjects into a single group of unpredictable subjects may mask such important differences. They propose instead that *two* separate moderators be developed, one for distinguishing the underpredicted from the low hits and the other for distinguishing the overpredicted from the high hits.

The prediction situation studied by Hobert and Dunnette involved the forecasting of managerial effectiveness from a battery of standardized predictor measures. A sample of 443 managers from a large corporation were divided into a derivation sample of 222 subjects and a cross-validation sample of 221 subjects. The criterion to be predicted, y, consisted of a composite measure of several criterion variables. The predictor, x_1, was a score yielded by a cross-validated multiple-regression equation based on a number of aptitude, personality, and background variables. In the derivation sample, subjects were divided into four groups on the basis of median scores on predictor and criterion, as illustrated in Figure 2.3. Separate moderators were then developed to separate underpredicted from low-hit subjects and to separate overpredicted from high-hit subjects. The item pool in which moderators were sought consisted of the three standardized background, personality, and aptitude tests which were originally most predictive of the criterion. That is, the moderators were developed from the most valid portion of the predictor score itself, x_1.

A 16-item scale was found to be the most effective discriminator of underpredicted from low-hit subjects, and a 12-item scale was found to be the most effective discriminator of overpredicted from high-hit subjects. In the derivation sample, the investigators found a cutting score for each of the two moderators that maximized correct identification. These cutoff scores were then applied to the cross-validation sample to eliminate unpredictable subjects. By elimination of 25 percent of the subjects in the cross-validation sample, those classified as unpredictable, it was possible to raise the validity coefficient from .65 to .73, a statistically significant difference.

Although the development of two separate moderators by off-quadrant analysis appears, at first glance, to represent a promising new approach to moderated prediction (Owens and Jewell, 1969), closer scrutiny of the procedure itself indicates that it is not properly classified as a moderated prediction technique (Abrahams, 1969) and that the apparent predictive gain is illusory (McNemar, 1969a). The reasons will become evident from inspection of Figure 2.4, in which the shape of the joint distribution of predictor and criterion scores is represented by an ellipse of the form that would be expected for this degree of correlation: $r_{x_1 y} = .65$. Inspection of the distribution of scores within each of the four groups indicates that the groups differ from one another, not only in terms of their mean criterion scores, but in terms of their *mean predictor scores* as well (Abrahams, 1969).

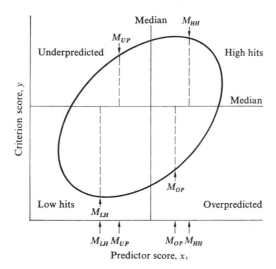

Fig. 2.4 Mean predictor scores for subgroups. (After Abrahams, 1969, p. 67.)

Note that the mean predictor score of the low-hit group, M_{LH}, is lower than the mean predictor score of the underpredicted group, M_{UP}. For this reason, differences between these groups on the "moderator" variable will reflect, primarily, differences between the groups on the original predictor variable. Since the "moderator" variable which Hobert and Dunnette used to differentiate these two groups was composed of scales from the original predictor composite, their procedure represents little more than a reweighting of the original predictor composite (Abrahams, 1969). This would also be the case in differentiating high-hit subjects from overpredicted subjects, as can be seen from Figure 2.4. More generally, McNemar (1969a) has demonstrated that improved prediction, of the kind reported by Hobert and Dunnette, can always be obtained by simply excluding cases from the center of the distribution of *predictor scores*. Although the validity coefficient in the reduced sample will increase, the standard error of estimate will remain the same, and the apparent gain in prediction will be illusory.

Although the application of off-quadrant analysis described above does not appear to qualify as a technique for developing moderators, as traditionally defined, there are other applications that do. Ghiselli's (1963) original method of contrasting unpredictable (overpredicted plus underpredicted) groups with predictable (low-hit plus high-hit) groups is simply an approximation to the procedure of forming groups on the basis of differences between actual and predicted criterion scores: $D = |y - y'|$. Similarly, should one wish to develop *separate* moderators for underpredicted and overpredicted subjects, the appropriate contrasts would be underpredicted versus predictable (low-hit plus high-hit) and overpredicted versus predictable (low-hit plus high-hit). Whether these contrasts are made by use of D-score methodology or by off-quadrant analysis depends on the priorities assigned to accuracy of estimates and economy of computations, respectively.

HIGHER-ORDER FUNCTIONS

The moderator (Saunders, 1956) or linear joint function (Ezekiel and Fox, 1959) represents only one of an extremely large family of possible equations for expressing a criterion variable as a function of two or more predictors. In the conventional multiple-regression equation, the estimated criterion score, y', is expressed as a function of two predictors, $f(x_1x_2)$, in which $f = b_1x_1 + b_2x_2$. In the case of moderator or linear joint-functional relationships, $f(x_1x_2)$ is interpreted as $f = b_1x_1 + b_2x_2 + b_3x_1x_2$.

More complex functions, involving higher-order expressions, could just as easily be assumed. In a squared joint-functional relationship, $f(x_1x_2)$ may be interpreted as $f = b_1x_1 + b_2x_2 + b_3x_1x_2^2 + b_4x_1^2x_2$. A still more complex interpretation of $f(x_1x_2)$ might be as a second-order parabolic joint function. In the parabolic case, $f(x_1x_2)$ is interpreted as $f = b_1x_1 + b_2x_2 + b_3x_1x_2 + b_4x_1x_2^2 + b_5x_1^2x_2$.

There is, of course, no limit to the complexity of interpretation placed on the function $f(x_1x_2)$ in relating the predictor variables to the criterion. The computational labor involved in solving these complex equations for a given set of data is no longer prohibitive as it was before the advent of the computer. Might we not, then, as some writers have suggested, be on the verge of a "new era" of predictive science which will employ models of sufficient complexity to do justice to the complexities of variables assessed in personality research? Perhaps, but only if two conditions are met.

First, we shall require sufficiently articulated theories of personality-trait organization to point the direction for selecting appropriate mathematical-prediction models from the myriad possibilities that exist. Second, we shall require solid and extensive demonstrations that such models do indeed provide predictive increments over the usual multiple-R and that these increments are of practical significance (Sechrest, 1963). Although the presence or absence of such conditions cannot be established on the basis of a single study, the investigation to be reported next represents one of the most thorough investigations of these issues that has yet been conducted.

Ward's Prediction Study

Ward (1954) concerned himself with the prediction of five criteria of proficiency in radio operation from four relatively independent predictors of such criteria. Predictor and criterion measures were available for 871 airmen who had completed the Air Force radio operator course at Lackland Air Force Base. Ward selected four test variables which represented relatively independent factors that had been consistently replicated in a series of factor analyses of the Airmen Classification Battery. The tests were: (1) Word Knowledge, (2) Dial and Table Reading, (3) Numerical Operations, and (4) General Mechanics. Four criterion variables were selected from 14 available phase grades in such a way as to represent diverse kinds of activities rated at different periods during the training course. The names of the four criterion variables, representing different aspects of the proficiency criteria, are given in Table 2.4 along with "final grade" in the course, which was at least partially based on these criteria.

The four methods of prediction employed by Ward are listed in the first column of Table 2.4. They are: (1) the usual multiple-regression equation, (2) a linear joint function, (3) a squared joint function, and (4) a second-order parabolic joint function. The form of these expressions has already been briefly described. In each case, a different interpretation of $f(x_1 x_2)$ is made in the prediction model, and the models are ordered in terms of the complexity of the relationships assumed among the independent variables. Note that for each degree of order assumed, additional terms (variables) are required in the prediction equation.

For each of the four equations, regression weights were determined by the method of least squares for the separate prediction of each of the five criteria of proficiency. In the case of the usual multiple-regression equation, this involved the simultaneous determination of regression weights for four predictors in each of five prediction situations. In the case of the second-order parabolic joint-function equation, this involved the simultaneous determination of regression weights for 22 separate terms for each of the five criteria to be predicted. Needless to say, these computations were done on a computer.

As indicated in Chapter 1, when predictor variables are *fixed*, as in the present example, the anticipated shrinkage in multiple-Rs can be estimated by applying a correction for shrinkage formula to the multiple-Rs obtained from the *total* sample (in this instance $N = 871$). However, Ward (1954) chose to employ a cross-validation design in which regression weights derived from half of the sample ($N = 436$) were applied to the other half ($N = 435$). Since care was taken to ensure that Sample A and Sample B were determined randomly, and since comparisons were between different prediction equations applied to the same samples, his results may be used to illustrate the point at issue.

Subjects' scores were substituted in the regression equations, and predicted scores were obtained for each of the five criteria by the four types of equations in the first sample of 436 airmen (Sample A). In order to compare the predictive validities of the different types of equations, product-moment correlations were computed between predicted and obtained scores for each of the five criteria. Table 2.4 presents these correlations between predicted (y') and obtained (y) scores in the first sample.

Table 2.4 Correlations between predicted and obtained scores for four prediction equations in the original sample (A) of 436 airmen. (After Ward, 1954.)

Prediction equations	Proficiency Criteria				
	Final grade	Type-writing	Radio-telegraph	Morse code	Flight simulation
Multiple regression	.598	.159	.440	.205	.320
Linear joint	.608	.215	.450	.213	.332
Squared joint	.610	.208	.467	.224	.357
Parabolic joint	.619	.259	.474	.230	.373

For the sample presented in Table 2.4, the prediction of final grade in the radio operator's course by the usual multiple-regression equation is correlated .598 with actual grade achieved. Prediction of this criterion by the linear joint-function equation is correlated .608 with final grade. The use of the squared joint-function equation raises the correlation to .610, and the second-order parabolic joint-function equation achieves the highest correlation, .619. With one very slight exception (typewriting grade) this pattern of increasing predictive accuracy with increasing complexity of the prediction equation holds in each of the five criterion situations. From a statistical standpoint, this increment in prediction over the usual multiple-regression equation was consistently significant ($p < .05$) for only the most complex of the equations employed, the second-order parabolic.

Recall that the original sample of 871 airmen was divided randomly into two groups: Sample A ($N = 436$) and Sample B ($N = 435$). When regression weights in Sample A had been derived and their effectiveness evaluated, the next step was to evaluate the accuracy of the *same* weights when applied to the predictors in Sample B. Subjects' scores from Sample B were substituted in the regression equations, and predicted scores were obtained for each of the five criteria by the four types of equations. The correlations between predicted and obtained scores for each of the prediction equations are presented in Table 2.5.

As would be expected, the correlations between predicted and obtained scores in Table 2.5 are generally lower than those in Table 2.4, where the sample employed was that from which the regression weights were derived. Of greater importance, however, is the apparent reversal of order of accuracy

Table 2.5 Correlations between predicted and obtained scores for four prediction equations in a cross-validation sample (B) of 435 airmen. (After Ward, 1954.)

Prediction equations	Proficiency Criteria				
	Final grade	Type-writing	Radio-telegraph	Morse code	Flight simulation
Multiple regression	.532	.162	.380	.136	.294
Linear joint	.534	.123	.374	.124	.282
Squared joint	.509	.120	.354	.113	.260
Parabolic joint	.520	.144	.352	.107	.225

of the prediction equations in each of the prediction situations. Although this reversal is not so orderly as the data in Table 2.4, it is nonetheless striking and seemingly illustrative of the following principle: *Increases in the complexity of prediction equations may result in corresponding decreases in predictive accuracy when the equations are applied to an independent group of subjects.* Table 2.5 shows that this principle holds completely for three of the five criterion situations (radio-telegraph, Morse code, flight simulation) and is generally, though not completely, true for the other two.

A legitimate question here is whether or not one might *expect* the complex relations among independent variables, assumed by the equations employed in Ward's study, to be in any way characteristic of the organization of the actual variables employed in his study. Ward notes: "If the relations that are represented by the equations actually exist in the population, the more complex equations might maintain better predictive efficiency on subsequent samples" (p. 10). This point is well taken and returns us to our original question: Where, or under what conditions, might one expect departures from the usual multiple-regression equation to be appropriate mathematical models of the prediction situation? Again, we cannot overemphasize the need for theories that point the appropriate direction for future research. As Ward's study clearly illustrates, the availability of computers is not enough.

SUMMARY

The predictive limits that seem to have been reached in applications of the basic prediction model to personality data have inspired experimentation with alternative models. Of the many possible alternative models available, the moderator, or linear joint function, has received the most attention. *Differential predictability* may be said to have occurred when the relationship between a predictor and a criterion, r_{x_1y}, varies directly as a function of classification on a moderator variable, x_2. Frederiksen and Melville (1954) presented evidence suggesting that "compulsiveness," x_2, moderates the relationship between engineering interest, x_1, and achievement, y. Replications of this study indicated that evidence for the differential predictability of high- and low-compulsive students is suggestive at best. Saunders (1956) applied a linear joint function, $y' = b_1x_1 + b_2x_2 + b_3x_1x_2$, to the Frederiksen-Melville data, using a third term to express the interaction between the predictor and moderator variable, $b_3x_1x_2$. Although this form of *moderated multiple regression* was found, in some instances, to be superior to conventional multiple regression, the increments in predictive validity were small and the relationships judged to be unstable.

Ghiselli (1960b) has proposed a method whereby moderator variables may be developed for a specific prediction situation. In a derivation sample, the absolute differences between predicted and actual criterion deviation scores, $D = |y - y'|$, are obtained for each subject. Subjects are then divided into high and low groups on the basis of this index of predictability, D. An item analysis is conducted to identify items that discriminate between high- and low-predictable subjects. The resultant items are combined in a *predictability scale*, x_2, that functions as a moderator. In a cross-validation sample, subjects are ordered on the predictability scale, and predictions from the original variable, x_1, are made for the most predictable subset of subjects. As predictions are restricted to increasingly smaller proportions of the total sample on the basis of x_2 scores, the predictive validity of Test x_1 approaches unity. Ghiselli has provided a number of convincing demonstrations of the utility of this approach and of variations on it. Because such predictability variables tend to be highly specific and possibly unstable, it is not clear that they provide a strong alternative to the development of better predictors in conventional multiple regression. Nevertheless, this approach has shown considerable promise and appears to warrant further investigation.

An extensive study by Ward (1954) provided an empirical demonstration of some limitations on the use of the linear joint-function and higher-order equations in applied prediction problems. In a large sample of airmen, an attempt was made to predict five criteria of proficiency in radio operation from four relatively independent predictors. In a derivation sample, the four predictors were combined according to four mathematical models ranging in complexity from the usual multiple-regression equation to a second-order parabolic joint function. In the derivation sample, it was clear that increases in the complexity of the prediction equations were associated with corresponding inrceases in predictive accuracy. However, when the same regression weights were applied to predictors in a cross-validation sample, increases in the complexity of the prediction equations were associated with corresponding decreases in predictive accuracy. With few exceptions, the usual multiple-regression equation outperformed the more complex models. We raised the question whether or not one might expect such complex relations among independent variables to obtain in any given body of data. At present, theories of personality structure do not appear to be sufficiently articulated to guide the selection of appropriate mathematical prediction models from the myriad possibilities that exist.

CHAPTER 3

ALTERNATIVE PREDICTION MODELS:
II. CONTINGENCY TABLES AND
ACTUARIAL PREDICTION

The multiple-regression equation (Chapter 1) and its variants (Chapter 2) are the principal methods employed for combining continuous predictor variables (test scores, ratings) in the forecasting of continuous criterion measures (supervisors' ratings, work production). However, there are many situations in which predictor variables are categorical in nature (sex, marital status, diagnosis) and in which the prediction desired is one that states the *probability* that an individual with a given combination of predictor attributes (40-year-old, unmarried, paranoid schizophrenic) will achieve a given criterion status (improvement in psychotherapy). Procedures that derive probability estimates of criterion status from contingent-frequency tables of predictor attributes will be referred to as *actuarial prediction* procedures. Such procedures are in no way limited to prediction problems involving categorical or noncontinuous predictors. In many situations it might be deemed appropriate to transform continuous variables into categories so that actuarial methods may be employed. In this sense, actuarial prediction is always an *alternative* methodology to multiple-regression analysis.

The present chapter is concerned with the nature and logic of actuarial prediction and with the manner in which actuarial techniques have been employed in personality assessment. Although the work of many authors will be considered, the chapter relies heavily on the formulations of Sines (1966), who has written a comprehensive survey of actuarial prediction in psychology. Sines defines actuarial prediction as "the empirical determination of the regularities that may exist between specified psychological test data and equally clearly specified socially, clinically, or theoretically significant non-test characteristics of the persons tested" (p. 135). Sines's definition stresses the fact that actuarial prediction is based on *known* empirical relationships and that such predictions are generated according to explicit mathematical *rules*. Such a definition distinguishes actuarial prediction procedures from clinical prediction procedures, which will be considered later (Chapters 4 and

5). The definition does not distinguish actuarial from multiple-regression procedures, however. In our more narrow usage, actuarial prediction will refer only to procedures that involve the derivation of probability estimates from contingent-frequency tables.

INSURANCE RATES AND ACTUARIAL PREDICTION

The most familiar example of the use of actuarial prediction methods is found in the insurance industry. In the early days of Lloyds of London, the establishment of insurance rates was a "clinical" speculative enterprise. With the availability of accurate census and demographic data and the development of statistical techniques, the insurance industry rapidly became an enterprise based on facts rather than intuition. The continued success of insurance companies, both in this country and abroad, is a tribute to the validity of actuarial prediction methods. Although clinical prediction may continue to be employed for years to come in personality assessment, it is unlikely that insurance companies will ever revert to this method of data combination.

An applicant for auto insurance is requested to fill out a background questionnaire indicating such characteristics as his age, sex, marital status, place of residence, etc. Within the context of our consideration of actuarial prediction, these variables may be considered as psychological test data which will serve as *input* to an actuarial prediction system. Give this input information, the actuary will consult an actuarial table similar to Table 3.1, which presents fictitious data on the accident history of a large and representative sample of individuals classified on the various predictor measures.

As Table 3.1 shows, younger people tend to have a large number of minor accidents and older people tend to be involved in major accidents. It is also clear that female drivers are better risks than male drivers. Similarly, married individuals tend to have fewer accidents than either single or divorced individuals. It would be possible to determine insurance rates based on the single variable of age. Under such circumstances, rates would be higher for younger people than for older. It would also be possible to set rates on the basis of sex alone, marital status alone, geographical location alone, etc. Clearly, however, the most accurate prediction of accident rate would be based on some *combination* of these predictor variables. The goal of actuarial prediction in this instance would be to find the most narrowly defined basis for classification that would yield stable enough frequencies to allow for reliable predictions. That is, we might wish to consider age, sex, marital status, geographical location, and type of community simultaneously. Under such a classification system, it might turn out that there are too few individuals in the actuarial table who are over 56, female, divorced, and resident in a rural area of the Southwest. Under such circumstances, we

Table 3.1 Actuarial table for automobile accidents ($N = 10,000$)

	No. of accidents per five years			No. of major accidents per five years		
	0	1	>2	0	1	>2
Age:						
16–21	524	921	130	1121	398	56
22–25	1456	1315	350	1918	1126	77
26–35	1565	598	121	1997	198	89
36–44	1671	121	60	1711	101	40
45–55	804	110	55	821	98	50
>55	101	51	47	109	46	44
Sex:						
Male	1641	2782	577	2873	1893	234
Female	4327	492	231	4719	183	98
Marital:						
Married	4851	1349	312	5221	993	218
Single	996	1562	289	1695	982	170
Divorced	345	212	84	549	101	40
Geographical:						
Northeast	1122	727	198	1414	521	112
Southeast	2416	684	164	2534	612	
Midwest	1987	588	112	2284	371	
Northwest	473	828	182	1711		
Southwest	194	296	29	592		
Community:						
Urban	4852	2014	498			
Rural	1340	1109				

might wish to reduce the number of predictor variables so that the subclasses thus formed were large enough to provide a basis for more stable predictions. Regardless of the number of predictor variables employed for classification, it should be noted that the actuarial method does not provide a rationale for the initial *choice* of predictor variables (Gough, 1962, p. 530). Once actuarial data are available, it becomes apparent that some categories are more differentiating than others. However, the choice of variables for study is initially intuitive.

On the basis of input data and their relation to the criterion (number of accidents) as represented in Table 3.1, it might be that young, unmarried, male drivers from urban northeastern communities must pay higher insurance rates than middle-aged married female drivers from rural midwestern areas.

Such differential rates are not meant to discriminate against individuals who are members of the first group. Rather, the rates are determined by *empirical* facts which reflect the different probabilities of accidents in those two groups. By and large, the general public has accepted the practice of assigning different rates to different "kinds" of drivers, probably because the predictor variables involved usually make intuitive sense. Considerations of public relations aside, there is nothing in the actuarial method that requires highly predictive input variables to make intuitive sense. Given a sample large enough to provide stable probability estimates, it might be found that left-handed divorced redheads from Arkansas constitute a highway menace. Similarly, it might be found that blue-eyed karate instructors from Peoria, Illinois, are almost never involved in highway accidents. The assignment of very high rates to the former group and very low rates to the latter might result in a more equitable distribution of insurance rates in the population at large. Unfortunately, such a practice would be viewed by the general public—and in particular, left-handed divorced redheads from Arkansas—as discriminatory. In personality assessment, the combinations of predictor variables employed often do not make intuitive sense. Input or predictor variables are evaluated solely by the extent to which they differentiate criterion groups rather than by their appeal to common-sense considerations. Unfortunately, this sanguine view of the content of predictor variables is not shared by the general public (American Psychological Association, 1965).

ACTUARIAL PREDICTION IN PSYCHOLOGY

As previously stated, actuarial prediction in psychology consists of the empirical determination of relationships existing between psychological test data and certain socially important nontest behaviors. In terms of the insurance example presented in Table 3.1, psychological test data would be analogous to the demographic characteristics of age, sex, etc. The nontest characteristics to be predicted would be analogous to the accident classifications presented in the columns of Table 3.1. The prediction problem may now be stated somewhat more formally by use of the notation suggested by Dawes (1962). The psychological test or predictor variables may be represented by the symbols $R_1, R_2, \ldots, R_j, \ldots, R_m$. The nontest or "criterion" behaviors to be predicted may be represented by the symbols $C_1, C_2, \ldots, C_i, \ldots, C_n$. In the insurance example, the various criterion-group possibilities are represented by: C_1 = zero accidents in five years; C_2 = one accident in five years, etc. The prediction problem for both insurance companies and psychologists is of the following form: "Given a series of test responses, $R_1, R_2, \ldots, R_m$, what is the probability that an individual with this pattern of responses will be a member of a given criterion group, $C_1, C_2, \ldots, C_n$?"

The problem then becomes one of estimating the probability of criterion-group membership from the observed frequencies in the actuarial table.

Although the form of the actuarial prediction problem is identical for both insurance companies and psychologists, the full implications of this identity have only recently been recognized. In both insurance practice and clinical practice, the type of inference required is of the form $P(C_i \mid R_j)$, which is read: "Given a particular pattern of test responses (or demographic characteristics), what is the probability that an individual who gave this response pattern is a member of a specific criterion group (e.g., successful physician or high-risk driver)?" The answer to this probabilistic question can be found only within a table that gives the frequency of incidence of the criterion behavior for specific subcategories or combinations of the predictor variables. The type of inference of the form $P(C_i \mid R_j)$ is not peculiar to actuarial prediction. In his psychodiagnostic practice, the clinician operates in precisely the same fashion: "Given a particular pattern of Rorschach test responses, what is the probability that this patient will make a suicide attempt?" Instead of an actuarial table, the clinician may be relying on his clinical experience with patients who have given that particular pattern of Rorschach responses in the past to estimate the probability that the present patient is a member of the criterion group of suicidal patients. Despite the obvious similarity of actuarial prediction in insurance and in clinical prediction, it is only recently that psychologists have begun to recognize that the prediction problem is properly stated in this form (Dawes, 1962; Sines, 1964; Sines, 1966).

Despite the need for an actuarial analysis of information in personality assessment of the kind contained in Table 3.1, the sources of validity information that are currently available present the basic data in a form which differs substantially from that required by the actuarial prediction problem (Sines, 1966). The validity of a psychological test or pattern of test scores is expressed by the degree of relationship that exists between the psychological test data and the nontest criterion behaviors. The form in which these data are presented in test manuals and journal articles is typically that shown in Table 3.2.

The hypothetical data in Table 3.2 bear on the validity of a "schizophrenia index" in predicting the nontest criterion of schizophrenic diagnosis. In this particular example, a group of diagnosed schizophrenics and a group of normal subjects were both administered the schizophrenia index. The mean scores indicated a significant difference between the two criterion groups. Other frequently reported information bears on the degree of *separation* (or "proportion of overlap") between two criterion groups achieved by such indices. Regardless of the statistical format of the presentation of validity data, note that the prediction *problem* is here stated in a different form.

Table 3.2 Reported validity of a schizophrenic index

	Schizophrenic sample ($N = 100$)	Normal sample ($N = 500$)
Mean score on schizophrenia index	78.90	50.25
Standard deviation of schizophrenia index	12.96	11.25
Discrimination between criterion groups	$CR = 20.61$ ($p < .001$)	

From validity information of the kind provided in Table 3.2, it is possible to make inferences of the following form: "Given that an individual is a member of a criterion group (schizophrenics), what is the probability that he will obtain a certain score on the schizophrenia index?" In the example of the schizophrenia index illustrated in Table 3.2, we might say: "Given that an individual is a member of a specified criterion group (normals), it is extremely unlikely that he will achieve a score as high as 80 on the schizophrenia index." But note the form of inference involved: "Given that an individual is a member of a criterion group, what is the probability that he will emit this pattern of test responses?" Stated more formally: $P(R_j \mid C_i)$. A comparison of this expression, $P(R_j \mid C_i)$, with the form given earlier, $P(C_i \mid R_j)$, indicates that the prediction problem has now been stated in a quite different way.

From a practical standpoint, it should be apparent that the *form* of the prediction problem represented by the validity information in Table 3.2 is not the same as the form in which we initially stated the actuarial prediction problem. The information "Given that an individual is a member of a criterion group, the probability of his emitting a specified test pattern is .90" may be of limited value to the clinician or actuary who is trying to *predict* criterion-group membership. If such membership were known in advance, there would be little point in attempting to predict it from psychological test data.

From the points developed thus far, it should be apparent that the usual sources of validity information available for psychological test scores and response patterns are relevant to the actuarial prediction problem if and only if

$$P(C_i \mid R_j) = P(R_j \mid C_i).$$

Dawes (1962) has called attention to the fact that the two expressions above are not mathematically equivalent[1] and that stating the prediction problem in the form represented by the right side of the equation is illogical and contrary to clinical practice. There are special circumstances under which the two probability values may be equal, but such an equivalence can never be assumed. Sines (1966) has argued that the equivalence of the expressions above is an empirical matter and that there are few known instances in the literature in which the values yielded by the two expressions would be the same. To the extent that the values are not equivalent, the type of validity information presented in test manuals can be *misleading* with respect to the practical utility of the testing instrument involved.

A hypothetical example serves to illustrate the confusion that may be generated when a discrepancy exists between the usefulness of a test suggested by validity data, $P(R_j \mid C_i)$, and the actual utility of a test in making diagnostic decisions, $P(C_i \mid R_j)$. Let us consider a specific criterion-group category, namely, that group of psychiatric patients who have a history of making suicide attempts, C_1. Let us further assume that the presence of extreme elevation on three particular scales from the Minnesota Multiphasic Personality Inventory[2] has been found to be an almost infallible predictor of criterion-group membership in the class of people who have attempted suicide. To make the example extreme, we shall assume that the clinical utility of the suicide index comprising three MMPI scales is: $P(C_1 \mid R_1) = .99$. In other words, given the presence of extreme elevation on three MMPI scales, R_1, the probability that an individual giving that response is a member of the criterion group of potential suicides is almost unity. Under these circumstances, if this MMPI index occurs in the record of any patient, that patient must surely be regarded as an extremely high suicide risk.

For reasons that will be justified later, we shall further assume that *more than one pattern of test response* is associated with membership in the criterion group of suicide attempters. Specifically, we shall assume that a particular depression score on a mood check list and the presence of shading responses on the Rorschach inkblot test are also associated with membership in the critical criterion class, C_1. This situation is illustrated in Table 3.3. Moreover, we also assume that no single suicide index, for example, R_1, characterizes *all* members of the criterion group, C_1. As presented in Table 3.3, the MMPI index, R_1, is assumed to occur in only 10 percent of suicidal patients.

---

1. The relationship between these two probabilities is expressed by Bayes's theorem of inverse probability. Calculation of the value on the left requires additional probability information that is usually not available.

2. The Minnesota Multiphasic Personality Inventory (MMPI) is described in Chapter 9. For a more complete description of this instrument, which is referred to frequently throughout the present text; see Dahlstrom and Welsh (1960).

Table 3.3 Validity and clinical utility of three suicide indices

Suicide indices	Clinical utility $P(C_i \mid R_j)$	Validity data $P(R_j \mid C_i)$
R_1: Elevation on 3 MMPI scales	$P(C_1 \mid R_1) = .99$	$P(R_1 \mid C_1) = .10$
R_2: Depression on mood check list	$P(C_1 \mid R_2) = .60$	$P(R_2 \mid C_1) = .60$
R_3: Shading responses on Rorschach	$P(C_1 \mid R_3) = .10$	$P(R_3 \mid C_1) = .90$

Therefore, if we were to conduct the typical validity study of the form $P(R_j \mid C_i)$, we would be forced to conclude that, given membership in the criterion group of suicide attempters, the probability of occurrence of the MMPI index is only .10. Since such an index occurs in only 10 percent of the records of suicidal patients, it appears not to be a very practical predictive index. However, from the clinical utility of this index, $P(C_1 \mid R_1)$, it is clear that, given the presence of the MMPI index, R_1, the probability that the patient who obtained that index will attempt suicide is almost a certainty (.99). Despite the relative infrequency of occurrence of this index among suicidal patients ($P = .10$), prediction of suicide from the presence of the index will have almost perfect validity ($P = .99$). Considering the critical social importance of the criterion category involved, C_1, such an index could hardly be ignored in clinical practice. Nevertheless, the validity data presented in the final column of Table 3.3 might suggest that the MMPI index be ignored.

Other possible relationships between clinical utility and validity data for indices based on the mood check list and on the Rorschach test appear in Table 3.3. In the case of the mood check list, the conventional validity study suggests that the index is potentially useful ($P = .60$) and that this suggestion is, to some extent, borne out by the moderate degree of clinical utility of the instrument ($P = .60$). The situation with respect to the Rorschach test is exactly the opposite from that encountered with the MMPI index. Shading responses occur in 90 percent of the Rorschach records of individuals who have attempted suicide. However, note that, given the presence of shading responses, R_3, the probability that an individual will be a member of the critical criterion class, C_1, is only .10. Although shading responses are characteristic of suicide attempters, C_1, such responses are also characteristic of patients in general and therefore could equally well be associated with membership in a variety of other criterion classes, $C_2, C_3, \ldots, C_n$. Although the validity data of Table 3.3 suggest that shading responses on the Rorschach test provide a useful index of suicidal tendencies, the actual clinical utility of such an index is negligible.

The data presented in Table 3.3 are hypothetical—and somewhat extreme—but they are not unrealistic. In fact, there are certain logical considerations which lead us to expect that large discrepancies between clinical utility and validity data would be more often the rule than the exception. These considerations relate to the nature and composition of socially defined criterion groups, C_i, and the nature and composition of groups formed on the basis of psychological test responses, R_j.

The Composition of Socially Defined Criterion Groups

In our initial definition of actuarial prediction, we indicated that the behavior to be predicted consisted of nontest characteristics of the persons tested and that these characteristics were socially, clinically, or theoretically "significant." In developing a psychological theory or engaging in basic psychological research, one commonly employs criterion categories that possess intrinsic theoretical relevance. In most problems of applied personality assessment, however, the criterion categories are much more likely to possess *social* relevance. Socially relevant criterion categories are those which are held to be important by one or more segments of our society.

In Chapter 9 we shall consider the suggestion of Berg (1957) that all socially relevant criterion classifications are based on the notion of statistical deviance. That is, every member of a criterion group is by definition "deviant" in that he is different from individuals who are not members of that criterion group. In this sense, the criterion groups of suicide attempters, successful physicians, high–grade-point-average students, and brain-damaged patients are *all* deviant because members of these groups have been designated as being different from the norm or average. The important point with respect to deviant groups is that they are *socially* defined, rather than defined on the basis of psychological theory. Becker (1963) has made this point dramatically with respect to the sociology of such deviant groups as drug addicts, homosexuals, prostitutes, etc. Becker's point is that the critical condition for being assigned to membership in a deviant group is not a psychological condition of the individual but the circumstances which lead to labeling on the part of society. Hence, when we study "murderers," we are studying not a psychologically homogeneous group of individuals but rather a group of individuals who have been *convicted* of the crime of murder by one jury or another. Similarly, a "drug addict" is an individual who either has voluntarily applied for treatment or has been apprehended in connection with laws relating to narcotics usage. The variety of definitions of such criterion classifications as "alcoholic" (Jellinek, 1962) underscores the wide variations that exist in social-labeling procedures for defining group membership.

Once it is recognized that groups formed by social definition are highly heterogeneous, it should be clear that criterion-group membership may tell us little or nothing about the *psychological* characteristics of the group members. Knowing that an individual has a high grade-point average does not necessarily enable us to describe his personality. The reason, of course, is that a wide variety of personality factors may be associated with membership in the criterion group of high–grade-point-average students. Although members of a criterion group are homogeneous with respect to the defining characteristics of the criterion class, they are most likely heterogeneous with respect to personality characteristics.

The Composition of Psychologically Defined Groups

Most psychological tests are developed in an attempt to measure individual differences with respect to theoretically meaningful dimensions of behavior. A psychological test of "extraversion," for example, attempts to classify individuals in terms of the varying degrees to which the underlying psychological trait of extraversion is manifested in their behavior. In the process of developing such a test, it is possible to select for study individuals who are known to vary in outgoing behavior. The normative or reference group for such a test may be equally clearly specified by appropriate sampling procedures. Consequently, individuals who are later classified on the basis of sharing common patterns of test responses may be considered homogeneous with respect to a relatively clearly defined and theoretically meaningful dimension of behavior. Presumably, membership in such a class should be associated with a variety of behaviors that are theoretically associated with this underlying dimension. However, psychological classifications that possess theoretical relevance may possess little or no "social" relevance in a given applied prediction problem. Such relevance must be demonstrated empirically for each prediction problem.

On the basis of the considerations above and others, Sines (1966) has argued that actuarial classification should be based on patterns of meaningful psychological characteristics, rather than on the inconsistent designations of socially defined criterion groups. That is, instead of classifying subjects on the criterion variable of suicide attempters, C_1, and non–suicide attempters, C_2, and looking for patterns of psychological test responses that are associated with these two categories, we should first classify subjects on the basis of meaningful patterns of psychological test responses, $R_1, R_2, \ldots, R_m$, and then explore the possible relationships between the original psychological classifications and membership in certain criterion groups, $C_1, C_2, \ldots, C_n$.

Because of the manner in which psychological tests have been developed historically, Sines's proposal appears at first glance to *reverse* the normal procedure in actuarial prediction, but in fact, it does not. Returning to the original example of actuarial prediction in the setting of insurance rates (Table 3.1) we can see that the normal procedure for actuarial prediction is precisely the one suggested by Sines. In actuarial prediction, subjects are assigned to a class defined by their pattern of response to predictor variables (age, sex, marital status, etc.). The frequency of criterion classifications (accidents) within these classes of predictor variables is then used as a basis for setting insurance rates. As we have indicated several times, the nature of clinical prediction in psychology takes precisely this form. Actuarial prediction of the form $P(C_i \mid R_j)$ is called "prediction from taxonomic classes." We shall now consider this method of prediction in more detail.

SPECIAL REQUIREMENTS OF ACTUARIAL PREDICTION

Actuarial prediction systems require the collection of measures on a large and representative sample of the subject population to which the system will eventually be applied. Systems designed for very general use must be based on either well-chosen or extremely large samples of the potential populations to which the systems are to be applied. Life insurance rates set by insurance companies are based on U.S. census data and public records, which constitute, in effect, an almost total sampling of the population involved. Prediction problems in personality assessment are more limited in scope and generally are confined to smaller segments of the total population. Nevertheless, the lack of availability of the kinds of data required for even highly specialized prediction systems has, until very recently, prevented the implementation of actuarial systems in the practice of personality assessment (Meehl, 1956).

The situation in personality assessment is slowly changing, however, and the prospects of future actuarial systems are becoming brighter. The possibilities of developing actuarial systems for the prediction of academic success have been enormously increased by the availability of extensive data on 500,000 high school students who participated in Project Talent (Flanagan *et al.*, 1962). MMPI records and demographic data have been collected on a sample of more than 150,000 medical patients (Swenson, 1965). The stringent and expensive sampling requirements of large-scale or nationwide actuarial prediction need not preclude the development of "local" and highly specialized systems intended for limited use. In fact, in the absence of large-scale data banks, the most frequent application of actuarial systems of the future will probably be local and specialized in nature. Such specialized systems are financially feasible, and they can represent a considerable economy, particularly when the output of the system is applied repetitively over a period of time.

Data Collection

For purposes of illustration, we will first consider the development of a hypothetical actuarial prediction system designed for use in psychiatric practice. Later we will consider examples of actual systems that have been developed for this purpose. Our example will involve the implementation of an actuarial system in a state mental hospital with approximately 3,000 inpatients. Data will be obtained for *all* testable patients for whom complete records are available. Once developed, the system will be used for the diagnosis and clinical disposition of all future patients who are admitted to the hospital.

When data are collected for the establishment of an actuarial prediction system it is generally appropriate to gather all potentially relevant data at the same time. This procedure may result in the collection of some classes of data that are of limited practical utility. Nevertheless, because of the expense involved in re-collecting data, it is better to err in the direction of over-collection rather than undercollection. The classes of data which are collected simultaneously may be arbitrarily designated as: (a) predictor variables, (b) criterion data, (c) personality descriptors, (d) demographic data, and (e) miscellaneous data.

Predictor variables. In the establishment of an actuarial prediction system, the most critical decision involves the choice of the variables that will eventually be employed in the formation of taxonomic classes. Once these predictor variables have been selected, the prediction system is essentially "set" and the eventual success of the system will be almost entirely a function of the relevance of the predictor variables to the classes of non-test behaviors to be predicted. The considerations involved in the selection of psychological test variables for any given assessment task are too detailed to be treated at this point. However, certain general considerations may be mentioned. Generally speaking, an appropriate set of predictor variables should be: (1) available, (2) objective, (3) reliable, (4) multidimensional, (5) valid, and (6) theoretically relevant. In most practical situations, actuarial prediction systems will be developed on *available* data. This may result in the restriction of predictor variables to those psychological tests that have been routinely administered to all subjects over a period of time. Under ideal conditions, in which actuarial systems are designed independently of current practice and data are gathered over a period of years, one is more likely to select the "best" set of predictor variables. In the more realistic situation, one is restricted to data which have already been collected. Further, one must select variables that have been routinely administered to all subjects. In the present instance, it will be assumed that the MMPI has been routinely administered to all patients, and that test will therefore be the one chosen for use as a source of predictor variables. Although the number of predictor variables that may be chosen is frequently large, the number that can actually be employed to define taxonomic classes is relatively small. (These practical constraints will be discussed below.) Nevertheless, despite faith in a given instrument or set of instruments, it might be advisable to collect data on second-choice instruments in the event that one's first choice turns out to be less effective than was anticipated.

For practical reasons, it is desirable that predictor variables be *objective* in the sense that they can be quantified with a minimum of human judgment. Self-description inventories and other "objective tests" lend themselves readily to this type of quantification. Note that actuarial prediction in no way precludes the use of predictor variables that require human judgment (e.g., interviews and projective techniques). However, since economy is one of the presumed virtues of actuarial prediction, such elaborate procedures could be justified only under highly specialized circumstances. Recall that the predictor variables used in the establishment of the actuarial prediction system must continue to be employed in future applications of the system.

Although *reliability* is a desirable characteristic in all psychological tests, it is an especially important property of predictor variables that will form the basis of taxonomic classes. In actuarial prediction, predictor variables are typically employed *in combinations*, sometimes of a highly configural nature. The combinations of patterns of predictor variables that are eventually employed for taxonomic classification will almost certainly be less reliable than the individual tests or scales that contribute to the patterns. For this reason predictor variables that are employed in actuarial prediction must be especially reliable.

The issue of *dimensionality* with respect to predictor variables involves considerations of both representativeness and redundancy. Although it is clearly not possible to measure all dimensions which underlie human behavior, it may be possible to measure some of the major dimensions. Given that only a few dimensions can be assessed, it follows that the dimensions chosen should be relatively independent of one another. Aside from considerations of reliability, it would not be efficient to employ five predictor variables that are highly intercorrelated. That this issue has been given insufficient attention is apparent from the frequent choice of MMPI clinical scales as predictor variables in actuarial systems. The MMPI clinical scales provide redundant measurement of a very small number of personality dimensions. Future attention might better be focused on inventories that have been specifically constructed to be multidimensional in nature (e.g., the Sixteen Personality Factor Questionnaire of Cattell and Eber, 1962).

The *validity* of a personality test or pattern of test scores generally refers to the extent to which the test is correlated with nontest criteria of interest. If two tests are equal in all other characteristics, preference should clearly be given to the more valid test. In practice, however, tests are seldom equal on all other characteristics, and the problem of validity in actuarial prediction must be construed somewhat differently than it is in other assessment paradigms. In actuarial prediction, the validity of a test or scale is less an issue than the validity of a taxonomic classification based on a combination of individual scales or tests. Since the particular combinations of psychological tests that will define the taxonomic classes are seldom known in advance, it is unlikely that validity information will be available for any particular combination of tests prior to the development of the prediction system. To take an extreme example, it is possible that a particular combination of test scales might form a highly valid taxonomic class even though the individual scales that went into that combination were not especially valid in the usual sense of that word. Development of taxonomic classes on the basis of any set of predictor variables will almost inevitably lead to the discovery of *new* combinations of variables, and this possibility should be recognized with an open-minded and experimental attitude toward the kinds of predictor variables that might be initially included.

A final consideration in the selection of predictor variables has to do with the *theoretical relevance* of the variables to the prediction task at hand. Even before all the preceding conditions for predictor variables have been met, it is appropriate to give attention to the theoretical basis on which one might expect a given set of predictor variables to relate to the criterion behaviors of interest. However, as was true of validity considerations, considerations of theoretical relevance must be tempered by recognition that new combinations of variables may be involved in taxonomic prediction. It is easier, of course, to interpret the significance of new patterns or combinations of predictor variables when the theoretical nature of the original scales is well understood. Under these circumstances, a by-product of an actuarial prediction system might be a basic contribution to personality theory.

Criterion data. At the same time that predictor variables are recorded, information is gathered that is relevant to all foreseeable criterion categories. If gathered from existing records, it will be immediately available even though it was originally recorded at a time subsequent to the recording of the predictor variables. Although a given actuarial system may be designed for the purpose of making only one or two criterion discriminations, it is wise to anticipate other possible criterion categories that might be of interest in the future. For the system we are developing here, the most important criterion categorization seems to be that of psychiatric diagnosis. In addition, it would be useful to gather data on other criterion designations, such as prognosis for recovery, response to therapy, and length of hospitalization. Since accurate prediction of criterion designations is the eventual aim of any actuarial system, it is important that such data be recorded carefully and in detail. Although the eventual categorization of criterion variables may be broad (e.g., psychotic, neurotic, etc.), it is best to record the original criterion information in finer categories (schizophrenic reaction; acute, undifferentiated type).

Personality descriptors. An especially interesting class of data to be collected is that which may be called "personality descriptors." Such descriptors are based primarily on direct observation of patient behavior by physicians, psychologists, attendants, and nurses. These data may be gathered in the form of adjective check lists, rating scales, or Q-sort descriptions.[3] Personality descriptors are of two general classes: those based on relatively simple behavioral observations ("slow personal tempo," "has few friends on ward") and those requiring inferences from behavior ("has considerable repressed hostility," "is characterized by latent homosexual tendencies)". Experience and research with such descriptors indicate that the direct behavioral ratings are more reliable and useful than highly inferential ratings (Sines, 1966).

In addition to personality variables, it is useful to gather data on the characteristic symptoms and complaints of the patient. These data may be gathered by means of symptom check lists, or they may be extracted from clinical reports. Unfortunately, few hospitals employ behavioral rating scales, adjective check lists, or Q-sorts on a systematic basis. Such data are more likely to be available when institutional record-keeping systems are designed for use in an actuarial prediction system. A convincing case for the use of existing hospital records as a source of personality descriptors has been made by Sines (1966).

Demographic data. The files of hospitals and similar institutions will typically contain records of such demographic characteristics as age, sex, marital status, place of birth, number of siblings, birth order, socioeconomic class, education, occupation, etc. Since actuarial prediction systems are seldom designed in such a fashion as to control for demographic variables, it is essential that such variables be recorded for both descriptive and predictive purposes. Once taxonomic groups have been assembled, demographic data should be consulted to define the characteristics of the particular sample of subjects employed and thereby estimate the probable reduction in validity to be encountered if the system is employed outside its original context. Further, it is likely that demographic characteristics will interact both with taxonomic classification and with the prediction of criteria from such classification. Careful recording of as many demographic characteristics as possible will ensure the detection of such interaction patterns and facilitate their interpretation.

———————

3. In the Q-sort method (Block, 1961; Stephenson, 1953), judges are asked to sort a set of cards containing descriptive statements into a number of piles or categories ranging from "least" to "most" descriptive. Frequently, the number of cards placed in each pile is fixed, so that the resultant distribution of descriptive statements is normal in form.

Miscellaneous data. When actuarial prediction systems are derived from existing hospital records, it is important to be sensitive to other data sources that might clarify or facilitate the predictive systems. Psychological tests that are more or less routinely administered can often provide additional information that will help to clarify the nature of taxonomic groups. Some form of intelligence estimate is often available, and it should be recorded routinely. Results of any other psychological tests that lend themselves readily to quantification should also be included. Records of medical and neurological examinations are an equally fertile source of potentially useful information. In some actuarial prediction systems, such records may provide a source of criterion data, and in almost all, they will constitute a useful supplement to the other kinds of data available. Since every hospital setting has aspects that are unique, it is difficult to specify all potentially useful classes of miscellaneous data. It is therefore important to familiarize oneself with all available sources of recorded information when first implementing an actuarial system.

Identification of Groups

The goal of taxonomic classification is to provide a manageable number of (a) homogeneous and (b) mutually distinct classifications that occur with (c) sufficient frequency to provide a basis for reliable predictions. Before considering the methods whereby this goal might be attained, one must give some thought to the role of *a priori* expectations in the formation of taxonomic classes. Recall that most predictor variables are selected for taxonomic classification on the basis of their possessing some criterion validity, at least of the form $P(R_j \mid C_i)$. Consequently, there are certain predictor-criterion relationships expected on an *a priori* basis, and these relationships may or may not be taken into account in establishing the taxonomic classes. In the MMPI, there are a number of profiles, or constellations of predictor scores, that are known to be related to such criterion classifications as psychiatric diagnosis. Actuarial prediction systems based on the MMPI have varied in their emphasis on such *a priori* categorization, from very heavy emphasis (Gilberstadt and Duker, 1965) to none whatsoever (Sines, 1966).

A *priori* classifications are not necessarily compatible with the overall goal of taxonomic classification and, in some instances, may be incompatible. Profile classifications with known or expected criterion relationships (a) may not be homogeneous within a profile class, (b) may not be mutually exclusive, or (c) may not occur with a practical degree of frequency. Further, imposing *a priori* limitations on a taxonomic classification system may obscure predictor-criterion relationships that are stronger than those already known or assumed. When one is deciding on the role of *a priori* considerations in taxonomic classification, a conflict arises between ignoring known or assumed predictor-criterion relationships on the one hand and precluding still undiscovered relationships on the other. Because actuarial prediction is a relatively new technique in personality assessment, there is a tendency for new systems to preserve at least some of the information from earlier research with the predictor variables. Although such a strategy is not necessarily the most logical in principle, it does guarantee a more widespread acceptance of the system among practitioners who have had experience with the predictor variables in earlier application or research.

Simple versus complex classifications. Given a set of predictor variables, such as the ten standard clinical scales of the MMPI, the possible ways of forming taxonomic groups are almost unlimited. Since the goal of taxonomic classification itself involves a compromise between specificity (group homogeneity and independence) and reliability (sufficient numbers of subjects in taxonomic classes), any taxonomic system will itself be a compromise between these two competing requirements. The resultant system may be thought of as falling on a continuum ranging from quite simple classifications (which may combine large numbers of possibly heterogeneous subjects) to highly complex classifications (which may sacrifice reliability for specificity).

With respect to the ten standard MMPI clinical scales, the simplest taxonomic system might involve classification of each profile in terms of the highest scale score in that profile. Thus, if an individual obtained his highest score on the first scale, he would be assigned to the taxonomic class of 1's, if on the second scale, to the class of 2's, etc. Such a system would have no more than ten categories and it might have fewer since there is no guarantee that at least one subject in a given group will obtain a highest score on each of the ten scales. Further, there is no guarantee of large frequencies in each of the possible classes because high scores on some scales may be relatively rare. Nevertheless, it is possible by this method to find a set of scales that will exhaustively classify all subjects in the original sample. With ten or fewer scales being employed, the number of cases in each category can be quite large, and the *reliability* of predictions is almost certain to be acceptable. Note, however, that such an extremely simple classification system does little to ensure either homogeneity of subjects within a class or distinctiveness between subjects in different classes. Under this simple system it is possible for subjects in different taxonomic groups to have *identical* scores on nine MMPI scales. Not only may subjects in different taxonomic groups be highly similar, but subjects within a given taxonomic classification may be quite different from one another since it is possible for them to be at the opposite ends of continua on as many as nine scales.

Defining a taxonomic class on the basis of similarity in elevation on one out of the ten standard MMPI clinical scales is unlikely to result in homogeneous and mutually distinct classifications. Moving up the continuum of complexity of classification, let us consider classification of profiles in terms of the two highest scale scores. Individuals whose profiles share the common characteristic of elevation on two scales are certainly more similar to one another than are those with only one. Nevertheless, with a classification system based on the two highest scales (65 = highest score on scale 6, next highest score on scale 5) it is still possible for subjects in different taxonomic groups to have identical scores on eight MMPI clinical scales and for subjects within a given classification to be at the opposite ends of continua on as many as eight scales. Moreover, using permutations of two scales at a time (12, 21) would result in 90 potential categories of classification. Even with a very large sample of subjects, there is no guarantee that a set of categories may be found that contains classifications of sufficient frequency to provide a basis for reliable predictions.

It should be apparent that even very simple bases of classification generate an extremely large number of potential classes. Clearly, if one were to consider rigorously the concept of similarity of MMPI profiles, one would be concerned with defining profile similarity on the basis of all ten standard clinical scales. Considering only the possible relative orderings of scale elevation on ten MMPI scales, we would have 10! = 3,628,800 potential taxonomic categories to contend with! As we shall see in the next section, the relative ordering of scales represents an extremely gross categorization that allows for considerable variability among individual profiles within a taxonomic class. Classification on the basis of relative ordering ignores such essential aspects of profile similarity as elevation, shape, and scatter. Profile classification systems which do not attend to the elevation, shape, and scatter of a profile cannot be considered as even minimally complex in nature. Yet the number of possible taxonomic classes that can be formed on the basis of even reasonably complex classification is astronomical. Fortunately, there are a number of procedures that have been developed for coping with this seemingly insurmountable problem.

Principles of profile classification. Two basic strategies may be employed in the discovery or definition of taxonomic classes (Cattell, Coulter, and Tsujioka, 1966). The first involves the definition of all possible combinations of values on the predictor variables (e.g., the 3.6 million possible permutations of ordered MMPI scales in the example above) followed by an actual counting of the number of instances of each classification observed in the initial sample. Not only is this strategy prohibitively laborious, but it is inefficient as well. The more common strategy, which is employed in almost all psychological taxonomy, involves the *empirical* determination of "clusters" of subjects defined in terms of their profile similarities. That is, by direct comparison of subjects' profiles, an attempt is made to discover groupings of subjects' profiles that are (a) homogeneous, (b) mutually distinct, and (c) of sufficient frequency to provide a basis for reliable predictions. There are many ways of defining profile similarity (Cronbach and Gleser, 1953) and many ways of discovering clusters of profiles (Sawrey, Keller, and Conger, 1960). Rather than review this technical and controversial literature, we shall use a simple illustration that is representative of current practice.

The two profiles in Figure 3.1 can serve as a geometric example of differences that might occur between the ten-variable MMPI profiles of two patients. The variables in these profiles, 1, 2, ..., 10, are presented in *standard* form $(X - M_x)/\sigma_x$, to facilitate comparison. Standard scores on MMPI variables are called T-scores (Hathaway and McKinley, 1951). The three main parameters along which profiles may differ are *elevation, shape,* and *scatter.* Elevation refers to the overall *mean* level of the profile, and in the MMPI, it is associated with the extent to which the profile deviates from normality. Shape refers to the overall *configuration* of the profile as determined by the relative elevation among the scales. Scatter, a measure of the *variability,* σ, of scales within a profile from the overall mean of that profile, represents an "accentuation of shape" (Cattell, Coulter, and Tsujioka, 1966). Comparing the two profiles in Figure 3.1, we can see that although the profiles differ markedly in overall elevation, they are highly similar in shape. However, it is also clear that the scatter of the bottom profile is greater than that of the top.

An obvious first approximation to an index of profile similarity would be to *correlate* the two profiles in Figure 3.1 across the ten values of the

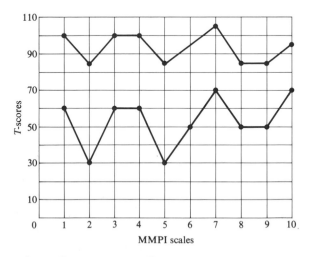

Fig. 3.1 Comparison of two MMPI profiles.

MMPI scales. This statistic may take the form of the standard Pearson product-moment correlation (Stephenson, 1952) or the rank-order correlation coefficient (Holland *et al.*, 1953). However, as Cronbach and Gleser (1953) have noted, definitions of profile similarity based on correlations ignore both the *elevation* and *scatter* components of profile similarity. In the example presented in Figure 3.1, the two profiles are very highly correlated, though obviously *different* in both elevation and scatter.

An index of profile similarity that takes elevation, shape, and scatter into consideration is the "generalized distance function" (Mahalanobis, 1936), which was introduced to psychologists by Osgood and Suci (1952) and Cronbach and Gleser (1953). The generalized distance function is defined as the sum of the squared differences between all variables for any two profiles. To calculate the generalized distance between the profiles in Figure 3.1 we simply subtract the scores between the two profiles on each of the ten variables, square them, and sum them: $D^2 = (100 - 60)^2 + (85 - 30)^2 + \cdots + (95 - 70)^2 = 17,175$. One shortcoming of the D^2 index of profile similarity is the assumption that the variables of the profile are themselves uncorrelated (Cattell, 1949; Nunnally, 1962). A more elaborate technique of computing profile similarity, which takes into account the problem of correlated variables and the number of dimensions involved, is the "pattern similarity coefficient" proposed by Cattell (Cattell, 1949; Cattell, Coulter, and Tsujioka, 1966). For purposes of illustration, the more commonly used D^2 statistic will be employed here.

Given a means of defining profile similarity by use of the D^2 statistic, there are a variety of alternative methods that may be employed for discovering or defining clusters of individuals for purposes of defining taxonomic groups (Haggard *et al.*, 1959; Sawrey, Keller, and Conger, 1960; Cattell, Coulter, and Tsujioka, 1966). In our present MMPI example, we shall illustrate a method proposed by Sawrey *et al.* (1960) and actually implemented in an MMPI prediction study by Sines (1966).

Let us assume that we have scores on the ten standard MMPI clinical scales for some 3,000 psychiatric inpatients. The means and standard deviations of the ten scales for the entire sample are given in Table 3.4. Let us further assume (and it will soon become clear why) that we have access to a high-speed computer. We first compute the index of profile similarity, D^2, between all possible pairs of the 3,000 MMPI profiles. Although this will involve approximately 4.5 million separate D^2 calculations, bear in mind that the computer is performing these operations for us. We can further program our computer to perform a cluster definition and search routine that would be almost impossible by hand.

Given our indices of profile similarity, D^2, between all possible pairs of MMPI profiles, we must now decide, somewhat arbitrarily, on a definition

89514

Table 3.4 Means, standard deviations, and variance indices for ten MMPI scales

	MMPI profile scales ($N = 3,000$)									
	1	2	3	4	5	6	7	8	9	10
Mean	56.3	65.6	54.2	58.3	51.3	60.1	70.2	72.4	63.0	51.1
σ	11.1	12.2	9.8	10.2	13.2	14.2	11.6	14.0	10.6	11.4
σ^2	123.2	148.8	96.0	104.0	174.2	201.6	134.6	196.0	112.4	130.0

Computations

$$\sum_{i=1}^{10} \sigma^2 = 1421$$

$$\tfrac{1}{2}\sum \sigma^2 = 710$$
$$\tfrac{1}{3}\sum \sigma^2 = 474$$
$$\tfrac{1}{4}\sum \sigma^2 = 355$$

of the maximum amount by which two profiles may differ in D^2 and still be called "similar" profiles. The arbitrary definition suggested by Sawrey *et al.* (1960) is based on the standard deviations of each of the test scores in the entire population. Returning to Table 3.4, we can see that a standard deviation, σ, has been computed for each of the ten MMPI scales in the total sample. The variance, σ^2, of each of the scales appears beneath each standard deviation. Summing the variances across all scales

$$\left(\sum_{i=1}^{10} \sigma^2 = 123.2 + 148.8 + \cdots + 130.0 \right)$$

gives an index of the total variance of all the scales in the profile, which, as the lower left of Table 3.4 shows, is equal to 1421. An arbitrary maximum of profile similarity may be set at half of this value: $\tfrac{1}{2}\sum \sigma^2 = 710$. That is, to be classified as similar, two profiles cannot differ by more than half of the sum of the standard deviations of all scales in the profile. Profiles whose D^2 value is 710 or less are classified as similar, and profiles whose D^2 value exceeds this amount are classified as different.

For each of the 3,000 patient profiles we record those profiles whose D^2 value from that profile does not exceed the arbitrary amount of 710. Table 3.5 shows a portion of such a record. Next to Johnson's name we record the names of all patients whose D^2 profile difference from Johnson's profile is 710 or less. Table 3.5 shows that Benson, Feldman, and Davis, among others, all have profiles that are within 710 D^2 points of Johnson's profile. In fact, there are 273 patients whose profiles meet this definition of similarity to Johnson's profile. The same procedure is followed for Brown's profile, which is similar to the profiles of May, Hess, Goldstein, and others. The

Table 3.5 Portion of recording sheet listing similar ($D < 710$) profiles

Profile	Similar profiles	Total number of similar profiles
Johnson	Benson, Feldman, Davis, etc.	273
Brown	May, Hess, Goldstein, etc.	230
Coulter	Harris, Fry, Crane, etc.	200
Jennings	Donovan, Morris, Benson, etc.	150
⋮		⋮
Adcock		0

profiles are ordered in terms of the number of similar profiles with which they are associated. In its entirety, Table 3.5 would contain 3,000 rows, each representing one of the patients in the total sample. The last rows of the table carry the names of individuals whose profiles are not similar to any other profiles in the sample, e.g., Adcock. Note that such a listing will not result in groups of mutually exclusive similar profiles. A profile similar to Johnson's can equally well be similar to Brown's or Coulter's. For example, Benson's profile is defined as similar to those of both Johnson and Jennings.

The next step in classification involves the selection of "potential nucleus groups" (Sawrey *et al.*, 1960) that will form the eventual basis of taxonomic classification. The profile associated with the largest number of other profiles is taken to represent the first potential nucleus group—in the present example, Johnson's. All profiles similar to Johnson's (Benson, Feldman, Davis, etc.) are then eliminated from consideration in other potential nucleus groups. That is, any name in Johnson's row is deleted from any of the succeeding rows. In the present example, Benson's name would be deleted from the fourth row because it appears in Johnson's potential nucleus group. The next potential nucleus group is represented by the profile with the second largest number of associated profiles—in the present instance, Brown's. All names in Brown's row (which have not already been eliminated because they were also in Johnson's row) are now deleted from the rows for Coulter, Jennings, etc. This procedure is continued until a set of *mutually exclusive* nuclear groupings is achieved, the smallest group containing, let us say, only two similar profiles and the largest group (Johnson) containing 273 profiles. Let us assume that we have identified 175 such potential nucleus groups. Having selected groups which are homogeneous and mutually exclusive, we now direct our attention to the problem of making these potential nucleus groups as maximally *dissimilar* as possible.

The 175 potential nucleus groups are now considered in relationship to one another. A matrix is formed by which to compare the D^2 value of each nuclear profile with that value of every other nuclear profile in the total groups. Table 3.6 represents a portion of a 175 × 175 matrix, the entries of which represent the D^2 differences between the profiles involved. Recall from Table 3.5 that the profiles of Johnson, Brown, Coulter, and Jennings were selected as potential nuclear profiles on the basis of their being associated with a large number of other profiles in the population. In Table 3.6, we now directly compare the D^2 differences between the nuclear profiles of Johnson, Brown, and Coulter and the 172 other nuclear profiles. Looking at the D^2 entries in the body of Table 3.6, we can see that Johnson's profile differs from Brown's by a D^2 value of 2,525, Brown's from Coulter's by a D^2 value of 1,962, etc. The entries of Table 3.6 thus represent the D^2 differences between all possible pairs of the 175 nuclear profiles.

Table 3.6 Portion of matrix giving D^2 differences between 175 nuclear profiles

Profile	Johnson	Brown	Coulter	Jennings		Smith
Johnson	0	2,525	1,562	1,250	· · ·	4,328
Brown	2,525	0	1,962	2,750	· · ·	2,122
Coulter	1,562	1,962	0	1,816	· · ·	1,786
Jennings	1,250	2,750	1,816	0	· · ·	2,005
⋮	⋮	⋮	⋮	⋮		⋮
Smith	4,328	2,122	1,786	2,005	· · ·	0
Column sum	426,200	157,268	392,414	121,626	· · ·	226,342

If we sum the *columns* of Table 3.6, we will arrive at an index of the *dissimilarity* of the profile represented by that column to all other profiles included in the potential nuclear classifications. Summing Johnson's column across all 175 entries, we arrive at a grand total of 426,200. Summing Brown's column, we obtain 157,268. The next step will involve a procedure for profile elimination that begins with the profile having the largest sum of differences across all other profiles, $\sum D^2$.

Before we can proceed to eliminate profiles, we must decide on an arbitrary *minimum* definition of profile *dissimilarity*. One such suggested minimal definition of dissimilarity is the sum of the squared standard deviations of all ten MMPI clinical scales, $\sum \sigma_i^2$. Table 3.4 shows that this value is 1,421. Recall that we took half of this value ($\frac{1}{2}\sum \sigma^2 = 710$) as our definition of profile *similarity* in the selection of nuclear profiles. We now adopt as our definition of profile *dissimilarity* the sum of all variances of MMPI scales. This is, of course, a relatively liberal definition of dissimilarity.

Returning to the 175 × 175 matrix of potential nuclear profiles in Table 3.6, we proceed to eliminate profiles that are too similar to each other, i.e., those whose mutual D^2 value is less than 1,421. We start with the nuclear profile that has the largest $\sum D^2$ column (i.e., is the most dissimilar to other potential nuclear profiles). In the present example, Johnson's profile is the most dissimilar. Reading across Johnson's row, we eliminate each profile whose D^2 value is less than 1,421. It is eliminated not only from the nuclear profile group of which it is a member, Johnson's, but from all other groups in the matrix. Table 3.6 shows that the D^2 value of Jennings' profile falls below the minimum value of dissimilarity to Johnson's profile (1,250 < 1,421). We therefore eliminate the entry for Jennings from Johnson's row. Further-more, we eliminate the entire fourth row of the matrix, which was based on Jennings' nuclear profile. We continue the procedure with the next most dissimilar potential nuclear profile, eliminating profiles that are too similar to it from all subsequent considerations. In Table 3.6, Coulter's row would be the next one considered.

The foregoing procedure has the effect not only of reducing the number of profiles in a given nuclear group associated with a nuclear profile, but of eliminating some nuclear profile groups entirely (such as Jennings'). As a consequence, we now have a reduced set, let us say arbitrarily, of 100 potential nuclear profile groupings, which are maximally distinct from one another and which may be thought of as "prototype profiles" (Sines, 1966). They are used as a basis for defining potential nuclear clusters of profiles that exist within the entire sample of 3,000 profiles.

We now have a set of 100 prototype profiles, each of which is associated with varying numbers of similar profiles defined by our original index of profile similarity. The number of similar profiles associated with each prototype profile will vary considerably. We might now wish to eliminate those prototypes which are associated with a small number of similar profiles. For example, we can decide to eliminate prototype profiles that are similar to fewer than 15 other profiles in our reduced sample. Let us assume that this arbitrary decision results in the further reduction of prototype profiles to 50.

For each of the 50 prototype profiles, we compute the mean scale value on all ten MMPI scales for all the similar profiles associated with that prototype. In other words, for each prototype group, we average profiles among similar members to obtain 50 mean prototype profiles. They are of the kind originally presented in Table 3.4, but they are now based on varying numbers of cases falling within each prototype group. The mean prototype profiles are now employed in a regrouping procedure designed to increase the number of profiles in a prototype category while maintaining dissimilarity between the prototype profile groupings. At this point, all the remaining profiles that have not been classified as falling within the 50 prototype groups are compared with the mean scale scores of each of the 50 prototype groups by means of the D^2 statistic. That is, for a given profile not included in one of the groupings, D^2 is computed between that profile and the mean profiles of Prototype I, Prototype II, etc.

Next it is necessary to develop a somewhat more rigorous definition of profile similarity. Whereas previously our definition of profile similarity was $\frac{1}{2} \sum \sigma_i^2 = 710$, our current definition might be $\frac{1}{4} \sum \sigma_i^2$. The value of this more rigorous definition, as Table 3.4 shows, is 355. On the basis of the new definition, a profile whose D^2 distance from a given mean prototype profile is less than 355 becomes a member of that prototype profile group. (Any profile that can be classified in more than one of the 50 prototype groups is temporarily set aside.) When this procedure is finished, the original 50 prototype groups have been enlarged by inclusion of additional similar profiles, under a rigorous definition of profile similarity. The mean MMPI scale profile is *recomputed* for each of the 50 enlarged prototype groups. This procedure yields 50 new mean profiles that can serve as revised prototypes for further classification. Profiles that were not included in the regrouping of prototype clusters just described may now be compared with the revised mean profiles of each of the new prototype groups. For this purpose it is necessary to use a somewhat less rigorous definition of profile similarity. One such definition might be $\frac{1}{3} \sum \sigma_i^2$, the value of which is computed in Table 3.4. This procedure may continue indefinitely with successively less rigorous definitions of profile similarity ($\frac{1}{2} \sum \sigma_i^2$, $\frac{3}{4} \sum \sigma_i^2$, ..., $\sum \sigma_i^2$, etc.). After each new classification attempt, the augmented prototype profile group mean is recomputed for use in the subsequent step.

The extent to which prototype profile groups are augmented by inclusion of additional profiles is at the discretion of the taxonomist. Appropriate guidelines here would be those originally stated as the goals of taxonomic classification, namely, the determination of a manageable number of (a) homogeneous and (b) mutually distinct classifications that occur with (c) sufficient frequency to provide a basis for reliable predictions. As has been indicated several times, homogeneity and distinctiveness are somewhat at odds with reliability as considerations in the determination of taxonomic classes. The particular compromise the taxonomist selects will vary with the relative emphasis he places on purity of classification as opposed to practicality of classification. By purity we mean the homogeneity and distinctiveness of taxonomic classifications that ensure psychological similarity between individuals classified in the same taxonomic class. By practicality we mean the recognition of the hard fact that a taxonomic system that can classify only 1 percent of a given population is of little value, regardless of its purity.

Let us assume that we have wrestled with these problems and decided on a final taxonomic classification system based on 25 distinct MMPI profile types. Let us further assume that these types are relatively pure and that they classify 75 percent of the present patient population (i.e., 2,250 patients). Finally, let us assume that there are at least 50 patients represented in each of the 25 separate taxonomic categories.

Construction of Actuarial Tables

Once the taxonomic categories have been formed, it becomes possible to construct actuarial prediction tables from the criterion data, personality descriptors, demographic data, and miscellaneous data already gathered. The frequency of occurrence of different categories of the criterion and other data are tabulated separately for each of the taxonomic classifications. These frequencies in turn may be converted to percentages within each taxonomic class to form a table of the type illustrated by Table 3.7.

Table 3.7 is a portion of a much larger actuarial table that might be formed in the hypothetical MMPI study under discussion. The columns of such a table would identify the 25 taxonomic categories previously derived. The rows would list the different classes of criterion data that might be entered. In the present illustration, the criterion data are categorical and can therefore be expressed as frequencies, which are converted in turn into percentages. Entries in the actuarial table need not be categorical in nature, as we shall see in a moment. However, one advantage of categorical data, which can be expressed as percentages, is that the percentages are subject to direct interpretation as probabilities. Thus we can make direct probability statements of the form $P(C_i \mid R_j)$, which may be stated as: "Given that an individual is classified as falling within the taxonomic category of Profile Type I, the probability that he will receive the psychiatric diagnosis of psychotic is .80."

In the interpretation of actuarial probabilities, it is important to take into account not only the probability of occurrence of the criterion classification *within* a given profile type, but the overall probability of its occurrence in the entire population ($N = 3,000$). Consideration of the latter probability enables the test interpreter to avoid the "Barnum effect,"[4] which gives the impression of descriptive accuracy by generating statements that are true of virtually *all* people of the type considered (Meehl, 1956). Because such statements are true of all people, they give the illusion of accuracy when applied to an individual case. A Barnum-type personality description: "Under stressful circumstances, this person occasionally experiences some feelings of self-doubt."

In hospitalized psychiatric patients, anxiety and depression are so common that the attribution of either anxiety or depression to a given patient is

---

4.   Paterson, D. G. "Character reading at sight of Mr. X according to the system of Mr. P. T. Barnum." Unpublished paper, University of Minnesota, Minneapolis.

Table 3.7 Actuarial table for psychiatric prediction

	Profile type I	Profile type II	Profile type III
Criterion data			
Psychiatric diagnosis			
Psychotic	80*	20	15
Neurotic	10	70*	02
Character disorders	04	05	01
Organic	00	03	78*
. . .	. .	. .	. .
Length of hospitalization			
3 months or less	05	45*	01
6 months	05	35*	05
1 year	10	15	14
2 years	10	10	20
3 years	15	05	25
More than 3 years	55*	00	35
. . .	. .	. .	. .
Personality descriptors			
Anxious	70	92*	68
Withdrawn	90*	02	33
Confused	65	05	64
Assaultive	15	01	03
. . .	. .	. .	. .
Demographic data			
Age			
15–21	10	60*	05
21–25	10	30	10
25–35	05	02	02
35–45	10	03	03
45–55	15	02	10
Over 55	50*	03	70*
Marital status			
Single	30	12	05
Married	55	50	65
Divorced	10	38*	10
Widowed	05	00	20*
. . .	. .	. .	. .
Miscellaneous data			
Neurological findings			

unlikely to contribute information that will enable him to be discriminated from any other hospitalized patient. In the present example, Table 3.7 shows that 70 percent of patients classified within Profile Type I are described as "anxious." However, if the personality descriptors attributed to the entire population of patients ($N = 3,000$) indicate that some 78 percent of patients in general are described as anxious, little weight should be given to that personality descriptor as a unique characteristic of individuals in Profile Type I.

To avoid Barnum-type statements, it is standard practice to calculate the relative frequency of occurrence of categories of criterion data in the entire sample under consideration. Such data may be used as a base line against which to assess *significant departures* from overall group trends. In Table 3.7, for example, actuarial categories within a profile type that significantly ($p < .01$) depart from the group average are indicated by asterisks. For the personality descriptor "anxious," note that a significant departure from the group norm, 78 percent, occurs in Profile Type II, in which 92 percent of the patients are described by that term. Similar asterisks identify other criterion categories which depart significantly from the norm of the entire sample. In classifying departures from group norms, one must indicate not only those percentages which are significantly above the group norm, but also those which are significantly below. Further, it is sometimes desirable to attempt to quantify the degree of deviation ($p < .05$; $p < .01$; $p < .001$). The method employed by Marks and Seeman (1963) employs plus signs to indicate significant deviations above group norms ($+$; $++$; $+++$) and minus sign for deviations significantly below ($-$; $--$; $---$).

Entries in actuarial tables are not limited to categorical data; they may include data based on means, medians, or any other descriptive statistic. In fact, the form in which data are entered need not be subject to the limitations that are occasionally present when data for a group of patients are averaged. In constructing actuarial tables for prediction from the MMPI, Marks and Seeman (1963) made extensive use of personality descriptors based on Q-sorts. Psychologists and psychiatrists were asked to describe their patients by placing each of 108 descriptive statements in one of nine categories, according to the judged degree of relevance of each statement to a given patient. Instead of computing the *mean* placement of each item for each taxonomic class, Marks and Seeman selected the "most homogeneous" members of each class by correlating the Q-sort descriptions of all patients within a given class and selecting only those who formed a homogeneous cluster on the personality descriptors. The mean score values of the descriptors for this subsample of patients were then entered in the actuarial table, along with indications of the extent to which they represented significant deviations above ($+$) or below ($-$) the mean for the entire patient population.

Actuarial tables of the type illustrated by Table 3.7 may be consulted directly by a clerical worker, or they may be stored on a computer tape for access by automation. Although the system may be intended primarily for local use, it is almost certain to be of interest to other workers, and it should therefore be published, if possible (Marks and Seeman, 1963; Gilberstadt and Duker, 1965). For large-scale repetitive use, storage of the actuarial table on a computer tape is appropriate, not only because such handling facilitates interpretation, but because the kind of individual profile classification to be discussed next is accomplished most easily with the help of a computer.

Use of Actuarial Tables

Once an actuarial system has been assembled, it may be put into actual diagnostic practice by routinely applying it to all new patients admitted to the hospital. In the present instance, all new patients admitted to the hospital would be administered the MMPI, and their profiles of clinical scale scores would be determined. A given patient's profile would then be compared with each of the 25 profile types previously established. Its similarity would be assessed by the D^2 statistic. Recall that a given profile is considered most similar to that profile type which, on comparison, yields the smallest D^2 value.

Again, it is necessary to specify an arbitrary maximum value of D^2 for the purposes of defining similarity. On the basis of experience with the original sample (Table 3.4) one might select a value which represents some fraction of the sum of the variances of profile scales in the total original sample, for example, $\frac{1}{2} \sum \sigma^2 = 710$. Although this value is arbitrary, it is not to be taken lightly. By selecting a very small maximum value (e.g., 400 or below) one ensures a rigorous classification of profile types and maximizes the likelihood of psychological similarity between the patient being diagnosed and members of the profile type to which he is assigned. Unfortunately, the more rigorous the definition of profile similarity, the less likely it becomes that the patient will be assigned to any profile type, and consequently, the actuarial system becomes applicable to only a very small proportion of new patients. On the other hand, very broad definitions of profile similarity (e.g., 1,500) ensure the wide applicability of the actuarial system at the risk of assigning patients to profile types to which they are not psychologically similar. For our example, we might select the arbitrary value of 700 as the most appropriate compromise.

When the patient has been assigned to a profile type, actuarial prediction may proceed in two quite distinct directions. Depending on the diagnostic problem, the system may be used in an attempt to predict "fixed criteria" or "free criteria." It is important to understand the distinction between these two kinds of prediction and to recognize that an actuarial system of the type described is capable of predicting either or both.

Prediction of fixed criteria. By far the most widely recognized use of actuarial prediction systems is found in the prediction of fixed categories of social, clinical, or economic importance. The use of actuarial methods by insurance companies is restricted to the prediction of fixed criteria, such as number of accidents, time of death, number of fires, etc. In personnel selection, most of the fixed-criterion categories represent different definitions of job "success," such as number of products sold, supervisors' proficiency ratings, etc. In clinical psychology, the most frequently predicted fixed criteria relate to prognosis or the probable outcomes of various types of treatment.

In the actuarial system under consideration, certain fixed-criterion categories of Table 3.7 would be of special interest in a psychiatric hospital setting. If a patient's profile was assigned to Profile Type I, it would be predicted that the most likely ($P = .80$) psychiatric diagnosis is that of "psychotic," the length of hospitalization is likely to be quite long (more than three years), and the response to conventional psychotherapy may be rather poor. For patients assigned to Profile Type II, the most likely psychiatric diagnosis is that of "neurotic," the anticipated length of hospitalization is quite short, and response to conventional psychotherapy is likely to be good. Actuarial systems are ideally suited for prediction of such fixed categories, and their use to date has been largely restricted to this kind of prediction.

Prediction of free criteria. Frequently in clinical practice, the psychologist is asked to provide a general personality description or characterization of a person without reference to any fixed categories of prediction. The process involved may be thought of as the prediction of "free criteria" (Gleser, 1963; Sines, 1966). The derivation of a general personality characterization from psychological test responses has traditionally been viewed as a somewhat artistic enterprise, heretofore almost exclusively the province of the individual clinical psychologist. However, since any characterization or classification of a person that is based on a presumed relationship between test response and personality characteristics is a *prediction*, there is no need to view this process as mysterious. In fact, actuarial prediction systems of the type we have been describing lend themselves readily to such predictions.

Recall that in collecting data for the actuarial prediction system, we made an attempt to obtain personality descriptors based on behavior ratings and judgments made by professional personnel. As indicated in Table 3.7, such descriptors are entered in the criterion data matrix and may be utilized in precisely the same fashion as the more fixed criteria. When a patient's profile is classified as belonging to Profile Type I, the computer may be instructed to print out all personality descriptors that are *significantly* associated with membership in this profile type (e.g., withdrawn). The elaborateness of such personality characterization is limited only by the number of descriptors originally collected and the number of descriptors that are significantly associated with membership in a given profile type. Assuming that a large and representative sample of personality descriptors was initially available, the number of descriptive statements that can be made on the basis of profile-type membership is a function of the number of empirically justifiable statements that can be made about patients of that profile type. Typically, the personality descriptors generated by the computer form the basis for a psychological report or personality evaluation that is prepared by a clinician. Moreover, one can program the computer itself to write the entire psychological report by storing a relatively small number of declarative statements that allow the generation of English sentences containing the descriptors as adjectives.

Understandably, the image of a computer writing a relatively complex personality evaluation is viewed with some alarm by both clinicians and the general public. Such a procedure may seem to be a "dehumanization" of what is basically a humanistic process. Regardless of its humanistic merits, or lack thereof, it should be clear that the prediction of free criteria by actuarial procedures is a highly objective process that is solidly grounded in empirical observation. Presumably, the personality characterizations developed by clinical psychologists are similarly grounded in some sort of empirical observation. The objectification of such a procedure by the use of an actuarial prediction system seems to enhance the *accuracy* of such predictions and thereby increase the efficiency with which the assignment process serves its purposes. In any event, the prediction of free criteria should not be considered the exclusive domain of the clinician, since it is a natural outgrowth of the logic of actuarial prediction.

SOME ACTUARIAL PREDICTION SYSTEMS

After description of the general characteristics of actuarial prediction systems in psychology and illustration of a somewhat "idealized" hypothetical system for use in psychiatric settings, it seems appropriate to consider some actual systems that have been developed for clinical practice. Actuarial prediction systems are still somewhat new in clinical psychology, and the number of examples that can be found in the literature is quite small. Since the early demonstration study by Halbower (1955) and the preliminary descriptive coding system developed by Drake and Oetting (1959), there have been only three major examples of actuarial prediction systems that have been reported in the literature. All these systems have employed the Minnesota Multiphasic Personality Inventory as the basis for forming taxonomic groups.

The systems developed by Gilberstadt and Duker (1965), Marks and Seeman (1963), and Sines (1966) are of special interest because they represent successive degrees of departure from conventional clinical interpretation of psychological test data. The system of Gilbertstadt and Duker is deeply rooted in the tradition of clinical interpretation and relies heavily on the accumulated wisdom gained by clinical practitioners. The system of Marks and Seeman also retains roots in clinical interpretation but represents a significant departure in the direction of actuarial methods. The recent system of Sines represents an example of a "pure" actuarial system that departs completely from traditional clinical interpretation. The major characteristics of each of these systems will now be briefly summarized.

The Gilberstadt-Duker System

Derivation of profile types. The taxonomic procedure employed in this system resembles the "classic case" approach employed in clinical psychology and psychiatry. Rather than classifying MMPI profiles on the basis of their empirical similarities and differences, Gilberstadt and Duker attempted to locate prototypical examples of profile types that represented "classic" case history characteristics. Such classic cases were those that exhibited most of the characteristics thought to be associated with a given profile type. Records were obtained from the files of the Minneapolis Veterans Administration Hospital for the years 1952–1957. The authors consulted case history material and made a preliminary rating of the goodness of fit of the record to the "classic case" picture suggested by the profile. They devised preliminary rules to specify the profile configurations that seemed to best characterize the classic cases. After reading records for the years 1952 and 1953, they effected some refinement of the rules for profile specification. Next, they read records for the years 1954, 1955, and 1957 in an attempt to match the profile rules to the case history material. They then read case records of patients from 1957 through 1960 as a further check on the accuracy of the now narrowly defined profile specification rules. Finally, they defined 19 profile types in terms of mean profiles of groups of case records which were judged to represent classic cases. Each profile type included a minimum of nine cases. Table 3.8 gives the MMPI mean profile type and specification rules for the first Gilberstadt-Duker taxonomic class.

Table 3.8 Gilberstadt-Duker MMPI profile type 1-2-3

Mean profile	Hs	D	Hy	Pd	Mf	Pa	Pt	Sc	Ma	Si
($N = 11$)	92	85	80	57	54	51	62	59	53	58

Rules

1) Hs, D, and $Hy > 70$
2) $Hs > D > Hy$
3) No other scales > 70
4) $L \leq 65$; $F \leq 85$; $K \leq 70$

Criterion data. For each of the 19 MMPI profile types, the authors provided both a "diagnosis" and an "alternative diagnosis." The diagnosis was the authors' recommendation based on an intensive after-the-fact study of the cases found in the profile type. The alternative diagnosis represented the most frequent diagnosis given at discharge by the psychiatric staff. The authors felt that their own diagnoses were preferable in that they bore a closer relationship to diagnostic constructs in the literature and eliminated individual biases that often enter into discharge diagnoses given by a psychiatric staff.

Personality descriptors. Case history records for 266 patients, who formed the basis for the 19 profile types, provided a source of information on characteristic complaints, traits, and symptoms associated with each type. Using a check list devised by Cantor (1952), three judges independently rated each case history record for the presence or absence of the various items on the list. An item was counted as being present if two of the three judges agreed on its presence in the case history material. Statistical comparisons were then made between the profile type sample and a "general abnormal" sample that was considered representative of all patients admitted to that hospital (Rosen, 1952). Only those items which appeared with a significantly greater frequency ($p < .05$) in the profile type sample were entered in the actuarial table. "Barnum-type" statements about patients in a given profile type were thus avoided. Check list items which appeared with high frequency in *both* the profile type sample and the general abnormal sample were also included in the system, but they were clearly indexed as "high-base-rate" items so that they would not be considered as differentiating a particular profile type.

Cardinal features. For each profile type, the authors provided a brief descriptive summary which attempted to convey the salient characteristics associated with membership in that type. Largely clinical in nature, the summary constituted an attempt to communicate concisely the clinical impressions that were formed on the basis of reading the case history material associated with a given profile type.

Miscellaneous data. For each profile type, the authors provided a discussion section which presented material from the case history on such items as background and early history, educational and vocational adjustment, heterosexual and marital adjustment, and clinical appearance and trait makeup. In the discussion section an attempt was made to integrate the material discussed with the published literature of the MMPI. That section was thus meant to serve both a practical and a theoretical purpose.

Application of the system. Since the Gilberstadt-Duker actuarial system was designed with the individual clinical practitioner in mind, the authors compiled all the relevant material in a small *Handbook* (Gilberstadt and Duker, 1965). Nevertheless, the rules for profile classification are sufficiently explicit to be easily translated into computer language (Payne and Wiggins, 1968), and the criterion data, personality descriptors, and cardinal features may be similarly stored for automated use. Procedures for hand scoring are relatively simple, though somewhat laborious. After scoring a given MMPI profile, the clinician attempts to visually locate similar profiles among the 19 types illustrated in the *Handbook*. When he locates a similar profile type, he finds a series of rules (such as those shown in Table 3.8) to apply. If a given profile satisfies all the rules for the type, the clinician classifies it as falling within that profile grouping and then consults the actuarially derived characteristics for that grouping.

Although the rules for profile classification are themselves strict, clinicians are not discouraged from interpreting profiles which almost meet the rules for a given profile type. Considerable experience and clinical sophistication appear to be requisites for interpretation of MMPI profiles with the Gilberstadt-Duker system. To some, this feature makes it the most appealing of available actuarial systems. Although the Gilberstadt-Duker system is primarily actuarial in method, it is clearly clinical in spirit. Such a compromise system has great appeal among those who are unwilling to break from the rich and extensive tradition of clinical interpretation of the MMPI.

When the rules defining profile type membership are rigidly enforced, the Gilberstadt-Duker system appears to be applicable to only approximately 28 percent of psychiatric hospital samples (Klett and Vestre, 1968; Payne and Wiggins, 1968). Relaxation of one rule (other than the first) for the profile types, results in the classification of approximately 57 percent of a psychiatric hospital sample (Payne and Wiggins, 1968).

The Marks-Seeman System

Derivation of profile types. The MMPI profiles of 248 patients admitted to the Department of Psychiatry of the University of Kansas Medical Center were examined for possible profile types based on scale elevations. Nine profile types were tentatively identified and an attempt was made to specify rules for profile classification. The nine tentative categories were then applied, the following year, to the records of 387 psychiatric patients. The application of the categories to the new sample resulted in a refinement of profile rules, as well as the addition of seven other profile types. A minimum of 25 patients (irrespective of sex) was initially required for definition of a profile type. Later, a large ($N = 826$) two-year sample of patient profiles was judged to be stable with a minimum of 20 patients in each of the 16 types. A representative MMPI profile type, along with classification rules, appears in Table 3.9.

Comparison of the profile specification rules of Table 3.9 with those of Table 3.8 makes it apparent that the MMPI profile types of Marks and

Table 3.9 Marks-Seeman MMPI profile type 2-7-8

Mean profile	Hs	D	Hy	Pd	Mf	Pa	Pt	Sc	Ma	Si
(N = 20)	70	93	73	70	60	70	90	89	54	73

Rules
  1) D, Pt, and $Sc > 70$
  2) $D - Hs > 15$
  3) $D - Sc < 15$
  4) $Pt - Pd > 10$
  5) $Pt - Pa > 10$
  6) $Sc - Pt < 5$
  7) Pt and $Sc > Hs$ and Hy
  8) $Ma < 70$
  9) $Si > 70$
  10) L and $K < 70$; $F < 80$

Seeman are much more narrowly and specifically defined than those of Gilberstadt and Duker. In their utilization of the "classic case" approach, Gilberstadt and Duker tended to emphasize certain aspects of a profile while allowing considerable latitude in classification of other aspects. Although Marks and Seeman placed heavy emphasis on *a priori* theoretical considerations, they specified their profile types so narrowly that the number of them which met the criterion of 20 patients per type was dictated more by empirical than by theoretical considerations. Consequently, the Marks-Seeman system more closely approximates the "pure" actuarial system described earlier in this chapter.

Criterion data. The Marks-Seeman system is notable for the care and precision with which criterion data have been reported for each of the 16 profile types. Entries in the actuarial tables are coded in categorical form, which allows presentation of the percentage of incidence of each category associated with each profile type. These percentages are further qualified by plus and minus signs that indicate the extent to which each obtained percentage deviates from the percentage for that category in the *entire sample* of psychiatric patients. A plus sign indicates that the obtained percentage is above the third quartile for all patients, and a minus sign indicates that it is below the first quartile of the entire sample. Double and triple plus and minus signs indicate even more marked departures from the percentage of occurrence in the entire sample. Criterion data relating to psychiatric diagnosis are further broken down by the age, sex, and inpatient or outpatient status of the subjects. The percentage of occurrence of the major categories of psychiatric diagnosis (psychoneurotic, psychotic, brain disorder, personality disorder) are given along with the most frequent specific diagnosis that occurs within each of the major categories (e.g., schizophrenic, paranoid). Detailed categorical breakdowns are also provided for several categories related to the present illness and course of treatment in the hospital.

Personality descriptors. The primary source of descriptor data was 108 phenotypic (descriptive) and genotypic (dynamic) *Q*-sort items which had been screened for their empirical applicability from a pool of over 2,000 items. As with other characteristics, *Q*-sort statements associated with each profile type were presented as percentages qualified by plus and minus signs. Professional staff familiar with the patient in question placed each *Q*-sort item in one of nine categories to indicate its degree of applicability to that patient. Nine or ten patient records were selected for each profile type. The personality descriptions of these patients were then intercorrelated, and the five who were most similar psychologically were selected as a defining group for that profile type. The mean placement of each *Q*-sort item was then computed on the five patients in each of the 16 profile types. Case histories, hospital records, and therapy notes were rated by three staff psychologists on 225 items originally selected from a larger pool. Descriptive data on symptoms, complaints, and mental status were presented in terms of categorical percentages qualified by plus and minus signs.

Demographic data. Demographic data (age, sex, birth, sibling status, marital status, number of children, etc.) were also collected as part of the case history rating procedure.

Miscellaneous data. Case folders contained test scores and standardized behavior ratings on the patients for each profile type. These data included a detailed breakdown of intelligence test scores and categories of ward behavior obtained from a standardized rating form.

Application of the system. It is possible to use the Marks-Seeman system either on an individual, hand-scoring basis or by an automated computer procedure. Procedures for hand scoring are similar to those of Gilberstadt and Duker. First, the clinician selects the most similar profile from the 16 available types and then tests directly the applicability of each of the several rules. When all rules of a given profile type are satisfied, he consults the extensive output data for *significant* characteristics associated with profile type membership. Because the coding system for actuarial data is highly detailed, the Marks-Seeman system lends itself especially well to computer programming.

Although Marks and Seeman reported a classification rate in excess of 80 percent for their original sample, subsequent applications have reported much lower rates. In other samples, classification rates have varied from 17 percent to 28 percent (Huff, 1965; Pauker, 1966; Payne and Wiggins, 1968; Schultz, Gibeau and Barry, 1968; Sines, 1966). Relaxation of one rule (other than the first) can raise the classification rate from 27 percent to 47 percent in a psychiatric sample (Payne and Wiggins, 1968). The *joint* application of both the Gilberstadt-Duker and the Marks-Seeman systems to the same population results in considerably higher rates of classification (Payne and Wiggins, 1968; Schultz *et al.*, 1968). Whereas either system alone classifies approximately 28 percent of a patient population, joint application results in an overall classification rate of 49 percent. Joint application, with relaxation of one rule (other than the first), results in an overall classification rate of 74 percent, a figure that is satisfactory for most clinical applications.

The Sines System

Derivation of profile types. The actuarial system of Sines was developed for use in the Medical Psychology Section of the University of Missouri Medical School. As we shall see, the procedures followed in the development of this system parallel closely those described earlier in the hypothetical example of a "pure" actuarial prediction system. The derivation of profile types was similar at many points to the procedure of Sawrey, Keller, and Conger (1960) outlined earlier in this chapter. In the initial sample of MMPI profiles, each profile was compared to every other profile, and the D^2 value of the sum of the squared differences was obtained between MMPI scales. When the D^2 value between two profiles was equal to or less than 625, the identification number of the two profiles was noted, as well as the individual scale on which the largest D^2 value occurred. The largest set of profiles associated with a given profile, with a D^2 value of 625 or less, was then selected as a "target" profile. All profiles whose D^2 values with this profile were 400 or less were then set aside. Profiles that related to this set of profiles with D^2 values of 625 or less were then located. A matrix of D^2 values was formed which compared each profile in this group with every other. Profiles were successively eliminated until only those remained that related to at least 60 percent of the other profiles in the group with D^2 values of 625 or less. All profiles meeting this criterion were then *averaged*, and the mean profile was computed for "prototype 1."

The prototype profile was then compared with every other profile in the original sample to identify profiles related to the prototype with D^2 values of 484 or less. All such profiles were removed from the sample, and a similar procedure was followed in the development of the second profile cluster. The actuarial system of Sines has not been completely developed at the time of this writing. Current plans include the development of profile types in which a limit is set on the magnitude of the d^2 value of a single scale that can be tolerated within a specified profile class. To date, 11 MMPI profile types have been identified by the preceding method of analysis (Sines, 1966).

Criterion data. The output data for the actuarial system developed by Sines were gathered from institutional records of the patients in the various profile types. Initially, the total contents of institutional records for some 80 patients were read, and all descriptive information was dictated for stenographic transcription. Each behavioral statement was typed on a separate card, yielding a group of some 40,000 cards. Two psychologists, working independently, categorized the statements into ten broad categories and then recategorized them into subareas under each of the broader categories. Specific statements relating to fixed-criterion data included such categories as diagnosis, response to treatment, suicide risk, reaction to staff, and ward behavior. In classifying criterion data for the patients in the profile types, the psychologists read the institutional records and coded each relevant statement in terms of the master coding system developed on the initial sample of 80 patients.

Personality descriptors. Statements of a personological nature were similarly coded. Three general categories of personality descriptors were used: phenotypic statements, genotypic statements, and statements relating to social relations.

Demographic data. Statements relating to a variety of demographic categories were also coded in the initial classification scheme. From this system it is possible to derive information on such categories as age, religion, and education of patients in a given profile type.

Miscellaneous data. Since all information available from institutional records was included in the initial classification scheme, regardless of its relevance to actuarial prediction, a variety of miscellaneous data were made available for each profile type. Categories of miscellaneous data include specific behavioral statements relating to such categories as childhood, health, parents, spouse, work, social behavior, and siblings.

Application of the system. Although the actuarial prediction system of Sines is still under development, we may clearly anticipate its eventual use from the manner in which data have been gathered. Once the profile type has been identified, the profile group and a control group are compared for the frequency of occurrence of statements, from a potential pool of approximately 2,500. Statements which occur with significant frequencies in the profile group are coded as such and printed out when an individual profile is classified as belonging in that profile group. Table 3.10 illustrates a typical profile type classification. The MMPI profile of a newly admitted patient is

Table 3.10 Sines MMPI profile type 4-3

Mean profile	Hs	D	Hy	Pd	Mf	Pa	Pt	Sc	Ma	Si
($N = 16$)	56	56	62	75	53	56	59	59	53	45

Rule

D^2 value ≤ 625

compared by means of the D^2 statistic to all existing profile types. If such a profile is related to the illustrated 4-3 profile with a D^2 value of less than 625, classification is automatic and the descriptive statements associated with this profile type are then printed out. Although the final form of this system is not certain at this writing, it is clearly one which lends itself to completely automated actuarial prediction.

SUMMARY

In actuarial prediction, probability estimates of criterion status are derived from contingency tables relating predictor and criterion variables. Such procedures are especially useful when predictor variables are categorical in nature, although actuarial procedures are not limited to such situations. The most familiar example of actuarial prediction is the setting of insurance rates on the basis of observed contingencies between demographic characteristics (age, sex, marital status) and the criterion insured (automobile accidents). The form of such predictions may be represented by the expression $P(C_i \mid R_j)$, which is read: "Given a particular pattern of demographic characteristics (age, sex), what is the probability that an individual with this pattern is a member of a specific criterion group (high-risk driver)?"

Although the form of actuarial prediction in psychology is the same as that employed in the insurance industry, most studies of the validity of psychological tests provide information that is relevant only to the problem $P(R_j \mid C_i)$, which is read: "Given that an individual is a member of a criterion group, what is the probability that he will emit this pattern of test responses?" Although $P(R_j \mid C_i)$ is mathematically related to $P(C_i \mid R_j)$, the two probabilities cannot be assumed to have equal values in a given prediction situation. Examples are provided of situations in which values of $P(R_j \mid C_i)$ may give misleading impressions of the clinical utility of a test.

Socially defined criterion groups are likely to comprise persons who are heterogeneous with respect to personality characteristics. For this reason and others, it has been proposed that actuarial prediction systems be established for groups of persons classified on the basis of their psychological similarity. The goal of such taxonomic classification is to provide a manageable number of homogeneous and mutually distinct psychological classifications that occur with sufficient frequency to provide a basis for reliable predictions. Predictions from such taxonomic classifications may be either "fixed" (socially important criterion categories) or "free" (general personality descriptions).

The mechanics of actuarial prediction are described with reference to data collection, identification of taxonomic groups, and the construction and use of actuarial tables. Examples are provided of the major actuarial prediction systems that are currently employed in clinical psychology.

CHAPTER 4

CLINICAL PREDICTION

Thus far, our consideration of prediction models in personality assessment has been limited to the more common statistical techniques for combining predictor variables to forecast human behavior. Despite the variety of forms that these models assume, they share in common the property that combination of predictors is determined entirely on the basis of *known* empirical relationships. In this sense, all statistical methods of prediction may be thought of as alternative ways of expressing known regularities that exist between predictor variables and criterion measures. Although we have considered the major *statistical* methods of combining predictor variables, we have overlooked the most common of all methods employed in the prediction of human behavior. This method, which antedates all the others and which we employ every day of our lives, has come to be called the *clinical* method of data combination.

Assume that you are late for a prearranged luncheon date with a friend and that when you arrive at the restaurant, your friend is not there. As you reason through this common situation, many alternative courses of action occur to you, all of which involve certain expectations (predictions) about the probable behavior of your friend under a number of possible circumstances. Assuming that your friend arrived on time, you may consider it appropriate to look for him in the bar, call his home or office, remain where you are, etc., depending on your expectations of your friend's most likely behavior under this set of circumstances. Assuming that your friend has not yet arrived, you might try the bar across the street, call his home or office, etc., again depending on your best prediction of his behavior, given this set of circumstances. Intuitively, it should be clear that the best prediction, given a set of circumstances, would be based on your past knowledge of your friend's behavior under similar circumstances. Of course, it is unlikely that you have made systematic observations of your friend's reactions to many such circumstances or that you are certain about which of your friend's personal characteristics are most likely to determine his behavior in this particular situation.   Nevertheless, you make an "educated guess" and behave accordingly.   In fact, if you were to reflect on your day-to-day social transactions, it would become apparent that such predictions constitute a major portion of your daily life.

A student, uncertain as to his eventual vocation, consults a college counselor.   After a series of personal interviews and a number of aptitude and vocational interest tests, the counselor may venture a prediction as to the most appropriate vocational goals for this student.   The information available to the counselor is extremely heterogeneous in nature.   He has formed certain impressions of the student on the basis of the personal interviews.   In inspecting the test results, the counselor perceives a "pattern" of personality and interest variables which seems consistent with his interview impressions.   Based on his clinical experience with similar (but certainly not identical) students, he renders an opinion.   Note that the counselor has not employed a regression equation, consulted an actuarial table, or perhaps even paid much attention to the "norms" on which the various tests are based.   Rather, he has *combined* all this information "intuitively" to come up with an educated guess that he feels will be helpful to the student.

A college admissions officer consults an application folder and finds that the applicant's weighted admission index (based on a multiple-regression equation) falls one point short of that required for admission to the college. The admissions officer then consults the letters of recommendation which accompanied the student's application and finds them highly favorable. Under these circumstances, he decides that the empirically determined regression equation may be wrong *in this instance* and decides to accept the student's application for admission.   By so doing, the admissions officer is "overruling" the regression equation and relying on his *own* judgment in making the final decision.

The three preceding examples differ widely in content but have in common the defining characteristic of clinical prediction.   In each instance, *human judgment* was involved in the determination of the manner in which predictor variables would be combined to forecast a given outcome.   In the restaurant example, very little "hard" data were available, but whatever data were available were combined intuitively.   The college counselor had access to a great deal of relevant information, but the manner in which it was combined was intuitive rather than statistical.   In the instance of the admissions officer, an actual statistical prediction was involved, but the overruling of such a statistical prediction constituted an intuitive judgment that was qualitatively identical to those in the other two examples.

The examples we have been discussing have very little to do with "clinics" in the ordinary sense of the word and it is appropriate to inquire into the use of the words "clinical judgment" in situations where "human judgment" may seem more precise. The reasons for the choice are more historical than logical and reflect a long-standing controversy in behaviorial science (Lundberg, 1941; Sarbin, 1944), which became focalized in the area of personality assessment with the publication of Meehl's *Clinical versus Statistical Prediction* in 1954. In this seminal monograph, Meehl posed a number of penetrating questions relating to the use of human judgment in the practice of clinical psychology. Much of this chapter and the next will be concerned with the theoretical and empirical literatures that have developed in response to Meehl's statements. The implications of the issues raised by Meehl and subsequent workers extend well beyond the original context of clinical psychology. Nevertheless, because the issues were originally raised with respect to the practice of clinical psychology, it has become standard practice for psychologists to speak of "clinical prediction" when describing the activities of human judges who may or may not be clinical psychologists.

In any consideration of either clinical or statistical prediction methods, it is important to distinguish between the manner in which data are *collected* and that in which data are *combined* for purposes of prediction (Meehl, 1954; Sawyer, 1966). This distinction between "measurement" and "prediction" is illustrated in Figure 4.1. Psychological test responses are measurements which serve as input to a predictive system which combines data in such a way as to produce estimates of future criterion behavior. The predictive system is logically distinct from its source of input data. Before considering the manner in which data are combined, we will focus on the measurement or data-collection component of the prediction paradigm.

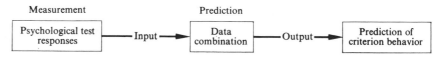

Fig. 4.1 Measurement and prediction in the prediction paradigm.

JUDGMENTAL MEASUREMENT

When the collecting, recording, or scoring of input data involves human judgment, we may speak of the *judgmental measurement* of predictor variables. With reference to Figure 4.1, it may be stated that *any* procedure which occurs to the left of the box for data combination and which involves human judgment will *by definition* categorize the measurement procedure as judgmental in nature. In Part 2 of the present book, we will indicate the wide range of techniques of data collection involved in measurement via observational, structured, and unstructured techniques. For our present purposes, the various techniques of data collection can be conveniently divided into those which rely on human judgment for obtaining data (judgmental) and those which do not (mechanical). It is important to note that the distinction between judgmental and mechanical measurement is not equivalent to the distinction between quantifiable and nonquantifiable data. In the ensuing discussion it will be assumed that all data (judgmental and mechanical) are potentially quantifiable. A distinction is thus made between quantifiable data which require human judgment and quantifiable data which do not.

The open-ended interview is representative of data collection techniques which are classified as judgmental. A clinician talks with a client for an hour and pursues topics that appear to be relevant at the moment. At the end of such an open-ended interview, the clinician may rate the client on significant dimensions of personality, such as extraversion, anxiety, and desire for improvement. Although such ratings may be highly quantified, they are not mechanical, in the sense that human judgment is required to obtain them. Note also that the distinction between judgmental and mechanical measurement is not based on the reliability of response-recording. Test-scoring machines are not perfectly reliable, and a small margin of scoring error is to be expected with such machines. On the other hand, clinicians can, in principle, be trained to record their clinical impressions with very high reliability. In an extreme example, judgmental measurement might be more reliable than mechanical measurement. No matter how reliable, any measurement that relies on human judgment is, by definition, judgmental measurement.

When judgment is a source of input data in the prediction paradigm illustrated in Figure 4.1, the clinician is essentially functioning as a measuring or recording instrument. As with any other recording device, the clinician is subject to evaluation in terms of such characteristics as *reliability* and *accuracy*. Given the complex nature of the stimuli on which such judgments are based (i.e., human beings), it is difficult to obtain objective (nonjudgmental) criterion measures against which to validate the judgments. Consequently, many experimental appraisals of the reliability and accuracy of judgmental measurement have been conducted under highly contrived or artificial circumstances. Despite their shortcomings, such experimental investigations provide the only scientific evidence available on the reliability and accuracy of the human judge as a recording instrument.

Characteristics of Good Judges of Others

The accuracy and sensitivity of the human judge as a recording instrument have been studied in a variety of contexts by a number of different experimental procedures. The experimental procedures are traditionally classified under five general categories (Notcutt and Silva, 1951; Taft, 1955), as illustrated in Table 4.1. These experimental procedures are subject to a variety of conceptual and methodological pitfalls (Taft, 1955; Cronbach, 1955; Gage and Cronbach, 1955). Nevertheless, the studies emanating from them provide the only available empirical basis for estimating the characteristics of good judges of others.

Table 4.1 Major methods of studying judgmental accuracy. (After Taft, 1955)

Judging task	Typical data source	Typical criteria of accuracy
Rating emotional expressions	Photographs, drawings, movies, and models	Intention of models, consensus of psychologists
Rating and ranking traits	Acquaintance, information about subject	Pooled peer ratings, judgments of observers, test results
Writing personality descriptions	Interview, observation of subject, descriptive material	Judgments of "experts"
Matching two sources of data from the same subject	Acquaintance, information about subject	Degree of agreement
Predicting subjects' responses to test items, and predicting subjects' life-history data	Acquaintance, information about subject	Degree of agreement

An early and frequently cited review of the literature represented by the experimental approaches listed in Table 4.1 was conducted by Taft (1955). Although recognizing the methodological and conceptual difficulties inherent in many of the studies, Taft nevertheless felt that *some* general conclusions could be drawn about the characteristics of good judges of others. He concluded that ability to judge others was positively correlated with *age* (in children but not adults), *intelligence, esthetic interests* (particularly dramatic and artistic), *self-insight, emotional adjustment*, and *social skill*. More generally, accurate judgment should occur when the judge possesses appropriate judgmental norms, has high judging ability (a combination of general and social intelligence), and is motivated and free to make accurate judgments about the subject (Taft, 1955).

Methodological Problems in the Study of Judgmental Accuracy

Shortly after the appearance of Taft's (1955) review of the literature, a series of papers by Cronbach (1955, 1958; Gage and Cronbach, 1955) challenged the drawing of conclusions from existing studies of judgmental accuracy. Cronbach called attention to the fact that previous studies were based on *global* indices of judgmental accuracy which did not lend themselves to straightforward interpretation. When such global, or overall, indices of judgmental "accuracy" are analyzed into their components, the processes affecting the global indices frequently involve rater biases and mathematical artifacts which bear little conceptual resemblance to constructs such as "empathy" and "social sensitivity."

In a typical judgmental accuracy experiment, a judge is required to predict the responses of others to a variety of self-report items. The self-description of other o on item i may be represented as x_{oi}. The corresponding *prediction* of this item response by a given judge may be represented as y_{oi}. Where there are k items and n others, the overall accuracy of a judge's prediction of others' responses is expressed by the squared error of prediction:

$$\frac{1}{kn} \sum_o \sum_i (y_{oi} - x_{oi})^2.$$

That is, judgmental accuracy is expressed as the squared difference between the predicted and actual responses of others, summed over all items and all others.

Cronbach (1955) has shown that a judge's overall accuracy score may be expanded and rewritten as a sum of four separate components, as indicated in Table 4.2. The four components, which sum to the total accuracy score,

Table 4.2 Components of overall judgmental accuracy score. (After Cronbach, 1955)

Expansion of overall accuracy score	Name of component
$\dfrac{1}{kn} \sum_o \sum_i (y_{oi} - x_{oi})^2$	Overall accuracy
$= (\bar{y}_{..} - \bar{x}_{..})^2$	Elevation, E
$+ \dfrac{1}{n} \sum_o [(\bar{y}_{o.} - \bar{y}_{..}) - (\bar{x}_{o.} - \bar{x}_{..})]^2$	Differential elevation, DE
$+ \dfrac{1}{k} \sum_i [(\bar{y}_{.i} - \bar{y}_{..}) - (\bar{x}_{.i} - \bar{x}_{..})]^2$	Stereotype accuracy, SA
$+ \dfrac{1}{kn} \sum_o \sum_i (y'_{oi} - x'_{oi})^2$	Differential accuracy, DA

are designated as elevation (E), differential elevation (DE), stereotype accuracy (SA), and differential accuracy (DA). Since these components have varying degrees of relevance to the concept of "judgmental accuracy," it is important to consider each one in turn.

Elevation

The elevation component, E, expresses the difference between the *average prediction* of the judge and the *average response* of others:

$$E^2 = (\bar{y}_{..} - \bar{x}_{..})^2,$$

where

$\bar{y}_{..}$ = grand mean prediction summed over others and items,

$\bar{x}_{..}$ = grand mean of self-descriptions summed over others and items.

Any difference between the manner in which the judge uses the prediction scale and the way in which the average other uses it will be reflected in the elevation component. Therefore, this component reflects the manner in which the judge uses the rating scale, more or less independently of his "accuracy." As Cronbach (1955) points out, "a judge who happens to use the same region of the response scale as other persons (elevation is small) need not have superior insight." Similarly, a judge who consistently uses a higher region of the response scale, as compared with the persons judged (elevation is large), is not necessarily lacking in insight.

Differential Elevation

The differential elevation component, DE, reflects the extent to which the judge's average prediction for a given other corresponds to that other's deviation from his own mean:

$$DE^2 = \frac{1}{n} \sum_o [(\bar{y}_{o.} - \bar{y}_{..}) - (\bar{x}_{o.} - \bar{x}_{..})]^2,$$

where

$\bar{y}_{o.}$ = average prediction for each *other* summed over items,

$\bar{x}_{o.}$ = average self-description of each *other* summed over items.

In other words, the differential elevation component represents the judge's ability to judge *deviations* of others' elevations from their central tendencies. As Cronbach (1955) has indicated, this component may be rewritten as the variance of a difference:

$$DE^2 = \sigma^2_{\bar{y}_{o.}} + \sigma^2_{\bar{x}_{o.}} - 2\sigma_{\bar{y}_{o.}}\sigma_{\bar{x}_{o.}} r_{\bar{x}_{o.}\bar{y}_{o.}}.$$

The variance term $\sigma^2_{\bar{y}_{o.}}$ indicates the extent to which judged differences among others are large or small. Cronbach refers to this term as the "assumed dispersion in elevation" on the part of the judge. Such a term is more indicative of a judge's rating tendencies than of this accuracy. The correlation term $r_{\bar{x}_o.\bar{y}_o.}$, however, indicates the judge's ability to judge *which* others score highest on the elevation scale. This "differential elevation correlation" term is therefore more closely related to the concept of "judgmental accuracy."

Stereotype Accuracy

The stereotype accuracy component, SA, reflects the judge's ability to predict the *norm* or average response of all others:

$$SA^2 = \frac{1}{k} \sum_i [(\bar{y}_{.i} - \bar{y}_{..}) - (\bar{x}_{.i} - \bar{x}_{..})]^2,$$

where

$\bar{y}_{.i}$ = average prediction for each *item* summed over others,

$\bar{x}_{.i}$ = average *item* self-description summed over others.

The component may also be rewritten as the variance of a difference:

$$SA^2 = \sigma_{\bar{y}_{.i}}^2 + \sigma_{\bar{x}_{.i}}^2 - 2\sigma_{\bar{y}_{.i}}\sigma_{\bar{x}_{.i}}r_{\bar{y}_{.i}\bar{x}_{.i}}.$$

The variance term $\sigma_{\bar{y}_{.i}}^2$ represents the extent to which predicted *variation* in item means is large or small. The correlation term $r_{\bar{y}_{.i}\bar{x}_{.i}}$ indicates the judge's ability to predict item means or item "difficulty level." Although the ability to predict a stereotype or "generalized other" has been shown *empirically* to affect accuracy of prediction, such a component is not usually included in the *concept* of "interpersonal sensitivity" or "judgmental accuracy." In fact, we tend to think of a "sensitive" judge as one who can depart from stereotypes and thereby recognize individual differences in personality. Consequently, global measures of accuracy that are primarily determined by the stereotype accuracy component are not properly interpreted as measures of "interpersonal sensitivity."

Differential Accuracy

The differential accuracy component, DA, reflects the extent to which a judge is able to predict differences among others on each trait or item considered separately:

$$DA^2 = \frac{1}{kn} \sum_o \sum_i (y'_{oi} - x'_{oi})^2,$$

where

y'_{oi} = prediction expressed as a *deviation score*[1] from both item mean and other mean,

x'_{oi} = self-description expressed as a *deviation score*[2] from both item mean and other mean.

---

1. $y'_{oi} = y_{oi} - \bar{y}_{o.} - \bar{y}_{.i} + \bar{y}_{..}$.
2. $x'_{oi} = x_{oi} - \bar{x}_{o.} - \bar{x}_{.i} + \bar{x}_{..}$.

Rewriting this component as the variance of a difference, we obtain

$$DA^2 = \sigma^2_{y'_{oi}} + \sigma^2_{x'_{oi}} - 2\sigma_{y'_{oi}}\sigma_{x'_{oi}}r_{y'_{oi}x'_{oi}}.$$

The variance term $\sigma^2_{y'_{oi}}$ represents the "assumed dispersion on any item," with elevation held constant (Cronbach, 1955).   The correlation $r_{y'_{oi}x'_{oi}}$ indicates the judge's ability to predict *which* others have the highest score on an item, when the score is expressed as a deviation from others' mean. This "differential correlation" appears to be closest in meaning to what is usually implied by "judgmental accuracy" or "interpersonal sensitivity."

To summarize, Cronbach (1955) has made an invaluable contribution to the study of judgmental accuracy by calling attention to the fact that the several components which enter into global indices of "accuracy" do not have equal status as indices of the behavior of interest. The components of elevation, *E*, and differential elevation, *DE*, appear to reflect the extent to which judges interpret the words defining a scale in the same manner as subjects do. Such congruences seem to have little to do with the concept of "interpersonal sensitivity" and therefore should be controlled or eliminated in studies of judgmental accuracy. The stereotype accuracy component, *SA*, provides important information on the possible *reasons* for judgmental accuracy in a given study. However, such tendencies are seldom included in the concept of "interpersonal sensitivity," and consequently, their presence can lead to interpretative ambiguity. The correlational components of differential elevation and differential accuracy appear to be much closer to the common notion of "interpersonal sensitivity." When properly extracted from global accuracy measures, such terms can serve as a basis for evaluating a judge's sensitivity to individual differences in personality.

The early literature on judgmental accuracy is replete with examples of interpretative ambiguity introduced by a failure to consider the separate components of global accuracy measures (Cronbach, 1955; Gage and Cronbach, 1955; Cline, 1964). Subsequent research treating global accuracy measures analytically has tended to support the importance of such distinctions (Gordon, 1957; Crow, 1957; Cline and Richards, 1960; Hatch, 1962). Although differential accuracy has continued to be the preferred index of interpersonal sensitivity, research by Cline and Richards (1960, 1962) and Richards and Cline (1963) has demonstrated a shortcoming of this measure. The research of these authors suggests that certain procedures for *scoring* responses can produce ambiguities which make the interpretation of differential accuracy measures difficult.

The response measure to be predicted in studies of judgmental accuracy is frequently in the form of statements to which the subject indicates his agreement (e.g., "Strongly agree") or disagreement (e.g., "Strongly disagree") along a five- or seven-place rating scale. Such statements may be scored for "agreement" (regardless of what it is that is agreed with), or they may be scored as "pro" or "con" with respect to the issue at hand (regardless of whether agreement indicates pro or con attitudes). Depending on which scoring system is used, the differential accuracy component and its correlation and variance terms will take on different values, and there appears to be no criterion for establishing which values are the most appropriate measures of judging ability (Cline, 1964). For this reason, Cline and Richards (1962) have suggested a measure of interpersonal accuracy, IA, composed of correlation and variance terms that are *not* based on deviation scores, as are the corresponding differential accuracy terms. The authors claim that such an index is independent of the manner in which response measures are scored.

The Generality of Judgmental Accuracy

In speaking of *the* accuracy of a given judge, we are making an implicit assumption about the generality of accuracy as a trait or characteristic of judges. It makes intuitive sense to speak of judgmental accuracy, or "interpersonal sensitivity," as a personality trait or dimension of individual differences among people. Our linguistic habits are such that we speak of certain individuals as being interpersonally sensitive and therefore good judges of others, and of other individuals as lacking in this characteristic and consequently being poor judges of others. To speak of interpersonal sensitivity as a trait is to imply that such a trait has *generality* over both persons and situations. One would expect an individual who possesses a high degree of sensitivity to be an accurate judge of different kinds of people over a wide variety of judging situations. That judgmental accuracy is, in fact, a general trait has been extremely difficult to establish empirically.

Allport (1937) suggested that the ability to judge others, like other artistic abilities, is neither entirely general nor entirely specific. He concluded, however, that to view judgmental accuracy as entirely specific would do an injustice to the facts. In his review of the earlier literature on judgmental accuracy, Taft (1955) found that Allport's position was generally supported by available data: "The degree to which a person can make accurate judgments about others is a function of his general ability to judge and of specific situational and interactional factors, but the greater his general ability to judge, the less will be the relative influence of the specific factors" (p. 6). Bruner and Tagiuri (1954) reached a similar conclusion.

Conclusions drawn from the early experimental literature on the generality of accuracy are severely limited by the methodological and conceptual defects of the studies themselves. A lack of comparability among measures, traits judged, and the composition of both judge and subject groups makes it difficult to compare the results of one study with another. Further, as Vernon (1964) notes, not only are the separate judgment measures of questionable consistency and stability, but the difference scores on which most measures of accuracy are based are implicitly unreliable. Of greatest importance is the lack of attention given to the individual components of accuracy scores in comparisons of one accuracy measure with another. Thus, when consistency among accuracy measures is found, it is not clear whether the consistency can be attributed to differential accuracy or whether it is a function of some artifact, such as stereotype accuracy.

An analytic study of the generality of judgmental accuracy was conducted by Crow and Hammond (1957). Films of ten patients being interviewed by doctors were viewed by senior medical students, who were asked to judge the patients' responses to the MMPI, the Strong Vocational Interest Blank, and a self-rating form. Analysis of the agreement among some 15 measures of judgmental accuracy failed to yield any consistent evidence of the generality of judgmental accuracy. Further, when the same judgments were repeated after a period of six months, little evidence was found for the temporal consistency of judgmental accuracy components—with the exception of the stereotype accuracy score.

A more recent and extensive series of studies by Cline and Richards (1960, 1961) has provided modest but positive evidence for the generality of judgmental accuracy. A carefully selected set of interviews, filmed in color and sound, constituted the input information for judges. A variety of judgment tasks was presented to large numbers of undergraduate students. The tasks included a behavior-postdiction test, a sentence-completion test, an adjective check list, an opinion-prediction test, and a trait-rating test. The results have been analyzed for convergences among global-accuracy measures and among the components of elevation, differential elevation, stereotype accuracy, and differential accuracy (Cline, 1964). Although the data provided some support for the notion of judgmental accuracy as a generalized trait, several qualifications must be placed on such a conclusion. Analysis of the interrelations among the judgment measures in terms of Cronbach's components of judgmental accuracy showed that stereotype accuracy accounted for a large portion of the apparent generality of judgmental accuracy. However, when that component was held constant, there was still some generality, which appeared to be related to the differential accuracy component, a more meaningful definition of judgmental accuracy. In fact, stereotype accuracy and differential accuracy appeared to operate relatively independently of each other.

The relative independence of stereotype accuracy and differential accuracy had been previously noted (Bronfenbrenner, Harding, and Gallwey, 1958) and was interpreted by Cline (1964) as reflecting the operation of two independent factors of judgmental accuracy. That judgmental accuracy is factorially complex does not preclude its generality across instruments.

However, it does illustrate the complexities of conceptual and methodological analysis which plague the field of judgmental-accuracy research. In light of the contradictions, complexities, and confusions in that field, it seems appropriate to conclude that the question of the generality of judgmental accuracy has not been conclusively answered.

The Clinician as Expert Judge

Despite the paucity of empirical data suggesting that accuracy is a general trait, it seems reasonable to suppose that professional decision makers, such as clinical psychologists, are generally more accurate in their judgments of others than are laymen or those without specific psychological training. Presumably our society entrusts the making of important decisions to those who are best qualified to make them. Professional clinicians, such as psychiatrists, social workers, and clinical psychologists, are more or less "certified" by our society as individuals qualified to help make important life decisions. The presumed superiority of the clinician as an expert judge is based on special qualifications he is thought to possess, qualifications that stem from training, experience, and utilization of input data.

It is widely assumed, for example, that the psychologist's academic background prepares him for making accurate judgments of others. Similarly, the experience the clinician develops in dealing with hundreds of individual cases and making hundreds of individual decisions should substantially contribute to his overall accuracy as a judge. Finally, by virtue of his training and experience, the clinician is assumed to utilize data in a special way. He is considered able to integrate large amounts of input data in a complex fashion in order to arrive at a judgment or prediction about a single individual that is more accurate than judgments based on smaller amounts of information. Surprisingly, there is little empirical evidence that justifies the granting of "expert" status to the clinician on the basis of his training, experience, or information-processing ability.

Training

In an early study of the judgment of emotion from facial expressions, students who had completed at least one psychology course were less accurate than students just taking their first course (Buzby, 1924). Another early study found no relationship between training in psychology and ability to predict subjects' answers to inventory items from biographical data (Hanks, 1936). As part of a large-scale assessment study, which we shall consider in more detail in Chapter 11, Kelly and Fiske (1951) compared the judgmental accuracy of advanced graduate students in clinical psychology with beginning graduate students, who had less training. The students were required to predict the inventory responses of psychiatric patients to whom they had already administered a variety of psychological tests. The results showed no differences in accuracy between the advanced and beginning graduate students in clinical psychology. Although the findings of earlier studies are not always consistent (e.g., Polansky, 1941), there is little to suggest that training in psychology increases the accuracy of clinical judgment.

A recent study by Kremers (1960) provides a somewhat more substantial basis for this pessimistic conclusion. A single subject was selected from a group of subjects on the basis of the consistency (over one-month intervals) of his responses to a series of items indicating how he would behave in a variety of situations. For this particular subject, there was complete agreement between his own indication and that of his close acquaintances of how he would react to the situations. Thus, although the criterion subject may not have been representative, his responses (which formed the target of prediction) were consistent and realistic. Six groups of undergraduate and graduate students, majoring in psychology, classics, and natural sciences, served as judges. After observing the subject giving a ten-minute speech, the judges were asked to predict his responses to the given situations. Accuracy scores for each judge consisted simply of the number of "correct" predictions of responses. No differences in the accuracy scores were found between undergraduate and graduate students or among the students in the separate disciplines represented. Thus, among both undergraduate and graduate students, there was no relationship between selection of psychology as a major and ability to judge others.

Experience

Given the "academic" nature of most psychology courses and the relative youth and inexperience of most students of psychology, it may not be surprising that no relationship has been established between educational background in psychology and judgmental accuracy. Professional *experience* in making clinical appraisals seems a more relevant variable on several counts. First of all, those who hold Ph.D.'s in clinical psychology represent a highly selected group, one of the criteria for selection presumably being judgmental skills. Second, the day-to-day experience of meeting and diagnosing patients in a clinical situation seems to be more valuable as an educational experience than simply taking formal academic courses in psychology. Finally, there is no reason to assume that the clinical judgments made by undergraduates—and even graduate students—resemble in any way the decisions made by practicing clinicians. Consequently, it should follow that when experienced clinicians are asked to make diagnostic judgments of the kind usually encountered in clinical practice and on the basis of the information typically available to them, their superior accuracy over other groups of judges should become apparent. Goldberg (1959) performed an early and classic study meeting these requirements.

Goldberg selected a judgment procedure that was a familiar part of most clinicians' daily diagnostic practice: the diagnosis of organic brain damage from the Bender-Gestalt test. This test (Bender, 1938) consists of a series of nine geometric forms which are presented to the patient, one at a time, with instructions to reproduce them on a single piece of paper. Because this task is highly dependent on visual-motor coordination, the test is widely held to be useful in diagnosis of organic brain damage. Protocols of 30 patients were selected from the files of a Veterans Administration general medical and surgical hospital. Half of them were produced by patients who had been independently diagnosed as "organic" on the basis of neurological examinations. The remaining 15 protocols were produced by psychiatric patients with no neurological or other symptoms of brain damage (nonorganics). The 30 protocols were presented to judges in sets of 10, with instructions to diagnose the patient as either "organic" or "nonorganic." In addition, the judges were asked to indicate the degree of *confidence* they had in each diagnosis on a five-point rating scale.

Three groups of judges were selected to represent clear-cut points on the continuum of appropriate clinical experience: (a) four psychology staff members with Ph.D.'s and four to nine years of clinical experience with the test; (b) ten psychology trainees with MA degrees and one to four years of experience with the test; and (c) eight hospital secretaries with no training in psychology and no previous experience with the test. The professional judges were encouraged to arrive at their diagnoses in the manner that they typically used in clinical practice. Since the secretaries were totally unfamiliar with the test, it was administered to them, and they were then told the nature of the diagnostic problem. All judging groups were asked to diagnose each protocol as organic or nonorganic as well as to indicate the degree of confidence they placed in each diagnosis. The mean percentage of correct judgments for each of the judging groups is shown in Table 4.3.

Although there was a slight tendency for the secretaries and the psychology trainees to do better than the experienced psychology staff members, none

Table 4.3 Diagnostic accuracy of three judging groups. (After Goldberg, 1959)

Group	N	Mean correct, %	Range, %	Differing from chance: No. (%)	
Psychology staff	4	65	60–70	1	25
Psychology trainees	10	70	60–77	6	60
Secretaries	8	67	57–73	5	62
All groups	22	68	57–77	12	54

of the differences were statistically significant. The results are particularly sobering when we recall that the level of chance expectancy was 50 percent (15 organics and 15 nonorganics). Only 12 judges exceeded chance expectancy in their diagnosis of patients and, as the final column of Table 4.3 shows, the highest proportion of non-chance judgments was in the group of secretaries. Although there were no significant differences in accuracy, there were substantial differences with respect to confidence. As a group, the experienced clinicians tended to be the *least* confident in their judgments, the secretaries the most. However, no significant relationships were found between accuracy and degree of confidence in this clinical judgment task.

A single study such as that of Goldberg (1959), no matter how well conducted, is insufficient to support the generalization that the amount of professional training and experience of a judge are unrelated to his judgmental accuracy. However, both earlier studies (Estes, 1938; Wedell and Smith, 1951; Luft, 1950; Kelly and Fiske, 1951; Soskin, 1954) and subsequent studies (Hiler and Nesvig, 1965; Goldberg, 1965a; Johnston and McNeal, 1967; Levy and Ulman, 1967; Schaeffer, 1964; Stricker, 1967) lend support to such a generalization. Even in those studies in which experienced clinicians were shown to have greater judgmental accuracy than totally inexperienced laymen, brief supplementary training of the inexperienced judges tended to raise their level of performance to that of the highly experienced clinicians (Oskamp, 1962; Goldberg, 1968b).   The argument that the clinician's presumed expertise is based on his professional training and experience has found little empirical support in studies to date.

Utilization of Input Data

In addition to his purportedly superior interpersonal sensitivity, the clinician is believed to qualify as an expert judge on the basis of his ability to integrate large amounts of input data in such a way as to arrive at an accurate personality formulation. Though at first primarily an "intelligence tester," the clinical psychologist later achieved professional prominence on the basis of his ability to administer and interpret batteries of personality tests. The superiority of clinical measurement based on extensive and complex input data has been assumed from the beginning:

It is maintained, however, that in the present state of our knowledge of personality and maladjustment—in which the interrelationships of functions are so obscure—the clinical psychologist is on much safer ground when he has a battery of tests, rather than but a few, on which to base his diagnosis. The use of full batteries of tests is the more recommendable since only such practice yields the kind of experience and material on which to rear a better theoretical understanding of, and better testing practices for, the interrelationships and autonomy of different functions in adjustment and maladjustment. (Rapaport, Gill, and Schafer, 1946, p. 8)

A typical battery of clinical diagnostic tests would include a case history, or other biographical information; a structured personality test, such as the MMPI; and unstructured personality assessment devices, such as the Rorschach inkblot test, the Thematic Apperception Test (TAT), or a sentence-completion test. In bringing such an extensive battery of tests to bear on a single diagnostic problem, such as the clinical assessment of neuroticism, the clinician finds himself confronted with a wide array of complex and often conflicting data. The process whereby the clinician integrates this mass of data into a consistent clinical impression is believed to be extraordinarily complex (e.g., Schafer, 1954). On the basis of an elaborate theory of personality structure and dynamics, the clinician attempts to reconcile conflicting evidence from different levels of personality structure by testing a series of hypotheses against available evidence. The assumptions underlying the process are that the clinician is able to process large amounts of input data, and that his reliability and accuracy are a direct function of the amount of input data available to him.

To subject the above assumptions to empirical test, it is necessary to: (a) select a representative group of clinical judges, (b) select an appropriate group of subjects or patients to be judged, (c) obtain verified criterion information on the subjects, (d) provide the clinician with varying amounts and combinations of appropriate input data, and (e) evaluate the results in terms of the relationship between accuracy of clinical judgment and varying amounts and combinations of input data. Three empirical studies meet these criteria and provide considerable insight into the ability of clinicians to process input data. Each study will be briefly described.

The Kostlan (1954) Study

Judges. The judges selected for the study were 20 clinical psychologists, each of whom had at least two years of psychodiagnostic experience and each of whom was familiar with both the patient population and the psychological tests employed. They were assigned at random to four groups of five each, in accordance with an experimental design which called for presentation of input data of differing kinds and amounts.

Patients. The patients were five male veterans of World War II who had been given a complete diagnostic work-up and who had received individual psychotherapy from the Oakland Veterans Administration Mental Hygiene Clinic.

Criteria. In the attempt to establish valid information against which clinical judgments could be evaluated, two sources of criterion data were employed. *Internal* criterion information was established by the agreement of eight highly experienced clinicians to a series of check-list items on the basis of exposure to *all* input data employed in the study. *External* criterion information was established by compiling a check list of items from the progress notes kept by the patients' therapists. Internal and external check-list items, combined in a single list for presentation to the judges, were analyzed separately.

Input data. The input information consisted of a social case history (obtained by a social worker), the Rorschach inkblot test, the MMPI, and a sentence-completion test. This battery was presented to judges under five experimental conditions, representing different combinations of the data. In the first four conditions, judges were presented with different combinations of three tests. For example, in one condition, judges received the social case history, the Rorschach, and the MMPI, but *not* the sentence-completion test. In another condition, the judges received the case history, Rorschach, and sentence-completion test, but not the MMPI, etc. In the fifth condition, the judges were given only face-sheet information consisting of age, marital status, occupation, education, and source of referral to the clinic. This fifth condition served as a control for psychological test information and as a test of the ability of clinicians to make better than chance inferences on the basis of identifying information alone. Each judge was exposed to all five patients and all five experimental conditions, but neither a patient nor a condition was repeated for any judge. This Latin-square design (Grant, 1948) was necessary, since judges would be likely to remember characteristics of the same patient from one experimental condition to another.

Results. In all analyses performed, the results obtained with internal criterion measures were comparable to those obtained with external criterion measures, and therefore these two validity criteria need not be considered separately. It was found that clinical judges were able to make more accurate predictions than could be expected by chance on the basis of face-sheet information alone (age, marital status, etc.). Since this condition was a control condition that did not involve the use of psychological tests, it provided an appropriate base line against which to evaluate the relative accuracy of predictions under the other conditions. Only two experimental conditions yielded accuracy scores that exceeded those obtained from face-sheet information alone: the test battery which included the social case history, MMPI, and sentence-completion test and that which included the social case history, MMPI, and Rorschach. These two batteries have in common the social case history and the MMPI. Under conditions in which the test battery excluded the MMPI or the social case history, judgmental accuracy did not exceed that obtained under conditions of face-sheet information alone.

Clearly then, it cannot be concluded that all additional test information increases the accuracy of the clinical judge. The addition of some tests led to increments in accuracy of prediction whereas the addition of other tests did not. Kostlan's design did not allow for an evaluation of whether the social case history or the MMPI was the "best" source of information for clinical prediction.   It did show, however, that different combinations of input data led to different degrees of accuracy of clinical prediction.

In addition to finding differences among combinations of psychological tests, Kostlan found significant differences among *judges* in their ability to make clinical predictions from different combinations of tests.   Thus the effects of increased information on judgmental accuracy may vary according to the judge studied.   Finally, Kostlan found significant differences among *patients* with respect to the accuracy with which they could be predicted. In sum, generalizations about the effects of increased information on accuracy must be qualified with respect to the particular tests, judges, and subjects employed.

The Sines (1959) Study

Judges.   The judges were five clinical psychology trainees at different levels of training who had been employed by the Veterans Administration for at least one year.   Each judge interviewed, and administered a Rorschach test to, each of the six patients for whom he was to make predictions.   Since the data were made available to the clinicians in differing sequential orders, the points at which the interview and Rorschach administration were conducted were determined by the experimental design.

Patients.   The patients were 30 male veterans of World War II who had received a complete diagnostic work-up and 10 or more hours of individual psychotherapy at the Fort Snelling Veterans Administration Mental Hygiene Clinic.   Two-thirds of the patients had been diagnosed as having some neurotic condition, and one-fifth had been diagnosed as having some psychotic condition.   The median age of the patients was 32.5 years.

Criteria.   A set of 97 *Q*-sort items, describing both phenotypic and genotypic personality characteristics, was selected from a larger pool of 295 items on the basis of judged relevance to the input data with which the judges were provided.   Thirteen psychotherapists rated the degree of descriptive relevance of each statement for each of their patients after ten hours of therapy. Correlations between judges' predictions and therapists' ratings on the 97 *Q*-sort items constituted the criterion of predictive accuracy.

The same set of *Q*-sort items was also used to obtain a Mean Average Patient, or stereotype score.   Eleven clinical psychology trainees performed a *Q*-sort describing their conception of a typical patient in a mental hygiene clinic.   The mean values of these sorts formed the basis for the stereotype score.   In addition, each of the five clinical judges who participated in the study was asked to sort the same items according to his conception of a typical mental hygiene patient.   Thus both general and individual stereotype measures were available.

Input data. Each of the five clinical judges was provided with a biographical data sheet for each of the six patients he was to examine prior to any contact with the patient. He was asked to make Q-sort ratings on the basis of this information alone. Each clinical judge then either interviewed the patient, administered the Rorschach, or interpreted an MMPI, and he made a Q-sort on the basis of the biographical data sheet plus one of these diagnostic techniques. The clinician was then given his third set of information (interview, MMPI, or Rorschach) and required to make predictions based on three data sources. Finally, the clinician received the fourth information source (interview, MMPI, or Rorschach), and he was asked to make predictions based on the complete battery. The order in which data sources were given to the clinician was randomized across clinicians and patients. This design permitted an evaluation of the effects on judgmental accuracy of varying amounts of input data. It also permitted an evaluation of the relative contribution of different data sources to the accuracy of the clinical judgments.

Results. The experimental design employed by Sines permitted a number of analyses to be made of the contributions of individual data sources and of the sequential effects of adding different data sources in relation to the overall accuracy of prediction. Only the major analyses will be considered here. The average validity coefficients for each of the data sources are presented in Table 4.4.

For each combination of input data, a correlation was computed between the Q-sort placement of items by the clinician after a given input and the Q-sort placement by the patient's therapist after the tenth hour of psycho-

Table 4.4 Average validity coefficients of different combinations of input data. (After Sines, 1959)

Input data	N	Average validity coefficient
Biog. + interview + MMPI	10	.595
Biog. + interview	10	.566
Biog. + interview + MMPI + Rorschach	30	.480
Biog. + interview + Rorschach	10	.450
Biog. + MMPI + Rorschach	10	.403
Biog.	30	.396
Biog. + MMPI	10	.378
Biog. + Rorschach	10	.368
Stereotype Q-sort	30	.340
Clinicians' average patient Q-sort	30	.289

therapy. Table 4.4 shows that all combinations of input data provided a more accurate basis for prediction than did the average patient stereotype. The data in Table 4.4 are based on averages, however, and it should be noted that in nine of the thirty sorts made by clinicians, the stereotype description exceeded the validity of the final clinical sort. Note also that predictions made on the basis of the biographical data sheet alone were more valid than those made on the basis of the biographical data sheet plus the MMPI and the biographical data sheet plus the Rorschach. Of greatest importance is the fact that only the first two combinations of data listed in Table 4.4 (Biog. + Interview + MMPI; Biog. + Interview) yielded validity coefficients that were *significantly* different from the biographical data alone or the stereotype alone. The complete battery of tests did not significantly exceed biographical data alone. However, when the Rorschach was *excluded* from the total battery, the highest average validity coefficient was obtained. Moreover, when only the interview was added to the biographical data, the average validity coefficient was almost as great as that attained with the interview and the MMPI.

The importance of the interview as a source of input data for this type of prediction was further established by a sequential analysis of the point at which different input data were introduced. Only on the addition of the interview was there a demonstrated increase in validity over that obtained on the basis of previous data. Sines's study is untypical in providing positive evidence for the validity of clinical interviews as assessment devices (see Kelly, 1954). However, it is important to note that, in this study, the interview represents a "sample" of the criteria (Wernimont and Campbell, 1968) in that therapists' criterion ratings were based on ten interviews.

The relationship between the amounts of data provided the clinician and the accuracy of the clinician's predictions is given in Table 4.5. Recall that

Table 4.5 Relationship between ordinal position of *Q*-sorts and their average validity coefficients. (After Sines, 1959)

Q-sort	Mean validity coefficient
Clinicians' average patient sort	.289
Stereotype sort	.340
First clinical sort	.396
Second clinical sort	.446
Third clinical sort	.477
Fourth clinical sort	.480

the first clinical Q-sort was made on the basis of the biographical data sheet alone, the second on the basis of biographical plus one additional data source, the third, biographical plus two additional sources, etc. Clearly the relationship between the amount of information available to the clinician and the accuracy of his judgments is a positive one. Despite this trend, however, the absolute improvement from the first clinical Q-sort (biographical data alone) to the final one was quite small. In a sequential analysis of the data, Sines discovered a tendency for clinicians to rapidly crystallize or "freeze" their impressions of patients. That is, the clinician tended to change his impression of a patient less and less as further input data were added. This tendency of clinicians has been noted in other contexts (Dailey, 1952; Meehl, 1960). One may conclude that the relationship between the amount of information available to the clinician and the accuracy of his judgments is complex rather than linear, and it varies according to the particular data source made available to him.

The Golden (1964) Study

Judges. Of 30 experienced clinical psychologists selected as judges, 25 were Ph.D.'s with an average of 4.6 years of clinical experience beyond the doctorate, and the others were clinical psychology trainees with an average of 4.8 years of clinical experience. All judges were highly experienced in using the particular data employed, and several were acknowledged experts with one or another of the tests. Each judge was assigned to one of six experimental conditions in which he received, successively, different combinations of input data for different patients. As in the Kostlan study, no subject or experimental condition was repeated for any judge. In addition, the judges were asked to complete the various experimental tasks a week apart.

Patients. Five male patients at a Veterans Administration hospital were selected from a larger pool of patients employed in a previous study (Little and Shneidman, 1959). One was a nonpsychiatric patient. Of the others, two had been diagnosed as neurotics, one as a psychophysiologic disorder, and the fifth as a psychotic.

Criteria. Forty-eight highly experienced psychotherapists were asked to indicate whether or not approximately 100 criterion statements were true of a given patient on the basis of their reading of extensive case history material. Each therapist made judgments about two patients, and each patient was judged by four therapists. The pooled judgments of the four therapists served as the validity criterion. The average level of agreement between the therapists was 88 percent.

Input data. All judges were first given a face sheet containing identifying data (age, sex, race, religion, education, and service status) and asked to make predictions on this basis alone. Then, at one-week intervals, each judge was given four sets of data representing different combinations of the MMPI, Rorschach, and TAT. One group of judges received the following sequence: (1) MMPI; (2) Rorschach; (3) MMPI plus Rorschach; (4) MMPI plus Rorschach plus TAT. Two other experimental groups received different orders and combinations of the same tests. No subject or experimental condition was repeated for any individual clinical judge. This complex Latin-square design enabled Golden to study both the reliability and the validity of single tests, and combinations of tests, in clinical prediction. The reliability measure was based on the amount of *inter-judge* agreement among clinicians who judged the same patient-data combination. The validity measure was based on the extent of agreement between the judges and the criterion psychotherapists.

Results. The average percentages of agreement between clinical predictions based on identifying data alone and the criterion judgments of psychotherapists did not exceed chance expectations. However, the average percentages of agreement between clinical judgments based on psychological tests, singly and in combination, and the criterion judgments of psychotherapists were greater than would have been expected by chance. When agreements based on identifying data alone were compared, by means of analysis of variance, with agreements based on psychological test data, significant differences were found. However, comparisons among judgments based on different psychological tests, singly and in combination, produced no significant differences. Hence, it could not be concluded that any particular test or combination of tests led to increased accuracy of prediction.

Examination of inter-judge agreement among the clinicians showed that better than chance agreement occurred both for predictions made from identifying data and for predictions made from the various psychological tests. However, no differences in reliability could be attributed to the use of any test, singly or in combination. Golden concluded:

The results of the present study do not *support the view that clinical inferences based on a battery of tests are more reliable and valid than those based on individual tests. With a variety of types of* Ss, *with experienced clinicians interpreting different combinations of three frequently used psychological tests—the Rorschach, TAT, and MMPI—reliability and validity did not increase as a function of increasing amounts of test data, nor were there any differences in this respect among individual tests or pairs of tests.* (p. 444).

Conclusions

The studies of Kostlan (1954), Sines (1959), and Golden (1964) provide evidence that clinicians can utilize psychological test data to make better predictions than they could make on the basis of identifying information alone. However, whereas Kostlan and Sines found that the addition of certain tests to the battery resulted in increased predictive accuracy, Golden did not obtain this finding. One must conclude that the postulated relationship between amount of input data and accuracy of clinical judgments does not always hold and that when it does, the relationship is complex rather than linear. Further, it seems likely that marked individual differences will be found among clinicians, both in their accuracy and in the manner in which they utilize specific input variables for specific patients.

CLINICAL PREDICTION

When human judgment enters into the combination of input data for the forecasting of criterion behaviors, we speak of *clinical prediction*. As Figure 4.1 indicated, the combination of data (prediction) is logically distinct from the source of such data (measurement). In our attempt to evaluate the reliability and accuracy of the clinician as a *measuring* instrument, we considered a number of studies that might be more accurately classified as instances of clinical *prediction*. Similarly, in our consideration of clinical prediction, it will be necessary to consider instances of judgmental measurement. Both judgmental measurement and clinical prediction have in common the process of human *judgment*, which constitutes the major topic of the present chapter. When *judgment* is the central topic of concern, the distinction between measurement and prediction may be rather academic. However, when *prediction* is the topic at issue (Chapter 5), the distinction between measurement and prediction must be carefully maintained.

Despite its central importance as both a practical and a theoretical issue in personality assessment, the process whereby clinicians combine input data to arrive at predictions is still largely not understood. Until recently, the "cognitive activity of the clinician" (Meehl, 1960) has been viewed as inaccessible or private and therefore not subject to logical or empirical analysis. Practicing clinicians themselves have contributed substantially to this mystique, frequently maintaining that they are unable to "verbalize" the complex and, at times, inaccessible processes that enter into data combination. The demarcation of clinical judgment as an area outside the purview of scientific analysis has led to several unfortunate consequences. On the one hand, individuals with a strong professional or ideological identification with clinical judgments have used the alleged "inaccessibility" of clinical judgment as a rationalization for practices which are both nonoptimal and inaccurate. On the other hand, those who are strongly predisposed toward statistical methods of data combination have argued that the apparent inaccessibility of clinical judgment constitutes sufficient grounds for its rejection as a method of data combination. In the material that follows, we will attempt to provide a somewhat more balanced perspective on clinical judgment by considering the current status of both logical and empirical investigations of the clinical judgment process.

Some Theoretical Considerations

A topic as complex as clinical judgment does not lend itself readily to empirical formulation. It is unlikely that the "nature" or "utility" of clinical judgment will be decided on the basis of a single experiment, or even on the basis of a series of experiments. Under such circumstances, it is advisable to approach the issue from a logical or theoretical rather than an empirical perspective. For example, if it can be shown that, in principle, a human judge can *never* combine data more accurately than a computer, the practical contribution of clinical judgment to personality assessment will be seriously questioned. On the other hand, if it can be demonstrated that, in principle, it is possible for a human judge to combine data more accurately than a computer, it behooves us to identify the circumstances under which this may take place. An impressive first step toward the logical reconstruction of clinical activity has been achieved by Meehl (1954). In the material that follows, we will attempt to gain a perspective on the nature of clinical judgment through a consideration of the theoretical contributions of Meehl and others.

The Clinician as a Second-Rate IBM Machine

There is little ambiguity about the manner in which the basic prediction model (Chapter 1) and its alternatives (Chapters 2 and 3) are applied in statistical prediction. On the basis of empirically established relationships between predictor and criterion variables, the predictors are combined and weighted in such a fashion as to yield a mathematically optimal forecast of the criterion scores. In the case of prediction via multiple-regression equations, the input data are weighted on the basis of their correlations with the criterion variable and with each other: $y' = b_1 x_1 + b_2 x_2 + \cdots + b_n x_n$. The weights assigned in multiple regression are optimal under a least-squares criterion and will therefore yield predictions with the least possible error. Alternatives to the multiple-regression model are based on the same principle. The actuarial method of prediction combines data on the basis of empirically established contingencies between predictor and criterion frequencies. Actuarial tables are frequency tables which indicate the number of occurrences of the criterion variables for classes of the predictor variables. Actuarial predictions are stated in terms of probabilities (for example, $P = .40$), whose accuracy is limited largely by the size of the sample observed.

Given the fact that statistical prediction by means of multiple-regression equations or actuarial tables is mathematically optimal, in what sense might we expect a clinician to improve on such predictions by an alternative combination of input variables? Critics of the clinical method of data combination (e.g., Lundberg, 1941; Sarbin, 1944) have argued that under *no* circumstances can the clinician be expected to improve on the mathematically optimal data-combination techniques of statistical prediction. From this point of view, the clinician is, at best, a "second-rate accounting machine" (Meehl, 1954) and, at worst, a producer of totally inaccurate predictions. It has been maintained that given the *same* input information, the clinician is unable to improve on mathematically optimal methods of data combination and, in the light of the literature on the manner in which clinicians process complex input information, he is unlikely even to approximate the accuracy of statistical prediction.

Proponents of the clinical method of data combination (e.g., Allport, 1937; Holt, 1958; Parker, 1958) have argued that a comparison of the clinician with an IBM machine is invidious, and it overlooks those aspects of clinical judgment which result in predictions that are superior to those of a machine. Proponents hold that the advantages of clinical prediction, as opposed to statistical prediction, reside in: (a) the fact that the clinician makes predictions for the *individual case* rather than for groups of individuals; (b) the ability of the clinician to detect among input variables *unique patterns* which would be overlooked by statistical techniques; and (c) the fact that the clinician almost always possesses *additional information* not available to the computer.

Critics of the clinical method are reluctant to accept the assertion that the differences between the computer and the clinician are qualitative rather than quantitative. They hold that everything the clinician does, or claims to do, can, *in principle*, be duplicated by the statistical approach. Consider the clinician's argument that he predicts for *individuals* rather than for groups of people. First, it must be recognized that *all* predictions are probabilistic rather than deterministic. The probability that a prediction from a multiple-regression equation is correct may be stated with reference to the standard error of prediction. The probability that a clinical prediction is correct may be subjectively expressed in terms of the clinician's degree of confidence in his prediction or more rigorously expressed in terms of the empirical success rate that a given clinician enjoys for a certain class of predictions. In either instance, a probability statement is involved.

Probability statements are made with reference to the relative frequency of occurrence of a given event in a class of events. When the class of events is a *group* of persons, the probability statement is expressed in terms of the relative frequency of occurrence of the criterion behavior in that group. To say that one is "predicting" for an *individual* is to imply that such probability statements are made with reference to a class. One such class of events might be the lifetime of a single individual. Under this definition, it is possible to state the relative frequency of a given event over the lifetime of a single individual. Such "individual" predictions can be made with equal ease by a computer or a clinician. However, to assert that predictions made on the basis of the relative frequency of occurrence of an event in the life of a single person are *intrinsically* superior to predictions based on the relative frequency of occurrence in a group of persons is to provide a premature answer to an empirical question (Meehl, 1954, pp. 19–23). If indeed the clinician bases his probability statements on events in the life of a single individual, the computer can, in principle, do the same thing.

The clinician's purported ability to extract a unique pattern from a given set of input data has been one of the mainstays of the argument for the inherent superiority of clinical inference over statistical data combination. This argument is made primarily with reference to *rare events*, which tend to be overlooked by statistical methods. In determining the weights to be assigned to variables in a regression equation or the probabilities to be assigned to actuarial frequency statements, the computer gives the greatest weight to relationships that are *statistically* significant. An event that has occurred only once in a thousand instances is unlikely to be included in an actuarial table or to be given weight in a multiple-regression equation. However, should the input data for a given individual represent an instance of this one occurrence in a thousand, the clinician who is able to recognize such a unique pattern will weight it heavily *in this particular case* and make a prediction that will be superior to one that would have been made by a computer.

In addition to being generally skeptical about the ability of clinicians to remember or "store" such a variety of rare events, the critics of clinical judgment reject the weighting of unique events on the grounds that such weightings are mathematically nonoptimal. From a statistical standpoint, a given event or pattern of predictor variables is either *significantly* related to the criterion of interest or it is not. If significantly related, it will occur in a sufficient number of cases to justify its inclusion in a regression equation or actuarial table. If it does not occur with sufficient frequency, then its inclusion in data-combination procedures could only be *nonoptimal*. Statistical prediction is based on rules for data combination which are mathematically optimal in the sense of making the smallest sum of (squared) errors in prediction. Departures from this model can result only in increases in error. If one grants the suspicion that the clinician is unable to combine input data in a mathematically optimal fashion to begin with, further departures from optimality seem likely to result in even greater error.

In clinical practice, the clinician almost always has available to him information other than that employed in most systems of statistical prediction.

Such information may come from formal or informal contacts with the patient, from friends or relatives of the patient, or from other psychological data which are not employed in formal prediction. It is maintained that the clinician, under these realistic circumstances, has a "natural" predictive edge by virture of his access to data that are unavailable to the computer. Again, in addition to their general skepticism regarding the ability of clinicians to process large amounts of input data, critics of the clinical method are also skeptical of the predictive value of such additional data. They argue that, in principle, any additional information available to the clinician could be coded in such a way that it could be included in statistical data combination. If such additional "impressions" are difficult to "verbalize," as clinicians frequently assert, then it is difficult to understand how clinicians verbalize this information to themselves when they are combining their input data for prediction. That clinicians frequently have *access* to information not available to a computer is conceded. However, critics argue that the clinician would spend his time more profitably in attempting to convert this information to a form that would allow its optimal utilization by a computer than in jealously guarding information which may or may not be of any predictive significance.

In summary, early critics of the clinical method (Lundberg, 1941; Sarbin, 1944) attempted to establish logical grounds for rejecting clinical judgments *in principle*, based on the view of the clinician as a second-rate IBM machine. Since all prediction is assumed to be based on inference from class membership, no qualitative difference between clinical and statistical data combination can be established. Given the fact that statistical methods of data combination can be demonstrated to be mathematically optimal, there is no way in which the clinician can improve on predictions generated by a computer. When the clinician's claims to distinctive methods of data combination are examined, they turn out to be either not distinctive or simply nonoptimal strategies. Independently of *empirical* evidence supporting or refuting the clinician's claim to predictive prowess, critics of the clinical method have concluded that, in principle, the clinician is, at best, a second-rate IBM machine.

Meehl's Logical Reconstruction of Clinical Prediction

The arguments of statistically minded psychologists are convincing, and it may very well be that in functioning as a combiner of data, the clinician can never expect to be more than a second-rate computer. Nevertheless, to practicing clinicians at least, there is something about this line of reasoning that seems over simplistic and that fails to do justice to the complexity of clinical inference as subjectively perceived. Such feelings of dissatisfaction with the statistical argument led Meehl (1954) to attempt his own logical reconstruction of clinical prediction. Meehl tried "to show that in *principle* there could be situations in which the Sarbin-Lundberg analysis does not hold up as a description of what takes place, leaving open the question as to whether what does take place 'pays off' in terms of an increase in objective success-frequency" (p. 38).

This effort by Meehl must surely represent the most original and stimulating aspect of his famous monograph, *Clinical versus Statistical Prediction*. Most of the widespread reaction to the monograph has been directed toward the chapter in which the empirical studies of clinical versus statistical prediction were summarized. Although almost twice as many pages were devoted to a logical analysis of clinical activity, that aspect of Meehl's contribution has been less widely recognized. Nevertheless, this important theoretical effort by Meehl deserves the attention of all who are concerned with prediction in psychology.

Contexts of Discovery and Justification

In describing the descriptive function of epistemology (the study of knowledge), Reichenbach (1938) distinguished between the *context of discovery* and the *context of justification*. The context of discovery (of knowledge) refers to the *psychological* thought processes as they actually occur in scientific discovery or inference. The context of justification refers to a *logical* or "epistemological" analysis of the truth or verifiability of the knowledge discovered. This distinction would apply, for example, to the difference between the manner in which a mathematician discovers or arrives at a theorem and the manner in which he presents it to fellow mathematicians. In Reichenbach's view, the context of discovery is the province of psychology, and the context of justification is the province of epistemology.

Meehl has applied Reichenbach's terms to distinguish two separate analytic problems in the realm of clinical prediction. In Meehl's usage, the context of justification refers simply to the usual scientific procedures for establishing the empirical validity of a prediction. Regardless of how they came about, the validity of clinicians' predictions must be established by the same empirical standards that are applied to statistical predictions. A given clinical prediction can be unambiguously established as true or false, and the set of predictions of a given clinician may be designated as mostly true or mostly false.

An equally legitimate but distinct set of questions may be raised regarding the manner in which the clinician arrives at his prediction. In the context of discovery, we are concerned not with the empirical truth or falsity of clinical predictions but with the psychological processes that give rise to such predictions. In this context Meehl has attempted a logical reconstruction of clinical activity, in which he seeks to discover whether the clinician could, *in principle*, have access to information that would enable him to improve on actuarial prediction. Whether or not clinicians do in fact have access to such sources of information is less important for Meehl's argument than whether or not they *could* have. A successful a priori argument for the superiority of clinical prediction would bring into question the previous a priori argument that the clinician can *never* function more effectively than a computer.

The failure to separate the contexts of discovery and justification has led to a number of misunderstandings between proponents of the clinical and of the statistical methods of prediction. At this point in time, it seems fair to observe that available empirical studies of clinical and statistical prediction (context of justification) appear to be overwhelmingly in favor of statistical prediction methods (Chapter 5). This fact has led to a number of unjustified statements about the context of discovery. For example, when confronted with the existing negative evidence for clinical prediction, the clinician is prone to respond that the complex working of the human brain can never be forced into the rigid mold of a multiple-regression equation. Such a statement clearly fails to separate the context of discovery (complex workings of the human brain) from the context of justification (statistical validation of clinical prediction). Similarly, when proponents of statistical prediction interpret the negative findings from empirical studies (context of justification) as indicating that the clinician is using multiple-regression equations with nonoptimal weights (context of discovery) they are guilty of a non sequitur. The two contexts are logically independent, and the results of analyses in one context cannot be used as a basis for interpretations in the other.

Lawfulness and Uniqueness

In addition to the difficulties arising from a failure to distinguish between the contexts of discovery and justification, much of the current confusion regarding the nature of clinical prediction may be traced to an improper perspective on the relationship between general (nomothetic) laws, which hold for groups of individuals, and specific (idiographic) laws, which hold for single individuals. The distinction between nomothetic and idiographic lawfulness has polarized much of contemporary thought into opposing camps and generated a high ratio of heat to light (Allport, 1962; Beck, 1953; Eysenck, 1954; Falk, 1956; Holt, 1962). Meehl (1954) offers a balanced and highly useful formulation of this issue, which avoids the difficulties inherent in the view that the existence of one type of lawfulness (nomothetic) necessarily *precludes* the existence of the other (idiographic). Meehl is in general agreement with Allport (1937) that general laws do not preclude uniqueness but rather that general laws describe how uniqueness comes about. More specifically, Meehl's view is that behavioral laws are: (a) nomothetic in their *form* for a given group, (b) idiographic in their *parameters*, and (c) strongly idiographic in their *end terms*, which refer to response properties of the organism. (Meehl, 1954, p. 64).

Meehl provides an example of these properties by considering the well-known law of learning which states that habit strength is related to number of reinforcements by a positive growth function. Although this law is stated in the terminology of stimulus-response reinforcement theory, Meehl's argument presumably holds for any theoretical framework. The effect of reinforcement on habit strength is frequently demonstrated by placing a rat in a Skinner box and dispensing food pellets each time the animal depresses a lever. Although for any *group* of rats the form of the learning curve is clearly a smooth growth function, different rates of acquisition may be found for individual rats. Thus the form of this law is nomothetic for the group but idiographic in its parameters. Whereas the conditions of reinforcement and, to some extent, the previous history of the animals are under the control of the experimenter, the *end term* of the law (lever press) is under the control of the individual rat. Consequently, no matter how the response "lever press" is defined by the experimenter, there will be marked individual differences among rats in its properties.

The response "lever press" was originally selected because this response class was shown to have lawful relationships with the experimental operations of reinforcement. Although such lawful relationships are nomothetic in form, they may be strongly idiographic in terms of the properties of the response itself. Thus, for example, a "lever press" may involve depressing the bar with the left front paw, the right front paw, or both paws, or even sitting on the bar. These *individual differences* in response topography are overlooked in the general statement of the law, since the law holds in spite of them.

In addition to being idiographic in its end terms, a nomothetic law which is true for a group of animals may not hold precisely for a given animal in the group. Although every attempt is made in the laboratory to provide constant conditions for each animal, it is almost certain that the life experiences of any two rats will not be *identical*. Further, it is possible, in principle, to devise an experimental situation that appears to have the form of a general nomothetic law but that in fact is based on a unique pattern of individual experiences. A rat previously trained to depress a lever to avoid shock may demonstrate the usual nomothetic acquisition curve when given food. However, the actual determinants of the animal's response acquisition may be those of its shock rather than its food experience. Although such a phenomenon is unlikely in the typical laboratory experiment, an ingenious experimenter can in principle demonstrate instances in which a given final response is an exception rather than an illustration of a general nomothetic law.

Idiographic exceptions to nomothetically stated laws become highly plausible when we consider the complex nature of learning in humans. Whether speaking of response acquisition or any other aspect of human personality, we know that no two individuals have identical life histories. When considering the end terms or human behaviors of interest to the clinician, we become even more aware of the idiographic components of nomothetic laws. The *response classes* employed in the description of human behavior include a wide variety of specific responses which bear no topographic resemblance to one another. Consider the following behaviors: being purposely late for an appointment, criticizing a friend's manner of dress, striking a child on the head, giving a stranger false directions. Although the form these responses take have nothing in common topographically, they *may* all be instances of the response class of *aggression*. Further, whether or not such responses are classified as aggressive will depend on the *context* in which they occur.

Although it may be nomothetically true that aggression is a consequence of frustration (Dollard *et al.*, 1939), the conditions which are perceived as frustrating and the form in which the aggression is expressed will vary widely from one individual to another. Thus, although it is *convenient* for purposes of nomothetic prediction to state that the generic stimulus class of "frustration" is related to the generic response class of "aggression," such a generalization overlooks the diversity of contexts in which this relationship might occur as well as many individual instances in which the nomothetical law is not strictly true. Regardless of their utility (context of justification) for clinical prediction, idiographic laws must be recognized as components of, and particularly as possible exceptions to, general nomothetic laws. The question now becomes one of the extent to which a clinician might have *access* to the detailed information which describes the causal development of an idiographic law.

Returning specifically to clinical prediction, we should recognize that the clinician typically does not have direct access to information describing the development of the behavior to be predicted (Meehl, 1954, p. 45). He has before him such information as can be gained from an interview, an MMPI, a Rorschach, or other psychological test data. It cannot be argued that such data *cause* the behavior to be predicted (response to psychotherapy) in any literal sense of causation. It is true that the input variables may be lawfully related to other variables, which in turn are lawfully related to the behavior to be predicted. However, given our current fragmentary knowledge of such relationships, it seems that the only information available to the clinician would be the crude (and noncausal) correlations known to exist between input variables and the criterion. It is for this reason that proponents of statistical prediction argue that the clinician has no more information available to him than would a computer which stores such correlations. If this is true, it seems unlikely, as we have already indicated, that the clinician could combine such input data as optimally as a multiple-regression equation. Thus, even though we have conceded the possible existence of idiographic laws, it is necessary to specify the manner in which the clinician could, in principle, capitalize on such laws for predictive purposes. Meehl describes a possible way as "forming an impression of the person."

Forming an Impression of the Person

In describing the manner in which they utilize input data to arrive at a prediction of some future behavior, clinicians use a variety of expressions which may be categorized under the general heading of "forming an impression of the person." On the basis of psychological test data and interview impressions, the clinician *invents a hypothesis* concerning the state of certain hypothetical variables which constitute the clinician's theory of personality.   From his assessment of the nature and arrangement of these hypothetical variables in a particular patient, the clinician then attempts to deduce their consequences for the behavior to be predicted. Thus, instead of predicting on the basis of known regularities between predictor data and the criterion to be predicted, the clinician uses such data to estimate the patient's status with respect to hypothetical variables, and he then uses this theoretical model as a basis for his prediction. The sequence is illustrated in Figure 4.2. Again, since Meehl's argument is developed in the context of discovery, the validity of predictions generated by personality theory is not at issue.   What is at issue is the possibility that the clinician utilizes data-combination procedures that could not, in principle, be duplicated by a computer.

Proponents of statistical prediction might maintain that, despite the apparent complexity of the chain of inference represented in Figure 4.2, such predictions could, in principle, be achieved by a computer. The argument would be based on the assumption that the presumed lawful relations that exist at stages 1, 2, and 3 must have been arrived at *inductively*. Unless he is

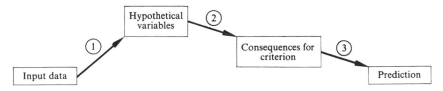

Fig. 4.2 Clinical predictions based on personality theory.

clairvoyant, the clinician must base his inferences on regularities that have been observed in the past between input data construed theoretically and the consequences of such theoretical constructions for the behavior to be predicted. This point would be conceded by Meehl, since it cannot be denied that all laws are based on inductions (Meehl, 1954, p. 46). Further, it could be argued that *given* the status of an individual on certain hypothetical variables, one could write a computer program that would derive the consequences for the criterion of interest (stage 2) and generate predictions on the basis of these consequences (stage 3). Although it is unlikely that this could be accomplished in fact, it must be conceded as a possibility, in principle.

According to Meehl, the critical point in the chain of inference is that of stage 1, the point at which hypotheses are *invented* concerning the state of hypothetical variables in the patient. As currently practiced, the invention of clinical hypotheses seems to lie more in the realm of art than of science. Even if one grants that such inferences are arrived at inductively, it is extraordinarily difficult, if not impossible, to specify the rules under which a given hypothesis is invented. Published examples of clinical intuition (Berne, 1949; Reik, 1948), as well as examples given by Meehl himself (pp. 48–50), are sufficiently complex to discourage even the most sophisticated computer programmer from attempting to reconstruct them statistically.

Basically, clinical intuition involves the ability to invent particular hypotheses that exemplify a general principle in a specific and often fragmentary instance of that principle. A slip of the tongue, a phrase, or a movement in a specific *context* is recognized as an instance of a more general psychodynamic law. That aspect of clinical hypothesis formation which makes it most refractory to statistical analysis is the fact that a given specific instance in a given specific context may never have been previously observed by the clinician or may, in principle, never have been previously observed by anyone.

To say that a clinician is able to recognize a unique event as an instance of a general class of behaviors which have lawful relations with criterion measures is not to imply that he is clairvoyant. Clearly, the clinician operates on the basis of *rules* for class recognition, even though they may be extraordinarily difficult to verbalize. If such rules exist, could they not be made explicit, studied empirically, and presented to a clerical worker along with statistical tables containing relevant information on frequencies of occurrence? Meehl's answer to this question is central to his entire argument:

It seems to me that even if we acquaint the clerical worker with the statistical frequencies and make sure that she understands the meaning of all the concepts involved, we still have to create in her a readiness to invent particular hypotheses that exemplify the general principle in a specific instance. And when we have done this last, which I do not think can be done wholly *by stating general rules, we have trained a clerical worker to the point that she is now actually a skilled clinician.* (Meehl, 1954, p. 50.)

Thus the invention of clinical hypotheses is considered to be an attribute of clinical prediction that cannot be duplicated by mechanical means. If this is true, then the chain of inference pictured in Figure 4.2 represents an alternative method of combining input data that need not be, in principle, inferior to the statistical combination of data by multiple-regression equations. However, even though at this point we are not concerned with the context of justification, it is still necessary to demonstrate that, in principle, predictions based on personality theory could be more accurate than predictions based on statistical combinations of input data.

Structural-dynamic Hypotheses

According to Meehl, there is a formal difference between the process of prediction involved in statistical combination and that in clinical hypothesis formation. In statistical prediction, deductions, though probabilistic in nature, follow directly from classification of the input data. In clinical prediction, on the other hand, the hypothesis is not a straightforward formal consequence of these data. Once the hypothesis has been stated, the original data are seen as entailed by it, but someone has to state the hypothesis in the first place. In order to demonstrate that such hypotheses could in principle lead to more accurate prediction, Meehl offers a physical analogy of the prediction problem. Although analogical arguments are not the strongest form of proof, the particular example offered by Meehl is highly compelling.

Figure 4.3 depicts an opaque box which has a series of colored lights on the front and rows of buttons on the back. By a complex arrangement of gears, wires, and pulleys, the buttons are connected to the lights. Pressing different combinations of buttons will result in the illumination of different patterns of lights. The internal mechanisms (represented by dashed lines) are not visible from the outside. Even with the relatively small number of buttons and lights indicated, different combinations of buttons pressed, say three at a time, will of course result in hundreds of combinations of lights being illuminated. Let us assume that this particular box is a member of a large class of similar but not identical boxes, all of which are wired internally in a somewhat different fashion.

Let us imagine that we present this box to a statistical psychologist and allow him to make a finite number of observations of the "stimulus-response" relations between different combinations of buttons and different combinations of lights. On the basis of such a finite set of observations, he notes a

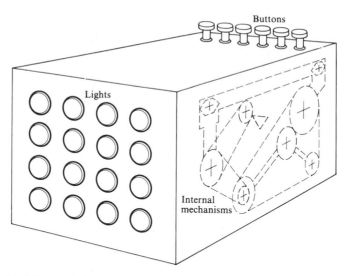

Fig. 4.3 Meehl's prediction analog.

number of classes of approximate relationships between different combinations. Our statistical psychologist may have made similar observations on other boxes whose mechanisms were similar (but not identical) to the present box. After he has gathered his data concerning the probabilistic relations that exist between classes of button presses and classes of light displays, we ask him to predict the outcome of pressing still another combination of buttons. Although he has never pressed this particular combination of buttons, he is able to classify it as belonging to a class of button presses whose relations with the light displays he knows. On the basis of the probabilities suggested by his frequency table, he makes a prediction of the most likely occurrence.

Now let us suppose that we present the same box to a skilled mechanic who has had considerable experience in dismantling and repairing boxes of this type, as well as in observing the relationships between button pressing and light display. Unlike our statistical psychologist, the skilled mechanic adopts a "trouble-shooting" approach to the problem. On the basis of a relatively small number of carefully chosen button presses, he attempts to arrive at a hypothesis concerning the internal structural arrangement of this particular box. Although he may never have encountered a box wired exactly like this one, he is nevertheless able to invent a hypothesis about its internal structure on the basis of his experience with similar boxes. When asked to predict the outcome of pressing a combination of buttons he has never tried, the skilled mechanic bases his prediction on his hypothesis regarding the most likely internal structure of the box.

In the context of justification, the skilled mechanic's hypothesis may turn out to be incorrect and his prediction of the light pattern erroneous. On the other hand, it is conceivable that his hypothesis is in fact correct and he will therefore be able to predict the outcome of any combination of button presses with complete accuracy. Thus it is possible, in principle, for the skilled mechanic to make predictions based on structural-dynamic hypotheses whose accuracy will exceed that of predictions based on the rough probabilistic relationships observed by the statistical psychologist.

Meehl's analogy, of course, is designed to illustrate the manner in which a skilled clinician, who has had experience "taking people apart and putting them back together," is able to invent structural-dynamic hypotheses that could, in principle, form a better basis of prediction than the frequency tables of the statistician. The hypothetical variables of most dynamic personality theories are, for the most part, structural variables of this kind, whose parameters differ from individual to individual. Whereas the statistical psychologist has access only to probabilistic relationships that exist between stimuli (buttons) and responses (lights), the clinical psychologist has access to a theory which attempts to explain the structural relationships that exist between stimuli and responses.

Although several objections might be raised to Meehl's analogy, the most crucial one concerns the alleged inability of the statistical psychologist to make use of information regarding structural relationships. We could, for example, provide the statistician with a table of relative frequencies pertaining to different arrangements of gears, pulleys, etc., for all the boxes that the skilled mechanic had dismanteld. Under such circumstances, Meehl contends, it would be extremely unlikely that the statistician would be able to *invent* the correct hypothesis concerning the structural arrangement of the box for which predictions are to be made. As before, one could appropriately train the statistician to invent hypotheses in a specific instance. But again, as Meehl argued in the case of the clerical worker, we would no longer have a statistical psychologist (clerk); rather, we would have created a skilled mechanic (clinician).

Thus, if Meehl's line of argument is correct, the distinguishing feature between statistical and clinical prediction lies in the invention of structural-dynamic hypotheses by the clinician. Although such hypotheses entail the available data, they do not stem from it in any straightforward statistical fashion. Meehl has attempted to demonstrate that such clinical activity is plausible in the context of discovery and that such prediction can surpass the accuracy of statistical prediction in the context of justification. Remember that Meehl's logical reconstruction of clinical prediction was offered as a reconstruction of how clinical prediction *might* occur, in the absence of data suggesting how it *does* occur. Nevertheless, we must recognize that reconstructions of the clinician's activity which conclude that he is a second-rate

IBM machine are equally speculative. Thus the issue can be ultimately resolved only with reference to *data* on the nature of clinical prediction (context of discovery) and on the accuracy of clinical prediction (context of justification).

Empirical Studies of the Nature of Clinical Prediction

The Brunswik Lens Model

As was apparent from even a brief consideration of Meehl's reconstruction of clinical activity, the study of clinical judgment involves more than an isolated applied problem. The issues involved in clinical judgment are the same as those involved in human judgment in general, and they implicate such basic fields of investigation as cognition, perception, and learning. Hammond and his associates (Hammond, 1955, 1966; Hammond, Hursch, and Todd, 1964; Hursch, Hammond, and Hursch, 1964) were the first to emphasize the relevance of Brunswik's (1955, 1956) "probabilistic functionalism" to the study of clinical inference. Brunswik maintained that the environment is an uncertain, probabilistic one in which the organism makes inferences based on probabilistic data. Brunswik represented this situation in terms of a convex lens describing the relationship between human judgments, environmental cues, and the objects to be judged. An application of the Brunswik lens model to the clinical prediction paradigm is presented in Figure 4.4.

In the center of the lens, the typical predictor data or, "cues," are represented by x_1, x_2, x_3, and x_4. In clinical prediction, they would typically take the form of data from psychological tests, such as the Rorschach, MMPI, or of case history variables. At the far left of the lens are the criterion scores, y_c, to be predicted from the available input data. At the far right are the actual predictions of the clinician, y_j. From the standpoint of research on clinical prediction, the aspect of the lens model which raises it from an interesting conceptual formulation to a powerful research tool is the suggestion that the

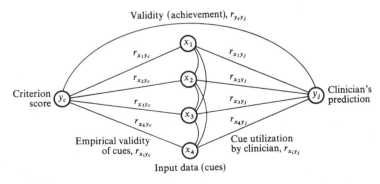

Fig. 4.4 Clinical prediction paradigm schematized by Brunswik's lens model. (After Hammond, Hursch, and Todd, 1964)

relationships among predictions, cues, and criteria may be specified by means of correlational analysis (Brunswik, 1947; Todd, 1954; Hammond, 1955; Hoffman, 1960).

Empirical Validity of Cues

In correlational terms, the left side of the lens represents the empirical validity of input data or cues which can be described by the basic prediction model developed in Chapter 1. The prediction of a given criterion score, y_c, from a set of predictor variables, x_1, x_2, x_3, x_4, may be accomplished by straight-forward application of the multiple-regression model:

$$y'_c = {}_cb_1x_1 + {}_cb_2x_2 + {}_cb_3x_3 + {}_cb_4x_4.$$

The subscript preceding each regression weight, c, indicates that the regression weight was determined with reference to the *criterion*. As indicated in Chapter 1, the regression weights for predicting the criterion score from input data are determined by the intercorrelations that exist among the predictor variables, $r_{x_1x_2}$, $r_{x_2x_3}$, etc., and the correlations or empirical validities of the input data with the criterion, $r_{x_1y_c}$, $r_{x_2y_c}$, $r_{x_3y_c}$, $r_{x_4y_c}$. This aspect of the lens model has already been considered in some detail and need not be elaborated further at this point.

Cue Utilization by Clinician

The right side of the lens represents a kind of correlational analysis that we have not yet considered, namely, the relationship between input data, x_1, x_2, x_3, x_4, and the *prediction* made by the clinician, y_j. Application of multiple-regression analysis to this half of the lens enables us to "predict the prediction" of the clinician:

$$y'_j = {}_jb_1x_1 + {}_jb_2x_2 + {}_jb_3x_3 + {}_jb_4x_4.$$

Here the subscript preceding each regression weight j, indicates that the regression weight was determined with reference to the judgment made by the clinician. As before, the prediction of the clinician's prediction from the input data is a function of the intercorrelations among the cues, $r_{x_1x_2}$, $r_{x_2x_3}$, etc., and the relationships between the cues and the clinician's judgment, $r_{x_1y_j}$, $r_{x_2y_j}$, etc. Although this type of regression analysis is mathematically straightforward, it is *conceptually* quite novel and requires rather special consideration. Note that the correlations between cue values and the clinician's predictions are being used as a basis for predicting—or more accurately, "describing"—the manner in which the clinician utilizes the cues. We can perhaps best describe this procedure by reference to a concrete experimental situation.

Let us assume that we are interested in the manner in which a given clinician utilizes an MMPI profile of scales in arriving at a diagnosis of "psychotic" versus "neurotic." Let us further assume that the cues represented in Figure 4.4 constitute the first four clinical scales of the MMPI, x_1, x_2, x_3, x_4. We select 100 such profiles from the case files of a psychiatric hospital and give them to the clinician, one at a time. We ask him to inspect each one and make a differential diagnosis of "psychotic" or "neurotic." Thus, on each *trial* we can record the values of the four MMPI scales in question, x_1, x_2, x_3, x_4, as well as the specific prediction, y_j, the clinician makes when confronted with this particular constellation of values of the four scales. When this procedure is completed for the 100 MMPI profiles, we have obtained all the information necessary for computing the desired regression equation:

$$y'_j = {}_jb_1x_1 + {}_jb_2x_2 + {}_jb_3x_3 + {}_jb_4x_4.$$

Note that this type of analysis is not concerned with the *accuracy* of the clinician's predictions. Rather, by an examination of the relative size of the regression weights, ${}_jb_1, {}_jb_2, {}_jb_3, {}_jb_4$, it may be possible to gain some insight into the manner in which the clinician utilizes these particular cues in arriving at his overall prediction. To the extent that we are able to devise a regression equation that accurately predicts a particular clinician's judgments, it may be said that we have "described" the manner in which he utilizes the cues in this prediction situation. We will return to the implications of this type of analysis later, but for the moment we will refer to the right side of the lens as that which describes "cue utilization" by the clinician.

Validity of Clinical Inferences

The top of the lens in Figure 4.4 illustrates the relationship between the clinician's predictions and the actual criterion scores, $r_{y_cy_j}$. This relationship, of course, is an indication of the clinician's *validity*, often referred to as the clinician's "achievement" in Brunswik's terminology (e.g., Hammond *et al.*, 1964). Perhaps the most notable contribution of Hammond and his collaborators (Hammond *et al.*, 1964; Hursch *et al.*, 1964) lies in their demonstration that the usually unanalyzed statistic of clinical validity, $r_{y_cy_j}$, may be analyzed into its component parts. As Figure 4.4 shows, the components entering into the validity of clinical inference involve the interrelationships among the cues, the empirical validity of the cues, and the manner in which the cues are utilized by the clinician.

In its most general form, the validity of clinical predictions may be analyzed into the following components[3] of the lens model:

$$r_{y_cy_j} = GR_cR_j + C\sqrt{1 - R_c^2}\sqrt{1 - R_j^2},$$

---

3. The present notation is based on Tucker's (1964) suggested modification of Hammond *et al.*'s (1964) lens model equation.

where

$r_{y_cy_j}$ = the validity coefficient (achievement) of the judge: the correlation between the judge's predictions and the actual criterion values;

G = the linear component of judgmental accuracy: the correlation between predicted scores from the linear model of the judge and predicted scores from the linear model of the criterion, $r_{y'_cy'_j}$;

R_c = the linear predictability of the criterion: the multiple correlation between the cues and the criterion scores, $R_{y_c \cdot x_i}$;

R_j = the linear predictability of the judge: the multiple correlation between the cues and the clinician's predictions, $R_{y_j \cdot x_i}$;

C = the nonlinear component of judgmental accuracy: the correlation between the residual values of the criterion and the residual values of the judge's predictions, after linear components in both the criterion and the judge have been removed.

The expression $(1 - R_c^2)$ represents the amount of *residual variance* in the criterion that is linearly unpredictable from the cue values. Should the criterion values be perfectly predictable from a linear combination of cues ($R_c^2 = 1.00$), the residual variance would be zero. In like manner, the expression $(1 - R_j^2)$ represents the amount of residual variance in clinical judgments that is linearly unpredictable from the cue values. As noted above, the C term represents the *correlation* between the residual values of the criterion and the residual values of the judgments. Although "residual variance" is traditionally assumed to be random and thereby uncorrelated with other residual variances, it need not be so (Siddiqui, 1960).

There are, in fact, several situations in which the residual values of the criterion and the residual values of the judgments might be correlated. One possibility occurs when the clinician is basing his judgments on cues other than those enumerated in the lens model. Although such a finding might occur in a naturalistic study in which the clinician has access to cues not defined by the experimenter, most experimental studies of clinical prediction restrict the clinician's cues to the extent that such a possibility may be ruled out (Hoffman, 1960; Hursch *et al.*, 1964). A second possibility occurs when the clinician is clairvoyant (Reichenbach, 1938) and is forecasting the future on the basis of supra-environmental cues. Such a possibility is assigned rather low priority as a contemporary scientific explanation. The third and by far the most interesting possibility occurs when the clinician is correctly utilizing a *nonlinear* relationship between the cues, x_1, x_2, x_3, x_4, and the criterion, y_c.

In Chapter 2, we considered a number of alternatives to the simple linear combination of input data in forecasting criterion scores. One such model would be the linear joint function:

$$y'_c = {}_cb_1x_1 + {}_cb_2x_2 + {}_cb_3x_1x_2.$$

Let us assume that the optimal combination of cues to forecast the criterion scores is given by some such linear joint function. Let us further assume that the clinician weights the cues in terms of such a joint-functional relationship. In this situation, the overall achievement or validity of the clinician, $r_{y_cy_j}$, would be high, but the empirical validity coefficient, R_e, and the cue utilization coefficient, R_j, would be low because they are computed on the basis of linear multiple-Rs which fail to detect the joint-functional relationships. Residual variance terms would be large for both criterion, $1 - R_e^2$, and judgments, $1 - R_j^2$, and to the extent that the clinician's predictions exactly match the empirical validity of the cues, the C term would approach unity. Under these circumstances, the C term becomes an index of the degree of nonlinearity present in the predictive system.

Application of the Lens Model

As previously indicated, the principal contribution of Brunswik's lens model to the study of clinical prediction resides in the analytic possibilities of applying correlational analysis to the study of cue utilization in carefully designed judgment experiments. The lens model guides both the design of such judgment experiments and the manner in which the results are analyzed.

Situational Components

In the *experimental* study of judgmental responses to multiple cues, the experimenter is able to control the environmental input that is made available to the judge. Several choices exist for determining the arrangement among cues, and each choice has implications for the overall validity (achievement) that the judge might be expected to attain. The first consideration has to do with the degree of intercorrelation that is allowed among the cues. Thus cues may be completely uncorrelated ($r_{x_1x_2}, r_{x_2x_3}, \ldots = 0$) or varying degrees of correlation may be allowed ($r_{x_1x_2}, r_{x_2x_3} \neq 0$). The degree of intercorrelation that exists among the cues has implications for the most appropriate strategy of prediction adopted by the judge, and the mathematical implications of cue intercorrelations for the total lens model have been specified in detail by Hursch *et al.* (1964). From the standpoint of environmental realism, the most representative case is that in which some degree of intercorrelation among the cues is allowed.

The second decision the experimenter faces is the degree of empirical validity to be assigned to individual cues, $r_{x_iy_c}$. Since the clinician has access only to cues, $x_1, x_2, \ldots$, etc., and not to criterion scores, y_c, the limits of his achievement are set by the degree of empirical validity which the cues possess. The most realistic representation of the empirical validity of cues would be one in which at least some cues are related to the criterion and in which the cues differ from one another in their validity.

A final consideration, which is not independent of the first two, has to do with the size of the multiple correlation that exists between the cues and the criterion scores, R_c. When there is no correlation among the cues $(r_{x_1x_2}, r_{x_2x_3}, \ldots = 0)$, optimal prediction may be obtained by an additive combination of the cues weighted in terms of the empirical validity and standard deviation of each of the cues. However, to the extent that cues are correlated, optimal weighting must simultaneously take into account both the empirical validity of the cues and their intercorrelations. Further, when the relationship between cues and criterion scores is best expressed by a *nonlinear* combination of cues, the size of the multiple correlation, R_c, will be attenuated. Thus the experimenter must decide what degree of nonlinearity he wishes to introduce into the environmental side of the lens model. Although there is some skepticism about the extent of nonlinearity that exists between psychological test variables and criterion scores (Chapter 2), it is frequently of interest to study clinical judgment in response to a nonlinear environmental arrangement of cues and criterion scores.

Judgmental Components

Correlational analysis of the judgmental side of the lens model has contributed greatly to our understanding of the nature of clinical prediction. By reanalyzing earlier studies of clinical judgment (e.g., Grebstein, 1963; Todd, 1954; Newton, 1965), as well as studies of their own design (Hammond and Summers, 1965; Peterson, Hammond, and Summers, 1965; Summers and Hammond, 1964; Todd and Hammond, 1965), Hammond and his associates have been able to illuminate the components of clinical prediction in a manner that was not previously possible. Although the substantive findings of this research program are too detailed to be reviewed here, it is instructive to consider briefly some of the components of clinical judgment that have been subjected to correlational analysis. In so doing, we will find helpful a restatement of the validity or achievement of the clinician in terms of the correlation model:

$$r_{y_cy_j} = GR_cR_j + C\sqrt{1 - R_c^2}\sqrt{1 - R_j^2}.$$

Limits of achievement. Hursch *et al.* (1954) have classified six different relations that may exist between statistical properties of the environment and statistical properties of the response system of the judge. These six cases are based on consideration of the intercorrelations among cues and of whether, or to what extent, the clinician's utilization of cues "matches" the empirical validity of the cues. Within each of these six cases, Hursch *et al.* (1964) have been able to specify mathematically both the upper and lower limits of achievement, $r_{y_c y_j}$, that obtain under the constraints of cue intercorrelation and cue utilization by the clinician. The degree to which a clinician could be expected to *improve* the accuracy of his predictions is related to these constraints. Thus, in an analysis of the performance of an actual clinician, it is frequently demonstrated that the clinician's achievement, $r_{y_c y_j}$, though not outstanding, is close to the maximum that he could have achieved, given the circumstances. "What is to be remembered is that the upper limit of achievement is not *uncritically* to be assumed to be unity" (Hammond *et al.*, 1964, p. 441).

Linearity of judgment. The multiple correlation, R_j, provides an index of the extent to which a clinician's judgments may be described by a linear model. Correspondingly, the multiple correlation, R_c, provides an index of the extent to which criterion scores are linearly predictable from the cues. As R_c approaches unity, it is clearly appropriate for the clinician to combine cues in a linear manner. However, linearity alone on the part of the clinician, R_j, is not sufficient to ensure high achievement, $r_{y_c y_j}$. For high achievement, it is necessary that the weights assigned by the clinician to each cue, $_j b_i$, "match" the corresponding empirical weights of each cue, $_c b_i$. The degree of *matching* of cues in the two linear systems is given by G, the correlation between the predicted scores from the linear model of the judge and those from the linear model of the criterion (Tucker, 1964).

When R_j is small, it is clear that the clinician's judgments are poorly described by a linear model and that considerable residual variance, $1 - R_j^2$, remains to be accounted for. There are two possible reasons for such an occurrence, and they are of considerable theoretical and practical importance. One, already mentioned, is that the clinician is behaving in a *systematic* nonlinear fashion that is poorly described by a linear model. Another possible reason is that the clinician is behaving in a more or less *random* manner that cannot be predicted from *any* model.

When the optimal combination of cues to predict criterion values is nonlinear, it is clearly appropriate for the clinician to combine cues in a nonlinear fashion. As before, however, "nonlinearity" alone on the part of the clinician is not sufficient to ensure high achievement, $r_{y_c y_j}$. For high achievement, it is necessary that the nonlinear assignment of weights by the clinician to each cue *match* the optimal nonlinear assignment of empirical weights to each cue. The degree of *matching* of cues in the two nonlinear systems is given by C, the correlation between residual values in the two systems (Tucker, 1964). Should C be high, it is reasonable to infer that the clinician is behaving in a systematic nonlinear fashion that is appropriate to the judgment task.

What of the situation in which the optimal empirical weighting of cues is linear but the clinician combines cues in a nonlinear fashion? Obviously the clinician's achievement, $r_{y_c y_j}$, would be limited in such a situation, and his judgments would be poorly described by a linear model, R_j. Since there is little residual variance in the model for the empirical validity of cues, $1 - R_c^2$, it is unlikely that such variance would be systematically associated with residual variance in the model of the judge, $1 - R_j^2$. Hence the C term is likely to be zero. Under these circumstances, there is no term in the lens-model equation that would enable us to evaluate the extent to which the clinician is behaving in a systematic (nonrandom) manner. Additional evidence on the *reliability* of the clinician's judgments, when the same judgments are repeated several times, would lend credence to the assertion that the clinician is behaving in a systematic manner. Similarly, the demonstration that a particular nonlinear model provides an adequate and reliable "description" of the judge would also support the contention that the clinician's judgments are systematic and nonlinear in nature. The implications of the latter type of demonstration will now be considered in more detail.

Paramorphic Representation of Clinical Judgment

In the preceding discussion of Brunswik's lens model, we indicated the manner in which clinical judgments could be "described" by multiple regression of cues on the judgments produced by the clinician. Although we have thus far used the word "described" uncritically, we now call attention to the fact that a basic philosophical issue is involved in the use of the word "description" in connection with this methodology. The issue is set in the context of discovery and involves the extent to which a mathematical simulation of clinical judgment can be considered a description of the manner in which clinicians "really" make clinical judgments (Green, 1968).

In an early important paper on clinical judgment, Hoffman (1960) characterized the multiple-regression approach to the analysis of clinical judgment as a "paramorphic representation." Recognizing that investigations of the nature of clinical judgment take place within the context of discovery, Hoffman emphasized that they are in some sense investigations of the "mental processes" of the clinician. As Hoffman and many others before him have observed, the equating of mental processes with "private experience" places such processes outside the usual realm of scientific investigation. Similarly, the equating of mental processes with a physical (neurological, biochemical) event is scientifically more palatable but of little practical value in the current absence of suitable physical measurement techniques. A third approach to the investigation of mental processes involves an attempt at *description* by means of mathematical models:

That is to say, in controlled situations wherein the input (information) and the output (judgment) are known or capable of quantification, one may postulate functional relationships between input and output and assess their adequacy by determining the accuracy with which each is capable of predicting judgment. (Hoffman, 1960, p. 117.)

In this usage, "mental process" refers to the functional relationship between consistencies in judgment and different patterns of input information. Mental processes in clinical judgment are considered to be described when a given mathematical model is highly effective in predicting judgment from a given set of cues. Although such mathematical models are considered representational, they are not assumed to bear any resemblance to "real" events occurring either inside or outside the organism.

Hoffman has borrowed the term "paramorph" from mineralogy to illustrate the thesis that a mathematical representation of clinical judgment constitutes only one of several possible levels of explanation. In mineralogy, when conventional chemical analysis shows that two substances have the same chemical structure, but optical and other analyses show that they differ in molecular structure, one substance is said to be a *paramorph* of the other. In this analogy, mathematical representations of human judgment are considered to be on the level of chemical descriptions of minerals. Although such formulations may provide useful descriptions, they are never complete in that other levels of analysis may provide alternative descriptions.

The [mathematical representation] may never be said conclusively to exemplify the cognitive processes it is supposed to represent, but may be assessed in terms of parsimony, predictive accuracy, construct validity, etc., and revised and embellished as broader degrees of generality of the phenomena are included within the theoretical framework. (Hoffman, 1968, p. 53.)

It should be clear that Hoffman does not view the clinician's activity (in the context of discovery) as the workings of a second-rate IBM machine. On the other hand, it should be equally clear that Hoffman believes that the study of clinical judgment (in the context of discovery) must be *empirical*, and that mathematical models are useful tools in the organization of empirical observations.

The Linear Model

On the grounds of parsimony and other considerations of research strategy, Hoffman (1960, 1968) has advocated that the linear or multiple-regression model of cue utilization be employed as a first approximation to the description of clinical judgment. The research question to be investigated is not so much whether or not the clinician actually combines cues in a linear fashion but the more empirical question of how adequate the linear multiple-regression model is as a paramorphic description of the clinical judgment process. More specifically, how much of the variance in the clinician's judgments can be accounted for by the multiple correlation between input cues and clinical predictions?

Relative weights. When a clinician is presented with a set of profiles or input variables, $x_1, x_2, \ldots, x_n$, and asked to predict the criterion status of the individuals who produced each profile, y_j, it is possible to represent the relationship between input data and clinical predictions by means of a linear multiple-regression equation:

$$y'_j = {}_jb_1x_1 + {}_jb_2x_2 + \cdots + {}_jb_nx_n.$$

The degree to which such a linear model provides an adequate description of the clinician's judgmental behavior may be assessed by the multiple correlation between the clinical judgments and cues, $R^2_{y_j \cdot x_1x_2 \cdots x_n}$, when such a multiple-$R$ is properly corrected for the shrinkage to be expected upon cross-validation. When the corrected multiple-$R = 1.00$, we have provided a complete, though not necessarily unique, description of the clinician's cue-utilization behavior.

The regression weights associated with each predictor variable, ${}_jb_1$, ${}_jb_2, \ldots, {}_jb_n$, are of theoretical interest because they indicate, within limitations, the emphasis or importance attached to each of the cues by the clinician. Within limits, large regression weights signify that the cue in question is considered important by the clinician in this prediction situation, and small regression weights signify that the cue is of lesser significance. Unfortunately, regression weights as conventionally defined are not comparable from one judge to the next, do not permit an exact interpretation in terms of relative weighting, and do not account for all the predictable variance involved.

In an attempt to circumvent the interpretive difficulties involved in the use of conventional regression weights, Hoffman (1960) has suggested the use of *relative weights* in the assessment of the contributions of the predictor variables. A relative weight is defined as follows:

$$_jw_i = \frac{{}_jb_i r_{x_iy_j}}{R^2_j},$$

where

$\quad {}_jb_i =$ the regression weight for the ith cue in predicting y_j;

$\quad r_{x_iy_j} =$ the correlation between the ith cue and the clinical judgments;

$\quad R^2_j =$ the squared multiple-R reflecting the best linear combination of the cues in predicting the clinician's judgments.

By the use of weights expressed as proportions of the best linear combination of cues, it is possible to evaluate the relative emphasis placed on a given cue by a given judge, to compare weights given to the same cues by different judges, and to do so with respect to the total variance expressed by the best linear combination of cues. It should be noted that the assessment of the "independent" contribution of cues is meant to apply only to the predictable variance of clinical judgments as expressed by the multiple correlation of a specified set of cues with clinical judgments (Hoffman, 1962). It should also be noted that even this limited interpretation has not been widely accepted (Hammond *et al.*, 1964; Darlington, 1968; Ward, 1962).

As an illustration of the application of the linear model to clinical judgment, Hoffman (1960) presented detailed results for two judges who were asked to predict "intelligence" from profiles of nine cues for 100 subjects. A sample profile is illustrated in Figure 4.5. On each of 100 trials the judge was presented with a profile of the nine cues (x_1 = high school rating; x_2 = status scale, etc.) and asked to predict the intelligence of the individual represented by the profile on the nine-point judgment scale illustrated in Figure 4.5.

For each of two judges, the multiple correlation was obtained between the nine cue values and the intelligence predictions across 100 trials. For

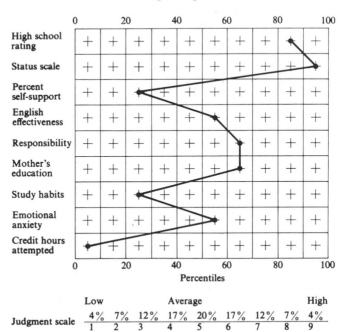

Fig. 4.5 Sample profile for the judgment of intelligence. (After Hoffman, 1960)

Judge A, the squared multiple correlation between judgments of intelligence and the nine cues, R_j^2, was .948 when corrected for the shrinkage expected to occur upon cross-validation. For Judge B, the corresponding multiple-R^2 was .829 when similarly corrected. Test-retest estimates of the reliability of judgments for the two judges were .876 and .836, respectively. When the multiple-R^2 was corrected for attentuation due to unreliability of judgment, the estimated coefficient for Judge A was 1.00 and for Judge B, .907. Thus one can see that, within the limits of reliability of judgment, the linear model of judgment reproduces the behavior of Judge A with almost complete certainty. On the other hand, within the limits of reliability of judgment, the linear model is able to account for approximately 82 percent of the variance in the judgments of Judge B. Clearly then, one may be confident that the linear model provides an excellent paramorphic representation of Judge A while providing a somewhat less adequate paramorphic representation of the judgmental behavior of Judge B.

Subjective weights. Although the linear multiple-regression model provides an adequate paramorphic representation of the clinician's judging *behavior*, it is also of interest to inquire as to the correspondence between the paramorphic model and the clinician's intuitive perceptions of his own judgmental processes. The clinician's own perceptions of the manner in which he combines cues in arriving at his predictions are referred to by Hoffman as *subjective weights.* If it were possible to obtain a measure of the clinician's subjective weights that could be evaluated on the same scale as his relative weights, it would be posssible to evaluate directly the correspondence between the paramorphic representation of the clinician's judgments and his intuitive perceptions of them.

To obtain measures of subjective weights, Hoffman utilized the remarkably straightforward procedure of providing each judge with 100 points and asking him to distribute them among the cues in the manner that best reflected their relative importance in his predictions. In the case of the intelligence judgments, Hoffman asked each judge to distribute the 100 points among the cues of high school rating, x_1, status scale, x_2, percent self-support, x_3, etc. According to Hoffman (1960, p. 126), his judges were satisfied with this method of representing their cue-utilization behavior and appeared quite unconcerned about the violence such a procedure does to the notion of configural combination of cues. Consequently, Hoffman was able to compare subjective weights, in which the clinicians expressed confidence as being representative of the manner in which they combined the cues, with relative weights, which provide a paramorphic representation of the manner in which they actually utilized the cues. Figures 4.6 and 4.7 present the comparison of relative and subjective weights for Judge A and Judge B, respectively.

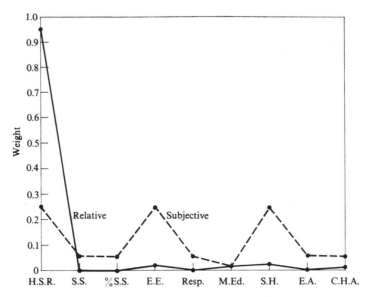

Fig. 4.6 Comparison of relative and subjective weights for Judge *A*.   (After Hoffman, 1960)

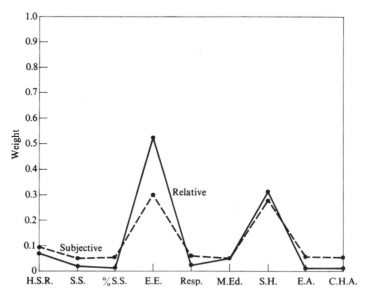

Fig. 4.7 Comparison of relative and subjective weights for Judge *B*.   (After Hoffman, 1960)

Figure 4.6 indicates a marked discrepancy between Judge A's verbal report of the manner in which he utilized the cues and the manner in which the paramorphic model represents his use of the cues. This apparent inability of judges to verbalize the manner in which they combine input cues has also been reported in other contexts (Todd, 1954; Rommetveit, 1960). Although the full implications of these findings will not be discussed here, it should be mentioned parenthetically that such findings call into question those strategies of judgment research which attempt to build mathematical models that "simulate" the *verbal report* of the judge (e.g., Clarkson, 1962). Although such simulation models may accurately describe the verbal reports of judges, they may be less accurate in describing the manner in which the judges make decisions.

Examination of the relative and subjective weights for Judge B (Figure 4.7) reveals that this judge was quite accurate in verbalizing the manner in which he utilized cues, as described by the paramorphic model. With the exception of the fourth cue (English effectiveness), there is very little discrepancy between the relative and subjective weights for Judge B. The relationship between relative and subjective weights for a given judge can be assessed directly by the correlation coefficient between those weights across the cues, r_{rs}. Such a variable may well be an individual-difference variable that should be investigated in terms of its relationship to other components of the judgmental process. In the present example, the linearly more predictable judge was the one who was less able to verbalize his own judgmental behavior. Whether or not such a tendency would persist in an adequate-sized sample of judges is an empirical question worthy of further investigation.

Configural Model

To the extent that the linear-regression model is incapable of providing an adequate paramorphic representation of clinical judgment, serious consideration must be given to the alternative of utilizing more complex mathematical models to represent nonlinear or configural tendencies on the part of clinicians. As previously mentioned (Chapter 2), there is little limit on the complexity of mathematical forms that may be employed, and the availability of high-speed computers has dramatically reduced the computational labors involved in implementing such models. The problem still remains, however, of selecting that mathematical function which might be considered an appropriate representation of the manner in which clinicians combine cues. Hoffman (1960) provides an interesting example of one such approach from a study of clinical judgment performed by Martin.

Martin (1957) presented five counseling psychologists with the task of predicting "sociability" from eight scales of the Edwards Personal Preference Schedule (Edwards, 1954). Each judge was first asked to provide a detailed verbalization of the manner in which he would utilize the eight EPPS scales in the assigned task. Most of the judges claimed that sociability could be predicted from the EPPS scales only by means of a "patterned" or configural approach.

Clinician D, for example, provided a highly detailed report of the manner in which he would utilize the eight EPPS scales (Hoffman, 1960, p. 128). From the verbal statements of Clinician D it was apparent that he combined certain EPPS scales in an interactive or multiplicative manner whereas he combined others in a nonlinear manner best described by an exponential function (these scales being important only when their values are very high). On the basis of Clinician D's verbal statements, EPPS scales were transformed to interactive (for example, $x_1 x_2$) and configural (for example, x_3^2) variables, and optimal regression weights were determined according to least-squares procedures. As was the case with the linear model, relative and subjective weights were assessed in terms of a common metric.

Figure 4.8 shows that a sizeable discrepancy exists between the paramorphic representation of the manner in which Clinician D actually utilized input information and the manner in which he subjectively perceived that he did. In particular, note that Clinician D overestimated his reliance on the first and third predictor variables, which were interactive terms. In a sense, the clinician stated that he was more complex than he actually was.

Application of the configural model for describing Clinician D's judgments showed that the multiple-R, corrected for shrinkage, was .88. Although

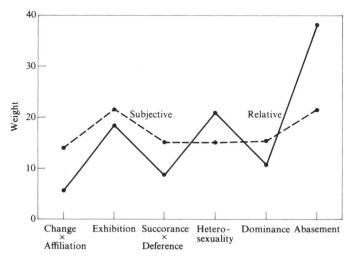

Fig. 4.8 Comparison of relative and subjective weights for Clinician D from Martin's (1957) study. (After Hoffman, 1960)

this appears to be a relatively adequate paramorphic representation of Clinician D's judgmental behavior, application of the *linear model* to the same data resulted in a corrected multiple-R of .91. Thus the application of a configural model to a self-professed configural clinician resulted in a loss of descriptive validity of approximately 5 percent.

In summary, when Clinician D was questioned about the manner in which he combined these cues, his self-description was that of a configural data processor. However, comparison of Clinician D's relative and subjective weights (Figure 4.8) suggests that he may be less configural than he thinks he is. Further, in an attempt to give a paramorphic representation of the judging behavior of Clinician D, it was found that the simple linear model provided a more accurate representation of his cue utilization than did the more complex configural model. The example provided by Clinician D is somewhat representative of results that have been found in other research contexts. However, the general issue of linear versus configural paramorphic representation of clinical judgment is sufficiently complex to require more detailed consideration.

Linear versus Configural Models of Clinical Judgment

The Empirical Evidence

The clinical prediction of psychosis versus neurosis from the MMPI. The differential diagnosis of psychosis from neurosis by means of MMPI profiles is an important and representative clinical prediction task. It is also generally viewed by clinicians as highly configural in nature (Meehl, 1959, p. 104). This task has been the subject of numerous investigations of clinical prediction, primarily because of the availability of an extensive body of data, which includes clinical judgments, MMPI profiles, and criterion diagnoses (Meehl, 1959; Meehl and Dahlstrom, 1960). In one such analysis of these data, Wiggins and Hoffman (1968) directed their attention to the issue of linear versus configural representations of these clinical judgments.

Judges. The judges were 29 clinicians from the Minneapolis area who had varying degrees of experience in MMPI interpretation. The group included 13 Ph.D. clinical psychologists recruited from the faculty of the University of Minnesota and from local hospitals and clinics and 16 predoctoral clinical trainees at the University of Minnesota.

Patients. The patients were 861 male psychiatric patients, each of whom had received a primary psychiatric diagnosis of either psychosis or neurosis. They came from a variety of clinical sources, located primarily in the Midwest and the San Francisco Bay Area. The seven different samples were from state, federal, and private hospitals and outpatient clinics. As a combined group, this sample is the largest ever employed in a study of clinical prediction.

Criteria. The official hospital or clinic psychiatric diagnosis served as a basis for criterion definition. The procedures for arriving at this final psychiatric diagnosis varied from sample to sample. The degree of "criterion contamination," i.e., the extent to which MMPI protocols influenced psychiatric diagnosis, also varied considerably from institution to institution. Descriptions of the institutions involved and the likely degree of criterion contamination that existed may be found in Meehl and Dahlstrom (1960) and Goldberg (1965a).

Input data. The cues consisted of sets of profiles of 11 MMPI scales (*Mf* and *Si* excluded), which were presented without identifying information. The clinical judges received the profiles in seven sets, corresponding to the seven institutions represented in the total sample. They were told only that the patients were males under psychiatric care, each of whom had been diagnosed as neurotic or psychotic. For each sample group, the judges were required to sort the profiles on an 11-point forced normal distribution ranging from "neurotic" through "neutral" to "psychotic."

Analysis. For each of the 29 judges, Wiggins and Hoffman compared the adequacy of three paramorphic models as representations of the 861 judgments made by each clinician in response to the MMPI profiles. The first model employed was the standard linear multiple-regression model. The other two were configural in nature and were designated as "quadratic" and "sign."

The standard linear-regression model needs little description. In the two-variable case, the regression equation is expressed as follows:

$$y'_j = {_j}b_1x_1 + {_j}b_2x_2.$$

Since Wiggins and Hoffman used 11 MMPI input variables, there were 11 such independent terms in their linear model.

The quadratic model included linear terms, second-degree nonlinear terms, and interactive terms. In the two-variable case, the quadratic model is as follows:

$$y'_j = {_j}b_1x_1 + {_j}b_2x_2 + {_j}b_3x_1^2 + {_j}b_4x_2^2 + {_j}b_5x_1x_2.$$

The linear terms, x_1, reflect the clinician's tendency to use the MMPI input variables in an independent and additive fashion. The nonlinear terms, x_1^2, reflect his tendency to weight variables more highly when their values are extreme. The configural terms, x_1x_2, reflect his tendency to use variables in an interactive or moderating fashion. Since Wiggins and Hoffman used 11 MMPI scales, there were 77 terms in their quadratic model.

The sign model consisted of a linear combination of 70 clinical signs which clinicians had reported, either privately or in the literature, as being relevant to the discrimination of psychosis from neurosis on the MMPI (Goldberg, 1965a). The signs varied in complexity from simple linear combinations of single MMPI scale scores (e.g., $Pt - Sc$) to highly complex configural formulas, such as the Meehl-Dahlstrom (1960) sequential rules. Although both the quadratic and sign models are configural in nature, there is an important difference between the two. Whereas the quadratic model provides a description of the manner in which the clinician *might* utilize input cues, the sign model includes a variety of configural expressions which many clinicians *say* that they use. The terms in the sign model include both theoretical combinations of scales and combinations which have been empirically derived to discriminate psychosis from neurosis on the MMPI.

Wiggins and Hoffman assessed the adequacy of each of the three paramorphic models in describing the judgmental behavior of each of the 29 judges by means of the cross-validation design illustrated in Figure 4.9.

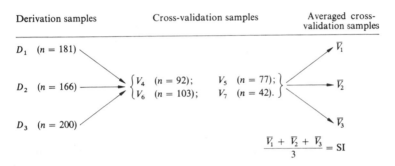

Fig. 4.9 Cross-validation design showing derivation of overall simulation index (SI) for a given judge. (After Wiggins and Hoffman, 1968)

Three samples of MMPI profiles were employed in the *derivation* of regression weights for each model. Figure 4.9 shows that derivation sample 1, D_1, contained 181 profiles, D_2 contained 166, and D_3 contained 200 profiles. The regression weights obtained from each derivation sample were then cross-validated on the remaining four validation samples, V_4, V_5, V_6, and V_7. The multiple-regression weights from the derivation samples were applied to the four cross-validation samples, and a multiple-R was computed for each. The *average* cross-validated multiple-R for the four samples was then determined: $\overline{V}_i = (V_4 + V_5 + V_6 + V_7)/4$. Thus the regression weights from each of the three derivation samples were cross-validated on four samples, and their average cross-validity was determined. The result was three estimates of the average cross-validity of a given model, $\overline{V}_1$, $\overline{V}_2$, and $\overline{V}_3$. The mean of these three averaged cross-validities was designated as an "overall simulation index," or SI. It is important to bear in mind that this complex cross-validational design was employed for each of the three models and applied to *each* of the 29 clinical judges.

Results. In examining the fate of each of the paramorphic models under the rigorous cross-validational procedures employed, the authors found that the multiple correlations between cues and judgments for all three models held up extremely well (Wiggins and Hoffman, 1968, pp. 73–74). This result indicates that the models were reasonably descriptive of the judgmental processes involved, and that the behavior of the judges was reasonably consistent from sample to sample.

Of greatest relevance to the present issue is a comparison of the overall simulation indices for each model for each judge. As indicated in Figure 4.9, the overall simulation index (SI) is an index of the adequacy of a given model as a paramorphic representation of a given judge, as estimated from a rigorous cross-validation design. The cross-validated simulation index (SI) for each of the three models for each of the 29 judges is presented in Table 4.6. The final column of the table presents the authors' judgment as to which of the three models provided the "best fit" of the clinician's judgmental behavior. The "best" model for a given judge was taken to be that with the highest average cross-validated multiple-R. By this criterion, the sign model predicted 13 of the clinical judges best, the linear model 12, the quadratic model three, and the sign and the linear model predicted one judge equally well.

Recall that the sign model included a variety of terms, ranging from simple linear to highly complex configural expressions. To establish that judges classified as using the sign model were, in fact, utilizing configural terms in their predictions, the authors examined the individual regression weights for each judge. They found that for the 16 judges classified as "configural" (sign or quadratic model), the best-fitting regression equation contained at least one heavily weighted configural term. Moreover, for these "configural" judges, either highly configural or nonlinear signs appeared with the largest regression weights in the equations. Thus the characterization of 16 of the 29 judges as "configural" was an accurate description of the manner in which they utilized input cues.

Although Wiggins and Hoffman interpret their findings as evidence for the descriptive validity of configural models in providing a paramorphic representation of clinical judgment, they add a note of caution to this generalization: "Though the differences [between linear and configural judges] appear reliable, their magnitude is not large; the judgments of even the most seemingly configural clinicians can often be estimated with good precision by a linear model" (1968, pp. 76–77). This point is given heavier emphasis by Goldberg (1968b):

. . . the most overwhelming finding from this study was how much of the variance in clinicians' judgments could be represented by the linear model. For example, if one compares the judgment correlations produced by the linear model with those from each of the two configural models [Table 4.6], one finds that (a) the linear model was equal to, or superior to, the quadratic model for 23 of the 29 judges (and at best, for the most configural judge, the quadratic model produced a correlation with his judgments which was only .03 greater than that of the

Table 4.6 Overall simulation index (SI) for linear, quadratic, and sign models. (After Wiggins and Hoffman, 1968)

Judge	Linear SI_L	Quadratic SI_Q	Sign SI_s	Best-fit model
1	.602	.604	.638	Sign
2	.829	.788	.848	Sign
3	.712	.664	.684	Linear
4	.674	.684	.651	Quadratic
5	.763	.749	.763	Sign-Linear
6	.778	.776	.741	Linear
7	.745	.760	.709	Quadratic
8	.815	.808	.833	Sign
9	.837	.830	.858	Sign
10	.698	.706	.731	Sign
11	.863	.843	.872	Sign
12	.744	.698	.720	Linear
13	.730	.688	.563	Linear
14	.543	.561	.533	Quadratic
15	.819	.800	.830	Sign
16	.845	.830	.860	Sign
17	.697	.655	.649	Linear
18	.821	.839	.847	Sign
19	.799	.775	.778	Linear
20	.784	.774	.782	Linear
21	.866	.830	.854	Linear
22	.805	.797	.819	Sign
23	.742	.672	.656	Linear
24	.656	.602	.672	Sign
25	.871	.875	.891	Sign
26	.794	.763	.784	Linear
27	.715	.658	.597	Linear
28	.755	.781	.787	Sign
29	.752	.734	.738	Linear

linear model); *and* (*b*) *the linear model was equal to, or superior to, the sign model for 17 judges* (*the superiority of the sign model being but .04 for the single most configural judge*). (pp. 490–491.)

The interpretation one places on the Wiggins and Hoffman results is of critical importance to the issue of linear versus configural representation of clinical judgment. The study was based on an extensive sample of realistic clinical judgments made by experienced clinicians with respect to a socially important (though admittedly unreliable) criterion. Both the highly sophisticated cross-validational design and the equally sophisticated correlational analyses are difficult to fault. Hence the results of the study are probably the most representative available with respect to how clinicians actually behave in diagnostic practice. Depending on one's theoretical predilections, the results may be interpreted as establishing the configurality of clinical judgment (Wiggins and Hoffman, 1968), or as demonstrating the descriptive potential of the linear model in providing a paramorphic representation of clinical judgment (Goldberg, 1968b).

Other studies. There now exists a considerable body of literature that relates to the adequacy of the linear multiple-regression model in providing a paramorphic representation of the cue-utilization behavior of human judges. Considered in its entirety, this literature provides almost overwhelming support for the adequacy and generality of the linear model as a representation of human judgment (Goldberg, 1968b; Hammond and Summers, 1965; Hoffman, 1968). That linear models serve as quite adequate paramorphic representations has been documented in such diverse realms as those of *clinical inference* (Grebstein, 1963; Hammond, 1955; Hammond, Hursch, and Todd, 1964; Hoffman, 1960, 1968; Hursch, Hammond, and Hursch, 1964; Naylor and Wherry, 1965; Todd, 1954), *quasi-clinical tasks* (Lee and Tucker, 1962; Newton, 1965), *multiple-cue probability studies* (Peterson, Hammond, and Summers, 1965; Rappoport, 1963; Smedslund, 1955; Summers, 1962; Todd and Hammond, 1965; Uhl, 1963), and *impression formation* (Anderson, 1962). In the face of such diverse and well-documented evidence, one might be tempted to conclude that clinicians utilize cues in a linear fashion (despite what clinicians *say* they do) and to move on to more interesting topics. However, within the context of discovery, we may still wish to make a distinction between what clinicians really do and how well what they do can be approximated by a linear model. This distinction may be forced on us by certain mathematical and statistical properties of the linear regression model itself.

The Statistical Problem

There are several statistical limitations that must be borne in mind when attempting to describe clinical judgment by regression procedures involving

nonlinear or configural expressions.   The first limitation is one with which
we are already familiar from our consideration of Ward's (1954) study in
Chapter 2.   Namely, the greater the complexity of the prediction equation,
the greater is the shrinkage in accuracy of prediction when that equation is
applied to an independent sample of observations.   In addition, there are
very practical limitations involved in the investigation of complex mathematical functions involving many terms.   As the number of terms in the
prediction equation increases, the number of cases necessary for cross-
validation and estimates of statistical significance increases geometrically.
An adequate statistical assessment of a reasonably complex regression equation requires that literally tens of thousands of cases be available (Hoffman,
1968).   Finally, configural relations, by definition, involve a high degree of
interdependence of terms, and that fact in turn increases the possibility of a
given function capitalizing on chance.   In Hoffman's words:

*Under such circumstances, the rare but significant configural parameter lies
imbedded in a sea of chance relationships, from which it cannot reliably be
distinguished.   Thus, the failure to discover configural models which maintain
their superiority over linear models under adequate cross-validation may be due
to the fallibility of statistical methods rather than due to inherent lack of
configurality in behavior.   (1968, p. 63.)*

Configural models may also come off second-best because of what might
be termed the general "robustness" of the linear multiple-regression model.
In Chapter 1 we demonstrated that the linear regression model is *the* best
representation (in the least-squares sense) of a composite of input variables
which combine in an additive fashion.   What we have not yet directly considered is the power of the linear regression model in representing *nonlinear*
relationships.   The linear model is a very general one and will frequently
provide an excellent "approximation" to the most nonlinear of functions.
Green (1968) provides a graphic example of the extent to which a clearly
quadratic function may be fitted by a straight line.   Yntema and Torgerson
(1961) have demonstrated that a linear model may account for 94 percent of
the variance of a completely configural function.   In light of this consideration
and others, Goldberg (1968b) has concluded that:

*. . . judges can process information in a configural fashion but . . . the general
linear model is powerful enough to reproduce most of these judgments with very
small error.   (p. 491.)*

Positive Indications

Hammond and Summers (1965) have observed that the vast majority of
studies of clinical inference and probability learning have employed cues
which are primarily linearly related to the criterion.   In a sense, the deck has

been stacked in the direction of linearity, and the expectation of configural cue utilization on the part of the clinician may not have been reasonable. In a highly specialized laboratory study involving only two cues, Hammond and Summers were able to demonstrate that subjects could utilize cues in a nonlinear fashion when provided with sufficient information concerning the task.

Similarly, using artificial data, Slovic (1966) was able to demonstrate that subjects weight input cues differentially according to their perceived "consistency." That is, when two cues which the judge believed to be highly correlated were consistent (both high or both low) they were both weighted heavily in the judgment task. However, when the two cues believed to be correlated were inconsistent (one high and one low), judges tended to rely on only one of them. Moreover, when a discrepancy existed between the two cues, judges tended to utilize other cues to a greater extent than when no discrepancy existed between the two most salient cues. Such differential cue utilization is clearly nonlinear in nature.

Dudycha and Naylor (1966b) also reported that highly correlated cues were weighted more uniformly than cues with low correlations. The main purpose of their study was to investigate the effects of departures from the "true" (real data) correlations among cues on the paramorphic representation of judgment. Their conclusions are of special interest:

If one is interested in obtaining information about the judgmental policies of individuals toward a certain class of stimulus objects he needs to be certain that the underlying cue-R matrix for his experimental stimuli is representative of the R matrix describing the population of stimuli of which his sample is assumed to be a subset. Otherwise, his ability to generalize is obviously going to be limited. (Dudycha and Naylor, 1966b, p. 602.)

It is interesting to juxtapose the conclusion of Dudycha and Naylor with the observations of Hammond and Summers:

It is possible to demonstrate pure cases of either process [linear or nonlinear cue utilization], however, only in very peculiar circumstances such as psychological experiments. While laboratory demonstrations of either process in pure form may be of some interest, the very peculiarity of the circumstances necessary to elicit them makes their relevance dubious. (1965, p. 222.)

The point to be made is that instances of configural cue utilization can be demonstrated under the contrived circumstances of laboratory experimentation. However, there is good reason to believe that judgmental behavior toward real data is different from judgmental behavior toward artificial data (Dudycha and Naylor, 1966b). Therefore, the laboratory demonstrations of nonlinear cue utilization are of interest to the general study of cognitive processes, but they may have little relevance as analogues of the clinical prediction process as exemplified in the prediction of psychosis and neurosis from MMPI profiles.

Conclusion

The evidence from realistic studies of clinical judgment is almost overwhelmingly in favor of the linear multiple-regression model as a paramorphic representation of the manner in which clinicians utilize cues. Where evidence of configural cue utilization has been found, its paramorphic representation does not statistically exceed that of the more parsimonious linear multiple-regression equation. The superiority of the linear model may in part be attributed to purely statistical considerations, which favor the more robust linear model over configural models. Although it is possible to demonstrate nonlinear cue utilization in contrived laboratory situations, it is doubtful whether models of judgments of artificial data may be generalized to models of judgments of clinical data. The eloquently stated conclusion of Goldberg (1968b) seems almost inescapable:

Consequently, if one's sole purpose is to reproduce the responses of clinical judges, then a simple linear model will normally permit the reproduction of 90%–100% of their reliable judgmental variance, probably in most—if not all— clinical judgment tasks. While Meehl (1959) has suggested that one potential superiority of the clinician over the actuary lies in the human's ability to process cues in a configural fashion, it is important to realize that this is neither an inherent advantage of the human judge (i.e., the actuary can include non-linear terms in his equations), nor is this attribute—in any case—likely to be the clinician's "ace-in-the-hole." If the clinician does have a long suit—and the numerous clinical versus statistical studies have not yet demonstrated that he has—it is extremely unlikely that it will stem from his alleged ability to process information in a complex configural manner. (p. 491.)

SUMMARY

Judgmental Measurement

When the collection, recording, or scoring of input data for prediction involves human judgment, we speak of judgmental measurement. Past research suggests that the good judge of others uses appropriate norms, has both general and social intelligence, and is motivated and free to make accurate judgments. Much of this research is based on global indices of judgmental accuracy which are heavily influenced by rater biases and mathematical artifacts. More appropriate indices of judgmental accuracy distinguish an ability to differentiate among subjects from a reliance on stereotypes and other response biases.

The ability to judge others is frequently construed as a general trait of the judge that is relatively independent of the persons or qualities judged. However, evidence for the generality of judgmental accuracy is far from conclusive. Similarly, it is frequently asserted that professional decision-makers, such as clinical psychologists, are generally more accurate in their judgments of others than are laymen. This presumed superiority of the clinician is thought to stem from his training, his experience, and his ability to integrate large amounts of input data. Available evidence suggests that claims of superior judging ability for clinicians must be viewed with considerable skepticism.

Clinical Prediction

When human judgment enters into the combination of input data for the forecasting of criterion behaviors, we speak of clinical prediction. The nature of clinical prediction may be considered from both logical and empirical perspectives. Early critics of clinical prediction have argued that all prediction is based on inference from class membership, and thus no qualitative distinction can be made between clinical and statistical methods of data combination. Given the fact that statistical methods of data combination are mathematically optimal, the clinician is, at best, a second-rate IBM machine. More recently, Meehl has argued that by virtue of being able to invent hypotheses concerning the state of hypothetical variables in a given person, the clinician is able to utilize personality theory in such a manner as to generate predictions by a process that is qualitatively distinct from statistical combination. Further, to the extent that the clinician is able to specify the precise structural nature of stimulus-response relationships in a given person, his predictions could, in principle, surpass those made by statistical methods.

Empirical studies of the nature of clinical prediction have been greatly facilitated by the conceptual framework provided by Brunswik's lens model. The accuracy of clinical prediction is depicted as a function of the empirical validity of input data, or "cues," the relationships among the cues, and the relationship between the cues and the clinician's judgments. The relationship between input cues and the clinician's judgments may be expressed as a multiple-regression model that provides a "paramorphic representation" of clinical judgment. Although some evidence suggests that clinicians may combine input cues in a complex nonlinear fashion, the most parsimonious paramorphic representation of clinical judgment is achieved by a linear multiple-regression model. However, because the linear multiple-regression model provides an adequate approximation of even markedly nonlinear relationships, nonlinear or configural cue utilization on the part of clinicians cannot be decisively ruled out.

CHAPTER 5

CLINICAL VERSUS STATISTICAL PREDICTION

COMPARISON OF CLINICAL AND STATISTICAL PREDICTION

From the standpoint of applied personality assessment, the fundamental question underlying our detailed consideration of clinical and statistical prediction methods may be stated simply: "Which is better?" As Meehl (1954, pp. 6–7) has indicated, the question is far from trivial or academic. In the first place, as Meehl notes, the psychologist's orientation on this matter has a considerable impact on his clinical practice, particularly with respect to the distribution of his time. If it were true that statistical prediction is equal or superior to clinical prediction, the clinician might better spend his time in therapeutic and research activities. Second, the clinician's opinion on this matter will influence the manner in which he makes clinical decisions. In those instances in which an actuarially generated prediction conflicts with the intuitions of a clinician, the relative weight that the clinician places on one or the other prediction will depend on his assessment of the relative validity of the two methods. Finally, the clinician's answer to this question will influence both his professional identity (diagnostic testing usually being considered the exclusive province of the clinical psychologist) and the character of the research in which he engages.

Questions as to the relative validity of clinical and statistical prediction methods must be raised in the *context of justification*. Meehl has observed: "Always, we might as well face it, the shadow of the statistician hovers in the background; *always* the actuary will have the final word (1954, p. 138). Although this remark has been widely misinterpreted, Meehl's intention was to underscore the inevitability of *empirical* resolution of the issue. Within the context of justification, the validity of clinical prediction can be established only through empirical investigations of the *accuracy* of clinical predictions. Having considered, in some detail, the nature of both clinical and statistical prediction methods, we must now consider the proof of the respective puddings in the context of justification.

The Empirical Literature

The most widely publicized and influential aspect of Meehl's (1954) monograph was that portion of it devoted to a consideration of the empirical literature involving comparisons of clinical and statistical prediction methods. Although the issue of clinical versus statistical prediction is an old one (see Gough, 1962, for a scholarly historical review), there was a remarkable dearth of studies for Meehl to review in 1954. Almost all the available studies suffered from serious defects of design, thus precluding a rigorous comparison of the relative efficiency of the two methods. Although there has been an extraordinary amount of controversy surrounding the proper conduct of a clinical versus statistical investigation, the basic design of such a study is really quite simple. The *same* input data are given to a clerical worker (or a computer) and a clinician, and each is asked to make specific predictions concerning a socially relevant criterion. This design is illustrated diagrammatically in Figure 5.1.

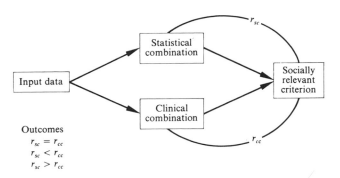

Fig. 5.1 Basic design for comparison of clinical and statistical prediction.

From the design in Figure 5.1, it is possible to obtain the validity correlation between statistical predictions and the criterion, r_{sc}, and that between clinical predictions and the criterion, r_{cc}. When the two validity coefficients are compared, there are three possible outcomes to the study: (a) statistical and clinical data-combination procedures are equally effective in predicting the criterion ($r_{sc} = r_{cc}$); (b) statistical data combination is inferior ($r_{sc} < r_{cc}$) or (c) statistical data combination is superior ($r_{sc} > r_{cc}$).

In reviewing the literature prior to 1954, Meehl was able to unearth 20 studies which might reasonably be considered relevant to the comparison of statistical and clinical data-combination procedures. Most, if not all, of these studies failed to meet the simple design standards illustrated in Figure 5.1. Some provided the clinician with input data not available to the actuary and thus biased the design in favor of clinical prediction. Others were similarly biased in favor of clinical prediction in that *optimal* statistical weights were not always applied to the input data (e.g., the weights sometimes were subjectively determined). Finally, although the prediction domains involved could all be considered socially relevant in the sense that they had relevance for society, many were not *clinically* relevant, in the sense that the clinician was required to make predictions of criterion behaviors that fall outside the realm of his typical concerns (Holt, 1958; McArthur, 1968). Many clinicians feel that asking them to predict grade-point average in college from an aptitude test and high school rank is a statistical parody of typical clinical judgments.[1] With all their shortcomings, the 20 studies reviewed by Meehl constituted the *only* body of evidence that was then available for the evaluation of clinical prediction in the context of justification.

Meehl's famous "box score" tabulation of the outcomes of studies comparing statistical and clinical data-combination methods is summarized in Table 5.1. In 1954, Meehl reviewed some 16 to 20 studies that were relevant to the issue, depending on the stringency of the criterion of relevance allowed. The prediction domains included success in academic or military training, recidivism and parole violation, and recovery from psychosis. Of the 20 studies reviewed, 11 were classified as indicating the relative superiority of statistical over clinical data combination, 8 were classified as "ties," in which clinical prediction did not statistically exceed actuarial prediction, and one study was classified as evidence favoring the superiority of clinical over statistical data combination. Unfortunately, the sole study indicating the superiority of clinical prediction was based on a faulty statistical analysis (McNemar, 1955) and was later reclassified by Meehl (1965) as a tie. Thus, of the 20 early studies reviewed, there was not a single instance of clinical prediction exceeding statistical prediction, and the bulk of the evidence seemed to favor statistical data combination as the superior procedure.

The impact of Meehl's review on clinical psychologists was nothing less than devastating. The professional reaction to this single review was almost unprecedented (e.g., de Groot, 1961; Gough, 1962; Harris, 1963; Holt, 1958; Holzberg, 1957; Humphreys, 1956; Hutt, 1956; Kogan, 1955; Mann, 1956; McArthur, 1956a, 1956b, 1968; Richards, 1963; Sanford, 1956; Sawyer, 1966; Sydiaha, 1959; Tiedeman, 1956; Zubin, 1956).

In addition to creating such a critical and theoretical flurry, Meehl's review was responsible for the fact that several new studies were designed and executed to provide additional empirical evidence for the evaluation of clinical prediction. By 1957, Meehl was able to evaluate some 27 studies,

---

1. Nevertheless, such predictions are made routinely by some college admissions personnel and some college professors.

Table 5.1 Meehl's "Box Scores" of studies comparing clinical with statistical prediction

Source	No. of studies	Prediction domain	"Box score" Stat > clin	Stat = clin	Stat < clin
Meehl (1954)	16–20	Success in academic or military training; recidivism and parole violation; recovery from psychosis.	11	8	1*
Meehl (1957)	27	Success in academic or military training; recidivism and parole violation; recovery from psychosis; personality description; outcome of psychotherapy.	17	10	0
Meehl (1965)	51	Success in academic or military training; recidivism and parole violation; recovery from psychosis; personality description; outcome of psychotherapy; response to shock treatment; formal psychiatric nosology; job success and satisfaction; medical (non-psychiatric) diagnosis.	33	17	1†

* See McNemar, 1955; Meehl, 1965.
† See Goldberg, 1968a.

which now included the prediction domains of personality description and outcome of psychotherapy. The "box score" for the 1957 tally is also presented in Table 5.1, which shows that, of the 27 studies reviewed, 17 indicated the superiority of statistical over clinical data combination, 10 were rated as ties, and no study was interpreted as evidence favoring clinical over statistical prediction.

The decade following the publication of Meehl's original monograph was characterized by an increased amount of research activity directed toward providing a more substantial empirical basis for evaluating clinical prediction within the context of justification. Thus, in 1965, Meehl was able to tally the "box score" of more than 50 empirical investigations. By that time, the predictive domain had been expanded to include studies of continuance in psychotherapy, response to shock treatment, formal psychiatric diagnosis, job success and satisfaction, and medical diagnosis. Meehl's tabulation of this literature is also presented in Table 5.1. Of the 51 studies considered, 33 were judged to demonstrate the superiority of statistical over clinical data combination, 17 were judged to be ties and one study (Lindzey, 1965) was judged to be the first example of clinical prediction exceeding statistical prediction. Again, however, the sole study favoring the clinical method turned out to be a rather bad example, which should be considered at best a tie (Goldberg, 1968a).

Considering the range of predictive domains involved in Meehl's (1965) most recent tally, it can no longer be asserted that the data favoring statistical prediction come from narrowly defined realms of little clinical relevance. Further, the fact that clinical prediction *equaled* statistical prediction in approximately one-third of the studies reviewed provides little solace for the practicing clinician. Obviously, from the practical standpoints of cost, efficiency, and utilization of clinical time, the statistical method of data combination would be preferable to clinical prediction in any cases where the two have been shown to be approximately equal in validity.

A Representative Study

It is instructive to consider in some detail the extensive study of Goldberg (1965a) as representative of the typical findings in clinical versus prediction studies. From the standpoint of rigor of design, clinical realism, extensiveness, and clarity of outcome, Goldberg's study is not so much "representative" as "exemplary."

Goldberg utilized the data collected by Meehl (Meehl, 1959; Meehl and Dahlstrom, 1960) in his study of the prediction of psychosis versus neurosis from MMPI profiles. Since these data were described in some detail in Chapter 4, they will be only briefly reviewed here. MMPI profiles were collected from 861 male psychiatric patients, who came from seven different clinical settings and who had received a primary psychiatric diagnosis of either "psychosis" or "neurosis." The clinical judges were 13 Ph.D. staff members and 16 predoctoral clinical trainees, who were required to sort each profile on an 11-point forced normal distribution ranging from "neurotic" through "neutral" to "psychotic." The accuracy of each clinical prediction was validated against the official psychiatric diagnosis of hospital or clinic for each patient. A more complete description of these data may be found in Goldberg (1965a).

Diagnostic Signs

In evaluating *statistical* prediction, Goldberg assessed the predictive validity of 65 "diagnostic signs" that represented a variety of combinations of 11

MMPI scale scores. Goldberg operationally defined a sign as "any index which can be programmed for a computer." Of course, such signs can also be scored with relative ease by a clerical worker. The signs included single scale scores, simple linear combinations of single scale scores, configural combinations of a few scales, and complex, often highly configural "rules," some of which were applied in a sequential strategy in arriving at a decision.

The diagnostic signs came from three general sources: (a) the published literature of both clinically and empirically derived rules, (b) suggestions of MMPI experts based on both clinical and empirical experience, and (c) signs which were specially derived for this study. Two of these signs are of particular interest: the elaborately derived sequential strategy for differentiating psychotic from neurotic MMPI profiles developed by Meehl and Dahlstrom (1960) and the empirically derived linear combination of MMPI scales developed by Goldberg (1965a). Both signs were developed on a *separate* sample of 402 cases (Meehl and Dahlstrom, 1960), which will be referred to as the *derivation sample*.

The complex, sequential rules developed by Meehl and Dahlstrom are the product of an intricate interweaving of both clinical and empirical procedures:

The skilled clinical eye was employed as a searcher and idea originator: statistical runs were employed both as searchers and as checks upon the deliverances of the clinical eye. (Meehl and Dahlstrom, 1960, p. 377.)

The end product of the Meehl-Dahlstrom collaboration was a complex, sequential decision-making strategy, with many branches along the way, resulting in the ultimate classification of a given profile as psychotic, neurotic, or indeterminate. Since the authors recommended that predictions not be made for profiles falling in the indeterminate category, Goldberg presented his findings both for the smaller determinate sample and for the total sample of profiles.

Using the same derivation sample of 402 cases employed by Meehl and Dahlstrom, Goldberg developed a number of diagnostic signs by purely empirical procedures. Single MMPI scales and combinations of MMPI scales which showed the greatest promise in the forecasting of psychosis and neurosis in the derivation sample were employed in a series of linear regression analyses (Goldberg, 1965a, pp. 17–19). Five MMPI scales, which both singly and in combination tended to have the highest regression weights in the multiple-regression prediction of the criterion, were combined into a simple nonweighted linear composite: $(L + Pa + Sc) - (Hy + Pt)$.

All the diagnostic signs employed in Goldberg's study were first validated on the derivation sample of 402 cases, and 43 signs achieved significant validity coefficients in the differentiation of psychosis from neurosis in that sample.

Cutting scores for each sign were determined from the derivation sample and subsequently applied to the larger cross-validation sample.

Comparison of Diagnostic Signs with Diagnosticians

Diagnosticians. The 13 Ph.D. staff members and 16 predoctoral trainees were presented with 861 MMPI profiles and asked to record their judgment of the presence of psychosis or neurosis on an 11-point scale. The 11-point scale could be utilized either as a complex psychological dimension (psychoticism-neuroticism) or as a scale indicating the degree of probability of a given profile's belonging to a given category. This recording procedure permitted the characterization of each prediction in dichotomous terms (psychotic or neurotic) as well as the establishment of a "doubtful" or indeterminate category for comparison with those statistical methods which included such a category.

For each clinical judge, a validity coefficient was computed between the 11-point continuous scale of psychoticism-neuroticism and the dichotomous criterion of "psychotic" and "neurotic" across the 861 profiles. In addition, the number of "hits" for each judge was expressed as the percentage of correct identifications achieved in the entire sample. Finally, the percentage of correct identifications was calculated for determinate cases when an indeterminate category was allowed. That is, allowing 31 percent of the clinical predictions to be classified as indeterminate, the percentage of correct identifications of the remaining 591 cases was calculated. The latter procedure provided a degree of clinical realism in that clinicians are seldom able to predict for all cases with equal confidence. When an indeterminate category is permitted, the percentage of correct identifications should presumably increase for the cases for which predictions are made.

Diagnostic signs. Validity correlations were computed between each of the 65 diagnostic signs (scored by a computer) and the psychiatric criterion of "psychotic" and "neurotic." In addition, the percentage of correct identifications in all 861 cases was calculated on the basis of cutting scores determined in the derivation sample of 402 cases. Finally, the percentage of correct identifications was computed under conditions in which an indeterminate category was permitted. The overall percentage of indeterminate cases allowed (31 percent) was determined by the proportion of cases so classified by the Meehl-Dahlstrom rules. To some extent, then, the Meehl-Dahlstrom rules had a slight advantage in that they were allowed to determine the proportion of cases excluded for all other signs.

Results. The major results of the Goldberg study are presented in Table 5.2. The first 9 rows present the overall achievement of the clinical judges in forecasting the psychiatric criterion. The remaining 14 rows present

Table 5.2 Validity coefficients and accuracy percentages for diagnosticians and diagnostic signs. (After Goldberg, 1965a)

Predictors	Validity coefficients (N = 861)	Accuracy percentage for all cases (N = 861)	Accuracy percentage with indeterminate category (N = 591)
Diagnosticians			
13 Staff			
Range	.17–.35	59–65	62–71
Average	.28	62	66
16 Trainees			
Range	.14–.39	55–67	60–73
Average	.28	61	66
29 Total judges			
Range	.14–.39	55–67	60–73
Average	.28	62	66
Diagnostic signs			
$(L + Pa + Sc) - (Hy + Pt)$	.44	70	74
Meehl-Dahlstrom rules	.39	66	74
Two-point rules	.38	67	71
$Sc - (Hs + D + Hy)$	.36	67	71
Number of Taulbee-Sisson signs	.34	64	69
$(Pt - Sc)$	.33	65	67
High-point rules	.32	66	69
$(Hy - Pa)$	.31	61	67
Number of Peterson signs	.31	60	68
$\bar{N} - \bar{P}$	.31	63	67
$Pa - (Hs + D + Hy)$	.30	62	66
$\bar{N}/\bar{P}$	.30	63	68
$(Hs - Sc)$	.30	61	67
$(Pd + Pa) - (Hs + Hy)$	.30	63	68

comparable figures for the achievement of various diagnostic signs in statistically predicting the psychiatric criterion.

Examination of the achievement of the clinical judges makes it clear that there were virtually no differences between the predictive abilities of the Ph.D. staff members and those of the predoctoral trainees. The average Ph.D. staff member achieved a validity coefficient of .28, correctly classified 62 percent of all cases, and was able to identify correctly 66 percent of predicted cases when an indeterminate category was permitted. The comparable figures for the average trainee are virtually identical. Examining the *range* of accuracy scores, we find a slight tendency for somewhat greater variability among trainees (scores are both higher and lower than those of staff members), although the variability may be attributable to the fact that there were a few more trainees than staff members. As indicated in Chapter 4, it is not unusual to find a lack of relationship between experience and clinical judgment.

Of greatest relevance to the issue at hand is the relative accuracy of clinical (diagnosticians) versus statistical (diagnostic signs) prediction. As is apparent from Table 5.2, there are at least fourteen actuarial rules which exceed the validity of clinical prediction in the present data. The first two diagnostic signs, the Goldberg linear composite and the Meehl-Dahlstrom rules, exceed the performance of the *best* clinician in the combined staff and trainee groups. The remaining twelve diagnostic signs clearly exceed the validity of the average clinical judge. When the results of this study are entered into the "box score" tabulation they should clearly be tallied as an instance of the superiority of actuarial over clinical prediction.

The relative validities of the various MMPI diagnostic signs represent a rather specialized problem which need not be considered here in great detail. However, the performance of Goldberg's empirical index, $(L + Pa + Sc) - (Hy + Pt)$, and the configural Meehl-Dahlstrom rules are of special interest. Note that the simple, unweighted *linear* composite of five MMPI scales outperforms every clinician in the study, as well as the highly configural Meehl-Dahlstrom rules. The implications of this fact for the issue of clinical versus statistical prediction should be readily apparent. The implications for the issue of linear versus configural combination of data in *statistical* prediction are more complex, and they are discussed in detail by Goldberg (1965a, 1969).

Methodological Considerations

The practical superiority of statistical over clinical methods of data combination seems well established by the empirical literature reviewed by Meehl. Nevertheless, for many years following the publication of Meehl's monograph, clinicians felt dissatisfied with both the argument and the evidence. Holt (1958) remarked:

Clinical students in particular complain of a vague feeling that a fast one has been put over on them, that under a great show of objectivity, or at least bipartisanship, Professor Meehl has actually sold the clinical approach up the river. (p. 1.)

Holt felt that Meehl had done the clinician a disservice by polarizing the clinical and statistical prediction issue with respect to the manner in which data are combined. According to Holt (1958), Meehl failed to take into account the fact that clinical judgment may enter into all phases of the total prediction paradigm. Consequently, Holt suggested an extended typology that included prediction situations more favorable to the clinician.

Pure actuarial prediction refers to the situation in which mechanical data are used to predict a clear-cut criterion by means of statistical combination in the absence of clinical judgment.

Naive clinical prediction refers to the situation in which judgmental measurements (of unknown validity) are used intuitively to predict a criterion of unknown characteristics. In this type of prediction, clinical intuition is relied on at all stages in the prediction paradigm.

Sophisticated clinical prediction refers to the situation in which the clinician receives both judgmental and mechanical data, whose relations to the criterion are known, and is asked to predict a well-understood criterion. This type of prediction involves a job analysis, pilot studies, item analysis, and cross-validational procedures.

It is Holt's contention that the studies reviewed by Meehl (1954) tended to pit pure actuarial against naive clinical prediction. Such studies tend to put the clinician at a disadvantage. Some of Meehl's studies, according to Holt, were actually comparing naive clinical with sophisticated clinical prediction and could not be considered as pure examples of "clinical versus statistical" comparisons.

Holt's proposed reclassification of clinical and statistical prediction studies blurs the important distinction between measurement and prediction that is necessary for the scientific evaluation of clinical prediction in the context of justification. Nevertheless, Holt's very general reaction to Meehl's analysis contains within it several specific points which are worthy of separate consideration. These points have been raised by others, in various forms, but they may be conveniently categorized as involving the issues of: (a) task appropriateness, (b) handicapping the clinician, (c) cross-validation, and (d) judgmental measurement.

Appropriateness of Prediction Task

Both McArthur (1956a, 1956b) and Holt (1958) were quick to point out that many of the early "clinical versus statistical" studies reviewed by Meehl involved prediction tasks that were both inappropriate and untypical of what the clinician does in practice.

Thus, the statistician takes advantage of the foolish boast of the clinician, "Anything you can do, I can do better," and plans the contest on his own grounds. The clinician ends up trying to predict grade-point average in the freshman year by a "clinical synthesis" of high grades and an intelligence test. This is a manifest absurdity: under the circumstances, how could the clinician do other than operate like a second-rate Hollerith machine? (Holt, 1958, pp. 5–6.)

Although this criticism applies to some of the earlier studies reviewed by Meehl (1954), it does not apply to many of the later studies, such as that of Goldberg (1965a). The burden of proof here seems to be on the clinician to provide definitions of "appropriate" prediction tasks that can be studied experimentally. Recent increases in the number of such relevant situations studied have done nothing to offset the final "box score" reported by Meehl (1965). Nevertheless, the continued classification of purportedly irrelevant studies under the "clinical versus statistical" rubric has led McArthur (1968) to comment on a recent study:

To predict grades is scarcely a brain-worthy assignment, nor is it part of the guidance man's job. What duffer in the trade doesn't answer that question by turning to his handy-dandy experience table? Why study experimentally a task nobody performs? (p. 172.)

The suggestion of both McArthur and Holt is that the clinician be allowed to predict the criterion of his own choice, using his own methods. The implication here is that there are many clinical criteria that do not lend themselves to actuarial prediction. Although this may be *practically* true for certain specialized situations (e.g., the practice of psychotherapy), it is not logically necessary, as can be seen from the ease with which actuarial systems can predict "free criteria" (Chapter 4).

Handicapping the Clinician

Implicit in Holt's (1958) objections and those of many other writers is the feeling that the artificial nature of any experiment in clinical versus statistical prediction unduly handicaps the clinician by depriving him of information that is typically available in a realistic clinical setting. These objections sometimes stress the *kind* and sometimes the *amount* of information with which the clinician is provided. Both forms of the objections relate to the issue of judgmental *measurement* rather than that of clinical prediction (Sawyer, 1966).

In typical clinical practice, the clinician frequently gains information from impressions formed during *face-to-face* contacts with the patient. Since the actuary (or computer) does not have access to such information, impressions formed from direct testing and interviewing of the patient are typically excluded from clinical versus statistical prediction experiments. Note that there is nothing in the design of such studies that excludes coded or rated interview impressions (gathered by another clinician) as a source of input data for clinical or statistical combination. However, it is precisely those "uncodable" impressions gained from direct patient contact that the clinician feels give him a predictive edge over the actuary.

Although we must leave open the possibility that "uncodable" impressions combined in an "unverbalizable" fashion may lead to prediction that exceeds actuarial prediction, such a possibility cannot be evaluated directly by the rigorous standards of the context of justification. It is possible to investigate the assertion that the accuracy of clinical prediction increases with the *amount* of information available to the clinician, and to some extent, this has been done (Chapter 4). To compare clinical and statistical prediction in the context of justification, however, requires that input variables be restricted to those that can be coded and verbalized. What is required is more ingenuity in the design of clinical versus statistical studies to provide the clinician with information that is typical of that available in clinical practice.

Cross-validation

Holt (1958) and others have argued that the clinician faces an unfair advantage when his *initial* predictions are compared with those of a *cross-validated* regression equation. Although there is some merit to this argument, one must bear in mind that cross-validation is a two-edged sword in studies comparing clinical and statistical prediction. Meehl (1954) has insisted from the beginning that clinical prediction be subjected to the same cross-validational procedures as actuarial prediction. This suggestion has seldom been followed in practice.

Both Holt (1958) and Lindzey (1965) have presented data which they interpret as demonstrating the superiority of clinical prediction over cross-validated actuarial indices. However, as Hammond, Hursch, and Todd (1964) observed, small sample studies in which the regression equation is cross-validated but the clinician is not place the regression equation at a distinct disadvantage. Regression weights which are determined on a small and unrepresentative sample will shrink considerably on cross-validation because of both random and *systematic* error in generalizing from one sample to another. Holt's clinicians were not required to hold strictly to weights developed in a validation sample (Hammond *et al.*, 1964), and the cross-validated performance of Lindzey's clinicians was not adequately assessed (Goldberg, 1968a). Hence the superior cross-validating characteristics of clinicians, or superior "validity generalization" (Meehl, 1965), has yet to be demonstrated.

The extensive study of Goldberg (1965a) may be more subject to Holt's criticism. In that study, extensively cross-validated MMPI predictive indices were compared with clinical predictions that were not systematically cross-validated. One might speculate, of course, that the differentiation of psychotic and neurotic MMPI profiles is such a typical clinical task, that the expert judges employed must have had considerable, though informal, "cross-validational" experience prior to participation in Goldberg's study. Whether such a speculation is correct or not is irrelevant, however, in view of Goldberg and Rorer's (1965) demonstration that extensive cross-validational experience with "feedback" concerning right and wrong predictions does little to improve the accuracy of experienced clinicians in differentiating psychosis from neurosis on the basis of MMPI profiles. Since Goldberg and Rorer's clinicians were trained on the *same* MMPI profiles employed in Goldberg's (1965a) original study, the generalization appears warranted. Thus, although cross-validational procedures have seldom been applied appropriately in studies of clinical versus statistical prediction, it appears that their inclusion in experimental designs would have had little effect on "box score" statistics that have been compiled to date.

Judgmental Measurement

Meehl's original monograph stimulated a number of legitimate criticisms of clinical versus statistical experimental designs, which relate to such specific issues as the fallibility of criterion measures (Humphreys, 1956) and the use of appropriate statistical comparisons (McHugh and Apostolakas, 1959). For the most part, however, the vague feeling that clinical skills have somehow been sold up the river may be traced to Meehl's relative neglect of the importance of judgmental measurement. Although the *source* of input data must clearly be distinguished from the manner in which data are combined, Meehl's exclusive focus on methods of data combination has somehow given the impression that judgmental *measurement* procedures are also lacking in merit. For example, Meehl's oft-repeated suggestion that clinicians might more fruitfully spend their time in therapeutic and research activities than in psychodiagnosis has tended to denigrate the role of the clinician as *data gatherer* (Holt, 1958; Sawyer, 1966).

Although it is necessary to separate measurement and data combination for purposes of experimental analysis, the two should not be separated when the total diagnostic contribution of the clinician is being evaluated. Sawyer criticized Meehl's "box score" for clinical prediction on the grounds that prediction (combination) cannot be evaluated *independently* of its source (measurement). His point is of sufficient importance to be considered in some detail.

The Importance of Judgmental Measurement

Sawyer (1966) has suggested a *joint* classification of prediction methods that takes into account both the source of input data (measurement) and the manner in which data are combined. Thus what was a confounding factor in Meehl's (1954) analysis is used as a source of systematic evaluation by Sawyer. The eight-fold classification system of prediction methods, which takes into account both measurement and combination, is presented in Table 5.3. The rows list the sources of input data, and the columns indicate

Table 5.3 Sawyer's classification of prediction methods.   (After Sawyer, 1966.)

Mode of data collection	Mode of data combination	
	Clinical	Statistical
Judgmental	1. Pure clinical	2. Trait ratings
Mechanical	3. Profile interpretation	4. Pure statistical
Both	5. Clinical composite	6. Mechanical composite
Either or both	7. Clinical synthesis	8. Mechanical synthesis

the methods of combination, clinical and statistical.   The entries contain suggested titles for eight methods of prediction.

Pure clinical prediction involves both judgmental measurement and clinical data combination.   In this type of prediction, the clinician may interview a patient and then proceed to make a prediction without having access to any test or objective information.

Trait ratings refer to judgmentally collected data which are combined statistically.   Thus, after interviewing the patient, the clinician attempts to rate him on objective personality dimensions.   Instead of making predictions, however, the clinician turns his ratings over to a clerk, who combines them statistically on the basis of their known relationships with the criterion to be predicted.

In *profile interpretation*, mechanical data (e.g., MMPI profiles) are used as a basis for prediction by the clinician.   This was the type of clinical prediction studied by Goldberg (1965a) in connection with the diagnosis of psychosis versus neurosis from the MMPI.

In *pure statistical* prediction, mechanically collected data are combined by a computer or an actuary.   Goldberg's (1965a) "diagnostic signs" correspond to this type of statistical prediction.

In the *clinical composite* method of prediction, both judgmental and mechanical data are provided to the clinician, who integrates them and comes up with a prediction of the criterion.   This method is used in what is probably the most typical clinical situation, in which predictions are based on a combination of interview, observation, test scores, and biographical information.

In the *mechanical composite* method of prediction, both judgmental and mechanical data are integrated by a clerk or computer in terms of their known relationships with the criterion to be predicted.

In the *clinical synthesis* method of prediction, judgmental and mechanical input data, singly or in combination, are processed in the manner illustrated at the top of Figure 5.2. Judgmental and/or mechanical input data are fed into a computer, which then makes a prediction on the basis of a multiple-regression equation. This prediction, in turn, is *given to the clinician* as an additional source of input information. Note in Figure 5.2 that the clinician also has access to the input data in raw form. In this prediction method which is analogous to Holt's (1958) "sophisticated clinical prediction," the clinician is free to: (a) ignore the prediction made by the computer and follow his own clinical intuition, (b) modify his clinical impression on the basis of information provided by the computer, or (c) abandon his clinical intuition in favor of the actuarially generated prediction.

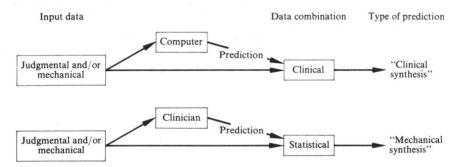

Fig. 5.2 Prediction methods of clinical and mechanical synthesis.

The *mechanical synthesis* prediction method is illustrated at the bottom of Figure 5.2. Judgmental and/or mechanical input data are "fed in" to a clinician, who combines the data clinically and generates a prediction with respect to the criterion, which is then made available to the computer. The computer also has access to the original input data. In this prediction method, the computer has the same options as did the clinician in the method of clinical synthesis: (a) predictions can be based exclusively on the clinician's recommendations; (b) clinical predictions can be used to modify actuarially generated predictions; or (c) clinical predictions can be ignored. Note, in the method of mechanical synthesis, that the decision as to which of the three options to choose is determined *actuarially*. That is, clinical predictions are weighted in terms of their empirical validity. Should the clinical predictions have a zero correlation with the criterion, they would receive a zero weight in prediction by the method of mechanical synthesis.

Sawyer (1966) employed this eight-fold classification of prediction methods as a basis for reanalyzing the results of the published literature on

clinical versus statistical prediction. He found 45 published studies that met
the following standards: (a) scores of individuals were predicted on a pre-
specified criterion, (b) quantitative information was furnished concerning the
relation of the predictors to the criterion, (c) more than one prediction
method was employed, and (d) more than one predictor was employed in
statistical combination. This literature is essentially the same as that reviewed
by Meehl (1965) in his most recent "box score" tabulation. In each of the 45
studies reviewed, each prediction method employed was classified as belonging to one of the eight types specified in Table 5.3. In many of the studies,
more than two types of prediction were employed.

For each study it was determined whether a given prediction method was
superior, equal to, or inferior to the other method(s) employed in the study.
In the 45 studies reviewed, this procedure involved a total of 75 comparisons
between different prediction methods. Approximately 37 percent of the 75
comparisons revealed a clear-cut superiority of one method over another.
In the remaining 63 percent, the methods compared were found to be
approximately equal in predictive efficiency. However, there was a remarkable
consistency to the comparisons in which significant differences were found
between methods:

. . . not one single conclusion directly opposes another—*that is, there is no
pair of methods for which one study found one method better while a second
study found the other method better.* (Sawyer, 1966, p. 191.)

An almost equal consistency was found when all comparisons for a given
method were considered. That is, except in one comparison, there was no
prediction method that was superior in some comparisons and inferior in
others. Thus significant differences between methods compared were more
the exception than the rule, but when such differences occurred, they occurred
with remarkable consistency.

Space limitations preclude a detailed consideration of all 75 comparisons
between prediction methods. However, Sawyer (1966, p. 192) has provided
a succinct summary of his overall findings, which is representative of trends
that would be revealed by a more detailed analysis. For each prediction
method (e.g., *pure statistical*), he tallied the number of comparisons in which
the method proved superior and to that value added one-half the number of
comparisons in which the method was found to be equal to another. For
example, of 41 comparisons in which the pure statistical method was pitted
against one of the other seven methods, 11 indicated that this method was
superior and 30 that it was equal to the method with which it was compared.
Adding half of the cases in which the pure statistical method was found to
be equal ($30 \div 2 = 15$) to the number in which it was found to be superior
(11) gives a result of 63 percent ($26 \div 41 = 63$). Thus the index 63 percent

is an index of the relative superiority of the pure statistical method which "splits the difference" of those studies in which the pure statistical method was found to be equal to another method. Comparable indices for each of the eight prediction methods are given in Table 5.4.

Table 5.4 Results of Sawyer's review of 45 studies of clinical versus statistical prediction. (After Sawyer, 1966.)

Mode of data collection	Mode of data combination			
	Clinical		Statistical	
Judgmental	1. Pure clinical	20%	2. Trait ratings	43%
Mechanical	3. Profile interpretation	38%	4. Pure statistical	63%
Both	5. Clinical composite	26%	6. Mechanical composite	75%
Either or both	7. Clinical synthesis	50%	8. Mechanical synthesis	75%

Two limitations of these percentages must be kept in mind. First of all, they are based on comparisons of a given method with a variety of other methods. Second, the number of comparisons on which the percentages are based varies widely from method to method. Nevertheless, given these limitations, it is still possible to draw certain conclusions that would not be contradicted by more detailed analyses.

Comparing adjacent column entries in Table 5.4, we can see that for each measurement method, statistical data combination is superior. That is, when judgmental measurement is the input, statistical combination exceeds clinical combination by a margin of 23 percentage points. When mechanical data are the input, statistical exceeds clinical combination by a margin of 25 points. Thus, regardless of the nature of input data, statistical combination is superior to clinical. These findings demonstrate that Meehl's (1954) general conclusion about data combination holds independently of the nature of the input data.

For either method of data combination, judgmental measurement is the weakest source of input data. Thus, within the clinical mode, all combinations of input data involving mechanical measurement exceed those involving judgmental by margins ranging from 6 to 30 percentage points. Within the statistical mode, all combinations involving mechanical exceed judgmental measurement by margins ranging from 20 to 32 points. Thus judgmental measurement alone as input should be avoided, regardless of the method of data combination.

Within each mode of data combination, there is a trend toward the association of predictive superiority with the availability of *both* judgmental and mechanical input data. Thus, as the column of statistical combination indicates, having both judgmental and mechanical data available is superior to having either judgmental or mechanical data alone. A striking exception to this trend is apparent within the clinical mode at "clinical composite." Thus, within the clinical mode of data combination, having both kinds of data (26 percent) is little better than having only judgmental data (20 percent) and is *worse* than having only mechanical data (38 percent).

A particularly interesting aspect of Sawyer's results appears in the "synthesis" method. The most effective method of clinical data combination (clinical synthesis) is that in which the clinician is provided with the actuarial prediction of the computer (see Figure 5.2). Considering the superiority of the clinical synthesis method to the clinical composite, one might conclude that when the clinician is furnished with both judgmental and mechanical input, he would do well to rely on the computer's integration of these data rather than on his own. Although the "sophisticated" method of clinical synthesis is superior to other clinical methods of data combination, it is also inferior to any statistical method of data combination which has access to mechanical input (pure statistical, mechanical composite, mechanical synthesis).

The most efficient of the prediction methods in Table 5.4 is clearly the mechanical composite. The finding of no difference between the mechanical composite and mechanical synthesis methods suggests that the computer will generally opt to ignore clinical predictions (assign them zero weights) when provided with this additional source of information. Since the availability of clinicians' predictions appears to add nothing to the method of statistical combination of judgmental and mechanical measurement inputs, the elaborate method of "mechanical synthesis" seems to have little practical value.

The most striking finding from Sawyer's analysis is the extent to which the mechanical composite method exceeds all other prediction methods, not only all clinical methods of data combination, but also the statistical methods involving judgmental or mechanical data alone. It therefore seems safe to conclude that the "best" method of prediction is one in which *both* judgmental and mechanical input data are available for statistical combination. Sawyer concludes:

This suggests that the clinician may be able to contribute most not by direct prediction, but rather by providing, in objective form, judgments to be combined mechanically. (1966, p. 193.)

Sawyer's analysis reinforces Meehl's (1954) conclusion that the clinician is a highly inefficient *combiner* of data, but it also underscores the heretofore neglected contribution of the clinician as a valuable *source* of input data.

Though far from conclusive, Sawyer's analysis does give substance to the clinician's vague feeling that Meehl's analysis and conclusions somehow denigrated his clinical talents and sold him up the river. Instead of suggesting that clinicians abandon their psychodiagnostic activities and move on to more promising fields, such as psychotherapy and research, we might more appropriately suggest that they attempt to refine their observational talents in their role as data collectors. Clinicians need not view themselves as second-rate IBM machines unless they choose to engage in activities that are more appropriately performed by such machines. In the realm of clinical observation and hypothesis formation, the IBM machine will never be more than a "second-rate clinician."

AUTOMATED CLINICAL PREDICTION

Automated Clinical versus Actuarial Prediction

It should be clear from the foregoing section that a variety of prediction methods are subsumed under the general categories of clinical and statistical prediction. Sawyer's (1966) classification is not exhaustive, however, and still another type of prediction method must be considered before conclusions can be drawn about the relative merits of the various approaches. In fact, the method of *automated clinical prediction* has recently become so widely used that it warrants separate and detailed consideration.

In the method of *automated clinical prediction*, clinical *interpretations* of input data are standardized to such an extent that they may serve as the basis for a computer program which will automatically generate the interpretations when provided with appropriate input data. Thus, on the basis of published research, clinical hypotheses, and clinical experience, a skilled clinician assembles a set of interpretations that are uniquely associated with different values of the input data. Once these statements have been programmed for a computer, the process of test interpretation is automated from beginning to end. It is thus possible to generate a complete psychodiagnostic report for a patient who has never been seen by a clinical psychologist.

Automated clinical prediction differs from actuarial prediction in several important respects. Although these differences have been repeatedly emphasized (Sines, 1966; Seeman, 1964; Fowler, 1969), there appears still to exist a widespread confusion of the two methods among practicing clinicians. Since practicing clinicians are increasingly turning to automated clinical prediction as an efficient adjunct to diagnostic practice, it is important to note that the many victories of actuarial prediction over clinical prediction cannot be interpreted as necessarily supporting the method of automated clinical prediction.

Both automated clinical and actuarial prediction share in common the feature of *statistical* combination of input data for the generation of predictions. However, statistical combination of input data qualifies as "actuarial prediction" if *and only if* the combination is completely determined by empirical regularities that have been demonstrated to exist between the input data and the criterion to be predicted (Sines, 1966). In automated clinical prediction, input data are combined on the basis of clinical theory relating input variables to criteria, rather than on the basis of known empirical regularities between input data and criteria. Consequently, it is misleading to refer to automated clinical prediction as "actuarial." This distinction is clearly recognized by most of the clinicians who have developed automated clinical prediction systems, although it does not always appear to be recognized by clinicians who use such systems.

Automated clinical prediction is probably best viewed as a highly practical *interim* procedure in current clinical practice (Fowler, 1969). As was noted in the preceding chapter, there are currently only a handful of pure actuarial prediction systems that are available for clinical use. Moreover, available systems tend to classify a relatively small percentage of the populations to which they are applied. Consequently, the practicing clinician is faced with the disposition of large numbers of patients who cannot be assessed by actuarial techniques. Under these circumstances, the use of automated clinical prediction may be defended on the grounds of efficiency, consistency, and its general actuarial spirit. With respect to the latter justification, it should be pointed out that several automated clinical prediction systems are actuarial in more than spirit. That is, certain "mixed" automated clinical prediction systems are, *in part*, based on known empirical relationships that are truly actuarial in nature. As more actuarial data become available, it will be possible to extend and refine automated clinical prediction systems to the point where they become actuarial prediction systems (Fowler, 1969). Until such modification of existing automated systems becomes possible, however, it is necessary to maintain a careful distinction between the two types of prediction.

Automating Clinical Lore

The interpretive rules employed in automated clinical prediction are based on a variety of sources, which include published research, theoretical writings, and the cumulative experience of one clinician or of many. We shall use the term "clinical lore" to refer to the total body of information available to the clinician who designs an automated prediction system. "Lore" is *not* here used in a pejorative sense but rather in the general sense of connoting "knowledge or wisdom gained through study or experience." The probability that any given bit of lore has a "factual" basis, in the actuarial sense, varies widely from one interpretation to another. There are perhaps even greater variations in credibility between clinical lores associated with different psychological tests.   Our respect for the clinician as an observer and as a *source* of clinical hypotheses should dissuade us from precipitously rejecting all such clinical lore as unfounded.   On the other hand, we cannot grant tenure to interpretive procedures that lack an empirical basis.   As with any other prediction system, the ultimate value of automated clinical lore lies in its ability to predict socially relevant criteria.

The Origins of Clinical Lore

Almost any psychological test that has enjoyed widespread clinical use will have associated with it a specific body of lore that represents a peculiar interweaving of facts, hypotheses, and convictions.   In part because of the lack of a generally accepted theory of personality, and in part because of the biases which predispose a clinician toward one type of test rather than another, the lore surrounding a given test tends to be stated in a language and theoretical system which is peculiar to that test.   The reasons for this development and the manner in which it came about would constitute a fascinating chapter in the history of psychodiagnostics.   For our purposes, we can only briefly comment on two extremes of clinical lore that have been traditionally associated with the use of structured and unstructured tests, respectively.

The MMPI is not only the prototypic structured test but also a prototypic example of a structured test that has accumulated a considerable body of clinical lore.   The lore of this instrument (Cottle, 1953; Dahlstrom and Welsh, 1960; Gough, 1953; Hathaway and Meehl, 1951a, 1951b; Welsh and Dahlstrom, 1956) is for the most part grounded in empirical facts recorded in a variety and multitude of investigations.   To a lesser extent, MMPI lore is founded on clinical observation and experience, a situation which has led to the development of hypotheses of a rather low order of abstraction.   In the clinical interpretation of the MMPI, an attempt is made to generate hypotheses which are not incompatible with existing facts.   Although empirical justifications may be given to most standard MMPI interpretations, the particular study or studies on which such interpretations are based are frequently not impressive in terms of the size and representativeness of the sample employed and in terms of the magnitude of the effect observed.   Trends observed in the literature are prone to become laws within the general lore surrounding the MMPI.

The lore surrounding such unstructured instruments as the Rorschach and the TAT tends to be couched in the language of personality theory— frequently, but not exclusively, psychoanalytic theory.   The lore surrounding the Rorschach (Beck, 1950; Klopfer *et al.*, 1954; Ogden, 1967; Phillips and Smith, 1953; Piotrowski, 1957; Shafer, 1948, 1954) and the TAT (Lindzey, 1952; Shneidman, 1951; Stein, 1955; Tomkins, 1947) is more concerned with the development and refinement of theoretical constructs than with the statement of lower-order empirical regularities based on specific studies. Consequently, it is extremely difficult to estimate the validity of a specific set of Rorschach interpretations for a given assessment problem. Whereas MMPI interpretations may be too specific to be generally useful, Rorschach interpretations are typically too general to apply to a specific assessment problem.

The Mayo Clinic Program

The earliest and most widely used system of automated clinical prediction was that developed by the psychology staff of the Mayo Clinic (Pearson *et al.*, 1964, 1965; Rome *et al.*, 1962, 1965; Swenson, 1965; Swenson and Pearson, 1964a, 1964b; Swenson *et al.*, 1962, 1965). The system was developed in an attempt to provide physicians with summary personality interpretations based on the MMPI. Because a very large number of patients are typically seen in this medical setting, an emphasis was placed on techniques of *automation* that would enable the processing of large numbers of patients in a relatively short period of time.

The Mayo staff developed a new form of the MMPI, which required the patient to record his responses (*true* or *false*) on special IBM cards that could be read directly by a computer. The patient's responses, along with identifying data, were then fed into a computer, which scored a minimum of 14 MMPI scales. A "library" of interpretive statements, associated with elevations on the MMPI scales, was stored in the memory of the computer. When a given MMPI scale elevation corresponded to the range of elevations associated with an interpretive statement, the computer printed out the library statement in the form of a psychological report. The total machine time involved was approximately 35 seconds per patient record (Rome *et al.*, 1962). A psychological report was typically available to the consulting physician within 24 hours after the patient had been given the MMPI. Within this automated system, the clinician has been entirely superseded by a computer.

The library of interpretive statements was compiled by two clinical psychologists (Swenson and Pearson, 1964a) on the basis of their own experience in interpreting the MMPI in this medical setting. Elevations on MMPI scales were divided into five categories ranging from "low" to "marked." Associated with each degree of scale elevation was a set of "characteristic" statements that are ascribed to individuals whose MMPI scale score falls within that range. In general, these descriptive terms are compatible with those found in the early MMPI studies that provide the empirical basis for standard MMPI interpretive lore (see Dahlstrom and Welsh, 1960, p. 159).

For illustrative purposes, descriptive statements associated with two

MMPI scales are presented in Table 5.5. Although these particular statements were taken from an early version of the Mayo program, which has since been extensively revised, they serve to indicate the general logic underlying this approach. If a given patient's *Pt* scale score was within the marked range (> 42), the computer printed out "Agitated, ruminative, and fearful.

Table 5.5 Sample library statements from an early Mayo Clinic program

Scale elevation statements

	Scale	
Range	*Pt*	*Sc*
Low	Probably not a worrier. Tends to be relaxed regarding responsibilities.	Strong interests in people and in practical matters.
Normal	Has sufficient capacity for organizing work and personal life.	Has a combination of practical and theoretical interests.
Mild	Conscientious, orderly, and self-critical.	Tends toward abstract interests such as science, philosophy, and religion.
Moderate	Rigid and meticulous. Worrisome and apprehensive. Dissatisfied with social relationships. Probably very religious and moralistic.	Probably somewhat eccentric, seclusive, and withdrawn. Many internal conflicts.
Marked	Agitated, ruminative, and fearful. Probable obsessions, compulsions, and phobias. May have religious preoccupation and guilt.	Probably feelings of unreality, bizarre or confused thinking and conduct. May have strange attitudes and false beliefs. Consider psychiatric evaluation.

Configural modifications

Rule 8: If *Pt* > 31 (male) or > 34 (female) and *Ma* = 22 to 28, do not print *Pt* and *Ma* descriptions. Print instead:

"Restless or agitated. Active mentally or physically but lacks sense of accomplishment."

Rule 9: If *Pt* > 37 (male) or > 43 (female) and *Ma* > 28, do not print *Pt* and *Ma* descriptions. Print instead:

"Very restless and agitated. Probable flight of ideas and press of speech. May alternate between grandiose ideas and obsessive self-condemnation. Consider psychiatric evaluation."

Probable obsessions, compulsions, and phobias. May have religious pre-occupation and guilt."

The interpretive system illustrated in Table 5.5 does not take patterns or "configurations" of scale scores into account. There has been a long-standing conviction associated with MMPI lore that the interpretation placed on a given scale will change considerably as a function of patterns of eleva-tions on other scales. The bottom of Table 5.5 illustrates the manner in which configural modifications may be introduced into an automated inter-pretive system. For example, if *Pt* (of a male) is greater than 31 and *Ma* is within the range 22–28, another statement is substituted for the usual state-ments associated with *Pt* and *Ma*. The origins of such configural rules for MMPI interpretation are to be found in early studies and clinical reports of the significance of specific patterns of scale elevations (e.g., Guthrie, 1950; Gough, 1946).

The Mayo Clinic program began with approximately 49 statements associated with single-scale elevations (Rome *et al.*, 1962) and 11 statements regarding configural patterns. In its present revised form, there are approxi-imately 62 statements related to scale elevation and 38 statements which impose configural modifications on the statements. A portion of an early Mayo Clinic "clinical report" is illustrated in Table 5.6. In general, the number of interpretive statements printed by the computer will vary with the source of the referral. For routine screening purposes, it may be sufficient to print out interpretive statements associated only with unusually low elevations or with marked elevations. Nevertheless, there are many occasions on which the consulting physician would prefer to have a series of normal statements for purposes of discussing the analysis with the patient (Swenson and Pearson, 1964a).

The Mayo Clinic automated clinical prediction program was developed for large-scale data processing in a rather specialized medical setting. The emphasis to date has been on methods of automation and the general recep-tion of the program within this setting. There is little doubt that the Mayo program is both totally automated and highly efficient. Moreover, the system has been well accepted by both patients and physicians in clinical practice (Swenson *et al.*, 1965). Despite the enormous efforts that have been expended in the development and execution of the Mayo Clinic program, *there has been no attempt to evaluate the validity of the predictive system which has been automated.* Thus, although the system has now been employed in the interpretation of more than 50,000 MMPI records at the Mayo Clinic alone (Swenson, 1965), there has been virtually no attempt to ascertain the validity of the statements generated in the automated personality descriptions of these 50,000 patients. Although future data of an actuarial sort have been promised (Swenson, 1965) they do not appear to be in any way related to the descriptive library now in routine use. Clearly, much of the effort of the

Table 5.6 An early Mayo Clinic psychological test report

226–32–21					03/15/64		49		M	F09	B		
Q	L	F	K	HS	D	HY	PD	MF	PA	PT	SC	MA	SI
2	5	2	27	6	24	28	18	23	11	5	1	10	23	RAW
4	53	49	78	72	66	71	74	55	59	68	60	48	48	T

BR	3	CONSIDER PSYCHIATRIC EVALUATION.
K		HIGHLY DEFENSIVE. MINIMIZES OR UNDERSTATES PROBLEMS IN SOCIAL AND EMOTION ADJUSTMENT.
PD	4	SOMEWHAT REBELLIOUS OR NONCONFORMIST. AVOIDS CLOSE PERSONAL TIES. DISSATISFIED WITH FAMILY OR SOCIAL LIFE.
HS	1	CONSIDERABLE NUMBER OF PHYSICAL COMPLAINTS. PROMINENT CONCERN WITH BODILY FUNCTIONS.
HY	3	PROBABLY SOMEWHAT IMMATURE, EGOCENTRIC, SUGGESTIBLE AND DEMANDING.
PT	7	CONSCIENTIOUS, ORDERLY AND SELF-CRITICAL.
D	2	MILDLY DEPRESSED OR PESSIMISTIC.
SC	8	TENDS TOWARD ABSTRACT INTERESTS SUCH AS SCIENCE, PHILOSOPHY AND RELIGION.
PA	6	SENSITIVE. ALIVE TO OPINIONS OF OTHERS.
MFM	5	NORMAL MALE INTEREST PATTERN FOR WORK, HOBBIES, ETC.
MA	9	LOW ENERGY AND ACTIVITY LEVEL. DIFFICULT TO MOTIVATE, APATHETIC.
SI	10	HAS CAPACITY TO MAINTAIN ADEQUATE SOCIAL RELATIONSHIPS.

psychologists at the Mayo Clinic has been directed toward "public relations" (Goldberg, 1965b). Now that they have "sold" automation, one can hope that future efforts will be directed toward utilizing the enormous potential of this data source for genuine actuarial prediction.

Earlier, we commented on the necessity of maintaining a clear distinction between actuarial prediction and automated clinical prediction. The importance of maintaining this distinction is well illustrated in the manner in which the Mayo Clinic program has been adopted for other uses. The publishers of the MMPI have recently announced the availability of an automated clinical interpretation service based on the Mayo program. They have advertised this service as follows:

The library of interpretive statements used in the computer was developed over a five-year period during which MMPI records were obtained from more than 150,000 patients at the Mayo Clinic in Rochester, Minnesota. (American Psychologist, 1967.)

Although the personality assessment specialist may be well aware of the distinction between automated clinical and actuarial prediction, the typical *consumer* of MMPI test interpretations may not. Such a consumer might reasonably be expected to infer from this advertisement that there is some relationship between the automated prediction program and the fact that it has been *employed* in more than 150,000 instances. This is, of course, not at all true. The library of interpretive statements constituting the Mayo Clinic program is based on clinical lore that has not been firmly validated on this or on any other existing population. Continued use of the program, in the absence of systematic evaluation, does not lend credibility to its initial correctness. Although there are many reasons to believe that the system has promise, the possibility exists that an unknown number of errors of interpretation have been made—not once, but 150,000 times. Such a possibility should not form the basis of an advertising campaign for the commercial use of the system.

The Alabama Program

A somewhat more elaborate program for automated clinical prediction, based on the MMPI, has been developed by Fowler (1964, 1965, 1966, 1969). Although conceived under the same philosophy as that of the Mayo Clinic program, the Alabama program differs in two important respects. In the first place, the major interpretive statements are based on characteristics believed to be associated with elevations on *two* scales rather than on a single scale. It is Fowler's (1969) contention that clinical interpretation is typically based on configurations of two or more scales, rather than on single scales considered one at a time. There is, indeed, a considerable body of MMPI lore based on interpretations of the two highest scales in the profile (Dahlstrom and Welsh, 1960, p. 165–212). Second, the interpretive statements are stored in the computer as *paragraphs* summarizing the essential characteristics of individuals with elevations on the two scales in question. For this reason, as well as for other innovations in programming "verbal" material, psychological reports "written" by the Alabama Program bear a very close resemblance to reports prepared by clinicians in their daily practice.

In developing the library of statements for the Alabama program, Fowler prepared a basic interpretive paragraph for each combination of two high scales that had been noted in clinical lore. Variations in these paragraphs were then prepared to reflect variations in the level of elevation of the scales involved. Since the interpretive significance of the two highest scales is believed to be influenced by other profile characteristics, additional paragraphs were written to take into account other scale elevations and configurations. In addition, such factors as sex, age, and marital status were considered in preparing alternative paragraphs. Finally, additional statements were prepared to reflect elevations on scales not accounted for in the basic two-scale configurations. The end result of this procedure was an elaborate set of interpretive rules and an extensive library of alternative paragraphs and statements which took into account variations in the two-scale profile configurations.

The Alabama program has been adapted for commercial use by the Roche Psychiatric Service Institute (Fowler, 1966). The first page of a sample report (Table 5.7) shows the manner in which descriptive paragraphs, stored in the library, are assembled into a coherent psychodiagnostic report. Subsequent pages of the report provide such technical information as scores on the standard MMPI scales plus 14 other special scales for which norms are available. "Critical items," i.e., items expressing serious symptoms which have been answered in a symptomatic direction, are also listed.

The Alabama program appears to be a promising clinical instrument that has been carefully and responsibly made available for clinical use. Studies are in progress (Fowler, 1969) which will shed some light on the validity of the program as currently written. Although such validity is far from established, the Alabama program has the virtue of operating in very much the same fashion as expert clinicians do when interpreting MMPI profiles (Dahlstrom and Welsh, 1960). The program is designed for psychodiagnostic evaluation in a psychiatric setting, and it is in this type of setting that it will no doubt prove maximally useful.

The Kentucky Program

By far the most ambitious of all automated MMPI interpretive programs to date is that developed by Finney (1965c, 1966a) for use by professional psychologists and psychiatrists.

For this reason it is designed to get the maximum information out of the data. It intends to tell all that can be told about the person. (Finney, 1965c.)

The Kentucky program is designed in terms of Finney's own view of the nature of mental illness (Finney, 1962), and it places heavy emphasis on certain underlying dimensions of the MMPI (Finney, 1961) as well as on a large number of special scales developed by the author (Finney, 1965a, 1965b, 1966b).

The program first attempts to describe the individual in terms of three major dimensions which are assumed to underlie the test. Also included are paragraphs derived from the literature of the two highest scale scores, which formed the basis of the Alabama program. A series of specially derived "process" scores are considered in all possible combinations. Finally, a total of 96 MMPI scales, for which interpretive statements are available, is stored in the computer library.

Table 5.7 Sample Roche psychological test report

ROCHE PSYCHIATRIC SERVICE INSTITUTE

MMPI REPORT

CASE NO: 00000   RPSI NO: 0000
AGE 37 MALE

THE TEST ITEMS APPEAR TO HAVE BEEN ANSWERED TRUTHFULLY WITH
NO EFFORT TO DENY OR EXAGGERATE.

THIS PATIENT APPEARS TO BE CURRENTLY DEPRESSED AND ANXIOUS.
HE SHOWS A PATTERN WHICH IS FREQUENT AMONG PSYCHIATRIC PATIENTS.
FEELINGS OF INADEQUACY, SEXUAL CONFLICTS AND RIGIDITY ARE ACCOM-
PANIED BY A LOSS OF EFFICIENCY, INITIATIVE AND SELF CONFIDENCE.
INSOMNIA IS LIKELY, ALONG WITH CHRONIC FATIGUE. HE IS ANXIOUS,
TENSE, AND OVERLY SENSITIVE. SUICIDAL THOUGHTS ARE A POSSIBILITY.
IN THE CLINICAL PICTURE, DEPRESSION PREDOMINATES. PSYCHIATRIC
PATIENTS WITH THIS PATTERN ARE LIKELY TO BE DIAGNOSED AS DEPRESSIVE
REACTION OR ANXIETY REACTION. THE CHARACTERISTICS ARE RESISTANT
TO CHANGE, ALTHOUGH SYMPTOMATIC RELIEF MAY BE OBTAINED WITH BRIEF
TREATMENT.

HE TENDS TO BE PESSIMISTIC AND COMPLAINING, AND IS LIKELY
TO BE DEFEATIST, CYNICAL, AND UNWILLING TO STICK WITH TREATMENT.
HE MAY NEED FREQUENT REASSURANCE ABOUT HIS MEDICAL CONDITION. DY-
NAMICALLY, HE IS A NARCISSISTIC AND SELF-CENTERED PERSON WHO IS
RIGID IN THOUGHT AND ACTION AND EASILY UPSET IN SOCIAL SITUATIONS.

REPRESSION AND DENIAL ARE UTILIZED AS A DEFENSE AGAINST AN-
XIETY. IN PERIODS OF HEIGHTENED STRESS HIS ANXIETY IS LIKELY TO BE
EXPRESSED IN SOMATIC SYMPTOMS. HE MAY RESPOND TO SUGGESTION AND
REASSURANCE.

HE IS A SELF CONTROLLED CAUTIOUS PERSON WHO MAY BE SOMEWHAT
FEMININE IN HIS INTEREST PATTERNS. HE IS IDEALISTIC, SOCIALLY
PERCEPTIVE, AND RESPONSIVE. HE SHOWS SOME SELF AWARENESS, BUT HE
IS SENSITIVE AND PRONE TO WORRY. HE IS VERBALLY FLUENT, PERSUASIVE
AND ABLE TO COMMUNICATE IDEAS CLEARLY.

THIS PERSON IS HESITANT TO BECOME INVOLVED IN SOCIAL SIT-
UATIONS. HE MAKES AN EFFORT TO CONSCIENTIOUSLY CARRY OUT HIS RE-
SPONSIBILITIES, BUT HE IS RETIRING AND SOMEWHAT WITHDRAWN FROM IN-
TERPERSONAL RELATIONSHIPS.

Considerable effort has been directed toward generating paragraphs and statements from the large library in such a manner that they bear some resemblance to a typical clinical report. The use of transitions (e.g., "and," "but," "although") between statements, as well as a number of other "verbal" reporting techniques, have achieved this goal to some extent. A problem, common to all automated programs but most acute in the case of the Kentucky program, is that of "contradictory statements." With more than a hundred scales and indices scored for the MMPI and approximately a thousand statements available in the program library, contradictions are almost inevitable. Many of these contradictory statements are viewed as reports at different "levels" of personality, and some attempt has been made to present them in this fashion. Others may simply be presented as contradictions: "There is conflicting evidence about the possibility that this person is psychotic" (Finney, 1966a).

Automated clinical reports generated by the Kentucky program are too rich and detailed to be fully illustrated here. Table 5.8 presents a fragment of a typical Kentucky report for illustrative purposes. As Table 5.8 indicates, Kentucky reports tend to be stated in smooth, though somewhat redundant prose. The system is capable of generating 18 different types of reports, depending on the referral source and the amount of detail desired. Thus different reports may be written for personnel workers, counselors, physicians, correctional workers, clinical psychologists, psychotherapists, and the persons tested. Both the content and style of these reports are adopted to the type of reader.

Although the program generates reports that contain more information than any other available program, it does not appear to have gained widespread acceptance as a diagnostic tool for routine clinical use. This fact may be due, in part, to the reliance of the program on Finney's own specially derived scales (Finney, 1962a, 1965b, 1966b), which themselves have not yet gained wide acceptance among practicing clinicians. Nevertheless, the Kentucky program represents an interesting and creative endeavor that has contributed considerably to the technology of automated clinical prediction.

Automating the Expert Clinician

The automated clinical prediction systems just discussed rely on clinical lore as the basis for interpretations which may be programmed into a computer. Although clinical lore typically represents the cumulated wisdom of many clinicians, its validity is seldom firmly established. Granted that clinical lore is a quite reasonable source of interpretive hypotheses, it is still extraordinarily difficult to estimate, in advance, the overall accuracy of such a body of knowledge.

Table 5.8 Portion of a Kentucky psychological report

86	MP		
1680		6	LET US CONSIDER HOW SHE STANDS IN THE PERSONAL QUALITIES THAT HAVE
		23	TO DO WITH SUCCESS IN THE WORLD OF WORK.
1695		23	FOR MANY WOMEN, MARRIAGE AND MOTHERHOOD ARE A CAREER, AND SO THESE REMARKS ABOUT JOBS AND CAREERS MAY OR MAY NOT MATTER GREATLY TO HER.
1700		3	AT THIS TIME, BEING EITHER SOMEWHAT UPSET OR CONFUSED, OR PERHAPS
1706		2	ONLY TOO FRANK, SHE GIVES THE IMPRESSION THAT SHE IS SOMEWHAT LACKING IN
1710		2	WHAT IT TAKES TO DO WELL IN MOST KINDS OF WORK. BUT SHE CAN DO BETTER
1707		3	THAN THAT. IN THE LONG RUN, IT MAY BE FAIRER TO SAY THAT SHE HAS GOOD, NORMAL ABILITY TO DO WORK. SHE CAN DO AS WELL AS ANY AVERAGE, NORMAL
1719		0	PERSON IN MOST KINDS OF WORK. SHE DOES WELL ENOUGH IN THE PERSONAL QUALITIES THAT MAKE FOR SUCCESS AT WORK. OF COURSE, SOME KINDS OF WORKING SITUATIONS FIT HER BETTER THAN OTHERS.
1723		0	HER STRONGEST POINT, THE ONE THAT CAN HELP HER THE MOST TO SUCCEED
1771		94	IN HER WORK, IS HER SELF-RELIANCE IN HER WORK, AND ABILITY TO USE GOOD
94	AI	4	JUDGMENT ABOUT IT. WITHIN NORMAL RANGE, SHE SEEMS TO USE GOOD JUDGMENT IN HER WORK. SHE CAN DO WELL ENOUGH IN A JOB THAT CALLS ON HER TO TAKE
1725		94	RESPONSIBILITY FOR GOING AHEAD WITH THE WORK AND SOLVING PROBLEMS FOR
1761		94	HERSELF, KEEP WORKING CONSTRUCTIVELY WITHOUT BEING SUPERVISED, AND USE SOUND JUDGMENT IN MAKING DECISIONS ABOUT THE WORK.
1726		32	ANOTHER STRONG POINT THAT CAN HELP HER IN HER WORK IS HER AMBITION AND URGE FOR ACHIEVEMENT.
1732		0	YOU WILL BE WISE TO HELP HER CHOOSE A LINE OF WORK THAT CALLS ON HER STRONG POINTS. IN THE RIGHT LINE OF WORK, AND IN THE RIGHT WORKING CONDITIONS AND SETTING, PEOPLE WILL APPRECIATE HER FOR HER BEST QUALITIES.
1733		99	ONE OF HER WEAK POINTS, SOMETHING THAT MAY HANDICAP HER IN HER WORK,
1776		99	IS SOME LACK OF WILLINGNESS TO CONFORM TO THE CUSTOMS AND EXPECTATIONS OF
99	SO	6	SOCIETY. SHE IS SOMETHING OF AN INDIVIDUALIST. SHE HAS HER OWN OPINIONS, AND SHE MAY NOT ALWAYS BE POLITE TO PEOPLE THAT DISAGREE WITH HER. SHE

The same is not true of individual clinicians. In almost all studies of the accuracy of clinical prediction, large individual differences have been found within the group of clinicians studied. If we put aside the issue of generality of accuracy, it seems that for specific prediction tasks, some clinicians are clearly more accurate than others. One apparent solution to the problem created by the generally poor predictive accuracy of clinicians is to assign particular prediction problems to those clinicians who have *demonstrated* a superior flair for them. Unfortunately, such a solution is not *practical*, since the number of individuals so gifted is slight in relation to the number of diagnostic decisions demanded in routine clinical practice. A possible solution to the dilemma may be found in the potentialities of *automating* the judgments of expert clinicians. To the extent that the judgments of an expert clinician may be simulated by a computer, his judgmental processes may be "frozen" within a computer program and performed repetitively with thousands of new cases.

Kleinmuntz (1963) has provided interesting preliminary evidence on the possibility of simulating the judgments of an expert clinician by means of a computer program. The prediction task was to identify the adjustment level of college students from their MMPI profiles. The profiles were collected from a group of 126 undergraduates who were known, by other criteria, to be either "maladjusted" or "adjusted." A *counseling group* comprised 65 students who had received counseling of one kind or another at the student counseling center. Independent ratings by two counselors resulted in the classification of 28 of them as maladjusted and 37 as adjusted. A *fraternity-sorority group* consisted of 31 students who had been nominated by their fraternity and sorority members as being the least or most adjusted members of their group. Of these students, 17 were judged by their peers to be the most maladjusted and 14 the least maladjusted. A *normal group* comprised 30 students randomly selected from freshman test files. None of this group had been seen at the counseling center, and hence all of them were judged to be adjusted. The total sample thus comprised 126 college students, 45 of whom were judged to be maladjusted and 81 adjusted.

The MMPI profiles of all 126 were given to ten experienced MMPI interpreters, who were instructed to order the profiles along a 14-step distribution ranging from "least adjusted" to "most adjusted." The predictive accuracy of this group of clinicians was assessed by calculating the percentages of correct identification of the maladjusted and adjusted students. It was then possible to select the "best" clinician in terms of his overall percentages of identification. The best clinician was able to identify 80 percent of the maladjusted students and 67 percent of the adjusted students in the total sample of 126 cases. On repeating his classifications for the same cases, the expert achieved a test-retest reliability coefficient of .96. Because of his demonstrated expertise (relative to the other judges in the study), the best judge was selected for intensive study in an attempt to capture the rules that formed the basis for his decisions.

Kleinmuntz provided the expert with small samples from the larger group of profiles and asked him to "think aloud" into a tape recorder as he placed the profiles into adjusted and maladjusted categories. Approximately 60 hours of tape-recorded material were edited and compiled in an attempt to construct a set of decision rules. As Kleinmuntz (1963, p. 9) pointed out, this procedure cannot be considered a "pure" simulation of human thought by a computer (Newell and Simon, 1961). Rather, it was an attempt to ascertain the logic underlying a large number of verbalizations. From our viewpoint, this procedure qualifies as "simulation" in that the judge's *verbal behavior* was simulated in the absence of concern for the *accuracy* of the judgments themselves. As such, it is to be considered automated clinical prediction rather than actuarial prediction.

A content analysis of the verbalizations of the expert judge suggested 16 sequential rules which he employed in arriving at a final decision as to whether a given profile indicated that the student was adjusted or maladjusted. The first six rules are presented in Table 5.9, along with sample verbalizations that gave rise to them. The protocol on the left represents the judge's verbalization of the bases for his interpretive procedures. The associated rules on the right represent attempts to formalize the verbalizations.

The rules derived from the expert clinician's verbalizations were programmed into a sequential decision-making procedure, written in the language of the computer. Table 5.10 is a flowchart that represents the basic logic underlying the computer program. Following the flowchart, we see that the computer "reads" the MMPI profile and "decides" whether or not a given rule is applicable. If a rule is considered applicable, the program "branches" to a decision of either "adjusted" or "maladjusted." If not, the program passes on to the next rule. The flowchart in Table 5.10, which corresponds to the six rules covered in Table 5.9, represents only a portion of that employed by Kleinmuntz.

Having access to a computer program which purports to simulate the cognitive activity of the clinician, we are now interested in inquiring into how well such a program fares in the *empirical* discrimination between adjusted and maladjusted college students from their MMPI profiles. The total sample of 126 profiles was submitted to the computer for diagnosis by means of the program illustrated in Table 5.10. The percentages of correct identification of maladjusted and adjusted college students were compared with those achieved by the expert clinician himself. Data relevant to this comparison are presented in Table 5.11.

Table 5.11 compares the expert clinician with the computer program

Table 5.9 Verbalizations of expert clinician and underlying rules.   (From Kleinmuntz, 1963, p. 10)

Verbalizations of expert clinician	Underlying rule
1. Now I'm going to divide these into two piles . . . on the left [least adjusted] I'm throwing all mults with at least four scales primed.	1. If four or more clinical scales $\geq T$ score 70, call maladjusted.
2. I'll throw all mults to the right [most adjusted] if there's no clinical scale above a T score of 60. I'll let Ma go up as high as 80 . . . maybe a raw score of 10 on Mt would be playing it safe . . . so I'm looking at three things now and sorting according to these conditions.	2. If scales Hs, D, Hy, Pd, Mf, Pa, Pt, Sc, and Si are ≤ 60 and if $Ma \leq 80$ and $Mt \leq 10$, then call adjusted.
3. If either Pd, Pa, or Sc is primed, I'm putting it on the left side [least adjusted] . . . it would also be nice to have all of these scales slightly more elevated than the others.	3. If the first two coded scales include Pd, Pa, or Sc, and at least one of these is ≥ 70, then call maladjusted (if Mf is among the first two scales, then examine the first three scales in the code).
4. If the elevations are lopsided to the right with the left side of the profile fairly low, I'm throwing the mults to the left [least adjusted].	4. If Pa or $Sc \geq 70$ and Pa, Pt, or $Sc \geq Hs$, D, or Hy, call maladjusted.
5. Here's a paranoid character. I wish his K score were not quite so high and he could use more Mt . . . when that Mt score is less than 10, I figure something must be stabilizing him. I like an inverted V with F high on the validity scales.	5. Call maladjusted if $Pa \geq 70$ unless $Mt \leq 6$ and $K \geq 65$.
6. Boy, I don't know, that Mt is too low to call her maladjusted. I'll settle for calling them adjusted if Mt is at a raw score of 6 or lower.	6. If $Mt \leq 6$, call adjusted.

Table 5.10 Computer flowchart of rules underlying verbalizations of expert clinician. (After Kleinmuntz, 1963)

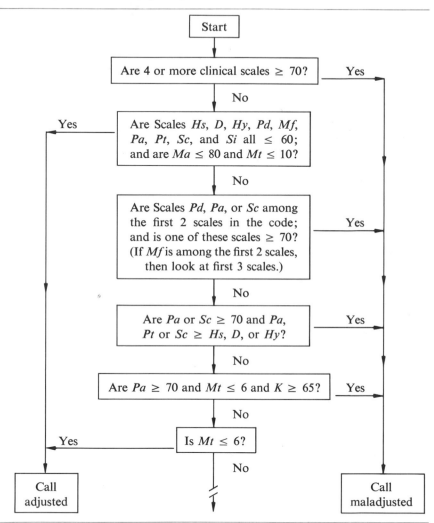

(generated by the expert clinician) in terms of percentages of correct identification achieved in the counseling sample, the fraternity-sorority sample, and the total sample, which includes the 30 "normal" records, as well as those of the two separately evaluated groups. Note that the computer fared especially well in correctly identifying both maladjusted and adjusted students in the counseling sample. It seems reasonable to assume that in this sample the criterion designations of "maladjusted" and "adjusted" were most meaningful. In the fraternity-sorority sample, in which peer nominations served as

Table 5.11 Relative accuracy of clinician and clinician-generated computer program in identifying maladjustment from the MMPI. (After Kleinmuntz, 1963)

			Correct identification, %		
Sorter	Group	N	Mal-adjusted	Adjusted	Phi coefficient*
Clinician	Counseling	65	75%	70%	.448
Computer	Counseling	65	96%	81%	.768
Clinician	Fraternity-sorority	31	65%	64%	.289
Computer	Fraternity-sorority	31	35%	100%	.445
Clinician	Total sample	126	80%	67%	.447
Computer	Total sample	126	63%	88%	.521

* Calculated by the present author.

validity criteria, the computer did less well in identifying the maladjusted cases but made no errors in the identification of adjusted cases. The results for the total sample indicate that the expert clinician had a tendency to call more students maladjusted and consequently made more errors in the identification of adjusted students.

From a statistical standpoint, the most appropriate comparison lies in the *correlation* of predictions with criterion status. For dichotomous data, such as we have here (maladjusted versus adjusted), the correlation coefficient is called a *phi coefficient*. Comparing the phi coefficients between the expert clinician and the computer (see Table 5.11), we can see that the computer was superior to the clinician in all instances. This superiority is most evident in that group of cases for which professional criterion judgments were available, the counseling group. There is little doubt that in this instance, a clinician-generated computer program outperformed the clinician himself in the diagnosis of adjustment and maladjustment from MMPI records of college students. The implications of these findings will be considered subsequently.

In discussing these findings, Kleinmuntz (1963, p. 13) tends to de-emphasize the superiority of the computer by pointing out that the expert clinician's bias toward the overdiagnosis of maladjustment is a desirable procedure in this clinical setting. Although this may be true, it is a relatively simple matter to adjust the computer program so that the desired degree of bias is achieved. What is more important is the fact that a clinician-generated program outperformed the clinician himself. Since this clinician was selected from a group of 10 as the "expert" among them, it is safe to infer that the clinician-generated computer program outperformed all 10 clinicians in the present task.

Subsequently, Kleinmuntz (1967, 1969) modified the clinician-generated computer program by including additional variables and revising the rules in accord with a series of cross-validated *empirical* studies. Thus the automated clinical prediction program formed the basis for an *actuarial* prediction program whose effectiveness was evaluated on new samples. Not unexpectedly, the actuarial prediction program was later shown to be superior to predictions made by highly expert clinicians, and one may presume—though this comparison was not actually made—that it was superior to the original clinician-generated program itself.

Two findings from Kleinmuntz's study deserve special emphasis. First, it appears that the automation, or "computerization," of the verbalizations of expert clinicians provides a valuable *source* of interpretations which can be incorporated into an *actuarial* prediction system. From our consideration of the literature on clinical versus statistical prediction, it should be apparent that the final actuarial prediction system will be most likely to have greater accuracy than either clinical prediction or automated clinical prediction. Nevertheless, the role of the clinician as a generator of *hypotheses* must not be ignored, since it is unlikely that the computer would uncover such hypotheses in hundreds of hours of empirical search. The second finding to be stressed is that an automated prediction program (generated by a clinician) was found to *outperform* the clinician who generated it. Although this finding may seem strange at first, it will later be demonstrated that such an outcome is *almost inevitable*. The reasons for this paradoxical inevitability will be examined in detail in the next section.

Automating Paramorphic Models

Kleinmuntz's (1963) findings suggest that an automated prediction program, based on the verbalizations of an expert clinician, tends to outperform the clinician himself. Assuming that there is some stable relationship between what the clinician *says* he does and how he actually makes predictions—an assumption that is not always justified, however (Hoffman, 1960)—such a finding may not be as paradoxical as it at first appears. Since the judge himself is not a machine, he is subject to such human shortcomings as distraction, fatigue, boredom, etc. Such momentary and random deviations from typical performance are viewed as "random error" from the standpoint of prediction (Chapter 7). Since random error decreases reliability, it must decrease validity as well. Consequently, any procedure which tends to reduce the amount of random error associated with prediction is likely to increase the overall achievement of the prediction system.

One of the salient features of a computer is its *consistency*, or reliability, in performing repetitive operations. Once the computer has been instructed (programmed) to perform a series of repetitive operations, it will do so with perfect reliability. Consequently, to the extent that a simulation procedure is successful in capturing the judgmental strategy of a clinician, the computerization of this strategy is likely to perform as well as or better than the clinician himself over time. This point has been noted by a number of writers (Dudycha and Naylor, 1966a; Naylor, Dudycha, and Schenck, 1967; Naylor and Schenck, 1966; Yntema and Torgerson, 1961). Dudycha and Naylor (1966a) have provided an empirical demonstration of this phenomenon. They conclude:

. . . humans tend to generate "correct" strategies but then, in turn, fail to use their own strategy with any great consistency. . . . One is left with the conclusion that humans may be used to generate inference strategies but that once the strategy is obtained the human should be removed from the system and replaced by his own strategy! (p. 127.)

Goldberg (1970) has suggested an ingenious approach to automated clinical prediction which capitalizes on both the ability of computer programs to generate reliable predictions and the ability of paramorphic models (Chapter 4) to capture the rating strategies of clinicians. Whereas Kleinmuntz (1963) utilized a *simulation* of a clinician's verbalizations in subsequent automated clinical prediction, Goldberg (1970) employed a paramorphic model of clinical judgment as a basis for subsequent automated prediction. Since neither approach made use of information concerning the *accuracy* of the judgments involved, both qualify as examples of automated clinical prediction.

Goldberg (1970) once again utilized the data collected by Meehl (Meehl, 1959; Meehl and Dahlstrom, 1960) in his study of the prediction of psychosis versus neurosis from MMPI profiles. These data were described earlier in this chapter in connection with Goldberg's (1965a) study of clinical versus statistical prediction, as well as in Chapter 4 in connection with the study of Wiggins and Hoffman (1968). As the reader will recall, 29 clinical psychologists of varying experience and training were asked to make judgments of psychosis versus neurosis from 861 MMPI profiles collected from seven diverse samples of hospital and clinic patients. A linear paramorphic model was constructed for each of the 29 judges by regressing the MMPI scale scores on the judgments across all 861 profiles. The "paramorphic validity" of each model for each judge is given by the multiple correlation between judgments and input cues, R_j. These values (Table 4.6, second column) indicate that a linear paramorphic model was generally quite successful in capturing the rating strategy of each of the 29 judges.

The linear multiple-regression equation derived for each judge may be viewed as a paramorphic model of that judge's rating strategy:

$$y'_j = {}_jb_1x_1 + {}_jb_2x_2 + \cdots + {}_jb_nx_n.$$

The question raised by Goldberg (1970) pertains to the relative accuracy or achievement of such a model in diagnosing psychosis versus neurosis from the MMPI. That is, if we were to program a computer to weight each of the MMPI scales according to the regression weights obtained in the above equation, how accurately would this model perform in comparison with the clinician on whom the model is based?

Goldberg's unique approach to automated clinical prediction requires further elaboration. First, we are concerned with a clinician who makes clinical predictions on the basis of multiple-input cues. The accuracy or achievement of this clinician is referred to as the validity of *clinical prediction*. Second, we are concerned with a *model* of this clinician which is derived by multiply regressing input cues on clinical judgments *without consideration for the outcome or accuracy of the judgments*. The extent to which this paramorphic representation captures the strategy of the judge is reflected in the size of the multiple correlation of input cues on clinical judgments. The latter index may be referred to as the "paramorphic validity" of the model. Finally, we employ the paramorphic model as a *prediction system* by programming a computer to weight input variables according to the regression weights specified in the paramorphic model. This procedure enables us to compare the achievement of clinical prediction (validity of clinical prediction) with the achievement of the paramorphic model used as a predictor (validity of automated clinical prediction).

When the validity of the clinical judges was compared with the corresponding validity of automated models of clinical judgment, across all 861 predictions, it was found that the model bested the man in 25 out of 29 comparisons. In those four instances in which judges outperformed their paramorphic models, the differences in validity coefficients were so slight that calculation to the third decimal place was required to reveal them. However, it should also be stressed that the absolute amount by which models improved on men was quite small. The average validity of clinical prediction across 29 judges was .28. The average validity of automated clinical prediction across 29 models was .31. From the standpoint of incremental validity (Sechrest, 1963), it cannot be argued that automated paramorphic models represent a significant improvement over clinical prediction. However, from a practical standpoint, which will be considered in more detail below, it should be noted that automated paramorphic models represent a satisfactory substitute for clinical prediction. A conservative interpretation of Goldberg's (1970) results would be that he clearly demonstrated that automated paramorphic models perform *at least* as well as the judges on whom they are based.

Goldberg (1970) also demonstrated that the superiority of paramorphic models to the judges who produced them was not limited to paramorphic models constructed from a large sample without concern for cross-validation.

He employed a cross-validational design which involved dividing the total sample of 861 profiles in half; constructing paramorphic models separately for each half; cross-validating the models on the opposite half, using the same regression weights; and then averaging the two resultant cross-validities. The same design was repeated, dividing the sample into three equal parts, constructing paramorphic models based on a third of the cases, calculating cross-validities on the remaining two-thirds, and then averaging the three indices of cross-validity. In fact, Goldberg repeated this procedure for derivation samples of $\frac{1}{4}, \frac{1}{5}, \frac{1}{6}, \frac{1}{7}, \frac{1}{8}, \frac{1}{9}$, and even $\frac{1}{10}$ of the original sample size. In each instance, the averaged cross-validity estimates were compared with the clinical validity achieved by the judge in the cross-validation sample. In a sense, such a comparison favors the clinician in that his performance is contrasted with a *cross-validated* model that is subject to shrinkage. (There is, of course, no comparable way in which the clinician could be "cross-validated" since the "weights" which the clinician presumably uses are not available.)

When the paramorphic model was based on half the sample, its cross-validity exceeded the validity of clinical prediction in 86 percent of the cases. When the paramorphic model was developed on $\frac{1}{7}$ of the sample, its average cross-validity still exceeded the validity of clinical prediction in 79 percent of the comparisons. Even when the paramorphic model was developed on $\frac{1}{10}$ of the total sample size ($n = 86$), its average cross-validity exceeded that of clinical prediction in 72 percent of the comparisons. Clearly, the relative superiority of automated paramorphic models over clinical judges represents a general phenomenon which is not restricted to large samples nor attenuated by cross-validation.

As in earlier study (Goldberg, 1965a), Goldberg was interested in the clinical predictive accuracy of the "average judge" and the "composite judge." The clinical validity of the average judge is simply the average validity attained by the 29 judges ($\bar{r} = .28$). The corresponding validity of the "average model" is simply the average validity of the 29 paramorphic models ($\bar{r} = .31$). Note, however, that the average validity of the composite judge is obtained by *pooling* the judgments of all 29 judges across 861 cases and calculating the validity of the composite pool. The validity of the composite judge was found to be .35, that of the paramorphic model which described him only .33. As would be expected, the unreliability which attenuated the validity of individual judges was reduced by pooling the judgments of all clinicians. When the number of judges pooled is this large ($n = 29$), apparently no further predictive gain can be achieved by modeling this more reliable composite.

The practical significance of Goldberg's demonstration of the relative superiority of automated paramorphic models over individual clinical judges lies in the fact that the models were developed in the complete *absence* of criterion information. There are many practical prediction situations in which clinical measurements (of unknown validity) are used intuitively to predict a criterion of unknown characteristics. Goldberg (1970) cites as an example the clinical psychologist employed by a municipal suicide-prevention center who uses cues from telephone interviews to assess the probability that each of his callers will try to kill himself. Holt (1958) labeled this type of prediction "naive clinical prediction," and it has generally been considered the exclusive province of clinical prediction. Certainly, in the absence of criterion information and knowledge of the relationships between predictors and criterion, it is not possible to employ actuarial prediction techniques. However, as Goldberg's (1970) work suggests, it may well be both practical and appropriate to employ automated paramorphic models in such naive clinical prediction situations.

Despite the absence of criterion information and despite the lack of knowledge of the empirical relationships existing between predictors and criterion variables, Goldberg's study seems to suggest that an automated paramorphic model would not do worse than a clinician and in all likelihood might do better. Further research is needed on the validity of automated paramorphic models in prediction situations other than that studied by Goldberg. Nevertheless, from the evidence available, it appears that Goldberg may have discovered a rational solution to the long-standing and widespread problem of naive clinical prediction.

Considering Goldberg's (1970) results in conjunction with other empirical studies considered in this and preceding chapters, it is possible to formulate some tentative "rules of thumb" which may serve as guidelines for the clinical practitioner.

1. When criterion information exists, collect it and use it to construct statistical models of data combination. [This allows clinicians to spend their time refining their observational talents in their appropriate role as data collectors.]

2. When criterion information does not exist and there are many clinical judges with experience in the task, use their composite judgments as a basis for prediction. [This assumes that the cost of such a large expenditure of professional time can be justified.]

3. When criterion information does not exist and there are many clinical judges with experience in the task, pool their judgments, find the clinician who correlates most highly with this composite, model him (by linear regression techniques), and use the model for prediction. [This assumes that the cost of (2) cannot be justified.]

4. When criterion information does not exist and there is a clinical judge
   with experience in the task, capture his policy (by linear regression
   techniques) and use the model instead of the man. [This frees a staff
   member for other duties or allows the short-term employment of an
   outside consultant.]

SUMMARY

Clinical versus Statistical Prediction

Questions as to the relative validity of clinical and statistical prediction
methods are raised in the context of justification. To compare the two, the
same input data are given to a clerical worker (or a computer) and a clinician,
and each is asked to make specific predictions concerning a socially relevant
criterion. Early comparisons of clinical and statistical prediction methods
tended to give unfair advantage to one or the other method. Nevertheless,
in reviewing the 50 available studies, Meehl concluded that 33 of them
demonstrated the superiority of statistical over clinical data combination, and
the remaining 17 studies indicated that the two methods were approximately
equal in predictive accuracy. Other writers have challenged this conclusion
on methodological grounds. They point out that many of the studies reviewed
by Meehl: (a) involve prediction tasks that are inappropriate for clinicians
(b) deprive the clinician of information that is typically available to him;
(c) unfairly compare the clinician with cross-validated statistical procedures;
and (d) fail to recognize the contribution of judgmental measurement.

Of the foregoing methodological criticisms, the failure to recognize the
contribution of judgmental measurement is the most telling. Sawyer reconsidered 45 of the studies reviewed by Meehl and classified them by jointly
considering both the method of measurement (judgmental or mechanical)
and the method of prediction (clinical or statistical). As before, statistical
prediction was equal or superior to clinical prediction in all instances.
However, the best prediction method appeared to be that in which *both*
judgmental and mechanical input data were available for statistical combination. This finding underscores the heretofore neglected contribution of the
clinician as a valuable *source* of input data.

Automated Clinical Prediction

In the method of automated clinical prediction, clinical *interpretations* of
input data are standardized to such an extent that they may serve as the
basis for a computer program which will automatically generate the interpretations when provided with appropriate input data. Automated clinical
prediction differs from actuarial prediction in that in the former, input data
are combined on the basis of clinical lore, in the latter, on the basis of known

empirical regularities between input data and criteria. To date, the most widely used programs of automated clinical prediction have been based on MMPI clinical lore. These programs differ from one another primarily in the elaborateness of the final computer-written psychological report.

Kleinmuntz has provided interesting preliminary evidence on the possibility of simulating the judgments of an expert clinician by means of a computer program. His data suggest that predictions generated by a computer program which simulates the clinician's judgments tend to be more accurate than the clinician himself. Subsequently, Goldberg demonstrated that predictions generated by multiple-regression models of clinicians' judgments tended to be more accurate than predictions of the clinicians themselves. Such a finding has implications for "naive clinical prediction" in situations where criterion information is not available. This and other practical implications of the preceding chapters are summarized in the form of tentative "rules of thumb," which are meant to serve as guidelines for the clinical practitioner.

CHAPTER 6

THE OUTCOMES OF PREDICTION: PERSONNEL DECISIONS IN SELECTION, MULTIPLE SELECTION, AND CLASSIFICATION

We have now considered in some detail the roles of measurement and prediction in the basic prediction paradigm in personality assessment. We have assumed, implicitly, that the goal of measurement (data collection) is to furnish precise estimates of subjects' scores on personality and background variables relevant to criterion performance. Similarly, we have described the goal of prediction (data combination) as the minimization of squared predictive error in the forecasting of criterion status. Under optimal measurement and prediction procedures, the correlation between predicted and obtained criterion scores, $r_{yy'}$, will approach the maximum value possible for a given prediction problem.

Until fairly recently, concern with the technical problems of measurement and prediction has resulted in a relative neglect of the broader context in which such problems arise, namely, the optimal assignment of men to jobs or treatments. Within this broader context, which is the overriding concern of personality assessment, the *outcomes* of prediction are of paramount importance to the individuals involved and to the society in which they live. From this standpoint, measurement and prediction are simply technical components of a system designed to make *decisions* about the assignment of personnel to jobs or treatments (Cronbach and Gleser, 1965). Thus, although measurement and prediction may be evaluated by formal psychometric criteria, such as reliability and validity, the outcomes of personnel decisions must be evaluated in terms of their consequences for individuals and institutions within our society.

By emphasizing measurement and prediction rather than the outcomes of decisions, traditional assessment psychologists have accepted classical test theory (Gulliksen, 1950; Lord and Novick, 1968) as providing the standards for evaluating the worth of a psychological test or assessment procedure. From this standpoint, the role of assessment psychologists in making personnel decisions is limited to the development of assessment procedures that possess the highest possible predictive validity. By emphasizing the outcomes of personnel decisions and their consequences for institutions and individuals, Cronbach and Gleser (1965) have adopted standards for evaluating the worth of a psychological test that may differ considerably from those of classical test theory. From their standpoint, the role of assessment psychologists in making personnel decisions is broadened to include the evaluation of institutional gain and loss as a consequence of adopting different possible decision strategies.

In this chapter, we will first introduce some elementary notions of decision theory and provide a description of the major types of personnel decisions. Next, we will consider the major types of personnel decisions from the standpoint of classical validity. Finally, we will introduce the alternative concept of discriminative efficiency and give detailed examples of the manner in which the expected utilities of personnel decision strategies may be maximized.

DECISION THEORY AND PERSONNEL ASSIGNMENT

The Decision Maker

To shortcut an extremely involved sociopolitical argument (e.g., Churchman, 1961), we axiomatize: "Someone has to make decisions." Experience with ultrademocratic institutions, such as academic departments, has led some to the cynical corollary that such decision makers are better selected on the basis of demonstrated decision-making ability than of willingness to serve in this capacity. Willingness to assume responsibility is perhaps a necessary, but certainly not a sufficient, qualification for effective performance as a decision maker. Given a choice between acts (placements) in the face of uncertain outcomes (performance), the effective decision maker behaves in such a fashion as to maximize the values (profits) of the institution he represents. In the role of employee, a decision maker may accept or be indifferent to the values implicit in institutional gain, but if he is an applied scientist, he is thoroughly committed to the principle of maximization. Assessment psychologists who drag their feet or are otherwise indifferent to the principle of maximization are implicitly supporting irrational behavior in areas of great social importance.

Personnel decisions center around the assignment (or nonassignment) of one or more individuals to treatments whose outcomes are of importance to an institution or to the individuals so assigned. If the decision maker knew in advance how well each individual was qualified for each treatment and could thereby anticipate the outcome of any assignment, there would be no problem and, for that matter, no such book as the present one. Lacking such information, the decision maker must *predict* in the sense in which this term has been discussed in preceding chapters. At the outset, certain information may be available that will enable the decision maker to make better-than-chance assignments. This type of information, called a priori information, will be considered later. In addition, the decision maker is willing to utilize any other information that will enable him to forecast outcomes more accurately. Data from psychological tests and assessment procedures are one such source of additional information. When the a priori information is collated with assessment data, probability values or indices of predictive efficiency may be attached to the outcomes of selection or placement decisions. Whereas this step has sometimes been considered the final contribution of personality assessment, it, in fact, only sets the stage for the decision problem.

Classical test theory does not give sufficient emphasis to the fact that the multitude of assignments that are made in any decision situation are seldom of equal importance (value). That the outcomes of some selection decisions are more important than others is intuitively evident when we consider a specific industry or institution. Consider the crew members of a modern jet airliner, who have a number of diverse, though interrelated, job functions. Public relations seem to be an important aspect of the airline industry, and airline stewardesses are carefully selected with this fact in mind. However, when we board a jet at an airport, we find ourselves praying for the success of the decision maker who selected the pilot. Clearly, different values may be attached to the outcomes of different placement or selection assignments within a given program. The task of the decision maker is to collate the predictions from a priori and assessment data with the values placed on the several possible outcomes in such a way as to maximize the overriding purpose of the organization for which he is working.

The Nature of Decision Theory

Modern decision theory owes a great debt to the late Abraham Wald, whose formalization of the decision process has had far-reaching applications in statistics and the behavioral sciences. Cronbach and Gleser (1965) were the first to emphasize that personnel decisions represent a special case within Wald's (1950) more general statistical model. By considering the total contribution of a test in making decisions over *all* outcomes, Cronbach and Gleser (1965) have arrived at highly challenging implications for such things as test design, construction of selection batteries, the meaning of validity coefficients, and the use of tests for selection. It is not our intent to give a comprehensive review of statistical decision theory, game theory, or even Cronbach and Gleser's contribution to the science of personnel decisions. What we will emphasize are some of Cronbach and Gleser's results, and the serious reader is directed to the original work.[1]

---

1. The original monograph (Cronbach and Gleser, 1957) has been revised to include relevant papers by others and a guide to recent literature (Cronbach and Gleser, 1965). A paperback edition of the revision is also available.

Figure 6.1 is a schematic representation of the decision process as it will be conceived in this chapter. As previously indicated, *information* about an individual consists of any data prior to testing, as well as assessment data (test scores, peer ratings, interviewer's impressions) which are believed to be relevant to the personnel assignment problem at hand. The relationship between this kind of information and outcome (at the right of the diagram) is usually thought of as "validity" information, $r_{yy'}$. This relationship is not depicted in the diagram, because validity information is only one kind of information entering into the box labeled "strategy." A *strategy* is a formal rule for arriving at decisions, which indicates the steps to be taken in light of the information available. The *decision* is a course of action that is dictated by the strategy.

The *outcome* of a decision is a situation that arises when certain actions are taken in the face of certain states of nature. Let us consider a very simple decision process in order to illustrate the general nature of outcomes. An individual living in a semitropical climate faces each day the problem of whether or not to wear a raincoat. Let us assume that he adopts the following rule, or strategy, for arriving at this decision: "If the weather report on the radio indicates that the probability of precipitation is .50 or greater, wear a raincoat. If the probability is less than .50, don't wear it." The decisions or *actions* (wear, not wear) dictated by this strategy and the possible *states of nature* (rain, not rain) in which actions are taken result in the following *outcomes*:

	Actions	
States of nature	Not wear coat	Wear coat
Rain	O_3 = Wet	O_1 = Dry
Not rain	O_4 = Comfortable	O_2 = Hot

This example shows that a distinctive outcome is associated with each of the actions under each of the possible states of nature. To identify these distinctive outcomes, we have labeled them O_1 = Dry, O_2 = Hot, O_3 = Wet, and O_4 = Comfortable. If the individual keeps track of the frequency of these outcomes over the course of a year, he may express each outcome as a *probability*, by dividing its frequency by the total number of actions taken during the year ($N = 365$).

The admission or nonadmission of students to college is a familiar personnel decision problem. Scholastic aptitude tests are frequently employed in an attempt to distinguish those students who are likely to graduate from

Data   Decision   Outcome   Utility

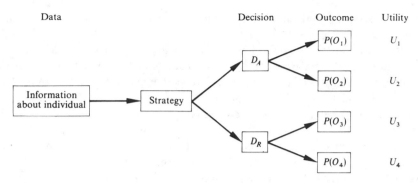

Fig. 6.1 Schematic representation of the decision process.

those who are not. A typical personnel decision strategy might be as follows: "If an individual's aptitude test score falls above a certain level, admit him to college. If his score falls below, reject him." The actions (accept, reject) and the possible states of nature (graduate, not graduate) result in the following outcomes:

	Actions	
States of nature	Reject	Accept
Graduate	O_3	O_1
Not graduate	O_4	O_2

Again, there are four distinctive outcomes: O_1 indicates that a student graduates successfully from college; O_2 that a student fails to complete his college career; O_3 that a student would have graduated if he had been admitted; and O_4 that a rejected student would not have graduated. A properly conducted validity study, in which all applicants are admitted to college, regardless of their aptitude test scores, would yield frequencies for each of the four outcomes. Dividing these frequencies by the total number of subjects would yield the probability values indicated in Figure 6.1: $P(O_1)$, $P(O_2)$, $P(O_3)$, and $P(O_4)$. Such probabilities would be of considerable use in deciding on an appropriate strategy for college admissions.

Associated with each outcome in Figure 6.1 is a *utility* value that indicates the relative worth or favorableness of an outcome for an institution (or for the individuals involved). The most favorable outcome in our example is O_1, in which an accepted applicant becomes a college graduate. Since some outcomes are more favorable than others, it is likely that we would wish to adopt a strategy that enabled us to maximize the probability of *favorable* outcomes.

Our discussion thus far has deviated only slightly from the classical description of the personnel assignment problem (Thorndike, 1949). It is the unique contribution of decision theory to personnel selection (as applied by Cronbach and Gleser) to insist on a thoroughgoing and explicit analysis of the adjective "favorable," which we have just slipped past the reader. In speaking of the "likelihood" of an outcome, we use the word "probability," which is assumed to have a uniform and precise meaning for all readers. When we associate that word with an event, we do not mean that it is "highly likely" or "pretty likely" to occur. We mean, for example, that the event in question is expected to occur 37 times out of 100 ($P = .37$), 22 times out of 100 ($P = .22$), or not at all ($P = .00$). Similarly, when we speak of the "favorableness" of an outcome (*utility*), we are hoping eventually to rise above such expressions as "very desirable" and "not too desirable" and to replace them with such units of value as $2,371.22, $1.98, or 1.58 utiles. As a matter of fact, the evaluation of the utility of an outcome can be achieved precisely only to the extent that such "utility scales" can be developed.

As Cronbach and Gleser (1965, p. 121) note, "The assignment of values to outcomes is the Achilles' heel of decision theory." Let us anticipate the conclusion of our discussion for a moment and state that the goal of a satisfactory decision function (strategy) is one that maximizes the expected utilities of outcomes across all possible outcomes. That is, we hope to arrive at a strategy which will, on the average, emphasize decisions which have the highest utility for the institution or individuals involved. There are two requisites for this goal. First, we must be able to specify exactly the utilities involved (represented in Figure 6.1 by U_1, U_2, U_3, and U_4). Second, in order to optimize an *average* of utilities, such values must be expressed in terms of comparable units which permit averaging. The problem is two-fold: (a) devising methods for encouraging consistent introspection on the part of institutional officials with respect to "intangibles" and (b) scaling these intangible values in such a way that they may enter into mathematical computations. To further complicate the issue, some decision situations require the reconciliation of institutional values with those of individuals living within the society (American Psychological Association, 1965; Arrow, 1963).

For many business and industrial situations, the "dollar criterion" appears to be the most appropriate standard by which the value of personnel decisions may be assessed (Brogden and Taylor, 1950). However, for certain other settings (especially psychiatric), the use of such a crass yardstick for evaluating the impact of personnel decisions does not seem appropriate.

Even within the field of economics, measures of "subjective utility" are frequently preferable to measures of "objective utility" (Edwards, 1961).

There are two basic methods of determining utility functions, which more or less parallel the differences between introspective and behavioristic psychology. The introspective (explicit) approach asks the subject how much money is worth to him (Stevens, 1959) or how much an institutional value is worth in business (Churchman and Ackoff, 1954). Behavioristic approaches attempt to infer values from the decisions actually made by an individual (Davidson, Suppes, and Siegel, 1957; Edwards, 1961). Neither approach has proved entirely satisfactory thus far, and furthermore, the two do not give equivalent results.

Another issue in utility analysis centers around the relative merits of ordinal versus cardinal (numerical) utility scales. Although cardinal units of measurement seem to be most satisfactory for a situation which requires the maximization of averages, ordinal scales appear to be generally more useful (Edwards, 1954). Without denying the central importance of utility measurement to the personnel decision process, nor the very primitive current state of such measurements, we consider it appropriate to point out that the battleground of current theoretical warfare is somewhat removed from the practical applications with which we are here concerned. That is, whereas economists, statisticians, and the majority of psychologists are concerned with developing models which will describe (explain) the economic, political, or social behavior of man, we are primarily concerned with helping decision makers to behave rationally, regardless of whether their behavior is rational in other areas.

Having indicated the importance of utility measurement, we now return to Figure 6.1, where the probability of an outcome, $P(O_1)$, is evaluated in terms of the utility for that outcome, U_1. Decision making, for example, in the college admission situation we have been discussing, can now be seen as an attempt to maximize institutional gain across a variety of outcomes by choosing a strategy which takes into account not only the probability of the outcome but the utility associated with it. There are many ways in which utility can be maximized, depending on the risks which the individual or institution prefers to take. The science of such risk-taking behavior owes much to the work of von Neumann and Morgenstern (1947), who pioneered the area currently referred to as "game theory." In general, institutions will prefer to maximize their overall utility across a variety of outcomes. The appropriate strategy for this situation would be one which maximizes a function involving the sum of the products of each outcome probability and its associated utility: $\sum U_i \cdot P(O_i)$.

In the gaming situations described by von Neumann and Morgenstern, the individual faces an uncertain situation involving a competitive opponent who will attempt to defeat him at every turn. In such a situation, where only one person can win (zero-sum game), conservatism is an appropriate strategy. That is, the player should adopt a strategy which attempts to minimize large losses (minimax) or, alternatively, maximize small gains (maximin). Wald (1950) has interpreted the scientific enterprise as a two-person zero-sum game between the scientist and nature. Under the assumption that nature will attempt to mislead us at every opportunity, Wald suggests a conservative strategy for making statistical evaluations of the outcome of experiments. His point of view has been challenged as unrealistic, since nature is presumably indifferent to the consequences of our scientific enterprise. Similarly, most personnel assignment situations do not seem to involve open warfare between the decision maker and his outcomes. The most appropriate strategy here seems to be one which attempts to maximize overall utility with an emphasis on production. We will encounter exceptions to this strategy, however, in realistic military selection situations in which a war "game" is actually involved. Within this context, the assignment of both counter-espionage agents and Peace Corps volunteers may be viewed as situations in which the conservative minimax strategy is an appropriate one.

SELECTION, MULTIPLE SELECTION, AND CLASSIFICATION

Personnel decisions are made in a variety of different contexts, and these contexts may be classified on the basis of many parameters, which vary from one type of decision-making situation to another (Cronbach and Gleser, 1965). For the sake of simplicity, we may single out two characteristics of decision problems: (a) what the *number* of different positions available is and (b) whether *rejection* is a permissible option. With respect to the number of positions available, it is convenient to distinguish situations in which only one kind of position is available from those in which two or more kinds are open. With respect to the second characteristic, either applicants can be rejected, or all candidates must be hired. Figure 6.2 depicts the four possible situations that are defined by joint consideration of number of positions and the rejection option.

	Rejection allowed	All Ss retained
One position	Selection	(*Acceptance*)
Two or more positions	Multiple selection	Classification

Fig. 6.2 The major personnel decision problems.

When only one position is available and rejection is allowed, we speak of *selection*. When two or more positions are available and rejection is allowed, we speak of *multiple selection*. When two or more positions are available and all subjects are retained, we speak of *classification*. When only one position is available and all subjects are retained, no decision problem exists, and we may speak of *acceptance*. The category of acceptance is less trivial than it sounds, and although it will not be formally treated as a decision problem, it should always be kept in mind as an alternative to selection. When the number of applicants is close to the number of jobs and when training procedures are inexpensive, it may be appropriate to accept all and see how they actually perform on the job. The possibility of also testing everyone should not be automatically ruled out, since testing may provide a unique opportunity to gather the kind of realistic validity data which is seldom available.

Cronbach and Gleser (1965) have emphasized a number of additional considerations which characterize, in more detail, a given personnel decision situation. The values or utilities which are maximized in a decision function may be oriented toward an *institution* or toward a single *individual*. Institutional values (broadly conceived) will be our main concern here, since it is only such specialized situations as counseling or vocational guidance which require maximization of a single individual's welfare. As a matter of fact, the extension of decision theory to such individual cases may not be appropriate, since the decisions faced are not repeatable and it is not clear across which class of events utility is maximized. A more germane parameter of a decision situation has to do with whether or not a *quota* is imposed on the treatments to which individuals are assigned. The selection paradigm which sets fixed proportions on the number of individuals who may be accepted has important implications for the usefulness of a test or assessment procedure of a given level of validity (Taylor and Russell, 1939). Similarly, in multiple selection and classification, fixed quotas in one or more of the different treatments involved will affect the manner in which decisions are made about individuals.

In some decision situations, a single individual may be assigned to more than one treatment so that the optimization problem becomes a complex one. Most of the personnel decisions we will consider involve assigning individuals to single treatments. It should be borne in mind, however, that there are other specialized situations, such as academic advising, in which single individuals may be considering different combinations of *multiple treatments*. The nature of the data on which decisions are based affects the decision process, and here we may distinguish between situations in which decisions are made on the basis of univariate data and those in which decisions are made on the basis of multivariate data. In practice, situations involving multivariate data are simplified by combining such data (e.g., via multiple-regression equations) in such a way as to provide a single score on which decisions may be based. Although this procedure is more practical, there is no reason to assume it is necessarily the best.

Cronbach and Gleser distinguish between *static* and *sequential* decision strategies. In a static (single-stage) decision strategy, the individual is assigned to a treatment (or rejected) and left in this state regardless of his future performance. Sequential (multiple-stage) strategies provide the option of making investigatory decisions to obtain additional information prior to a terminal decision. The many advantages of sequential decision strategies appear not to have been fully recognized in practice. A final, and perhaps most important, distinction of Cronbach and Gleser's has to do with *fixed* versus *adaptive* treatment procedures. In the past, the most common role of the psychologist in institutional decisions has been strictly that of a selection or classification specialist. Once a terminal decision has been reached, the individual is assigned to a fixed treatment, under which he must swim or sink. Adaptations of treatments (i.e., fitting the job to the man) have traditionally been the concern of educators and human engineers of one sort or another. Cronbach (1957) has convincingly called attention to the fact that selection or classification may be greatly improved where treatment adaptations are possible. To the extent that adaptations of the treatment are possible, the role of selection in a decision process may be minimized.

CLASSICAL VALIDITY

One index of the worth of a psychological test or assessment procedure is the predictive validity of an instrument or a battery of instruments for forecasting criterion performance. As we noted in preceding chapters, such indices as the square of the correlation coefficient and the standard error of estimate indicate the extent to which such prediction is possible in a given situation. Although the multiple-regression equation forms the basic model for selection, multiple selection, and classification, its implementation varies with the different decisions required by each of these situations.

Selection

In the basic paradigm of selection a subgroup of applicants, considered qualified for a single job, is selected from a total pool of applicants. An attempt is made to forecast the criterion performance of all applicants by means of a selection battery which orders the applicants in terms of their probable degree of success on the job. Tests and assessment procedures are sought which have high correlations with criterion performance, r_{xy}, and low correlations among themselves, $r_{x_1 x_2}$. The combination of these measures into a regression equation yields a single composite score for each individual which may be expressed by:

$$y' = b_1x_1 + b_2x_2 + \cdots + b_nx_n.$$

Here we have n predictors, each weighted in terms of its correlation with the criterion and its independence from other predictors. Additional predictors may forecast different components of criterion variance and lead to greater accuracy of prediction. However, for most assessment situations, it is not likely that more than three or four truly independent predictors will be found. In terms of classical validity, the "best" selection battery is that which yields the highest correlation between predicted and obtained criterion scores, $r_{yy'}$, and hence yields the fewest errors in selection.

The weights which enter into a multiple-regression equation are determined entirely by statistical considerations. Tests which have high correlations with criterion performance and are relatively independent of other predictors are given the largest weights. Tests which have relatively low correlations with criterion performance or are highly related to other predictors are given correspondingly smaller weights. Although the statistical weightings are constant for all individuals, the test scores, $x_1, x_2, \ldots x_n$, will vary widely from individual to individual. Hence it is possible for individuals with widely differing profiles of predictor scores to obtain identical scores for the criterion being predicted.

Let us assume that we are selecting pilots on the basis of a test of "pilot aptitude," x_1, and a test of visual acuity, x_2. The test of pilot aptitude may be the "best" predictor of pilot success because of its high correlation with the criterion. Since there may be little variability in visual acuity among applicants for pilot training, the correlation of this measure with the criterion may be slight, though positive. This relationship is expressed by the regression equation

$$y' = .40x_1 + .10x_2.$$

If Applicant A has acceptable visual acuity but only modest pilot aptitude, his equation may be

$$y'_a = .40(5) + .10(20) = 4.00.$$

If Applicant B has greater pilot aptitude but is functionally blind without glasses, his regression equation may be

$$y'_b = .40(10) + .10(0) = 4.00.$$

Despite the modest size of the regression weight for visual acuity, which is given by the statistical solution of the regression equation, we must consider visual acuity "important," since pilots with poor vision would make decidedly poor risks. Applicants A and B are clearly not equivalent in their potential for flying success, despite the fact that the multiple-regression equation for each yields the same score for the predicted criterion.

The type of regression equation we have been describing allows for a *compensatory* interaction of abilities. Individuals scoring low on one predictive index may compensate by scoring high on another. Although such compensation is often permissible, we frequently encounter situations, such as the example just given, in which weights determined by purely statistical methods are not satisfactory. An alternative to the "compensatory" model is one which has been termed the "multiple-cutoff" approach. When a given predictor is considered "important" (independently of its psychometric properties), a *minimal level* of acceptable performance is set, and all applicants below this level are automatically rejected. Selection then takes place within the group of applicants who meet minimal standards on the basis of successive predictors.

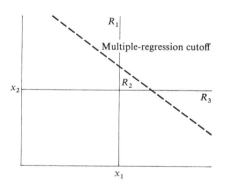

Fig. 6.3 Decisions made by multiple-cutoff and multiple-regression models. (After Thorndike, 1949)

Figure 6.3 is a scatter plot (with observations omitted) of the joint distributions of Tests x_1 and x_2. In the first stages of selection, all subjects who failed to score above the minimal cutoff on Test x_1 are eliminated from further consideration. In the second stage, all subjects who failed to score above the minimal cutoff on Test x_2 are eliminated. Although this illustration involves the use of only two predictors, subsequent selection could occur by setting up additional hurdles with predetermined cutoffs. In the example given, subjects are retained only if they fall in the upper right quadrant, defined by the intersection of cutting scores of the two selection tests. To compare this selection model with the more usual multiple-regression model, we have inserted a broken line to represent the multiple-regression cutoff[2] which might be employed on the basis of the equation $y' = b_1 x_1 + b_2 x_2$.

A comparison of cases selected by the two methods indicates that there are basically three kinds of situations in which the models yield different decisions. Subjects falling in the triangular area indicated by the letter R_1 are rejected by the multiple-cutoff approach and accepted by the usual multiple-regression approach. These subjects have extremely high aptitude on the second test, x_2, but fail to meet the minimal qualifications of the first screening test x_1. Subjects falling in the triangular area represented by R_2 are accepted by the multiple-cutoff approach but rejected by the usual multiple-regression procedure. Such subjects were able to "squeeze through" the multiple-cutoff procedure, but their overall capability was judged to be insufficiently high by the multiple-regression model. Subjects falling in the triangular area represented by the letter R_3 are accepted by the multiple-regression model but rejected by the multiple-cutoff model on the basis of insufficient potential on Test x_2. In the present example, the multiple-cutoff approach is the more conservative of the two. Reduction of cutting scores in the multiple-cutoff could of course result in much less conservative selection.

In general, no satisfactory analytic solution has been developed for the multiple-cutoff model. Cutoff scores must be determined by trial and error on a fixed sample on the basis of numerous external considerations, such as the supply of candidates available and the kinds of predictive errors that will be tolerated. Fixed cutting scores for a given sample are apt to be inappropriate for other subject groups, and the extent of such shrinkage cannot be estimated so precisely as in the multiple-regression model. When multiple-cutoff selection occurs on more than two or three variables, determination of optimum cutoffs becomes extremely laborious and generality to new samples is even more unlikely.

In terms of such considerations as flexibility, efficiency, and preciseness, the multiple-cutoff procedure cannot be considered a serious competitor to the multiple-regression model (Thorndike, 1949). The use of the multiple-cutoff model has occasionally been defended on the grounds of its superiority in selection situations in which predictor-criterion relationships are non-linear in form. As indicated in Chapter 2, multiple-regression prediction is not limited to linear relationships. Further, the replicability of nonlinear relations from sample to sample must always be subjected to careful scrutiny (Thorndike, 1949). In our original example of pilot selection, we encountered

---

2. This line is not to be confused with the regression line. It represents the *minimum* score necessary to qualify for selection. This single score may be achieved by many different combinations of the two weighted predictor scores, as illustrated in the figure.

a situation in which statistical weights were not commensurate with administrative decisions. Such a situation does not necessarily call for an abandonment of the mathematical model of prediction. Rather it might suggest a different decision strategy for dealing with the data yielded by the model.

Multiple Selection

In multiple selection, applicants are simultaneously evaluated for assignment to two or more treatments. Under this definition, multiple selection may be thought of as the general case of selection. Although the decision strategy for multiple selection may be based on several additional parameters, the basic statistical model is the same. One method of coping with the problem of multiple treatments is to develop a *separate* selection battery for each treatment. Thus, if we face the problem of selecting applicants for admission to graduate programs in experimental psychology and clinical psychology, we might develop one battery for predicting success in experimental psychology based on Tests x_1, x_2, and x_3 and a separate battery for forecasting success in clinical psychology based on Tests x_4, x_5, and x_6. The goal in each case would be simply to determine optimum weights for each of the batteries separately. Applicants to the two curricula would be given different sets of three tests, and their success would be forecasted from two separate regression models. In practice, when several treatments are being considered simultaneously, they often have features in common. Even when this is not strictly true, considerations of economy have led to attempts to develop a single test battery which would serve several purposes.

Let us represent the treatment of admission to a graduate program in experimental psychology by A and the treatment of admission to graduate work in clinical psychology by B (many readers will of course recognize these treatments as *investigatory* decisions). The multiple-regression equations may be represented as follows:

$$y_a' = {}_ab_1x_1 + {}_ab_1x_2 + \cdots + {}_ab_nx_n,$$
$$y_b' = {}_bb_1x_1 + {}_bb_2x_2 + \cdots + {}_bb_nx_n.$$

Because there may well be common elements in the criterion components in experimental and clinical psychology, we are attempting here to forecast success in both fields by use of the same set of tests, $x_1, x_2, \ldots x_n$. We also anticipate that these components of criterion behavior will be *differentially* related to the tests so that separate regression weights are developed for the two selection problems. The subscript preceding the regression weight indicates that the regression weight was determined from an analysis of the relevance of that predictor to the treatment in question. The weight ${}_ab_1$ indicates the amount by which Test x_1 is to be weighted in selecting for experimental psychologists. The weight $_bb_1$ indicates the contribution of Test x_1 to the selection of clinical psychologists.

When one is assembling predictors for the single-treatment situation, it is often appropriate to include samples of behavior that are as close to the actual criterion behavior as possible. The extreme example of this type of predictor is the "job sample," which attempts to simulate, insofar as possible, the actual working conditions of the treatment. Where selection must be concerned with two or more treatments, job-sample approaches often introduce an element of specificity which seriously limits the usefulness of the battery for multiple selection. Thus, in our example, a measure of "interpersonal sensitivity" might prove to be of value in the selection of clinical psychology graduate students but of little use in the selection of successful experimental psychologists. For this reason, tests and assessment procedures included in multiple-selection batteries more often represent attempts to tap broad abilities or traits which are thought to be widely applicable. The use of factored ability tests and factored personality inventories in multiple selection would be one such example. Although such general traits or abilities may be present in many criterion behaviors, there is no guarantee that they will be of importance in any one of them. Therefore, assembling tests for a multiple-selection battery is often a compromise between job sample and general trait measurement. When the measurement of general traits proves unprofitable, the possibility of developing separate selection batteries for each treatment should be given serious consideration. There is nothing in the multiple-selection *model* which requires the use of a single battery for different selection problems.

The shortcomings of the multiple-cutoff model for single-treatment selection are magnified in multiple selection. As the number of treatments increases, additional predictors are usually required, and the clerical labor alone may become prohibitive. Although the determination of optimal regression weights for many variables and many treatments once posed a serious computational problem in multiple-regression approaches, there are few practical multiple-selection situations which would seriously tax the capacity of modern computers.

In our discussion of the multiple-selection model, we have implicitly assumed that success on all treatments is *equally* relevant, and we have made no mention of such restrictions as treatment quotas and the optimum utilization of available manpower. When these restrictions enter into multiple selection, they may have profound effects on the ultimate decision strategy. As in the case of simple selection, however, such considerations are external to the mathematical model of multiple selection and must be treated in a broader context of decision making.

Classification

In classification, the rejection option is not available, and the number of individuals to be assigned to jobs or treatments is equal to the number of applicants available. Such a problem is typically found in military, educational, and other settings involving a "captive" population. The question of a minimal level of qualification for assignment to a given treatment is less important here than in multiple selection, since all individuals must be assigned, regardless of their quality. To maximize the overall effectiveness of the organization, one must distribute the available talent in such a way that each individual is assigned to that treatment for which he shows the greatest aptitude *relative* to all other treatments.

"Talent" may be thought of as a normally distributed continuum ranging from Renaissance Men to a group of individuals who seem unable to do anything well. Closer scrutiny of the pattern of talents of the latter group may reveal that, level notwithstanding, they are able to perform some tasks less poorly than others. It is clearly in the overall interests of the organization to assign these individuals to tasks for which they are *relatively* qualified. When only two treatments are available for classification assignment, an analytic solution to the problem exists. Unfortunately, the majority of classification problems encountered will involve many more than two treatments, and the two-treatment model has not as yet been generalized to these cases. Nevertheless, careful consideration of the two-treatment model will yield insights into the nature of the problems involved in the n-treatment case.

Where two treatments are available (A and B), but no rejection option is allowed, the quantities to be maximized are no longer simply $r_{y_a y_a'}$ and $r_{y_b y_b'}$ as was true in multiple selection. With no rejection option, it is necessary to develop a composite score that will indicate an individual's *relative* fitness for Job A over Job B. Such an index may be a difference score expressing the amount by which the individual's performance in Job A is predicted to exceed his performance in Job B: $D = y_a' - y_b'$. Given such an index of expected differential success, it is possible to order all applicants, in terms of their scores on this index, from high to low. If half the applicants are to be assigned to Job A and the remaining half to Job B, the 50 percent of applicants with the highest D scores are simply assigned to Job A. Variations in quotas for Jobs A and B are reflected in the proportion of individuals with high D scores who are assigned to the first treatment.

The multiple-regression model based on *differential* performance takes a form different from that of the more usual model involved in multiple selection:

$$(y_a' - y_b') = (_ab_1 - _bb_1)x_1 + (_ab_2 - _bb_2)x_2 + \cdots + (_ab_n - _bb_n)x_n.$$

In classification, test scores are weighted by the differences between the regression weights for Job A and those for Job B. Thus assessment procedures which have high and identical regression weights for the two treatments will not be weighted heavily in this expression. Tests which have moderate but different regression weights for the two treatments will be given more weight. The desirability of employing independent, "factor-pure" predictor variables, noted in the context of multiple selection, is even more apparent in classification. In multiple selection, we had the option of developing separate test batteries for each treatment. This is obviously not feasible for classification, since differential performance must be predicted. Similarly, whereas the multiple-cutoff approach was a possible option for selection and multiple selection, the classification problem requires a continuous score for purposes of ordering individuals in terms of their differential proficiency.

The quantity which is maximized, in the least-squares sense, by the expression above is the correlation between predicted differences and actual differences in performance on the two criterion treatments. Following Thorndike (1949), we may express this validity estimate by the formula for the correlation of sums and differences:

$$r_{(y_a' - y_b')(y_a - y_b)} = \frac{(r_{y_a' y_a} - r_{y_a' y_b}) + (r_{y_b' y_b} - r_{y_b' y_a})}{\sqrt{1 - r_{y_a' y_b'}} \sqrt{1 - r_{y_a y_b}}}.$$

The correlation between predicted and obtained differential performance in two treatments is a function of the difference between treatment-*relevant* validity coefficients ($r_{y_a' y_a}$, $r_{y_b' y_b}$) and *irrelevant* validity coefficients ($r_{y_a' y_b}$, $r_{y_b' y_a}$). The actual level of the relevant validity coefficients is less important than the size of the differences between the relevant and irrelevant validity coefficients. An examination of the denominator of the validity coefficient for the classification problem reveals a somewhat paradoxical relationship. High correlations between predictors, $r_{y_a' y_b'}$, and between criterion scores, $r_{y_a y_b}$, tend to *increase* the validity of classification. Thorndike provides us with the following explanation.

In using scores for classification purposes, it is desirable that the errors of measurement and other completely non-functional variance in the several score composites be as highly correlated as possible. *This non-functional variance tends thereby to be held constant for the different job categories and to be more or less partialed out of any difference score.* (Thorndike, 1949, p. 225.)

The two-treatment classification model we have been discussing is unrealistic, not only in terms of the number of treatments available, but also in terms of such realistic constraints as treatment quotas and the differential importance (utilities) of the treatments. As we have already indicated, the accurate classification of pilots may be of much greater importance to an airline than the accurate classification of ancillary personnel. As with multiple selection, such parameters must be considered along with the results of the multiple-regression analysis, although the situation with regard to classification is somewhat embarrassing since analytic models have yet to be developed for complex situations. In practice, a few rules of thumb have been developed as guidelines. For example, when treatments can be ordered in terms of importance (utility), successive selection in terms of the criticalness of the treatment may be an optimum strategy (Flanagan, 1948). Again, such considerations are more in the realm of decision making (to be considered later) than in the realm of classical validity.

Differences in application of the multiple-regression model to selection, multiple selection, and classification are recapitulated in Table 6.1. *Selection* involves the optimal weighting of a set of independent predictors to maximize the correlation between predicted and actual criterion performance in a single treatment. *Multiple selection* may involve the development of two or more independent selection batteries, but more typically it involves the use of a single battery for two or more purposes. Again, correlation between predicted and obtained criterion performance in each treatment is maximized separately for all treatments available. In *classification*, the differences in performance among two or more treatments must be optimized in such a way that predicted differences are highly correlated with actual criterion differences in performance. In the classification paradigm, the actual level of validity coefficients is less important than the size of the difference between relevant and irrelevant (other treatments) validity coefficients. Whereas analytic solutions have been developed for maximizing the classical validity coefficients for selection and multiple selection, the classification model has not as yet been satisfactorily generalized. External parameters, such as quotas, utilities, and worker satisfaction, are problems of decision theory rather than of classical test theory. Such considerations will be discussed in later sections.

Table 6.1 Applications of the multiple-regression model in classical validity

Selection:	$y'_a = {}_ab_1x_1 + {}_ab_2x_2 + \cdots + {}_ab_nx_n$
Multiple selection:	$y'_a = {}_ab_1x_1 + {}_ab_2x_2 + \cdots + {}_ab_nx_n$
	$y'_b = {}_bb_1x_1 + {}_bb_2x_2 + \cdots + {}_bb_nx_n$
Classification:	$(y'_a - y'_b) = ({}_ab_1 - {}_bb_1)x_1 + ({}_ab_2 - {}_bb_2)x_2$
	$+ \cdots + ({}_ab_n - {}_bb_n)x_n$

DISCRIMINATIVE EFFICIENCY

Classification of Test Predictions by Their Outcomes

Although the classical validity coefficient, $r_{yy'}$, we have been discussing is obviously a useful index, there are many ways in which it falls short of telling the whole story of predictive success. From a practical point of view, the *number of correct decisions* made by a psychological test or assessment procedure is a more important piece of information than the degree of association which exists between predicted and obtained criterion scores. The more or less standard terminology for discussing the outcomes of test predictions will be presented in this section. A slight but useful distinction will also be made between outcomes expressed as frequencies and outcomes expressed as probabilities.

Outcomes Expressed as Frequencies

A multiple-regression equation gives rise to a continuous distribution of predicted outcomes, y', which are "cut" at some point as a practical method of making personnel decisions. The distribution of actual criterion performance (when available) is similarly cut at some point to enable a distinction between "successful and "unsuccessful" performance. The joint frequency distribution of predicted and actual criterion scores is presented in Figure 6.4, where the actual cases in the scatter plot have been omitted in the interests of readability. This figure is simply the familiar scatter plot of the regression of obtained on predicted criterion scores.

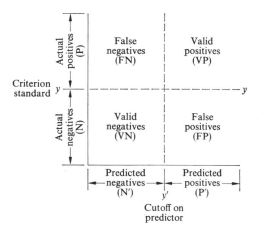

Fig. 6.4 Classification of test predictions by their outcomes.

Four possible outcomes of a prediction may be delineated. When success is predicted and success results, we refer to the individuals so classified as *valid positives* (VP). When success is predicted and failure results, we speak of *false positives* (FP). When failure is predicted and failure occurs, we have a group of *valid negatives* (VN). And finally, when failure is predicted but success obtains, we are dealing with *false negatives* (FN). In Figure 6.4, these various outcomes are represented in frequency form. Thus the symbol

VP stands for the number, or frequency, of individuals who may be classified as falling in the upper right quadrant.

Since the polarity of the outcomes above (positive versus negative) may be confusing, a note on the origin of this terminology may be in order. The use of the word "positive" to indicate the *presence* of a trait or characteristic is a convention borrowed from the terminology of medical laboratory tests. When results of a laboratory examination (Wasserman positive) suggest the presence of disease (syphilis), the diagnosis may be correct (valid positive), or a false alarm may have been raised (false positive). This medical analogy has been carried over into the field of clinical psychology in the diagnosis of such "diseases" as schizophrenia. For consistency, we shall employ this terminology to refer to the presence of *desirable* traits or characteristics as well (creativity, success, etc.).

Returning to Figure 6.4, we reemphasize the distinction between the cutoff on the predictor variable, y', and the cutoff on the criterion measure, y. The cutoff on the predictor represents a more or less arbitrary score above which success is predicted and below which failure is predicted. It can be varied by moving it to the right (more conservative prediction) or to the left (less conservative). Once the cutoff score is set, however, definite numbers of predictions of success and failure are made. As will become apparent later, the number of predictions of success is usually limited by the number of applicants that can be hired, the number of patients that can be treated, etc. As Figure 6.4 shows, the total number of *predicted* positives, P', may be calculated from: VP + FP. Similarly, the total number of *predicted* negatives, N', is given by: FN + VN.

The cutoff on the criterion measure is made with reference to external standards which define performance above a certain level as successful and below as failure. Because criterion standards are set by others, they are often regarded as absolute or "real," as opposed to arbitrary. In principle, such standards may be quite arbitrary, although in practice, they should usually be regarded as fixed and not subject to manipulation. Thus we speak of the number of "actual positives," P, that exist in the total sample and may calculate it from: P = FN + VP. Similarly, we may calculate the number of "actual negatives," N, that exist in the total sample from: N = VN + FP.

An alternative representation of the outcomes of test prediction is illustrated in Figure 6.5. Here we consider the frequency distributions of two kinds of people, namely, actual positives (successes) and actual negatives (failures). Figure 6.5 indicates that the success of a psychological test or assessment procedure in separating positives from negatives is a function of the *degree of overlap* that exists between the two hypothetical distributions under consideration. When the overlap of the two distributions is complete, the predictor battery cannot improve on the strategy of flipping a coin for assignment purposes. When there is no overlap between the two parent

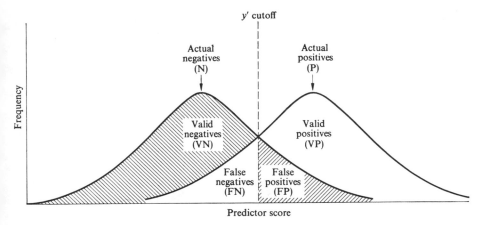

Fig. 6.5 Alternative representation of classification of test predictions by their outcomes.

populations, there exists a cutting score on the predictor battery which will make possible the complete separation of the two groups and, consequently, perfectly accurate prediction. The extent to which a predictor battery is able to separate and classify outcomes accurately (valid positive and valid negative) is referred to as the *discriminative efficiency* of the battery. Because the correlation coefficient does not express the degree of overlap that exists between the two populations to be distinguished, indices of discriminative efficiency are considered more practical guidelines for personnel decisions.

Outcomes Expressed as Probabilities

Thus far, we have emphasized the *frequencies* of occurrence of each of the four possible outcomes of test prediction. Such frequencies reflect the total sample size, and they would obviously vary in samples of different size. To facilitate comparison of prediction outcomes in samples of varying size, it is preferable to express frequencies as simple *probabilities* or proportions of the total sample size. One does so by dividing the frequency of a given outcome by the total number of people in the sample. Thus the probability of occurrence of a valid positive, for example, is given by: $P(VP) = VP/(P + N)$. This probabilistic representation of the outcomes of test prediction is given in Figure 6.6. When outcomes are expressed as probabilities [$P(VP)$, $P(FP)$, $P(VN)$, $P(FN)$], they are referred to as "hit rates." Such hit rates reflect the "batting average" of a psychological test in a given prediction game and may be compared directly from one sample to another.

The row and column totals of Figure 6.6 are also expressed as probabilities. Because these marginal totals are of critical importance in the evaluation of test predictions, they have been given special names. The

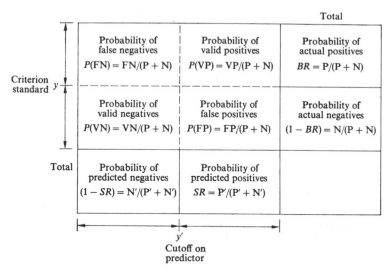

Fig. 6.6 Outcomes of test predictions expressed as probabilities.

probability or proportion of actual positives that exist in the total sample of applicants is called the *base rate* (*BR*). This probability may be calculated directly $[BR = P/(P + N)]$ or from the probabilities of two outcomes $[BR = P(FN) + P(VP)]$. The expression "base rate" usually has reference to the base rate of the *positive* class. The probability or base rate of failure in the total sample is given by the expression: $1 - BR$.

The probability or proportion of predicted positives among the total sample of applicants is called the *selection ratio* (*SR*). This probability may be calculated directly $[SR = P'/(P' + N')]$ or from the probabilities of two outcomes $[SR = P(VP) + P(FP)]$. The importance of these two marginal probabilities, base rate and selection ratio, cannot be overemphasized. But before we turn to a detailed consideration of the influence of these two probabilities on the outcomes of prediction, it will be necessary to review some simple algebraic relationships.

Calculating Validity Coefficients from Outcomes[3]

Figure 6.6 may be thought of as a 2 × 2 contingency table that shows the degree of association between predicted and obtained criterion scores. When

3. The computational approach presented here was suggested to the author by Lewis R. Goldberg. Those who are familiar with other expositions of this material (e.g., Meehl and Rosen, 1955) may appreciate the computational and conceptual simplicity of this particular approach.

two variables are expressed in dichotomous form (success-failure, select-reject), the correlation between them is given by the *phi coefficient*. A simplified computational formula for the phi coefficient (McNemar, 1969b, p. 225) is as follows:

$$\varphi_{yy'} = \frac{P(VP) - BR \cdot SR}{\sqrt{BR(1 - BR)SR(1 - SR)}}.$$

The value of $\varphi_{yy'}$ is identical to $r_{yy'}$ when the latter is computed on values of 0 and 1 for the two dichotomous variables.

The remarkable simplicity of the computational formula for $\varphi_{yy'}$ is due to the fact that the values in the 2×2 contingency table are not entirely independent of one another. In the first place, the values in adjacent rows and columns must sum to their marginal totals. More important, once the values of three outcomes are known, the fourth value is known—a situation referred to as "one degree of freedom." The computational formula for $\varphi_{yy'}$ capitalizes on these dependencies and permits the calculation of the validity coefficient from only three values: (1) the probability of a valid positive, $P(VP)$, (2) the base rate, BR, and (3) the selection ratio, SR.

There are other, more ominous, implications of the fact that one degree of freedom is involved in the contingency of predicted and actual outcomes. For example, *the marginal totals (BR and SR) constrain the degree of association that can exist between predicted and obtained outcomes.* A numerical example will clarify this point. Consider the situation in which $BR = SR = .60$ and its tabular representation:

	Reject	Accept	
	$P(FN)$	$P(VP)$	
Success			$BR = .60$
	$P(VN)$	$P(FP)$	
Failure			$1 - BR = .40$
	$1 - SR = .40$	$SR = .60$	

Perfect prediction of the criterion by test scores would obtain if the cell entries were

	P(FN)	P(VP)	
	.00	.60	$BR = .60$
	P(VN)	P(FP)	
	.40	.00	$1 - BR = .40$

$$1 - SR = .40 \qquad SR = .60$$

and

$$\varphi_{yy'} = \frac{P(VP) - BR \cdot SR}{\sqrt{BR(1 - BR)SR(1 - SR)}} = \frac{(.60) - (.60)(.60)}{\sqrt{(.60)(.40)(.60)(.40)}} = 1.00.$$

Now consider an extreme example, in which BR remains .60, but $SR = .01$. The *maximum* possible predictability in this situation is

	P(FN)	P(VP)	
	.59	.01	$BR = .60$
	P(VN)	P(FP)	
	.40	.00	$1 - BR = .40$

$$1 - SR = .99 \qquad SR = .01$$

and the *maximum phi* is

$$\varphi_{yy'} = \frac{(.01) - (.60)(.01)}{\sqrt{(.60)(.40)(.01)(.99)}} = .08.$$

Thus, regardless of the validity of a particular test in other situations (with other base rates and other selection ratios), the validity of *any* test in *this* situation ($BR = .60$; $SR = .01$) can never exceed $\varphi_{yy'} = .08$.

We will return to the implications of these marginal constraints on test validity several times during the course of the present chapter. For the moment, it can be stated that *a test or assessment procedure can achieve perfect validity* ($\varphi_{yy'} = 1.00$) *if, and only if, BR = SR*. As the base rate and selection ratio become more discrepant from each other, the potential of a test for making optimal decisions becomes more and more constrained.

Calculating Outcomes from Validity Coefficients

The computational formula for the phi coefficient,

$$\varphi_{yy'} = \frac{P(VP) - BR \cdot SR}{\sqrt{BR(1 - BR)SR(1 - SR)}},$$

can be solved for the probability of valid positives:

$$P(VP) = BR \cdot SR + \varphi_{yy'} \sqrt{BR(1 - BR)SR(1 - SR)}.$$

This expression is especially useful in evaluating the outcomes of test prediction. Given the validity of a test, $\varphi_{yy'}$, the base rate of the positive class, BR, and the proportion of individuals to be selected, SR, it is possible to specify completely the outcomes of prediction. For example, consider the following parameters: $\varphi_{yy'} = .30$, $BR = .50$, $SR = .50$. The value of $P(VP)$ may be obtained from

$$P(VP) = (.50)(.50) + (.30)\sqrt{(.50)(.50)(.50)(.50)} = .325.$$

The following values may now be entered in the contingency table.

P(FN)	*P*(VP)	
	.325	*BR* = .50
P(VN)	*P*(FP)	
		1 − *BR* = .50

1 − *SR* = .50   *SR* = .50

The remaining three cells may then be filled in by simple subtraction.

Probability tables can be easily transformed to frequency tables when a specific population is considered. For example, applying the proportions above to a population of one thousand applicants would yield the following frequency table.

	FN		VP
	175		325
	VN		FP
	325		175
	500	500	1000

Now that we have specified the computational mechanics of evaluating the outcomes of prediction, it is possible to return to the more substantive implications of base rates and selection ratios for assessment in general.

The Effects of Base Rates on Outcomes

The base rate of a sample indicates the number of positives that may be expected from a total sample of applicants. This quantity is determined by the nature of the applicant sample and therefore cannot be varied by statistical manipulations. The proportion of mentally retarded individuals (positives) one would expect to find in a state colony for mental retardates might be close to .99 (autistic children are occasionally misclassified). The proportion of mentally retarded individuals one would expect to find in a state university (contrary to faculty suspicions after examinations) must certainly be less than .01. In an outpatient diagnostic clinic specializing in mental retardation, the base rate of retardation might be close to .50. Such variations in base rates will have considerable effects on the outcomes of test prediction in these different settings.

Meehl and Rosen (1955) were the first to provide a formal statement of the effects of base rates on the outcomes of prediction. They called attention to the fact that validity coefficients reported in test manuals and in research articles have reference to selection in a population with a given base rate and that such validity coefficients should not be generalized to populations with markedly different base rates. An example, cited and analyzed by Meehl and Rosen, will serve as a concrete illustration of this principle.

Psychiatric Screening of Military Personnel

Danielson and Clark (1954) developed a personality scale to identify men who would not complete basic training in the Army because of psychiatric problems or unauthorized absences from training. The personality scale was administered to a group of 504 men, of whom 415 subsequently made an adequate adjustment to training and of whom 89 were later independently identified as psychiatrically unfit for military service. At a given cutting score on the personality scale, the outcomes of prediction were

	Retain	Reject	
	FN	VP	
Poor adjustment	40	49	89
	VN	FP	
Good adjustment	336	79	415
	376	128	504

Examination of the frequency of the outcomes of prediction suggests that the personality scale may be of some value as a screening device for military service. The scale correctly identified 49 of the 89 men in the poor-adjustment group (positives) and 336 of the 415 men in the good-adjustment group (negatives). In order to examine other properties of the scale in question, it is convenient to convert the frequencies of outcomes into probabilities of outcomes. One does so by dividing each frequency by the total number of cases in the sample (504).

	Retain	Reject	
	$P(FN)$	$P(VP)$	
Poor adjustment	.079	.097	$BR = .176$
	$P(VN)$	$P(FP)$	
Good adjustment	.667	.157	$1 - BR = .824$
	$1 - SR = .746$	$SR = .254$	

We note first that the *selection ratio* employed by Danielson and Clark (1954) was .254. Although in some selection situations, the selection ratio may be varied at the discretion of the tester (Meehl and Rosen, 1955), this value must be considered as fixed in the majority of practical settings. In the present example, it is assumed that the nation's need for military manpower can be met by accepting 75 percent of available men for military service. Although that selection ratio may not be realistic, it should be emphasized that it is in no sense arbitrary. As we will see in a later section, application of a psychological test to a setting with a markedly different selection ratio will result in quite different outcomes of prediction.

It is also apparent from the probability table that the *base rate* of poor adjustment was .176 in the sample employed by the scale authors. Meehl and Rosen (1955) called attention to the fact that this estimate of the base rate of psychiatric disability is probably unrealistically high. In an unselected population of inductees, the base rate of psychiatric disability is likely to be closer to .05, or less. Consequently, the present outcomes cannot be generalized to the typical psychiatric screening situation.

It is also appropriate to ask just *how much* the personality scale contributed to the personnel decision problem to which it was applied. This question concerns the *incremental validity* (Sechrest, 1963) of the personality scale. That is, how many more correct decisions were made by using the present scale than would have been made by an alternative procedure? An obvious alternative procedure is one that involves no psychological testing at all. Given the selection ratio of .254, what would be the effect of simply eliminating 25 percent of the applicants *at random* and inducting the remaining 75 percent? Since the base rate of poor adjustment is .176, we know that approximately 18 percent of the men randomly rejected would be genuine rejects (positives) and approximately 18 percent of the men randomly inducted would be false negatives. In this situation, $\varphi_{yy'} = 0$, and $P(VP) = BR \cdot SR = (.176)(.254) = .045$. Consequently, the outcomes of *random selection* would be

	Retain	Reject	
	P(FN)	P(VP)	
Poor adjustment	.131	.045	$BR = .176$
	P(VN)	P(FP)	
Good adjustment	.615	.209	$1 - BR = .824$
	$1 - SR = .746$	$SR = .254$	

The overall probability or *proportion of correct decisions* made under random selection is given by: $P(VP) + P(VN) = (.045) + (.615) = .660$. The overall proportion of correct decisions made by use of the personality scale was: $P(VP) + P(VN) = (.097) + (.667) = .764$. Hence the use of the personality scale resulted in approximately 10 percent more correct decisions than would have resulted from random selection. If the cost of such a testing program is small, it may be deemed advisable to employ the test in order to increase the number of correct decisions by 10 percent.

A More Realistic Example

The personality scale developed by Danielson and Clark had only modest incremental validity in their particular sample. It is all the more important, therefore, to inquire about the incremental validity of the scale when applied to an unselected sample in which the base rate of maladjustment would be closer to .05. To do so, it is helpful to calculate the validity coefficient of the personality scale in the original sample.

$$\varphi_{yy'} = \frac{P(VP) - BR \cdot SR}{\sqrt{BR(1 - BR)SR(1 - SR)}} = \frac{(.097) - (.176)(.254)}{\sqrt{(.176)(.824)(.254)(.746)}} = .317.$$

With this value of phi, it is possible to estimate the probability of a valid positive in a new sample with a maladjustment base rate of .05:

$$P(VP) = BR \cdot SR + \varphi_{yy'}\sqrt{BR(1 - BR)SR(1 - SR)}$$

$$= (.05)(.254) + (.317)\sqrt{(.05)(.95)(.254)(.746)} = .043.$$

The probabilities of the various outcomes may now be determined by subtraction.

	Retain	Reject	
	$P(FN)$	$P(VP)$	
Poor adjustment	.007	.043	$BR = .05$
	$P(VN)$	$P(FP)$	
Good adjustment	.739	.211	$1 - BR = .95$
	$1 - SR = .746$	$SR = .254$	

The probability table above shows that when the personality scale of Danielson and Clark is applied to an unselected sample, the overall proportion of correct decisions is: $P(\text{VP}) + P(\text{VN}) = (.043) + (.739) = .782$. If selection had been done on a purely *random* basis, then $P(\text{VP}) = BR \cdot SR = (.05)(.254) = .013$, and the overall proportion of correct decisions would have been: $P(\text{VP}) + P(\text{VN}) = (.013) + (.709) = .722$. Hence, in a selection situation with a more realistic base rate, the increment in correct decisions, over random selection, is only 6 percent. The value of such testing becomes even more questionable as the base rate becomes more extreme.

Random Selection versus Selection with a Test

Meehl and Rosen (1955, p. 196) have called attention to an additional feature of these data which, though technically correct, may be quite misleading to the practitioner. They point out that, under a selection ratio of .254, the overall proportion[4] of correct decisions made by the test is .782. However, if the selection ratio is changed to *zero* (no rejections, all applicants retained) and no test is employed then, $P(\text{VP}) = .00$, $P(\text{VN}) = .95$, and the overall proportion of correct decisions is .95. This procedure is sometimes referred to as "predicting from the base rate" since it capitalizes on the fact that the base rate of, in this case, the negative class is extremely large. However, Meehl and Rosen make the point that the use of a psychological test has *reduced* the proportion of correct decisions from .950 to .782. Nonetheless, the comparison is not appropriate, because the selection ratio is zero (no rejections) in the random case and .254 in the case where the test is employed. Further, this particular example appears to have given rise to a widespread misconception that the use of a psychological test can result in a *decreased* proportion of correct decisions, as compared with random selection.

The relationship between random selection and selection with a test can be seen from a reconsideration of our computational formula for the probability of valid positives:

$$P(\text{VP}) = BR \cdot SR + \varphi_{yy'}\sqrt{BR(1 - BR)SR(1 - SR)}.$$

Under random selection, $\varphi_{yy'} = .00$, and the probability of a valid positive is determined solely by the product of the base rate and the selection ratio. The larger the latter product, the more correct decisions can be made on a random basis. Such a situation exists when base rate, selection ratio, or both are considerably greater than .50. But random selection can never outstrip selection with a test that has a validity equal to or greater than zero.

---

4. The present calculations differ slightly from those of Meehl and Rosen, who employed a selection ratio of .208 (rather than .254) in the realistic example.

It is conceivable, however, that the incremental validity of tests employed in situations of extreme base rate will be so slight that the costs of testing would be considered unjustified. It should also be clear from our examples that the outcomes of prediction reported for a given base-rate situation cannot be generalized to situations with markedly discrepant base rates. Finally, it should be evident that knowledge of the validity coefficient of a test, $\varphi_{yy'}$, and the proportion of individuals to be selected, SR, is not sufficient to enable a decision maker to estimate the probable outcomes of prediction. Knowledge of the proportion of positives to be expected in a given sample, BR, is *essential* to rational decision making.

The Effects of Selection Ratios on Outcomes

Most practical selection or multiple-selection situations involve a *quota* on the total number of applicants that may be accepted for treatment. This circumstance is obvious in the case of astronaut selection and perhaps less so in military selection. As we indicated earlier, the ratio of the number of applicants who can be accepted to the total number of available applicants is referred to as the selection ratio. Taylor and Russell (1939) seem to have been the first to call attention to the importance of the selection ratio as a parameter that constrains the discriminative efficiency of a test.

When the number of applicants to be accepted by quota is large in relation to the total number of applicants, we speak of the selection ratio as being *high*. The selection ratio is generally high in new firms, for military service during war, and for special treatments which have little general appeal. In some circumstances (such as the selection of Kamikaze pilots in Japan toward the end of World War II), the selection ratio may be very close to 1.00. The utility of employing a psychological test in situations involving high selection ratios must always be subject to careful scrutiny. In those situations where the number of applicants greatly exceeds the quota to be accepted (low SR), there is likely to be more utility in employing a psychological test. The population explosion, coupled with advances in automation, has resulted in many treatment situations that involve low selection ratios. This has become increasingly true of institutions of higher education during the past decade.

The importance of the selection ratio as a marginal total constraining the outcomes of prediction should already be apparent from our earlier consideration of probability tables. From a mathematical standpoint, the selection ratio constrains the outcomes of prediction in *exactly* the same manner as does the base rate, the contingency table being indifferent to the label assigned to a row or column marginal total.

From a psychological standpoint, however, the selection ratio is usually treated as a different kind of variable in personnel decisions. Many authors have held out the hope that the selection ratio will not be considered as a fixed quota and that it may be varied to suit the purposes of the tester (Cronbach and Gleser, 1965; Cureton, 1957; Dawes, 1962; Meehl and Rosen, 1955; Rimm, 1963; Rorer, Hoffman, and Hsieh, 1966a; Rorer et al., 1966b). Under such conditions of flexibility, one may either decrease the selection ratio (more conservative selection) or increase it (less conservative selection). The problem then becomes one of determining the *optimal cutting score* on the predictor battery that will yield the desired distribution of outcomes of prediction. Raising the cutting score will decrease the probability of false positives while increasing the probability of false negatives. Lowering the cutting score will decrease the probability of false negatives while increasing the probability of false positives. A great deal of attention has been devoted to this problem, and quite satisfactory solutions may be found in the writings of the authors just cited.

Unfortunately, examples of practical selection situations in which the tester is free to vary selection ratios do not readily come to mind. The decision to admit a patient to a hospital is certainly constrained by the number of available beds. Conversely, the decision not to admit a patient to a hospital cannot be made independently of the fact that hospital budgets are affected by the number of beds that are filled. Patients cannot be assigned to a particular kind of psychiatric treatment if there are no therapists available who are qualified to administer such treatment. Not everyone can be admitted to college, nor can government, industry, or even the military employ all qualified applicants. By the same token, nevertheless, colleges, governments, industries, and military services do require a minimum number of students or employees to fulfill the purposes of the organizations involved.

It is true, of course, that the discriminative efficiency of a given test will be greater under some selection ratios than under others. Given a fixed test battery, it is reasonable to seek populations with optimal selection ratios. An academic aptitude battery may be less efficiently applied in the setting of a new community college (with a relatively small number of applicants) than in the setting of an older, more established community college. But the same is true of base rates. Although base rates within a population cannot be varied, the population to which a test is applied can be. Selection of riot-control policemen who are familiar with upper-middle-class values would be more efficiently accomplished on college campuses than in large cities.

Taylor and Russell (1939), as well as most subsequent writers on the subject, have emphasized the fact that selection becomes increasingly efficient as the selection ratio becomes smaller. Even a test of very modest validity may be relatively successful in selecting the "cream of the crop." This generalization bears closer examination, and a numerical example will help to provide the full picture of the effects of variation in selection ratios on the outcomes of prediction. Consider a test with the quite modest validity of $\varphi_{yy'} = .18$ that is applied to a population in which the base rate of success is .40. Figure 6.7 illustrates the outcomes of prediction when the test is employed under selection ratios of .95, .50, and .05. The values in Figure 6.7 were calculated in the same manner as in previous examples relating to base rates. The probabilities of valid positives were estimated from the formula

$$P(\text{VP}) = BR \cdot SR + \varphi_{yy'}\sqrt{BR(1 - BR)SR(1 - SR)},$$

and the remaining cell entries were determined by subtraction.

Under a selection ratio of .95 (Fig. 6.7a) the overall proportion of correct decisions is .448, which represents an increment over random selection of only .038. Under a selection ratio of .50 (Fig. 6.7b) the overall proportion of correct decisions is .900, which represents the considerable increment of .400 over random selection. Although the extremely small selection ratio of .05 (Fig. 6.7c) yields an overall proportion of correct decisions of .628, the tiny increment of .038 over random selection is identical to that achieved under a selection ratio of .95. This puzzling set of findings does not seem consistent with the generalization that selection becomes more efficient as the selection ratio becomes smaller.

The reason for the apparent contradiction lies in the fact that Taylor and Russell used the word "efficient" in a more restricted sense than we have been using it. Instead of considering the overall proportion of correct decisions made by a test, $P(\text{VP}) + P(\text{VN})$, Taylor and Russell emphasized *the proportion of selected applicants who are subsequently judged to be successful*. This probability is estimated by dividing the probability of valid positives by the selection ratio: $P(\text{VP})/SR$. As Figure 6.7 indicates, under a selection ratio of .95, 42 percent of those selected turn out to be successful. When the selection ratio is reduced to .50, this proportion increases to 49 percent. And finally, when the selection ratio is .05, a test of quite modest validity identifies 78 percent of successful applicants from among those selected. It is in this sense that smaller selection ratios are said to result in more efficient selection.

In industrial selection, it is quite common to *ignore* the outcomes of rejection. Applicants who should not have been hired, VN, and even those who "would have been" successful, FN, have no obvious effect on the subsequent productivity of the industry involved. That is, the outcomes of rejection have no positive *utility* for the firm. From the standpoint of utility, industries are more concerned about the productivity of successful employees, VP, and the costliness of hiring unsatisfactory employees, FP. For this reason, the "hit rate" of $P(\text{VP})/SR$ is of greater interest than indices based on all possible outcomes of selection.

But there are many other selection situations in which the outcomes of rejection are of considerable importance. The most dramatic examples are found in medical and psychiatric diagnosis. If the "positive class" to be identified is schizophrenia, brain damage, cancer, or suicide, the proportion

Fig. 6.7 Outcomes of prediction under different selection ratios ($BR = .40$; $\varphi_{yy'} = .18$).

(a)

P(FN)	P(VP)	
.001	.399	$BR = .40$
P(VN)	P(FP)	
.049	.551	$1 - BR = .60$

$$1 - SR = .05 \qquad SR = .95$$
$$\text{Overall} = .448$$
$$\text{Random} = .410$$
$$\text{Increment} = .038$$
$$P(\text{VP})/SR = .420$$

(b)

P(FN)	P(VP)	
.156	.244	$BR = .40$
P(VN)	P(FP)	
.656	.256	$1 - BR = .60$

$$1 - SR = .50 \qquad SR = .50$$
$$\text{Overall} = .900$$
$$\text{Random} = .500$$
$$\text{Increment} = .400$$
$$P(\text{VP})/SR = .488$$

(c)

$P(\text{FN})$	$P(\text{VP})$
.361	.039
$P(\text{VN})$	$P(\text{FP})$
.589	.011

$BR = .40$

$1 - BR = .60$

$$1 - SR = .95 \qquad SR = .05$$
$$\text{Overall} = .628$$
$$\text{Random} = .590$$
$$\text{Increment} = .038$$
$$P(\text{VP})/SR = .780$$

of false negatives who do not receive the required treatment is of the utmost concern. For example, if Figure 6.7c were used to select brain-damaged patients, the proportion who would be operated on is 78 percent. But 90 percent of the patients in need of treatment would not receive it!

The validity coefficient of a psychological test does not tell the whole story of predictive success, and it is therefore necessary to consider the discriminative efficiency of a test in terms of the four possible outcomes of prediction. But even knowing the probabilities of the various outcomes does not enable us to evaluate the worth of the test unless we are able to specify the *utilities* associated with such outcomes.

MAXIMIZING THE EXPECTED UTILITIES OF PERSONNEL DECISION STRATEGIES

We have now developed the terminology and notation necessary for discussing the outcomes of personnel decisions in terms of institutional gains and losses.   Figure 6.8 presents, in schematic form, the illustrative personnel decision strategy considered earlier in the chapter. The strategy, or rule for personnel assignment, is as follows: *Administer Test A to all applicants. Accept all applicants whose scores fall above the cutting score (C_a) and reject all whose scores fall below.* Typically, the cutting score on Test A will be determined by the selection ratio. The decision to accept, D_A, results in two possible outcomes that are expressed as probabilities, $P(\text{VP})$ and $P(\text{FP})$. The two possible outcomes of the decision to reject, D_R, are also expressed as probabilities, $P(\text{FN})$ and $P(\text{VN})$.   Associated with each outcome is a

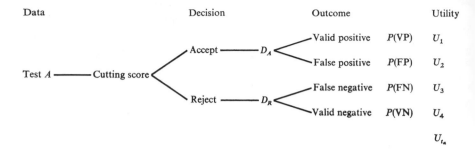

Fig. 6.8 Outcomes and utilities of a personnel decision strategy.

utility, U_i, that indicates the expected institutional gain, $+U_i$, or loss, $-U_i$ that is anticipated as a consequence of each outcome. In addition, there is a utility, U_{t_a}, associated with the costs of administering Test A which is almost always a negative value.

The decision strategy depicted in Figure 6.8 may be evaluated in terms of its *overall utility* for the institution involved. The general formula employed for evaluation of the expected utility, EU, of a decision strategy is

$$EU = U_1 \cdot P(\text{VP}) + U_2 \cdot P(\text{FP}) + U_3 \cdot P(\text{FN}) + U_4 \cdot P(\text{VN}) - U_t.$$

From this expression, we can see that the expected utility of a decision strategy is equal to the sum of the products of the probability of each outcome and its associated utility, minus the cost of testing.

The Estimation of Utilities

Considerations in Utility Estimates

Although the assignment of utility values to outcomes may very well be the "Achilles' heel" of decision theory, it is not a problem that can be ignored by any institution that makes personnel decisions. Whether an institution wishes to acknowledge it or not, there are specifiable outcomes to any personnel decision, and some are more profitable for the institution than others. As Rorer, Hoffman, and Hsieh (1966a) put it, "If an individual is unable to construct a table representing his values with regard to specific decision outcomes, then he has no rational basis on which to make that decision, with or without the test" (p. 368).

The first task confronting the decision maker is the determination of the *relative* values to be assigned to seemingly quite diverse outcomes. The unit of measurement is not at issue here, since all that is required is that the outcomes be evaluated on a common interval scale. The assumption of an interval scale will probably not be strictly justified in some situations. Note, however, that it is not necessary to express each outcome in relation to every other outcome. Rorer, Hoffman, and Hsieh (1966a) have called attention to the fact that the *gain* associated with a personnel decision strategy may be expressed as

$$\text{Gain} = \frac{U_{\text{VP}} - U_{\text{FN}}}{U_{\text{VN}} - U_{\text{FP}}}.$$

Consequently, it is necessary only to specify the difference in utility between the valid positive and false negative outcomes in relation to the difference between valid negative and false positive outcomes.

There remains the difficult task of estimating the utility or cost of testing on the same scale as that used for estimating the relative utilities of outcomes. Since testing costs may be expressed in terms of dollars, it is tempting to employ objective utility estimates. But how does one evaluate the loss involved in the misdiagnosis of a fatal disease in relation to a diagnostic procedure that costs $57 in equipment and personnel time? Clearly, there are some situations in which testing costs should be estimated subjectively, relative to the net utility of outcomes. But there are many other situations, especially in business and industry, in which all utilities may be estimated by relatively objective cost-accounting procedures. A number of discussions of utility estimation are available (e.g., Alf and Dorfman, 1967; Arthur, 1966; Cronbach and Gleser, 1965; Darlington and Stauffer, 1966; Diggory, 1969; Rimm, 1963; Rorer, Hoffman, and Hsieh, 1966a), including a discussion of situations in which direct estimation may be bypassed (Buchwald, 1965).

A Numerical Example

For purposes of illustration, we will consider a hypothetical selection situation in which a group of applicants is to be considered for a single treatment. We first set the utility of a valid positive equal to $+1.0$. This arbitrary unit expresses the gain which the institution anticipates will accrue from the acceptance of a qualified applicant. The monetary gain associated with a valid positive may be $10,000, but the arbitrary unit of $+1.0$ is sufficient for computational purposes.

We next consider the utility of rejecting an applicant who "would have been" successful, if hired (false negative). Although many institutions are indifferent to false negatives ($U_3 = 0$), let us assume that ours is not. A large number of false negatives is apt to result in poor public relations as a consequence of the "unfairness" of the institutional testing program. It cannot always be safely assumed that the eventual status of false negatives will remain in doubt, since they may go on to successful careers in comparable institutions. In addition, competing institutions may now have access to a desirable source of manpower, despite the fact that the initial recruiting efforts of our institution were greater than theirs. The utility of a false negative is thus a negative one and, although its absolute value is not equal to that of a valid positive, our institution may consider it at least half as important. We thus assign a value of $-.5$ to a false-negative outcome.

Although the utility associated with the correct identification of a negative (valid negative) may be considerable in medical and psychiatric diagnosis, the utility of valid negatives in industrial selection is frequently zero (Cronbach and Gleser, 1965, pp. 36–37). The decision that a healthy patient does not require a dangerous brain operation is quite different from the decision that an untalented candidate should not be hired. In the present example, we shall assume that we are indifferent to valid-negative outcomes and assign a value of zero to the fourth outcome of prediction.

It is frequently costly for an institution to accept applicants whose subsequent performance turns out to be unsuccessful. Not only are men placed in positions that could have been occupied by more productive applicants, but a situation is created that is likely to result in decreased employee morale and poor public relations. In our hypothetical example, we will assign a utility of -1.0 to a false positive decision. This assignment need not imply that the absolute value of a false positive decision (-1.0) is equal to that of a valid positive decision $(+1.0)$. It does imply that the difference in utility between a valid negative and a false positive is twice as great as the difference in utility between a valid positive and a false negative. Recall the expression of Rorer, Hoffman, and Hsieh:

$$\text{Gain} = \frac{U_{\text{VP}} - U_{\text{FN}}}{U_{\text{VN}} - U_{\text{FP}}} = \frac{(1.0) - (.5)}{(0) - (1.0)} = \frac{.5}{-1.0} = -.5.$$

From the values above it might appear that the institution is doomed to lose, since the gain associated with personnel decisions is negative in sign. That is not true, however, since the *probabilities* of the various outcomes have not yet been considered. Nevertheless, in such a situation, institutional loss is quite possible, and hence the overall utility of any personnel decision strategy must be carefully scrutinized.

As we have indicated, the cost of testing is almost always a negative utility. In the present example, we will assume that two tests or selection procedures are available and that they differ in both validity and cost. Test A is a relatively inexpensive screening device of modest validity: $r_{ay} = .30$. The fixed cost of administering Test A is .02 per applicant: $U_{t_a} = -.02$. In terms of our arbitrary utility scale, if the utility of identifying a valid positive $(U_1 = +1.0)$ is thought of as a monetary value of $10,000, the cost of testing one applicant on Test A would be $200. That cost estimate is based on considerations of professional, administrative, and clerical salaries, as well as the less expensive cost of test booklets and answer sheets.

Test B is a considerably more valid assessment procedure ($r_{by} = .60$) that is also, not surprisingly, more costly: $U_{t_b} = -.20$. Test B might be a contrived situational task that closely resembles the criterion performance. Applicants are placed in a simulated job situation for three days and their performance is observed and rated by high-level supervisors. The cost of such elaborate situational testing could easily be $2,000 per applicant, and the validity of such a procedure might well be .60. We shall assume further that Test B is only slightly related to Test A ($r_{ab} = .18$) and that when the common criterion variance of the two tests is removed, or "partialled out," the two tests are virtually uncorrelated: $r_{ab \cdot y} = .00$. The latter assumption will make our subsequent numerical examples much simpler.

We have now assigned numerical values to the utilities involved in our hypothetical example. It must be strongly emphasized that these particular values are not to be generalized to any specific selection situation. Each decision maker must estimate the values of his own institution on the basis of his familiarity with the goals of that institution. Such a highly subjective procedure is neither easy nor rigorous, but it is both necessary and rational. In order to apply our hypothetical utilities to a concrete example, we must specify several population parameters. Let us assume that we have an applicant sample of 1,000 cases from which we must select 500, and that half of our applicants would be successful, if hired ($SR = BR = .50$). The preceding sections of this chapter should have made it clear that the outcomes of selection in this situation cannot be generalized to situations involving markedly different base rates and/or selection ratios.

The parameters of our hypothetical selection situation are summarized in Table 6.2. Given these values, we are now in a position to consider the several possible *personnel decision strategies* that might be employed under these circumstances.

Table 6.2 Parameters of hypothetical selection situation

Population parameters	Outcomes	Associated utilities
$N = 1,000$	Valid positives	$U_1 = +1.0$
$BR = .50$	False positives	$U_2 = -1.0$
$SR = .50$	False negatives	$U_3 = -.5$
	Valid negatives	$U_4 = 0$

Test A	Test B
$U_{t_a} = -.02$	$U_{t_b} = -.20$
$r_{ay} = .30$	$r_{by} = .60$

$$r_{ab} = .18$$
$$r_{ab \cdot y} = .00$$

Personnel Decision Strategies

Cronbach and Gleser (1965, pp. 72–74) have distinguished a number of different personnel decision strategies that may be applied to our hypothetical selection situation.   Their most fundamental distinction is that between *single-stage* (nonsequential) and *multistage* (sequential) decision strategies (pp. 14–15). The principal distinction between these two classes of strategies lies in the nature of the decisions made on the basis of testing. In single-stage strategies, the cutting score on the test battery is used to make *terminal decisions*. Individuals are either selected or rejected, and no further decisions are made. In multistage strategies, the cutting score on the test battery may be used to make *investigatory decisions*. A group of applicants may be provisionally accepted and assigned to further testing to determine whether or not they should be permanently accepted. This process is diagrammed in Figure 6.9. The investigatory decisions may continue through a number of stages of subsequent testing before terminal decisions are made regarding all applicants.

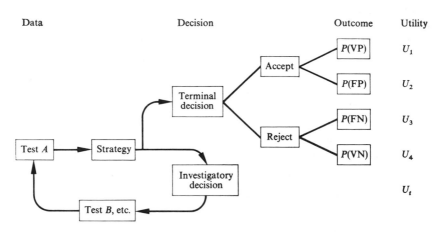

Fig. 6.9 Function of terminal and investigatory decisions in multistage strategies. (Adapted from Cronbach and Gleser, 1965, p. 18)

Single-Stage Decision Strategies

A priori strategy. Discussions of the value of pyschological tests in selection frequently fail to take into account the fact that *some* sort of selection procedure exists, even in institutions that have no formal assessment program. Applicants are interviewed, letters of recommendation are perused, records of past performance are consulted, and a variety of other data may be brought to bear on the decision problem at hand. Whether or not such procedures are formal or consistent, it is necessary to estimate their discriminative efficiency in order to provide a *base line* against which to evaluate the incremental validity of any alternative procedure.   In our hypothetical selection situation, we will employ a *random strategy* as the base line for evaluating the incremental validity of alternative strategies.   It seems likely that such a strategy provides an underestimate of the discriminative efficiency of most, but not all, a priori strategies employed in practice.

Single-stage strategies.   The general form of a single-stage decision strategy was depicted in Figure 6.8.   A test or test battery is administered to all applicants, and on the basis of a cutting score, usually determined by the selection ratio, applicants are assigned to the terminal decision categories of accept or reject.   Within this general form of strategy, we may distinguish three alternatives that may be employed in our present hypothetical selection situation: (1) Test *A* may be given to all applicants, (2) Test *B* may be given to all applicants, or (3) Test *A* and Test *B* may be given to all applicants and the cutting score determined by multiple-regression procedures.   Which of the three strategies is optimal will depend on the relative costs of the two tests, their relative validity and independence, and the utilities associated with different outcomes.

Double-Stage Strategies

Under a double-stage strategy, terminal decisions are made for a portion of applicants on the basis of Test *A*, and the remaining applicants are administered Test *B*.   Terminal decisions are then made for the remaining applicants on the basis of Tests *A* and *B* combined.   In one variant of this double-stage strategy (Figure 6.10) all applicants are administered Test *A*, and on the

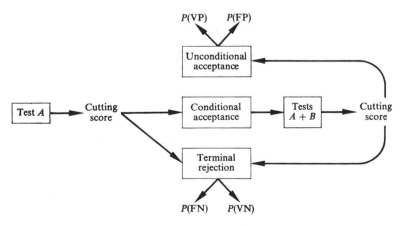

Fig. 6.10 A pre-reject, double-stage selection strategy.

basis of a cutting score, some are terminally rejected and others are provisionally accepted. The provisionally accepted applicants are then administered Test B, and on the basis of a cutting score determined by multiple regression of Tests A and B on the criterion, they are either unconditionally accepted or terminally rejected.

There are three variants of the double-stage selection strategy. That illustrated in Figure 6.10 is called *pre-reject* (Cronbach and Gleser, 1965, p. 73). Here terminal rejection decisions are made on the basis of Test A alone, and the remaining applicants are evaluated on Tests A and B. In the *pre-accept* variant, unconditional acceptance decisions are made on the basis of Test A alone, and the remaining applicants are evaluated on Tests A and B. Pre-reject and pre-accept are equivalent sequential strategies, although one may be more administratively feasible than the other in a given selection situation. A *complete* double-stage strategy is illustrated in Figure 6.11. Here it is necessary to determine two cutting scores on Test A that is, C_1 and C_2. Those applicants whose scores on Test A fall above C_1 are unconditionally accepted, and those whose scores fall below C_2 are terminally rejected. Applicants whose scores fall between C_1 and C_2 are provisionally accepted, and their final disposition is made on the basis of Tests A and B. Because it makes full use of the validity of Test A, the complete double-stage strategy will always be more efficient than either pre-select or pre-reject.

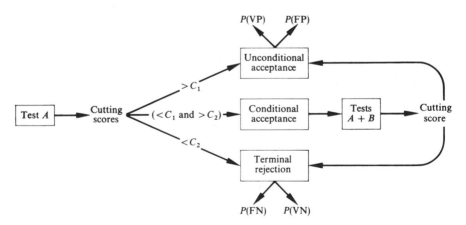

Fig. 6.11 A complete double-stage selection strategy.

Evaluating the Expected Utility of Personnel Decision Strategies

Given the hypothetical selection situation indicated by the parameters in Table 6.2, and given the several alternative strategies that may be employed, which strategy is the best? *The strategy to be used is the one that maximizes the expected utility for the institution across all possible outcomes.* In the present instance, that strategy will now be determined by evaluating the expected utility of the several alternative personnel decision strategies.

Strategy I: Random Selection

As a base line from which to estimate the incremental contributions of other strategies, we will evaluate a random-selection procedure. Given the selection ratio of .50 (see Table 6.2), the decision rule is: *Select 500 cases at random.* Given the base rate of .50 (Table 6.2), the results of random selection would be as follows:

	Reject	Accept	
	FN	VP	
Success	250	250	500
	VN	FP	
Failure	250	250	500
	500	500	

The expected utility of this strategy may now be evaluated:

$$EU = U_1 \cdot P(\text{VP}) + U_2 \cdot P(\text{FP}) + U_3 \cdot P(\text{FN}) + U_4 \cdot P(\text{VN}) - U_t,$$

$$EU_1 = (+1.0)(.25) + (-1.0)(.25) + (-.5)(.25) + (0)(.25) - (0) = -.125.$$

Strategy II: Single-Stage Selection on Test A

As previously indicated, the decision rule is: *Administer Test A to all applicants. Accept all applicants whose scores fall above C_a, and reject all applicants whose scores fall below C_a.* From Table 6.2, we recall that the validity of Test A is .30 and that the cost of administering it is $-.02$ per applicant. The probability of a valid positive is estimated from the now familiar formula

$$P(\text{VP}) = BR \cdot SR + \varphi_{yy}\sqrt{BR(1 - BR)SR(1 - SR)}$$
$$= (.50)(.50) + (.30)\sqrt{(.50)(.50)(.50)(.50)} = .325.$$

The frequencies of the outcomes are determined by subtraction,

	FN	VP	
Success	175	325	500
	VN	FP	
Failure	325	175	500
	500	500	

and the expected utility is evaluated:

$$EU = U_1 \cdot P(\text{VP}) + U_2 \cdot P(\text{FP}) + U_3 \cdot P(\text{FN}) + U_4 \cdot P(\text{VN}) - U_{t_a},$$

$$EU_{\text{II}} = (+1.0)(.325) + (-1.0)(.175) + (-.5)(.175) + (0)(.325) - (.02)$$
$$= +.043.$$

Strategy III: Single-Stage Selection on Test B

The decision rule is: *Administer Test B to all applicants. Accept all applicants whose scores fall above C_b, and reject all applicants whose scores fall below C_b.* The validity of Test B is .60, and the cost of administering it is $-.20$ per applicant.

$$P(\text{VP}) = BR \cdot SR + \varphi_{yy}\sqrt{BR(1 - BR)SR(1 - SR)}$$

$$= (.50)(.50) + (.60)\sqrt{(.50)(.50)(.50)(.50)} = .400.$$

	FN	VP	
Success	100	400	500
	VN	FP	
Failure	400	100	500
	500	500	

As before, the expected utility is evaluated:

$$EU = U_1 \cdot P(VP) + U_2 \cdot P(FP) + U_3 \cdot P(FN) + U_4 \cdot P(VN) - U_{t_b},$$
$$EU_{III} = (+1.0)(.400) + (-1.0)(.100) + (-.5)(.100) + (0)(.400) - (.20)$$
$$= +.050.$$

Strategy IV: Single-Stage Selection on Tests A and B

Administer Test A and Test B to all applicants. Determine cutting score by multiple-regression of Test A and Test B on criterion. Accept all applicants whose scores fall above C_{a+b} and reject all applicants whose scores fall below C_{a+b}. The multiple correlation of Tests A and B with the criterion may be estimated from

$$R_{y \cdot ab} = \sqrt{\frac{r_{ay}^2 - 2r_{ab}r_{ay}r_{by} + r_{by}^2}{1 - r_{ab}^2}}.$$

All these correlations are known and may be substituted:

$$R_{y \cdot ab} = \sqrt{\frac{(.30)^2 - 2(.18)(.30)(.60) + (.60)^2}{1 - (.18)^2}} = .63.$$

This estimate of the correlation between the two tests and the criterion may now be substituted in the formula.

$$P(VP) = BR \cdot SR + \varphi_{yy'}\sqrt{BR(1 - BR)SR(1 - SR)}$$
$$= (.50)(.50) + (.63)\sqrt{(.50)(.50)(.50)(.50)} = .407.$$

	Reject	Accept	
	FN	VP	
Success	93	407	500
	VN	FP	
Failure	407	93	500
	500	500	

$$EU = U_1 \cdot P(VP) + U_2 \cdot P(FP) + U_3 \cdot P(FN) + U_4 \cdot P(VN) - U_{t_a} - U_{t_b},$$
$$EU_{IV} = (+1.0)(.407) + (-1.0)(.093) + (-.5)(.093) + (0)(.407) - (.02)$$
$$- (.20) = +.048.$$

Strategy V: Double-Stage Selection (Pre-reject)

The decision rule for this strategy involves two stages. In the first stage, a portion[5] of the applicant sample is provisionally accepted on the basis of the first test, and the remaining applicants are terminally rejected. In the second stage, terminal decisions are made concerning the provisionally accepted applicants on the basis of both tests. *Administer Test A to all applicants. Set the cutting score, C_a, such that 77 percent of all applicants fall above. Reject all applicants whose scores fall below C_a. Administer Test B to all applicants whose scores fall above C_a. Determine cutting score by adjusted multiple regression of Tests A and B on criterion. Accept all applicants whose scores fall above C_{a+b}, and reject all applicants whose scores fall below C_{a+b}.*

Stage 1. Since 77 percent of all applicants are provisionally accepted on the basis of Test A, the selection ratio now equals .77.

$$P(\text{VP}) = BR \cdot SR_2 + \varphi_{yy'}\sqrt{BR(1 - BR)SR_2(1 - SR_2)}$$

$$= (.50)(.77) + (.30)\sqrt{(.50)(.50)(.77)(.23)} = .448.$$

	Reject	Provisionally accept	
	FN	VP	
Success	52	448	500
	VN	FP	
Failure	178	322	500
	230	770	
		(to Stage 2)	

---

5. The proportion of applicants provisionally accepted by the first test is not arbitrary and should be determined in relation to the parameters of the second stage of selection. The particular proportion chosen for this example was determined by a computerized trial-and-error procedure (Goldberg and Chaplin, 1970) that need not concern us here.

Stage 2. Test *B* is now administered to the 770 applicants provisionally accepted in the first stage. Here an estimate is required of the multiple correlation of the two tests with the criterion in the reduced sample of 770 applicants. From the computations for Strategy IV, we know that this multiple-*R* is estimated to be .63 in the entire *unselected* sample of 1,000 applicants. Correcting for the fact that the variance on Test *A* is attenuated in the present sample, we adjust the estimate[6] of the multiple correlation to .61 and use this value in estimating the probability of a valid positive in the second stage.

$$P(\text{VP}) = BR \cdot SR + \varphi_{yy'}\sqrt{BR(1 - BR)SR(1 - SR)}$$

$$= (.58)(.65) + (.61)\sqrt{(.58)(.42)(.65)(.35)} = .520.$$

The frequency of valid positives among 770 applicants is $(.520)(770) = 400$.

	Reject	Accept	
	FN	VP	
Success	48	400	448
	VN	FP	
Failure	222	100	322
	270	500	

Note that both the base rate and the selection ratio change in the second stage.

In order to estimate the expected utility of Strategy V, it is necessary to consider the overall outcomes of selection from both stages. Among the 500 applicants unconditionally accepted in the second stage, 400 were successful (VP) and 100 were not (FP). Among the 500 applicants rejected in one or the other stage, there were $178 + 222 = 400$ valid negatives and $52 + 48 = 100$ false negatives. The overall outcomes of selection are

---

6. A general discussion of the effects of restriction of range on validity coefficients may be found in Thorndike (1949, pp. 169–180).

	Reject	Accept	
	FN	VP	
Success	100	400	500
	VN	FP	
Failure	400	100	500
	500	500	

$$EU = U_1 \cdot P(VP) + U_2 \cdot P(FP) + U_3 \cdot P(FN) + U_4 \cdot P(VN) - U_{t_a}$$
$$- U_{t_b}(SR_2)$$

$$EU_V = (+1.0)(.400) + (-1.0)(.100) + (-.5)(.100) + (0)(.400) - (.02)$$
$$- (.20)(.77) = +.076.$$

Evaluating the Personnel Decision Strategies

We have now calculated the expected utilities of five possible personnel decision strategies for our hypothetical selection situation in order to provide a basis for comparison among the strategies. We are committed to the principle of employing the strategy that maximizes the expected utility for the institution across all possible outcomes. The strategy of choice is evident from an inspection of Table 6.3, which summarizes the expected utilities from the preceding calculations.

Recall that our equation for calculating expected utilities was expressed in terms of the gain or loss associated with a decision regarding a single applicant. Since our hypothetical selection situation involved 1,000 individuals, the expected utility values in Table 6.3 have been multiplied by that

Table 6.3 Expected utilities of five personnel decision strategies

Strategy	Expected utility	Increment over random selection
I Random selection	−125	000
II Single-stage selection on Test A	43	168
III Single-stage selection on Test B	50	175
IV Single-stage selection on Tests A and B	48	173
V Double-stage selection (pre-reject)	76	201

number. The final column in the table expresses the increment over random selection that is contributed by a given strategy. In evaluating the data in Table 6.3, we must bear in mind several characteristics of the original utility scale. Although we assumed that our original arbitrary utility scale had interval properties, we could still make a choice from the expected utilities in Table 6.3 even if we assumed only *ordinal* properties. That is, the *EU* of Strategy V is clearly greater than that of Strategy III, which is in turn greater than that of Strategy IV. Since we granted interval properties to our utility scale in the first place, however, the calculation of the increments over random selection is justifiable.

From Table 6.3, it is clear that the double-stage pre-reject strategy is the preferred one in this selection situation. Despite its high cost, Test *B* was a remarkably effective instrument, as we can see from the *EU* for Strategy III. Adding Test *A* to single-stage selection, as in Strategy IV, is less efficient than using Test *B* alone. The use of Test *A* alone in single-stage selection is the least efficient testing strategy. Even that strategy, however, is considerably more profitable than random selection, which results in substantial institutional losses. Translating our original utility unit of +1.0 into a monetary value of $10,000, we can see that a random-selection strategy would produce an institutional loss of $1,250,000. Use of a double-stage selection strategy, on the other hand, would produce an institutional gain of $760,000, an amount that exceeds the negative result of the random strategy by more than $2,000,000.

Such monetary units cannot be taken literally, however, and it would be misleading to attempt to sell a testing program to an institution on the basis of claims for specific monetary gains. In our hypothetical example, we have made many assumptions, both statistical and factual, at every stage of our calculations. The statistical assumptions can be improved on by gathering empirical data and by employing more precise computational techniques. But the factual assumptions regarding utilities remain the Achilles' heel of the entire enterprise. Nevertheless, there can be little argument with the claim that, *given our assumptions*, decisions should be made on the basis of a double-stage testing program.

How widely may we generalize the results of our hypothetical selection example? From the number of parameters involved in the calculations, it should be clear that we can generalize very little, if at all. Slight changes in base rates, selection ratios, test validities, intercorrelations among tests, and especially utilities of outcomes may result in changes in the relative efficiency of the various strategies. In order to arrive at generalizations about the relative efficiency of personnel decision strategies, it is necessary to (a) determine the mathematical relationships that exist among the many parameters involved and (b) program a computer to take these relationships into account in evaluating the expected utility of different strategies under varying parameter values. A pioneering first step in this direction has been taken by Cronbach and Gleser.

In addition to providing a thorough mathematical exposition of the use of psychological tests in personnel decisions, Cronbach and Gleser (1965) present empirical examples of the relative expected utilities of decision strategies under different selection ratios (pp. 76–85). Although their results are dependent on certain mathematical assumptions and limited to certain assumed parameter values, certain generalizations are possible. Their most striking conclusion is that a complete double-stage selection strategy is equal or superior to all other strategies at all selection ratios (p. 78). We have already indicated that a complete double-stage strategy is, by necessity, equal or superior to pre-reject or pre-accept double-stage strategies. But the *general* superiority of complete double-stage selection has much broader implications for personnel selection.

SUMMARY

Until fairly recently, concern with the technical problems of measurement and prediction has resulted in a relative neglect of the broader context in which such problems arise, namely, the optimal assignment of men to jobs or treatments. Within this broader context, which is the overriding concern of personality assessment, the *outcomes* of prediction are of paramount importance to the individuals involved and to the society in which they live. From this standpoint, measurement and prediction are simply technical components of a system designed to make *decisions* about the assignment of personnel to jobs or treatments. Thus, although measurement and prediction may be evaluated by formal psychometric criteria, such as reliability and validity, the outcomes of personnel decisions must be evaluated in terms of their *utilities* for individuals and institutions within our society.

The major types of personnel decisions may be distinguished from one another on the basis of: (a) what the number of different positions available is and (b) whether rejection is a permissible option. When only one position is available and rejection is allowed, we speak of *selection*. When two or more positions are available and rejection is allowed, we speak of *multiple selection*. When two or more positions are available and all subjects are retained, we speak of *classification*. From the standpoint of classical validity, the multiple-regression equation forms the basic model for prediction in all these types of personnel decisions. However, the implementation of the multiple-regression model varies with the different decisions required by each situation. In selection, optimal weights are assigned to a set of independent predictors so as to maximize the correlation between predicted and actual criterion performance in a single treatment. In multiple selection, two or more separate test batteries may be optimally weighted to maximize validities in two or more treatments, although typically a single battery is employed for two or more purposes. In classification, the differences in performance between two or more treatments must be optimized in such a way that predicted differences in performance are highly correlated with obtained criterion differences. The actual level of validity coefficients is less important here than the size of the difference between relevant and irrelevant (other treatments) validity coefficients.

From a practical standpoint, the number of correct decisions made by a psychological test or assessment procedure (discriminative efficiency) is a more important piece of information than the degree of association that exists between predicted and obtained criterion scores (classical validity). From a scatter plot of the joint frequency distribution of predicted and obtained criterion scores, it is possible to distinguish four outcomes of prediction: (a) success is predicted and success obtains (valid positives); (b) success is predicted and failure obtains (false positives); (c) failure is predicted and success obtains (false negatives); and (d) failure is predicted and failure obtains (valid negatives). The frequencies of cases in each of these four outcomes may be expressed as probabilities by dividing each by the total number of cases in the sample of applicants. Thus the outcomes of prediction may be expressed as a 2×2 contingency table with marginal totals.

	Reject	Accept	
	P(FN)	P(VP)	
Success			BR
	P(VN)	P(FP)	
Failure			$1 - BR$
	$1 - SR$	SR	

The elements of this table are referred to as "hit rates" since they represent the overall probability of correct decisions in the total sample, P(VP) + P(VN), as well as the overall probability of incorrect decisions, P(FP) + P(FN). The marginal totals, BR and SR, constrain the degree of association that can exist between predicted and obtained outcomes. The base rate of a sample, BR, indicates the proportion of positives that may be expected from a total sample of applicants. The overall proportion of correct decisions made by a psychological test will vary considerably as a function of the population base rate. It is possible that the incremental validity of tests employed in situations of extreme base rate will be so slight that the costs of testing would be considered unjustified. The ratio of the number of applicants who can be accepted to the total number of available applicants is referred to as the selection ratio, SR. The selection ratio constrains the outcomes of prediction in exactly the same manner as does the base rate. In most industrial settings, selection with a psychological test becomes increasingly efficient as SR becomes smaller.

The four possible outcomes of decisions will typically have different utilities for the institution involved. The first task of the decision maker is the specification of the relative values to be assigned to these diverse outcomes. This task involves the estimation of the difference in utility between valid positive and false negative outcomes in relation to the difference between valid negative and false positive outcomes. The utility or cost of testing must also be estimated on the same scale as that used for estimating the relative utilities of outcomes. The overall decision problem then becomes one of selecting the personnel decision strategy that will maximize expected utilities across all four outcomes. The expected utility, EU, of a personnel decision strategy is given by the sum of the products of each outcome probability and its estimated utility, minus the cost of testing: $EU = \sum U_i \cdot P(O_i) - U_t$.

In single-stage (nonsequential) decision strategies, a cutting score on the test battery is used to make terminal decisions. Individuals are either selected or rejected, and no further decisions are made. In multistage (sequential) decision strategies, a cutting score on the test battery may be used to make investigatory decisions. A group of applicants may be provisionally accepted and assigned to further testing to determine whether or not they should be permanently accepted. Such investigatory decisions may continue through a number of stages of subsequent testing before final decisions are made regarding all applicants.

A numerical example was provided in which the expected utilities of five personnel decision strategies were evaluated. Fixed values were assumed for such parameters as the base rate, selection ratio, utilities associated with outcomes and the validities, intercorrelation, and costs of two tests. The personnel decision strategies compared were: (a) random selection without testing, (b) single-stage selection on Test A, (c) single-stage selection on Test B, (d) single-stage selection on Tests A and B, and (e) double-stage selection, in which applicants were pre-rejected at the first stage. The results of this example cannot be generalized to situations involving different values of the many parameters involved. However, it is generally true that complete double-stage selection will be superior to other strategies, and this finding has broad implications for personnel selection.

Part II

TECHNIQUES OF DATA COLLECTION IN PERSONALITY ASSESSMENT

CHAPTER 7

OBSERVATIONAL TECHNIQUES: I. GENERALIZABILITY AND FACETS OF OBSERVATION

In his comprehensive survey of observational methods, Weick (1968) offers the following definition of an observational method:

. . . the selection, provocation, recording, and encoding of that set of behaviors and settings concerning organisms "in situ" which is consistent with empirical aims. (p. 360.)

Selection is emphasized to call attention to the fact that *all* behavioral observations are focused on some fragment of the total behavioral episode recorded. *Provocation* is included in the definition to emphasize the fact that the observational setting may be manipulated in such a way as to increase the probability that the behavior of interest will emerge. *Recording* calls attention to the fact that many observational techniques require extensive records of the behavior observed. *Encoding* refers to the process whereby observations or records are transformed to a more usable form by means of such devices as rating scales and frequency counts. The phrase "in situ" refers to the natural setting in which behavior typically occurs, which is approximated in widely varying degrees by different observational techniques.

That observational methods are *consistent with empirical aims* is perhaps the most important feature of Weick's definition for our purposes. There are a wide variety of observational methods that play an important role in almost every field of psychology. Our concern will be limited to those observational methods which are consistent with the empirical aims of personality assessment, namely, the prediction of socially relevant criterion measures. We will first consider issues relating to the *reliability* of observational methods and the procedures that have been proposed for assessing such reliability by classical test theory and the more recent theory of generalizability. Next, we will consider a number of *facets* that influence the dependability of observational methods and, in particular, those of settings, observers, instruments, occasions, and attributes.

RELIABILITY OF OBSERVATION

The Nature of Measurement Error

It should be intuitively obvious that any measurement procedure is subject to "error." In observational measurements, many different sources may contribute to such error. In personality assessment, the observer is typically a human observer and is thus subject to a variety of human frailties. He may become bored or fatigued, he may be careless or inattentive, or he may not be consistently highly motivated to do a good job. Similarly, the observer is typically provided with some type of rating form to help him in "encoding" his sensory impressions. This form may be difficult to read or confusing, or it may require discriminations that are beyond human capacity. The *conditions* under which observations are made may also contribute error. Observing the subject in a noisy or distracting environment may impede accurate observation. Observations made at different *times* of the day or year may be unrepresentative and hence inaccurate. All these factors which militate against accurate observation seem to be properly classified as "error."

If a given observation, x, is subject to error, e, then the observation without the error, $x - e$, must represent a completely accurate or "true" observation, t. In fact, this deceptively simple formulation,

$$x - e = t,$$

is the fundamental assumption in the psychometric theory of mental test scores (Gulliksen, 1950; Lord and Novick, 1968). Although few would quarrel with the intuitively obvious notions of observed score, x, and error, e, the notion of a "true" score has given rise to issues of a philosophical nature.

Within the so-called classical theory of reliability, at least three different conceptions of true score may be delineated (Lord and Novick, 1968, pp. 28–29). One conception relies on the ordinary language connotation of the word "true" in the sense that there is a "real," though unobservable, value for each observation that is obscured by errors of measurement. Because of certain similarities to the philosophical school of idealism, this conception has recently come to be referred to as the "Platonic" true score (Sutcliffe, 1965). Such a conceptualization makes many psychologists uncomfortable (e.g., Thorndike, 1964) in that the basic equation of classical test theory appears to contain an element, t, that can never, in principle, be observed.

A second and more widely used conception of true score is based on a probabilistic sampling notion. If a large—in principle, an infinite—number of observations of the same attribute are made, the *mean* or average value of these observations will converge to a constant, which may be thought of as the "true" score of the person being observed. The probabilistic interpretation of true score as the average of an infinite number of repeated observations is much more compatible with the conceptions of modern statistics than is the notion of a Platonic true score. A third definition of true score, and the one which has been most thoroughly explicated, is that employed by Gulliksen (1950) and Lord and Novick (1968). Certain relationships are *defined* among true and error scores, and these definitions are considered mathematically convenient and conceptually useful. "Specifically it is assumed that corresponding true and error scores are uncorrelated and that error scores on different measurements are also uncorrelated" (Lord and Novick, 1968, p. 29). From these definitions and/or assumptions have emerged the most mathematically rigorous and detailed explication of mental test theory to date (Lord and Novick, 1968).

It is important to note that the three conceptions of true score employed in classical test theory share in common the assumption of a *specific* true score (Lord and Novick, 1968, p. 43). That is, it is assumed that for a *specific* set of conditions, there is a single true score which represents accurate measurement under that set of conditions. This notion of a specific true score stands in contrast to the concept of a *generic* true score which forms the basis of the modern theory of "generalizability" (Cronbach, Rajaratnam, and Gleser, 1963). Rather than to a single set of conditions, generalizability theory has reference to a "universe" of conditions which involves differences in such things as stimuli, observers, occasions, and situations of observation. In generalizability theory, the true score is conceived of as a "universe score," which is the mean of observations over all conditions in the universe. Although differing only slightly in mathematical details, the theories of classical reliability and generalizability are sufficiently different in conception to warrant separate consideration. Hence we shall first consider the definitions of reliability that have been offered by classical test theory and then turn to a consideration of the liberalization of these concepts that has been introduced in the theory of generalizability.

Classical Reliability Theory

As indicated above, all theories of reliability conceive of observed scores as comprising some "true" component, variously defined, plus an error component:

$$x = t + e.$$

The basic equations of reliability theory can be derived from either a definition of true score or a definition of error score (Gulliksen, 1950). Since the concept of measurement error is perhaps the more intuitively familiar, we shall derive our definition of reliability from considerations based on the nature of error.

Definition of Error

Errors of observation may be thought of as falling into two general classes. *Constant* or systematic errors are errors which are systematically associated with a measurement procedure. A ruler whose origin is one inch rather than zero will yield measurements consistently smaller than those obtained with a standard ruler. Since the error in this case is systematically associated with the measurement procedure, it is considered to be a constant. *Random* or chance errors, on the other hand, reflect momentary variations in the circumstances of measurement which are unrelated to the measurement procedure itself. Such errors are assumed to be random, and it is this property which permits their definition in statistical terms. Classical reliability theory is concerned exclusively with random errors.

It is assumed that if we make a sufficiently large number of observations of the same phenomenon, random errors will cancel each other out. Thus it is reasonable to assume that over a sufficiently large number of observations the average error will be zero. For a large number of observations, then, we may define the mean error score as being equal to zero. Since random error is, by definition, unrelated in any systematic way to the phenomenon under observation, it is also reasonable to assume that over a sufficiently large number of cases there will be no systematic relationship between error scores and true scores. More rigorously, the theoretical *correlation* between true and error scores is assumed to be zero. Finally, since errors are random by definition, there is no reason to assume that error present on one occasion will be related in any systematic way to error present on another occasion. More formally, over a large number of observations it is assumed that errors of measurement are *uncorrelated*. Hence random error has the following defining properties:

$$M_e = 0,$$

$$r_{te} = 0,$$

$$r_{e_1 e_2} = 0.$$

Variance of Observed Scores

Our fundamental definition of an observed score expresses it as the sum of true and error components: $x = t + e$. The variability, or variance, in such observed scores must then be a function of variability in the sum of these composite scores. Stating the variance of observed scores in terms of the variance of a composite, we obtain

$$\sigma_x^2 = \sigma_{t+e}^2 = \sigma_t^2 + 2r_{te}\sigma_t\sigma_e + \sigma_e^2.$$

However, since the correlation of true and error scores has been defined as zero ($r_{te} = 0$), the middle expression drops out and we have

$$\sigma_x^2 = \sigma_t^2 + \sigma_e^2.$$

Thus the variance of observed scores may be expressed as the variance of true scores plus the variance of error scores. This result, which simply follows from a definition of error, represents a fundamental equation in classical test theory.

Definition of Parallel Tests

All conceptions of reliability involve the notion of *repeated* measurements, and it is necessary for each conception to provide a working definition of what is meant by this expression. Clearly the notion of repeated measurements includes more than the concept of an identical measurement procedure being repeated exactly. On the other hand, the idea of repeated measurement is not so general as to embrace the comparison of fundamentally different measurement procedures designed to assess different attributes. Thus the reliability of observations of length is not restricted to measurements obtained from a single (presumably standard) ruler. Such reliability must embrace measurements obtained from a large set or class of (presumably standard) rulers. On the other hand, of course, it makes little sense to compare measurements obtained with a ruler with measurements obtained with a bathroom scale. The measurements obtained must in some sense be "comparable," though not necessarily identical.

To resolve this apparent dilemma, classical test theory has relied heavily on the notion of *parallel tests*. Such tests are conceived of as comparable or equivalent with respect to the measurement of an attribute, but not necessarily identical in format. Intuitively, tests may be said to be parallel when "it makes no difference which test you use" (Gulliksen, 1950). More formally, two tests may be said to be parallel if their true scores are identical and if the variability of errors is identical:

$$t_1 = t_2,$$

$$\sigma_{e_1} = \sigma_{e_2}.$$

Classical reliability theory postulates that regardless of the degree of random error present, the true score of an individual on an attribute of one test is equal to his true score on that attribute on a parallel test. Because errors have been defined as being uncorrelated, we cannot say that the error score on one test is equal to the error score on a parallel test. However, we can assume that the standard deviation of errors on two parallel tests are equal without violating the assumption of uncorrelated error. Although parallel tests may be defined in terms of the equivalence of true scores and the standard deviation of error scores, such a definition is theoretical and is of little help in ascertaining the extent to which any two tests are, in fact, parallel. However, given this formal definition of parallel tests, it can be shown to follow (Gulliksen, 1950, pp. 12–13) that

$$M_{x_1} = M_{x_2},$$

$$\sigma_{x_1}^2 = \sigma_{x_2}^2,$$

$$r_{x_1x_2} = r_{x_1x_3} = r_{x_2x_3} = \cdots$$

That is, scores on parallel tests are defined as having equal means, variances, and intercorrelations. Further, it is conceptually useful to think of parallel tests as involving similar content, item types, and instructions to subjects (Gulliksen, 1950, p. 14) although such additional properties are in no way part of the mathematical definition of parallel tests (Cronbach, Rajaratnam, and Gleser, 1963, p. 139). The assumptions made with respect to the definition of parallel tests have varied considerably (Lord and Novick, 1968), ranging from relatively restrictive assumptions (Gulliksen, 1950) to practically none at all (Tryon, 1957). Regardless of the restrictions placed on the definition of parallel tests, the classical definition of reliability rests on the concept of the *correlations* among parallel tests.

Correlations Among Parallel Tests

From the fundamental definition of the components of an observed score, $x = t + e$, it is possible to express the correlation between two parallel tests in terms of their true and error components:

$$r_{x_1x_2} = r_{(t+e_1)(t+e_2)} = \frac{\sum (t + e_1)(t + e_2)}{N\sigma_{x_1}\sigma_{x_2}}.$$

That is, the correlation between observed scores on two parallel tests may be thought of as the correlation of the composite of true and error scores on the two tests. From the expression for the variance of observed scores, $\sigma_x^2 = \sigma_t^2 + \sigma_e^2$, and from the definition of correlated errors, $r_{e_1e_2} = 0$, it can be shown (e.g., Ghiselli, 1964, p. 226) that

$$r_{x_1x_2} = \frac{\sigma_t^2}{\sigma_x^2}.$$

Thus we can define reliability as the correlation between parallel tests and interpret this reliability as the *ratio of true-score variance to observed-score variance*.

This very general formulation of reliability provides both a theoretical statement of the idea underlying the concept of repeated observations and a practical means whereby the concept may be directly assessed. The right side of the reliability equation expresses the concept of reliability as the ratio of specific true-score variance to observed-score variance. When a true score is defined as $x = t + e$, it follows that $\sigma_t^2 \leq \sigma_x^2$. Therefore, the ratio of true-score variance to observed-score variance can assume values from 0 to 1.00. When observational procedures are completely random, no component of the true score is involved, and the reliability of observation is zero. When random error is totally absent from observation, $\sigma_x^2 = \sigma_t^2$, and the associated reliability is 1.00. The left side of the reliability equation above provides an operational definition of reliability as the correlation between parallel tests.

Coefficients of Reliability

Since the classical definition of parallel tests is mathematical, there is little substantive restriction on the types of measurement procedures that may be called parallel. Thus, for many years, it was considered desirable to distinguish among several different experimental designs for the comparison of parallel tests. In the original version of the American Psychological Association's (1954) "Technical Recommendations," three types of designs were distinguished: (a) internal consistency, (b) equivalence, and (c) stability. When different parts of data obtained on a single occasion are considered parallel, a *coefficient of internal consistency* may be computed by "split-half" methods or by the procedures developed by Kuder and Richardson (1937). When parallel forms of a test are administered on a single occasion or close together in time, the correlation between forms is known as a *coefficient of equivalence*. When the same test form is administered on two occasions separated by an interval of time, the correlation between the obtained scores is known as a *coefficient of stability*.

The distinctions above were meant to convey the idea that "reliability is a generic term referring to many types of evidence" (APA, 1954, p. 28). Clearly, different designs for determining the reliability of parallel observations take account of quite different sources of error. Thus, although reliability may be defined as the ratio of true-score variance to observed-score variance, the error that enters into observed scores differs from one design to another. Internal-consistency procedures involve the estimation of error due to the selection of a given set of items or observations. Depending on the time interval between administration of parallel forms, equivalence procedures may estimate error due to selection of specific items and/or to response variability of subjects. Stability procedures provide an estimate of response variability in subjects as well as of the effect of differences in conditions of test administration or observation.

Such distinctions among different types of reliability coefficients have had two undesirable consequences. Though meant to be general, the distinctions have taken on connotations of specificity. Hence one frequently encounters references to *the* coefficient of internal consistency, *the* coefficient of stability, etc., with the emphasis implying that there is a single definition of error associated with each general type of coefficient. Second, the very attempt to classify specific types of reliability coefficients has resulted in a restrictive terminology that does not do justice to the many different sources of error that may be of interest in observational or testing programs. As a consequence, the revised edition of the American Psychological Association's (1966) *Standards* recommends that these distinctions be discarded (pp. 26–27). In lieu of estimating specific types of reliability coefficients, the *Standards* emphasize:

The estimation of clearly labeled components of error variance is the most informative outcome of a reliability study. . . . The analysis of error variance calls for the use of an appropriate experimental design . . . the choice of design for studying the particular test is to be determined by its intended interpretation and by the practical limitations upon experimentation. (p. 26, emphasis omitted.)

Although not identified as such, the statement above seems to represent an advocation that the theory of generalizability replace classical reliability theory as a framework for evaluating observational and testing procedures. With this in mind, we now turn to a consideration of the theory of generalizability.

The Theory of Generalizability

The Concept of Generalizability

The classical concept of reliability is based on the notion that every test or observation has a single specific true score, belongs to only one family of parallel tests, and may be expressed in terms of a single reliability coefficient. This limited conception of reliability has been criticized by several writers (e.g., Guttman, 1953; Tryon, 1957). More recently, Cronbach and his associates (Cronbach and Azuma, 1962; Cronbach and Gleser, 1964; Cronbach, Rajaratnam, and Gleser, 1963; Cronbach, Ikeda, and Avner, 1964; Cronbach, Schönemann, and McKie, 1965; Cronbach, Gleser, Nanda, and Rajaratnam, in press; Gleser, Cronbach, and Rajaratnam, 1965; Rajaratnam, 1960; Rajaratnam, Cronbach, and Gleser, 1965) have consolidated previous objections to the limited specific-true-score view of reliability theory within the broader context of a theory of generalizability. According to their view, an interest in the "reliability" of a given measure is based on a desire to *generalize* from the observation involved to some other class of observations.

An interest in "rater agreement" may actually be an interest in the degree to which we can generalize from a given set of ratings to those that other raters might make. An interest in the "reliability" of the score on an anxiety scale may actually be an interest in the extent to which such a score is representative of scores that might have been obtained on other anxiety scales constructed by the same method. Since a given measure may be generalized to many different "universes," the investigator must be able to specify the universe in which he is interested before he can study "reliability."

Persons

Psychological tests and observations are applied to a specific sample of persons. The sample is assumed to be a subset of a larger *population* to which the test results or observations may be generalized. Although this point may appear obvious, it is often overlooked (Loevinger, 1965). To determine the reliability of a psychiatric screening device, we would wish to obtain a random sample of persons who would presumably be representative of the population of persons (psychiatric patients) to whom we would like to generalize. Clearly, assessing the reliability of a psychiatric screening device on a sample of college sophomores would violate this principle.

Conditions

To Cronbach, Rajaratnam, and Gleser (1963), who use the term in a very general sense, *conditions* may refer to particular test items, test forms, stimuli, observers, occasions, or situations of observation. In estimating the reliability of a specific set of conditions, we are interested in the extent to which we can generalize from that set to the universe of which our conditions are a sample. The generalization desired may be quite limited, as when our interests lie in the extent to which we can generalize from the ratings of one observer in one set of conditions to the ratings of the *same* observer in another set. On the other hand, the degree of generalization desired may be extremely broad, as when our interest lies in the extent to which we can generalize from peer ratings of "academic competence" to faculty ratings of "academic competence." Note that the latter is traditionally thought of as a "validity" generalization. That is, peer ratings are generally viewed as "predictors" and faculty ratings as a "criterion." Nevertheless, the extent to which one can generalize from one sample of raters to the other falls within the realm of the theory of generalizability. Thus the theory of generalizability purposely blurs the traditional distinction between "reliability" and "validity" (Cronbach *et al.*, 1963).

The Universe Score

For a given sample of persons, p, and a given set of conditions, i, we obtain an observed score for a given person on a given condition, X_{pi}. For each person we define a *universe score*, M_p, as the mean of X_{pi} over all conditions in the universe. The assumptions underlying this definition are: (a) The universe can be unambiguously described, so that it is clear what conditions fall within it. The universe may be conceived of as encompassing either a finite or an infinite number of conditions. (No assumptions are made about the content of the universe or about the statistical properties of the scores within conditions.) (b) Conditions are experimentally independent; the person's score in condition i is independent of his being observed under other conditions. (c) The observed scores, X_{pi}, are numbers on an interval scale. (d) Conditions are *randomly* sampled from the universe of conditions, and the persons observed are *randomly* sampled from the pertinent population.

The Generalizability Study

A distinguishing and valuable feature of the approach of Cronbach and his associates is the requirement of a generalizability study (G study) in the investigation of the relationship between an observed score and a universe score. A G study is specifically designed to assess the measuring technique of interest in terms of the relationship between the observed scores and the universe scores to which they are to be generalized. Among its other valuable features, the G study forces the investigator to specify the universe of scores to which he would like to generalize.

To speak of the generalizability of a measure is obviously an incomplete statement until the speaker indicates what construct is being generalized to; he is forced to be explicit about what has often been implicit and therefore lost from sight. The so-called error of measurement becomes a discrepancy between the measurement and a universe score, and the question "What universe?" follows naturally. (Cronbach *et al.*, 1963, p. 156.)

In the generalizability study, the number of conditions sampled is designated by n_i.

The Decision Study

The decision study (D study) provides the basic data from which decisions about individuals or groups are made. Thus, in the typical personality assessment paradigm, the decision data represent the input on which actual dispositions, diagnoses, or classifications are made. Therefore, from a practical point of view, it is the decision data whose dependability is of primary interest. Frequently, the same set of data may be used both for an analysis of generalizability (G study) and for decision making (D study).

Thus the G and D studies may be the same. However, they may be separate and may be based on quite different experimental designs. In order to assess the dependability of employing only one observer as a source of data for decisions (D study), it may be necessary to employ several different observers in the G study. Here it is assumed that the person or persons in the D study come from the same population as those in the G study. The actual number of conditions employed in a D study is designated by n_i'.

An Illustrative Generalizability Design

As part of a diagnostic procedure, a single observer rates the sociability of a group of children during a free-play period. On the basis of a random time-sampling procedure, he observes each child for approximately the same amount of time during the single period. Since this observer is the one who provides the observational data on which decisions will be based, the issue of generalizability relates to the dependability of his observations when they are based on only a *single* period of observation. Although we are willing to restrict our generalizations to ratings made by a particular observer, we would like to know to what extent ratings made on a single occasion will generalize to other occasions. The assessment of this aspect of generalizability requires a design in which the rater in question observes a group of children on several different occasions. Such a design is represented schematically in Table 7.1.

Table 7.1 Basic data matrix for a generalizability study

Persons	Conditions 1	2	3	$\cdots$	n_i	Means
1	X_{11}	X_{12}	X_{13}	$\cdots$	X_{1n_i}	$\bar{P}_1$
2		X_{22}	X_{23}	$\cdots$	X_{2n_i}	$\bar{P}_2$
3			X_{33}	$\cdots$	X_{3n_i}	$\bar{P}_3$
$\vdots$			$\vdots$			$\vdots$
n_p			X_{n_p3}			$\bar{P}_{n_p}$
Means	$\bar{I}_1$	$\bar{I}_2$	$\bar{I}_3$	$\cdots$	$\bar{I}_{n_i}$	$\bar{M}$

The Basic Data Matrix

A total of n_p persons have been observed under n_i different conditions. The rows of Table 7.1 represent the persons, $1, 2, 3, \ldots, n_p$, and the columns represent the conditions, $1, 2, 3, \ldots, n_i$. The body of the table consists of the scores of each person observed under each condition: X_{11} is the rated total sociability score of Person 1 observed under Condition 1; X_{23} is the rated score of Person 2 under Condition 3, etc. Summing the scores of each person across conditions and dividing by the number of conditions produces a mean score for each person. The symbol $\bar{P}_1$ denotes the average score of Person 1 over all conditions of observation. It is also possible to obtain a mean score for each condition of observation by summing the scores for each condition across persons and dividing by the number of persons. The symbol $\bar{I}_1$ denotes the average score of all persons observed under Condition 1. By summing across *both* persons and conditions, one can obtain a "grand mean," $\bar{M}$, for all observations in the study.

Sources of Variation

When observational data are arranged as in Table 7.1, it is possible to specify the sources of variation, or components of variance, that contribute to an observed score for a given person under a given condition of observation. One accomplishes this result by expressing a score for a given person under a given condition, X_{pi}, as a sum of *deviation scores* about the several means involved:

$$\begin{matrix} \text{Grand} & \text{Person} & \text{Condition} & \text{Residual} \\ \text{mean} & \text{effect} & \text{effect} & \text{effect} \end{matrix}$$

$$X_{pi} = \quad \bar{M} \quad + (\bar{P}_p - \bar{M}) + (\bar{I}_i - \bar{M}) + (X_{pi} + \bar{M} - \bar{P}_p - \bar{I}_i).$$

The *grand mean* represents the average sociability score in the entire sample of observations and serves as a base line against which other effects are evaluated. The *person effect* compares the average score of the single individual of interest with the average person in the sample. Should the individual's average score be less than that of the average person, this term would have a negative value. The *condition effect* compares the average score for the condition of interest with the average score for all conditions. Should the condition of interest yield higher scores than other conditions, this term would have a positive value. The *residual effect* includes any source of variation in the observed score that cannot be attributed to person or condition effects. In the present instance, this would mean that the observed score, X_{pi}, is higher or lower than would be predicted from a knowledge of the corresponding person and condition means. Such an effect is usually called an *interaction*, in this case between a person and a condition.[1]

Analysis of Variance

Having specified the sources of variation that may influence a single observed score, we now return to the question that prompted our generalizability study: To what extent can we depend on this observer's ratings that are typically

---

1. In this particular example, all persons are observed under all conditions by a single rater, so that persons and conditions are completely "crossed" or "matched." For "unmatched" experimental designs, a "within persons" source of variation must be considered.

based on a single period of observation? Such a question requires estimates of the components of variance that contribute to the observed scores of all persons under all conditions rather than simply the effects that determine one person's score under one condition. The method for calculating such sources of variation by conventional analysis-of-variance procedures is summarized in Table 7.2. A detailed description of analysis-of-variance procedures is not necessary at this point, since they are adequately covered elsewhere (Lindquist, 1953; Winer, 1962; Scheffé, 1960) and since estimation of generalizability does not involve the use of conventional significance tests.

Table 7.2 Sources of variation for data in Table 7.1

Source of variation	Degrees of freedom, df	Sum of squares	Mean squares
Between persons	$(n_p - 1)$	$n_p \sum_{p=1}^{n_p} (\bar{P}_p - \bar{M})^2$	MS_p
Between conditions	$(n_i - 1)$	$n_i \sum_{i=1}^{n_i} (\bar{I}_i - \bar{M})^2$	MS_i
Residual (error)	$(n_p - 1)(n_i - 1)$	$\sum_{p=1}^{n_p} \sum_{i=1}^{n_i} (X_{pi} + \bar{M} - \bar{P}_p - \bar{I}_i)^2$	MS_r
Total	$(n_p n_i - 1)$	$\sum_{p=1}^{n_p} \sum_{i=1}^{n_i} (X_{pi} - \bar{M})^2$	

As Table 7.2 indicates, the total variation in observed scores for all persons can be broken down into that between persons, between conditions, and remaining, or residual. Associated with each analysis is a term indicating the number of "degrees of freedom," df, or simply the number of *independent* observations on which the variation is based. The "sum of squares" for each analysis is calculated by summing the squared deviations from the mean of the source of variation of interest. The between-persons sum of squares is calculated by summing the squared deviations of each person's mean, $\bar{P}_p$, from the grand mean, $\bar{M}$, and the between-conditions sum of squares is calculated in an analogous fashion. The residual variation may be calculated directly, as indicated, or determined by subtracting the between-persons and between-conditions sums of squares from the total sum of squares.

When a sum of squares is divided by its associated degrees of freedom, a mean of the squares, or *mean-squares* term, is obtained. Thus MS_p represents the mean, or average, of the squared deviations between person means and the grand mean, MS_i the mean-squares term for the variation between conditions, and MS_r the mean-squares term for residual, or interactive, variance that cannot be accounted for by variance due to persons or conditions.

Intraclass Correlation

Traditional formulations of reliability that are based on an analysis-of-variance model express the reliability coefficient as the ratio of the variance of "true" scores to the variance of observed scores, an expression known as an *intraclass* correlation. In generalizability theory, the sources that contribute to observed-score variance will vary according to the definition of the problem.   In our present example, the coefficient of generalizability of interest takes the form:

$$\alpha_{(1)} = \frac{MS_p - MS_r}{MS_p + (n_i - 1)MS_r}.$$

In the numerator, the variance due to universe ("true") scores is estimated as the mean squares due to persons minus the residual mean squares due to person-by-condition interaction.   The observed-score variance expressed in the denominator indicates the "expected value" of observed-score variance for a single condition of observation.   Hence the coefficient indicates the extent to which we can depend on this observer's ratings when they are based on a single period of observation.

Coefficients of Generalizability

The intraclass correlation described in the preceding example provided an estimate of the generalizability of observations for a specified universe of conditions within a particular experimental design for a generalizability study. Other questions regarding generalizability will require different definitions of the universe and possibly different experimental designs.[2]   In order to illustrate this principle, we will now consider a more general expression for estimating the coefficient of generalizability and then provide examples of some of its possible applications to familiar "reliability" problems.

Generalizing From an Unspecified Number of Conditions

Frequently, an investigator may wish to inquire about the generalizability of an unspecified number of conditions to be employed in a D study. This can happen when he does not know in advance which conditions will be employed in the D study or when a particular condition of interest cannot be included in a G study.   Here the interest is not in the generalizability of a single condition, but in the generalizability of conditions in general.   The question involves the extent to which we can generalize from conditions in a decision study, n_i' to a random sample of all possible conditions, as represented

---

2.   The present discussion will be restricted to "matched" or "crossed" experimental designs.

in the generalizability study, n_i. The *general form* of the intraclass correlation may be written

$$\alpha_{(n_i')} = \frac{n_i'(MS_p - MS_r)}{n_i'MS_p + (n_i - n_i')MS_r},$$

where n_i = the number of conditions in the generalizability study, and n_i' = the number of conditions to be employed in the decision study.

Generalizing From One Condition

We have already considered the situation in which the generalizability of a particular observer's ratings from a single period of observation is at issue. In that instance, there is only one condition in the decision study ($n_i' = 1$), and the general form of the intraclass correlation given above becomes

$$\alpha_{(1)} = \frac{MS_p - MS_r}{MS_p + (n_i - 1)MS_r},$$

which is the formula employed in our original example.

The "Internal Consistency" of Observations

Thus far, we have considered situations in which observations are made for persons on several separate occasions. Suppose, however, that the only data available are ratings of sociability for a group of children on a single occasion of observation. On the basis of a time-sampling procedure, a single observer has made a number of subobservations of a group of children, so that a total score for sociability is available for each child. Up to this point, we have been concerned with the generalizability of such total scores across other occasions. Now our interest lies in the homogeneity or "internal consistency" of the total scores themselves. That is, to what extent can we depend on a particular set of subobservations as representative of all possible subobservations that might constitute a total score?

In this instance, we may define the *conditions* of interest as different *subobservations* (items) that contribute to a total score on observed sociability for a single occasion. The basic data matrix then becomes a matrix of persons by subobservations. Since there is only one occasion in our generalizability study ($n_i = 1$) and one occasion in our decision study, the general form of the intraclass correlation becomes

$$\alpha_{(n_i)} = \frac{MS_p - MS_r}{MS_p}.$$

This formula is equivalent to the "generalized" formula of Kuder and Richardson (KR 20) for estimating the average correlation of all possible "split-halves" of items from a single test (Cronbach, 1951). Note that the formula is derived from generalizability theory by considering as "conditions" subobservations (items) instead of occasions of observation. It has been repeatedly emphasized that the term "conditions" is employed very broadly in generalizability theory. In that theory, the estimation of internal consistency does not require a special definition of reliability (e.g., "split-half reliability"); internal-consistency estimation represents only one of many universes to which an investigator may wish to generalize.

Increasing the Number of Observations

It is well known that increasing the number of subobservations made during a single period of observation will increase the generalizability of the total score involved. If an investigator is dissatisfied with the generalizability of an observational procedure based on n_1 observations (where the generalizability is symbolized by α_1), he may wish to estimate it based on n_2 comparable observations (α_2). Where $k = n_2/n_1$, or the fraction by which the number of subobservations is increased, the generalizability of the lengthened observational procedure is estimated by the expression

$$\alpha_{(n_2)} = \frac{k\alpha_{(n_1)}}{1 + (k - 1)\alpha_{(n_1)}},$$

which is the well-known formula developed by Spearman (1910) and Brown (1910) for estimating the effect of increased test length on reliability. Solving the Spearman-Brown formula for k, with a fixed value of $\alpha_{(n_2)}$, will enable the investigator to estimate the number of additional observations (items, observers, etc.) that must be employed to achieve a desired degree of generalizability.

Multifacet Designs

Our presentation of generalizability theory has been limited thus far to the simple situation in which n_p persons are observed or tested under n_i conditions (see Table 7.1). Although we have emphasized that the condition considered may be alternatively interpreted as involving different observers, different stimuli, or different situations of observation, we have nevertheless confined our examples to the single-condition case. As a consequence, the formulas developed are little different from those employed in classical estimates of test reliability. A distinguishing feature of generalizability theory is its *simultaneous* treatment of components of variation arising from two or more conditions. The various conditions which might influence observation are referred to as "facets," which, alone or in combination, define the universe of interest (Cronbach *et al.*, in press). Typical observational studies involve the observation of a given *attribute* on a given *occasion* within a specified *setting* by certain *observers* employing certain *instruments*. The intersect of some or all of these conditions, or facets, defines the universe of generalizability.[3]

Consider the two-facet generalizability study illustrated in Figure 7.1. Ten persons are observed by four observers (Facet I) on three different *occasions* (Facet II). The facets of settings, instruments, and attributes are held constant for all observations in this particular study.[4] Thus the universe of generalizability is defined by persons, observers, and occasions. The "cell entries," X_{pij}, represent the rating assigned a person, p, by a particular observer, i, on one of the occasions, j.

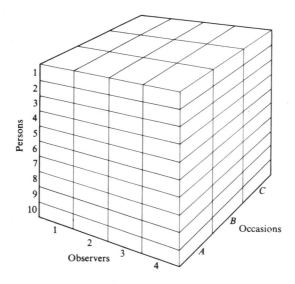

Fig. 7.1 Two-facet generalizability design.

The largest universe of generalizability involves the mean for each person over all possible observers and occasions in the universe sampled, M_p. Alternative definitions of the universe of generalizability may be of interest. One may wish to estimate the generalizability of a person's rating across

3. Cronbach (personal communication) does not consider attributes or instruments as falling within the current scope of generalizability theory. Questions relating to the generalizability of instruments (method variance) and to the generalizability of attributes (construct validity) are usually considered questions of "validity," and for this reason, they will be reconsidered as such in Chapter 9.

4. Cronbach *et al.* (in press) call attention to the importance of such "fixed" facets in defining the universe score. Although there is no way to estimate generalizability over a fixed facet, such a facet provides a partial definition of the universe score. Definitions of the universe should be qualified with this in mind.

observers for one specific occasion.   Or one may wish to estimate the generalizability of ratings given by one particular observer across occasions. From a practical viewpoint, it may be of interest to establish the number of observers (or occasions) that need to be included to achieve a coefficient of generalizability of a given magnitude.   Although any single decision study is unlikely to require estimates of all these variously defined components of variance, the generalizability study that makes them available will be the one most useful to other investigators.   The general logic that underlies the computation of generalizability coefficients for components of variance from two, three, or even ten facets is the same as that we have presented for the one-facet case.   The computational complexities are considerable, however, and the interested reader should consult the forthcoming book by Cronbach *et al.* (in press).

Implications of Generalizability Theory

The theory of generalizability developed by Cronbach and associates has far-reaching implications of both a theoretical and a practical nature.   The theoretical proofs and implications of generalizability for classical reliability theory, which are not treated here, can be found in the original writings of Cronbach and associates.   It should be apparent, however, that generalizability theory has provided a more precise and intuitively satisfying conception of the nature of reliability.   It is also important to note that the computational formulas for estimating reliability need not be restricted by assumptions regarding strictly parallel forms.   Finally, the various coefficients of reliability (internal consistency, equivalence, stability) and the somewhat equivocal distinctions to which they refer can be easily subsumed under the notion of generalizability:

Any idea that could be expressed by naming coefficients distinctively can be expressed more precisely by designating the universe to which each coefficient refers. (Cronbach, Rajaratnam, and Gleser, 1963, p. 159.)

The *degree* of generalizability desired for a given observational procedure is, to some extent, an option of the individual investigator (Cronbach *et al.*, 1963).   Consider, for example, playground observations of aggression in children obtained during a period of free play.   One investigator may wish to regard such observations as representing the child's "general aggressiveness" in all interpersonal situations.   Another investigator may wish to distinguish between home and school environments and expect to generalize only over school situations.   A third investigator might expect generalizability only if he narrows the universe of concern to certain free-play situations within the school situation in which the teacher maintains certain supervisory attitudes.   It is possible to design a generalizability study that will indicate the degree of generalizability across the several universes mentioned. Nevertheless, the definition of the universe of interest still remains at the discretion of the theorist. Some theorists may prefer a single score for aggressiveness, even though greater generalizability could be attained with multiple scores from a number of subuniverses (Cronbach *et al.*, 1963, p. 158).

It should now be clear that investigators are obligated to specify and define the nature of the universe to which they would like to generalize their observations. Such considerations can no longer be left to "the statistician." It should also be clear that test constructors and those who develop standardized observational procedures are obligated to specify the universe to which they would generalize their instruments and to provide empirical evidence of such generalizability in the form of generalizability coefficients or estimates of the components of variance involved. To the extent that such obligations are honored in the future, we can anticipate advances in clarity and rigor of conceptualization in the field of behavior observation.

FACETS OF OBSERVATION

As we have just seen, a variety of conditions, or facets, alone or in combination, contribute to the universe score, M_p, of the person observed. Somewhat arbitrarily, we may partition potential universes of interest into the facets of: (a) settings, (b) observers, (c) instruments, (d) occasions, and (e) attributes. The design of a generalizability study may require systematic sampling of any or all of these sources of variation, depending on the purposes and preferences of the investigator. Facets which are ignored ("fixed") are present, nevertheless, and their contribution to the definition of the universe should be acknowledged. In the sections to follow, we shall consider the characteristics of each of these facets, all of which limit or enhance the generalizability of behavior observations.

Settings

The environmental settings in which behavior observations occur may be roughly ordered in terms of the degree of *control* that is exercised over the events which occur in the environment observed. This dimension ranges from completely uncontrolled observations made in the "natural" setting of real life to the highly controlled observations that may be made in the psychological laboratory.

Naturalistic: Immediate

When behavior is observed *in situ*, in the absence of artificial constraints, the observational procedure is referred to as "naturalistic." The anthropological field study is perhaps the best known example of naturalistic observation in the behavioral sciences (Mead, 1964). Naturalistic observation has also been championed by a number of psychologists, notably Lewin (1936) and his students (Barker and Wright, 1955; Cartwright, 1959; Festinger, Riecken, and Schacter, 1956). Examples of naturalistic observation in psychology include the observation of a single child for a full day (Barker and Wright, 1951) and the observation of family interaction patterns in the home setting (Patterson and Harris, 1968).

The defining characteristic of *immediate* naturalistic observation is the planned or "preprogrammed" nature of the observations. Although the observer has little or no control over the behavior observed, he has complete control over that *aspect* of behavior to which he will attend. Consequently, it is possible to obtain considerable generalizability across observers by use of carefully constructed encoding devices which program the observer to behave systematically in the face of an unpredictable environment. The behavior of interest is recorded as it occurs and is not subject to the vagaries of the observer's recollection or memory of the event.

Naturalistic observational techniques are usually considered to be those which achieve "realism" at the expense of environmental control. Although the prediction of behavior in real-life situations is usually assumed to be the goal of most psychological measurement procedures, "realism" may not be equivalent to "naturalism" in personality assessment. In the forecasting of college achievement, for example, the criterion measure may be performance on comprehensive examinations taken during the senior year of college. Comprehensive examinations represent a highly controlled situation although they may be completely "real" for this particular criterion. As attempts are made to predict longer-range or "ultimate" criteria (Chapter 1), the criterion setting becomes increasingly naturalistic. The performance of a "good physician" in a community is subject to few environmental controls. Consequently, observations made in relatively naturalistic settings (internship performance) may have greater generalizability to the ultimate criterion than would more controlled observations (performance in preclinical laboratory courses).

Naturalistic: Retrospective

When an observer is called on to reconstruct or recollect an earlier observation made in a naturalistic setting, we may speak of *retrospective* naturalistic observation. A defining quality of such observation is the absence of planning or preprogramming of the original observations themselves. A college student is asked to rate the degree of dominance in a fellow fraternity member. Such a *peer rating* requires the observer to reconstruct occasions (of his own choosing) on which the trait of interest may have been observed. An elementary school child is asked to indicate which of his classmates is the class "bully." Such a *peer nomination* requires the observer to recall which of his classmates has performed in an aggressive manner on the largest number of occasions (selected by the observer). A mother is asked to indicate the extent to which her child engages in solitary activity and daydreaming. In such a *parent interview*, the observer must again recall those occasions (of her own choosing) on which the behaviors of interest have occurred.

Elaborate and highly sophisticated encoding devices have been developed to aid the informant giving peer ratings, peer nominations, and parent interviews. Such devices, no doubt, have contributed to the substantial degree of generalizability across *different observers* that have been reported in studies of peer ratings, peer nominations, and parent interviews. Nevertheless, as will become apparent in a later section of this chapter, generalizability across observers in, for example, a peer-rating task does not imply that the peer ratings would themselves be generalizable to immediate naturalistic observations made at the time at which the behavior of interest occurred. This is a particularly troublesome point, and it has led to considerable confusion in the observational literature. Despite the psychometric advances that have been made in the development of peer ratings, peer nominations, and parent interviews, it must not be forgotten that the observations themselves are *retrospective* in nature and hence highly dependent on characteristics of the observer. Immediate naturalistic observations, on the other hand, are *preprogrammed* and can be recorded in such a way as to minimize the effects of observer characteristics.

Paradoxically enough, it has become customary to view retrospective naturalistic observations as somehow more "rigorous" than immediate naturalistic observations. This is due, in large part, to the controlled circumstances under which retrospective observations may be obtained and to the psychometric refinements that have been introduced in the coding and scoring of retrospective measuring devices. However, the ease with which retrospective observations may be obtained and scored should not distract us from the fact that such observations are both remote and highly selective.

Sophisticated advocates of retrospective observations tend to view peer-rating and peer-nomination devices as indices of social reputation or social-stimulus value and to view parent interviews as providing indices of parent perceptions of the child. Such a view seems to be a tacit admission that retrospective observational devices may provide more information about observers than observees. From the standpoint of generalizability, it is often argued that criterion measures themselves frequently reflect social-stimulus value and hence retrospective observations may be generalized to many criterion situations of social importance. This is no doubt true for many applied assessment problems. However, it seems likely that an equal number of assessment problems involve criterion measures that are influenced by immediate naturalistic observation. We refer here to situations in which an employer, a superior, or a psychiatrist conducts a series of preplanned immediate observations to determine the criterion status of a given employee, subordinate, or patient. When criterion measures are based on immediate observation conducted by significant others, the observer characteristics present in retrospective measures may contribute only error to the ultimate prediction.

Controlled

Observation of behavior in a laboratory setting or under special circumstances created by the observer is classified as controlled observation. A clinician manipulates the environment of a playroom by stocking it with aggressive objects and observing the aggressive behavior of children toward these objects. Emotionally arousing stimuli are presented on slides to a subject and his physiological reactions are recorded. Subjects are purposively made angry, and their reactions to frustration are then observed. In all these situations, the experimenter has control not only of the stimulating conditions but of the categories of possible response the subject might make. It is this type of control that distinguishes controlled observation from naturalistic observation.

The advantages of controlled observation should be evident. Stimulus control ensures the relevance of the behavior observed by increasing the probability that the response class of interest will be emitted during the period of observation. Limitation of the environment decreases the range of possible responses the subject might make and thereby makes it more likely that the behavior observed will be easily classified within a preplanned system of coding. Perhaps most important, the standardization of the stimulating environment minimizes the influence of extraneous factors which tend to decrease generalizability across different times and different occasions. From the standpoint of classical reliability theory, the controlled experiment is the technique par excellence of behavior observation.

Despite their many desirable features, controlled observations are subject to the charges of being "artificial" and "untypical." The allegedly artificial character of controlled observations lies in the simulated nature of the stimulating environment, and the allegedly untypical aspects are features of the behaviors elicited in such a situation. To assert that controlled observations are artificial is to assert that they differ in significant ways from "real" observations that might be made under naturalistic conditions. Certainly the novelty of the psychological laboratory and the presence of an observer and of experimental instructions and apparatus which limit modes of responding are not part of naturalistic settings. On the other hand, the recall of unplanned observations in retrospective naturalistic observation seems to be equally remote from the "real" behavior of interest, and the physical presence of observers in immediate naturalistic observation seems to contribute a substantial element of artificiality to such real-life observations (Patterson and Harris, 1968; Webb *et al.*, 1966).

In defense of controlled observation, Aronson and Carlsmith (1968) distinguish "experimental realism" from "mundane realism." Experimental realism is achieved "if the situation is realistic to the subject, if it involves him, if he is forced to take it seriously, if it has an impact on him" (p. 22). Mundane realism, on the other hand, refers only to the degree to which the laboratory events are likely to occur in the real world of everyday social transaction. Clearly, all events which occur in the real world are not guaranteed to be of interest or importance to the assessment task at hand. On the other hand, there are many laboratory situations that, despite their lack of mundane realism, provide samples of highly significant behavior that cannot be obtained by any other means. As Bandura and Walters (1963) observe, "experiments are not designed to reproduce the stimulus events that occur in real-life situations and they would be superfluous if they were" (p. 41). Rather, controlled observations are made of phenomena which do not lend themselves to precise observation in naturalistic settings.

Contrived

Contrived observational situations attempt to retain the rigorous control of laboratory procedures while avoiding the unnatural atmosphere usually created by a controlled setting. An observational setting which is apparently (to the subject) natural is, in fact, under the control of the observer. After a particularly grueling interview, a job candidate strikes up a conversation with a fellow candidate in the waiting room. However, the "fellow candidate" is actually a stooge who is observing his postinterview reactions. A candidate for a sensitive overseas position is presented with a construction test which ostensibly tests his ability to direct two helpers in building a frame structure out of simple wooden materials. In fact, the two "helpers" have been preprogrammed to provide situations which will test the candidate's emotional stability, frustration tolerance, energy, initiative, and social relations (Office of Strategic Services, 1948). Given the shortcomings of both naturalistic and controlled observations, it is possible that certain contrived settings may elicit behavior that is more generalizable to criterion situations than any that might result from use of either of the more conventional techniques.

Contrived observations may possess a high degree of both experimental and mundane realism. However, two rather serious shortcomings of contrived observational procedures relate to their ethical status and their security. Assessment procedures which violate the subject's privacy without his consent are viewed unfavorably both by the general public and by many social scientists (American Psychological Association, 1965; Baumrind, 1964; Kelman, 1967; Lovell, 1967; Shils, 1959; Willingham, 1967). The possible risk of unfavorable public or professional response to contrived observational procedures may be enough to offset their advantages. Similarly, although contrived observational procedures require that subjects be unaware of the experimental manipulation, it is not always possible to guarantee the security of such deception. Subjects may "psych out" the experimenter and see through the ruse. Or they may be informed of the true nature of the observational situation by former subjects or by others who have knowledge of the purpose of the experiment. Thus there is always the risk that a contrived setting, no matter how ingenious, may backfire and provide professional or interpretative problems for the investigator.

Observers

The most obvious dimension of generalizability in observational studies is that of generalizability across comparable observers and across different types of observers. Perhaps the most central concern in personality assessment is the extent to which predictor observations (e.g., peer ratings) may be generalized to criterion observations (e.g., supervisor's ratings). A less obvious but equally important dimension of generalizability relates to the extent to which the observer himself intrudes on or interferes with the behavior being observed (Weick, 1968). Measurement procedures which influence and thereby change the behavior of the subject are called "reactive" (Webb *et al.*, 1966). Situations which are highly reactive in terms of observer effects are not likely to be generalizable to situations in which such effects are minimal. This reasoning is implicit in the widely made distinction between *participant* and *nonparticipant* observation.

Participant Observation

It is convenient to define participant observation as that in which the observer is clearly visible to the subject being observed. Although such a category includes procedures which vary markedly in the extent or degree of observer participation, the definition serves to distinguish such observations from those in which observers are not physically present. The reactive effect of the observer's presence may vary from virtually none at all to a great deal, as in the situation in which the observer is the principal stimulus for the subject's behavior.

Observations conducted in naturalistic settings by an observer who maintains a passive and nonparticipating role are generally thought to be the least reactive in terms of observer effects. In the classic study of Barker and Wright (1955), in which observations were made of children in natural settings, the presence of the ubiquitous observers was eventually accepted as part of the natural environment. The reactive effects of observation were also reported to be quite slight with younger children. On the other hand, studies of delinquent children (Polansky *et al.*, 1949), nursery children (Arsenian, 1943), and families observed in their homes (Patterson and Harris, 1968) have reported considerable reactive effects of observation in a naturalistic setting.

Despite the attempt by an observer to blend into the natural setting, his mere presence may be sufficient to invoke the "guinea pig effect" (Selltiz *et al.*, 1964), which makes for self-conscious behavior, or the "role selection effect" (Webb *et al.*, 1966), in which subjects select from many possible roles the one they believe to be appropriate to the purpose of observation. Frequently, the inactivity or nonparticipation of the observer makes him a conspicuous person in groups for which nonmember role patterns do not exist (Weick, 1968, p. 370). While the reactive effects of observation in naturalistic settings are not to be denied, such effects may be quite localized in nature and may be reduced when the extent and kind of interference is accurately assessed (Weick, 1968).

Although the observer in a controlled laboratory setting is considered part of the standard environment, there is abundant evidence that the experimenter-subject relationship is a highly reactive one. Such demographic variables as the experimenter's sex, race, religion, and status, as well as such personality variables as likability, warmth, adjustment, hostility, anxiety, and authoritarianism, have all been found to affect subjects' responses (Rosenthal, 1964). Perhaps the most dramatic reactive effect of experimental observers is what Rosenthal has identified as the "experimenter expectancy effect." In a series of ingenious and pioneering studies, Rosenthal demonstrated the manner in which an observer's *expectation* of the outcome of an experiment exerts a subtle influence on the results obtained. Although the reactive effects of observation appear to be extensive in controlled settings, the very nature of such settings makes it possible to manipulate or to control those effects with considerable precision.

The semistructured interview or "polling" observational technique has been the subject of numerous studies of reactive characteristics contributed by the interviewer. Such factors as age (Erlich and Riesman, 1961), sex (Benney, Riesman, and Star, 1956), race (Cantril, 1944), and socioeconomic background (Katz, 1942) have long been known to influence the subject's responses. Similarly, the interviewer's own attitude toward the subject matter will strongly influence the opinions obtained (Cahalan, Tamulonis, and Verner, 1947). Recognition of such biasing effects and the proper training and selection of interviewers can do much toward eliminating these interference effects (Cannell and Kahn, 1968).

Unstructured interviews, particularly of a psychiatric or psychotherapeutic nature, have in recent years come to be regarded as a fertile source for
the study of observer effects. In the case of the psychotherapeutic interview,
therapist variables have come to represent a rather specialized area of study
(Bergin, 1967; Bordin, 1966; Gardner, 1964; Strupp, 1962). The emphasis
here is not so much on controlling reactive effects as on finding the optimal
combination of therapist characteristics that will lead to successful treatment
(Truax and Carkhuff, 1967). Unstructured interviews that are conducted for
assessment purposes are equally susceptible to such intrusive effects. Idiosyncratic characteristics of the interviewer will contribute to a lack of
generalizability of the observations obtained. By its very nature, the unstructured interview represents an observational situation in which the observer
is maximally intrusive. Because the interviewer provides the primary
stimulation to which the subject responds, it might be appropriate to view
the unstructured interview as a "setting" as well as an example of participant
observation.

Nonparticipant Observation

Situations in which a human observer is not visible to the subject might
appear, at first thought, to be relatively free of the reactive effects of observation. Prominent in this category are concealed observations, in which the
observer is not physically visible to the subject, and observations by means
of audiovisual recording devices in place of a human observer. Nonparticipant observations may be made with or without the knowledge of the subject
under observation.

When the consenting subject is observed through a one-way mirror or
by means of a microphone or movie camera, the reactive effect of the invisible
observer may still be considerable. Tape recording, for example, has been
demonstrated to have an intrusive effect on observees (Roberts and Renzaglia,
1965). On the other hand, studies in which subjects were outfitted with radio
transmitters (Purcell and Brady, 1965; Soskin and John, 1963) have reported
that the incidence of self-conscious comments about observation dropped off
almost to zero after the first day of recording. Nevertheless, it still could be
argued that such a sensitive recording device heightens the threat of observation (Weick, 1968, pp. 372–373). It is commonplace that individuals
behave in a stilted and unnatural fashion at first contact with tape recorders
and movie cameras. The critical question is the extent to which individuals
adapt to such intrusions and become engrossed in the activities under
observation.

Recent developments in nondetectable audiovisual recording techniques
have considerably enlarged the possibilities of nonparticipant observation
without awareness (Webb *et al.*, 1966; Weick, 1968). Some will remember the

"Candid Camera" television program, which provided dramatic illustrations of contrived nonparticipant observation. However, the use of technical equipment introduces technical problems which may themselves be intrusive. Taking motion pictures, for example, involves certain film-making conventions, which may drastically alter the conclusions drawn from such films (Michaelis, 1955). Such problems as lighting (Macoby *et al.*, 1964), angle, camera movement, and duration of exposure (Michaelis, 1955) can affect conclusions based on observation of the films. Nevertheless, nondetectable audiovisual recording represents one of the potentially most fruitful approaches to behavioral observation in naturalistic settings. As with contrived situations in general, the problems of such observations are more ethical than technical at the present time.

Classification of Observations

The degree of control exercised over observational *settings* and the degree of intrusiveness introduced by the presence or absence of an *observer* permit a tentative classification of observational techniques in terms of these two dimensions, given in Table 7.3. From the examples in the table, it should be clear that both participant and nonparticipant observational techniques may be applied in all the settings we have considered. This classification is not meant to be exhaustive, although it does indicate the variety of procedures

Table 7.3 Classification of observational procedures

	Observers	
Settings	Participant	Non-participant
Naturalistic: immediate	Anthropologist living with Indian tribe One child observed for 24 hours	Children observed in classroom through one-way mirror
Naturalistic: retrospective	Peer ratings Peer nominations Parent interview	Unobtrusive (nonreactive) measures Analysis of personal documents
Controlled	Structured interview Typical psychological experiment	Child's reactions to teaching machine observed through one-way mirror
Contrived	Observer posing as peer	"Candid Camera" incident Hidden observer watching reactions to "rigged" situation

that fall within the heading of observational techniques. A more complete classification of observational techniques would be achieved by consideration of the additional, and equally important, facets of instruments, occasions, and attributes.

Instruments

For observations to be of practical value they must be translated into some form of permanent record which may be analyzed subsequently. Such records may be the automatic product of mechanical recording devices, or they may be the end product of coding procedures employed by human observers in translating their sensory impressions into a permanent record. In either instance, there is a considerable degree of *selectivity* involved in the processing or encoding of raw observations into permanent records. In addition, there are certain peculiarities or characteristics about the instruments themselves that color the final form of the observation. Sources of variation that are associated with a given instrument, rather than with the behavior observed, have been referred to as "method variance" (Campbell and Fiske, 1959).[5] Characteristics of observation that may be attributed directly to the instrument, rather than to the setting, the observer, the occasion observed, or the attributes observed, qualify as "method variance." The implication is that different characteristics would have been recorded if a different instrument had been employed. The dimension of generalizability involved is that of *instruments* (methods), and the question to be raised is that of the generalizability of a given observation across different classes of instruments. Specific techniques for assessing generalizability across methods (Campbell and Fiske, 1959) will be considered in detail in Chapter 9. The present section focuses on components of method variance that are involved in the use of mechanical recording devices and the use of encoding devices by human observers.

Mechanical Devices

A variety of instruments have been developed which permit audio, visual, or polygraphic recording of human performance and thereby circumvent the shortcomings of human observers. There are also a number of mechanical devices which assist the human observer in recording his sensory impressions (e.g., a manually operated counter), although these would be more properly classified as encoding devices. Of interest here are those techniques which do not rely on human judgment and which may be either visible to the subject (and hence may be potentially reactive) or not visible to the subject (and hence may involve ethical problems).

---

5. For Campbell and Fiske, "method variance" denotes *all* systematic effects associated with a given measurement procedure, including the effects attributable to different types of observers. In the present exposition, "method variance" denotes only instrument effects (Wiggins, 1962, 1968).

The majority of such techniques have focused on the auditory recording of aspects of human speech. We have already mentioned tape recording procedures for obtaining records of *verbal* behavior, and a number of other devices focus on *vocal* aspects of human speech in social interaction situations. The Automatic Vocal Transaction Analyzer (Cassotta *et al.*, 1964) permits automatic recording and classification of vocal interaction patterns without human intervention. Voice records are made on tape, which is automatically sampled at rapid intervals for both the presence and the intensity of sound patterns. The resulting transcript provides a detailed analysis of vocal interaction patterns over an extended period of time. Measures of general noise level have been obtained with tape recorders in studies of the effects of drugs on hospital patients (Heusler, Ulett, and Blasques, 1959). Eye movements have been employed as indices of subject interest in specific classes of stimuli (Walters, Bowen, and Parke, 1963), as have measures of pupil dilation (Hess and Polt, 1960). These examples should suffice to indicate the kinds of behavior that are subject to recording by mechanical devices.

In a highly stimulating monograph, Webb *et al.* (1966) described classes of observational methods that are both unobtrusive and nonreactive. In particular, they emphasized the use of physical "erosion" and "accretion" measures, as well as of publicly recorded "archives." These measures are nonreactive in the sense that subjects are unaware of the fact that they are making records at the time of the behavior. They are retrospective in that, for the most part, measurements are obtained at a time subsequent to the behavior in question. In Table 7.3, such unobtrusive measures have been classified under nonparticipant, retrospective naturalistic observation.

Erosion measures are based on the degree of selective wear on some material of interest. For example, activity level in children may be measured by the rate at which they wear out their shoes. Accretion measures are based on the deposit of materials of interest. One example would be the content analysis of garbage cans in a residential dwelling. Although public archival records are of greatest interest to sociologists and political scientists, the use of such personal documents as diaries and letters has long been advocated as a fertile source of data in personality assessment (Allport, 1942). The variety and ingenuity of such unobtrusive measures in behavioral-science research can be appreciated only by a perusal of the monograph by Webb and his colleagues (1966).

Mechanical devices contribute a special kind of method variance to behavior observations. Because the devices are mechanical and objective, the question of generalizability of "specific true score" is seldom raised. Thus it is assumed that within permissible instrument error, the recording of vocal transactions on a single machine may be generalized to other similar machines. The generalizability of mechanical devices is limited not so much by method variance peculiar to a given machine as by the *aspect* of behavior measured by that class of mechanical devices. Mechanical devices, by their very nature, are highly *selective* in their recording and tend to focus on attributes of behavioral events that are most susceptible to mechanical recording. Thus the question of generalizability of method is closely related to the problem of generalizability of attribute. That is, to what extent do vocal interaction patterns, eye movements, and measures of shoe wear generalize to more molar classes of criterion behaviors? Bear in mind that the problem of method or "instrument" variance is not peculiar to the field of personality assessment. In the field of learning, for example, there has been considerable difficulty in reconciling theories of response acquisition based on performance in T-mazes (Hull, 1943) with those based on performance in Skinner boxes (Skinner, 1938).

Encoding Devices

Encoding devices are formats which aid the observer by providing a systematic frame of reference for recording his sensory impressions of the attribute in question. Observational schedules provide a set of *rules* for making and recording observations. Rating scales provide a *metric* for quantifying observations by degree or kind. As was true of mechanical devices, the critical dimension for encoding devices is that of generalizability across methods. To what extent will observations made under the rules of a given observational schedule generalize to those made under the different rules of different observational schedules? Similarly, to what extent will ratings made with reference to the metric of a given rating scale generalize to those made with reference to the different metrics of different kinds of rating scales?

Observational Schedules

Observers are seldom turned loose to swim in the "stream of behavior" (Barker, 1963) represented by ongoing psychological events. *Systematic* observations are preprogrammed in the sense that observers have agreed or been instructed as to what, how, and when to observe. There are a wide variety of observational schedules or rules for observations, which reflect the many different purposes of systematic observations. There are many possible ways of distinguishing among different kinds of observational schedules, but a broad and useful distinction may be made between "sign systems" and "category systems" (Medley and Mitzel, 1963, pp. 298–305). Although these two types of observational schedules are conceptually distinct, they may best be thought of as representing end points of a continuum since the characteristics of both systems may be represented by intermediate types.

Sign systems. An observed behavior may be viewed as a "sign" or as a "sample" of other behaviors (Goodenough, 1949; Loevinger, 1957). In viewing an observed behavior as a sample, one assumes that it bears a close similarity to the behavior to be predicted. In viewing an observed behavior as a sign, on the other hand, one assumes that it is an "indicant" of criterion behaviors which may be topographically quite dissimilar. Thus certain behaviors of a child in a playroom may be regarded as signs of interpersonal maladjustment. An observational schedule that is based on signs is limited to a list of specific incidents or behavioral acts which may or may not occur during the period of observation. The observer has a list of such specific behaviors ("yells," "cries," "laughs"), and he is asked to record their incidence during the period of observation. Typically, the list includes a wide variety of acts or incidents, although they are seldom considered to be exhaustive of all possible behaviors that might occur during the period of observation. The observer does not attempt to classify all behaviors that occur but rather notes the occurrence of specific behaviors listed in his observational schedule.

Patterson and associates (Patterson, Ray, and Shaw, 1968) have developed a sign system for coding sequences of family interactions in the naturalistic home setting. Trained observers, instructed to be as inconspicuous as possible, are present in the home during periods of family interaction. According to a prearranged schedule, the observer concentrates his attention on a single family member and records the patterns of interaction of that individual with other family members during a limited time period. Interaction sequences are coded in terms of 29 behaviors, or "signs," which include 18 specific behaviors and 11 specific consequences of these behaviors. A typical observational schedule is given in Figure 7.2.

At the top are the 18 behaviors of interest, as well as the 11 consequences that these behaviors might have in terms of the responses they elicit from other family members. The distinction between behavior and consequence is not rigid but is suggested as a conceptual scheme to help the rater think in terms of *interaction* units. In the area for recording behavior sequences, the wider space of each line is for codes indicating the behaviors, and the narrow space is for subscripts indicating to whom the subject's behaviors were directed (Mo = Mother, Fa = Father, etc.). The first two lines of the record sheet in Figure 7.2 represent the following behavior sequence:

Billy is in the living room watching T.V. This gets coded as normative social activity, NO, and it is consequated by NR since no one else is responding to Billy. As Mother walks by Billy's chair he touches her on the arm (TH) and says, "Mother, what are we having for supper?" (TA) Mother replies, "Baked

BEHAVIOR RATING SHEET

Subject __BILLY__   Observer __D. SMITH__   Date __10/10/67__ No. __1__

Behavior codes				Consequence codes			
CM	Command	IN	Indulgence	AT	Attention	DI	Disapproval
TA	Talk	SS	Self-stimulation	AP	Approval	HU	Humiliate
NO	Normative	TH	Touching, Handing	CO	Compliance	NC	Non-compliance
DP	Dependency	CN	Command (negative)	PP	Positive Physical	PN	Negative Physical
PL	Play	PX	Proximity		Contact		Contact
TE	Tease	RC	Receive	LA	Laugh	NR	No Response
YE	Yell	HR	High Rate			IG	Ignore
CR	Cry	WK	Work				
DS	Destructiveness	NE	Negativism				

1 | NO — NR — TH & TA — Mo TA — AT — Mo CM — CO — Mo AP
   | MO   Mo   Mo

2 | WK — Mo WK — Jo↓ — Jo TE — PN — Jo YE — Fa DI & CN — CO & NE — Fa DI
   | Mo   Jo   Fa

3 | DS — Mo YE PN & CN — CO — ↑Bi↓ — NO — NR — NO — NR — NO — NR —
   | Fa   Fa

4 | NO — NR — NO — NR — NO — NR — NO — NR — NO — NR —

5 | NO & SS — NR — NO & SS — NR — TA — Fa PP & TA — TA — all LA —
   | Fa   Fa

6 | Fa TA — AP — TA — Fa AP — HR — Fa DI — Fa CM — CO —
   | Fa   Fa   Fa

7' | TH — Jo RC — PL — Jo PL — PL — Jo PL — PL — Jo PL — YE — Jo HU & CN —
    | Jo   Jo   Jo   Jo   Jo

8 | NC — Jo PN — CR — Mo TA & PP — TA — Mo CM — NC —
   | Jo   Mo   Mo   Mo

9 | PX — Mo NR — PX — Mo NR — TA — Mo IG — TA — Mo IG — TA — Mo IG
   | Mo   Mo   Mo   Mo   Mo

10 | TA — Mo TA — CM — Mo NC & CM — CR & DP & NC — Mo DI
    | Mo   Mo   Mo

Description _____
_____
_____
_____

Fig. 7.2 Schedule for observation of family interaction.

ham, green beans, and rice." (TA) Billy is watching her as she talks and is no longer looking at the T.V. (AT) "Come help me set the table and we'll be able to eat sooner," Mother says. (CM) Billy begins setting the table. (CO) Mother says, "Thank you, Billy." (AP) [At this point the observer takes a break to catch up on coding. Upon resetting the timer and beginning to code again, the observer puts a vertical mark at the start of the next line to indicate that the interaction is not continuous.]

Billy is now in the kitchen helping Mother serve supper. (WK–MoWK) Johnny comes in from outside. (Jo↓) Johnny says, "Look at Miss Billy cooking supper." (TE, his teasing tone of voice makes it clear that he is baiting Billy) Billy responds by punching him hard on the arm. (PN) Johnny yells, "Ouch, you didn't have to hit me." (YE) Father says, "You know I don't like any messing around. Cut it out right now." (DI, CN) Billy stops, protesting, (CO) "You always pick on me " (NE) Father replies, "You shouldn't talk back to me." (DI) [Once again the observer takes a break indicated by the slash at the beginning of line number three.] (Patterson, Ray, and Shaw, 1968, p. 8.)

When coded properly, such observations may be scored in terms of the *frequency* of occurrence of specific behavior-consequence patterns. These signs may then be used, singly or in combination, to predict criterion behaviors of interest, such as childhood psychopathology. This type of record also permits a detailed analysis of family interaction patterns which may be of use in planning the treatment of a disturbed child (Patterson and Bechtel, 1971).

Category systems. Unlike sign systems, category systems are typically limited to one or just a few aspects of behavior. Such systems are developed when previous research and a well-elaborated theory indicate the importance of a single dimension or category of behavior for predictive purposes (Medley and Mitzel, 1963, p. 299). An attempt is made to construct a finite set of mutually exclusive categories which are believed to be *exhaustive* of the dimension of behavior under consideration. Unlike sign systems, category systems rest on the assumption that the behaviors represented by each category will occur with considerable frequency and that any aspect of this dimension of interest will be easily codable within the available categories. The final record of a category system enables the investigator to classify the observed behavior in terms of the frequency of incidence of each category in the system.

Withall (1949) developed a set of categories to reflect the "social-emotional climate" of classroom instruction. The behaviors of interest were *statements* made by teachers in the course of classroom instruction. It was assumed that all such statements could be classified along a seven-category continuum of "learner-centeredness" versus "teacher-centeredness." These seven categories are presented in Table 7.4. Although Withall (1949) used these categories as a method for coding typewritten transcripts of classroom behaviors, Mitzel and Rabinowitz (1953) used them as an observational schedule for direct assessment of ongoing teacher behavior.

Table 7.4 Categories for assessment of social-emotional climate. (After Withall, 1949, p. 349)

Category 1	*Learner-supportive* statements that have the intent of reassuring or commending the pupil.
Category 2	*Acceptant and clarifying* statements having an intent to convey to the pupil the feeling that he was understood and help him elucidate his ideas and feelings.
Category 3	*Problem-structuring* statements or questions which proffer information or raise questions about the problem in an objective manner with intent to facilitate learner's problem-solving.
Category 4	*Neutral* statements which comprise polite formalities, administrative comments, verbatim repetition of something that has already been said. No intent inferable.
Category 5	*Directive* or hortative statements with intent to have pupil follow a recommended course of action.
Category 6	*Reproving* or deprecating remarks intended to deter pupil from continued indulgence in present "unacceptable" behavior.
Category 7	*Teacher self-supporting* remarks intended to sustain or justify the teacher's position or course of action.

The categories listed in Table 7.4 illustrate several characteristic features of category observational schedules. First, the class of behaviors of interest (teacher statements) lends itself to exhaustive classification within the system outline. Second, a certain amount of *inference* on the part of the observer is required since the underlying dimension is one of teacher "intent." However, since the attention of the observer is entirely focused on a single, well-elaborated continuum of behavior, there is reason to believe that, with sufficient practice, he may record observations with satisfactory reliability. The results of this categorical study may be expressed in terms of the frequency and distribution of behaviors along the continuum of interest. Medley and Mitzel (1959) have shown that this dimension is related to supervisors' ratings of teacher effectiveness and to pupil rapport, as measured by a questionnaire.

Rating Scales

Rating scales provide a metric whereby the sensory impressions of the observer may be translated into quantifiable form. Although rating scales may be part of an observational schedule and may therefore be used for recording immediate observations, they are more frequently used as a method for recording impressions subsequent to the event. The elapsed time between observation and recording by means of rating scales may be relatively short, as when an interviewer rates his impressions of the interviewee on completion of the interview, or the amount of intervening time may be considerable, as in retrospective peer ratings. As with observational schedules, the dimension of primary concern is that of generalizability across different rating *methods*. Although different types of rating scales may bear a superficial similarity, there may be subtle differences in the perspective they provide for viewing the same behavior. Consequently, generalizability across different rating scales must be demonstrated rather than assumed (e.g., Madden and Bourdon, 1963).

Types of rating scales. Rating scales are among the oldest of techniques for data collection in personality assessment (Ellson and Ellson, 1953), and a wide variety of specific types have developed over the years. The classic taxonomy of rating scales is that of Guilford (1954, pp. 263–301), who distinguished four principal types: numerical, graphic, forced-choice, and cumulated-points. Figure 7.3 provides examples of these types with reference to the trait dimension of physical hostility.

Numerical rating scale

____ 10. Murderous
____ 9. Assaultive
_✓_ 8. Destructive
____ 7. Combative
____ 6. Hot-blooded
____ 5. Even-tempered
____ 4. Peaceable
____ 3. Harmless
____ 2. Inhibited
____ 1. Placating
____ 0. Cringing

Cumulated-points rating scale (partial list)

____ Adventurous	____ Bashful	_✓_ Calculating
_✓_ Aggressive	_✓_ Belligerent	____ Calm
____ Agreeable	____ Benevolent	____ Cheerful
_✓_ Angry	____ Bland	____ Cooperative
____ Anxious	____ Boring	____ Conscientious
____ Autonomous	____ Bright	____ Conservative

Forced-choice rating scale

____ Lazy
_✓_ Combative

____ Peaceable
_✓_ Self-sufficient

_✓_ Destructive
____ Dishonest

Graphic rating scale

____	____	____	_✓_	____
Cringing	Inhibited	Even-tempered	Destructive	Assaultive

Fig. 7.3 Four types of rating scales.

Numerical rating scales require the observer to translate his impressions into numerical form to represent the *degree* of the trait observed. The numbers may be supplemented by verbal "cues" or marker words which facilitate the numerical translation. Frequently, only terminal cues are provided ("murderous" and "cringing") to provide "anchors" of the dimension in question. Verbal cues should not be applied arbitrarily, however, and care should be taken to ensure that adjectival or adverbial markers correspond to the numbers to which they are assigned (Cliff, 1959). Numerical rating scales are among the most widely used of all types of rating scales, and perhaps for this reason, instances of their abuse are numerous.

Graphic rating scales provide a geometric representation of the dimension in question in the form of a straight line. Verbal cues are frequently displayed at various points along the line, as in Figure 7.3. A common variant of the graphic rating scale is the *continuous* scale, which provides the observer with an unbroken line. He may check any point along the implied continuum, and the number of discrete categories is limited only by the accuracy of the instrument which measures the distance from the end of the scale. This scale is probably the most widely used of all scales (Guilford, 1954), and there have been many ingenious variations on the basic design (e.g., Champney, 1941).

Cumulated-points rating scales do not require the observer to think in terms of either numerical or geometric concepts. Instead, on a list of attributes (see Figure 7.3 for part of such a list) he is asked to check those which apply. On the basis of a predetermined scoring key, items are assembled into scales whose total score can vary from zero to the number of items included. In the example of physical hostility, the total number of checked items which relate to hostility (aggressive, belligerent, etc.) forms the basis for the cumulated-points score. One advantage of the check-list format is that many personality traits can be assessed simultaneously. Since individual items are seldom weighted in such a procedure, it is assumed that the greater the number of items checked, the greater the intensity of the rated behavior.

Forced-choice rating scales were developed in an effort to overcome the well-known tendency of raters to assign only favorable adjectives to acquaintances. The observer's task is to select from a pair of items that which is more descriptive of the subject being rated. Typically, item pairs have been equated for "favorability" or "social desirability" (Edwards, 1957) although they differ with respect to their content or their predictive validity. Thus, in the examples provided in Figure 7.3, the item pairs have been equated for social desirability, but one member of each pair relates to the dimension of hostility. In other applications of the technique, items are paired for desirability, but the pair includes one item that has been empirically demonstrated to be related to the criterion of interest. A frequent variation of the forced-choice technique is one which provides the observer with four items (two high and two low in social desirability) and requests him to select the most and least descriptive. Many observers report dissatisfaction at being forced to make a choice between statements when *neither* statement appears to be strictly applicable. Consequently, the forced-choice technique is among the least popular rating scales from the standpoint of observers themselves.

Sources of error in rating scales. Special problems of distortion associated with the use of each of the four major types of rating scales are discussed in detail by Guilford (1954, pp. 263–278). In addition, Guilford enumerates a number of "constant errors" which are associated with this type of judgment task. The *leniency error* refers to the well-known tendency of raters to rate friends or close acquaintances higher on all traits. The *central tendency error* represents a widespread tendency of raters to use middle categories and thereby avoid extreme judgments. The *halo error*, or "halo effect," refers to the tendency to rate all traits in the direction of the general impression the rater has of the individual, rather than in terms of his specific standings on the given traits. The *logical error* refers to the tendency to give similar ratings for traits that seem "logically related," even though the traits, in fact, may be quite independent. The *contrast error* refers to the tendency to rate others in the opposite direction from the rater's own perceived position on the trait in question. Finally, the *proximity error* is reflected in spurious correlations between traits that appear close to each other on the rating schedule. A variety of special techniques have been developed for controlling these constant errors in human judgment (Guilford, 1954, pp. 278–294).

Occasions

Thus far we have given considerable attention to the following issues: (a) where and with what degree of control behaviors are observed (settings); (b) who is to do the observing and with what degree of intrusiveness (observers); and (c) what methods are to be employed to schedule and record observations (instruments). These issues are somewhat abstract and methodological and tend to divert attention from a more fundamental decision that lies at the heart of all behavior observation. Stated somewhat inelegantly, the question is: *How much* behavior is to be observed? More technically, what *sampling* procedure should be employed, and what is it that we are sampling?

Barker (1963) and his co-workers tend to view behavior observations as samples from a "stream of behavior." This metaphor is meant to call attention to the fact that the behavior of a person is a lifelong continuum that can never be seen in its entirety (Wright, 1960, p. 73). To observe this stream necessarily implies fractionation and thus the problem of sampling and representative units. Wright distinguishes two types of coverage that might be attempted by any sampling strategy. *Continuum coverage* has reference to the links or parts into which the "stream of behavior" is divided for purposes of observation. Consideration of units and extensiveness of observation has inspired the development of sampling techniques to ensure representativeness. Two broad classes of such techniques, time sampling and event sampling, are of special importance here. Wright's second type of coverage, *field unit analysis*, relates to strategies for defining units and time periods when continuous observations are made for extensive periods of time. Although such ecological studies are often referred to as census rather than sampling strategies (e.g., Kleinmuntz, 1967, p. 90), it should be clear that they do not constitute a census of the "stream of behavior" represented by an individual's life. The dimension of generalizability involved for all of these techniques is that of the representativeness of the sample of behavior observed.

Time Sampling

Time sampling procedures record "selected aspects of behavior if and as they happen within precise limited time spans" (Wright, 1960, pp. 73–75). The length, spacing, and number of intervals of observations employed are designed in such a way as to provide representative samples of the behavior of interest. Typically, two or more observers are preprogrammed to rotate their observations among subjects at fixed-time intervals. For example, in the previously mentioned studies of Patterson and associates (Patterson and Harris, 1968), on patterns of family interaction, each family member was observed for two nonsuccessive five-minute blocks during each observation session. Within each five-minute block, observations were divided into ten 30-second intervals, which were signaled by a light attached to a timing device built into the observer's clipboard. To minimize fatigue, the observer was permitted to take a 10-second break at the end of each 30-second interval, during which time he reset the timing device and prepared for the next 30 seconds of observation.

When multiple observers are used, it is possible to obtain estimates of inter-observer agreement by preprogramming observations in such a way that the same subject is observed by two or more observers during several time intervals. Once inter-observer agreement has been established, however, this procedure is not efficient, since multiple observers may be more fruitfully employed in obtaining larger samples of behavior than can be obtained by a single observer (Medley and Mitzel, 1963, p. 304).

Wide variations have been reported in the length, spacing, and number of observations made in different studies (Wright, 1960). The length of the observation period has varied from five seconds (Challman, 1932) to a full day (Barker and Wright, 1951). Spacing of observations may be daily, monthly, or even yearly. The number of observations may vary from a very few to many thousand. Such wide variations appear to reflect idiosyncracies of different investigators as well as solutions to specific sampling problems. A well-designed generalizability study should be able to answer the question of the length, spacing, and number of observations necessary to establish stable estimates of the attribute of interest. This number is likely to vary from attribute to attribute, as we will see in the discussion in the section on "attributes."

Although time sampling procedures are systematic and reliable, and they lend themselves to estimates of sampling adequacy, they are likely to violate "natural units" in the ongoing stream of behavior. Since the length of unit employed is typically small (five minutes or less), many naturally unfolding sequences of behavior are likely to be cut off in the middle as the observer shifts to his next object of observation. There is nothing in the fixed sequence of time sampling schedules to guarantee that events of interest will be observed or that they will be observed in their entirety. Concern for this shortcoming of time sampling procedures has led to the development of sampling procedures employing events rather than time as units.

Event Sampling

Where specific signs or categories of behavior are of interest, it is possible to program observations in such a manner that only instances of the relevant behaviors are observed. Thus the stream of behavior is structured into the "natural units" that define the event in question. With respect to our terminology, it is important to distinguish between "events" and the "settings" in which events or situations occur. Settings, as we have defined them, may vary in terms of the probability that a given event will be observed within them. In controlled and contrived settings, the environment is manipulated to ensure that the event of interest has a high probability of occurrence. Within naturalistic settings, it is desirable to select those naturally occurring environments which appear to be associated with the occurrence of the event of interest. But the "events" or situations themselves are not equivalent to the "settings" in which they are observed. As Wright (1960) noted:

The behavior of a child at a particular time does indeed depend more directly upon the situation [event] than upon the setting in which it takes place. (p. 77)

Thus it may be possible for a given event to have considerable generality across settings.

One of the earliest examples of event sampling involved naturalistic observation of spontaneous quarrels among preschool children on the playground over a period of four months (Dawe, 1934). Within this naturalistic situation, the play period was considered one in which the event of interest would be most likely to occur. Numerous other examples of the "opportunistic" use of naturally occurring settings for the observation of specific events are described by Webb *et al.* (1966). A contrived playground situation was utilized by Winder and Wiggins (1964) to study aggressive behavior in elementary school boys. A familiar game with slight modifications in the rules provided a maximum of frustration for the participants and hence a greater opportunity to observe aggressive behaviors. In observing deviant behaviors among children in family settings, Patterson and associates (Patterson and Harris, 1968) have found it convenient to observe families during dinner hour, a period of maximal social interaction, as well as during periods in which the father is absent. The defining characteristic of event sampling is not the setting in which events are observed but the choice of the event itself as the defining unit of observation.

In time sampling procedures, observer agreement is indicated by the convergence of ratings obtained within a predetermined time period. Event samplers are burdened by the additional problem of agreement as to the beginning, duration, and end of the event unit. This problem has not received much systematic attention (Wright, 1960, p. 107). Although inter-rater agreement is of importance in event sampling, the critical dimension of generalizability relates to the event itself. That is, to what extent does the event of "aggression" observed in one situation generalize to the event of "aggression" observed in critical criterion situations? Proponents of event sampling tend to be optimistic in this respect, primarily because the sampling method tends to do more justice to the "behavioral integrity" of the event than do other less natural procedures.

Field Unit Analysis

Most practical assessment problems seem to require that the behavior of interest be observed in the fractionated units of time sampling, event sampling, or a combination of the two. Special mention must be made, however, of the pioneering work of Barker, Wright, and associates (Barker, 1960, 1963, 1965; Barker and Wright, 1949, 1955; Barker and Gump, 1964) at the Midwest Psychological Field Station of the University of Kansas. These studies provide a conceptual and empirical foundation for the evaluation of more practical observational studies. From their painstaking observations of children in their everyday naturalistic settings have emerged the basic units of a psychological ecology. Their taxonomy of the naturally occurring stream of behavior distinguishes behavior *settings*, behavior *episodes* that occur within these settings, *association units*, which define the social context of behavior, and *environmental force units*, which describe the influence of the social context on behavior.

Behavior settings are the natural ecological units which provide the physical, temporal, and spatial coordinates of the stream of behavior. These settings are relatively stable patterns of extraindividual behavior whose identity and functioning are independent of the participation of particular persons (Barker, 1960, pp. 16–18). Typical settings for the people of "Midwest," Kansas, were Kane's Grocery, Pearl Cafe, and Denton's Drug Store (Barker and Wright, 1955). Although the behavior setting is a behavioral entity, its laws of operation are determined by a variety of nonbehavioral circumstances:

In the functioning of the Pearl Cafe in Midwest, for example, the availability and the price of food, the season of the year, the prevailing temperature, the size, lighting, and ventilation of the building, the state laws concerning hygienic practices, the customers, and the employees are all involved. We have only the beginning of an understanding of how these incommensurate phenomena are combined into the reliable non-erratic entity known so well to Midwest residents. (Barker, 1960, p. 18).

The complex relationships between people and settings provide a fascinating focus of investigation in psychological ecology (Barker and Wright, 1955; Barker, 1960).

Behavior episodes, which constitute the fundamental behavioral unit of observation in ecological investigation, are defined by the three criteria of directedness, size of behavior unit, and potency (Barker and Wright, 1955). *Directedness* refers to the fact that the behavior episode continues in one direction from its beginning to its end point or goal. The *size* of the behavior unit employed is determined by the portion of the behavior stream within which direction is to be determined. This segment of the behavior stream corresponds to the length of time during which people normally perceive that the behavior in question occurs. The *potency* of an episode refers to the fact that the total episode has greater potency than any of its parts. Thus, if any part of a behavior sequence exceeds or equals the whole in potency, that part becomes a separate episode. Typical behavior episodes are represented by such prosaic and easily recognizable units as "Walking down the street," "Playing with fountain pen," "Buying a soda," etc. Episodes are typically *overlapping* sequences of behavior which may be highly convoluted. Figure 7.4 illustrates a fragment of an observational record on Brett, a seven-year-old English boy who had just wandered into the "school yard" setting, where considerable noisy activity was in progress (Barker, 1963, p. 8). Within this relatively simple example of behavior episodes, we can see that the episodes "Watching cricket" and "Noting hurt child" are contained within the episode "Eating orange." Examples of more complex episodes are easily obtainable (Barker and Wright, 1955).

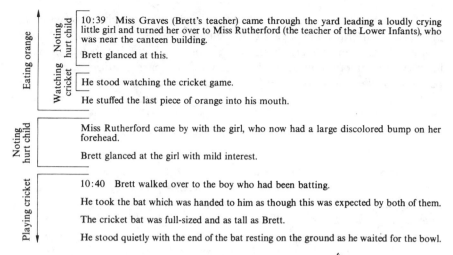

Fig. 7.4 Observational record on Brett in the school yard. (From Barker, 1963, p. 8)

Association units represent a natural and concrete way of categorizing the social context within which behavior episodes occur. An association unit is defined by a constancy in the number and identity of individuals who associate with the child during a period of time.

Associates are defined without conceptual or operational ado as individuals with whom the child becomes involved in any way. (Wright, 1960, p. 109)

Units are further analyzed for number, composition, and characteristic social action that occurs in the group. Because the behavior of an individual is influenced by the presence or absence of others, it is clear that, in many instances, there will be a close correspondence between association units and behavior episodes (Barker and Wright, 1955).

Environmental force units represent the "active efforts made by the child's social environment to penetrate his psychological world and to modify his behavior" (Schoggen, 1963, p. 42). In the same manner that behavior episodes represent the directedness of the child's behavior with respect to the persons and settings of his environment, these units attempt to specify the directed character of the social environment with respect to the child. The same three criteria used for defining behavior episodes serve in the definition of environmental force units. Such units are directed, fall within the range of units commonly perceived by people, and possess a relatively constant potency throughout their period of effectiveness (Schoggen, 1963, pp. 44–45). Examples of environmental force units initiated by a mother toward her four-year-old girl during a relatively brief period of time are as follows:

Getting S *to Bible School on time*
Questioning S *about cold*
Getting S *dressed*
Chatting with S *about haircurls*
Teasing S *affectionately* (Schoggen, 1963, p. 43)

One can gain an appreciation of the ingenuity and richness of the field observations made by Barker, Wright, and associates only by reading their detailed and encyclopedic records (e.g., Barker and Wright, 1951). It is unlikely that such methods will find immediate practical application in personality assessment procedures. Nevertheless, they may suggest modifications of existing techniques of time and event sampling that would make the latter procedures less arbitrary. Most important, the substantive findings of these studies may provide a base line against which the generalizability of more limited studies can be evaluated. An interesting example of such evaluation appears in Barker's own work (Barker, 1965, p. 5). As a student of Lewin, Barker carried out a classic series of studies of the consequences for children of frustration occurring in a controlled observational setting (Barker, Dembo, and Lewin, 1941). Some 20 years later, one of Barker's students (Fawl, 1963) looked for indications of the same findings in the elaborate behavioral records that had been accumulated by the Kansas Group. Fawl found that, in naturalistic settings, the incidences of frustration were considerably fewer than expected, and the consequences of frustration did not appear to be those observed in artificial laboratory situations (Barker, 1965, p. 5). The generalizability of other limited observational methods may also prove wanting when evaluated against the relationships obtained in naturalistic settings.

Attributes

Conceivably, any aspect of human behavior observed in any setting by any kind of observer would be grist for the data combination mill of personality assessment. Traditionally, however, personality psychologists, of both theoretical and applied persuasions, have tended to focus on relatively specialized classes of behavioral *attributes*. Although behavior is obviously the source of all observations, the observer's attention is directed toward attributes of behavior rather than to behavior itself (Torgerson, 1958). The *selection* of behavioral attributes for observation, largely a theoretical matter, is dictated by the personality model employed by the assessor (Chapter 10). The theoretical issue revolves on the proper choice of units in personality study (Allport, 1958). What has traditionally been considered the proper choice of units for personality study has recently been vigorously questioned (Goldfried and Pomeranz, 1968; Greenspoon and Gersten, 1967; Mischel, 1968; Kanfer and Saslow, 1965; Peterson, 1968; Wallace, 1967). The broader issue here centers on the relative merits of social-learning and multivariate-trait models of personality, and these two models appear to be in fundamental disagreement regarding the attributes of behavior which should be selected for observation.

The traditional choice of units for personality study has been the *trait* unit. Traits are organized dispositions within the individual which are assumed to have some generality in their manifestations across a variety of stimulus situations. On the basis of observed behavior, raters attempt to infer the position of the observee on the trait dimension in question. The rules for translating behavior observations into trait inferences are not always precise, and they rely heavily on the "ordinary language" of trait attribution. Thus the language of trait attribution is not unlike that employed by the novelist or the man in the street.

The choice of units in the more recent "behavioral analysis" approach to personality study is a *stimulus-response* unit. Limited segments of behavior are observed under carefully defined stimulus conditions, and the units are recorded with a minimum of inference on the part of the observer. Amplitude, frequency, and duration of response are recorded with reference to the stimulus conditions that preceded the response and the consequence of the response for the observee. Analysis of data of this sort permits statements about the stimulus conditions that "control" the response class of interest. Although the language of behavioral analysis is not that of the man in the street, the man in the street may be trained to make such observations.

From the standpoint of personality assessment, the "proper" units of observation are those which possess the highest degree of *criterion relevance* for the assessment problem at hand. Thus the critical dimension of generalizability with respect to the facet of attributes is one of criterion relevance. To what extent can the attributes observed be generalized to the attributes that define the criterion of interest?

Trait Attribution versus Performance Recording

The two most widely employed approaches to behavior observation in personality assessment are those which utilize retrospective *peer ratings* and those which employ immediate *behavior observations*. The issues involved in both approaches, which are sufficiently complex to require detailed consideration, are presented in the next chapter. For the moment we will limit discussion to the different attributes on which the two approaches focus and the extent to which these attributes may be considered relevant to socially important criterion measures. In practice, peer-rating and behavior-observation procedures form a continuum that includes many intermediate or mixed methods. In principle, it is possible to distinguish two extremes of methodology which would logically follow from two quite different choices of units for personality study. These hypothetical extremes will be designated "trait attribution" and "performance recording," respectively.

The distinction between performance-recording and trait-attribution approaches to behavior observation may be facilitated by consideration of the diagram in Figure 7.5, in which the behavior to be observed has been categorized into "stimuli" and "responses" in accordance with conventional psychological usage. The observational procedure outlined at the top of Figure 7.5 is what we have referred to as *performance recording*, or mechanical observation. The procedure outlined at the bottom is *trait attribution*, or judgmental observation.

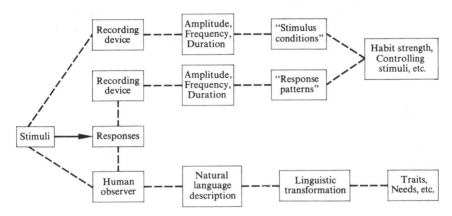

Fig. 7.5 Procedures of performance recording (top) and trait attribution (bottom) in behavior observation.

Performance recording. Under mechanical-observation procedures, a recording device is employed in order to provide a permanent record of certain attributes of both stimuli and responses. The attributes of interest are primarily physicalistic in nature, and hence the units of recording involve such quantities as amplitude, frequency, and duration of stimuli and responses. The devices for recording behavioral attributes may be mechanical equipment *or* human observers. Among proponents of mechanical observation, mechanical equipment appears to be preferable to human observers on the grounds of "reliability" in several senses of the word, which will be discussed below. In practice, particularly with respect to relatively complex behaviors, human observers are provided with special instructions and training that enable them to approximate the reliability of mechanical devices.

Ideally, a minimum of human judgment is involved in the translation of observations into the attributes of amplitude, frequency, and duration.

Operational definitions (Stevens, 1963) translate the quantitative attributes into the concepts of "stimulus conditions" and "response patterns," respectively. The *coordination* of these two sets of observations makes it possible to speak of higher-order constructs, such as "habit strength" and "controlling stimuli," in the language of S-R behavior theory. This theoretical coordination is typically not made by the observer; rather, it is made later on the basis of the observer's records.

Trait attribution. The judgmental or trait-attribution approach to behavior observation is outlined at the bottom of Figure 7.5. A human observer attends to certain attributes of the behavioral event. Although it is difficult to specify precisely which attributes are so attended to, it seems likely that they cover a broader range of possible qualities than do those which are recorded in mechanical observation. Further, although the human observer attends both to the setting or occasion for the behavior observed (stimuli) and to certain attributes of the reactions that occur within this setting (responses), we must emphasize that stimuli and responses are not recorded *independently.*

In Figure 7.5, the reactions of the human observer to the behavioral attributes observed are depicted as *descriptions* phrased in ordinary language. If called on to give a running account of the behavioral attributes in question, the observer would provide us with a narrative highly similar to descriptions of behavioral events in novels or in everyday social discourse. Typically, however, the human observer is not expected to provide a running narrative of his impressions; he is asked to make a rating in terms of an attribute, such as a personality trait. Note that in Figure 7.5 the transition between description and classification is labeled "linguistic transformation." The implication is that a set of observations, potentially describable in ordinary language, is *encoded* by the observer by means of a linguistic transformation which eventuates in the classification of the behavioral attributes in terms of a higher-order construct, such as a trait or a need. The important point here is that the observer must necessarily *interpret* the observed attributes in order to *categorize* them in terms of the system employed.

The sequence of judgmental observation outlined in Figure 7.5 has been described in terms of a layman making inferences in ordinary language. This example is of particular interest because of the widespread employment of "lay observers" in personality-assessment procedures involving such techniques as peer ratings and peer nominations. The observer could be a professional, however, and his language might be somewhat more specialized. However, whether the observer is a layman or a professional, he engages in a process of encoding of behavioral attributes which requires a transformation from discrete observations to a higher-order construct, such as that of a trait. There is general agreement that such an observational process involves an inference from attributes, but the description of such an inference as a "linguistic transformation" is somewhat peculiar to the present exposition.

Generalizability. The chief advantages of mechanical observation are held to reside in their objectivity, reliability, and descriptive power. The use of the word "objectivity" in connection with a behavior-observation procedure may imply either very high or very low generalizability. Where objectivity is used in the sense of "consensus," it implies that observations will be consistent across a broad universe of observers. Under these circumstances, the contribution of idiosyncratic human error is slight and the observational procedure is highly generalizable. To the extent that human observers become bored, fatigued, or otherwise distracted, it must be conceded that their observations are less objective than those of mechanical recording devices. Another use of the word "objective" distinguishes judgmental from non-judgmental observations. Where "objective" is contrasted with "subjective," the universe to which generalizations are made may be quite limited in scope. That is, observations may be generalized only across machines or nonhuman recording devices. Objectivity in this sense seems more a shortcoming than a virtue of behavior observations in personality assessment.

The description of mechanical observational procedures as "reliable" closely approaches the meaning of the word "precision" to engineers. Reliability is used here in the sense of *specific true-score* reliability. Behavioral observations with high specific true-score reliability are not necessarily those that will prove to be of greatest value in applied personality assessment. Specific true-score reliability represents the lowest order of generalizability. The question asked is: What would be the correlation of this behavior observation with an equivalent parallel-form observation (identical true and error scores) under equivalent conditions of observation? Such a generalizability study is difficult to design because it appears that, ideally, nothing would *vary* from observation to observation. Technical considerations aside, it appears that, intuitively, mechanical-performance-recording procedures would tend to have greater "reliability" in this sense than those of trait-attribution procedures in behavior observation. It should be recognized, however, that such specific true-score reliability is in no sense a guarantee of generalizability to a more broadly defined universe.

The "explanatory power" of mechanical observational procedures relates to the degree of criterion relevance that such observations are thought to possess. Mechanical observational procedures achieve an analytical integration of *both* stimulus conditions and response patterns. From the standpoint of personality assessment, the purported advantage of this method of observation would lie in the fact that future outcomes (response patterns) could be predicted for a given criterion (stimulus conditions). Although it is possible to *describe* virtually any prediction problem in the language of S-R behavior theory, it does not necessarily follow that it is possible to implement the procedures of mechanical observation in all such situations. Whether or not this is an intrinsic shortcoming of the mechanical approach to observation is an empirical question, however, and the extent to which such programs may be implemented may be limited only by the ingenuity of "behavioral engineers."

Judgmental recording procedures typically emphasize outcomes (responses) rather than the circumstances which brought them about (stimuli). The assumption here is that psychological traits are relatively enduring response dispositions which will manifest themselves in a wide variety of stimulus circumstances. Even if traits have this degree of generalizability, and that they have has been questioned by many, it is difficult to qualify or adjust the prediction of criterion outcomes in the absence of a detailed knowledge of the relationships between stimulus conditions and the responses they evoke.

In personality assessment, the universe of generalizability contains socially relevant criterion measures. Although such criterion measures are occasionally capable of expression in objective terms, they more typically involve the judgments, opinions, or ratings of certain "significant others" in our society. Consequently, it seems intuitively that trait attribution procedures may have greater generalizability to such criterion measures. Although the criterion, or "criterion problem," may itself be composed of relatively imprecise measures, it is nevertheless the universe to which we would generalize in applied problems. No amount of precision in behavior observations will compensate for a lack of generalizability to criterion measures, regardless of how imprecise the latter may be.

Molar versus Molecular Behaviors

The *size* of the behavioral unit selected for observation is closely related to the trait-attribution and performance-recording distinction. Trait-attribution procedures typically involve larger, more global units, whereas performance-recording procedures focus on more narrowly defined behavior segments. This relationship is not necessary, however, and decisions concerning unit size must be made within both approaches. The attributes of behavior considered in trait attribution may be relatively narrow in scope (is frequently late to appointments) or quite large (is basically a passive-aggressive personality). Similarly, performance-recording procedures may focus on highly delimited behavioral attributes (pencil tapping) or may require the recording of relatively complex chains of stimulus-response interactions (seeking approval from mother).

It is a generally accepted maxim that molecular units of behavior can be observed with greater generalizability across observers and occasions than can more molar units. Molecular attributes can usually be defined with greater precision, can be recorded with fewer categories of alternative response, and tend to require less inference on the part of the observer. Unfortunately, the relationship between unit size and criterion relevance cannot be stated so dogmatically. Narrowly defined behavioral attributes run the risk of a high degree of specificity, which may preclude the possibility of generalizability to criterion behaviors. On the other hand, units that are too global in nature may yield only vacuous statements that are true of everyone or of no one.

The choice of unit size is determined by, among other things, the total amount of information gathered from observations. When a given attribute is fractionated into a number of narrowly defined components and an extensive sampling of these components is obtained, the resultant *sum* of the components may have greater generalizability than a single global rating. Here we are assuming, of course, that the components represent a single homogeneous dimension. Another determinant of unit size is the nature of the criterion itself. Broadly defined criterion units (overall effectiveness as an officer) may necessitate the use of broadly defined observational units. Even here, however, the inclusion of more molecular categories should not be ruled out on a priori grounds. In fact, one of the problems associated with the use of highly trained observers, such as clinical psychologists, is the tendency of such observers to attend to criterion-irrelevant attributes when the criterion itself is narrowly defined. Stern, Stein, and Bloom (1956, p. 74) discuss the tendency of clinicians to focus on such irrelevant attributes as psychopathology or potential for therapy when the criterion of interest is simply academic performance. There are shortcomings to observing either more or less than is required by the criterion definition.

High versus Low Base-Rate Behaviors

An important dimension of behavioral attributes is their relative frequency of occurrence, or *base rate* over time. Some behavioral attributes occur with such high frequency that they are almost certain to be observed in any procedure involving time or occasion sampling (e.g., paying attention). Other attributes occur so rarely that they are unlikely to be observed in either extensive time samples or highly specialized occasion samples (e.g., setting fires). Inter-observer agreement on low base-rate attributes will tend to be low because such observations are, by their very nature, limited in number. Consequently, one might choose to exclude low base-rate attributes from consideration on purely methodological grounds. However, a number of studies suggest that low base-rate personality attributes may be precisely those which are of greatest interest (Goodenough, 1930; Murphy, 1937; Schoggen, 1954). This is especially true of deviant behaviors of critical social importance (Patterson, 1969). As Wright (1960, p. 100) put it: "Possibly there is something of a negative relation between the significance of behavioral events and their occurrence." To the extent that this conjecture is true, investigations which focus on high base-rate attributes because of their convenience will have limited generalizability to important criterion attributes.

The choice between high and low base-rate attributes for observation may, in part, be guided by consideration of the base rate of the criterion attribute of interest. Where habitual performance or typical behavior is a criterion, observation of high base-rate attributes seems appropriate, but there is some evidence that such high base-rate attributes may often be "oversampled." Cobb (1969), for example, found that highly stable estimates of high base-rate events in a classroom could be obtained from 11 minutes of observation. Other investigators have spent several hours observing the same high base-rate events with little gain in stability. Where the criterion attribute has a low base rate, as is true of most deviant behaviors of interest to clinicians, attention should be directed to the settings or stimulus conditions under which such attributes are most likely to be observed (Patterson, 1969). Unfortunately, some criterion behaviors are so infrequent (e.g., suicide) that they cannot be efficiently forecasted by any observational measures (Rosen, 1954).

SUMMARY

This chapter was concerned with those observational methods which are consistent with the empirical aims of personality assessment, namely, the prediction of socially relevant criterion measures. It considered issues relating to the *reliability* of observational methods and the procedures that have been proposed for assessing such reliability by classical test theory and the more recent theory of generalizability. Next, it considered a number of *facets* that influence the dependability of observational methods and, in particular, those of settings, observers, instruments, occasions, and attributes.

All theories of reliability conceive of observed scores as comprising some "true" component, variously defined, plus some "error" component, variously defined. In classical test theory, error is assumed to be uncorrelated with true scores and with error present on other occasions. The theory relies heavily on the notion of parallel tests, which are defined as having equal means, variances, and intercorrelations. Reliability is defined as the correlation between parallel tests and interpreted as the ratio of true-score variance to observed-score variance. Different designs for the comparison of parallel tests yield different types of reliability coefficients, such as those of internal consistency, equivalence, and stability. Such distinctions among different types of coefficients may be unnecessarily restrictive in that they imply a single definition of error associated with each coefficient and do not do justice to the many different sources of error that may be of interest in observational and testing programs.

The theory of generalizability maintains that an interest in the reliability of a given measure is based on a desire to generalize from the observation to some other class of observations. Persons are observed under a given set of conditions, which may comprise particular test items, test forms, stimuli, observers, occasions, or situations of observation. In estimating the reliability of a specific set of conditions, the investigator is interested in the extent to which he can generalize from his sample of conditions to the universe of conditions of which his are a sample. A universe score is defined as the mean of observed scores over all conditions in the universe. A decision study involves a measurement procedure that provides the basic data from which decisions are made with reference to dispositions, diagnoses, or classifications. A generalizability study is specifically designed to assess the measurement procedure of interest in terms of the relationship between observed scores and the universe scores to which they are to be generalized. The generalizability study requires the investigator to specify the universe of scores to which he would like to generalize.

In a properly designed generalizability study, the effects of various conditions on observed scores are evaluated by analysis-of-variance procedures. The dependability of a given measurement procedure may be estimated by an intraclass correlation that expresses the ratio of universe-score variance to observed-score variance. Specific interpretations of the general form of this generalizability coefficient permit the computation of the several types of reliability coefficients with which classical test theory has been concerned. Moreover, the general form of the analysis may be extended to situations in which several conditions, or "facets," may be treated simultaneously.

Typical observational studies involve the observation of a given attribute on a given occasion within a specified setting by certain observers employing certain instruments. The intersect of some or all of these conditions or facets defines the universe of generalizability. *Settings* may be classified in terms of the degree of control exercised over the events which occur in the environment observed. The physical presence or absence of *observers* introduces questions of the generalizability of the observational procedure as well as its reactiveness. The use of a given *instrument* introduces an element of selectivity of observation as well as method variance associated with the instrument itself. *Occasions* of observation are defined on the basis of sampling techniques and strategies for defining units and time periods within the stream of behavior observed. The selection of behavioral *attributes* for observation is largely a theoretical matter, but the critical dimension of generalizability is that of criterion relevance.

CHAPTER 8

OBSERVATIONAL TECHNIQUES:
II. TRAIT ATTRIBUTION AND
BEHAVIORAL ANALYSIS

In Chapter 7, we observed that peer-rating and behavior-observation procedures focus on quite different attributes of behavior. We also indicated that the choice of one or the other class of attributes for observation was based on considerations of sufficient complexity to warrant separate and extended discussion. In the present chapter, we examine some of the assumptions underlying the use of ordinary language in *trait attribution* and provide examples of peer-rating systems that have been developed for normal adults and for specialized populations. We then consider some recently suggested procedures for *behavioral analysis* that focus on attributes of behavior in relation to certain classes of environmental variables.

TRAIT ATTRIBUTION

Observational procedures that employ human observers are obliged to provide such observers with encoding devices for translating their sensory impressions, or retrospective observations, into quantifiable form. Although it is possible to devise specific encoding devices for each assessment problem encountered, it is desirable, on both theoretical and practical grounds, to consider the possibility of a general schema for organizing observations of personality attributes. It should come as no surprise that ordinary language provides a convenient tool for codifying sensory impressions in such a manner that they may be reduced to a finite set of categories (Brown, 1958; Bruner, Goodnow, and Austin, 1956). Ordinary language is, in fact, what all of us employ in observing, categorizing, and responding to our associates. We need hardly belabor here the *efficiency* of such a taxonomic system for everyday social intercourse. The *utility* of employing the natural language of everyday discourse as a basis for the scientific study and prediction of human behavior is the less obvious issue with which this chapter is concerned.

It is the assumption (stated or implied) of most large-scale systems of trait attribution that the ordinary language provides a convenient starting point for the development of encoding devices (Cattell, 1946, 1957; Norman, 1963b, 1967). Although this strategy is sometimes rationalized as being primarily a technical expedient (Cattell, 1957), there are less mundane reasons for adopting such an approach. In a sense, the ordinary language of personality trait attribution represents the accumulated wisdom of the species. Certainly a good portion of ordinary trait names are functional in the sense that they provide the basis for discriminations of profound personal and social importance. To describe another person as "untrustworthy" is to communicate an enormous amount of highly essential information in a very efficient manner. To categorize an individual as "possessing" a personality trait is to provide a framework which determines the nature of subsequent interactions with that individual. Although the ordinary language of personality trait attribution may be imprecise, ambiguous, and in some instances inaccurate, we can hardly afford to ignore such a storehouse of accumulated wisdom as a natural starting point for the study of behavioral attributes.

Our concern is not with the ordinary language system in its entirety (in this instance, the English language) but rather with that subset of descriptive predicates that refers to perceptible variations in human attributes (Norman, 1963b). Thus our concern is not with the natural language generally but with what might be called the natural language of personality. This language system, which is a subset of the larger system of ordinary language, must be initially distinguished from other language systems. In particular, the ordinary personality language system must not be thought equivalent to a scientific language system (Feigl, 1949). This point has been the source of considerable confusion among both proponents and critics of trait attribution.

It has been argued, for example, that employment of a natural language taxonomy for trait attribution reduces scientific psychology to the level of popular psychology by employing the imprecise and frequently inaccurate language of the man on the street. To avoid this confusion, it is necessary to recognize that systematic trait-attribution studies are designed for the purpose of utilizing the natural (nonscientific) language for scientific aims (prediction and control) rather than for the more subversive intent of replacing scientific language systems (e.g., symbolic logic) with the less precise language of everyday discourse. A language need not be scientific to be useful; nor is a language necessarily useful *because* it is scientific.

The Language of Personality

Although much has been written about trait-attribution systems in personality study, the greatest clarity seems to have been achieved by Norman (1963b, 1967). Norman observes that an adequate taxonomy of personality attributes should be: (a) exhaustive, (b) precise, and (c) well structured.

Norman's specifications for exhaustiveness (generalizability) provide a succinct and rigorous definition of the subject matter of trait attribution:

... the set of all perceptible variations in performance and appearance between persons or within individuals over a period of time and varying situations *that are of* sufficient social significance, *of* sufficiently widespread occurrence, *and of* sufficient distinctiveness *to have been encoded and retained as a subset of descriptive predicates in the natural language during the course of its natural development, growth, and refinement.* (Norman, 1967, p. 2)

Norman's definition of precision appears to involve several meanings of "meaning," which we will consider separately and at considerably greater length.

A priori considerations. It is possible, on a priori grounds, to eliminate a large number of descriptive predicates in the English language on the basis of their presumed inutility in a taxonomic system. In Norman's (1967) words

... terms are to be excluded whose meanings are grossly vague or ambiguous; whether by virtue of the existence of well-known but distinct and alternative usage for a given orthographic form, because the meaning derives from some obscure and generally unknown historical, literary or dialectic source, or because the term refers to a compound or broad composite of more primary and more separately distinguishable attributes. (p. 2)

All would agree that such terms would be inappropriate in a taxonomic system designed for general use, and the identification and subsequent elimination of such terms on a priori grounds need hardly be justified.

Lexical meaning. The lexical meaning of a word is contained in a definition, such as that found in a dictionary which provides a series of synonyms that may be used more or less interchangeably with the word defined. In a sense, such a definition is based on the *rules* of the language (syntax), which state the conditions under which a word may be properly employed. Syntactical rules do not tell us how words should be applied to objects (semantics). Rather, they provide the formal ground rules for language usage. Thus the dictionary tells us that in describing John as "hostile," we might equally well characterize him as "unfriendly" or "antagonistic." Whether John is "in fact" any of these is quite a different matter. Nevertheless, it is extremely important that items in our potential taxonomic system be *used* according to the same rules by most observers. Thus it is desirable to ask a representative sample of raters to provide lexical definitions of all words that are being considered as potential candidates for inclusion in an encoding system. Words for which there is wide variability in lexical meaning should be eliminated.

Affective meaning. The language of personality by its very nature, is a *personal* language. Although we may strive for objectivity in our observations of others, the ordinary language of personality itself has emotional overtones. The words "hostile," "generous," "untrustworthy," and "courageous" may be highly descriptive; yet there are few among us who can attribute such terms to others without feeling a slight twinge of anger, warmth, pride, or some other emotion. Although words with affective connotations are vigorously eschewed by those concerned with the development of a scientific language (Feigl, 1949, p. 7), such words seem to be part and parcel of the ordinary language system employed by people to describe other people. Thus there may be good reason to restrict the number of descriptors that are, for example, *solely* evaluative in their connotation ("good," "bad"), but it seems likely that all potential personality descriptors will carry some such affective connotation. In fact, personality descriptors that are totally devoid of affective connotation are unlikely to denote attributes of behavior of much social or personological significance. For example, the words "intelligent" and "adjusted" are heavily saturated with evaluative connotations. Nevertheless, when one is predicting intelligence and adjustment from peer ratings, it seems patently absurd to exclude such terms as potential descriptors.

Since words with affective connotations are part and parcel of the ordinary language of personality, an adequate taxonomic system should be designed in such a manner that it is broadly *representative* of the major dimensions of affective connotations involved in trait attribution. A system based exclusively on words with evaluative connotations might be of some use in assessing character traits but of little value in assessing temperament and other kinds of traits. Another important consideration involves the relative *consistency* in the affective connotations of a trait descriptor from one observer to another. While the descriptor "good" clearly implies an evaluative connotation when applied to an object (or person), the descriptors "nifty" and "cool" might be applied with less consistency. The determination of the major dimensions of affective meaning in trait attribution is no small task. Fortunately, the monumental work of Osgood and associates (Osgood, Suci, and Tannenbaum, 1957; Miron and Osgood, 1966; Snider and Osgood, 1969) has provided us with a technique for measuring affective meaning with considerable precision, and recent extensions of this work to the domain of trait attribution (e.g., Kuusinen, 1969) have provided valuable insights into the nature of the problem.

Osgood *et al.* (1957) conceive of the "meaning" of a word as a point in a multidimensional semantic space whose coordinates (axes) represent the major dimensions of affective meaning. The dimensions of meaning represented by the coordinates were discovered through an extensive investigation of the rules that underlie the use of descriptive predicates (adjectives) with respect to "concepts" (nouns). Great care was taken to compile a list of adjectives that were representative of common usage of the English language. As a first step, 40 nouns were selected from the Kent-Rosanoff Free Association Test and read aloud to 200 undergraduates, who were instructed to write down the first descriptive adjective that occurred to them (e.g., HOUSE-big; PRIEST-good; TREE-green). By this elicitation technique, it was possible to determine the relative frequency of occurrence of adjectives associated with a variety of nouns. A more extensive sampling of adjectives involved the selection of 280 adjectives and their opposites (antonyms) from *Roget's Thesaurus* on the grounds of familiarity and representativeness. By these procedures it was possible to assemble representative adjective pairs (good-bad; fast-slow; hard-soft) and to study the manner in which they are applied to a wide variety of concepts. The method whereby the concepts (nouns) are "differentiated" with respect to adjective pairs is called the *semantic differential technique.*

In the semantic differential technique, stimuli such as words (LADY, BOULDER, SIN, FATHER), physical objects (paintings), and sensory events (sonar signals) are evaluated for their "meaning" against bipolar adjective scales of the following type.

happy	___ : ___ : ___ : ___ : ___ : ___ : ___ : sad
hard	___ : ___ : ___ : ___ : ___ : ___ : ___ : soft
slow	___ : ___ : ___ : ___ : ___ : ___ : ___ : fast

Numerical values from 1 to 7 are assigned to points on the rating scale, and the resulting seven-place scales are then intercorrelated across a variety of concepts. The intercorrelations among adjectival scales may be reduced to their underlying dimensions by means of factor analysis. In a large number of studies employing a wide variety of concepts, scales, and raters, three factors have emerged with considerable regularity (Osgood *et al.*, 1957). These factors, or underlying dimensions of affective meaning, have been labeled *evaluation* (good-bad; pleasant-unpleasant; nice-awful), *potency* (strong-weak; hard-soft; heavy-light) and *activity* (active-passive; fast-slow; noisy-quiet). Thus the semantic space discovered by Osgood may be represented by three orthogonal (independent) dimensions, as illustrated in Figure 8.1.

Perhaps the most striking feature of the semantic space depicted in Figure 8.1 is its *generalizability* across raters, scales, and concepts and especially across cultures involving diverse language groups (Miron and Osgood, 1966; Osgood, 1962, 1964). Wherever and whenever reasonably heterogeneous samples of raters, scales, and concepts are employed, the ubiquitous dimensions of evaluation, potency, and activity emerge as the underlying coordinates of affective meaning. However, the structure of

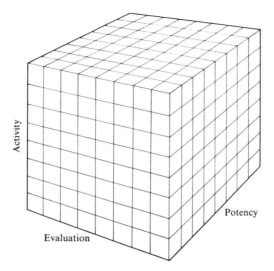

Activity

Potency

Evaluation

Fig. 8.1 Three-dimensional representation of "semantic space."

semantic space is not independent of the particular scales employed to rate particular concepts, and restrictions on either or both of these variables will result in underlying coordinates different from those in Figure 8.1. For example, Ware (1958) employed personality-trait descriptors as adjectives to rate persons as concepts and obtained a semantic space with many more coordinates than usual. An important consideration in such concept-scale interactions (Miron and Osgood, 1966) is the *relevance* of the adjectival scales for the concepts being rated. For example, the descriptor "high" seems to apply more directly to ratings of buildings than to ratings of persons. When a subject is required to rate the "highness" of a person or the "kindness" of a building, he is essentially being forced to respond *metaphorically*, and it is the affective dimensions of evaluation, potency and activity that are held to be the "common coin of metaphors" (Osgood, 1969).

Kuusinen (1969) has argued that an adequate set of trait descriptors should allow personality assessment in terms of *both* the broad dimensions of affective meaning identified by Osgood and the more specific dimensions uncovered by the more "relevant" personality scales, such as those employed by Ware. To demonstrate that this dual assessment is possible, Kuusinen had a variety of person concepts (self, others, well-known persons) rated on both the standard affective meaning scales of Osgood (e.g., gloomy-light) and on scales of greater personological relevance (e.g., moral-immoral). When the intercorrelations among scale ratings were subjected to a factor analysis, the resultant structure was heavily influenced by the affective meaning scales of Osgood, and the dimensions of evaluation, potency, and activity emerged with their usual clarity.

In order to investigate the nature of dimensions other than these three, Kuusinen *partialed out* the variance contributed by the affective meaning scales to the intercorrelations among scales. When the partialed matrix of intercorrelations was factored, a number of additional dimensions emerged, such as trustworthiness, rationality, uniqueness, and sociability. Since some of these additional dimensions were similar to those obtained by Ware (1958) in his study employing mainly "personality-relevant" scales, one may wonder why Kuusinen went to the trouble of administering the affective meaning scales and then partialing out their effects. His rationale was that "the affective *components* of meaning are assumed to be always present when judgments are made on any scales. Therefore, only by first including affective scales in the ratings and then partialing out their effects can the affective components be eliminated from the subjects' ratings." (Kuusinen, 1969, p. 187.)

The nature and significance of these additional dimensions of affective meaning is a subject of some controversy (Miron, 1969). Kuusinen is inclined to view the three broad dimensions of affective meaning as primarily "connotative" in nature and the more personality-relevant dimensions as somewhat "denotative" since they apply more specifically to personality. Osgood (1969) is reluctant to accept such a dichotomy, because "the traditions of philosophical usage of the terms 'connotation' and 'denotation' are already so befogged that to add a psychologically befogged distinction ... will eliminate any possibility of achieving a grasp on the nature of meaning" (p. 195). As previously indicated, Osgood (1969) maintains that, to the extent that a subject is provided with descriptors (e.g., gloomy-light) whose relation to the concept being rated (e.g., myself) is metaphorical, the subject will respond in terms of the major dimensions of affective meaning. As the relationship between scale and concept becomes less metaphorical, additional dimensions of affective meaning may emerge.

We have argued that an adequate taxonomic system of personality trait descriptors should be broadly representative of the major dimensions of affective meaning and that the affective connotations of the descriptors should be relatively consistent from observer to observer. To these general desiderata, we must now add the more applied concerns of personality assessment. *The dimensions of affective meaning represented by a set of trait descriptors should be those which have the greatest generalizability to criterion situations of social importance.* On a priori grounds alone, the dimension of evaluation seems to be one of considerable relevance to most criterion situations. The fact that our prediction tasks are variously described as "personality assessment," "personality evaluation," and "personality appraisal" seems to indicate an implicit awareness that most, if not all, of our trait attributions will involve the evaluative dimension of affective meaning. But the predictive significance or generalizability of other affective-meaning dimensions, both large and small, will have to be determined by empirical investigation. Although the problem has philosophical overtones, its solution is well within the realm of empirical investigation.

Implicative meaning. There is still a third sense in which personality trait descriptors should share a common meaning for observers who employ them as encoding devices. Implicative meaning refers to the relationship or structure that exists among a set of descriptive predicates. Lexical meaning establishes that certain trait names may be used more or less interchangeably (e.g., "hostile" and "unfriendly"). However, in the establishment of such synonymous relationships, no information is obtained about the relationships that exist among trait terms that are not strictly synonyms (e.g., "cautious" and "warm"). Similarly, although it is possible to establish the similarity between two traits in terms of their affective-meaning profile by means of the semantic differential, it cannot be assumed that because two words occupy the same position in semantic space, they will be *used* in an interchangeable fashion. Thus, while "nurse" and "sincere" may occupy the same region of the three-dimensional semantic space, there is no reason to assume that the terms will be used in the same manner, particularly with respect to their "denotative" referents (Weinreich, 1958).[1] What is required is a direct determination of the implicative relationships that exist among all members of a given set of trait descriptors.

A number of techniques have been devised for assessing trait-implicative meaning, each of which tends to emphasize a somewhat different aspect of the structural relations that exist among traits. One such procedure obtains direct ratings of the *meaning-similarity relationships* that exist among trait descriptors. For example, D'Andrade (1965) asked subjects to compare traits with respect to their similarity of meaning on the following scale.

Complaining; Resentful

Similar _____ : _____ : _____ : _____ : _____ : _____ : _____ : Contrary
unrelated

---

1. This particular example, which is frequently cited, may not be generally representative of the relationship that obtains between judged semantic differential "meaning" and judged implicative "meaning." Rowan (1954) found considerable convergence between "semantic space" and "implicative space" when concepts were judged by both methods. Similarly, Flavell (1961) reported substantial correlations between semantic differential profiles and implicative profiles of pairs of nouns and pairs of adjectives. The present distinction between "affective" and "implicative" meaning is used solely to distinguish two sets of *operations* that are commonly employed for judging meaning.

By this procedure it is possible to investigate the meaning-similarity relationship among all trait terms in a given set and, by means of factor analysis, to obtain groupings of terms which are judged to have similar "meanings." Later in this chapter, we will consider a specific application of this technique by D'Andrade (1965).

A more structured approach to the measurement of trait implication is found in those techniques which employ *conditional probability judgments* (Hays, 1958; Peterson *et al.*, 1965; Laabs and Dawes, 1969). Trait pairs may be presented to subjects in the following format:

> "Given that a person is *immodest*, how likely is it
> that he is also irreligious?"

Subjects are required to record their "likelihood judgments" on a ten-place scale with categories corresponding to probability of occurrence. Such implicative relationships may be thought of as the degree of "redundancy" that exists between traits (Dustin and Baldwin, 1966). The relationships may also be thought of as reflecting the structural relationships that exist within a given set of traits. Perhaps most important, framing the comparison within the context of probabilities enables investigators to examine the consistency of implicative relationships within subjects (Laabs and Dawes, 1969; Peterson *et al.*, 1965; Summers and Oncken, 1968). This approach also allows for the investigation of possible individual differences that may exist in judgments of trait similarity (Walters and Jackson, 1966). Although individual differences do exist, there is good reason to believe that, at least for certain sets of descriptive predicates, the implicative meaning of traits may be judged with considerable consistency (Laabs and Dawes, 1969). This is of course desirable, since it provides further evidence that observers utilize the natural language of personality in a consistent fashion.

Internal and external structure. Similarity of implicative meaning across a variety of judges is but one sense in which personality descriptors may be said to be "structured" (Norman, 1967). Another and perhaps more important sense of "structured" is the relationship that exists among trait descriptors when they are *applied* to real subjects in observational studies. This type of external structure has been the primary focus of investigation of the major systems of trait attribution developed to date (Cattell, 1946, 1957; Norman, 1963b, 1967). External structure may be assessed in peer-rating data when observers are asked to indicate the extent to which a set of trait dimensions is present in their acquaintances. Rating scales are correlated across subjects and factor-analyzed to reveal the external structure of the trait-attribution system as applied by observers. Consistency of the obtained factorial structure across a variety of subjects, observers, and trait terms is taken to be an indication of the structural stability of the system.

Whereas internal structure is established by demonstrating that the syntactical relationships among a set of personality trait descriptors are relatively uniform for a sample of judges, external structure is established by demonstrating that the syntactical relationships among traits are consistent from observer to observer when the traits are applied to external stimulus objects (peers). It should be apparent that a certain degree of internal structure is necessary for a set of personality descriptors to have a stable external structure. Personality descriptors must have the same connotative meaning for observers if they are to apply the descriptors with any degree of consistency. Thus it is desirable for personality trait descriptors to have common lexical, affective, and implicative meanings for all observers using the system. It does not necessarily follow, however, that such shared meaning will guarantee a consistent external structure when the adjectives are applied to real persons.

Semantic meaning. In its most general usage, "semantic meaning" refers to the relationship between terms (signs) and the objects to which they refer (significates) (Morris, 1946). For certain classes of words, such as nouns, this relationship can be established by pointing to the significate of a sign (e.g., pointing to a book to indicate the denotation of the word "book"). However, because adjectives are descriptive predicates, their semantic meaning must be appraised by examining the relationship between the sign (predicate) and the attribute or quality of an object to which it refers (thing-predicate). Consequently, to establish the semantic meaning of a trait descriptor, it is necessary to demonstrate high *inter-observer agreement* in the assignment or attribution of the term to qualities of the person being rated. That it is theoretically possible for a system to possess high connotative consistency and high structural consistency without possessing high semantic consistency is one of the recently discovered paradoxes of the language of personality (Norman and Goldberg, 1966). As we will see in later sections, the establishment of inter-observer agreement provides a partial means of resolving this paradox.

Peer Ratings of Normal Adults

Sampling Procedures

Although taxonomic systems that are based on the natural language may have many shortcomings, they lend themselves readily to an unambiguous definition of a finite universe of terms. The entire domain of interest is contained within the covers of the Webster unabridged dictionary. Thus the concept of the "total personality" may be represented by what Cattell (1957) designates the *language personality sphere*, which "captures all the particularity of behavior accumulated in our speech and dictionaries" (p. 71).

As early as 1936, Allport and Odbert set for themselves the formidable task of cataloguing all trait names that appeared in *Webster's New International Dictionary, Unabridged* (1925). At that time, they were able to uncover some 17,953 terms that could be reasonably considered trait names. By eliminating terms that referred to temporary and specific behaviors, those that had strictly evaluative implications, and those that were highly metaphorical and remote in connotation, the investigators were able to reduce this list to some 4,504 terms which, in their judgment, referred to "real traits." Such traits, in the judgment of Allport and Odbert (1936), represent "generalized and personalized determining tendencies—consistent and stable modes of an individual's adjustment to his environment" (p. 366). This basic sampling of the domain of personality descriptors has formed the basis for a number of systems of personality trait attribution, primarily because of its subsequent reduction by Cattell (1946).

More recently, the Allport-Odbert list has been revised and supplemented by Norman (1967) on the basis of scanning the entire contents of *Webster's Third New International Dictionary, Unabridged* (1961). New terms which had appeared in the quarter century separating the two dictionaries were added, and notations were made of terms that had been dropped in the later edition. The total pool comprising both the total Allport-Odbert list and all potential additions from *Webster's Third* was estimated to involve approximately 40,000 terms (Norman, 1967). By a detailed procedure, some aspects of which have already been mentioned, Norman (1967) has reduced this list to 2,797 personality trait descriptors whose characteristics are currently under study. It seems likely that this revised pool will serve as the source of items for trait-attribution systems for many years to come.

The Structure of Peer Ratings

Systematic studies of trait attribution typically evolve in several distinct stages. First, a procedure is developed for systematic sampling of the potential universe of trait descriptors contained in the ordinary language. Second, by means of both rational and empirical procedures, the initial list of terms is reduced to a more manageable set. Third, the apparent trait attributes involved are represented by bipolar rating scales ("talkative versus silent"). In a population of subjects, known to each other, these scales are administered in the form of peer ratings that require each subject to evaluate some or all of his peers with respect to these attributes. The intercorrelations among rating scales are used as a basis for determining underlying dimensions by means of factor analysis. On the basis of factor-analytic results, it is possible to group scales into sets according to the factors with which they are most highly associated. By summing scores on scales within a given factorial set, one can compute a total score on a given factor of trait attribution. The stability and generalizability of this factorial structure is then investigated in a variety of populations. Over the past quarter of a century a systematic and cumulative series of investigations of the structure of peer ratings may be traced. This work had its origins in the pioneering studies of Cattell (1946), found consolidation in the studies of Tupes and Christal (1961), and is currently represented by the work of Norman (1963b).

The Cattell studies. Starting with the 4,504 trait names assembled by Allport and Odbert (1936), Cattell (1946) reduced the list to 171 terms representing "synonym groups" on the basis of rational judgments of semantic meaning. These 171 terms were employed in a rating study of college students, and their intercorrelations were obtained. On the basis of a cluster analysis (a procedure similar to factor analysis), Cattell (1945) was able to identify 36 dimensions of personality, to which he added six further dimensions that, in his judgment, needed to be represented. These dimensions served as the basis for constructing 35 bipolar rating scales, which were, in turn, used in a series of peer-rating studies conducted in college, military, and clinical samples (Cattell, 1957). On the basis of a series of interrelated factorial studies, Cattell concluded that some 12 to 15 distinct factors are necessary to account for the intercorrelations among rating variables in the language personality sphere. These factors become the "primary personality factors" in Cattell's personality system and were subsequently extended to the domains of self-report personality questionnaires and objective or performance tests of personality (Cattell, 1957).

It should be noted that Cattell's primary personality factors are oblique, i.e., correlated among themselves rather than strictly independent (orthogonal). Further, their distinctiveness and reliability vary somewhat from sample to sample. Although Cattell (1957) maintains that at least 15 factors are necessary for a complete description of the language personality sphere, it does not necessarily follow that all these factors will prove to be useful as predictors of various criterion situations. Peterson (1965), for example, has argued that a smaller number of orthogonal (independent) factors may be sufficient for most prediction situations. Nevertheless, the factors isolated by Cattell appear to have some consistency across diverse samples (Cattell, 1945, 1946, 1948) and do not appear to be highly dependent on a particular set of raters (Fiske, 1949).

The Tupes and Christal studies. In a series of studies involving Air Force officer candidates and Air Force officers, Tupes (1957, 1959) found the Cattell ratings to be predictive of a number of performance measures and to have considerable stability under diverse rating conditions (Tupes and Christal, 1958). Consequently, Tupes and Christal (1961) conducted a series of studies designed to determine the number of reliable factors that could be isolated from peer-rating studies involving Cattell's 35 personality traits. Eight studies were compared (including two of Cattell's) that involved diverse rating situations:

These samples differed in length of acquaintanceship from three days to more than a year; in kind of acquaintanceship from assessment programs in a military training course to a fraternity house situation; in type of subject from airmen with only a high school education to male and female undergraduate students to first-year graduate students; and in type of rater from very naive persons to clinical psychologists and psychiatrists with years of experience in the evaluation of personality. (Tupes and Christal, 1961, p. iii)

In each of the diverse samples studied, five distinct orthogonal (independent) factors emerged with impressive consistency from study to study. These factors were labeled: (a) surgency (extraversion), (b) agreeableness, (c) dependability (conscientiousness), (d) emotional stability, and (e) culture. Of the 35 Cattell variables, six were related to the first factor, nine were related to the second, five to the third, six to the fourth, and four variables provided clear "markers" of the fifth factor. Thus it was argued, both on the basis of predictive validity and factorial consistency, that five independent factors were sufficient to represent the natural language of personality in peer-rating studies.

The Norman studies. Norman (1963b) reduced Cattell's list of 35 variables to 20 by selecting the four rating scales which were most representative of each of the five factors identified by Tupes and Christal (1961). Peer ratings on these 20 scales were obtained in four samples of male college students which comprised ROTC students, fraternity men, and residence hall men from all class levels. When the five factors extracted from the intercorrelations of rating scales in these four samples were compared, a remarkable consistency in factorial structure emerged (Norman, 1963b; Norman and Goldberg, 1966). The results from Norman's (1963b) fraternity sample of 215 men are presented in Table 8.1.

The first column of Table 8.1 lists the five factor labels (italicized) and the four rating scales[2] which presumably define each factor. For example, the rating scales "talkative–silent" and "frank, open–secretive" are presumed markers of the factor of *extraversion*. The rating scales of "good-natured–irritable" and "not jealous–jealous" are presumed markers of the second factor of *agreeableness*. The body of the table shows the loadings of each scale on each of the five factors extracted from the intercorrelations

---

2.   The rating scales indicated in Table 8.1 are *abbreviations* that Norman suggested for the more detailed rating scales of Cattell (1946) that were actually employed by both Norman and Cattell.

Table 8.1 Factor matrix of peer ratings in a fraternity sample (from Norman, 1963b, p. 579)

Scales	Factors				
	I	II	III	IV	V
Extraversion					
talkative–silent	90	02	−02	04	−00
frank, open–secretive	78	−08	07	−03	07
adventurous–cautious	79	15	−20	32	01
sociable–reclusive	86	01	−18	−01	−02
Agreeableness					
good-natured–irritable	17	80	17	12	07
not jealous–jealous	−10	64	20	49	07
mild, gentle–headstrong	−20	80	27	19	10
cooperative–negativistic	33	74	28	13	11
Conscientiousness					
fussy, tidy–careless	−33	−08	66	−35	20
responsible–undependable	−03	32	86	08	18
scrupulous–unscrupulous	−30	44	68	−02	20
persevering–quitting, fickle	−05	28	74	12	27
Emotional stability					
poised–nervous, tense	01	56	15	61	05
calm–anxious	06	21	−10	82	−07
composed–excitable	13	06	16	71	24
not hypochondriacal–hypochondriacal	21	27	−00	65	−09
Culture					
artistically sensitive–insensitive	−04	08	39	−10	75
intellectual–unreflective, narrow	−04	05	47	04	74
polished, refined–crude, boorish	15	25	53	16	46
imaginative–simple, direct	12	19	03	10	68

among scales. Such loadings may assume values from −1.00 to +1.00 and may be thought of as analogous (though not identical) to the correlations of each scale with the five underlying factors. An examination of the pattern of these factor loadings indicates that the variables are highly "structured." That is, the scales have high loadings on the factors they are supposed to mark and low loadings on the independent factors they are not supposed to mark. These results are highly replicable across samples and situations (Norman, 1963b; Norman and Goldberg, 1966).

What do Peer Ratings Measure?

From the foregoing, it should be apparent that the taxonomic system developed by Cattell and refined by Tupes and Christal and Norman, possesses a highly replicable external structure. Given this consistency and clarity of external structure, it seems appropriate to consider next the generalizability of the system in terms of the number of criterion attributes with which it is associated (predictive validity). Before doing so, however, we may find it instructive to consider the possible "meanings" of peer ratings in the several senses in which we have used that term. Our earlier distinctions between implicative and affective meanings will be especially useful here.

Implicative Meaning of Peer Ratings

D'Andrade (1965) conducted a direct test of the implicative meanings of the 20 scales employed by Norman (1963b) in his peer-ratings studies. A single term representing one pole was selected from each of the 20 scales (e.g., "silent," "good-natured"). Each of the 20 terms was compared with all other terms with respect to its "similarity of meaning" on scales of the following type.

Talkative: Irritable

Similar _____ : _____ : _____ : _____ : _____ : _____ : _____ : Contrary
unrelated

Ten students were asked to rate each of the 190 comparisons of two terms as to their similarity of meaning.

The average rated similarity value for each pair of terms was entered into the 20 × 20 matrix illustrated in Figure 8.2, which shows that the average rated value was the maximum degree of similarity (7) when each term was compared with itself (1 with 1; 2 with 2; etc.). The other values that were entered in the matrix represented mean similarity ratings between all possible pairs of the 20 terms. By correlating all possible columns of Figure 8.2, one can obtain the intercorrelations among the 20 trait terms with respect to their similarity of meaning. D'Andrade (1965) extracted five factors from these intercorrelations and obtained the factor matrix illustrated in Table 8.2.

The pattern of factor loadings in Table 8.2 is strikingly similar to the pattern of factor loadings given previously in Table 8.1. Recall that Table 8.1 illustrates the external structure of peer-rating scales when applied to real persons. Table 8.2, on the other hand, represents the structure of peer-rating terms which have been rated for similarity of implicative meaning. Of the 20 sets of terms in Table 8.2, only five are misplaced. The implicative

Terms

Terms	1	2	3	4 20		20
1. Talkative	7					
2. Secretive		7				
3. Adventurous			7			
.						
.						
.						
.						
.						
20. Imaginative						7

Fig. 8.2 Matrix of mean rated values of trait similarity.

meaning of these 20 terms must be considered similar, if not identical, to the external structure of similar terms when they are applied to real persons.

D'Andrade's (1965) study was intended as a demonstration, and it served that purpose well. Recall, however, that D'Andrade employed trait labels instead of the descriptive phrases used by Norman and that only 20 (of a possible 40) labels were rated. In addition, the results are based on the similarity ratings of only ten subjects. That these findings are generalizable to the full sample of trait descriptors and to larger groups of subjects is clear from the results of an elegant study conducted by Hakel (1969). A computer was programmed to select and print individual rating forms for each of 480 subjects (half men and half women). For each rating form, 100 pairs of trait descriptors were selected randomly from the complete matrix of 1,600 possible pairings of the 40 trait descriptors with the restrictions that no pair be repeated within the same rating form and that all pairs be represented equally across the 480 individual rating forms. Ratings were made on a seven-place probability of co-occurrence scale (Hays, 1958). Table 8.3 presents the five-factor solution obtained by a multidimensional scaling analysis of the probability of co-occurrence ratings. For consistency, only the loadings of the 20 positive pole descriptors are presented, although the pattern of the negative pole descriptors is equally clear. The internal structure

Table 8.2 Factor matrix of similarity of meaning ratings. (From D'Andrade, 1965, p. 224)

Scales	I	II	III	IV	V
Extraversion					
talkative–silent	86	−19	12	02	14
frank, open–secretive	93	04	18	12	15
adventurous–cautious	76	12	37	−30	14
sociable–reclusive	85	−11	−11	−29	−11
Agreeableness					
good-natured–irritable	−29	67	−38	−40	−19
not jealous–jealous	−14	87	08	−12	06
mild, gentle–headstrong	−70	36	−13	16	−41
cooperative–negativistic	32	04	−20	−43	−49
Conscientiousness					
fussy, tidy–careless	−80	03	−48	06	−18
responsible–undependable	−41	−02	−90	−05	00
scrupulous–unscrupulous	09	17	−72	43	25
persevering–quitting, fickle	−07	−07	−80	−36	−06
Emotional stability					
poised–nervous, tense	22	50	−18	−67	23
calm–anxious	−01	47	06	−79	21
composed–excitable	−59	44	−28	−52	16
not hypochondriacal–hypochondriacal	17	00	−15	−87	−09
Culture					
artistically sensitive–insensitive	−19	−11	01	36	−71
intellectual–unreflective, narrow	−14	−06	−30	−11	−90
polished, refined–crude, boorish	−53	−10	−20	11	−72
imaginative–simple, direct	−05	−02	79	24	40

obtained by Hakel is as clear as any external structure reported by Norman and associates.

Studies which demonstrate a high degree of consistency of implicative meaning of trait terms for observers have been interpreted by some writers (e.g., Mischel, 1968) as raising the possibility that personality traits exist in the constructs of the perceiver rather than in the characteristics of the perceived. It should be noted, however, that studies of the consistency of implicative meaning of trait terms can shed no direct light on this ancient

Table 8.3 Factor matrix of probability of co-occurrence ratings (adapted from Hakel, 1969, p. 404)

Scales	I	II	III	IV	V
			Factors		
Extraversion					
talkative–silent	84	−35	21	13	−15
frank, open–secretive	92	11	−24	−06	−31
adventurous–cautious	60	−51	48	−40	−38
sociable–reclusive	80	−59	20	−29	09
Agreeableness					
good-natured–irritable	−32	92	04	17	06
not jealous–jealous	13	84	−01	40	08
mild, gentle–headstrong	09	81	43	13	15
cooperative–negativistic	−61	65	31	31	16
Conscientiousness					
fussy, tidy–careless	05	−63	65	−49	09
responsible–undependable	−23	36	84	03	06
scrupulous–unscrupulous	−12	26	89	−14	07
persevering–quitting, fickle	−06	−09	80	38	19
Emotional stability					
poised–nervous, tense	−12	21	34	82	06
calm–anxious	05	24	−08	87	−37
composed–excitable	12	−45	42	70	−20
not hypochondriacal–hypochondriacal	−33	08	−23	85	06
Culture					
artistically sensitive–insensitive	08	−46	30	−26	80
intellectual–unreflective, narrow	−48	10	47	26	75
polished, refined–crude, boorish	−53	60	54	19	28
imaginative–simple, direct	−07	13	−11	−07	99

epistemological issue. If traits do, in fact, have existence in the "real world," it is necessary (but not sufficient) for the terms describing such traits to have consistent implicative meanings across observers, preferably as consistent as those found by D'Andrade (1965) and Hakel (1969). Otherwise, of course, there would be no guarantee that observers are describing the "same" traits. On the other hand, if there were no agreement among observers with respect to the implicative meanings of trait terms, it would be difficult to argue that traits exist *either* in the real world or in the minds of observers.

Although we have argued that a certain degree of internal structuring is a necessary condition for stable external structures to exist when trait descriptors are applied to real persons, we must also consider certain special cases in which internal structure is a sufficient condition for external structure. That is, are there rating situations in which trait attribution reflects "nothing but" the shared implicative meaning of the terms employed? A study by Passini and Norman (1966) suggests that there are indeed such situations and that they must be carefully distinguished from the more typical conditions under which peer ratings are usually obtained.

Passini and Norman obtained peer ratings from small groups of university undergraduates who were total strangers to one another. These subjects were in the same room for less than 15 minutes and had no opportunity for verbal communication. They were asked to rate one another on Norman's peer-rating scales as they "would imagine" one another to be. The ratings were intercorrelated, and five factors were extracted by the usual procedure. The resultant factor structure is presented in Table 8.4, which shows that the external structure obtained from peer ratings of complete strangers is highly similar to that obtained from close acquaintances (Table 8.1) and to the internal structure of the terms obtained from similarity ratings (Table 8.2) and probability of co-occurrence ratings (Table 8.3).

How are we to account for this degree of external structure among subjects who are total strangers to one another? One explanation is that the Passini and Norman procedure was simply a highly indirect way of assessing the implicative meaning of traits, and hence their internal structure, in the natural language. Thus, in rating a stranger, one is forced to rely on such superficial characteristics as dress, demeanor, physical size, movement, etc. Once a given rating has been made on this superficial basis, the remaining ratings are relatively "fixed" by the implicative structure that exists among trait terms. Thus, if a rater decides that a subject is "good-natured" (on whatever basis), it is likely that he will rate him as "cooperative," "mild, gentle," and "not jealous" as well. Another rater may decide that the same subject is "irritable" (on some trivial grounds), but once having made this decision, he is likely to rate him as "negativistic," "headstrong," and "jealous." One can enter the implicative system at almost any point and be guided by "consistent usage" of the descriptive language from then on. Since the superficial cues employed for initial trait ratings were likely to vary from rater to rater, it seems unlikely that substantial inter-rater consensus would exist in the rating of complete strangers. However, as raters become better acquainted with ratees, the cues on which ratings are based should be more valid, and substantial inter-rater agreement should obtain (Lay and Jackson, 1969).

An important study by Norman and Goldberg (1966) provides considerable support for the preceding explanation. Norman and Goldberg

Table 8.4 Factor matrix of peer ratings in a sample of strangers (from Passini and Norman, 1966, p. 46)

Scales	I	II	III	IV	V
Extraversion					
talkative–silent	80				
frank, open–secretive	67		−32		
adventurous–cautious	67		−42	37	
sociable–reclusive	85				
Agreeableness					
good-natured–irritable		67			
not jealous–jealous	−30	65			
mild, gentle–headstrong		70			
cooperative–negativistic	46	67			
Conscientiousness					
fussy, tidy–careless			72		
responsible–undependable		57	61		
scrupulous–unscrupulous		57	55		
persevering–quitting, fickle		36	63		
Emotional stability					
poised–nervous, tense		51		50	
calm–anxious				77	
composed–excitable				61	
not hypochondriacal–hypochondriacal			−33	58	
Culture					
artistically sensitive–insensitive					71
intellectual–unreflective, narrow			30		69
polished, refined–crude, boorish	54	36	32		20
imaginative–simple, direct					72

* Factor loadings less than .30 are omitted.

studied the external structure of peer ratings in groups varying in *length of acquaintanceship* from artificial groups based on random data, through strangers, to close acquaintances. The investigators used a "Monte Carlo" procedure, in which a computer generated random data of predetermined characteristics. Random numbers were selected for eight groups of seven "subjects" in such a manner that the correlations between raters (inter-rater agreement) were zero, but the pattern of correlations among scales (structure) was common for all raters. This Monte Carlo procedure represents the pure case in which structure is determined entirely by a shared implicative-meaning system and bears no relation to the "persons" rated.

The next body of data considered was that from the Passini and Norman (1966) study, in which the raters were totally unacquainted with the ratees. A third body of data came from a peer-rating study of ROTC seniors whose prior acquaintance was limited largely to "classroom and drill periods shared over a 1–2½ year period" (Norman and Goldberg, 1966, p. 685). A fourth peer-rating study was based on a group of Peace Corps trainees who had lived together, very closely, during a three-month period of intensive training. The fifth group, employed by Norman and Goldberg, consisted of senior fraternity men who had known one another and had lived together for periods varying from one to three years. The external structure of peer ratings in all of the groups was highly similar, even though the basis for the grouping was acquaintanceship of widely varying lengths. This study is consistent with others (e.g., Fiske, 1949) in indicating that the external structure of peer ratings is relatively independent of the length of acquaintanceship of the raters with the ratees.

In all the samples assembled by Norman and Goldberg, a number of raters rated a common group of ratees on 20 trait scales. Consequently, it was possible to compute indices of inter-rater agreement or rater generalizability in all samples studied. When inter-rater agreement was computed in the five samples that varied in length of acquaintanceship, a clear and consistent trend was found. The inter-rater agreement in the Monte Carlo results was approximately zero, as would be expected from the manner in which these data were generated by the computer. The inter-rater agreement in the Passini and Norman sample, whose members had had no prior acquaintanceship, was approximately .45. In the remaining three samples, with considerable lengths and intensities of acquaintanceship, indices of inter-rater agreement were near .70. Thus degree of inter-rater agreement consistently reflects the extent of acquaintanceship that exists between raters and ratees. It may also be taken as an indication of consistency in the *semantic meaning* of the trait terms across raters. Such an index is useful in distinguishing between peer ratings that are exclusively determined by the internal structure that exists among trait terms and peer ratings whose structure is determined by agreement by consensus of raters concerning perceived attributes of ratees. Norman and Goldberg conclude: "At the very least, there seems to be no good reason to fail to report coefficients of inter-rater agreement as a routine matter in future peer-rating studies of personality structure" (1966, p. 690).

As Norman and Goldberg note (p. 687), although substantial inter-rater agreement is a necessary condition for establishing the fact that the structure of peer ratings reflects attributes of ratees, it cannot be considered a sufficient one. However, the credibility of peer ratings as measures of ratee attributes may be further increased by appeal to *external* sources of evidence. Fortunately, such external criteria were available in both the Passini and Norman sample and in the sample of Peace Corps trainees. In both of these groups, subjects were instructed (a) to rate themselves on the 20 traits and (b) to *predict* the ratings that they would receive from their peers. In the Peace Corps sample, a moderate degree of generalizability was found for the peer ratings, which had correlations ranging from .27 to .54 with self-ratings and predicted peer ratings. In contrast, the corresponding values for the Passini and Norman subjects, who were not acquainted, were generally low and ranged from near zero to a high of .38. Thus it seems safe to conclude that peer-rating data obtained from close acquaintances will show not only a high degree of inter-rater generalizability but generalizability to other measures as well.[3] These two kinds of criteria seem to be essential for distinguishing peer ratings determined by external structure from those determined solely by internal structure. Peer-rating studies that fail to report such characteristics must always be treated with some skepticism.

Affective Meaning of Peer Ratings

Since personality trait descriptors almost necessarily have strong affective connotations, it is desirable that these connotations be relatively constant for different observers. Although there are admittedly some individual differences in the affective meaning of adjectival scales for different observers (Wiggins and Fishbein, 1969), the major findings of semantic differential research have provided evidence of considerable inter-judge *consistency* in the application of these scales across diverse populations and concepts (Osgood, Suci, and Tannenbaum, 1957). However, as with implicative meaning, the very consistency of application of trait terms has led to the suspicion that trait attribution in peer ratings may reflect "nothing but" dimensions of affective meaning. For example, Peterson (1965) has observed:

The invariant "personality" dimensions [neuroticism and extraversion] are rather easily construed as topical variants of more general ways of attributing meaning to objects, in this case human objects. "Adjustment" is good, "neuroticism" is bad. Extraversion "means" strong and active. (p. 57)

A number of other writers have also suggested that the major dimensions of trait attribution may be little more than dimensions of shared affective meaning of the terms themselves (Becker, 1960; Burke and Bennis, 1961; Ford and Meisels, 1965; Mulaik, 1964).

---

3.   One assumes, of course, that the nature of the acquaintanceship is *relevant* to the material to be rated (Freeberg, 1967).

Perhaps the most direct evidence available regarding the relationship between trait attribution and affective meaning appears in a study conducted by Hallworth (1965). In studying teachers' ratings of their pupils, Hallworth (1961) had earlier found that ratings on varied personality traits could be well summarized by the two factors of emotional stability and extraversion, factors which are similar to those isolated by Cattell (1957), Tupes and Christal (1961) and Norman (1963b) with adults. On the basis of the apparent similarity of the emotional stability and extraversion factors to the evaluation and activity factors of affective meaning, Hallworth (1965) designed a study to investigate the relationship between the two sets of factors. Six classes of preadolescent boys were rated by their teachers on 14 personality traits. The traits were rated on five-place scales. In addition, the teachers rated their pupils on 20 seven-place bipolar adjective scales that were known to mark the semantic differential factors of evaluation, potency, and activity. Thus both trait attribution and semantic differential ratings were obtained on a total group of 200 boys.

The 14 trait ratings and 20 semantic differential ratings were inter-correlated across the 200 boys, and four factors were extracted. The most relevant portion of this factor matrix is illustrated in Table 8.5. The scales have been arranged in such a manner that triplets of "personality" scales are followed by triplets of "semantic differential" scales. The first three scales mark the personality factor of emotional stability (trustworthiness, co-operation, emotional stability), the next three scales mark the (same) semantic factor of evaluation (good–bad; valuable–worthless; wise–foolish). The second factor of extraversion is equally well marked by the semantic scales for activity. Finally, the third factor of confidence appears to be equally well defined by the semantic scales for potency. The correspondence between "personality" and "affective meaning" dimensions is striking.

Are the major dimensions of trait attribution "nothing but" the major dimensions of affective meaning? Unfortunately, the design of Hallworth's (1965) study does not permit a direct test of this hypothesis. As will be discussed in more detail in Chapter 9, to demonstrate that two traits or qualities are "different" from one another, it is necessary to measure the two traits by two different methods (Campbell and Fiske, 1959). In the present instance, emotional stability and evaluation may appear to be the "same" traits when measured by a common method (five- and seven-place rating scales), but they may turn out to be "different" traits when measured by different methods. In fact, the conceptual distinction between trait attribution and affective meaning is blurred when both are defined by a common method. On what grounds can it be asserted that "trustworthy," "spontaneous," and "confident" are personality *trait* dimensions, whereas "wise," "rash," and "masculine" are affective *meaning* dimensions? The answer, of course, is that such a distinction cannot be made.

Table 8.5 Factor matrix of teacher ratings on trait and semantic differential scales. (After Hallworth, 1965, p. 164)

Scales	Factors		
	I	II	III
trustworthiness	85	05	05
cooperation	79	14	03
emotional stability	75	−07	34
good–bad	84	−08	06
valuable–worthless	83	16	28
wise–foolish	83	−14	22
spontaneity	−02	85	24
humor	00	83	08
sociability	09	76	31
moving–still	03	80	10
active–passive	23	69	23
rash–cautious	−50	68	−07
games ability	16	38	60
maturity	60	13	55
confidence	23	47	54
masculine–feminine	15	18	75
strong–weak	39	22	65
hard–soft	−25	06	62

More important than procedural problems, however, is the "chicken and egg" nature of the inferences that may be drawn from these data. If a person who is judged to be "trustworthy" is also judged to be "cooperative," is this because both terms are favorable (evaluative) or because they share a common *descriptive* quality such as "stability" which is evaluated favorably? Evidence and arguments bearing on this issue have been presented by Peabody (1967).

Peabody noted that previous arguments for the overwhelming importance of the evaluative component in trait attribution (Osgood, 1962; Podell, 1961) have been based on studies in which the evaluative and descriptive components of trait attribution have been confounded.

The problem is that a judgment is commonly at the same time both an estimate of the factual situation and an evaluation. For example, consider such contrasts as "kind–cruel" or "cautious–rash." The judgment that a person or action is "kind" or "rash" combines a descriptive aspect (e.g., that the action helps others, or involves very large risks) and an evaluative aspect (e.g., that the action is desirable or undesirable). In a single trait term (and its opposite) the two aspects are confounded since they always combine in the same way (e.g., helping as desirable, hurting as undesirable). (Peabody, 1967, p. 2)

Thus, to test the relative importance of evaluation and description in trait attribution, Peabody "unconfounded" these two components. On the basis of a study of such general sources as dictionaries of synonyms and antonyms, *Roget's Thesaurus*, and the Allport-Odbert (1936) listings, approximately 700 traits were classified into tentative sets. These sets were further reduced by the selection of terms that were common and that had relatively clear-cut evaluative ratings. A reduced list of 289 terms was given to 20 student judges, who made semantic differential ratings on the evaluative dimension. It was then possible to select sets of four terms in which both the "positive" and "negative" ends of the descriptive dimension were represented by both "positive" and "negative" values on the evaluative dimension. Table 8.6 illustrates four such sets.

Table 8.6 Sets of trait terms differing in evaluative meaning. (From Peabody, 1967)

+ .9	cautious	+1.1	bold
− 1.1	timid	−1.2	rash
+1.7	self-controlled	+1.1	uninhibited
−1.4	inhibited	− .3	impulsive
+ .9	thrifty	+1.8	generous
−2.0	stingy	− .8	extravagant
+ .5	skeptical	+1.8	generous
−1.4	distrustful	−1.4	gullible

Consider the set of four terms: cautious, timid versus bold, rash. In front of each term is the rated evaluative meaning as determined by semantic differential ratings. The "positive" pole is represented by both a high evaluation term ("cautious" = +.9) and a low evaluation term ("timid" = −1.1). Similarly, the "negative" pole is represented by both a high evaluation term ("bold" = +1.1) and a low evaluation term ("rash" = −1.2). For all sets of four terms there is a statistically significant difference between the high and low evaluation ratings given to the two terms marking each pole. From each set of four terms, it was possible to obtain meaning-similarity judgments of the following form:

CAUTIOUS

bold _____ : _____ : _____ : _____ : _____ : _____ : _____ : timid

The instructions read: "Assume a person with the characteristic given in capital letters. On the scale immediately beneath, you are to judge how likely it is that this person has one or the other of the traits given by the scale." (Peabody, 1967, p. 5.) Note that when the antecedent term (given in capitals) is compared with a bipolar scale from the same set, the usual confounding of evaluation and description is reversed. That is, if CAUTIOUS were judged to be similar to "timid," a high evaluation term (CAUTIOUS = +.9) would be related to a low evaluation term ("timid" = −1.1). The same would be true when CAUTIOUS is related to the dimension "timid–rash."

However, when a term is compared with a scale formed from outside its original set of four,

CAUTIOUS

skeptical _____ : _____ : _____ : _____ : _____ : _____ : _____ : gullible

it is possible to relate terms on the basis of their evaluative meanings without doing obvious injustice to their descriptive meanings. That is, evaluation and description may be confounded. In Peabody's study, all terms were employed as antecedent terms and evaluated against bipolar scales both within their original set of four (description and evaluation opposed) and against bipolar scales from other sets of four (description and evaluation potentially confounded). The design was an elaborate and carefully balanced one in which meaning-similarity ratings on 90 traits were made on 40 scales by 240 college students.

Of the total set of 3,600 ratings made, it was found that 67 percent were made in the direction of evaluative consistency. That is, when given the opportunity to relate terms on the basis of evaluation without doing obvious disservice to description, the subjects did so more often than not. However, within the critical set of 70 ratings in which evaluation and description were opposed, subjects rated in the direction of *description* on all of the ratings. The latter result may appear obvious if not trivial. However, considering the previous arguments that trait inferences are "nothing but" evaluation, Peabody (1967) observes:

To call these results obvious is to admit that the unlimited claims for evaluation are obviously wrong, once they are put more clearly. (p. 7)

Peabody then proceeded to intercorrelate the ratings made of the 90 antecedent terms and to extract the three largest factors. The factor loadings were examined in the light of both descriptive and evaluative hypotheses.

The central result is clear-cut; none of these large factors is evaluative. Instead, the substantial loadings systematically alternate according to the descriptive direction. Thus, removing the usual confounding between evaluation and descriptive aspects removes the possibility of interpreting any factor as evaluative. (p. 8)

Rosenberg and Olshan (1970) performed a different type of scaling analysis on the traits employed by Peabody (1967) and found that evaluation *was* an important dimension in accounting for the relationships among trait inferences. Subsequently, Peabody (1970) reevaluated his own earlier anlaysis and concluded that evaluation and description are of comparable importance as dimensions of trait attribution. Although both of these later studies represent a departure from the strong position originally taken by Peabody (1967), neither lends credence to the interpretation of trait inferences representing "nothing but" evaluation. The issue is far from resolved, however, and will no doubt continue to be a lively topic of investigation.

Implicit Theories of Personality

In recent years, it has become more or less standard practice to group the issues considered in the preceding sections under the general heading of "implicit theories of personality." We have purposely avoided using that expression for two reasons: (a) to the extent that the term "implicit theories of personality" refers only to the operations we have discussed for establishing the common implicative and affective meaning of trait terms, little is gained by the use of such an ambiguous phrase; and (b) to the extent that the term "implicit theories of personality" implies something more than the phenomena we have discussed, there seems to be little general agreement as to what is implied. Stating it more strongly, we can find little justification for concluding that the "meaning" of trait descriptors is *implicit*, resembles a *theory*, or is peculiar to the domain of *personality*.

An implicit theory of personality may be thought of as a relatively stable scheme of expectations and anticipations concerning the relations among traits of others that a rater brings to any trait-inference situation (Hays, 1958). Bruner and Tagiuri (1954) were among the first to emphasize the importance of studying such "naive" or "commonsense" schemes, and the investigations of implicative meaning, affective meaning, and trait ratings of strangers that we have discussed were conducted in response to their suggestion. The issue with respect to implicit theories of personality is not their existence but the extent of their possibly distorting influence on the perception of others. Vernon (1964), for example, views trait ratings "not so much as summaries of objectively observed behavior, as rationalizations abstracted from the rater's overall picture (his homunculus) of the subject" (p. 59). The implication here is that trait attributions are primarily determined by implicit schemata of raters and only secondarily by objective attributes of ratees. Lay and Jackson (1969), on the other hand, view implicit theories as veridical in the sense that inferential networks are acquired on the basis of experience and hence bear a close resemblance to the manner in which people are actually put together. They suggest further that raters who rely on implicit theories in predicting the behavior of others will tend to be relatively accurate, a point that is related to the concept of "stereotype accuracy" as discussed in Chapter 4.

To the extent that "implicit theories" are viewed as the *common* inferential network of lexical, implicative, and affective meanings held by the vast majority of English-speaking laymen, the term refers to the logical and empirical considerations of the preceding sections. Because this network of meaning relationships is so widely held and publicly verifiable, it is difficult to see in what sense it may be regarded as "implicit." Similarly, it is difficult to view the meaning relationships among a set of adjectives as constituting a "theory of language," like, for example, Chomsky's theory of language, or as a "theory of personality," like, for example, Freud's theory of personality. Finally, even granting that the meaning relationships among a set of adjectives constitute an "implicit theory," there is no reason to believe that such linguistic considerations apply uniquely to "personality." The same considerations would lead us to postulate a "theory of physical objects" or "a theory of vegetables" to refer to the "meaning" relationships among adjectives applied to other domains.

The expression "implicit theories of personality" can be, and to some extent has been, used in a quite different way. Instead of referring to the *common* network of meaning relationships held by most laymen, the word "theories" can refer to *individual differences* in meaning relationships among adjectives that exist from one person to another. This usage has the obvious advantage of being grammatically correct since it is not appropriate to speak of two or more individuals as holding common or identical "theories." In fact, this grammatical ambiguity has been a source of confusion in the literature since the term "theories" has been used to refer to both a common theory and to individual differences in theories.

The most clearly articulated statement of the individual-differences position with respect to the meaning of trait descriptors is found in the writings of George Kelly (1955). Kelly suggests that each man views life through a system of *personal constructs* that are a unique product of his own life experiences and that are not directly translatable into the different personal construct systems of other persons. This position is akin to that of Gordon Allport (1961), who held that *personal dispositions* are unique to each individual and that the so-called *common traits* refer to relatively arbitrary dimensions that are imposed on others. Although there is merit to both of these views, it should be noted that even in studies carefully designed to uncover individual differences in the meaning relationships of personality trait descriptors (e.g., Walters and Jackson, 1966), *communalities* in trait meanings are more striking than individual differences. This is, of course, consistent with the striking communalities in trait meanings uncovered by the studies cited in the preceding sections. In addition to certain logical difficulties inherent in the notion of "private languages" (Rhees, 1954), the evidence for a "public language" of personality cannot be easily dismissed.

Generalizability of Peer Ratings

The case for trait attributions reflecting characteristics of ratees, rather than consistencies of implicative and affective meaning structures, must be made with reference to external criteria. Theoretical considerations aside, the utility of peer ratings in personality assessment can be demonstrated only by reference to the generalizability of such ratings to criterion situations of social importance. For this reason, it is appropriate to comment briefly on the generalizability or "predictive validity" of peer ratings in representative personality assessment problems.

Two important types of generalizability to be expected from peer ratings are inter-observer agreement ("reliability") and generalizability of the factorial structure of ratings across diverse rating groups and conditions. Inter-observer reliability is a function of, among other variables, the *number* of raters employed. In observational studies, raters function very much as "items" in conventional tests function, reliability being related to the number of raters as given by the Spearman-Brown formula for test length (see Chapter 7). Thus, although ratings given by a single observer may be unreliable (.20 to .30), ratings obtained from a group of raters (10 to 20) yield quite satisfactory reliabilities (.80 to .90) (Tupes and Christal, 1961, p. 1). When certain technical considerations are taken into account, peer ratings have substantial generalizability across both observers and situations observed (Fiske, 1960; Fiske and Cox, 1960; Hollander, 1957; Suci, Vallance, and Glickman, 1954; Willingham, 1959). Further, as we have already indicated, the factorial structure of peer ratings is highly stable across diverse subject populations (Elliot, 1960; Ewart, 1960; Holdrege, 1961; Tupes and Christal, 1961; Norman, 1963b; Smith, 1967; Waters, 1960; Willmorth *et al.*, 1957).

A more practical concern is the generalizability of peer ratings to criterion situations of social importance. Peer ratings were first found to be of practical value in military personnel selection (Hollander, 1954a), and it is primarily in this area that they have continued to be employed. Within a military context, peer ratings have been found to be useful predictors of *officer effectiveness* (Haggerty, 1953; Hoffman and Rohrer, 1954; Tupes, 1957, 1959; Tupes and Kaplan, 1961; Williams and Leavitt, 1947), performance in *flight training* (Doll, 1963; Flyer, 1963; Flyer and Bigbee, 1954; Hollander, 1954b; Willingham, 1958), *leadership* (Bartlett, 1959; Kamfer, 1959; Robins, Roy, and deJung, 1958) and *disciplinary problems* (Klieger, deJung, and Dubuisson, 1962).

In other than military settings, peer ratings have found success in the selection of *supervisors* in industry (Weitz, 1958), in the prediction of *teacher effectiveness* (Isaacson, McKeachie, and Milholland, 1963), and in the forecasting of the performance of *Peace Corps volunteers* (Boulger and Colmen, 1964; Hare, 1962; Stein, 1963). A recent and somewhat novel application of peer ratings is to the prediction of *academic performance* within an educational setting (Astington, 1960; Smith, 1967; Wiggins, Blackburn, and Hackman, 1969). For example, Smith (1967) obtained peer ratings on the Cattell-Tupes-Norman scales for 348 college freshmen just prior to their first midterm examinations. These scales, along with a battery of more conventional predictors, were used in an attempt to predict grade-point average at the end of the first year of college. In the entire sample, the conscientiousness factor (quitting versus persevering) correlated $+.43$ with grade-point average. Although the magnitude of this correlation may not seem impressive, it should be noted that *none* of the conventional predictors of grade-point average (Scholastic Aptitude Test, Differential Aptitudes Test, Cooperative English Test, etc.) attained correlations in excess of $r = +.25$, and several tests had essentially zero correlations with the criterion.

Although peer ratings have only recently been used in formal academic prediction situations, Smith's (1967) finding is not atypical. Wiggins, Blackburn, and Hackman (1969) administered a battery of predictors along with peer ratings to two groups of first-year graduate students in psychology at the University of Illinois. Correlations of .51 and .49 with first-year grade-point average were obtained with a single peer-rating scale marking Norman's (1963) conscientiousness factor, providing considerable generalizability to Smith's (1967) finding. Direct peer ratings on such qualities as verbal aptitude, quantitative aptitude, and performance on prelims were equally impressive predictors. Moreover, such peer ratings have been found to be related to faculty ratings of competence obtained after three years in graduate school.[4] Again, for purposes of comparison, it should be noted that the highest correlation with grade-point average obtained with an aptitude predictor was .34, which was obtained with the Graduate Record Examination Psychology Scale (Wiggins *et al.*, 1969). Thus peer ratings may prove to be useful predictors of academic performance, particularly in groups that are highly homogeneous with respect to conventional aptitude test scores.

---

4. N. Wiggins, personal communication, 1970.

Peer Ratings of Specialized Populations

Trait-attribution systems developed from a systematic sampling of the natural language (e.g., Cattell-Tupes-Norman) appear to be applicable to a wide variety of criterion situations involving normal adults. Nevertheless, there are some criterion situations, and particularly some subject groups, that may require the development of specialized instruments for relatively circumscribed predictive tasks. As an example of such a specialized assessment problem, we shall consider the development of a peer-rating technique for assessing social maladjustment in preadolescent boys. Although the range of application of this particular instrument may be quite limited in scope, the principles underlying its development may be readily generalized to other specialized situations. For this reason, we will now consider the conception, development, and application of the Peer Nomination Inventory (Wiggins and Winder, 1961a) as illustrative of alternative approaches to the development of general systems of trait attribution.

Social Adjustment in Preadolescent Boys

The social adjustment of preadolescent boys is a matter of great practical concern for clinical, child, and school psychologists with an interest in identifying, and hopefully modifying, patterns of maladjustment that are detectable at an early age. Although most psychometric indices of adjustment in children are considered to be predictor variables, there are many situations in which peer ratings might be considered an appropriate *criterion* measure of this concept. The arguments for peer ratings as criterion measures have been made in other contexts (Wherry and Fryer, 1949), and such ratings have often formed a basis of evaluation for other instruments (Kamfer, 1959; Krumboltz, Christal, and Ward, 1959; Norman, 1961; Robins, Roy, and deJung, 1958). With respect to peer ratings as indices of social maladjustment in children, it has been argued:

The social stimulus value of a child to his peers is a source of observational data that has not been fully exploited as a criterion measure of adjustment. The opportunities for continuous observation over extended periods of time, both inside and outside the classroom, seem to qualify boys as highly informed witnesses of the behavior of their associates. In addition, judgments as to the appropriateness of any given social behavior might do well to include the opinions of members of the social group in question. (Wiggins and Winder, 1961a, p. 644)

Thus a peer-rating measure of adjustment with satisfactory measurement properties might provide a useful criterion measure against which psychological-assessment and behavior-modification procedures could be evaluated.

Sampling the Subcultural Language

The development of the Peer Nomination Inventory required a large pool of behavior descriptions that might be considered representative of social maladjustment as described by the peers of preadolescent boys. The eventual use to which the instrument would be put required that the dimensions of social maladjustment described by preadolescent boys bear some correspondence to the dimensions of adjustment which clinical and child psychologists believe to be important on both theoretical and practical grounds. Thus the developers had to choose between the extremes of: (a) imposing adult conceptions of social adjustment on children and (b) accepting children's conceptions of adjustment that might be of limited clinical or practical utility. The compromise they adopted was to develop items that were representative of the natural language employed by children of this age group and to assemble them in such a manner that their meaning would be clear to psychologists.

Potential items were collected in what might be considered a critical incident survey (Flanagan, 1954) of "preadolescent subculture," which utilized representatives of that subculture as "informants." A random sample of 8- to 12-year-old boys was drawn from 50 classes in seven public elementary schools representing several different socioeconomic levels. In this sample, 252 boys were interviewed individually by a team of interviewers who had had experience working in an elementary school setting. Each boy was seen in an individual tape-recorded interview that typically lasted 15 minutes. He was asked to think of boys in his class or other classes that were not making an adequate social adjustment (i.e., "not getting along too well with the other kids or with the teacher"). Once the respondent had named a boy (or more than one), he was encouraged to describe the boy's typical behavior ("What kinds of things does he *do*?"). No attempt was made to guide the direction of behavior description or to impose structure on the child's conception of adjustment.

Item Development

The 252 tape-recorded interviews obtained in the public school survey design were transcribed from tape by a pool of typists. Each transcription was a verbatim account of the interview. More than 1,500 pages of typed transcript were produced by this procedure. Three graduate students in psychology went through the transcript and circled each phrase or statement that was, in their opinion, a "behavior statement." "Behavior statements" referred to things that boys *did* rather than to irrelevant or highly inferential statements. Some 3,290 such behavior statements were identified and transferred to individual 3 by 5 cards. They were then sorted independently by three experienced judges into four substantive categories (aggression, dependency, withdrawal, depression) and a category of "other." The substantive categories were those that were considered to be of theoretical and practical importance in the diagnosis and modification of social maladjustment in children. The judges agreed in 80 percent of their category placements and thereby produced a total of 1,566 statements within the four substantive categories of interest.

Two experienced clinical psychologists examined the items within each category for distinct subcategories. Thus the raters agreed that there were 14 subcategories of aggression, 9 subcategories of dependency, etc. By eliminating obvious duplications and providing a reasonable sampling of all subcategories, they attempted to select 60 behavior statements for each of the four substantive categories. Although this was possible for aggression, dependency, and withdrawal, the category of depression yielded only 36 statements. These 216 behavior statements were then translated directly into peer-rating items. Although occasional modifications were made in the syntax of the items, they were essentially verbatim quotations phrased in the language peculiar to this subculture of preadolescent boys (e.g., "He's always fussing around").

Item Analysis

The 216 peer-rating items were randomly assigned to six preliminary forms of the Peer Nomination Inventory, each form containing ten items from each of the aggression, dependency, and withdrawal categories and six items from the depression category. In each of the six preliminary test forms, the items were arranged in an item by subject matrix, as illustrated in Figure 8.3. The task of each child was to consider the applicability of each statement to all members of his class (excluding himself). The preliminary forms were administered to 681 boys from ten different schools representing two broad categories of socioeconomic status. At the same time that the forms were administered to classes, they were also filled out by the teachers of those classes.

The 216 items were then subjected to an item analysis based on three successive criteria: (a) internal consistency, (b) difficulty level, and (c) concurrent validity. The criterion of internal consistency required that each item correlate at least .50 with the total scale (e.g., aggression) of which it was a member. Some 91 items were eliminated by this criterion. In the second stage of item analysis, an attempt was made to select items that were employed frequently enough to be of practical value and that were relatively stable in their difficulty level across different samples of subjects. Thirty percent of the items failed to meet this criterion, and the pool was further reduced to 88 items. The final criterion of item selection was based on the

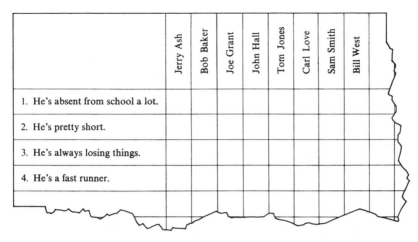

	Jerry Ash	Bob Baker	Joe Grant	John Hall	Tom Jones	Carl Love	Sam Smith	Bill West	
1. He's absent from school a lot.									
2. He's pretty short.									
3. He's always losing things.									
4. He's a fast runner.									

Fig. 8.3 Format of the Peer Nomination Inventory.

correlation between peer ratings and teacher ratings on each item ("concurrent validity"). The 12 items from each substantive category that had the highest correlation with teacher ratings were selected on this basis.

Administration of Final Scales

The 48 items that were derived from item analysis of the six original forms of the Peer Nomination Inventory constitute the basic item pool of that instrument. To this pool were added eight "likeability" items as well as several additional "filler" items to round out the inventory. This final form of the PNI is easily administered within a single class period. In order to evaluate the psychometric characteristics of the aggression, dependency, withdrawal, depression, and likeability "scales," the final form was administered to 710 boys from 52 classes in nine schools. Ratings on the same boys were also obtained from 50 classroom teachers. A year later the retesting of eight of the nine schools made it possible to obtain temporal stability data for 48 percent of the original sample.

The data from the normative sample of 710 subjects were used to assess such characteristics as internal consistency, difficulty level, concurrent validity, etc. The sample was large enough to allow investigation of the factorial structure of the peer nomination items as well. From a factor analysis of the intercorrelations among the 48 PNI items, four factors were identified as clearly interpretable. They were labeled: social isolation, hostility, crying, and attention-getting. On the basis of this factor analysis, corresponding factor scales were constructed to provide more precise representations of the underlying dimensions of peer ratings of social maladjustment.

Generalizability

Internal consistency. In the standardization sample of 710 boys, the internal consistency of the scales ranged from a low of .773 (depression) to a high of .944 (likeability). Internal consistency coefficients (odd-even) for the remaining three scales were in the high .80's and were considered to be highly satisfactory.

Temporal stability. The readministration of the PNI after a period of one year made it possible to compute temporal stability indices. However, not only were the retested boys in different grades, but many were among different classmates as well. Hence the readministration design confounds sources of unreliability due to the addition of new judges with the unreliability of groups of judges over time. This design is considered by many to be the most appropriate one for assessing the generalizability of observations (Medley and Mitzel, 1963). Temporal stability coefficients over a one-year period ranged from a low of .370 (depression) to a high of .519 (aggression). Although the temporal stability of the depression scale was considered unsatisfactory, the other results were considered generally encouraging, considering the developmental changes that might take place within a year at these age levels (Wiggins and Winder, 1961a, p. 667).

Concurrent validity. In the original administration design, the total scale scores on each of the four variables for teacher and peer ratings were correlated separately for each of 50 classes. The rank-order correlations between teacher and peer ratings ranged from a low of .42 (depression) to a high of .64 (dependency). These correlations were considered by the authors to be within the "desirable" range in that teacher ratings were not considered to be the *criterion* variable. In the development of a criterion measure of adjustment, correlations with a concurrent measure, such as teacher ratings, should be neither too high nor too low (Cronbach and Meehl, 1955).

Factorial stability. The factorial structure of the PNI, as determined from the original sample of 710 cases, was considered to be psychologically meaningful and generally clear-cut. Subsequently, this same factorial structure was demonstrated to be highly consistent in both similar (Sanner, 1964) and highly divergent (Siegelman, 1966b) samples.

Validation studies. Although the PNI may in some contexts be considered a "criterion" measure, its application can be justified only on the basis of demonstrations of its generalizability to attributes other than those narrowly defined by the ratings themselves. The basic item pool (Wiggins and Winder, 1961b) has proved a fruitful source of items and has provided a basis for extensions to preadolescent girls (Maccoby and Rau, 1962; Ferguson and Maccoby, 1966) as well as to the development of a teacher-rating instrument

(Ross, Lacey, and Parton, 1965) of considerable promise. Scores on the PNI variables have been related to parental attitudes and child-rearing practices in two quite different ways. Apparently, scores on PNI variables are "postdictive" of parental attitudes, as measured by parent interviews (Winder and Rau, 1962). PNI variables are also related to children's current *perceptions* of parental attitudes (Siegelman, 1966a). Perhaps the strongest justification for employment of the PNI as a criterion instrument comes from studies that have demonstrated its relationship to *behavior observations* obtained under highly controlled circumstances. Winder and Wiggins (1964) present evidence that PNI aggression scores are substantially related to independently obtained behavior ratings of aggression in a contrived naturalistic setting. The same investigators also demonstrated a relationship between PNI dependency scores and independently rated dependent behavior in a contrived classroom situation (Winder and Wiggins, 1964).

BEHAVIORAL ANALYSIS

As indicated in the preceding chapter, the choice of the trait unit as the primary attribute of behavior in personality study has recently been vigorously criticized. As is true of most issues in personality assessment, this question was originally raised in the context of the clinical diagnosis of behavioral pathology. During the last decade, it has become increasingly apparent that psychiatric treatment procedures based on social learning principles are more effective in the amelioration of certain classes of psychiatric symptoms (e.g., phobias) than are treatment procedures based on psychodynamic principles (Bandura, 1969; Franks, 1969; Krasner and Ullmann, 1965; Ullmann and Krasner, 1969). It has also become evident on both theoretical (Bandura, 1969) and empirical (Paul, 1969a, 1969c) grounds that traditional trait measurements are of little value in forecasting the outcomes of behaviorally oriented treatment procedures. As a consequence, radically new conceptions of the nature of clinical diagnosis and treatment have emerged, both with respect to criterion classifications (Kanfer and Saslow, 1965) and the assessment procedures employed for classification and prediction (Mischel, 1968; Peterson, 1968).

The "behavioral revolution" that occurred in clinical psychology in the sixties has resulted in a new climate of opinion regarding not only the nature of personality assessment in clinical practice, but the value of such assessment as well. There are two quite distinct issues here, and their differences have not been appreciated sufficiently. The first concerns the relative value of multivariate trait models and social learning models as frames of reference for guiding criterion analysis, selection of instruments, and prediction strategies (Chapter 10). This issue is perhaps best grasped by Goldfried and D'Zurilla (1969), who provide not only a convincing argument for the use of a social learning model in assessment, but ingenious procedures for criterion analysis and instrument development as well. The second issue, baldly stated, relates to whether or not clinical psychologists should be concerned with assessment and prediction at all. The latter issue has both scientific and professional ramifications.

In their zeal to dispense with "traditional" psychodynamic-trait *models*, many social behaviorists have advocated the abolition of "traditional" *principles* of personality assessment relating to the prediction of socially relevant criterion measures. The majority of social behaviorist writers have simply ignored the traditional personnel decision problem and concentrated on the development of assessment procedures for the single case. Given the availability of a number of effective treatments (desensitization, in vivo counterconditioning, etc.) and a large number of patients, *some* of whom can be so treated, it is not at all clear how the social behaviorist would solve the traditional personnel assignment problem. Moreover, the fact that many social behaviorists rely heavily on clinical impressions gained from interviews, construct self-report "surveys" of questionable psychometric properties, and generally operate without regard for decision-theoretic principles, seems to suggest that freedom from traditional models implies freedom from traditional psychometric principles as well.

In its professional aspect, this second issue concerns whether a clinical psychologist should spend his time treating patients or attempting to forecast the outcome of treatment procedures. This aspect is reminiscent of Meehl's (1954, p. 127) widely misinterpreted remark to the effect that clinicians could spend their time more profitably in research and psychotherapy than in trying to make "clinical" predictions of outcomes that could be more accurately forecasted by a computer. Meehl did *not* mean to imply that personality assessment and prediction are unsuitable activities for clinicians. One can hope that social behaviorists do not mean to imply this either, although it is more than clear what *their* preferred professional activity is. Goldfried and Pomeranz (1968) suggest that assessment activities may not be sufficiently "reinforcing" for social behaviorists, but surely one man's pellet may be another's cyanide capsule.

The positive contributions of social behaviorism to personality assessment lie in: (a) a set of clearly articulated and well-taken objections to the trait concept, (b) convincing arguments for the utility of viewing behavioral assessments as "samples" rather than as "signs" of criterion measures, (c) criterion analysis procedures for the classification of behavior that emphasize specificity and objectivity, and (d) strategies for the "functional analysis" of behavior that permit predictions to be qualified by the situation in which criterion behaviors occur. Each of these contributions will be touched on in the remainder of this chapter.

Objections to the Trait Construct

Although objections to the trait construct are hardly new (e.g., Lorge, 1935; Symonds, 1931), objections to the use of the trait unit in clinical assessment are of relatively recent origin (Bandura and Walters, 1963; Bandura, 1969; Greenspoon and Gersten, 1967; Kanfer and Saslow, 1965, 1969; Kanfer and Phillips, 1970; Mischel, 1968; Peterson, 1968; Wallace, 1966, 1967). The most extensive attack on the trait construct has been provided by Mischel (1968), who presented a selective review of research evidence casting doubt on some of the major assumptions of trait theories. One of the major thrusts of Mischel's arguments revolves around the notion that traits are primarily constructs of the observer rather than attributes of the observed, an issue that was discussed, in part, in earlier sections of the present chapter. Other objections may be classified under the headings of: (a) the consistency of traits, (b) traits as dispositional or causal variables, and (c) the neglect of the environment by trait theorists.

Consistency of Traits

Although traits, by definition, should be relatively stable dispositions, the empirical evidence for such consistency is far from conclusive. Relatively minor changes in the facets of settings, observers, instruments, or occasions may be sufficient to produce changes in the behavioral attributes observed. Typically, such evidence of instability is considered to be evidence of measurement error, which presumably could be reduced by methodological refinements within the various facets. An alternative interpretation would be that such instabilities are genuine as well as artifacts of method. Under this view, explanations of trait inconsistencies that are based on the notion of measurement error represent attempts to explain away instability on the grounds of instability (Mischel, 1968, p. 38). Even when evidence of trait consistency is positive, it does not necessarily follow that such consistency resides within the individual observed. When the occasions and settings of observation are held relatively constant, evidence of trait consistency may emerge, but such consistencies could, at least in part, be attributed to the constancy of occasions and settings rather than to the consistency of traits.

Several lines of evidence suggest that the behavioral consistencies which a human observer attributes to others may reflect cognitive and perceptual tendencies to see consistencies where none exist. Incompatible or contradictory cognitions create a state of "dissonnance" in the observer, which he may strive to reduce by making the cognitions compatible (Festinger, 1957). Although a variety of explanations have been offered to account for this tendency to seek cognitive consistency or balance (Abelson *et al.*, 1968), there is little doubt that such a tendency exists. In the realm of person perception, it has been demonstrated that subjects will misperceive or grossly distort facts to achieve a consistent view of themselves and of others (Gergen,

1968; Warr and Knapper, 1968). Constancies in person perception may be thought of as analogous to constancies in the perception of physical objects (Cantril, 1963; Heider, 1958). Just as objects will be perceived as the "same" when viewed from quite different perspectives, an individual's attributes may be perceived as the "same" when their manifestations are quite diverse. Thus a variety of cognitive and perceptual processes may be operative in producing what Mischel refers to as "constructed consistencies" in the behavior of others.

Traits as Dispositional Constructs

Perhaps the most objectionable feature of the trait construct, from the standpoint of social behaviorism, is the manner in which traits are construed as hypothetical entities which "cause" behavior. The objection is not to hypothetical constructs per se, although such constructs are held to a minimum in social behaviorism, but to hypothetical constructs that are animistic and circular, and that divert attention from lawful empirical relationships. The field of clinical psychodiagnosis is felt to be particularly vulnerable to such criticisms, although examples of such misuses of the trait construct can be found in other areas as well.

For many years the field of descriptive psychiatry, and much of clinical psychology, was dominated by the *disease* model of "mental illness." For example, a patient who displayed a given constellation of "symptoms" such as withdrawal, blunted affect, and poor reality contact would be diagnosed as suffering from the disease of schizophrenia. When pressed for an explanation of the presence of such deviant behaviors in a particular patient, a traditional clinician would indicate that the patient is suffering from the disease of schizophrenia. Thus the label ("schizophrenic") attached to the deviant behaviors is used as an *explanation* of the deviant behaviors, a procedure which is completely circular. One of the many adverse consequences of such reasoning is that it diverts attention from what a patient *does* to speculations about what he *has* (Mischel, 1968; Bandura, 1969).

Circularity in dispositional reasoning is not restricted to the field of descriptive psychiatry. To the extent that traits are viewed as "inner causes," significant environmental relationships may be overlooked. A person who relies heavily on others for support, reassurance, and guidance can be categorized as a "dependent" person. If his excessive help-seeking is, in turn, explained by his "need for dependency," the circularity of inference is no less than in the preceding psychiatric example. Again, the emphasis on what a person *has* may divert attention from significant aspects of his environment that are controlling and maintaining his help-seeking behaviors. For the social behaviorist, "explanation" consists of a specification of those factors in the social environment which brought about and which maintain the behaviors of interest.

Situational Factors

Although paying conventional lip service to the importance of "the environment," multivariate trait theorists have been guilty of a heavily one-sided emphasis on individual differences in behavioral attributes rather than on the environmental contexts in which such individual differences occur. Cattell (1966c), for example, has developed highly elaborate procedures for studying the stability and fluctuation of traits across different occasions, but he views behavior as primarily determined by individual differences in motives and traits which are, in turn, "modulated" by environmental factors (Cattell, 1963). Social behaviorists, on the other hand, have adopted a strongly "situationist" stance in explaining the dynamics of behavior. As a result, they have tended to emphasize the importance of environmental events which precede (antecedent) and follow (consequent) behavior and to minimize or even deny the role of individual differences in central traits or motives (e.g., Bandura and Walters, 1963).

An important series of studies by Endler, Hunt, and associates (Endler and Hunt, 1966, 1968, 1969; Endler, Hunt, and Rosenstein, 1962) has served to call attention to the relative neglect of situational factors by trait theorists. These authors constructed an *S-R Inventory of Anxiousness*, which permitted the assessment of the relative contributions of situations, responses, and individual differences to self-reported anxiousness on a personality questionnaire. For 11 situations (e.g., "You are going to meet a new date"), college students were asked to indicate their likely reactions in terms of 14 specific response modes (e.g., "mouth gets dry"). The item format permitted a quantitative estimate of the magnitude of each of the 14 responses under each of 11 situations:

You are going to go on a roller coaster.

Heart beats faster   1   2   3   4   5

Not at all   Much faster

The relative contributions of situations, responses, and individual differences to the determination of self-reports were assessed by analysis-of-variance procedures. Because the sample of response modes varied considerably in both expected frequency and social desirability ("get an uneasy feeling"; "having loose bowels"), one might expect the contribution of response modes to be substantial (Endler and Hunt, 1966, p. 340), and indeed it was (Endler *et al.*, 1962). Of greater immediate interest is the relative importance of situations and individual differences as determinants of self-reported anxiety. Endler, Hunt, and Rosenstein (1962) compared the relative magnitudes of mean squares in their analyses of variance and concluded that situations contributed a considerably greater amount of variance to self-report than did individual differences among subjects. This finding has been widely cited by social behaviorists (e.g., Mischel, 1968, p. 81) as evidence that individual differences are relatively unimportant in comparison with situations, even in self-report trait inventories.

It has been less widely reported that the original analysis (Endler *et al.*, 1962) was based on an inappropriate statistical model and that reanalysis of the same data (Endler and Hunt, 1966) and appropriate analyses of other data (Endler and Hunt, 1968, 1969) have led to quite different conclusions. When the estimated components of variance contributing to the total sum of squares are computed, it turns out that contributions of situations and individual differences are approximately equal *and both quite small* in comparison with the variance contributed by the several *interactions* between situations, responses, and individual differences. Although the adage that behavioral observations must consider the interaction between the persons observed and the situations in which responses occur may be a "methodological cliché" (Peterson, 1968, p. 27), it is one that is too frequently ignored by *both* trait theorists and social behaviorists. Regardless of the virtues or limitations of a strict "situationist" stance, the critical writings of the social behaviorists have served to underscore the relative neglect of situational factors by most trait theorists.

Observations as Behavioral Samples

Attributes as Signs of Traits

As we noted in Chapter 7, an observed behavior may be viewed as either a sign or a sample of other behaviors. For the most part, trait theorists view behavioral attributes as signs, or *indicants*, of underlying trait dispositions. A trait is thus a hypothetical construct which provides an organizing principle for relating a variety of superficially dissimilar behaviors under a single dispositional unit. Traits cannot be observed directly but must be inferred from their manifestations (Loevinger, 1957). A purported advantage of such a trait construct is that it provides an organizing principle for specifying relationships among behavioral attributes which are topographically dissimilar. Because the manifestations of a given trait are topographically dissimilar, it is contended that a physical description of environmental circumstances and response characteristics is not sufficient to indicate the relationships among manifestations of that trait.

Since traits are hypothetical constructs rather than observable entities, the usefulness of a trait construct must be demonstrated with reference to a complex set of procedures relating to the *construct validity*[5] of an instrument which purports to measure a trait (Cronbach and Meehl, 1955; Loevinger,

---

5. Procedures for establishing the construct validity of psychological tests are discussed in Chapter 9.

1957). Although some behaviorists (e.g., Bechtoldt, 1959) have objected to conceptualizations which rely on construct validation, it should be recognized that such conceptualizations are matters of preference or opinion rather than logical necessities (Peterson, 1968, p. 64). The telling criticisms of trait constructs are those which challenge the *manner* in which traits are conceptualized rather than those which challenge the use of hypothetical constructs in science. By the same token, justifications of the use of hypothetical constructs in psychology (MacCorquodale and Meehl, 1948; Cronbach and Meehl, 1955) should not be viewed as blanket endorsements of all such constructs.

Diverse behavioral attributes are considered manifestations of a single underlying trait when it can be demonstrated that such manifestations *co-vary* in groups of persons. Correlations among the observed or self-reported attributes of a group of subjects serve to identify clusters of attributes which may be manifestations of more basic trait units. The dimensions yielded by a factor analysis of such correlations are viewed as the principal trait dimensions on which individuals differ from one another (e.g., Cattell, 1957). The interrelationships among these principal trait dimensions are taken to be an indication of "personality structure" which, although defined with reference to groups of subjects, is thought to characterize the internal organizations of individuals within such groups. Thus most multivariate trait theories are "nomothetic" in the sense that trait dimensions discovered in groups serve as the basis for the prediction of future behaviors of individuals. Although some theorists have been distressed by the assumption that the structure or organization of *common traits* provides an adequate description of the organization of the *personal dispositions* (Allport, 1961) or *personal constructs* (Kelly, 1955) of individuals, the majority of trait theorists seem to accept this assumption with equanimity. The justification for such an assumption is usually held to reside in the extent to which individual differences in criterion attributes may be predicted on the basis of individual differences in common trait dimensions.

When a group of individuals is assessed with reference to a common trait dimension, an attempt is made to estimate each individual's position on the trait continuum with reference to that of others. The position of an individual on a trait dimension is thought of as his typical or characteristic disposition toward expressing the trait in question. Thus an individual may be characterized as mildly, moderately, or strongly aggressive in comparison with others. It is further assumed that an individual's characteristic disposition or need for trait expression is both *stable* within relatively short time periods and *generalizable* from one situation to another. Hence an individual who is moderately aggressive in the assessment situation is predicted to be moderately aggressive in most criterion situations. Situational variables, for the most part, are considered as exerting a moderating or "modulating" influence on *common* trait dimensions. Thus an attempt is made to identify environmental variables that influence the characteristic dispositions of individuals with respect to nomothetic dimensions of individual differences.

Attributes as Samples of Response Classes

Most social behaviorists view behavioral attributes as samples of response classes rather than signs of internal structures. To the extent that the ordinary language of personality is employed in behavioral observation, it is employed *descriptively* rather than inferentially. Bijou and Peterson (1971), for example, maintain that conventional trait attributions represent nothing more than giving two names to the same class of behavior. If a child is observed to strike another child, there is no reason to conclude that the child doing the hitting not only is aggressive but also has a "need for aggression." Behavioral attributes may be classified as instances of the response class of aggression without reference to internal dispositions toward aggression. Behaviors with aggressive attributes are classified in terms of their frequency, intensity, and duration rather than in terms of the degree to which they reflect an underlying disposition.

Diverse behavioral attributes are considered to be members of the same response class when it can be demonstrated that such attributes enter into the same functional relationships with antecedent, concurrent, and consequent stimulus conditions. Thus behavioral attributes that are under the control of the same set of stimulus conditions, particularly the consequent or reinforcement conditions, are considered as constituting a response class. Attributes are not classified as similar on the basis of their co-occurrence or co-variation in a group of persons. Instead, they are classified on the basis of the functional relationships they exhibit with the environmental conditions which "control" their occurrence. In principle, it would be possible to determine response classes, nomothetically, by identifying the environmental conditions which control response classes for groups of persons. In practice, social behaviorists, following Skinner (1938, 1953, 1959), have shown a strong preference for investigating the environmental conditions which control response classes in the lives of single organisms.

Because response classes are *defined* on the basis of their functional relationships with environmental conditions, the issue of environmental effects or modulating influences becomes superfluous. Similarly, the issues of *stability* and *generality* become empirical questions rather than assumptions. Given a change in stimulating conditions, particularly conditions of reinforcement, the frequency, intensity, or duration of the response class of interest should be predictable from a knowledge of the functional relationships between these attributes and the stimulus conditions which control them. Under these circumstances, it is more important to determine whether or not an individual is capable of performing a response, rather than trying to estimate the typical or characteristic level at which he responds. Wallace (1966, 1967) has proposed that personality traits are best viewed as abilities rather than dispositions toward action. Under this view, assessment is directed at the determination of an individual's *response capability*—that is, whether or not certain responses or behavioral tendencies exist within the person's repertoire. When an individual is observed to behave aggressively under certain circumstances, it may be concluded that he is capable of assuming an aggressive role. It cannot be concluded that the individual will behave aggressively in other situations and through other response modes, however, since his behavior in other situations will be determined by those environmental factors which tend to elicit and maintain this way of behaving. Thus an individual's *response performance* in the criterion situation to be predicted will be jointly determined by his response capability and the situational factors that are functionally related to the response class.

In sum, social behaviorists tend to view behavior observations as *samples* of response classes that are functionally related to environmental factors which elicit and maintain the responses in a class. Attributes are viewed not as dispositions but as capabilities whose probabilities of occurrence in criterion situations are determined by environmental factors. To the extent that the functional relationships between response classes and situational factors are lawful, problems of stability and generality become matters for empirical investigation rather than assumptions. This view, at least in part, provides an explanation for the situational specificity that has been found to characterize behavioral observations.

Attributes as Signs and Samples

The distinction made above between attributes as signs of trait dispositions and attributes as samples of response classes is not meant to imply that all personality psychologists may be divided neatly into multivariate trait theorists and social behaviorists. These two views of attributes are perhaps best thought of as end points that define a continuum of conceptualizations. Not all trait theorists attribute dispositional properties to the trait construct, and some social behaviorists include *R-R* relationships as part of the functional definition of response classes. Many intermediate or "mixed" views of attributes exist in the writings of personality psychologists.

Spielberger (1966) has emphasized the importance of making a distinction between trait and state constructs. Anxiety, for example, refers to a complex pattern of physiological and cognitive responses that may be viewed either as a *sample* of an individual's reactions to stress under specific stimulus conditions (state) or as a *sign* of an individual's predisposition toward acquiring or manifesting stress reactions in a variety of stimulus contexts (trait).   It is possible to define anxiety as a complex pattern of responses quite independently of the external or internal stimuli which elicit it (Martin, 1961).   Once the response pattern has been identified, samples of the response class may be studied in relation to situations which tend to elicit anxiety reactions.   Identification of the common features in situations in which anxiety responses typically occur permits a specification of the controlling stimuli for the pattern of responses (Bandura, 1969).

Attention may also be directed to the fact that there are individual differences in the likelihood that anxiety will be manifested under a variety of circumstances involving varying degrees of stress (Spielberger, 1966).   Thus some individuals are seldom aroused whereas others are chronically anxious. In a given stressful situation, some individuals react with considerable anxiety whereas others show few signs of discomfort.   Individual differences in the characteristic level of anxiety arousal reflect *anxiety proneness*, a dispositional trait construct.   This trait is assessed by studying the variety of situations in which the pattern of stress reactions is observed as well as the intensity of reactions in those situations.   The extent of anxiety proneness is determined, at least in part, by the number of situations an individual interprets as threatening.   A distinction between state and trait anxiety is made by *both* multivariate trait theorists (e.g., Cattell and Scheier, 1961) and social behaviorists (e.g., Paul, 1969b).

Classification of Behavior

As will become evident in the final chapter of this book, the major obstacle to the prediction of socially relevant criterion measures in personality assessment has been the vagueness with which such criterion measures are typically defined.   In attempting to forecast "overall effectiveness as an officer," "prognosis of recovery from mental illness," or "job satisfaction," the assessment psychologist has frequently resorted to predictor variables that are equally global and diffuse in nature.   In fact, as indicated in the preceding chapter, one of the principal justifications for the development of predictor variables couched in the ordinary language of trait attribution has been that criterion statements obtained from significant others are typically stated in the same language.   A number of procedures have been suggested for obtaining greater specificity and objectivity in criterion variables, most notably the critical incident technique of Flanagan (1954) and the procedures for criterion analysis suggested by Stern, Stein, and Bloom (1956), to be discussed in Chapter 10.   Although the procedures which social behaviorists advocate for achieving greater criterion specificity resemble these earlier procedures, they differ in several critical respects (Goldfried and D'Zurilla, 1969).   The major focus of criterion classification for social behaviorists is the *environmental conditions* which elicit and maintain the criterion attributes of interest.

Social behaviorism arose in the context of clinical psychology, and consequently, the schemes for classification of criterion behaviors that have been suggested (e.g., Ferster, 1965; Bandura, 1968; Kanfer and Saslow, 1969) relate to "deviant behaviors" that are considered to be in need of modification. Recall, however, that all criterion attributes are "deviant" in the sense that some socially defined attribute of performance ("successful physician," "high grade-point average student") has been singled out as being different from the norm or average (Berg, 1957). Thus the forecasting of "behavioral assets" such as academic competence (Goldfried and D'Zurilla, 1969) is no different, in principle, from the forecasting of "behavioral deficits" (e.g., social withdrawal) or "behavioral excesses" (e.g., compulsive hand-washing) (Kanfer and Saslow, 1969).

In common with earlier approaches to criterion analysis (Flanagan, 1954), social behavioristic approaches attempt to reduce global criterion evaluations ("lacks inherent flying ability") to *specific behavioral incidents* which exemplify the criterion. Similarly, in the same manner in which earlier assessment psychologists were sensitive to the implicit and explicit criteria employed by criterion judges (Stern, Stein, and Bloom, 1956), social behaviorists are concerned with the environmental conditions which control the "labeling behavior" of a criterion judge (Bijou and Peterson, 1971). Once the specific behavioral incidents have been identified, however, the approach of the social behaviorist diverges from earlier approaches. Whereas traditional assessment psychologists attempt to identify the broad trait dimensions which underlie the successful performance of specific behavioral incidents, social behaviorists attempt to identify the antecedent, concomitant, and consequent stimulus conditions which *control* these behavioral incidents.

The behavioral classification system of Kanfer and Saslow (1965, 1969) is representative of those employed by the majority of social behaviorists. The critical incidents of interest are the observed (or reliably reported) criterion behaviors. The environmental conditions which may potentially control such behaviors are: (a) antecedent events, (b) consequent events, (c) contingency-related conditions, and (d) the biological condition of the organism. Antecedent stimulus events are those which reliably precede the criterion behaviors, and they may be functionally related to them as "discriminative stimuli" (setting the stage for) or as "eliciting stimuli" (evoking the response). Consequent events refer to the new stimulus conditions which the criterion behaviors were "instrumental" in bringing about. The effects of criterion behaviors on the subject's internal and external environment are among the most important in determining whether or not the behaviors will recur. Contingency-related conditions refer to the temporal relationships of both antecedent and consequent events. Of major interest here are the "schedules of reinforcement" (Ferster and Skinner, 1957) under which response-contingent consequences occur. Although not given heavy emphasis by Skinnerians (e.g., Lindsley, 1964), the biological condition of the organism may be of importance as a controlling stimulus event for criterion behaviors which are facilitated or inhibited by the constitutional or physiological condition of the subject (Kanfer and Saslow, 1969).

In the analysis of *human* behavior, environmental conditions should be classified with reference to the units which have been identified by other disciplines (Skinner, 1953; Bandura, 1969; Peterson, 1968). Thus Kanfer and Saslow (1969) recognize that stimulus conditions may be considered as *systems* which include such potential variables as psychological, biological, economic, and social events. The individual's self-regulatory processes, the state of his health, his financial circumstances, and his relations with other individuals and social institutions may all be potent conditions which affect the acquisition and maintenance of criterion behaviors. Kanfer and Saslow suggest that all such potential variables be considered, without prior judgment about their order of importance, although most social behaviorists (e.g., Bandura, 1969; Peterson, 1968) tend to emphasize psychological and social systems.

Criterion behaviors, thus, can be considered to be fully classified only when the stimulus conditions which elicit and maintain them have been clearly identified. The social significance of such criterion behaviors is determined by significant others' judgments as to whether they are excessive, deficient, or adaptive. Since behaviors which are excessive or deficient in one situation may be adaptive in another, it is clear that such "labeling" is to some extent arbitrary (Bandura, 1969). But the functional relationships that exist between criterion behaviors and the stimulus conditions which control them are presumably lawful and permit the *prediction* of such criterion behaviors when it is possible to specify future stimulus conditions. Of great importance to psychotherapy, education, on-the-job training, and other "adaptive treatment" situations (Cronbach, 1957) is the fact that behavioral classification is, in effect, a specification of the conditions which will result in a *modification* of the criterion behaviors (Kanfer and Saslow, 1969). In addition, behavioral classification specifies the criteria which may be employed to *evaluate* the success or failure of any program of behavior modification. The extent to which criterion behaviors are *maintained*, by the individual or by environmental manipulations, is the extent to which a program of behavior modification has been successful (Bijou and Peterson, 1971).

Functional Analysis

The process whereby the environmental conditions that elicit and maintain criterion behaviors are discovered is called the *functional analysis* of behavior (Skinner, 1938, 1953, 1959). Traditionally, functional analyses have been conducted for purposes of basic research in human learning and for guiding and planning programs of treatment or behavior modification. There is no logical reason, of course, why the data yielded by a functional analysis of behavior should not be employed in the *prediction* of socially relevant criteria. In fact, when the results of a functional analysis are used to plan a program of treatment, there is an implicit prediction as to the probable success of the treatment selected, and this probability is most certainly less than unity.

As a prediction strategy, traditional functional analysis is *statistical* in the sense that it is based on *known* empirical relationships (Chapter 5). Whereas the statistical prediction strategies we have discussed thus far are based on empirical relationships between psychological test responses and theoretically significant non-test characteristics (*R-R* analysis), functional analysis is based on empirical relationships between environmental conditions and samples of criterion response classes (*S-R* analysis). Although based on different kinds of input data, both *R-R* and *S-R* prediction paradigms should be guided by the principles we have discussed thus far, including those related to methods of data combination and the evaluation of outcomes in terms of their utilities (see Bandura, 1969, pp. 99–111). However, whereas statistical predictions based on *R-R* relationships are usually expressed as forecasts of "typical" performance under varying criterion environments, those based on *S-R* relationships may be expressed as forecasts of response capabilities under *specific* criterion environments. The classical problem of predicting *what* environmental circumstances will prevail in future criterion situations (Taft, 1959) is common to both methods. But prediction systems based on *S-R* analyses seem to have the inherent advantage of being able to specify *which* aspects of the environment are relevant and *how* predictions should be adjusted accordingly.

Functional analyses performed under rigorous laboratory conditions or in semicontrolled naturalistic environments (Bijou *et al.*, 1969) provide empirical data on *S-R* relationships that could potentially be employed in the statistical prediction of criterion performances. Such data are typically presented as cumulative response curves that exhibit orderly changes as a function of experimental manipulations of environmental conditions (e.g., Ferster and Skinner, 1957). Since prediction has not been a central concern of functional analysis, there are few, if any, data available that would permit an assessment of the predictive potential of such *S-R* relationships in terms of such conventional indices as standard error of prediction, proportion of variance explained, or number of correct decisions. Thus, although there is every reason to believe that the lawful relationships uncovered by functional analysis in the laboratory and in semicontrolled naturalistic settings may have a considerable predictive edge over conventional *R-R* relationships, such an expectation at present is a matter of conviction rather than fact.

Surprisingly, most social behaviorists who advocate a functional analysis approach to personality assessment (Kanfer and Saslow, 1969; Bijou and Peterson, 1971; Mischel, 1968; Peterson, 1968; Goldfried and Pomeranz, 1968) also advocate methods of data collection and combination that are decidedly *clinical* (judgmental) in nature. Although in theory, procedures of functional analysis are based on *demonstrated* empirical relationships (Bijou *et al.*, 1969), in practice and particularly in clinical psychology, such relationships are frequently *estimated* on the basis of highly fallible measures. The major published descriptions of "functional analysis" in clinical practice (Kanfer and Saslow, 1969; Bijou and Peterson, 1971) suggest the use of interviews, self-report devices, and a variety of conventional psychological tests as methods of data collection, and they also place a heavy emphasis on the subjective evaluation of these data by the clinician as a method of data combination. Such procedures differ from conventional personality assessment only in the employment of a social learning *model*, rather than some other theoretical frame of reference (Chapter 10).

It is important to distinguish assessment procedures that employ social behavioristic principles as a frame of reference for clinical prediction from assessment procedures that employ functional analysis as a method of gathering data for statistical prediction. A complete functional analysis of behavior requires an *empirical* demonstration of the relationships between criterion attributes and the environmental conditions which control them. Such a demonstration requires, at a minimum, that reliably observed or recorded attributes of behavior (frequency, intensity, duration) exhibit lawful relationships with *experimentally manipulated* aspects of the stimulating environment. Experimental procedures of this type are by no means limited to conventional laboratory settings (Bijou *et al.*, 1969). But when these experimental procedures are applied to socially important criterion measures, their implementation is extraordinarily time-consuming and expensive. In addition to taxing the experimental skills and ingenuity of "behavioral engineers," such procedures frequently require direct, and to some extent unprecedented, interventions in the lives of subjects, peers, parents, teachers, spouses, and other associates. Finally, since rigorous procedures for functional analysis require the intensive study of single individuals (Bijou *et al.*, 1969), the economies of nomothetic procedures must be at least temporarily relinquished.

The major criticisms that have been leveled at the functional analysis of behavior, as opposed to conventional *R-R* analysis, are that it is usually impractical, unfeasible, or much too costly. The feasibility of such procedures is still an open question, however, and cost-accounting procedures have yet to be employed within a decision-theoretic framework.

Although the method proposed is more costly than current methods, we do not know how much more, for we have not yet ascertained from actual experience how many environmental situations in a given case would require sampling and how extensive each sample should be. (Bijou and Peterson, 1971, p. 78)

But many social behaviorists are so thoroughly disillusioned with the predictive power of conventional *R-R* analysis that they are willing to forge ahead at any cost.

How long can we tolerate a descriptive situation where our measures account for ten percent of accountable variance? How long can we go on seeking and failing to improve that score? How long will it be until we decide that there is no cheap way to study human behavior and begin looking as directly as possible at the behavior itself? (Peterson, 1968, p. 141)

SUMMARY

Trait Attribution

The ordinary language of personality trait attribution provides a convenient starting point for the development of a general schema by which to organize observations of behavioral attributes. As with any other coding system for organizing behavioral observations, it is important that the terms employed have common *meanings* for observers, in several senses: (a) lexical meaning refers to the rules for word usage as given in a dictionary; (b) affective meaning refers to the emotional connotations of words as represented by such dimensions as evaluation, potency, and activity; (c) implicative meaning refers to the structural relations that exist among a set of words as given by their probabilities of co-occurrence in the natural language.

The extent to which raters agree on the lexical, affective, and implicative meanings of a set of personality trait descriptors may be taken as an indication of the degree of *internal structure* that exists among the set of terms. The relationships that exist among a set of trait descriptors when applied to real persons in observational studies may be taken as an indication of the degree of *external structure* that exists among the terms. Under certain circumstances, it is possible for internal structure to be a sufficient condition for external structure. When this occurs, it may be properly asserted that trait ratings reflect primarily the common meanings of trait terms for observers rather than discriminable attributes of those observed. However, when it can be demonstrated that there is considerable inter-observer agreement in the application of trait descriptors to real persons and when such ratings can be shown to be generalizable to external criterion measures, the external structure of ratings may be thought of as reflecting veridical attributes of ratees.

Over the past quarter of a century, a systematic and cumulative series of investigations of the structure of peer ratings may be traced. This work was initiated by Allport and Odbert, who provided a list of all trait names that appeared in an unabridged dictionary. Cattell reduced that list to a manageable number of terms and, on the basis of cluster-analytic procedures, identified a smaller set of underlying dimensions. In a series of pioneering peer-rating studies, Cattell identified the major factors that underlie trait attribution. Subsequently, Tupes and Christal conducted a number of investigations designed to identify those of Cattell's factors which appeared with the greatest consistency and which had the greatest generalizability to socially relevant criteria. The factors identified by Tupes and Christal were further refined by Norman in a series of studies designed to illuminate both the internal and external structure of peer ratings.

In general, peer ratings have been shown to have substantial generalizability in terms of inter-observer agreement, generalizability of external structure across diverse rating groups and conditions, and generalizability to criterion situations of social importance. With respect to the last, peer ratings have been demonstrated to be predictive of officer effectiveness, performance in flight training, leadership ability, supervisory skill, teaching effectiveness, overseas performance of Peace Corps volunteers, and academic performance of both undergraduate and graduate students. Peer-rating procedures have also been applied successfully to specialized populations, as is evident from a series of studies designed to assess dimensions of social maladjustment in preadolescent boys.

Behavioral Analysis

The choice of the trait unit as the primary attribute in personality study has been criticized recently by behaviorally oriented clinical psychologists who have found trait measurements to be of little value in forecasting the outcomes of treatment procedures based on social-learning principles. It has been alleged that the *consistency* of traits is more apparent than real, that the causal or *dispositional* property of trait constructs has been inferred by circular reasoning, and that traits have been conceptualized without regard for the *situational factors* which determine their manifestations. As an alternative to observational procedures based on trait attribution, social behaviorists have proposed procedures which (a) view behavioral assessments as "samples" rather than as "signs" of criterion measures; (b) emphasize specificity and objectivity in criterion classification; (c) employ strategies for the "functional analysis" of behavior that permit predictions to be qualified by the situations in which criterion behaviors occur.

Social behaviorists view behavior observations as samples of response classes that are functionally related to environmental factors which elicit and maintain the responses in a class. Attributes are viewed not as dispositions but as capabilities whose probabilities of occurrence in criterion situations are determined by environmental factors. To the extent that the functional relationships between response classes and situational factors are lawful, problems of stability and generality become matters for empirical investigation rather than assumptions. This view, at least in part, provides an explanation for the situational specificity that has been found to characterize behavioral observations.

The major focus of criterion classification for social behaviorists is the environmental conditions which elicit and maintain specific behavioral incidents that exemplify the criterion. Environmental conditions which may potentially control such behaviors are: (a) antecedent events, (b) consequent events, (c) contingency-related conditions, and (d) the biological condition of the organism. These environmental conditions may be considered as systems which include such potential variables as psychological, biological, economic, and social events. Criterion behaviors, thus, can be considered to be fully classified only when the stimulus conditions that elicit and maintain them have been clearly identified.

The process whereby the environmental conditions that elicit and maintain criterion behaviors are discovered is called the functional analysis of behavior. As a prediction strategy, traditional functional analysis is statistical in the sense that it is based on known (experimentally verified) empirical relationships. Functional analysis is based on empirical relationships between environmental conditions and samples of criterion response classes (S-R analysis) rather than on empirical relationships between psychological test responses and socially significant non-test characteristics (R-R analysis). Prediction systems based on S-R analyses seem to have the inherent advantage of being able to specify which aspects of the environment are relevant to criterion behaviors and how predictions should be adjusted accordingly.

Although a complete functional analysis of behavior requires an empirical demonstration of the relationships between criterion attributes and the environmental conditions which control them, such relationships may be *estimated* on the basis of interviews, self-report devices, and a variety of conventional psychological tests. The latter procedure differs from conventional personality assessment only in the employment of a social-learning model, rather than some other theoretical frame of reference. It has been suggested that a complete functional analysis of behavior is usually impractical, unfeasible, or much too costly. The feasibility of such procedures is still an open question, however, and cost-accounting procedures have yet to be applied within a decision-theoretic framework. Moreover, many social behaviorists are so thoroughly disillusioned with the predictive power of conventional R-R analysis that they are willing to forge ahead at any cost.

CHAPTER 9

STRUCTURED TECHNIQUES

WHAT IS A STRUCTURED TEST?

In our usage a structured test denotes a series of stimuli (usually of a verbal nature) which are presented along with multiple-choice options, the responses to which have been restricted to the point necessary for scoring reliability to approach unity. Numerous other definitions of structured tests have been proposed (Watson, 1959), and several fairly elaborate classificatory systems have been offered to differentiate structured from unstructured and other testing techniques (Campbell, 1957; Rosenzweig, 1950; Leary, 1957; Bass and Berg, 1959). Distinctions have been made on the basis of (a) the nature of the stimulus, (b) the freedom of response involved, (c) the attitude, awareness, or set of the subject, and (d) the aspect or "level" of personality that is being measured. Although none of these bases for distinguishing structured from unstructured tests is entirely satisfactory, our emphasis on the scoring reliability of multiple-choice options appears to be the least ambiguous.

Paradoxically, speculations about the nature of the stimulus involved in personality tests can usually be reduced to aspects of *responses* to such tests. Structured stimuli are frequently spoken of as being unambiguous, clear, of uniform meaning for all subjects and for the same subject on different occasions. Unstructured stimuli, on the other hand, are described as ambiguous, unclear, and subject to a variety of interpretations among individuals, or even for the same individual on different occasions. Although some efforts have been directed toward specification of the physicalistic properties of test stimuli (Murstein, 1963, pp. 167–235), ambiguity is more typically inferred from responses of a population of subjects. Because the inkblots employed in the Rorschach test are "ambiguous" we would anticipate a greater variety of "meaning" being attributed to the stimuli and hence a greater variety of responses to a single stimulus than with a verbally stated true-false item of the inventory variety. Table 9.1 illustrates a pitfall of this line of reasoning.

Table 9.1 Hypothetical response frequencies to two personality items

Response frequencies to Card V of the Rorschach Inkblot Test		Response frequencies to MMPI Item 001: "I like mechanics magazines."	
Bat	90%	True	50%
Other	10%	False	50%

It seems reasonable to suppose that the initial response to Card V of the Rorschach might be "bat" for 90 percent of a normal population. Similarly, when the first item of the MMPI ("I like mechanics magazines") is presented to a normative population, 50 percent of the subjects may answer *true* while the remaining 50 percent answer *false*. In this example, which is admittedly untypical, it must be conceded that there is greater variability in response to the "structured" MMPI item than to the "unstructured" Rorschach item. Were we to employ a response definition of structure or ambiguity, we would have to conclude (in this particular instance) that the MMPI is a less structured, more ambiguous test than is the Rorschach.

Direct judgments of the "meaning" of the two stimuli might very well reveal the same paradox. The physical characteristics of Card V of the Rorschach are such that a bat is easily perceived as the "meaning" of the card under the instructions of the test. The stimulus "I like mechanics magazines," however, may clearly mean different things to different subjects. Does "like" imply fondness or tolerance? Does the statement imply that the respondent actually reads mechanics magazines? What are mechanics magazines? Are *Popular Mechanics* and *High Fidelity* both mechanics magazines? Would mechanics magazines include the trade journals of both automobile mechanics and electrical engineers? Does the statement refer to current or past tastes?

Clearly it is important to distinguish between the physical characteristics of the stimulus and the variability in response elicited by that stimulus (Murstein, 1963). One cannot be safely predicted from the other without reference to an empirically obtained distribution of responses. Although the stimuli of many structured tests may be more ambiguous in "meaning" than some found in unstructured tests, the restriction of response option (true-false or multiple choice) ensures the scoring reliability necessary for our definition of structured test.

The apparently greater freedom of response allowed the subject in unstructured tests is not in itself a distinguishing feature. Freedom of response relates to the number of different possible responses that may be made to a given stimulus. Levy (1963) has emphasized that the number of possible responses to an inkblot, though large, is not infinite in any psychologically meaningful sense. He makes the further point:

While it is true that any single *MMPI item permits of only two responses, if we shift our perspective to the response given to the test as a whole we find that with 550 items, each offering two response possibilities and each being a* constituent of the total response, *there are* 2^{550} *responses possible to the test as a whole—a not inconsiderable amount of freedom.* (p. 199)

The attitude of the subject and the conditions under which he takes the test have been proposed as additional distinguishing features between structured and unstructured techniques. In the oft-quoted words of George Kelly (1958), "When the subject is asked to guess what the examiner is thinking, we call it an objective test; when the examiner tries to guess what the subject is thinking, we call it a projective device" (p. 332). With respect to the "directness" of structured tests, Loevinger (1957) notes: "In a direct or undisguised test it is after all only the motives of the investigator, not those of his Ss, which are undisguised" (p. 649). Both of these remarks serve to illustrate the fact that the subject's attitude toward or interpretation of the testing situation cannot be defined on the basis of the stimulus materials alone.

Classification of personality tests in terms of what content or aspect of personality is being measured is, at present, a highly speculative enterprise which can be justified only by considerable research. Much of the present chapter will be concerned with the question of *what* it is that structured tests measure. We will face such issues as the following: (a) What is the meaning of a response to a structured test? (b) Why are such responses related to significant criteria? (c) What test-construction procedures ensure the measurement of desired and psychologically relevant personality traits?

WHAT IS THE MEANING OF A RESPONSE TO A STRUCTURED TEST?

The Correspondence or Rational Point of View

Personality, adjustment, and interest surveys typically ask the subject to report on his traits, symptoms, or interests through the restricted response options of "yes-no," "true-false," or "like-dislike." Personality assessment is hardly unique as a branch of psychology that deals with the verbal reports of subjects with reference to some "internal" state or attribute. Introspectionism was the first laboratory technique of experimental psychology, and it formed the cornerstone of structuralist and Gestalt theories of behavior. The task of observers in early experimental psychology was to give an accurate account of their interior sensations. Elaborate precautions were taken to ensure that such reports would be as accurate as possible by min-imizing certain linguistic and observational sets (e.g., "stimulus error") which might distort the veridicality of the reports. No matter how such a procedure is rationalized, it rests on the assumption of the existence of a one-to-one correspondence (or at least a probabilistic correspondence) of verbal reports to hypothetical internal states (Buchwald, 1961). Behaviorism arose, in part, as a protest to the fallibility of this type of measurement and the unrealistic epistemological assumptions on which it was based. Modern behavioral psychology is characterized by an exclusive concern for behavior and its correlates rather than subjective reports of states of consciousness. Psychophysics and perceptual psychology continued in the mainstream of the correspondence viewpoint, and it is only recently that such a view has been seriously challenged (Swets, Tanner, and Birdsall, 1961; Garner, Hake, and Eriksen, 1956).

The history of structured personality testing has an interesting parallel to that of experimental psychology, since the first personality inventories were developed under a definite "correspondence" point of view (Buchwald, 1961). Prior to World War I, the diagnosis of neurosis and other psychiatric conditions was achieved primarily by means of the psychiatric interview. The psychiatric interview, in its less sophisticated forms, can be considered a representative of the correspondence assumption, in that subjects are asked to report on the presence or absence of internal symptoms believed to be associated with categories of psychiatric illness. The mass psychiatric screen-ing required in the manpower mobilization for World War I made such individual psychiatric interviews impractical. As an alternative to the individual psychiatric interview, Woodworth (1917) proposed that the ques-tions typically asked be printed in inventory format and presented to large groups of subjects, who could indicate the presence or absence of such symptoms by checking *yes* or *no* on an answer sheet. Woodworth's Personal Data Sheet consisted of 116 questions concerning neurotic tendencies, of which the following are examples. "Have you ever had fits of dizziness?" "Do you wet your bed?" "Are you troubled with dreams about your work?" Subjects who answered in the affirmative were referred for further psychiatric evaluation; those who denied such neurotic symptoms were inducted into the army. The sole criterion for item inclusion was the presumed relevance of each item to neurotic symptomatology.

The assumptions underlying Woodworth's approach to the measurement of neuroticism must be seriously questioned. In order for "accurate" measurement to occur, the following conditions must hold: (1) The item has a common "meaning" among subjects and between the subject and the examiner. For example, what is "dizziness" for one subject must be "dizzi-ness" for another subject and must be related to the examiner's concept of "dizziness." (2) The subject is able to accurately assess his own internal states. Distortions due to defensiveness or insensitive observations must be held to a minimum. (3) The subject will honestly (and without fear of repercussion or induction) report these internal states to the examiner. (4) The items in question are, in fact, related to the concept of "neuroticism" as used by the psychiatrist.

Clearly, the conditions which must be fulfilled to meet the correspondence assumption are unrealistic even under the most optimistic view of the honesty of subjects and the semantics of verbal behavior. Personality inventories that have been constructed solely on the basis of the judged relevance of the items to the criterion to be predicted have enjoyed very limited success as predictive instruments (Ellis, 1946).

It is still possible to find in current use examples of inventories like Woodworth's that were constructed in complete absence of information regarding the external correlates of inventory scores. A more typical procedure today involves statistical refinement of items in the interests of "measurement." From almost the very beginning of inventory construction it was recognized that presumed indices of personality traits must possess certain statistical properties considered essential to sound psychological measurement. Foremost among such considerations was the statistical reliability, or internal consistency, of personality trait scales. If the various items from the Personal Data Sheet, for example, showed little consistent relationship among themselves or consistency from one test administration to another, it would be difficult to argue that a uniform measure of neuroticism was reflected in inventory scale scores.

Techniques of item analysis have been developed which enable investigators to purify total scale scores by eliminating items which exhibit little tendency to cluster with other items and retaining those items which do show such clustering. A typical scale-construction technique here would be to administer a large pool of rational items with unknown statistical properties to a preliminary population and then to correlate each item with the total score obtained by summing responses across the other items in the pool. By retaining only items which exhibit a high item-versus-total correlation and eliminating those which do not, the scale constructors obtain a reduced pool of items of high internal consistency. Such a procedure is related but not equivalent to selecting items which show consistency upon repeated administration. Both procedures are designed to ensure that the reduced scale will possess statistical properties implied by the concept of personality trait.

An additional statistical consideration which characterizes modern inventories has to do with the *dimensionality* of trait measurement. Returning to the example of the Personal Data Sheet, we might find that there are small groups of items which tend not to be correlated with one another but which exhibit internal consistency within their subgroup. Such a finding would suggest that what is being measured is multidimensional in nature and hence requires several separate groups of items to assess the several dimensions involved. Some contemporary personality inventories, such as the Sixteen Personality Factor Questionnaire (Cattell, Eber, and Tatsuoka, 1970), employ factor analysis both as a theoretical frame of reference guiding inventory development and as a technique for selecting items. However, the technique of factor analysis may be employed solely as a technique for item refinement under any view of item meaning, including the correspondence view.

Although statistical refinement by item analysis represents a considerable advance over very early inventories, it should still be emphasized that inventories so constructed, in the complete absence of information regarding external correlates, are being constructed under a correspondence philosophy. Statistical refinement of items, though desirable as a general principle in personality measurement, does little to guarantee the presumed correspondence between self-report and the internal state of the subject. Item analysis does guarantee that whatever is measured is measured consistently. Internal consistency is thus a necessary but far from sufficient condition for a one-to-one correspondence to obtain between verbal report and internal states.

The argument has been advanced that internally consistent personality scales increase the likelihood of measuring relevant dimensions of self-report. However, there are grounds for assuming that increasing the internal consistency among rational items may lead to increased measurement of intraverbal sets and habits which are *irrelevant* to the internal state under consideration (Meehl and Hathaway, 1946). In any event, tests that are developed in the absence of information regarding external correlates have no intrinsic guarantee of predictive success. Emphases on internal consistency and factorial purity have often obscured the fundamental issue with respect to the worth of such tests—namely, their correlates with external criteria. The use of the word "validity" to refer to such internal consistency measures has likewise served to obscure the real issue at hand (Meehl and Hathaway, 1946).

The Instrumental or Empirical Point of View

In the same way that Watsonian behaviorism may be viewed as a reaction to structuralism, the empirical approach in personality test construction may be viewed as a reaction to the correspondence point of view inherent in the earlier rational inventories (Meehl, 1945a; Buchwald, 1961). The earliest and most notable examples of empirically constructed tests are the Vocational Interest Blank developed by E. K. Strong at Stanford and the Minnesota Multiphasic Personality Inventory developed by Hathaway, McKinley, and

Meehl at the institution whose name it bears. From the empirical standpoint, responses to a personality inventory item gain "meaning" only through some demonstrated correlation with criterion variables. An empiricist does not assume the existence of a correspondence between verbal report and interior states of the subject; he views an inventory response as "an intrinsically interesting and significant bit of verbal behavior, the nontest correlates of which must be discovered by empirical means" (Meehl, 1945a). Such a position has been designated "instrumental" since verbal behavior is regarded as a neutral "tool" in research programs (Buchwald, 1961). The shift of emphasis between the two viewpoints has been stated by Buchwald as follows: "The psychologist who operates from the instrument viewpoint has his attention focused on what *he* can conclude about the subject on the basis of the subject's verbal utterances rather than on what the subject can tell him" (p. 464).

The empirical approach to test construction requires that the relevance of an item to the task at hand be demonstrated in advance and that the meaning of the item be restricted to this and other demonstrated instances of empirical relevance. The principal technique for demonstrating the relevance of an item to the task at hand has been the strategy of *contrasted groups*. In general, the goal of any personality measurement device may be thought of as the accurate distinction between two or more groups. We hope to distinguish those who possess the trait of "extraversion" from those who do not, on a continuous scale. We would like to be able to separate those who will succeed in college from those who will not. It would be of considerable importance to be able to specify in advance those individuals who will become psychologically maladjusted as contrasted with those who will not require psychological treatment. The strategy of contrasted groups is the statistical design which attempts to ensure this type of group discrimination.

The Strong Vocational Interest Blank

The measurement of vocational interest represents an area that, on initial consideration, may not seem especially susceptible to empirical analysis based on obvious external criteria. Rational approaches to interest measurement (e.g., Lee and Thorpe, 1956) assume a correspondence between a subject's stated preference for an occupation and his internally perceived interest in that occupation. The "meaning" or significance of this stated preference is accepted at face value. In contrast to this approach, E. K. Strong (1943) took the position that a stated occupational preference takes on importance only when it can be related to the stated occupational preferences of a well-defined occupational group. The stated occupational preferences of a specific occupational group, in turn, take on "meaning" only insofar as they are different from the stated preferences of people in general.

The basic item pool of the original Strong Vocational Interest Blank (SVIB) consisted of 400 items related to preferences for a variety of vocational and avocational activities. For a vocational stimulus such as "Actor," "Advertiser," or "Architect," the subject is asked to indicate whether he likes the occupation (L), is indifferent to it (I) or actively dislikes it (D). Samples of successful men in 45 different occupations were administered the items, and the proportion of subjects whose responses fell in each of the three options was tallied separately for each occupational group. In addition, response option tallies were collated for a large and heterogeneous group of individuals, from a variety of occupations, to represent the interests of "men-in-general."

Table 9.2 illustrates the manner in which the strategy of contrasted groups was employed to build an empirical interest scale for engineers. In

Table 9.2 Strategy of contrasted groups applied to the measurement of vocational interests (from Strong, 1943, p. 75)

Items	Control group percentage (men-in-general)			Criterion group percentage (engineers)			Difference in percentage between groups (criterion minus control)			Scoring weights for engineer key		
	L	I	D	L	I	D	L	I	D	L	I	D
Actor	21	32	47	9	31	60	−12	−1	+13	−1	0	1
Advertiser	33	38	29	14	37	49	−19	−1	+20	−2	0	2
Architect	37	40	23	58	32	10	+21	−8	−13	2	−1	−1

order to develop a scale that would reflect the unique interests of engineers, the 400 items of the SVIB were given to a group of professional engineers (criterion group) and a larger group of men-in-general representing a variety of occupations (control group). For each item, in each group, the percentage of subjects responding to each of the response options (like, indifferent, dislike) was tallied separately. Thus, in the control group of men-in-general, 21 percent indicated a liking for the stimulus "Actor," 32 percent indicated an indifference, and 47 percent indicated an active dislike. In contrast to the responses of men-in-general, only 9 percent of the group of professional engineers indicated a liking for the stimulus "Actor," 31 percent indicated an indifference, and 60 percent stated a definite dislike. The fourth major column of Table 9.2 indicates the *differences* between the control and criterion groups in percentage of item endorsement for each of the three response options. In comparison with the control group of men-in-general, engineers tend to like the stimulus "Actor" somewhat less (-12%), to have about the same degree of indifference (-1%), and to indicate more dislike ($+13\%$). The final column presents the empirical weights which Strong assigned to indicate the direction of such differences. The slight difference in liking is indicated by a weight of -1, the lack of difference with respect to the middle category by 0, and the slightly greater amount of dislike by the engineers by $+1$.

Ignoring for a moment such statistical considerations as the significance of such differences and their reliability, we can now state the rationale underlying this method of keying. Only those items for which one or more of the three options were assigned significant (nonzero) weights are considered relevant to the measurement of interest in the occupation of engineering. For those items on which significant differences occurred between engineers and men-in-general, both the extent and direction of these differences are indicated by weights ranging from -4 to $+4$. Summing across the weighted scores of all items involving significant differences, we arrive at a total score for an individual on the engineer scale of the SVIB. What is the meaning of such a score?

Subjects who receive a high score on the engineer scale can be said to be *more similar* (with respect to their pattern of self-report) to a group of professional engineers than to a group of men-in-general. This is an empirical and self-evident fact which may be thought of as constituting the "meaning" of a particular score on the engineer scale. The underlying rationale for the *interpretation* of a score with this meaning is based on a theory of stated vocational preferences. The theory states that an individual whose stated vocational interests are highly similar to the interests of a given occupational group is more likely to enjoy being a member of such a group than being a member of a group that has markedly different vocational preferences. Birds of a feather tend to flock together on the basis of a shared communality of stated preferences for certain activities and interests. Such a theoretical position makes no claim to the forecasting of ability (in this case, engineering ability). An individual may share common interests with engineers but have no relevant talent. However, if he has the talent *plus* a communality of interest, success would be forecasted. On the other hand, if he has the talent without the shared vocational interests, we might anticipate considerable vocational dissatisfaction, which in turn might result in less than optimal performance on the job.

Over a period of 40 years, the SVIB has been revised and refined extensively, and it is among the most useful and successful structured inventories available today (Campbell, 1968). The most recent revision of the men's form of the SVIB contains carefully validated and up-to-date scales for 54 specific occupational groups. The *Handbook for the Strong Vocational Interest Blank* (Campbell, 1971) summarizes results from over 100,000 adults in over 400 occupations, some of which were tested four times over 40 years. Given the success of the SVIB in the realm of vocational interest measurement, it is understandable that the empirical method of contrasted groups has also been attempted in the realm of personality measurement as well.

The Minnesota Multiphasic Personality Inventory

The Minnesota Multiphasic Personality Inventory (MMPI) is the prototypic example of empirical test construction in the realm of personality. Strictly speaking, the MMPI is a psychiatric inventory rather than a personality questionnaire. It was developed for the specific purpose of aiding psychiatrists in the diagnostic process which results in the assignment of patients to traditional categories of psychiatric classification (hypochondriasis, schizophrenia, paranoia). Although the MMPI is considerably larger in scope than Woodworth's Personal Data Sheet, the content of the items is similar to that employed by Woodworth in its emphasis on symptoms presumed to be related to psychiatric diagnoses. However, the test authors did not assume a one-to-one correspondence between self-report and possession of symptoms; instead, they viewed responses to items of symptomatic content as behavioral samples with as yet unknown behavioral correlates.

Although the reliability and validity of traditional psychiatric diagnostic categories have been challenged frequently (Ash, 1949; Bannister, Salmon, and Leiberman, 1964; Foulds, 1955; Seeman, 1953a; Mehlman, 1952; Wittenborn, Holzberg, and Simon, 1953), such categories provided a logical starting point for the development of a structured diagnostic device. Under the assumption that patients who are given the same diagnostic label by psychiatrists are more similar to one another than they are to patients given a different label, existing psychiatric diagnostic groups were selected as criterion groups for scale construction purposes.

A group of 724 visitors to the University of Minnesota Hospitals served as the normative or control group with which various psychiatric criterion groups were contrasted for scale development purposes. Subjects in this normal group were assumed to come from socioeconomic, educational, and age groups similar to those of the hospitalized patients. The normal subjects were requested to answer all items in the initial MMPI item pool, and the frequency with which they answered *true* or *false* to each of the items was tabulated. The same items were also administered to groups of psychiatric inpatients who were relatively clear-cut examples of various diagnostic categories. In the development of each clinical scale, the item responses of a psychiatric criterion group were contrasted with those of the normal control group.

Table 9.3 illustrates the manner in which the strategy of contrasted groups was applied in the development of a single MMPI scale, in this case the scale which was designed to measure the dimension of schizophrenia (*Sc*). Hypothetical responses are provided for only three of the 550 items that were originally contrasted in the control and criterion groups. On the item "I like mechanics magazines," the control group is evenly divided, half of the group answering *true* (50%) and the remainder answering *false* (50%). On this particular item the responses of the criterion group of schizophrenics are highly similar to those of the control group. The slight difference in percentage of response between the two groups does not attain the level of statistical significance usually required for inclusion in an MMPI scale (i.e., a percentage difference of at least twice the standard error). Consequently, this item is not a candidate for inclusion in the *Sc* scale, as is indicated by the zero weight assigned to both response options.

Table 9.3 Strategy of contrasted groups applied to the measurement of schizophrenia

	Control group ($N = 724$ normals)		Criterion group ($N = 50$ schizo- phrenics)		Difference in percentage between groups (criterion minus control)		Scoring weights for *Sc* scale	
Items	T	F	T	F	T	F	T	F
I like mechanics magazines	50	50	51	49	+1	−1	0	0
I hear strange things when I am alone	5	95	35	65	+30	−30	+1	0
I get all the sympathy I should	80	20	50	50	−30	+30	0	+1

A very small proportion of the control group (5%) admit to the item "I hear strange things when I am alone." Although only a minority of schizophrenics (35%) admit to this item, the difference in endorsement frequency percentage between the two groups (30%) is sufficient to justify the inclusion of this item in a preliminary *Sc* scale. Several preliminary weighting techniques were tried with MMPI items, but the authors of the test felt that the simple procedure of weighting either 1 or 0 for each option did sufficient justice to the data.[1]   Consequently a *true* response to this item is given the weight of *one* (i.e., scored in the schizophrenic direction).

With respect to the item "I get all the sympathy I should," the majority of the control group indicate that they do.   The schizophrenics are divided on this issue, however, with 50 percent of them answering *true* and the remainder answering *false*.   The difference of 30 percent in endorsement frequency for this item is sufficient for its inclusion, and a *false* response to the item adds one point to the *Sc* scale.   There were 78 items included in the final version of the *Sc* scale, each of which was found to exhibit a reliable difference in endorsement percentage between control and criterion groups.

Table 9.4 lists the 13 scales which constitute the standard MMPI profile. The first three are considered "validity scales" which reflect the test-taking attitudes and behavior of the subject.   The *L* scale consists of mildly undesirable items that are highly improbable when answered *false* ("I do not always tell the truth").   The *F* scale contains items that were answered in the scored direction by less than 10 percent of the normative sample ("Evil spirits possess me at times") and consequently may be indicative of carelessness, scoring errors, or pathological confusion, any of which would tend to invalidate self-report.   The *K* scale was developed by a complex set of procedures directed at the identification of psychiatric patients whose defensive style of self-presentation results in normal or false negative MMPI scale scores (Meehl and Hathaway, 1946).

The remaining ten scales are usually designated "clinical scales" even though the criterion groups on which *Mf* and *Si* were based were not hospitalized psychiatric patients.   The principal strategy for construction of the clinical scales was that of contrasted groups, but numerous additional considerations guided the selection of the final items for each scale.   Similarly, although the principal criterion groups listed in Table 9.4 served in the initial identification of items, empirical data from many different groups influenced final item selection.   The actual procedures involved in item selection were extraordinarily complex (see Welsh and Dahlstrom 1956, pp. 12–40, 60–123, 181–183) and have not been reported fully.

When a subject takes the MMPI, we tally the number of instances in which his pattern of responses agrees with that of each of the criterion groups employed in scale derivation.   What is the meaning of a high *Sc*

---

1.   Response option weighting schemes have not, in general, yielded results that are superior to unit weightings (Stanley and Wang, 1970). Although E. K. Strong was both a pioneer and a proponent of response option weighting, it is interesting to note that the range of scoring weights employed in the SVIB has decreased from ±30 in 1927, to ±15 in 1930, to ±4 in 1938, to ±1 in 1966 (Campbell, 1968, p. 123).

Table 9.4 The standard validity and clinical scales of the MMPI

Scale label	Principal strategy of derivation	Principal criterion group	No. of items	Typical interpretations of elevated scores
L	Rational	—	15	Denial of common frailties; "saintliness."
F	Statistical	—	64	Validity of profile is doubtful.
K	Empirical	50 psychiatric patients with low MMPI profiles	30	Defensive; minimizes social and emotional complaints.
Hs	Empirical	50 hypochondriacs	33	Numerous physical complaints.
D	Empirical	50 depressives	60	Severely depressed.
Hy	Empirical	50 hysterics	60	Immature, suggestible, egocentric, demanding.
Pd	Empirical	Unspecified number of psychopaths	50	Rebellious and non-conformist.
Mf	Empirical	13 male homosexuals	60	Artistic interests; effeminate.
Pa	Empirical	Unspecified number of paranoids	40	Resentful and suspicious of others.
Pt	Empirical	20 psychasthenics	48	Fearful, ruminative, agitated.
Sc	Empirical	50 schizophrenics	78	Withdrawn, seclusive; bizarre thinking.
Ma	Empirical	24 manics	46	Impulsive, expansive, distractable.
Si	Empirical	50 high and 50 low scorers on social introversion test	70	Introverted, shy, self-effacing.

score in this context? The adjective "high" implies a comparison, and certain normative facts must be available before a definitive answer can be given. If we know, for example, that the average or "normal" individual will answer 10 of the 78 *Sc* items in the keyed direction, what can we say about the subject who answers 33 of the *Sc* items in the keyed direction (two standard deviations higher than the average individual)? The meaning of such a test score is similar to that discussed with respect to scores on the Strong Vocational Interest Blank.

A subject who answers 33 of the 78 items in the keyed direction on the *Sc* scale is answering this psychiatric adjustment inventory in a manner more typical of hospitalized schizophrenics than of a normal control group.

It is thus self-evident that our subject is more *similar* to hospitalized schizophrenics than to nonhospitalized normals on whatever dimension or dimensions were involved in the original differences in *Sc* scores between those two
groups. Although the meaning of a high *Sc* score is thus defined, the application of that score or its utilization in decision making (e.g., calling the
subject "schizophrenic") requires additional kinds of empirical evidence.
Such evidence would include, among other things, the proportion of individuals with *Sc* scores this high or higher who are subsequently called
"schizophrenic" by psychiatrists. The *Sc* scale has been found to operate
in the proper direction (Rosen, 1958), but evidence to date suggests that a
great deal of caution is advisable in such a routine application of the scale.

It is of some importance to reflect on the reasons why the operational
meaning of an MMPI scale does not guarantee its successful application.
Returning to Table 9.3, we note that where significant differences in proportions of endorsement existed between the initial control and criterion groups,
the amount of overlap was considerable. More important, however, is the
fact that the *source* of the empirically observed differences cannot be specified.
Although some care was taken to match subjects on the basis of age, sex,
socioeconomic background and education, the influence of these and other
variables on MMPI scale scores has been amply documented (Dahlstrom
and Welsh, 1960). Innumerable differences of more subtle origin may be
contributing to the differences in verbal behavior between the control and
criterion groups. Here we are emphasizing that the particular control group
employed and the particular criterion group employed may be *different* in
many ways other than in the condition of being schizophrenic or non-
schizophrenic. Such differences will lead to false positive predictions. The
presence of such irrelevant variables in a given subject will not cause a
psychiatrist to label that subject as "schizophrenic." For this reason, there
is often a discrepancy between the apparent meaning of a scale and the
success with which that scale can be applied. Numerous and highly complex
interpretive procedures have been developed to circumvent such problems
in the clinical interpretation of the MMPI (Dahlstrom and Welsh, 1960).

Despite this restriction on application of empirically derived personality
scales, it should be apparent that the method by which they are constructed
guarantees a certain amount of success in criterion prediction. Carefully
constructed and cross-validated scales of this type are almost certain to
enjoy a reasonable amount of predictive success in similar populations and
under similar conditions. The last-mentioned restrictions are real ones,
however, and empirically constructed scales may be quite limited in their
generalizability. Empirically constructed scales faithfully mirror differences
that existed between the original criterion and control groups. Minor variations in the populations studied, the criterion employed, or the conditions

under which the test is administered may result in drastically reduced validity coefficients (Taft, 1959; Loevinger, 1957; Stern, Stein, and Bloom, 1956). Correcting for changes in the population or in the decision context is next to impossible when the scale has been developed by the method of "blind empiricism" that we have been describing. Since the meaning of the scale has reference only to unknown characteristics of the two original groups, it is not possible to specify which of these characteristics has resulted in validity shrinkage. The unfortunate and expensive alternative in such a situation is to repeat the entire process, starting with new criterion groups, new control groups, and a new item-analytic procedure. Procedures for avoiding a resort to such highly undesirable actions will be discussed later in this chapter.

Test Response versus Criterion Behaviors

From the examples of empirical item construction offered thus far, the reader might consider the empirical strategy to be simply an elaborate philosophical underpinning for a procedure that leads to selection of the same kinds of items as would be obtained from a rational approach. That this is clearly not true can be seen from a consideration of items which were finally included in the MMPI clinical scales.

Psychopathic personalities are traditionally considered to have grown up quite free from family rule and restraint (McCord and McCord, 1964). Nevertheless, the MMPI item "I have been quite independent and free from family rule" discriminates psychopathic personalities from normals when answered *false* (i.e., scored in the direction of psychopathy). Paranoids, as a group, are known to be highly suspicious of the motives of others. Note, however, that the item "I tend to be on my guard with people who are somewhat more friendly than I had expected" is answered *false* by a significantly larger proportion of paranoids than of normals. The "obvious" after-the-fact explanation that paranoids are suspicious with respect to the MMPI itself and tend to be guarded in their answers to items of paranoid content may seem at first to be plausible. Here, however, we must note that to the item "I believe that I am being plotted against" paranoids answer *true* significantly more than normals. Perhaps more impressive than these reversals of expectations from "rational" hypotheses, are the *subtle items* which turn out to be significant discriminators of psychiatric criteria (Wiener, 1948). The item "I sometimes tease animals" is answered *false* by a significant proportion of depressed patients when contrasted with nondepressed patients. The item "I enjoy detective or mystery stories" is answered *false* by a significant proportion of hospitalized hysterics.

Additionally, we might cite examples of items derived against non-psychiatric criterion groups that seem to bear no *rational* relation to the criterion discrimination. The item "My daily life is full of things that keep me interested" is answered *true* more frequently by neurodermatitis patients than by general medical patients. The item "I gossip a little at times" is answered *true* by individuals of high intelligence as contrasted with individuals of lower intelligence. The item "I do not like to see women smoke" is answered *false* more frequently by patients with low back pain of functional origin in comparison with patients whose low back pain has an organic basis. The item "I like poetry" is answered *false* by patients whose brain lesions have a parietal localization as contrasted with patients whose brain lesions are frontal. The item "I do not have a great fear of snakes" is answered *false* by prejudiced as compared with unprejudiced individuals.

In attempting to relate the apparent "content" of the preceding items to the empirical discriminations which they make, the reader no doubt has experienced a sense of frustration. Such an inability to predict the verbal behavior of criterion groups is quite widespread, however, as indicated by the fact that after a full quarter of study of the MMPI (under Professor Meehl himself) graduate students were still unable to predict the keyed response of such subtle items (Seeman, 1953b). The foregoing examples illustrate the fact that, familiar though we may be with characteristic *behavior patterns* of criterion groups, we do not as yet possess a sufficiently articulated theory of *verbal behavior* in the test situation to relate test responses to criterion behaviors. Although we know from observation that paranoids are suspicious, we do not as yet possess a theory of verbal behavior in the test situation which would allow us to predict their responses to the item "I tend to be on my guard with people who are somewhat more friendly than I had expected."

This principle is well illustrated in a classic study performed by Gough (1954) on the clinical concept of "neuroticism." Gough asked groups of advanced psychology students and professional clinicians to answer all the items in the MMPI as they would be answered by a patient "experiencing a psychoneurotic reaction." These groups were referred to as "dissimulators" because they were all normal subjects attempting to simulate the appearance of neuroticism, based on their professional opinion of the relationship between the verbal behavior of neurotics in a test situation and the characteristics of neurotics as observed in the clinic or studied in the classroom. To determine how genuine neurotics would answer the MMPI, Gough administered the inventory to samples of patients from local hospitals and clinics who had been given that diagnosis by psychiatrists. Thus it was possible to contrast the predictions or conceptions held by normals about the verbal behavior of neurotics with the actual verbal behavior of neurotics themselves. For each of the 550 items of the MMPI, Gough contrasted the proportion of dissembling normals who answered each item *true* with the proportion of genuine neurotics who answered the same item *true*. By the strategy of contrasted groups it was possible to determine on which items the normals guessed *significantly* wrong.

The item "I am sure I get a raw deal from life" was answered *true* by 79 percent of the normals who were attempting to simulate a neurotic response. Their reasoning, no doubt, was based on the frequent observation that neurotics complain bitterly about their misfortunes and bad luck. In fact, however, only 14 percent of the genuine neurotic group answered this item *true*. Here is clearly a discrepancy between popular conceptions of neuroticism and the verbal behavior of actual neurotics. To the item "I usually feel that life is worthwhile" only 25 percent of the neurotic dissimulators answered affirmatively, whereas 68 percent of the actual neurotics responded *true*. There were, in fact, 74 items which produced a significant difference in item endorsement between the dissimulators and the neurotics. These 74 items are of special interest in that they illuminate the areas of the misconceptions that professionals hold about the verbal behavior of neurotics on a personality test. In general, the dissimulators went wrong by overemphasizing such things as physical complaints, feelings of being misunderstood, irritability, dependency, dissatisfaction with family background, sexual conflicts, and eccentric ideas (Gough, 1954).

Having located these items, Gough proceeded to an additional application of the strategy of contrasted groups which nicely illustrates the ingenuity and flexibility of the empirical approach. The original procedure whereby items were located which differentiated dissemblers from actual neurotics is no different from that followed under any other empirical test-construction design. In this instance, the dissembling group served as a criterion group and the neurotics served as a normative sample from which they were to be discriminated. The 74 items which revealed significant differences between the two groups can thus be assembled into a scale which can be keyed in the direction of dissimulation (the direction of the more frequent answer by the dissimulators). Such a scale becomes, in effect, a "dissimulation scale" which may prove useful in discriminating genuine neurotics from individuals who might wish to appear neurotic for one reason or another. (Psychiatric screening at the time of induction into the army is one possible application of such a scale.)

To test the probable efficiency of such a scale in separating "fakers" from genuine neurotics, Gough repeated the experiment, employing a new group of 354 instructed fakers, a group of 915 hospital and clinic cases of neuroticism, and a group of 507 students who took the inventory under standard instructions. To be an effective screening scale, the dissimulation scale should enable us to separate fakers from genuine neurotics without confusing normals (students) with fakers. The score distributions of these three samples are presented in Table 9.5. The first column lists intervals of possible total score on the dissimulation scale. The remaining three columns indicate the proportions of dissemblers, clinical cases, and students whose total scale scores fell within the intervals. Note that 55 percent of the dissemblers achieved scores of 55 or greater, whereas none of the clinical cases or students achieved scores of that magnitude. A more realistic cutting score of 35 enables us to identify 93 percent of the dissemblers correctly while misclassifying only 6 percent of the clinical group and 2 percent of the students. How well this scale would work with populations of "real" fakers rather than instructed fakers is difficult to say. Nevertheless, the power and scope of the empirical strategy are well illustrated by this ingenious approach.

It should now be clear that the rational (correspondence) and empirical (instrumental) approaches to scale construction are based on different assumptions about the meaning of self-report, and they result, at least in some instances, in the selection of quite different types of items. The rational approach is based on the assumption that "the psychologist building the test has sufficient insight into the dynamics of verbal behavior and its relation

Table 9.5 Proportion of cases falling in scoring categories of Gough's dissimulation scale (from Gough, 1954)

Scores	Dissemblers (N = 354)	Clinical cases (N = 915)	Students (N = 507)
70–74	4.2		
65–69	15.2		
60–64	19.4		
55–59	16.9		
50–54	14.7	0.4	
45–49	11.0	0.8	0.2
40–44	7.3	1.8	0.6
35–39	4.2	2.6	1.2
30–34	3.7	5.3	4.5
25–29	2.0	7.2	7.5
20–24	0.6	12.5	14.8
15–19	0.3	17.5	23.2
10–14	0.3	21.5	24.6
5–9		19.8	19.3
0–4		10.1	3.9
Mean	54.13	15.94	15.88
σ	11.69	9.99	7.90

to the core of personality that he is able to predict beforehand what certain sorts of people will say about themselves when asked certain questions" (Meehl, 1945a). In contrast, the empirical approach accepts the *fact* that a person describes himself in a certain way but attaches significance to such a self-report only after its relation to personality or criterion variables has been established empirically. The strategy of contrasted groups is thus both a procedure for developing predictor scales and a method for studying the complex relations that may exist between test responses and criterion behaviors.

The Substantive or Construct Point of View

Although the rational and empirical approaches to scale construction differ with respect to the meaning assigned to test responses, neither viewpoint provides an explicit frame of reference for evaluating the *content* of such self-reports. The rational viewpoint appears to assume a one-to-one correspondence of verbal reports to hypothetical internal states (Buchwald, 1961), but the precise nature of such internal states and the manner in which one would assess their degree of correspondence to self-reports are not specified. The empirical viewpoint eschews the premature interpretation of the content of self-report and concentrates instead on the establishment of *R-R* relationships between test responses and criterion behaviors. In 1945, Meehl suggested that the puzzling relationships between the apparent content of self-report and the behavioral dynamics of a subject "be left aside for the moment as a theoretical question." However, proponents of the empirical approach have shown little inclination to investigate such theoretical questions in the ensuing 20 years (Wiggins, 1966).

From the substantive or construct viewpoint, a response to a structured test represents a manifestation of an underlying *personality construct*. This emphasis on the theoretical underpinning of test responses is of relatively recent origin. In 1954, a joint committee of educators and psychologists introduced the term *construct validity* to refer to the procedures involved in evaluating and interpreting psychological tests that are purported to measure specific conceptual entities (APA, 1954). The following year, two of the original committee members provided a more complete explanation of the logic of construct validity and explored its implications for test evaluation in greater detail (Cronbach and Meehl, 1955). Shortly thereafter, Loevinger (1957) radically extended the theoretical implications of construct validity by proposing that all scientific issues in test construction, validation, and use be evaluated from the construct point of view.

According to Cronbach and Meehl (1955), "a construct is some postulated attribute of people, assumed to be reflected in test performance" (p. 283). "A numerical statement of the degree of construct validity would be a statement of the proportion of the test score variance that is attributable to the construct variable" (p. 289). Procedures for determining the validity of a construct (or assigning the variance in test response to a construct) are "not essentially different from the general scientific procedures for developing and confirming theories" (p. 300). These procedures involve "examining the entire body of evidence offered, together with what is asserted about the test in the context of this evidence" (p. 284).

Assigning variation in test response to a construct presupposes the existence of a theory with respect to that construct. By "theory" we mean an interlocking system of laws which relate constructs to one another and to observable properties of the environment. This interlocking system of laws, which Cronbach and Meehl (1955) call a nomological network, is illustrated in Figure 9.1. The left-hand side represents the theoretical space (nomological network) and the extreme right-hand side represents "nature" or observables. The lines connecting the circles (constructs) represent definitions relating the constructs to each other or to the world of observables. Double lines represent operational definitions relating observable test responses to *indicants* of constructs, which are represented as C'. Here

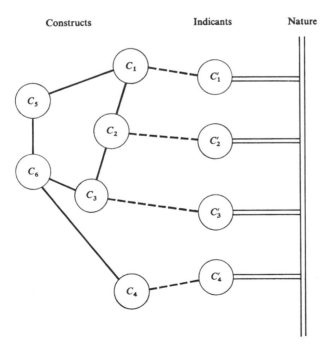

Fig. 9.1 Diagrammatic representation of a nomological network. (After Torgerson, 1958, p. 5)

we would assert, for example, that a total score on a set of personality items would define an indicant of "social extraversion." Broken lines connect indicants to constructs in the theoretical space. Here we might assert that our measure of "social extraversion" is equivalent to the theoretical construct of "social extraversion" employed by Jung. The line is broken to emphasize the fact that less than universal agreement exists in relating indicants to constructs, a state of affairs which distinguishes social sciences from more highly developed natural sciences (Torgerson, 1958). The solid single lines represent constitutive definitions which relate, by means of formal statements, one construct to another within the theoretical space. Notice that while some constructs (C_1, C_2, C_3, C_4) are related to observables—or at least to "indicants" of observable variables—others are not. In the illustration, constructs 5 and 6 are not directly linked to observables but are indirectly linked, through their constitutive definitions, with other constructs which are linked to observables. Hence it is not necessary for a construct to have direct ties with the empirical world. What is necessary, however, is "that it occur in a nomological net, at least *some* of whose laws involve observables" (Cronbach and Meehl, 1955, p. 290).

The process of establishing that variation in test response reflects variation in a theoretical construct involves a complex series of inferences based on tests of the postulated relationships illustrated in Figure 9.1. Since theory construction is hardly peculiar to the realm of personality assessment, we will not attempt a full delineation of that process at this point. The interested reader is directed to the article by Cronbach and Meehl (1955) and to the writers whom they recommend (Braithwaite, 1953; Carnap, 1953; Pap, 1953; Sellars, 1948; Feigl, 1950; Beck, 1953; Kneale, 1949; Hempel, 1952). We shall stress instead certain aspects of the process of construct validity, emphasized by Loevinger (1957), which seem directly relevant to the issues of test construction.

Although liberalizing the conventional grounds on which the merits of a psychological test are evaluated, Cronbach and Meehl carefully stated their arguments in the language of logical positivism, a language that is acceptable to most, though not all (e.g., Bechtoldt, 1959), contemporary behavior theorists. Indicants are defined by concrete operations, and constructs are specified by the interlocking system of laws which relate them to one another and to observable properties of the environment. In contrast, Loevinger finds a "naively realistic" view of constructs both more precise and more intuitively appealing.

Traits exist in people; constructs (here usually traits) exist in the minds and magazines of psychologists . . . . It is true that psychologists never know traits directly but only through the glass of their constructs, but the data to be judged are manifestations of traits, not manifestations of constructs. Cronbach and Meehl and their colleagues on the APA committee appear reluctant to assign reality status to constructs or traits. (Loevinger, 1957, p. 642)

Loevinger's view of the meaning of a structured test response is more *substantive* (belonging to the real nature or essential part) than the position of Cronbach and Meehl. Consequently, her recommendations for test construction provide the sharpest contrast with those stemming from the empirical point of view, as represented by Meehl (1945a) in his role of advocate of that position, and those stemming from the rational point of view, as represented by the early work of Woodworth.[2] Loevinger has emphasized three classes of considerations which must be taken into account in establishing the construct validity of a test score and which in turn have direct implications for test-construction procedures. These considerations are termed substantive, structural, and external.

Substantive Considerations

If variation in test response is to be attributed to variation in an underlying psychological construct, we cannot use simply any old kind of stimulus materials, as would be advocated by some authors (e.g., Berg, 1961). Item pools are usually not assembled "randomly" for the measurement of a given substantive domain since the universe of content from which such random sampling would take place is seldom specified. More typically, item pools are assembled on such fortuitous grounds as the availability of items from previous inventories or the idiosyncratic and often implicit theory of the test constructor. It seems desirable to substitute explicit theory for implicit theory and to sample systematically on the basis of that theory rather than to sample fortuitously. Although empirical considerations may be the final ones in item selection, empiricism need not take place in the dark. The item-selection procedure itself may be used as a testing ground for theory on the item level (Loevinger, 1957).

First, an attempt should be made to assemble a pool of items that is representative of the substantive domain delineated by the theory. If the construct is a general one, such as "adjustment," sampling may proceed on the basis of subareas of life importance or the symptomatology likely to be

---

2. Some writers (e.g., Edwards, 1970, pp. 29–37) equate the "rational" and "construct" points of view. It is likely that those who develop rational scales have some sort of construct in mind, but the construct is not specified clearly enough to be evaluated by the procedures advocated by Cronbach and Meehl and Loevinger. In this sense, rational scales may be thought of as "pretheoretical" or "preconstructural." The distinction between rational and construct scales is maintained here to call attention to the fact that the vast majority of available scales and inventories fall in the former category.

observed in a clinic. If the construct is defined more narrowly ("social extraversion"), an attempt should be made to give the heaviest representation to behaviors considered most salient by the theory. Thus far, our approach to assembling the item pool differs from that employed under a correspondence viewpoint only with respect to systematic sampling. In addition, however, we shall require that the initial pool include items whose relevance is dictated by competing theories as well as items judged to be irrelevant to the construct under consideration (Loevinger, 1957). By including items that on theoretical grounds would *not* be related to the criterion at hand, we provide the opportunity for a miniature test of our theory on the item level. Items which should be related to external criteria but are not may cause us to revise our theory or to examine more closely our method of measurement. Items which should not be related to our criteria but turn out to be so would lead to similar reconsiderations.

Given the content of the items specified by our theory, we must choose an appropriate *method of measurement*. Here again, it is possible to use the initial item pool in an exploratory fashion. Where the same item content is measured by several different methods (true-false, multiple choice, completion), it is possible to observe the moderating effect of item format on the relationship between content and external criterion measures. Here it is of considerable advantage to have prior knowledge of the relation between content and method or a theory of test response which indicates the appropriate method. In the absence of such prior knowledge, various combinations of form and content may be tried. Loevinger calls attention to the possible applicability to this problem of a design proposed by Guttman (1954). With each dimension of content and form considered as a "facet," it is proposed that "each value of each facet be paired with each value of every other facet, as in an analysis of variance design" (Loevinger, 1957, p. 660). Although such a design is perhaps too elaborate and therefore impractical for most test-construction purposes, it nevertheless illustrates the spirit behind the idea of utilizing the initial item pool as a fruitful source of information regarding both content and method variance in each area under study.

In summary, from the standpoint of substantive considerations, we would require that: (a) items be sampled systematically from a specified universe of content on the basis of their judged relevance to the theory; (b) the initial item pool be broader in scope than the anticipated test by inclusion of content dictated by competing theories as well as content judged to be irrelevant by one's own theory; and (c) more than one format be included in order to yield some information regarding the possible interactions of content and method. The final basis of item selection will still be empirical. Such empiricism, however, represents a considerable conceptual advance over that advocated by proponents of the instrumental viewpoint.

Structural Considerations

A structural consideration, according to Loevinger, "refers to the extent to which structural relations between test items parallel the structural relations of other manifestations of the trait being measured" (p. 661). Structural considerations are of two distinct kinds, one of which will be immediately recognizable and the other may be new to the reader. Loevinger has designated these two kinds of considerations "inter-item structure" and "structural fidelity." The notion of inter-item structure is the familiar one of scale homogeneity or internal consistency. We have frequently alluded to the notion that a high index of internal consistency, based on item-total or inter-item correlations, to some extent reassures the test constructor that his scale measures "something." We have also made the important point that the "something" measured may or may not be *relevant* to the construct of interest. We now add the further observation that the *degree* of inter-item structure need not be extremely high for all substantive domains. How much inter-item structure we may anticipate for a given substantive domain can be understood only by elaboration of the concept of structural fidelity.

From an empirical point of view, responses to structured test items are behaviors which are every bit as legitimate as any other class of verbal or nonverbal responses. From a construct point of view, it may be assumed that responses in the testing situation and outside the testing situation are manifestations, in varying degrees, of underlying organizations conveniently referred to as "traits" (Loevinger, 1957). Under this assumption, the determination of construct variance is not an enterprise relating test response to nontest response but rather an attempt to determine to what extent both classes of behavior represent manifestations of an underlying theoretical trait. This situation is represented diagrammatically in Figure 9.2.

To the extent that we have properly identified the construct which underlies criterion behaviors, we may anticipate substantial correlations between the construct and the criterion behaviors, r_{yt}. Similarly, to the extent that the test behaviors selected may be viewed as manifestations of the trait in question, we would expect high correlations between the trait and the test responses, r_{xt}. From a practical standpoint, our goal would

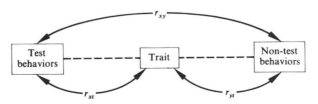

Fig. 9.2 Test behaviors and non-test behaviors as manifestations of an underlying trait construct.

be the prediction of criterion behaviors from test responses, and here the coefficient, r_{xy}, is simply the conventional validity coefficient. Note that in theory we are not assigning "causal" significance to the validity coefficient (Meehl, 1954, p. 45). A correlation exists between test responses and criterion behaviors because they are both manifestations of the same underlying trait (Lazarsfeld, 1954; Loevinger, 1957). Of course we can never *directly* compute the coefficients r_{xt} and r_{yt}, but they represent "convenient fictions" for conceptualizing the role of constructs in validity coefficients.

Assuming that the criterion behaviors are highly representative of the underlying construct (r_{yt}), the degree of interrelationship among criterion behaviors $(r_{y_1y_2}, r_{y_1y_3}$, etc.) will vary for different traits. The degree of interrelationship or structure that exists for a given behavior domain is called the "characteristic correlation" for that trait. Since test responses are manifestations of the same underlying trait, the characteristic correlation value for test responses $(r_{x_1x_2}, r_{x_2x_3})$ will be the same as that for the criterion behaviors (errors of measurement associated with the testing procedure itself are ignored). This characteristic correlation value may be thought of as an *upper limit* on the degree of structuring for a particular trait (Loevinger, 1957, p. 662), and the correlations among test items should not, in principle, exceed it.

The degree of intercorrelation among items is only one of a number of considerations that enter into determining the most appropriate method of combining items into scales to be used for trait assessment. There are a variety of procedures which have been suggested for combining items into scales, and these procedures may be thought of as "measurement models" (Messick and Ross, 1962, p. 2) which differ widely in their assumptions and implementation. Although a full consideration of such measurement models is well beyond the scope of the present discussion, it seems appropriate to differentiate among the three types discussed by Loevinger (1957, pp. 664–669) in order to illustrate the variety of ways in which items can be combined into scales.

The *cumulative* measurement model is the most familiar and widely used method of combining items into a single scale score. Here it is assumed that the number of occasions on which the trait is manifest is an index of the amount of the underlying trait that is present. For the hypothetical trait of extraversion, for example, it might be assumed that the individual who attends many social gatherings *and* speaks without hesitation in a group *and* prefers people to ideas is more extraverted than the individual for whom only one of these behaviors is true. Test items corresponding to these behaviors might then be cumulated to yield a total score reflecting the extent to which the first individual is more extraverted than the second. Even within the realm of cumulative measurement models, there are several distinct variants which tend to emphasize differing degrees of inter-item structure and different distributions of item difficulty levels (Loevinger, Gleser, and DuBois, 1953; Guttman, 1944; Tucker, 1955).

Class measurement models do not assume that the number of manifestations of a trait is indicative of the amount of that trait. The trait is assumed to be either present or absent, depending on the particular manifestations that appear together. To continue our previous example, the behaviors of attending social gatherings *and* speaking freely in a group may together indicate many possible classes (e.g., dominance); attending social gatherings *and* preferring people to ideas may also indicate several classes (e.g., affiliation); but the simultaneous presence of attending social gatherings, speaking freely, and preferring people to ideas may indicate extraversion uniquely. Although class models have not been employed with great frequency in personality assessment, their formal properties have been studied in detail (Lazarsfeld, 1959).

Dynamic measurement models may be appropriate where two or more "contradictory" behaviors are believed to be manifestations of the same underlying trait. In psychoanalytic theory, for example, direct expression of hostility toward others and an oversolicitous concern for the welfare of others may both be considered manifestations of the underlying trait of aggression. Special models are required when trait manifestations are mutually exclusive, negatively correlated, or related differently in different kinds of populations. Some definitions of personality rely heavily on the notion of consistency of trait organization (Lecky, 1945). Pathological groups may be differentiated from normals on the basis of their deviation from such consistency of pattern (Zubin, 1937). Other examples of dynamic measurement models are given in Loevinger (1957, pp. 668–669).

The concept of *structural fidelity* refers to how well the particular measurement model selected corresponds to the substantive domain under study. Structural characteristics of nontest manifestations of the trait should be faithfully mirrored in the structural characteristics of the scale employed to measure the trait. It is of great importance to note that once a particular measurement model has been chosen for selecting test items, the structural characteristics assumed by the model will *by necessity* obtain (Loevinger, 1957). Hence one should not seek to "discover" structural relationships among test items. The choice of measurement model should be determined by the structural relationships posited by the *theory* of nontest behaviors. Once again, we emphasize the importance of developing theories of personality trait organization that are sufficiently articulated to permit the selection of appropriate measurement models.

External Considerations

Prediction, as we have repeatedly emphasized, is the sine qua non of personality assessment, and the magnitude of the correlation between a personality scale and some outside criterion is an important index of the utility of the scale in question. Similarly, from the standpoint of construct validity, it is important that relationships between the personality scale and outside variables be demonstrated and that at least some of these outside variables be *nontest* behaviors (Loevinger, 1957). A less obvious but equally important requirement is that a *lack* of relationship between the personality scale and certain other variables be demonstrated. The full explication of the construct validity of a personality scale requires a demonstration of what the scale does *not* measure as well as what it measures.

Campbell and Fiske (1959) have introduced the terms *convergent* and *discriminant* to distinguish demonstrations of what a scale measures from demonstrations of what it does not. Evidence for convergent validity comes from the demonstration that the scale in question is correlated with another independent measure of the same trait. The convergent validity of a self-report measure of extraversion would be assessed by correlating the self-report measure with independently obtained peer ratings of extraversion. The discriminant validity of a self-report measure of extraversion might be assessed by demonstrating its *lack* of correlation with an irrelevant trait (achievement) measured by the same method (self-report) or by a different method (peer ratings). The variables of personality assessment represent trait-method units, in which a given trait (extraversion, anxiety, achievement) is measured by a given method (self-report, peer ratings, situational tests). To establish the construct validity of a given trait-method unit, one must demonstrate that the greater part of the variance in the unit represents trait variance, which acts in accord with theory, rather than method variance, which is peculiar to the measuring instrument employed.

Campbell and Fiske (1959) have also emphasized that in order to demonstrate both the convergent and discriminant validity of a personality scale, it is necessary to employ an experimental design involving more than one trait and more than one method. At the very least we must have two traits measured by each of two methods. The results of such a design may be evaluated in what Campbell and Fiske have called a *multitrait-multimethod matrix*, which contains all the intercorrelations involved in measuring several traits by each of several methods. Let us assume that we plan to measure three traits (extraversion, anxiety, and achievement) by each of three methods (self-report, peer ratings, and situational tests). Since the particular content of the study is of no great importance here, it is more convenient to refer to the three traits as trait *A*, trait *B*, and trait *C*. Similarly, we may call the three methods of measurement method 1, method 2, and method 3. Trait *A* will be measured by each of the three methods, and we may denote this fact by A_1, A_2, and A_3. Trait B will be measured by each of the three methods, B_1, B_2, and B_3. The three methods of measuring trait C will be C_1, C_2, and C_3. Figure 9.3 contains all possible intercorrelations resulting from the measurement of three traits by three methods. The correlation $r_{B_1A_1}$ represents the correlation between traits B and A, each measured by method 1.

The multitrait-multimethod matrix illustrated in Figure 9.3 permits the evaluation of both convergent and discriminant validities of the traits in question. *Convergent validity* is given by the boldface validity coefficients $r_{A_2A_1}$, $r_{B_2B_1}$, $r_{C_2C_1}$, etc., appearing in the diagonals of the different trait-different method matrices (broken-line triangles). These coefficients reflect the extent to which the same trait is predictable by different methods. From the standpoint of prediction, these convergent validity coefficients are the most important. They could indicate, for example, the extent to which peer ratings of extraversion are predictable from self-report measures of extraversion, or the extent to which situational measures of anxiety are predictable from peer ratings of anxiety. Which are predictor and which are criterion measures would depend on the particular assessment problem.

The matrix in Figure 9.3 also permits evaluation of at least three kinds of *discriminant validity*. The first kind represents a very minimal requirement although it is not always met in practice (Campbell and Fiske, 1959). Consider the predictive validity of peer ratings of extraversion in forecasting the

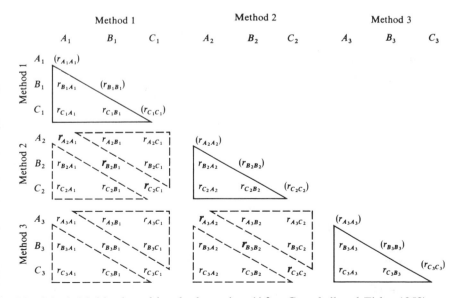

Fig. 9.3 A Multitrait-multimethod matrix. (After Campbell and Fiske, 1959)

criterion of self-reported extraversion. This convergent validity coefficient is based not on common methods of measurement but presumably on a common trait (extraversion), so that we would anticipate a substantial correlation. Further, we would expect this correlation to be greater than that between peer ratings of extraversion and self-reported anxiety, for example, or greater than the correlation between self-reported extraversion and peer ratings of anxiety. The last two correlations share neither trait nor method in common and hence would not be expected to be as high as a validity coefficient based on a commonly shared trait. More generally, a given convergent validity coefficient should exceed the correlations in the corresponding rows and columns of its different trait-different method matrix (broken lines) since the latter correlations share neither trait nor method in common. In Figure 9.3, we would require that

$$r_{A_2A_1} > r_{A_2B_1}, r_{A_2C_1}, r_{B_2A_1}, r_{C_2A_1},$$

$$r_{B_2B_1} > r_{B_2A_1}, r_{B_2C_1}, r_{A_2B_1}, r_{C_2B_1},$$

etc.

Little faith could be placed in measurement procedures that failed to meet this first minimal requirement of discriminant validity.

A second, more stringent requirement of discriminant validity is that correlations between variables presumably measuring the same trait (validity coefficients) exceed correlations between different traits which happen to be measured by the same method.[3] The correlation between self-report and peer-rating measures of extraversion, for example, should be greater than the correlation between self-report measures of extraversion and anxiety. More generally, a given convergent validity coefficient should exceed the correlations in the different trait-same method matrices (solid lines) which involve one or the other of the units entering into the validity coefficient. In Figure 9.3, we would require that

$$r_{A_2A_1} > r_{B_1A_1}, r_{C_1A_1}, r_{B_2A_2}, r_{C_2A_2},$$

$$r_{B_2B_1} > r_{B_1A_1}, r_{C_1B_1}, r_{B_2A_2}, r_{C_2B_2},$$

etc.

To the extent that convergent validity coefficients exceed correlations between different traits measured by the same method, we may accept the validity coefficients as evidence of construct validity for the trait in question. As the correlations between different traits measured by the same method

3. Although this requirement is an ideal one, it may be inappropriate to apply it too rigidly (Humphreys, 1960).

approach the corresponding validity coefficients, we are dealing with *method variance* in the sense in which this term was used in Chapter 7. Although method variance is to some extent unavoidable, clear-cut evidence for construct validity requires a demonstration that construct (trait) variance exceeds method variance in the situation under consideration.

The third and most stringent requirement of discriminant validity is that *patterns* of intercorrelations among traits be comparable, irrespective of the measurement procedures involved. If extraversion and anxiety are moderately correlated with each other but uncorrelated with achievement, we would expect this pattern of interrelationships among the three traits to obtain, regardless of the methods used to measure any of the traits. Thus the requirement would hold for patterns of trait interrelationships in both different trait-same method matrices (solid lines) and in different trait-different method matrices (broken lines). In the different trait-same method matrices of Figure 9.3, we would require comparability among the following patterns:

$$r_{B_1A_1} : r_{C_1A_1} : r_{C_1B_1} = r_{B_2A_2} : r_{C_2A_2} : r_{C_2B_2} = r_{B_3A_3} : r_{C_3A_3} : r_{C_3B_3}.$$

In the different trait-different method matrices, we would require comparability among the following patterns:

$$r_{B_2C_1} : r_{A_2C_1} : r_{A_2B_1} = r_{B_3C_1} : r_{A_3C_1} : r_{A_3B_1} = r_{B_3C_2} : r_{A_3C_2} : r_{A_3B_2}.$$

From the standpoint of construct validity, it is desirable that the pattern of relationships postulated among traits generally obtain over a wide range of interactions of trait and method variance. This is not to require that the values of the correlations be identical in different measurement situations, but rather to require that the pattern of intercorrelations be comparable despite fluctuations in the magnitude of the correlations.

The Personality Research Form

The Personality Research Form (PRF) developed by Jackson (1967b) is unquestionably the best example of a large-scale personality inventory developed under the construct point of view. Although various specialized instruments have been developed under construct-oriented procedures (e.g., Loevinger, 1962; Wiggins and Winder, 1961a) and the construct validity of numerous scales has been appraised after their development (e.g., Jessor and Hammond, 1957), the PRF is the only published multitrait personality inventory whose development was guided explicitly by the substantive, structural, and external considerations of the construct viewpoint. As applied to the development of the PRF, these considerations took the form of a set of four interrelated principles: (a) the overriding importance of psychological theory, (b) the necessity for suppressing response style variance,

(c) the importance of scale homogeneity, as well as generalizability, and (d) the importance of fostering convergent and discriminant validity at the very beginning of a program of test construction (Jackson, 1970, p. 63).

Substantive considerations. Jackson maintained that the system of variables emphasized in Murray's (1938) theory of personality possessed the advantages "of covering broadly, if not exhaustively, the spectrum of personality needs, states, and dispositions, of possessing carefully worked out published definitions, and of having a good deal of theoretical and empirical under-pinning" (Jackson, 1970, p. 67). Among the 20 Murray "need" variables selected for scale development were a number that had been the foci of considerable empirical research, such as achievement (McClelland *et al.*, 1953), affiliation (Schachter, 1959), and aggression (Buss, 1961). Many of these variables had also formed the basis for the construction of a variety of structured personality tests (Campbell, 1959; Edwards, 1959; Gough and Heilbrun, 1965; Stern, 1958). After reviewing the available research and theoretical literature on the 20 personality variables, Jackson developed a set of mutually exclusive, substantive definitions of each variable.

The final scales of the PRF were derived from a pool of approximately 3,000 items. Although the general principles which guided item creation and editing have been outlined (Jackson, 1967b, 1970, 1971), it is difficult to describe all the complex substantive considerations which guided the content and phrasing of each item. An attempt was made to delineate the potential universe of content by a grid of situations and behavior sequences considered relevant to each substantive domain. A heterogeneous team of item writers generated more than a hundred items for each trait. An attempt was made to generate an approximately equal number of items reflecting the positive (having the trait) and negative (not having the trait) pole of each of the traits. It was necessary, therefore, to delineate boundaries between trait dimensions and to determine which behaviors were *not* included within a particular trait definition. Hence a concern for both convergent and discriminant validities was present at the stage of *item writing*.

Although there are many issues of test construction philosophy on which the empirical and construct points of view are polarized, perhaps the greatest divergence of viewpoints occurs with respect to the concept of *subtle items*. Recall that the many examples of subtle items provided by Meehl (1945a) and others were used to illustrate the general point that the complex relation-ships between verbal reports and behavior patterns must be established empirically, rather than assumed. Although individuals may differ in the manner in which they interpret a given personality item, the fact that they differ may provide the basis for important discriminations among criterion behaviors. Jackson (1971) has challenged both the rationale and evidence for the existence of such subtle items: "It is my hunch that the great majority of subtle items uncovered with the MMPI, and considered a positive virtue by the proponents of empiricism, are present in MMPI scales due to errors in sampling items and subjects in the initial item-selection procedures of the MMPI" (p. 234).

Jackson (1971) maintains that item "subtlety" can be assessed only with respect to a clearly delineated substantive dimension. To judge an item as subtle is to do so with reference to a well-understood content. "Given a definition of a trait, it is possible to identify meaningful, valid, and relatively remote exemplars" (p. 238). An item is subtle if the respondent is not able to identify precisely the nature of the trait being measured. However, once the nature of the trait is made clear to the respondent, he will for the most part be able to recognize the content as a remote exemplar of the trait. Although few respondents could specify what is measured by the PRF item "I think newborn babies look very much like little monkeys," many would recognize it as an attitudinal exemplar of the negative pole of *nurturance* if they were told that this is the dimension being assessed. Jackson recognizes the virtue of such subtle items, particularly in the assessment of undesirable traits, but unlike the proponents of empiricism, he requires that the relationship between content and trait be recognizable once the trait is specified.

The statistical procedures employed in the final selection of items for the PRF were designed to ensure that the resultant scales had maximal convergent and discriminant *content saturation*. Provisional items were administered to groups of college students to obtain the item statistics necessary for item analysis and selection. As a preliminary test of the substantive homogeneity of the provisional item pools, internal consistency coefficients (Kuder-Richardson 20) were computed for each trait. The indices of homogeneity ranged from a low of .80 (for the trait of defendence) to a high of .94 for six of the traits (e.g., aggression). These values were interpreted as "characteristic correlations" among behaviors within a trait (Loevinger, 1957). For example, one would expect defensive people to admit defendence less consistently than aggressive people would admit aggression (Jackson, 1970). Having established that the provisional item pools appeared to represent homogeneous dimensions of content, Jackson then subjected the data to an elaborate, computer-based, sequential system of item analysis and selection.[4]

Each item was correlated with each of the 20 provisional content scales. If an item correlated higher with any content scale other than the one for

---

4. Since only selected aspects of these item-analytic procedures will be discussed in the present exposition, the reader with a special interest in the PRF, or in test construction in general, should consult the chapter by Jackson (1970).

which it was written, it was discarded on the grounds of possessing insufficient *discriminant validity*. Items with the highest correlations with their appropriate content scales were retained on the grounds that they had the greatest potential *convergent validity*. It is of interest to note that although there were approximately 5,700 opportunities for an item to be more correlated with an irrelevant than with a relevant content scale, such "misses" occurred only five times (Jackson, 1971). This finding is a tribute to the success of the substantively oriented item-writing procedures employed by Jackson and his collaborators.

In Jackson's view, *response styles* may operate in such a manner as to becloud or contaminate the substantive validity of a personality scale. Thus the tendency to respond to items in terms of their perceived social desirability or the tendency to acquiesce to statements irrespective of their content may decrease the *content saturation* of a personality scale by introducing sources of variance other than those specified by the substantive definition of a trait construct. In the construction of the final PRF scales, an attempt was made to minimize the potential contribution of acquiescence by requiring that half the items in each scale reflect the positive pole of the trait and half the negative. Of greater interest, however, is the manner in which Jackson attempted to minimize the contribution of social desirability variance to each content scale.

A group of college students rated the social desirability values of items that covered a broad and heterogeneous domain of contents. On the basis of these ratings, a group of highly desirable items (keyed true) and a group of highly undesirable items (keyed false) were assembled in a single *desirability scale* that was heterogeneous with respect to content. Because the content of the desirability scale was heterogeneous, it was assumed that subjects who attained high scores on the scale did so primarily on the basis of a tendency to respond to items in terms of their perceived desirability. Prior to item selection, each item in the provisional pool was correlated with the desirability scale. The correlation of an item with the desirability scale was compared with the correlation of the same item with its appropriate content scale by means of a *differential reliability index*,

$$\sqrt{r_{is}^2 - r_{id}^2},$$

in which the first term represents the correlation of an item with its provisional content scale, the second term its correlation with the desirability scale. Other things being equal, those items were selected which had the highest differential reliability index. This procedure represents still another attempt to maximize *content saturation* by excluding irrelevant or non-substantive sources of variance from the final content scales.

Structural considerations. The *cumulative* measurement model in scale con-struction assumes a linear relationship between items and a single underlying latent continuum. Jackson (1971) has argued that this model represents the "method of choice" in personality scale construction and that the evidence for the successful application of alternative models (e.g., dynamic and class models) is so slight that such alternatives have the status of "curiosities." In the adoption of a cumulative model for the measurement of 20 of Murray's needs, some concern was shown for considerations of both structural fidelity and inter-item structure (Loevinger, 1957). The interrelations among test items in the large provisional item pools for each trait were assumed to reflect the interrelations among *nontest* manifestations of the traits, as indicated by the interpretations placed on the relatively low homogeneity of items measur-ing defendence as opposed to items measuring aggression. Beyond this assumption of structural fidelity, however, no direct evidence has been presented on the extent to which relationships among test items mirror the relationships among nontest manifestations of the same traits.

Cumulative measurement models place a heavy emphasis on *homogeneity* in the inter-item structure of scales. The elaborate item-analytic procedures employed in the derivation of PRF scales were designed to ensure optimal levels of homogeneity within each scale. In addition, a variety of innovative procedures were utilized in an attempt to achieve homogeneity on the basis of *content saturation* rather than on the basis of substantively irrelevant response styles. Considerable evidence has been presented which indicates that the final PRF scales are relatively uncontaminated by sources of stylistic variance (Jackson, 1967b, 1970, 1971). Of greater methodological interest is a series of studies which demonstrate that the suppression of response style variance increases the content homogeneity of personality scales (Trott and Jackson, 1967; Jackson and Lay, 1968; Neill and Jackson, 1970).

External considerations. Regardless of the theoretical considerations which guide scale construction or the mathematical elegance of item-analytic procedures, the practical utility of a test must be assessed in terms of the number and magnitude of its correlations with nontest criterion measures. Because the PRF is a relatively new instrument, as compared with such established tests as the MMPI, it would be premature to interpret the promising but small body of evidence relating to its external validity (Jackson, 1967b). As might be expected of an instrument developed under the construct viewpoint, the initial validity studies of the PRF have placed a heavy emphasis on the investigation of both convergent and discriminant properties (Jackson and Guthrie, 1968; Jackson, 1969).

In one study, the PRF was administered to 202 male and female under-graduates, along with self-ratings and peer ratings of the same variables

(Jackson and Guthrie, 1968). For the self- and peer ratings, the PRF dimensions were identified by a key word (e.g., *aggressive* for aggression, *fun-loving* for play, etc.) and a paragraph describing the nature of the dimension to be rated. A nine-place rating scale was employed with instructions to identify points along the scale at which some person known to the subject might fall, in order to provide meaningful "anchors" for both the self- and peer ratings. The correlations between the 20 PRF scales and the self- and peer ratings are presented in Table 9.6. That table serves to identify the names of variables purportedly measured by the PRF, as well as to give an indication of the magnitude of convergent validites of the PRF scales with other methods of measurement.

Table 9.6 Convergent validity coefficients of 20 PRF scales with peer ratings and self-ratings (after Jackson, 1967b, p. 24)

PRF scale name	Peer ratings	Self-ratings
Abasement	.19	.33
Achievement	.46	.65
Affiliation	.40	.56
Aggression	.36	.38
Autonomy	.26	.44
Change	.22	.24
Cognitive structure	.18	.30
Defendence	.25	.23
Dominance	.38	.63
Endurance	.27	.52
Exhibition	.45	.43
Harmavoidance	.53	.58
Impulsivity	.30	.39
Nurturance	.27	.37
Order	.64	.76
Play	.42	.52
Sentience	.32	.31
Social recognition	.20	.56
Succorance	.20	.49
Understanding	.16	.29

In general, the PRF scales are more highly correlated with self-ratings than with peer ratings, although not too much significance should be attached to this result, since the peer ratings were provided by only one or two associates of the subjects. There is a considerable range of validity coefficients across different PRF variables, although all are statistically significant, and most are quite respectable in comparison with those typically reported for personality inventories (Jackson, 1967b).

It should be clear, even from the brief summary of procedures just reported, that the emphasis given to *substantive considerations* in the construction of the PRF distinguishes that instrument from both the MMPI and the Woodworth Personal Data Sheet. It is this construct-oriented emphasis, *not* the elaborate computer-based sequential item-analysis procedures, which distinguishes construct from empirical and rational inventories. The PRF was constructed more than 20 years after the MMPI and more than a half century after the Woodworth inventory. Modern psychometric theory and computer technology could be pressed into the service of both the rational and empirical viewpoints in the development of future instruments. The critical issue to be decided, of course, is which of the three viewpoints should guide the application of psychometric theory and computer technology. There is not as yet sufficient evidence to substantiate the assumption of the construct viewpoint that careful attention to considerations of substantive and structural validity will guarantee significant empirical validity as well. But this issue is among the most important facing personality assessment today (Wiggins, 1972).

CONTENT VERSUS STYLE IN STRUCTURED TESTS

The correspondence, instrumental, and substantive views of the meaning of a response to a structured test represent distinct orientations that implicate different approaches to the construction and interpretation of personality inventories. Although there are many specific points of disagreement among proponents of these views, the broadest point of contention relates to the issue of *what* is measured by the items of a structured personality test. The conceptual significance attached to the *content* of test responses ranges from atheoretical (instrumental) through pretheoretical (correspondence) to theoretical (substantive).

Although we hope that our categorization of the viewpoints above has brought order to the conceptual issues involved, it should not be considered an accurate characterization of the history of structured personality assessment as it has developed in the last 25 years. An accurate history of this period would have concentrated, instead, on the phenomena of response styles, sets, and biases, which have been the subject of more research and controversy than any other single topic in the field (McGee, 1967; Rorer, 1965). We chose, in effect, to "rewrite" the history of structured personality assessment on the grounds that the magnitude of research efforts during a given period is not an unfailing index of their significance. This is not to suggest that response styles are unimportant, nor to deny that the controversies surrounding their investigation were without foundation. Instead, we are asserting that the so-called "response style controversy" was not a novel issue in personality assessment, but a special instance of the more general disagreement over the *meaning* of responses to structured tests.

The Deviation Hypothesis

Over a period of years, Berg (1955, 1957, 1959, 1961, 1967) has formulated and refined a rationale for explaining the relationship between test response and criterion behaviors which is known as the *deviation hypothesis*. As stated initially, the hypothesis was:

Deviant response patterns tend to be general; hence those deviant behavior patterns which are significant for abnormality and thus regarded as symptoms are associated with other deviant response patterns which are in non-critical areas of behavior and which are not regarded as symptoms of personality aberration. (Berg, 1955, p. 62)

There are several terms in the hypothesis above which require elaboration before a full understanding of its implications is possible. We shall consider each of them in turn.

Deviant response patterns are defined solely on statistical grounds. There are two general forms of deviation: absolute and relative. *Absolute response deviation* involves departure from a statistically expected distribution, such as a normal curve or binomial distribution. For example, it has been reported (Goodfellow, 1940) that 80 percent of subjects will call "heads" on the first toss of a coin. This response clearly deviates from the statistically expected percentage of 50. At entrances to theatres and museums, three out of four patrons turn right, even though both paths arrive at the same point (Robinson, 1933). This too is an example of absolute deviation from statistical expectations.

Relative response deviation occurs with reference to expectations based on the performance of a specific population of subjects. Earlier in this chapter, we indicated that approximately 95 percent of a group of normal subjects answered *false* to the item: "I hear strange things when I am alone." An answer of *true* to this item is therefore a deviant response, with reference to the population of normals used as a base line against which to evaluate relative response deviation. Relative response deviation provides the statistical basis of the strategy of contrasted groups. It is also the type of deviation with which Berg and his students have concerned themselves almost exclusively. The cardinal point of the deviation hypothesis is that deviant response tendencies are *general*. Although there are many possible interpretations of "response generality" (Sechrest and Jackson, 1963) all of them seem to imply that individuals whose responses are deviant in one situation will have deviant responses in other situations as well.

Our society tends to view some behaviors as *critical* to its well-being and functioning, while other behaviors are considered *noncritical* or mainly irrelevant to the important values of the culture. In psychometric terms, critical behaviors are usually involved in the various criteria we attempt to predict (success in medical school, recidivism following parole), whereas the test behaviors typically employed to predict these criteria (answering *true* or *false* to an attitude item, stating an esthetic preference for an abstract drawing) are considered noncritical by society at large. "Putting it another way, a patient may be legally committed to a mental hospital because of significant deviant responses like delusions, but never solely on the basis of deviant responses to inkblots, designs, and such" (Berg, 1967, p. 152). It should be emphasized that the distinction between critical and noncritical behaviors is an evaluative rather than a scientific one.

The statement that deviant response tendencies are general applies to all deviant responses, wherever they happen to be classified as falling, whether in critical or in noncritical areas of social importance. Given that deviant response tendencies are general, *it is expected that deviant responses in critical areas of behavior will be associated with deviant responses in noncritical areas of behavior*. In Berg's view, in fact, this expectation constitutes the rationale for why complex criterion behaviors may be predicted from seemingly unrelated responses to test items.

Individuals who perform critical behaviors in our society (physicians, psychiatric patients, successful students) are by definition *deviant* in that their critical behaviors set them apart from other groups. Because of their deviance in critical areas of behavior, it is assumed, under the deviation hypothesis, that they will exhibit deviance in noncritical areas of behavior as well. This fact allows us to capitalize on the generality of deviant behavior by finding areas of noncritical behavior (test responses) which are associated with deviation in critical areas of behavior (criterion group membership). With reference to the numerous studies which have predicted diverse criteria by the strategy of contrasted groups, Berg states: "The Deviation Hypothesis offers an explanatory and unifying principle which is considered to account for the findings of huge numbers of disparate researches" (1961, p. 335).

There is an additional implication of the deviation hypothesis which has proved to be controversial: "Stimulus patterns of any sense modality may be used to elicit deviant response patterns; thus particular stimulus content is unimportant for measuring behaviors in terms of the Deviation Hypothesis" (Berg, 1957, p. 160). In reviewing the stimulus materials which have been used to discriminate groups, Berg was particularly impressed by their *variety*.

Such diverse materials as apparent movement of lights, spiral after effects, musical excerpts, embedded figures, and food preferences have been successfully employed as group-discriminative test items. Berg and his co-workers have demonstrated significant discriminations among psychiatric groups based solely on preferences for abstract designs (Barnes, 1955; Hesterley and Berg, 1958; Roitzsch and Berg, 1958). Berg's strongest statement of this position is:

. . . one should be able to construct MMPI scales from the Strong Interest Blank and the Strong occupational scales from the MMPI items by using the same technique. Or for that matter, one should be able to develop the scales of both tests from almost any hodge-podge of a similar number of items. . . . Given enough deviant responses and clean criterion groups, one should be able to duplicate any existing personality, interest, occupational and similar scales without regard to particular item content. (Berg, 1955, p. 70)

Such a strong statement with respect to the unimportance of test item content has not gone unchallenged:

In many ways this position is a restatement of the pragmaticism of the empirical movement (Meehl, 1945) with a non sequitur corollary which makes the blindness of blind empiricism a virtue. . . . The basis of the above inference is not clear since Berg is unable to provide even a rudimentary rationale whereby one might be able to predict the suitability of a given content for a given assessment. . . . To prejudge a given item pool requires a theory of content . . . and Berg's contribution to this enterprise has been mainly a negative one. (Wiggins, 1966, p. 2)

Norman (1963a) was the first to present evidence from an extensive and well-designed study which tended to refute Berg's contention that item content was unimportant. Employing carefully constructed peer ratings as criteria (see Chapter 8), Norman compared the discriminative effectiveness of three kinds of stimulus items, which varied on a continuum of content relevance: personality descriptive adjectives, occupational titles, and abstract figure drawings. His findings clearly supported the relevance of content in this prediction situation. In addition, he challenged the distinction between critical and noncritical behaviors:

. . . by any consistent adherence to the distinction implied by the conceptions of critical and noncritical areas of behavior, we will have explicitly precluded the development or construction of any theoretical system capable of yielding an adequate "explanation" of behavioral phenomena. What is the distinction, after all, between the terms critical and noncritical when applied to areas of behavior, but an admission of the incompleteness of our present knowledge? . . .

Whatever pragmatic virtue the Deviation Hypothesis might have for goading researchers to explore new possibilities for useful test stimuli, its purported theoretical value to account for or explain *specific behavioral phenomena or relationships is, at the very best, illusory.* (Norman, 1963a, p. 174)

The results of a study by Goldberg and Slovic (1967) provide additional negative evidence on the plausibility of Berg's assertions about the unimportance of item content. These investigators employed a complex experimental design that permitted the assessment of the relative predictive efficiency of content-relevant and content-irrelevant items, as well as the efficiency of verbal and nonverbal items. The criteria to be predicted consisted of two measures of academic achievement and four measures of social affiliation in a group of female college students. Four pools of items were employed in scale development: (a) 60 random geometric forms that had been employed in previous studies that purported to demonstrate the unimportance of item content (Berg, Hunt, and Barnes, 1949), (b) 60 self-report statements thought to be related to achievement, (c) 60 self-report statements thought to be related to affiliation, and (d) 60 self-report statements selected at random and thought to be irrelevant to both achievement and affiliation. The content-relevance or "face validity" of the 180 self-report statements for each of the six criterion measures was rated by a separate group of undergraduates. On the basis of these ratings, the self-report statements were further subdivided into categories of high, medium, and low face validity for each of the criterion measures.

Using the strategy of contrasted groups, Goldberg and Slovic (1967) built empirical scales for each of the criteria from nonverbal items and from verbal items differing in judged face validity. In the derivation samples which formed the basis for item selection, *all* scales had substantial and significant validity coefficients. Thus, if one is willing to accept evidence based on *non-cross-validated* scales developed by the strategy of contrasted groups, it appears that content is relatively unimportant. However, when Goldberg and Slovic assessed the validity of empirical scales in cross-validation samples, the validity of all nonverbal scales went to zero, and for five of the six criterion variables, *only scales built from items of the highest face validity had significant validity coefficients.* On the basis of the Goldberg-Slovic study it may be concluded that (a) verbal items are better predictors of intellective and social criteria than nonverbal items and (b) there is a substantial, though not perfect, relationship between the judged criterion-relevance of an item and its predictive validity.

There is good reason to question both the evidence for and the explanatory value of the deviation hypothesis. Nevertheless, this hypothesis has inspired considerable empirical research in applied areas (Adams and Butler,

1967), as well as thoughtful critiques of the measurement problems involved in contrasted-group research (Sechrest and Jackson, 1962, 1963). For our purposes, the deviation hypothesis rather clearly defines one pole of an attitude toward content in personality assessment. This pole is characterized by an indifference to theoretical considerations and an emphasis on pragmaticism as the proper concern of test constructors. The next identifiable position on this attitudinal continuum is occupied by the advocates of response style interpretations of personality tests.

The Response Style Controversy

The tendency for subjects to respond to personality items independently of their content has been variously referred to as "set" (Cronbach, 1946), "bias" (Berg, 1955), and "style" (Jackson and Messick, 1958). Although the definitions and implications of these terms have been variously and often inconsistently stated (Rorer, 1965), they share in common the property of representing either nonsubstantive or substantively irrelevant components of response to structured personality items. The major contributors to the extensive literature of response styles have not denied the possibility of measuring substantive dimensions of personality. Instead they have stressed the difficulty of measuring such dimensions independently of response styles and have taken the position that much of the variance in currently available inventories, such as the MMPI, is stylistic rather than substantive in nature. We have already touched on the response styles of social desirability and acquiescence as potential "suppressor variables" (Chapter 1) and, in connection with the PRF, as variables to be minimized in scale development. Here we will briefly sketch the nature of the arguments and counterarguments for the *pervasiveness* of response styles in personality inventories.

Social desirability. Edwards (1957) has defined social desirability response style as: "the tendency of subjects to attribute to themselves, in self-description, personality statements with socially desirable scale values and to reject those with socially undesirable scale values" (p. vi). Such a tendency qualifies as a *response style* because it refers to an organized disposition within individuals to respond in a consistent manner across a variety of substantive domains (Wiggins, 1968). This particular style is held to be different from, and to some extent independent of, tendencies to deliberately lie, dissimulate, or otherwise engage in "impression management" for ulterior motives (Edwards, 1970). Instead, social desirability response style, as defined by Edwards, involves an individual's typical or characteristic level of putting his best foot forward without special instructions or motivations to do so.

Most of Edwards' pioneering studies of the social desirability variable emphasized the correlates of a social desirability scale (*SD*) consisting of

39 MMPI items keyed in the socially desirable direction as determined by the unanimous opinions of ten judges. Although Edwards (1957) did not provide a precise statement of the universe of content sampled by the items on the *SD* scale, it has been repeatedly emphasized by others (e.g., Wiggins, 1958, 1968) that 22 of the 39 items in the scale were selected from the Taylor (1953) manifest anxiety scale. As a consequence, the *SD* scale is highly and negatively correlated with the Taylor scale and with a variety of other MMPI measures of anxiety and general maladjustment. Factor-analytic studies of the MMPI clinical scales have consistently uncovered a very large first factor which is marked by scales reflecting anxiety and general maladjustment (Wiggins, 1966). Perhaps not surprisingly, the *SD* scale is highly loaded on this factor and serves as an excellent marker of its negative pole (lack of anxiety).

The central role that Edwards assigns to social desirability as a stylistic determinant of response to the MMPI raises problems of interpretation rather than problems of fact. The substantial negative correlation of the *SD* scale with the MMPI clinical scales has been demonstrated on numerous occasions (Edwards, 1957). Similarly, the potency of the *SD* scale as a marker of the first factor of the MMPI has been established in a variety of different ways (Edwards and Diers, 1962; Edwards, Diers, and Walker, 1962; Edwards and Heathers, 1962; Edwards and Walsh, 1963, 1964). It is the interpretation placed on these empirical results that has led to controversy.

A reasonable conclusion is that to the degree to which MMPI scales also have high loadings on the first factor or to the degree to which they are correlated with the SD *scale, they must also be measuring the same trait as the* SD *scale regardless of the particular trait names which have been assigned to the MMPI scales.* (Edwards and Walsh, 1964, p. 59)

Thus, although most clinicians who employ the MMPI would interpret the scales which have high loadings on the first factor (e.g., *Pt, Sc*) as reflecting "fearfulness," "withdrawal," etc. (see Table 9.4), Edwards feels that a more parsimonious interpretation would be one that stressed patients' tendencies to attribute undesirable statements to themselves.

Edwards' interpretation of the first factor of the MMPI as a social desirability factor is plausible because of the nearly complete *confounding* of desirability and adjustment that is present in both MMPI items and scales. However, Block (1965) has observed:

Confounding is a blade that, if held too tightly, will cut its wielder. With the same logic advanced for social desirability as underlying [first factor] MMPI scales, one can argue that the [first] factor of the MMPI represents a personality dimension that is vital to an understanding of the SD *scale. Many of the [first factor] MMPI scales have empirical origins and demonstrable validity in separating appropriate criterion groups. The high correlations found between these scales and the* SD *measure therefore plausibly suggest—not an artifact or naivete in the construction of these earlier scales—but rather that the* SD *scale, wittingly or not, is an excellent measure of some important variable of personality.* (pp. 69–70)

In an attempt to unconfound content and social desirability in the MMPI, Block (1965) developed a "desirability-free measure of social desirability." He accomplished this by selecting a group of items that had substantial loadings on the first factor of the MMPI but that were *neutral* in terms of their rated social desirability values. These items were then assembled in an "ego resiliency–subtle" scale (*ER–S*), which presumably was relatively free of the confounding influence of social desirability. In nine separate and diverse samples of subjects, *ER–S* was shown to have acceptable, though not high, internal consistency and to be correlated with *SD* (range: .59 to .79) and *Pt* (range: −.61 to −.79), both of which scales are known to be markers of the first factor of the MMPI. It was Block's contention that a scale which is free of desirability, yet correlated with *SD* and other measures of the first factor of the MMPI, requires interpretation of the first factor in terms other than social desirability. On the basis of independent empirical correlates (clinicians' ratings) of high scores on the first factor of the MMPI in five diverse assessment samples, Block chose to interpret this factor as "anxiety proneness versus ego resiliency."

Edwards (1970) was unwilling to accept those arguments of Block which were based on the *ER–S* scale. Edwards argued that in the selection of items which were associated with the first factor of the MMPI but neutral with respect to social desirability ratings, it was necessary to reject precisely those items which were the best available markers of the first factor. As a consequence, it was likely that the items in the *ER–S* scale were associated with a factor other than the first factor of "social desirability." Edwards called attention to the fact that in samples independent of its derivation, *ER–S* had meager internal consistency and quite modest correlations with *SD* and *Pt*. Further, he noted that in published factor-analytic studies of MMPI scales, *ER–S* was found to be either a relatively poor marker of the first factor (Wiggins, 1966) or a marker of factors other than the first (Edwards and Walsh, 1964).

The problem of distinguishing social desirability from content in self-reports is similar, if not identical (Ford and Meisels, 1965), to the problem of distinguishing evaluation from description in peer ratings (Chapter 8). Because the MMPI was designed to measure dimensions of psychopathology that are negatively evaluated (viewed as undesirable) by society at large, it is hardly surprising that pathology and desirability are confounded at both the item and the scale level. Although there may be merit in both Block's (1965) and Edwards' (1970) *psychometric* arguments concerning the success with which Block was able to "unconfound" these two sources of variance, the broader issue involved centers on the heuristic value of the social desirability interpretation. In this connection, Block (1965) has given a spirited defense of substantive interpretations of the first factor of the MMPI, which is buttressed at many points by appeal to *external considerations* related to construct validity. Although it is somewhat unusual for an empirical instrument to be defended from a construct-oriented viewpoint (see Jackson, 1967c), the response style literature is replete with such anomalies.

Acquiescence. Acquiescence may be thought of as the tendency to agree to personality items as self-descriptive, independently of the particular content of the items. To qualify as a response stlye, such a tendency should refer to an organized disposition within individuals to respond in a consistent manner (*true, agree, yes*) across a variety of substantive domains. The problems encountered in the measurement of acquiescent response style are similar to those involved in measuring social desirability response style since the tendency to agree with items may be confounded with the particular content of the items. Consequently, measures of acquiescence should be developed from item pools that are demonstrably *heterogeneous* with respect to content and in which items are arbitrarily keyed *true* for purposes of measuring acquiescent response style. The alleged pervasiveness of the social desirability response style introduces still another complexity in the measurement of acquiescence; scales which purport to measure acquiescent response style must also be shown to be relatively free of the influence of social desirability.

In light of such constraints on the development of a "pure" measure of acquiescent response style, it is not surprising that this area of research has been beset by controversy. To rule out competing interpretations of social desirability, it seems appropriate to develop measures of acquiescence that comprise items of *neutral* rated social desirability values. The elimination of content variance from acquiescence measures is less easily achieved. Block (1965) has argued that "although it is possible . . . to formulate MMPI measures which unequivocally reflect content while excluding acquiescence, it is not possible to construct a measure of acquiescence wherein, *a priori*, content considerations are guaranteed to be uninvolved" (p. 24). The problem here is that "the agreement tendency itself has been defined with respect to *heterogeneous* and ambiguous items in such a manner that internal consistency in a presumed measure of acquiescence may itself be interpreted as content variance which would vitiate the acquiescence measure on logical grounds" (Wiggins, 1962, p. 235).

Wiggins (1962) has suggested that measures of acquiescent style be developed with reference to different *groups* of subjects that are known to differ in acquiescent tendencies on independent grounds. In a "normally" acquiescent population, the internal consistency of an acquiescence scale would be quite low, thus ruling out interpretations of content homogeneity. In a "highly acquiescent" population, the internal consistency of an acquiescence scale would be considerable, thus demonstrating the internal consistency of the response style. This suggestion has not been followed, possibly because of a reluctance to employ measures that are typically unreliable (Block, 1965) or because of the difficulty of identifying "highly acquiescent" subjects independently of such scales.

Jackson and Messick (1961, 1962a, 1962b) developed an MMPI measure of acquiescent response style that meets many of the requirements above. Sixty items of neutral social desirability values and of presumably heterogeneous content were arbitrarily keyed *true* in a 60-item scale called *Dy-3*. This scale, along with several specially derived measures of social desirability, was included in a factor analysis of the intercorrelations of MMPI clinical scales that had been divided into subscales of items keyed *true* and items keyed *false*. Thus, for example, the standard 48-item *Pt* scale was divided into a subscale of 39 items keyed *true* and a subscale of 9 items keyed *false*.

The resulting two-factor solution, which was replicated in three diverse samples of subjects, was interpreted in terms of a "social desirability" factor and an "acquiescence" factor. The social desirability factor, which was identified with reference to the social desirability scales, was substantially related to the average-rated social desirability scale values of the MMPI clinical subscales. The acquiescence factor, marked by *Dy-3*, achieved almost complete separation between *true*- and *false*-keyed clinical subscales. These exceptionally clear-cut factor structures appeared to warrant Jackson and Messick's conclusion that "In all three analyses, approximately three-fourths of the common variance and about one half of the total variance was interpretable in terms of the response styles of acquiescence and desirability" (1962a, p. 295). The implication, of course, is that very little variance in the MMPI clinical scales can be attributed to content. In Jackson and Messick's view, the MMPI appeared to be primarily a measure of the "rather massive response style effects" of social desirability and acquiescence.

Block (1965) challenged Jackson and Messick's interpretation of the influence of acquiescence in the MMPI on several grounds. First, he challenged the "purity" of *Dy-3* as a measure of acquiescence on statistical grounds and argued that the items in the scale represented consistent clusters of content. Second, he attempted to construct "acquiescence-free" MMPI clinical scales by balancing the number of *true*- and *false*-keyed items in each scale. Thus, for example, the 48-item *Pt* scale was reduced to a 9-item *true* scale and a 9-item *false* scale. On the basis of a factor analysis of these balanced and presumably "acquiescence-free" clinical scales, Block argued that the factor structure that emerged was the *same* as that obtained in the original Jackson and Messick studies and that these factors were therefore interpretable in terms of content rather than in terms of acquiescence. A consideration of Jackson's (1967a, 1967c) response to Block's arguments, Block's (1967) retort to Jackson, or various extensions of the controversy (Bentler, Jackson, and Messick, 1971, 1972; Block, 1971) would lead us well beyond the intended scope of the present chapter. As in most prolonged and polarized controversies, the "truth" is likely to fall somewhere between the two extreme positions.

COMPONENTS OF VARIANCE IN STRUCTURED PERSONALITY TESTS

Proponents of deviation, stylistic, and content interpretations of the meaning of a structured test response have tended to emphasize one aspect of response determination over others. Most of the research and theoretical writings concerning response styles posed issues in a "deviation versus content" or "style versus content" framework. In many respects this is reminiscent of the fable about the four blind men and the elephant. On the basis of touching different parts of the elephant (tail, leg, trunk, side), the four blind men were prepared to argue that an "elephant" had quite different physical characteristics. Similarly, those whose research has been most concerned with one aspect of structured test responses have overemphasized that component or been prone to argue that it is the sole defining property of such responses. But all behavior is *multiply determined*, and responses to structured test items are no exception. A complete understanding of the relations between test responses and criterion behaviors can come about only through recognition of each of the many components that determine response and an understanding of their relations to one another. This point has been stated succinctly by Loevinger (1957):

But in principle, all components of test variance must be valid for some purposes. The problem is that in life the various components of variance are confounded. The task of psychometrics is to isolate, to identify, and so far as possible, to measure separately the important components of variance. (p. 649)

In the way of review, we will now distinguish among several hypothetical components of variance that have entered into our consideration of structured inventories at different places in the present chapter. These components are not thought to be necessarily well established, mutually exclusive, or exhaustive of all possible facets of the domain involved. Nevertheless, such distinctions have previously provided a useful framework from which to view contemporary research on structured personality tests (e.g., Wiggins, 1968).

In principle, we may categorize sources of variance in personality inventories as: (a) by-products of the strategy under which a scale was constructed, (b) item characteristics which introduce method variance, (c) organized response styles which exist in individuals, and (d) manifestations of a particular content domain.

Components of Variance Due to Strategy

In discussing possible strategies for personality scale construction, we have focused on the major differences among rational, empirical, and construct approaches. There are, of course, many variations within each of these frameworks. Strategies of rational scale construction have ranged from relatively simple internal consistency analyses to highly complex multivariate procedures for item selection. The method of contrasted groups is a broad and flexible strategy that has been implemented with considerable ingenuity in a variety of assessment contexts. Although judgmental and statistical procedures for ensuring content saturation are relatively new, it is already clear that there are many different ways in which the construct approach can be implemented.

Although different strategies for scale construction have, historically, been associated with different views of the meaning of test responses, a given viewpoint does not necessarily imply a particular strategy. In fact, there appears to be a growing recognition of the virtues of employing "mixed" or "sequential" strategies in scale construction (Jackson, 1970). In the final analysis, it is the *purpose* or intended application of a scale that will determine the strategy selected (Butt and Fiske, 1968). In most practical situations, alternative strategies will exist for scale construction, and each available strategy may contribute unique characteristics which influence interpretations of the meaning of a test response. Sources of variance in test response which may be attributed to the overall strategy of scale construction (contrasted-group, internal-consistency, factor-analytic) may be thought of as conceptually distinct from other influences on test response.

Strategies and dimensions of interpretation. In contrasted-group strategies, items are selected on the basis of their ability to discriminate between a deviant criterion group and a normative group on whatever dimensions (specific or generalizable) are represented by differences between the actual groups employed. We have already emphasized that differences may arise between specific criterion groups and specific normative groups on dimensions other than those involved in the definition of the criterion group (age, sex, intelligence). In addition, the strategy of contrasted groups involves a statistical definition of deviance which is peculiar to that strategy. This definition arises at the item level and is imparted to the meaning of a total scale score by the fact that such a score represents an additive combination of these items.

We have already considered characteristics of individual items which qualify them for scales developed by the strategy of contrasted groups (e.g., Table 9.3). In arriving at a total scale score, one considers the number of instances in which the item response of the subject agrees with the predominant direction of the deviant group to be an overall measure of the similarity of the subject to that deviant group. Such instances are counted and combined into a total scale score bearing the name of the deviant group (e.g., schizophrenia). Since the items entering into the empirical scale vary widely in the extent to which they separate the two groups, the significance of a raw total scale score must be evaluated with respect to norms from the population to which the scale will be applied. A typical procedure in this instance would be to administer the newly formed scale to a large population of normals and to derive standard scores which would indicate the relative position of the subject with respect to the mean of this new normative distribution. Such a scale can now be applied in a relatively straightforward manner. A subject whose standard score is close to the mean of the normative distribution is considered to be more like "normals" on whatever dimension is measured by the scale than he is like the deviant criterion group. A subject whose score exceeds that of the average normative group (e.g., by two standard deviations or more) is considered more like the deviant criterion group. This situation is illustrated in Figure 9.4.

Figure 9.4 also illustrates the paradox that, whereas middle-range scores are indicative of "normality" (by default) and high scores are indicative of deviance (by reference to the original deviant criterion group), the meaning of a *low score* is undefined. What can we say about subjects whose scale scores fall significantly below (two standard deviations or more) the mean of the normative group? It should be clear that such subjects are very *unlike* the deviant criterion group and as such cannot be diagnosed by whatever label defined the criterion group. On the other hand, such subjects are very different from the "normal" group and cannot be classified as having similar characteristics to that group either. Subjects of this type have been referred to as "deviantly non-deviant" by Sechrest and Jackson (1963), and the possibility has been raised that such subjects may be characterized by exaggerated efforts to appear "normal" (Wiggins, 1962).

This paradox reveals a limitation on interpretation which has been imposed by the contrasted-groups strategy of test construction. On a scale so derived, significance (in terms of interpretation) can be attributed only to high scores. Middle-range scores are difficult to classify as having a *low* degree of the trait when, in fact, there is another group possible ("the deviantly non-deviant") with even lower scores. The situation represents not

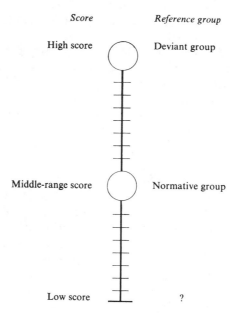

Fig. 9.4 The meaning of total scale scores under a contrasted-groups strategy.

so much a characteristic of the subjects involved as a characteristic of the strategy employed to measure the dimension of interest. Such a strategy may make the resultant scales especially vulnerable to the influence of social desirability response style (Wiggins, 1962).

Some theoretical frameworks attach special significance to possession of "too little" of a trait and thereby avoid the apparent paradox of scales constructed by the contrasted-groups strategy just discussed. In psycho-analytic theory, for example, pathological significance is often assigned to *both* extremes of a trait continuum. This conceptualization is represented graphically in Figure 9.5 for the variable of aggressiveness. Both extreme hostility and extreme (abnormal) concern for the welfare of others are interpreted as indices of maladjustment. This dynamic measurement model should not be confused with statistical artifacts introduced by the strategy of contrasted groups illustrated in Figure 9.4. To rigorously substantiate the dimension implied by Figure 9.5, one must provide evidence that three independently specified criterion groups (assaultive, assertive, oversolicitous) do, in fact, order themselves on this scale in the manner indicated by the figure. An example of the psychometric application of this line of reasoning may be found in Block (1953).

A somewhat complex example of the limitations of scale construction strategy on subsequent interpretation of total scale scores may be found in

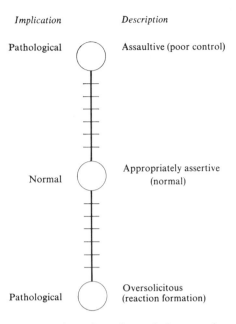

Implication   *Description*

Pathological   Assaultive (poor control)

Normal   Appropriately assertive
                                (normal)

Pathological   Oversolicitous
                                (reaction formation)

Fig. 9.5 Schematic representation of psychoanalytic reasoning.

the interpersonal system of personality diagnosis developed by Leary and associates (Chapter 10).   Leary (1957) devised a measure of interpersonal dominance by use of a construct-oriented strategy involving highly sophisticated structural and substantive considerations.   The interpersonal trait of dominance was considered a bipolar one characterized by extremely dominant behavior at one pole (autocratic) and extremely submissive behavior at the opposite pole (masochistic).   Such reasoning is characteristic of the conceptual framework illustrated in Figure 9.5.   In the standardization of this measure for application to clinic populations, however, Leary's normative reference group consisted of *psychiatric patients*.   The implied dimension represented by this strategy is illustrated in Figure 9.6.

The scaling strategy applied by Leary to his bipolar dominance measure makes interpretation extremely difficult.   Subjects scoring one or more standard deviations above or below the psychiatric norms are considered in both instances to be *more* pathological than the original psychiatric group. Judging a given subject to be "well off" when his score falls close to the psychiatric norm seems likely to result in a large number of false negative diagnostic decisions (Wiggins, 1965).   Similarly, such a frame of reference also fails to provide an appropriate base line for the evaluation of such psychiatric concepts as "improvement" (Baumrind, 1960).   The test construction strategy adopted by Leary seems to minimize sources of irrelevant

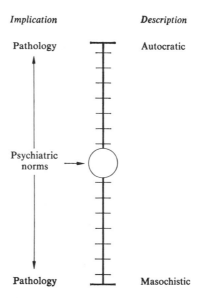

Fig. 9.6 The meaning of a dominance scale score in the interpersonal system of personality diagnosis.

variance which are often present in contrasted-groups strategies employing normal and psychiatric subjects. At the same time, however, it seems to give rise to interpretive problems of an equally troublesome nature.

Strategies and predictive validity. Proponents of different strategies of personality scale construction have presented convincing arguments for the relative superiority of their preferred strategy (e.g., Cattell, 1957; Loevinger, 1957; Meehl, 1945a; Travers, 1951). Implicit in these positions is the expectation that the preferred strategy will yield scales which are more highly correlated with relevant external criteria than scales developed by competing strategies. Despite the importance of such an assumption, it is only recently that systematic investigations of this topic have begun to be conducted (e.g., Crewe, 1967; Butt and Fiske, 1968; Alumbaugh, Davis, and Sweney, 1969; Hermans, 1969; Neill and Jackson, 1970).

An exceptionally extensive investigation of the relative predictive validities of different strategies of scale construction was conducted by Goldberg and Hase (Goldberg, 1972; Hase and Goldberg, 1967). Their research was directed to a broad and quite basic issue in personality assessment: "Given a large pool of personality items, by what strategy might item subsets be assembled to form a multiscale inventory that would be maximally efficient in predicting a diverse array of important social criteria?" (Hase and

Goldberg, 1967, p. 231). To shed light on this issue, the investigators contrasted the predictive effectiveness of sets of scales derived by different strategies from the 468 items of the California Psychological Inventory (Gough, 1957). Using a common item pool, they developed sets of scales under four major scale construction strategies and under two control strategies. The major strategies were: (a) factor-analytic, (b) contrasted-groups, (c) rational, and (d) theoretical.

The *factor-analytic* strategy involved the construction of scales which marked the principal dimensions accounting for the intercorrelations of the 468 CPI items. A sophisticated computational procedure avoided the bias often introduced by extreme item endorsements yet based the analysis on the total pool of items. The scales which represented the *contrasted-groups* strategy were originally devised by Gough (1957) to discriminate existing groups (e.g., delinquents versus nondelinquents) or to discriminate groups formed by peer and teacher ratings. It is important to note that these are cross-validated empirical scales that are known to possess some predictive power in forecasting most of the criteria employed by Goldberg and Hase.

Under the *rational* strategy, groups of items were assembled by one of the authors on the basis of their judged relevance to the dimensions presumably measured by the contrasted-groups scales. Several additional rational scales developed by Gough (1957) were also employed. The items in these rational scales were then purified by an internal-consistency analysis conducted in a separate sample of subjects. In the *theoretical* strategy, three judges assembled items on the basis of their judged relevance to the major constructs of a contemporary theory of personality—in this instance, Murray's (1938) theory of psychological needs. Only those items were included for which two of the three judges agreed that they matched the descriptions of personality variables provided by Murray. However, unlike many construct-oriented scales (e.g., Jackson, 1970), the scales in the Goldberg-Hase study were not subjected to internal-consistency analysis.

Control strategies were labeled "stylistic" and "random." Scales constructed under the *stylistic* strategy were based entirely on different combinations of the item characteristics of rated social desirability values and population endorsement frequencies, without regard to item content. Under the *random* strategy, items were selected and keyed on the basis of a table of random numbers. Stylistic and random strategies are not representative of scale construction procedures actually employed in practice, but they provided an essential base line for comparison of scales developed under the four major strategies.

Thirteen specific criterion measures were available for the 152 freshman women who served as subjects in the study. These measures fell in the general categories of: (a) social conformity, (b) peer ratings, (c) popularity, (d) academic achievement, and (e) academic interest.   In the words of the investigators: "It would be difficult to argue that these 13 criteria represent a random sample of all that might be of interest to psychologists. They are, however, meant to be a representative sample of important and diverse criteria related to problems that have been of interest to many investigators." (Hase and Goldberg, 1967, p. 239)

Eleven scales were developed under each of the six scale construction strategies, making a grand total of 66 personality scales developed from the same item pool.   Multiple-regression procedures were employed to assess the extent to which each of the 13 criteria was predictable from sets of 11 scales developed under different strategies. The sample of freshman women was divided randomly into two equal-sized groups within a double cross-validation design (Chapter 1). Regression weights derived from each group were applied to the other, and the average of the two cross-validated multiple-Rs was taken as an estimate of the validity of a given set of 11 predictor scales for predicting each of the 13 criteria.

The major results of the study involve the extent to which sets of scales developed under different strategies differ in their ability to forecast diverse criteria by means of multiple-regression equations.   An overview of these results may be gained by considering the *average* cross-validity coefficients (across the 13 criteria) obtained under the six different scale construction strategies.   Table 9.7 contains the average initial multiple-Rs obtained in derivation samples and the average multiple-Rs obtained upon cross-validation.

Table 9.7 Average initial and cross-validity coefficients in the prediction of 13 criteria by 11-scale sets constructed under different strategies (after Goldberg, 1972)

| | Strategies of Scale Construction | | | | | |
	Factor-analytic	Con-trasted-groups	Rational	Theoret-ical	Stylistic	Random
Initial multiple-R	.51	.48	.51	.48	.44	.40
Cross-validated multiple-R	.26	.25	.28	.26	.12	.09

As the table shows, moderate initial multiple-Rs were obtained under all strategies. Upon cross-validation, however, considerably greater shrinkage occurred under stylistic and random strategies. A statistical analysis of the results suggested that the four major methods of scale construction were *equally effective* in predicting the 13 criteria, and that all four methods differed significantly from the stylistic and random strategies (Hase and

Goldberg, 1967). This finding, emphasized in the initial report, is especially surprising in light of the previously mentioned arguments put forth by proponents of each strategy which implied that considerable differences would be found in the prediction of diverse criteria. If nothing else, one might expect the contrasted-groups scales, which are the standard scales of the California Psychological Inventory, to have at least a slight predictive edge, a result which clearly did not occur.

The results reported in Table 9.7 are based on *averaged* cross-validities across 13 quite diverse criteria. Although the sets of scales constructed under different strategies did not differ in their average effectiveness across these criteria, one would anticipate that the scale sets would differ in their predictive effectiveness for specific criteria. In fact, a comprehensive reanalysis of these data revealed an intriguing *strategy-by-criteria interaction* (Goldberg, 1972).

As one might expect, the 13 criteria differed considerably in their relative "predictability," as indexed by the average multiple-Rs for the four major sets of scales for each separate criterion measure. When the effectiveness of scale sets constructed under different strategies was examined in relation to the relative predictability of the criterion measures, an interesting pattern emerged. The factor-analytic, theoretical, and rational scales did very well in predicting "predictable" criterion measures, but the contrasted-groups scales possessed only moderate cross-validities. For example, in predicting the most predictable criterion measure employed in the study (peer ratings of "sociability"), the cross-validity coefficients were as follows: factor-analytic (.61), theoretical (.55), rational (.50), and contrasted-groups (.37). As the predictability of the criterion measures declined, the cross-validities of scale sets constructed under nonempirical strategies fell off rather sharply, whereas the contrasted-groups scales tended to "hold their own" at a relatively moderate level of validity. In other words, whereas the contrasted-groups scales tended to possess relatively moderate validity for the entire range of criteria, the other scale sets tended to do either very well or very poorly. This pattern held under a variety of prediction techniques, ranging from simple to highly complex, and for differing numbers of scales as predictors (Goldberg, 1972).

In the terminology of Cronbach and Gleser (1965), multiscale empirical inventories, such as the CPI and MMPI, appear to encompass a "broad band" of criterion variance, while possessing only moderate "fidelity" for the measurement of any one criterion variable. In contrast, inventories constructed under other strategies, such as factor-analytic and theoretical, appear to possess relatively high "fidelity" for the measurement of a "narrow band" of criterion measures. It must be emphasized that such an extrapolation is based on the single study by Goldberg and Hase. Whether such a generalization can be extended to other item pools, other scale sets, and other criterion measures is a matter for much-needed future investigations.

Components of Variance Due to Method

By *item characteristics* we refer to a broad class of quantifiable, nonsubstantive aspects of items employed under any test construction strategy. Variance which can be attributed to such characteristics, and particularly to their distributional properties within a scale or pool of items, will be referred to as *method variance*. The effects of such variation are manifested primarily in two ways: (a) item characteristics may interact with (or be confounded with) other sources of variance and thereby obscure the interpretation of the meaning of test responses, and (b) the distribution of item characteristics over the total pool of items may severely restrict or determine the kinds of scales that may be constructed from the item pool. Rather than attempting to present an exhaustive list of possible item characteristics, we shall consider only those which have received recent emphasis.

Social desirability. On several occasions we have referred to social desirability as a judged or *rated* property of a personality item. The procedure for scaling the desirability or favorability of personality test items was first introduced by Edwards (1953). A group of judges are requested to rate the desirability or undesirability of each member of a pool of items on a nine-place rating scale such as that illustrated in Figure 9.7. Ratings are averaged across judges to provide a mean or average social desirability scale value (SDSV) for each item, as well as an index of the dispersion of ratings for that item (Messick and Jackson, 1961).

Item: "To like to punish your enemies."

Undesirable								*Desirable*
—	X	—	—	—	—	—	—	—
Extreme	Strong	Moderate	Mild	Neutral	Mild	Moderate	Strong	Extreme
(1)	(2)	(3)	(4)	(5)	(6)	(7)	(8)	(9)

Fig. 9.7 Social desirability rating scale. (After Edwards, 1957, p. 4)

One of the more remarkable properties of such SDSVs is their stability across diverse cultural and subcultural groups. Although most SDSVs employed in assessment research have been based on ratings obtained from college students, such ratings are highly correlated with those obtained from groups of neurotics, schizophrenics, sex offenders, mental defectives, alcoholics, and novice nuns (Edwards, 1970, p. 91). Thus, although members of diverse subcultural groups may not themselves possess "desirable" traits, they are quite capable of recognizing what is generally considered desirable in our culture.

During the past 20 years, an unprecedented amount of research has been devoted to the item characteristic of social desirability scale value (Edwards,

1957, 1967, 1970). Note that we are distinguishing the rated *item* character-istic of social desirability value from the *subject* characteristic of social desirability response style. However, the two are closely related (Boe and Kogan, 1964), and the mean and variance of SDSVs in a given item pool will influence the extent to which social desirability response styles will be manifest in responses to a given inventory (Wiggins, 1962). If the distribution of the item characteristic of SDSV in a given pool of items is *bimodal* (extremely desirable and extremely undesirable), as in the MMPI, the opportunities for the emergence of social desirability response style will be enhanced (Edwards, 1967). Should the distribution of SDSVs in an item pool be flat and of neutral value, such opportunities are minimized. Although SDSVs have been studied in relation to several other item characteristics, the greatest amount of research effort has been expended in the investigation of the relationship between SDSVs and the item characteristic of endorsement frequency.

Endorsement frequency. The frequency or proportion of subjects in a given population who answer *true* to an item has been variously referred to as "probability of endorsement" (Edwards, 1953), "popularity" (Wahler, 1965) and "communality" (Wiggins, 1962). Unlike social desirability, endorsement frequency (EF) is not invariant under changes in the population of subjects, and therefore it must be defined with reference to a specific rating group. Although this characteristic is determined by both subjects and items, it represents a scalable characteristic of items which may be obtained without reference to item content. The distribution of EFs within a given item pool will have implications for both the internal consistency (Jones and Goldberg, 1967) and potential discriminant validity of scales constructed from that pool. For example, Ullmann and Wiggins (1962) found a large proportion of MMPI items to have consistently extreme endorsement percentages (e.g., 5%, 95%) across *both* normal and abnormal groups, and they concluded that such a pool was inefficient as a source of group-discriminative items.

In large and reasonably representative item pools, the correlation be-tween rated SDSVs and endorsement frequencies is close to .90 (Edwards, 1966b). As one would expect, items with high SDSVs tend to be endorsed by substantial proportions of subjects whereas items of low values tend not to be endorsed. This relationship can be manipulated by restriction of range of one or the other of these item characteristics or by selection of items in which these characteristics are unrelated or even negatively related (e.g., "I have never told a lie"). That these two characteristics place severe restrictions on response variance may be concluded from demonstrations that the principal dimensions of the MMPI may be reproduced by con-structing artificial scales solely on the basis of SDSVs and EFs (Edwards, 1966a; Wiggins and Lovell, 1965).

Keying direction. Responses to structured test items are typically restricted to such options as "true-false," "agree-disagree," or "yes-no." For items selected under a rational or construct-oriented strategy, there will be a definite association between item keying (*true* or *false*) and certain other item characteristics, such as the grammatical characteristic of positive versus negative phrasing and the presumed or rated content of the item. Even under an empirical strategy of item selection, these associations between keying, phrasing, and content will generally hold. The manner in which items are phrased by an item writer will determine, to a large extent, the *proportion* of true-keyed and false-keyed items in scales eventually developed from the item pool. A personality scale that has a disproportionate number of items keyed in a single direction (e.g., *true*) is likely to confound content with acquiescent response style. The classic example of such confounding is the California *F* scale, in which all items are keyed *true* and in which the closely related traits of acquiescence and authoritarianism are completely confounded (Bass, 1955; Messick and Jackson, 1958).

It has now become standard practice to attempt to restrict the acquiescence-eliciting potential of a scale by "balancing" the number of true- and false-keyed items. Although such balancing is a step in the right direction, it does not ensure that the resultant scale will be entirely unconfounded with acquiescence (Jackson, 1967c). The true and false halves of the scale may differ in means, variances, and item intercorrelations, and hence the true-keyed items, for example, may contribute differentially to the total score variance, and there may be a differential contribution of true-variance to the factorial structure of a scale or set of scales (Wiggins, 1968).

Other item characteristics. Among the item characteristics that have been the subject of recent interest are *item ambiguity* (Goldberg, 1963; Harris and Baxter, 1965), *item "objectionability"* (Butcher and Tellegen, 1966), *item stability* (Jones and Goldberg, 1967), *item serial position* (Cowen and Stiller, 1959), and a variety of *item grammatical classifications*, such as person, voice, tense, sentence structure, negation, relative temporal frequency, and sentence length (Wiggins, 1964b). The distribution of and interrelationships among item characteristics in a given pool may place severe restrictions on the kinds of scales that may be derived from that pool. Wiggins and Goldberg (1965) studied the interrelationships among a number of item characteristics in the MMPI item pool. They concluded that the over- and under-representation of certain classes of characteristics tend to make the pool unnecessarily homogeneous. Further, they indicated that the fortuitous confounding of such characteristics with substantive dimensions creates interpretative problems that may never be satisfactorily resolved within this particular fixed pool of items.

Components of Variance Due to Style

If nothing else, the recent response style controversy has sensitized us to the *possibility* that a variety of habitual response tendencies that operate independently of item content may significantly determine variance in response to structured test items. Examples of such styles would be tendencies to be critical (Frederiksen and Messick, 1959), acquiescent (Messick, 1967), socially acceptable (Edwards, 1957), or extreme (Hamilton, 1968) in one's manner of self-presentation. However, in order for such constructs to have referents other than the item characteristics just discussed, at least two conditions must be met: (a) within a reasonably heterogeneous population, *individual differences* among subjects should be observed in the expression of the purported style, and (b) across a broad range of content and a somewhat more restricted range of item characteristics, *response consistencies* must be observed (Wiggins, 1968). The first condition ensures that such constructs are nontrivial since dispositions that have the same constant value for all subjects have little explanatory power in differential psychology. The condition of generalizability demands that such constructs provide unique explanations. A "style to answer *true* to certain items relating to health on the MMPI" could never be unraveled from the content or method variance of the pool of items involved.

The final chapter on the response style controversy has yet to be written. At the present time, there seem to be at least several such purported styles that represent potential variance to be contended with in the construction of personality scales. Edwards' (1957) *SD* scale, which presumably measures typical or characteristic favorable self-presentation, appears to be so content-confounded that explanations of its correlates are not unique. However, Edwards (1970) has subsequently derived a variety of experimental social desirability scales which are less subject to this criticism and which exhibit the same properties. As indicated previously, the problem of distinguishing social desirability from content in self-reports is no different than the problem of distinguishing evaluation from description in peer ratings or in studies of impression formation in social psychology. Resolutions of this paradox in one area of psychology are likely to have salutary effects in other areas as well.

Tendencies to falsify self-report by dissimulating, lying, "faking good," role-playing, or impression management have been known to exist from the inception of personality inventories, and efforts were made early to identify and control such tendencies (e.g., Meehl and Hathaway, 1946). Among the more promising individual-difference measures of such tendencies are the Marlowe-Crowne social desirability scale (Crowne and Marlowe, 1964), Gough's (1952) good impression scale, and Wiggins' (1959) role-playing scale. The problem with such dissimulation scales, of course, is that one never *really* knows whether a high-scoring subject is a saint or a liar. Nevertheless, the aforementioned scales have all demonstrated some success in identifying subjects who have been instructed to create a favorable impression or who are thought, on other grounds, to be dissimulating.

The current status of acquiescence measures is less certain. In addition to the previously discussed problem of unraveling acquiescent style from content, various proposed measures of acquiescence have shown little generalizability across item characteristics, having tended to be virtually uncorrelated with one another, and they have been noticeably lacking in external correlates that would provide independent corroboration of their construct validity (Broen and Wirt, 1958; Forehand, 1962; McGee, 1962a, 1962b, 1962c; Rorer, 1965; Quinn and Lichtenstein, 1965; Siller and Chipman, 1963; Stricker, 1963). The lack of convergent validity among presumed measures of acquiescence has led some authors (Jackson and Messick, 1962b; Wiggins, 1964a) to suggest that there may be several "kinds" of acquiescence which are differentially mediated by different item characteristics. But Rorer (1965) wonders where this proliferation of acquiescence might end. In his view, consideration of all potentially relevant item characteristics would lead to a different acquiescence score for every item in an inventory.

Components of Variance Due to Content

Jackson and Messick's (1958) influential distinction between content and style in personality assessment was, at least in part, motivated by their desire to measure the former class of variables with greater precision. However, at one phase of their involvement in the response style controversy, they appeared to set the unfortunate precedent of defining content variance by default. In their factor analyses of MMPI clinical scales, content variance was identified as variance which survived after the extraction of two potent sources of content-confounded stylistic variance—acquiescence and social desirability (Jackson and Messick, 1962b). As Jackson (1971) has forcefully argued elsewhere, content is much more than what is "left over" when sources of strategic, method, and stylistic variance have been removed from a scale or inventory. Content is, in fact, what our scales are about, as distinct from how that "what" might be measured.

With the possible exception of Berg (1959),[5] no proponent of any strategy of scale construction has seriously denied the possibility of measuring substantive dimensions of personality. The authors of the early rational inventories were somewhat naive in their uncritical acceptance of face validity

---

5. In a more recent publication, Berg (1967) has indicated that his position on item content has "occasionally been misunderstood" and he acknowledges that his chapter title "The unimportance of test item content" may have been somewhat misleading (p. 174, footnote 4). Nevertheless, there is little in this more recent publication that serves to clarify what appears to be a widespread misunderstanding of Berg's position.

and tended to be conceptually vague, but they were convinced, nevertheless, that they were measuring "something." Although advocates of empirical strategies placed a heavy emphasis on external validity and were skeptical of the value of rational approaches, the nomological network of constructs presumably measured by MMPI scales is exceedingly rich (Dahlstrom and Welsh, 1960). But it was not until the implications of *construct validity* [as defined by Cronbach and Meehl (1955), extended by Loevinger (1957), and implemented by Jackson (1967b)] became apparent that the full possibilities of measuring substantive dimensions of personality were realized.

SUMMARY

We have chosen to define structured tests in terms of the restrictions placed on response options which lead to high reliability of scoring. Other emphases in definition are permissible although none, including this one, are entirely satisfactory. Historically, it is possible to distinguish three relatively divergent points of view regarding the "meaning" of responses to structured personality tests. The correspondence (rational) point of view assumes a direct correspondence between the verbal report of a subject and his internal states or feelings. The Woodworth Personal Data Sheet was described as an early example of a rational inventory. The unrealistic nature of the correspondence assumption was challenged by proponents of the instrumental (empirical) viewpoint. The latter point of view restricts the "meaning" of a structured test response to the demonstrated empirical correlates of such a response. Items developed under the instrumental viewpoint often bear little surface resemblance to the criteria they predict. Such discrepancies are assumed to reflect our current lack of knowledge of the relationships between verbal behavior in the test situation and criterion behaviors outside the test situation. The Strong Vocational Interest Blank and the Minnesota Multiphasic Personality Inventory were considered as representatives of empirical inventories.

The substantive (construct) point of view assumes that a response to a structured personality test represents a manifestation of an underlying personality construct. Tests developed under this point of view are evaluated with respect to their construct validity. Three classes of interrelated considerations enter into such an evaluation. (a) Substantive considerations require that items be sampled systematically from a specified universe of content, that the initial item pool include items of both relevant and irrelevant content, and that more than one response format be investigated. (b) Structural considerations require that the degree of intercorrelations among items in a scale reflect the homogeneity of external behaviors implied by the trait, and that the items be combined in a scale under a measurement model that mirrors the manner in which nontest manifestations of the trait are organized. (c) External considerations require that the resultant scale be correlated with relevant external manifestations of the trait (convergent validity) and uncorrelated with irrelevant or possibly confounding measures (discriminant validity). The Personality Research Form was discussed as an example of a test developed under the construct viewpoint.

A more accurate historical account of the development of personality inventories would place greater emphasis on the extensive body of research relating to response styles, sets, and biases in structured personality tests. The deviation hypothesis assumes that statistically deviant response patterns are general and that deviant behavior patterns in critical areas (criteria) will thereby be associated with deviant behavior patterns in noncritical areas (responses to structured tests). A corollary of this hypothesis is that the content of personality test items is relatively unimportant in the sense that discriminations between criterion groups in critical areas can be achieved on the basis of deviant response patterns to an almost infinite variety of test stimuli. Proponents of response style interpretations of scores on personality tests have called attention to a variety of habitual response tendencies that operate independently of item content and thus constrain the extent to which scales may be thought of as measuring substantive dimensions of personality. Social desirability response styles reflect organized dispositions within individuals to respond to personality items in terms of their perceived social acceptability across a variety of substantive domains. Acquiescent response styles reflect organized tendencies to agree to personality items as self-descriptive, independently of the particular content of the items.

A complete understanding of the relations between test responses and criterion behaviors can come about only through recognition of each of the many components that determine response and through an understanding of their relations to one another. A distinction was made among four hypothetical components of variance that seem to be involved in assessment via structured techniques. (a) Strategic variance refers to sources of variation which may be considered by-products of the particular strategy (rational, empirical, factor-analytic) under which a scale was constructed. (b) Method variance refers to a broad class of quantifiable, nonsubstantive aspects of items which may interact with other sources of variance or whose distribution within a given item pool may restrict or determine the kinds of scales that can be constructed. (c) Stylistic variance stems from organized dispositions within individuals to respond in a consistent manner across a variety of substantive domains. (d) Content variance represents the external manifestation of an underlying personality construct or trait. The complex procedures for estimating content variance (construct validity) must be implemented with due regard for possible sources of strategic, method, and stylistic variance as well.

Part III

THE PRACTICE OF PERSONALITY ASSESSMENT

CHAPTER 10

MODELS AND STRATEGIES
IN PERSONALITY ASSESSMENT

THE NATURE OF PERSONALITY THEORY

Historical Background

As a branch of scientific knowledge, *personality theory* occupies an ambiguous position with respect to related areas of behavioral science. Personality theory is that subdiscipline of psychology which is concerned with the development of a comprehensive theoretical framework for the understanding of human behavior. Such a goal is, of course, indistinguishable from the eventual aims of general psychology. Given what appear to be identical goals, it becomes necessary to inquire into the possible distinctions that might be made between personality theory and what might be called *general behavior theory*. To understand this subtle but important distinction, it is helpful to view both fields of inquiry within a historical context.

Speculations on the nature of man are as old as man himself, and the early writings on this subject by the classical philosophers may be considered as the origins of both personality theory and general behavior theory. With the advent of what is now considered to be "scientific psychology" and particularly during the early part of the present century, several distinctive and divergent approaches to the understanding of human behavior became discernible. At the risk of oversimplification, we may designate these trends as philosophical, theological, scientific, and humanistic. The grand traditions of philosophical inquiry into the nature of man are still present today in such specialized branches of philosophy as the philosophy of mind. Theology, which is concerned with man's salvation and his relation to a Higher Being, is still very much with us today, both as a specialized branch of knowledge and as a social movement. Although both philosophy and theology have had profound influences on the development of psychology (Kantor, 1953), they should be clearly distinguished from both scientific and humanistic disciplines.

443

Scientific psychology was the stepchild of nineteenth-century physiology and philosophy and the grandfather of contemporary behavior theory. Under the influence of Wundt and other pioneers in the German laboratories, the subject matter of human behavior was classified as falling within the domain of the natural sciences. Scientific psychology was dedicated to the principle of controlled observation and the collection of empirical facts which would lend themselves to the statement of general laws of human behavior. Having identified the subject matter of psychology as a specialized class of phenomena within the natural sciences, the early scientific psychologists adopted methods of inquiry which closely resembled those employed in the physical and biological sciences of that era. Scientific psychology became a laboratory-based science that concerned itself with phenomena that could be carefully and objectively studied under controlled circumstances. The experimental investigations conducted in early psychological laboratories produced a body of facts which influenced the direction of psychological laws and other theoretical conceptualizations.

Scientific psychology flourished in the period between 1898 and 1912 (Woodworth, 1931), and psychological laboratories were established in many parts of the world. Although early investigators shared a conviction that psychology was a natural science, the specific aspects of human behavior which were considered as starting points for controlled observation varied considerably from laboratory to laboratory. The diversity of opinion as to which aspects of human behavior were most central to the development of a science of human behavior served to consolidate different laboratories into "schools" or "systems" of psychology (Woodworth, 1931). Thus we can distinguish structuralism, functionalism, associationism, Gestalt psychology, and behaviorism as different constellations of viewpoints regarding the manner in which a comprehensive theoretical explanation of human behavior can best be attained. These schools or systems of psychology are the direct predecessors of modern theories of behavior.

The scientific psychologists of the nineteenth century were academic men pursuing their interests within university settings which were free from the pressures of the outside world (Hall and Lindzey, 1957). The subject matter of scientific psychology has traditionally been dictated by intellectual rather than social or commercial concerns. Those aspects of human behavior which are of greatest concern to society seem to be precisely those which do not lend themselves readily to controlled scientific observation. As a consequence, the subject matter of scientific psychology has tended to be somewhat far removed from the problems confronting human beings in the same period of history.

Because personality theory is that branch of psychology which has traditionally been most responsive to the exigencies of human existence, the trend represented by this field may be thought of as "humanistic," as distinguished from the more detached "scientific" pursuit of knowledge. As Hall and Lindzey (1957) have observed, it was no accident that the founders of modern personality theory (Janet, Charcot, Freud, Jung, and McDougall) were practicing physicians whose daily practice demanded a rationale and a set of procedures for coping with the psychological problems presented by their patients.

Those circumstances of nineteenth-century psychiatric practice which demanded an immediate comprehensive theory of personality gave rise to a kind of theorizing that was distinctively different from that of scientific psychology. Hall and Lindzey (1957) list the following five characteristics of personality theory which distinguish it from general behavior theory: (a) dissent from traditional academic theory, (b) concern with practical problems, (c) concern with causes of behavior, (d) treatment of the whole person, and (e) concern with integrating diverse findings. These characteristics of personality theory were dictated, not by the personal tastes or inclinations of the theorists, but by the demands of the medical practice they faced.

As would be expected from the different purposes and emphases of personality theory and general behavior theory, the two disciplines developed in relative isolation from each other. The subject matter of scientific psychology (reaction time, rote memory, etc.) was considered by humanistic psychologists to be contrived, sterile, and far removed from the everyday problems that confronted their patients. From the viewpoint of scientific psychologists, the subject matter of humanistic psychology (dreams, emotional conflicts, etc.) was too ephemeral and intuitive to form a basis for scientific investigation.

Both personality theory and general behavior theory underwent rapid development in the two decades following the turn of the century. By the late twenties, signs of an imminent "rapprochement" between the two disciplines were in evidence. In 1927, Henry A. Murray was appointed to the faculty of Harvard, at the suggestion of Morton Prince, and a new era of personality theory began. The subsequent appointment of Gordon Allport at the same institution and the gradual shift of interests of Gardner Murphy at Columbia set the stage for the development of an eclectic or middle-ground approach to theories of human behavior. It was the intent of these three famous academic personologists (Murray, Allport, and Murphy) to develop a theoretical framework for viewing human behavior that combined the rigor of the laboratory with the immediacy of the clinic. Scores of their students continue this enterprise today.

The gap between general behavior theory and personality theory was further narrowed by attempts from within the major theoretical systems of each camp to broaden their scope. Dollard and Miller (1950) sought to

reformulate the general behavior theory of Clark Hull (1943) in such a way
as to make it compatible with the personality theory of Sigmund Freud (1943).
Concurrently, certain developments within the personality theory of psychoanalysis (Hartmann, 1958; Rapaport, 1960) opened up new avenues of
communication between psychoanalysis and academic psychology (Gill,
1959).

Given the foregoing historical trends, one might anticipate that we are
on the threshold of the Golden Age of general psychological theory. Although
it would be premature to attempt to evaluate the age in which we live, it
does seem that quite the opposite trend is taking place. This observation is
based on the remarkably parallel developments that have recently taken
place in both general behavior theory and personality theory. Within general
academic psychology, Woodworth's (1931) "schools" of psychology became
more narrowly defined as "theories of learning" in Hilgard's (1948) classic
treatment of that subject matter. The two decades that followed the appearance of the latter work were characterized by increased experimentation and
decreased emphasis on general theories of behavior. Psychological theorizing
became narrower in scope and more precise in detail, as exemplified by the
mathematical "models" of limited behavioral phenomena. In other quarters
of experimentation, B. F. Skinner's (1950) decidedly antitheoretical viewpoint
gained wide acceptance, and experimental psychology became increasingly
"data-orientated."

Within the realm of personality theory, it is possible that Hall and
Lindzey's (1957) *Theories of Personality* served as an epitaph for grand-scale
theorizing in the humanistic tradition. In this connection it is interesting to
note that the authors state in their preface: "It is our hope that this volume
will serve a function in the area of personality similar to that served by
Hilgard's *Theories of Learning* in the area of learning" (Hall and Lindzey,
1957, p. vii). The decade following the publication of the Hall and Lindzey
text was one of increased experimentation and research in the area of
personality, accompanied by a decreased emphasis on grand-scale conceptualizations. As personality has become more firmly established as an
academic discipline, the model of the "academic personologist" has changed
from that of theorist to that of data gatherer. Contemporary personality
research is characterized by experimentation and increasingly precise
measurement in relatively limited behavioral domains (e.g., anxiety, authoritarianism, need achievement). It appears unlikely that a general integrative
theory of human behavior will be developed in the near future, and this is
not necessarily a cause for alarm. The balanced observation of Hall and
Lindzey remains true today:

*It is still not clear whether the path to a comprehensive and useful theory of
human behavior will proceed most rapidly from the work of those who have*

aimed directly at such a goal, or whether it will eventually owe more to the efforts of those who have focused upon relatively specific and delimited problems. (1957, p. 5)

Dimensions for Evaluating Personality Theories

Formal Dimensions

Although personality theories differ from general theories of behavior in the ways already discussed, they are nevertheless subject to evaluation by the same criteria that are applied to any theoretical system. Those criteria typically involve such features as the formal or structural characteristics of the theory, the particular methodology employed in generating hypotheses, and the extent to which the theory is related to empirical phenomena. An illustrative outline for appraising the formal aspects of a theory is given in Table 10.1. This particular outline was employed by the "Dartmouth group" (Estes, Koch, MacCorquodale, Meehl, Mueller, Schoenfeld, and Verplanck, 1954), who took upon themselves the task of evaluating the five major contemporary theories of learning. Although developed with reference to theories of learning (general theories of behavior), this outline might equally well be applied to any systematic formulation that aspires to be a theory. A similar outline was adopted by the American Psychological Association study group that undertook the task of evaluating all the major systematic positions in psychology (Koch, 1959, pp. 666–673).

By almost any of the formal criteria, theories of personality turn out to be rather poor theories. Theories of personality are generally lacking in clarity and explicitness, and they have not been sufficiently formalized to allow for the generation of hypotheses by formal axiomatic deduction. Because of the characteristic vagueness of personality theories and their lack of formalization, it is difficult to subject the systematic positions to empirical test. Further, since few personality theories seem to qualify even minimally as formal theories, it is difficult to make meaningful comparisons among personality theories on such criteria. The theoretical positions of Lewin (Cartwright, 1959), Cattell (1959), Murray (1959), Freud (Rapaport, 1960), and Rogers (1959) have been evaluated by the formal criteria adopted by the American Psychological Association study group. Although these analyses are among the most penetrating and illuminating that have been made of the systems involved, it was necessary to depart widely from the formal standards in order to give an accurate description of most of the theoretical positions involved.

Substantive Dimensions

It is difficult to compare theories of personality along the formal dimensions of theory construction, but it is quite meaningful to compare them with respect to their positions on certain issues that must be faced by any theory of

Table 10.1 Outline for the formal evaluation of theories (from Estes *et al.*, 1954, pp. xiii–xv)

I. Structure of the Theory

    A. Delineation of empirical area
        1. Data language
           Is the data language explicit and theoretically neutral?
           How does the theorist relate his empirical variables to the data language?
        2. Dependent and independent variables
           How does the selection of variables compare with those of other theories?
           What influence does the choice of variables exert upon the form of the theory?
        3. Relation between empirical areas covered and orientative attitudes exhibited by the theorist

    B. Theoretical concepts
        1. Primitive terms
           Are the primitive terms of the theory reducible to physical or object language?
           Is the usage of primitive terms fixed by implicit or explicit definitions?
        2. Principal constructs
           Do these serve only a summarizing function or are they related by definition or by hypothesis to terms of other disciplines (e.g., physiology)?
        3. Relations assumed among constructs
           How are the major theoretical variables interrelated in the foundation assumptions of the theory?
           How are such interrelations constructed from the observation base of the theory?
        4. Relations assumed or derived between constructs and experimentally defined variables

---

personality. Such an approach has been employed fruitfully by Hall and Lindzey (1957) in their classic text. The columns of Table 10.2 list the major substantive issues employed by Hall and Lindzey as a basis for comparing theories of personality. Whereas theories may be *evaluated* by formal criteria such as those listed in Table 10.1, the substantive dimensions found in Table 10.2 are primarily *descriptive* and therefore "neutral" from the standpoint of evaluation (Hall and Lindzey, 1957). The rows of Table 10.2 list 17 major personality theorists who have been classified as emphasizing (high), giving moderate emphasis to (moderate), or deemphasizing (low) each of the substantive issues. For example, Allport places heavy emphasis on the dimension of purpose, whereas Miller and Dollard tend to deemphasize it.

II. Methodologic Characteristics

    A. Standing of the theory on principal methodologic "dimensions"
        1. Explicit axiomatization
        2. Quantitativeness
        3. Consistency and independence of principal theoretical assumptions

    B. Techniques of derivation
       Are the empirical consequences of the theory developed by informal arguments or formal derivations?

III. Empirical Content and Adequacy

    A. Range of data for which interpretation or explanation in terms of the theory has been claimed

    B. Specificity of prediction demonstrated

    C. Obvious failures to handle facts in the area III A

    D. Tours-de-force
       Has it been possible to predict new experimental phenomena?
       Have any predictions of this sort been confirmed?
       Does the theory account for facts not predictable from computing theories in the same area?

    E. Sensitivity to empirical evidence

    F. Programmaticity

    G. Special virtues or limitations; techniques which may prove useful outside the context of the specific theory

Although the Hall-Lindzey table was constructed as a pedagogic device to facilitate comparison of theorists on substantive issues, it is tempting to assign numerical values to the ratings in their matrix for the purpose of discovering the principal dimensions underlying their comparisons of theorists. Cartwright (1957) was the first to yield to this temptation by factor-analyzing the correlations among the rows of Table 10.2. Subsequently, Taft (1960) and Schuh (1966) performed cluster analyses on the same data. As would be expected from the different multivariate procedures employed by Cartwright, Taft, and Schuh, the three solutions differed from one another in details. Nevertheless, a comparison of the results of the different analyses reveals that three factors may be clearly identified as emerging in each study.

Table 10.2 Substantive comparison of personality theories (from Hall and Lindzey, 1957, p. 548)

	Purpose	Unconscious determinants	Reward	Contiguity	Learning process	Personality structure	Heredity	Early developmental experience	Continuity of development	Organismic emphasis	Field emphasis	Uniqueness	Psychological environment	Self concept	Group membership determinants	Interdisciplinary emphasis — Biology	Interdisciplinary emphasis — Social science	Multiplicity of motives
Freud	H	H	H	M	L	H	H	H	H	M	L	M	H	M	L	H	M	L
Jung	H	H	M	L	L	H	H	M	L	H	L	M	M	M	L	H	L	M
Adler	H	M	L	L	L	M	H	H	H	M	H	H	M	H	H	M	H	L
Horney	H	H	M	L	M	M	L	M	M	M	M	M	M	H	H	L	H	L
Fromm	H	M	M	L	M	M	M	M	M	H	M	M	H	H	H	L	H	L
Sullivan	H	L	M	L	M	M	L	L	H	L	H	H	H	H	H	M	M	M
Lewin	H	L	L	M	L	M	M	L	L	H	H	H	H	M	L	L	M	H
Allport	H	H	M	L	L	H	M	L	L	H	L	H	M	H	M	H	L	H
Murray	H	H	M	L	L	H	H	H	L	H	L	H	H	M	L	H	H	H
Sheldon	L	M	M	L	L	H	H	L	H	H	L	M	L	L	L	H	L	L
Eysenck	L	L	H	L	H	L	H	L	M	L	L	L	L	L	L	H	H	L
Cattell	M	M	L	M	M	H	L	L	M	L	L	M	L	H	M	M	L	H
Miller and Dollard	L	M	L	M	M	L	M	M	H	L	M	L	L	L	M	H	L	M
Angyal	H	L	L	L	M	H	M	L	H	H	M	L	H	L	L	M	H	M
Goldstein	H	M	L	L	M	L	L	L	L	H	M	L	H	H	L	H	L	L
Rogers	H	M	L	L	M	L	L	L	M	H	M	M	H	H	L	L	L	L
Murphy	H	M	H	H	H	H	H	H	H	H	H	M	M	M	H	H	H	H

Key: H high (emphasized).   M moderate.   L low (deemphasized).

Factor I includes those neo-Freudian theorists who emphasized the social and cultural determinants of behavior, while giving only moderate emphasis to structural concepts (Adler, Fromm, Horney, and Sullivan). Factor II includes the self theorists whose organismic approach emphasized purposiveness in human behavior (Angyal, Goldstein, Rogers, and Allport). Factor III includes theorists who placed a heavy emphasis on personality structure, heredity, and the biological determinants of behavior, while tending to de-emphasize learning processes (Eysenck, Freud, Sheldon, Jung, and Murray).

The Hall-Lindzey table compares theorists within single substantive dimensions. It was not meant to compare substantive dimensions within theorists (e.g., How much emphasis did Freud place on purpose in comparison with unconscious determinants?) although at least one multivariate analysis appears to have been performed under this assumption (Schuh, 1966). Nevertheless, it is a common practice to classify theories on the basis of the substantive issues to which they give the greatest *relative* emphasis. Thus one may differentiate among self theories, social theories, cognitive theories, learning theories, constitutional theories, factor theories, developmental theories, etc. The classification of personality theories in terms of such substantive groupings has generally provided a more realistic basis for comparing theories than the use of more formal dimensions.

Metaphorical Dimensions

A third set of dimensions along which personality theories can be evaluated pertains to the metaphor, or analogy, employed by the theorist to describe human behavior. This aspect of personality theory cuts across both formal and substantive dimensions. The importance of the metaphor as a dimension for the evaluation of personality theories has received recent emphasis in the writings of Mehrabian (1968). The thrust of Mehrabian's argument seems to be that all personality theories are constructed with some metaphor, or analogy, in mind and that the structure of these theories may be better understood by making explicit what is often an implicitly assumed metaphor. This argument is perhaps best understood by considering the role of metaphorical reasoning in theory construction in general.

Metaphorical Reasoning and Theory Construction

Metaphorical reasoning involves the reconstruction of a given domain of objects and events in terms of another, often more familiar, domain of objects and events. For example, the interpretation of events in the brain and central nervous system as isomorphic with the events that occur in an electronic digital computer provides a new and useful way of viewing brain function (Ashby, 1960). Although such "reasoning by analogy" has long been resisted by logicians and philosophers of science, the achievements of certain representational "models" in both physics and psychology have recently led to a major reassessment of such approaches to theory construction. In fact, whereas "models" were once viewed as a rather specialized class of psychological theories, it is now held that no current psychological theory is free of analogical reasoning (Lachman, 1960).

A theory consists of a set of postulates or assumptions that, together with rules of inference, allow for the deduction of theorems. When theorems are interpreted or coordinated with behavioral events, the empirical validation of the theory becomes possible. Analogical reasoning may enter at any or all of these levels of theory. Analogical reasoning at the levels of (a) postulates, (b) rules of inference, and (c) empirical coordination has been termed "representation," "inference," and "interpretation," respectively (Lachman, 1960).

At the level of the basic assumptions of a theory, it might be asserted that the phenomenon in question is best *represented* or construed in terms of another domain of events. Thus one may construe brain events "as if" they were the events of an electronic digital computer. Once the basic postulates have been stated, rules of inference or propositional calculi are required to generate formal deductions or theorems. Although such rules of inference are typically verbal or mathematical in nature, analogical inference is equally possible and has become increasingly common. Thus the rules of *inference* of a computer may guide formal deduction at this point. Theorems, therefore, may be stated in verbal, mathematical, or analogical form (Simon and Newell, 1956), and a specific *interpretation* of these theorems must be made in order to coordinate them with empirical events so that their validity may be subjected to test. Analogical reasoning is perhaps the most common interpretation which guides the coordination of mathematically stated theorems with a given domain of events.

It is important to note that at no level of the theory is the "truth" of the model or analogue at issue. The consequences of adopting a particular model can be compared with the consequences of adopting a different model, but the validity of the model cannot be determined independently of such consequences. Although events may be "conceived" as existing independently of our constructs, there is no way of "knowing" events independently of our constructs about them (Kelly, 1955).

Metaphorical Reasoning in Personality Theory

The foregoing section was concerned with the *explicit* use of metaphorical reasoning in formal theory construction. Since we have already stated that personality theories fall short of meeting the rigorous requirements of formal theory construction, it might appear that an examination of the role of analogical reasoning in personality theory would be mainly an academic enterprise. To the contrary, however, Mehrabian (1968) has demonstrated that a deeper understanding of the nature of an existing personality theory may be obtained through careful consideration of the *implicit* metaphor that the theorist had in mind when he constructed his theory. Although formal theories, in their finished form, tend to be explicitly stated deductive systems, personality theories typically begin with observation and arrive at propositional statements inductively. This process is viewed by Mehrabian as involving the use of *metaphors*, at the level of observation, at the level of postulates, and at the level of rules of inference. He describes the process as follows:

Theoretical activity may typically proceed from a state in which an observer employs an implicit metaphor or analogy from an area more familiar to him in his attempts to develop concepts to order or make sense out of a novel set of phenomena. As the observer or theorist tries to communicate his observations to others, the translated categories which are based on his metaphor become more explicit because he describes the events by ordering them on the various categories. Furthermore, as he hypothesizes relationships between the categories on an a priori basis, that is, prior to systematic observation of experimentation, he may be asked about his rationale, and as he tries to explicate the rationale, the metaphor or analogy is alluded to explicitly. This is because the a priori propositional statements relating the categories are derived from the metaphor. (p. 8) *If the criteria for classification of phenomena into categories are found sufficiently reliable and valid, the theorist proceeds to test some of the propositional statements, derived from the metaphor, which relate the categories to each other. In actual experimentation, such propositional statements are frequently referred to as either basic assumptions of a theory, or hypotheses to be tested.* (p. 14)

In formulating the role of metaphors in personality theory, Mehrabian (1968) places a unique emphasis on the function of metaphors in behavioral observation. Behavioral events are not directly "perceived" by the observer; rather they are selectively *ordered* in terms of a priori constructs held by the observer. Mehrabian contends that the interpretation placed on events by the observer is influenced by an implicit metaphor, thought to be applicable to the events observed. In this connection, Mehrabian calls attention to the fact that language itself consists of a collection of categories and metaphors whose purpose is to provide their users with a system for organizing sense impressions (Whorf, 1956). Thus, not only may the same event be construed differently from the frameworks of different linguistic systems, but even within a given language, observation may be determined by the selection of one possible metaphor from among many alternatives.

According to Mehrabian, the selection of a given metaphor or set of metaphors imposes constraints on observation which, in turn, impose constraints on the categories that develop into propositional statements.

Mehrabian also seems to imply that the rules of inference employed to generate theorems from assumptions will also be constrained by the initial metaphor adopted by the theorist. This need not be true in formal theory construction for, as we have indicated, the use of analogical reasoning at any level of theorizing does not preclude the use of different analogies at other levels. However, the personality theorist is typically not operating under the formal rules of theory construction but rather is "discovering" phenomena which are guided by an implicit metaphor. Should this be the case, a detailed explication of a given personality theory in terms of the underlying metaphor should enhance considerably our understanding of the nature of the theory.

The central role of an implicit metaphor in a personality theory is nowhere better illustrated than in the elaborate spatial-hydraulic metaphor of psychoanalytic theory. Critics of this theory who have ridiculed its "reasoning by analogy" have overlooked the point that psychoanalytic theory has made explicit an analogical basis that is implicit in many competing theories. The current fascination with computer models of personality (Tomkins and Messick, 1963; Loehlin, 1968) may be taken as an indication of the extent to which the current climate of intellectual opinion regarding the role of models in personality theory has changed in the last decade. Whether this change reflects a fundamental reorientation among behavioral scientists or the generally positive regard in which computers are held is difficult to say. In any event, the explication of personality theories in terms of their underlying metaphorical dimensions seems to provide a fruitful basis for their evaluation.

PERSONALITY THEORIES AS ASSESSMENT MODELS

The Role of Theory in Prediction

The preceding rather cursory discussion of personality theories serves to set the stage for a more practical question: To what extent do personality theories facilitate the prediction of human behavior in applied settings? Our concern here is not with the issue of building a comprehensive theory of human behavior, but rather with the more practical consideration of the possibilities of using existing personality theories in realistic selection situations. Regardless of their merit as formal theories, personality theories were developed in a functional context to aid practitioners in making real-life decisions. Therefore, this body of wisdom from the past can hardly be ignored by current practitioners of personality assessment. There is good scientific reason to be skeptical of existing personality theories, however, and the first question to be asked is not *which* personality theory should be applied, but whether *any* personality theory can facilitate prediction.

As indicated in Chapter 1, the prediction paradigm in personality assessment involves several distinct steps, such as criterion analysis, selection of instruments, development of the prediction battery, combination of data, and application of the cross-validated battery. In our discussion of clinical prediction in Chapter 5, we indicated that human judgment may enter, in varying degrees, into each of the steps in the prediction paradigm. The question currently under consideration is whether, and to what extent, human judgment should be *guided* by explicit theoretical considerations at each step in the prediction paradigm. Since human judgment cannot be avoided in some steps, the issue becomes one that pits "common sense" against explicit theoretical orientations. Although this may seem no issue at all, note that "common sense" possesses certain homey virtues, and explicit theoretical orientations. may possess definite limitations. While providing an overall guiding framework for organizing personality data, personality theories, by their very nature, tend to focus on certain theoretically relevant aspects of behavior to the exclusion of others. Consequently, a given theoretical orientation may possess extremely limited predictive value when operating outside of its customary "focus of convenience" (Kelly, 1955).

In order for a personality theory to facilitate prediction at different steps of the paradigm, it must possess the characteristics of *relevance* and *explicitness*. To be useful in prediction, a theoretical formulation must be relevant to the criterion situation at hand, must be explicit enough to suggest the selection of specific testing instruments, must have definite implications for criterion performance, and must be capable of being evaluated. Because the implementation of a theoretical orientation inevitably involves costly personnel, the use of a personality model in a given assessment situation can be justified only if it can be shown to lead to an increment in predictive accuracy over that which would have been obtained in the absence of such a model. More important, and more likely, the use of a personality model can be justified if it can be demonstrated that the assessment procedures developed possess a greater generality of application (to other samples and other assessment situations) than does the use of procedures not guided by theoretical considerations. Finally, the development and implementation of a personality model may be justified on the grounds that a basic contribution to knowledge about human behavior has resulted from the use of the model.

Approaches to the Use of Models

Personality assessment programs can be ordered on a continuum expressing the extent to which an explicit personality model is relied on in generating predictions about human behavior. Such a continuum would be defined at one end by a heavy and explicit use of personality models, and at the other by a total lack of reliance on explicit theoretical considerations. Such a continuum could be applied to each step in the prediction paradigm, but the steps turn out to be correlated in practice although they need not be in principle. Since reliance on theoretical considerations at one step in the prediction paradigm tends to be correlated with reliance on theoretical considerations at other steps, it is possible to make a more global character- ization of personality assessment programs, in which highly theoretically oriented programs (at all steps in the prediction paradigm) are contrasted with programs that are not theoretically oriented.

One such useful classification of approaches to the use of models in personality assessment has been made by Stern, Stein, and Bloom (1956). These authors distinguish two approaches which define the ends of the continuum of reliance on theoretical models (analytic versus empirical) and a third approach (synthetic) which seems to fall in the middle. In a similar distinction made by Taft (1959), the categories of analytic, global, and naive empirical correspond roughly to the analytic, synthetic, and empirical approaches of Stern, Stein, and Bloom (1956), whose distinctions have served to clarify considerably the role of personality theory in assessment and will be considered here in some detail. For examples of these approaches in application and for further exposition of these important distinctions, the reader is referred to the original work (Stern et al., 1956).

The Analytic Approach

The analytic approach to personality assessment differs from other approaches in its heavy reliance on personality theory in defining the criterion, selecting instruments, and assessing candidates. It is the most elaborate of all approaches and consequently the most expensive. Stern et al. (1956) view the analytic approach as the "fundamental paradigm" from which all other methods can be derived. This approach involves several distinct stages, which are illustrated in Figure 10.1 by means of a flow diagram. As each stage of the analytic approach is considered in turn, the reader may find it helpful to refer to the sequential order indicated by the arrows in Figure 10.1.

Situational Analysis

Perhaps the most outstanding characteristic of the analytic approach is its attempted solution of the "criterion problem" (Chapter 1) by means of a theoretically guided criterion analysis. In formulating their solution to the "criterion problem," Stern et al. (1956) have made three distinctions which represent a considerable advance over earlier ways of viewing the problem; they involve the definition of "significant others," the distinction between explicit and implicit criteria, and a differentiation between standards of performance and psychological criteria.

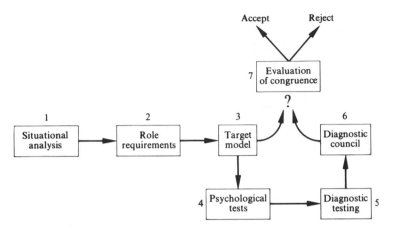

Fig. 10.1 The analytic approach.

Location of significant others. In many complex job situations, the assessor must rely on the ratings of employers or experts as a definition of criterion performance. Individuals whose ratings or opinions in effect *define* the criterion to be predicted are referred to as significant others. The opinions of significant others as to what constitutes "good" or "poor" performance may be widely at variance both with the intuitive standards the assessor holds for evaluating performance in this area and with the way society at large differentiates, or differentially rewards, "good" and "poor" perfor- mance. Although the bias, ignorance, or arbitrariness of a significant other may result in judgments of performance which are "wrong" in some broader context, the assessor cannot ignore the fact that these are the judgments to be predicted. Assessment programs which fail to incorporate the criterion standards of significant others are thereby doomed to failure. Stern *et al.* (1956) entreat the assessor to be a "realist" when operating under criterion standards over which he has no influence.

Although the location or identification of significant others within any organization or institution seems to be a relatively straightforward task, it is not always so. Titular heads of organizations and other "obvious" significant others may not be the ones who make the critical criterion deci- sions. Authority for such decisions may be delegated; or occasionally, there is a "power behind the throne" who assumes responsibility for criterion decisions in the absence of formal delegation of authority. The initial approach to the situational analysis thus involves two steps: the identification of significant others and an analysis of their criterion standards.

Explicit versus implicit criteria. In attempting to define the criteria employed by significant others, one must make a distinction between criteria which are verbalized and covert standards which are implemented in subtle ways. Although such a distinction is not always made by assessment psychologists, it is one the public at large clearly recognizes, as indicated by the number of jokes and cartoons that emphasize it.

In verbalizing his explicit criteria for evaluating performance in a typing pool, a personnel manager, or other significant other, may place heavy emphasis on typing skills, clerical ability, reliability, and emotional maturity. Examination of this significant other's past record of hiring and firing may reveal that performers he rated "good" and "poor" do not significantly differ on any of these characteristics. If the current pool of "satisfactory" typists bears a closer resemblance to a harem than to a business office, the assessor may well suspect that certain *implicit* criteria are operative. Implicit criteria are seldom this obvious, however, and may involve subtle interpersonal characteristics of the significant other. For example, although "independence" and "resourcefulness" may be verbalized as explicit criteria of good performance for graduate students by significant others (faculty), such terms may be implicitly qualified to mean "independence" and "resourcefulness" within a limited range of "proper" intellectual activity.

Standards of performance versus psychological criteria. When one is conceptualizing the nature of the criterion situation, it is important to distinguish between standards of performance set by significant others and the psychological job requirements of the criterion performance. Standards of performance represent *objective* definitions of a criterion, which may be stated in terms of ratings given by significant others or in terms of more objective criteria, such as grade-point average, passing of medical board examinations, and sales records. Although standards of performance are definitely the criteria to be predicted, it would be a mistake to assume that they constitute a *psychologically meaningful* set of distinctions. To say that one group of individuals has a grade-point average of A and that another group has an average of D does not convey any information about the personality characteristics of members of the two groups. Psychological criteria are: "psychological job requirements, stated in psychological terms" (Stern *et al.*, 1956, p. 33). These criteria involve the constellation of psychological traits and motives demanded by the job situation, and they constitute, in the view of Stern and his associates, the "true" criterion. Nonanalytic approaches to personality assessment (e.g., the empirical approach) are forced to restrict their attention to aspects of the standard of performance.

With the distinctions above in mind, the situational analysis is conducted by a team of assessors whose purpose is to clarify the nature of the job situation and to determine the psychological criteria which underlie performance in that situation. Interviews are conducted with significant others, both individually and in group discussions, in an attempt to determine both the explicit and implicit criteria of performance. Although initially broad and unstructured, the interviews become increasingly probing until the assessors are satisfied that they have a feeling for the job situation as perceived by the significant others. Where possible, some employees rated "good" and some rated "poor" in performance are observed and interviewed in an attempt to uncover the psychological demands of the job from the standpoint of the employee. Situational analysis does not involve a specific set of procedures; rather it involves a general approach to uncovering psychological job requirements, and thus the form of the analysis will vary from one situation to another. Regardless of the approach used, the end product of a situational analysis involves an explicit statement of the psychological *role requirements* of the job.

Development of the Target Model

Once the situational analysis has been completed, the assessment team attempts to translate the psychological role requirements into a *personality model* representing the constellation of personality characteristics of a hypothetical individual most likely to succeed in this job situation: ". . . the hypothetical model is an inductive system obtained from systematic examination of the requirements posed by the role previously formulated. It is a description of the type of person who can play the role, spontaneously and characteristically." (Stern *et al.*, 1956, p. 60.) In formulating personality models, Stern and associates prefer to use the transactional personality theory of Murray because of its emphasis on both situational (job conditions) and personal (employee) determinants of behavior. Although there is much to be said for this particular theoretical orientation, note that *any* theory of personality may be employed if the theory is sufficiently explicit to allow the translation of role requirements into a target model. With reference to the personality models to be considered in later sections of the present chapter, one might describe the target model in terms of drives and defenses (psychoanalytic), interpersonal dynamisms (interpersonal), needs and press (transactional), personal constructs (cognitive), ergs and traits (multivariate), or habits and rewards (social learning).

Diagnostic Testing

The main function of the target model is to suggest dimensions of personality that may be assessed by means of psychological testing. Hence an additional requirement of the particular theoretical orientation adopted is that the postulated psychological characteristics be specifiable in terms of testing procedures. Some theoretical orientations clearly lend themselves to this requirement more readily than others. The theoretical orientations considered in later sections of this chapter are those which appear to be potentially translatable into psychological testing terms. Table 10.3 presents illustrative examples of dimensions involved in different personality models and the psychological testing instruments that are typically used to assess such dimensions.

Table 10.3 Examples of instruments employed in assessing target dimensions under different personality models

Model	Typical dimension	Typical instrument
Psychoanalytic	Ego synthesis	Rorschach
Interpersonal	Docility	Interpersonal Check List
Transactional	Need achievement	Activities Index
Cognitive	Cognitive complexity	Role-Construct Repertory Test
Multivariate	Cyclothymia	16 Personality Factor Questionnaire
Social learning	Behavioral competence	Survey of Problematic Situations

Diagnostic testing in the analytic approach typically involves a large battery of instruments and interview procedures, which are administered individually to each candidate. The general philosophy of "multiple" personality assessments is that different testing instruments tap different aspects of personality, all of which may be relevant to the target model (Taft, 1959). A similar rationale underlies the use of multiple assessors, namely, that a more reliable consensus of opinion will be reached when more than one assessor has individual contact with the candidate (Taft, 1959). In the assessment programs conducted by Stern *et al.* (1956), the assessment staff typically consisted of representatives from social psychology, clinical psychology, educational psychology, and mathematical statistics. A typical battery of tests included interviews, biographical questionnaires, interest questionnaires, self-description, the Wechsler Intelligence Test, the Thematic Apperception Test, the Rorschach Test, and the Sentence Completion Test. The composition of the assessment staff and the nature of the testing battery will vary with the assessment problem and the particular theoretical orientation of the group.

The Assessment Conference

After potential job candidates have been assessed by the battery of tests just described, the test data are scored and evaluated and examined in a group meeting of the assessment team. The purpose of this meeting, which is called a "diagnostic council," is to assess, by group consensus, the *congruence* of a given candidate's personality (as inferred from diagnostic testing) with the hypothetical target model (derived from situational analysis). When the personality pattern of the candidate "fits" the hypothetical target model, success is predicted. When there is divergence, failure is predicted (Figure 10.1). The assumption, of course, is that candidates who are most like the hypothetical target model are most likely to succeed on the job.

It is difficult to describe the actual procedures employed in a diagnostic council under the analytic approach. One requirement of such a meeting is that all council members adopt, for the purposes of assessment, a common theoretical frame of reference, i.e., the theoretical frame of reference underlying the target model. Although each council member may represent a different speciality and a somewhat different point of view in assessment, it is necessary that he be able to translate his own specialty or point of view into terms which are meaningful in the context of the target model. It is especially important that material not directly relevant to the hypothetical target model be ignored (Stern *et al.*, 1956). For example, the clinical psychologist typically looks for (and finds) evidence of psychopathology in psychological test results. Such material should *not* be introduced in the diagnostic council unless it has direct bearing on the particular target model under discussion. This specialized orientation acts as a safeguard against prediction in terms of global categories, such as "ideal personality types," which have not been uncovered as relevant in the initial situational analysis. The specific manner in which decisions are reached about the congruence of a candidate's personality with the target model will depend on the theoretical orientation of the council as well as on the characteristics of individual members. In general, the approach to group decisions is "democratic," and there is a thorough airing of sources of disagreement. The final decision as to the "fit" of a candidate is usually unanimous.

Evaluating the Model

As with any assessment program, the overall success of the analytic approach is evaluated with reference to the number of correct decisions made by the assessment procedures (Chapter 6). Because of the expensive and time-consuming nature of the analytic approach, it is desirable to evaluate predictive outcomes as soon as possible. One method of obtaining early evaluation of the predictive success of a given model involves the "blind" assessment of current employees for whom criterion evaluations are already available. Significant others are asked to provide, for experimental purposes, a group of current employees that includes both "good" and "poor" performers on the job, without disclosing the actual criterion evaluations to the assessors. This group of current employees is then run through the diagnostic testing procedures, and each employee is evaluated in the diagnostic council.

Success is predicted for those employees whose diagnostic test results suggest a personality type that is congruent with the hypothetical target model; failure is predicted for those whose test results suggest a highly divergent personality type. The analytic approach is then evaluated in terms of the number of instances in which the predictions of the assessment team match the criterion judgments of significant others.

Because of the small number of experimental subjects typically involved in a blind validation study, and because of the high degree of success anticipated for the analytic approach, only a very small margin of error is tolerated. In a preliminary validation study of an analytic model for selecting theology students, Stern and his associates (1956) were able to identify correctly six out of six students provided by the faculty. An analytic model of teacher trainees was judged to be less successful when only eight out of ten trainees provided by the faculty were correctly identified by blind assessment procedures. Although the "hit rate" achieved in the latter study is well within the tolerance of other approaches, it was considered sufficiently low within the analytic approach to occasion a reevaluation of assessment procedures.

In addition to providing an estimate of the probable degree of success of a given analytic model when applied to a new population of applicants, blind validation studies provide a basis for *revisions* in the target model or in other aspects of the assessment approach. Regardless of the degree of success attained in any given validation study, the target model of the analytic approach is viewed as a tentative model subject to constant revision. Unlike other less theoretical approaches, the analytic approach is subject to modification in the light of validational evidence. Such revision is typically accomplished by an intensive study of predictive "failures."

In evaluating a given analytic approach, one must bear in mind that a two-stage inference process is involved (Taft, 1959). The first stage of inference involves the situational analysis, in which the role requirements of the environment are translated into psychological characteristics presumed to underlie successful performance (Figure 10.1). A faulty situational analysis may lead to an incorrect formulation of the role requirements and hence an inaccurate translation of role requirements into the psychological dimensions of the target model. The second stage of inference involves the translation of dimensions of the target model into psychological testing terms and the subsequent assessment of candidates in terms of their congruence with the hypothetical target model. A faulty interpretation of the target model in terms of psychological testing instruments or a faulty set of assessment procedures for evaluating the fit of a candidate to the target model will both contribute predictive error. Because there are several chains of theoretically mediated inferences involved in the analytic approach, the possibility of procedural errors is multiplied. Unlike other assessment procedures, the analytic approach requires both validation of the underlying model and validation of the assessment procedures.

From another perspective, however, it is precisely this reliance on psychological inference that gives the analytic approach a potential advantage over competing approaches. In the analytic approach, the *reasons* for predictive failure may be sought within the system itself. Intensive study of predictive failures in relation to the situational analysis, the target model, and the diagnostic assessment procedures may suggest revisions in any or all stages of the approach. Such revisions may, in turn, lead to a substantial increase in predictive accuracy upon application of the revised system to a new population. Although the analytic approach may require a continuous evaluation of all stages, it is nevertheless likely to lead to continuous improvements in predictive accuracy.

The flexibility of the analytic approach contributes to its most outstanding advantage, namely, its generality of predictive accuracy across samples of both individuals and situations. Even when a given assessment approach is utilized repetitively in the *same* criterion situation, the validity of the approach is subject to criterion "drift" (Taft, 1959). This "drift" may be brought about by subtle changes in the standards of significant others, changes in the requirements of the job situation, or changes in the characteristics of applicants for the job. Because the analytic approach is not "fixed," it is possible to seek out the sources of these subtle changes and modify the model or assessment procedures accordingly.

A more obvious stumbling block for any assessment approach involves the application of a given set of assessment procedures to populations or jobs other than those on which the approach was validated. Application of assessment procedures designed for selecting graduate students in psychology at the University of Illinois to the selection of graduate students in psychology at the University of Oregon would be likely to result in some validity shrinkage. Application of that set of procedures to the selection of graduate students in physics would almost certainly be even less successful. Whereas other assessment approaches appear to require the development of a new set of procedures for each new criterion, and even for each new sample of subjects (Loevinger, 1957), analytic models may frequently be tested and revised in such a manner that they are applicable to a wide variety of job situations and subject samples. Thus, although the analytic model may initially appear "inefficient" because of the time-consuming and expensive procedures involved, the successful application of an analytic model to a new sample of subjects or even to a slightly different job may more than repay the initial expense involved.

The Synthetic Approach

Frequently situations exist in which the elaborate situational analysis of the analytic approach may be bypassed. Such criterion situations may be familiar to assessors on the basis of personal experience, or on the basis of the writings and reports of others. Under such circumstances, an assessor may attempt to "intuit" the psychological requirements of the role required by the criterion rather than establish such requirements by means of an analytic situational analysis. Such an "armchair" situational analysis can never be justified on purely theoretical grounds, although considerations of time and economy may be invoked to justify such a procedure in a given practical situation. Few would argue that an armchair or "global" situational analysis is preferable to an analytic situational analysis based on actual observation. However, some would maintain that global appraisal is superior to other approaches that make *no* attempt at situational analysis. Although the situational analysis may be less accurate than that of the analytic approach, the underlying framework of the synthetic approach is, nevertheless, one that places heavy emphasis on *explicit* theoretical considerations in mediating predictions.

The theoretical elaboration of the analytic approach may be further bypassed, in some situations, when the global situational analysis suggests an already known hypothetical personality type that is relevant to the criterion situation. Such a hypothetical personality type or syndrome may be known to the assessor from previous analytic studies, or it may have been reported in the personality research literature. Regardless of its origin, such a synthetic model must be perceived, on some grounds, as having definite implications for performance in the criterion situation. If it is a positive model, then the assumption is that candidates whose personality characteristics are similar to those of the synthetic model will spontaneously and characteristically fulfill the role requirements of the criterion situation. If the model is negative, the assumption is that candidates whose constellation of personality characteristics is similar to the synthetic model will experience difficulty in meeting the psychological demands of the criterion situation. In either case, there are clear-cut grounds for predictions, which are predicated on the presumed relevance of a synthetic model to criterion performance.

Still more economy may be effected when the synthetic model chosen has been studied by structured testing procedures. Some synthetic models from previous analytic studies and most synthetic models from the research literature have been characterized in terms of subjects' performance on questionnaires or other structured techniques. When this is true, the elaborate diagnostic testing and assessment council procedures of the analytic approach may be bypassed in favor of group testing via structured tests.

The synthetic approach to personality assessment is outlined in Figure 10.2. A global appraisal of the role requirements of the criterion situation leads to the selection of a synthetic personality model which is believed to characterize the individual who will spontaneously and characteristically fulfill such role requirements. The synthetic model, in turn, has definite implications for testing via structured personality tests. Structured personality tests may be administered to groups of subjects, their test responses scored, and selection decisions made ("accept" or "reject") on the basis of appropriate cutting scores. When the components of the flow diagram in Figure 10.2 are compared with those of the analytic approach in Figure 10.1, it is apparent that a great reduction in the cost of assessment has been effected in the synthetic approach. The professional time required for situational analysis, formulation of a target model, individual diagnostic testing, and the diagnostic council has been almost completely eliminated.

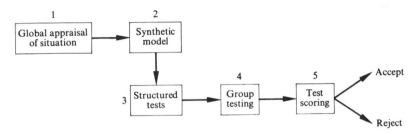

Fig. 10.2 The synthetic approach.

The particular variant of the synthetic approach outlined in Figure 10.2 is the one that shows the greatest amount of contrast with the variant of the analytic approach outlined in Figure 10.1. In practice, pure analytic approaches and pure synthetic approaches are rarely encountered. The two approaches are interchangeable at any step in the prediction paradigm, and combinations of the two are more the rule than the exception. Note in particular that the selection of a synthetic model in no way commits the assessor to a group testing program involving structured tests. After the synthetic model has been selected (Stage 2), the remaining steps may be those of the analytic approach illustrated in Figure 10.1. The same is true, of course, for the analytic approach.

An excellent example of the application of the synthetic approach may be found in the study of college freshmen reported by Stern *et al.* (1956, pp. 187–227), which was conducted in the undergraduate college of the University of Chicago during the early 1950's. The remarkable innovations in education that were introduced there during that period are probably well known to most readers. At that time, the college provided a liberal, intellectual atmosphere which was open to new ideas and experiences and which placed heavy emphasis on critical, abstract, and analytical thinking. During reflections on this criterion situation, it occurred to Stern and associates that a particular synthetic model, which had recently been reported in the literature, would have definite *negative* implications for success in this criterion situation. Although developed in quite a different research context, the *authoritarian personality* model (Adorno *et al.*, 1950) seemed to incorporate a constellation of psychological characteristics which would be incompatible with the role requirements of being a successful student at the University of Chicago at that period in its history. Consequently, this personality model was "borrowed" from its original context and employed in the context of academic prediction.

It was predicted that individuals who most resembled this synthetic model would experience difficulty in humanities and social science, would choose vocational careers that emphasized practical activity, would experience academic difficulty and emotional disturbance, and would be more likely to drop out of college than individuals who least resembled the synthetic model. A structured, attitudinal questionnaire was constructed on the basis of the same rationale that guided the construction of questionnaires in the earlier studies of the authoritarian personality (Adorno *et al.*, 1950). It was administered to large groups of students, and a cutting score was employed to differentiate those who most resembled the synthetic model from those who least resembled it. In this particular study, all the predictions were confirmed and the application of the synthetic personality model was judged to be highly successful.

An especially interesting feature of the study by Stern and associates was their attempt to *validate* the synthetic model by more analytic procedures. Twenty students, who had been classified on the basis of the structured attitudinal inventory as resembling or not resembling the synthetic model, were studied individually by means of interviews and other individual diagnostic testing procedures. The assessors, who were unaware of each student's classification on the attitude questionnaire, were provided with a description of the synthetic personality model and asked to predict whether that student resembled or did not resemble the model. They correctly identified 18 of the 20 students by this independent "blind" analytic assessment procedure. Such independent validation by analytic procedures tends to enhance the construct validity of the synthetic model and to lend credence to the implementation of the model by means of structured tests.

Although the advantages of the synthetic approach—economy and efficiency—are obvious, there are also limitations which may more than offset the apparent advantages.   While global appraisals of a criterion situation may occasionally approximate the accuracy obtained by an actual situational analysis, they will in general be less accurate, and they will frequently be misleading.   The selection of a particular synthetic model for a given criterion situation rests on two assumptions.   First, the model must be applicable to the criterion situation and have definite implications for success or failure in that situation.   Second, a significant proportion of successful applicants must be representatives of the personality type indicated by the synthetic model.   Even if personality types represented by the synthetic model are *always* successful in the criterion situation, the model is still not a practical assessment tool if the base rate of incidence of those personality types is less than five percent in the population of applicants.   For example, the synthetic model of the "self-actualized personality" (Maslow, 1954) may have definite implications for success in many complex criterion situations.   However, if the rate of occurrence of this syndrome in the general population is less than one in a thousand, the model is of little practical value, despite its validity.   Since structured test indices are frequently available for well-known synthetic models, group testing procedures are frequently employed in the synthetic approach.   The amount of information available from a single structured test may be considerably less than what could be obtained by individual diagnostic testing and use of a diagnostic council.   A single structured test may tap only one facet of the complex of behaviors implied by the synthetic model.

Although the synthetic approach is subject to correction in the light of predictive failures, it is less so than the analytic approach.   When a synthetic approach to a given assessment problem fails to show promise, it is difficult to pinpoint the source of inaccuracy.   Unfruitful synthetic approaches are likely to involve failures of intuition, but it is seldom clear whether the misjudgment occurred in the global appraisal of the criterion situation, in the selection of a synthetic model, or in the implementation of a given set of structured tests.   When synthetic approaches consistently fail, it is wise to adopt a more traditional analytic approach.

The Empirical Approach

Given a large number of candidates to be processed and a poorly understood criterion situation, it is often preferable to concentrate on the *standard of performance* rather than the *psychological criterion*.   The prosaic, yet practical, goal of the empirical approach is to discover some psychological test or assessment procedure that will reproduce an already established differentiation of subjects on a given standard of performance.   Stern and associates (1956) have called attention to a feature of such "standards of performance" which has tended to be overlooked by other writers.   In one sense, a "standard of performance" is an abstract concept existing in the minds of significant others, which symbolizes success or competence in performance in the criterion situation. In another sense, a "standard of performance" is an operationalized or concrete criterion measure which serves as a quantifiable representation of the abstract notion held by significant others. The abstract standard of "intellectual competence" may be operationalized in the more prosaic, but concrete, index of grade-point average. Whereas the analytic approach emphasizes a thorough investigation of the abstract standards held by significant others, the empirical approach, by its very nature, must restrict itself to concrete, quantifiable indices.

The importance of the distinction made by Stern and associates between abstract and concrete standards of performance becomes evident in the second stage of the empirical approach outlined in Figure 10.3. In the first

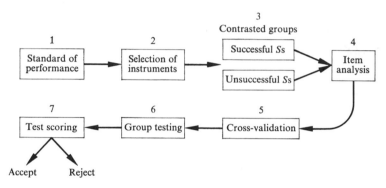

Fig. 10.3 The empirical approach.

stage of the empirical approach, the assessors select an operational index of the standard of performance that is easily quantifiable and as reliable as possible. Although this index may involve qualitative judgments, such as ratings by significant others, considerations of reliability often lead to the selection of more objective measures, such as grade-point average, work output, sales volume, etc. Once the operational definition of the standard of performance has been made, testing instruments are selected which are known to be or believed to be associated with that index. It is at this stage that the assessor must check his natural inclinations to think in terms of the abstract standard of performance, rather than in terms of the concrete index. Speculations about "skills" or underlying personality characteristics must be set aside in favor of empirically guided hunches concerning instruments which will be maximally correlated with the concrete index. Abstract considerations aside, grade-point average in college is likely to be best predicted by grade-point average in high school, regardless of the nature of the factors which determine these two indices. The success or failure of the empirical approach is determined entirely by the degree of correlation that exists between the instruments selected and the concrete index of criterion performance.

The third stage of the empirical approach (Figure 10.3) involves the implementation of the strategy of contrasted groups (Chapter 9). The concrete standard of performance is applied to an existing group of subjects on the job in such a manner that subgroups of "successful" and "unsuccessful" subjects may be identified. Both high-performing and low-performing subjects are administered a battery of tests for purposes of contrasted-group item analysis. Items (or tests) that exhibit a statistically significant difference between these contrasted groups are provisionally set aside as items that are capable of reproducing the original differentiation of the groups on the concrete standard of performance. Cross-validation of these items on another subject group is an essential next step in the empirical approach (Figure 10.3) that seeks to avoid capitalization on the idiosyncratic characteristics of the original contrasted groups.

Once the discriminating items or tests have been selected, they are assembled into a selection battery and administered to actual job applicants. Applicants who score high on this selection battery are considered to be most like the original criterion group of successful subjects, and they are selected for the positions. Applicants who score low are considered to be more like the original criterion group of unsuccessful performers, and they are rejected from consideration. After a period of time on the job, concrete criterion measures of performance become available on these placed candidates, and it becomes possible to assess the validity of empirical selection procedures. Evaluations of the validity of selection are ordinarily restricted to a consideration of false and valid positive hit rates, since potential false and valid negatives have been excluded from the program (Chapter 6).

Some predictive success is more or less *guaranteed* for the empirical approach since it is based on established empirical relationships between the selection battery and the concrete standard of performance. Frequently, however, the degree of success of empirical selection is considered to be less than optimal in terms of such considerations as hit rates, costs of testing, and selection ratios. It is precisely at this point that the disadvantages of the empirical approach become evident. When the success of an empirical assessment program is judged to be less than adequate, there are few alternatives to beginning the entire assessment program anew. Unlike the analytic and synthetic approaches, the empirical approach is not subject to self-correction on the basis of theoretical considerations. Cutting scores on the selection instrument may be modified to effect changes in the hit rates for different outcomes (Chapter 6), but there is no guiding theoretical rationale which can suggest the addition or deletion of items for purposes of maximizing the overall effectiveness of the instrument.

The *generality* of the empirical approach may be considerably less than that achieved by the other two approaches. The empirical approach is especially sensitive to idiosyncrasies that may exist in the original and cross-validation criterion groups. Application of the selection instrument to slightly different samples of subjects, under altered conditions of selection, may result in a dramatic shrinkage of validity coefficients. In principle, the empirical approach may become so specific that a new scale-derivation procedure is required for every assessment project (Loevinger, 1957).

Though limited in generality, the empirical approach is not without its advantages. In addition to being the most economical of approaches to personality assessment, the empirical approach, as we have indicated, carries with it a minimal guarantee of empirical success. Although the actual degree of discrimination achieved by an empirical approach may be relatively modest, it frequently surpasses the discrimination achieved in the initial phase of an analytic program. By avoiding the double stage of inference involved in analytic approaches, the empirical approach may achieve a more parsimonious solution of the prediction problem. Thus the empirical approach may be the approach of choice in "one shot" assessment programs and in situations in which the criterion is especially refractory to analysis. Finally, recall that the empirical approach is not simply a fixed sequence of testing procedures; rather, it is a *point of view* concerning the nature of assessment that can be implemented with considerable flexibility (Chapter 9). In the present context, for example, criterion groups defined by the standard of performance may be intensively studied by means of other empirical instruments. Such study may reveal other characteristics of the criterion groups and result in the development of an "empirical model" which, in turn, may suggest the inclusion of new items or tasks in the selection battery.

Some Representative Assessment Models

The Psychoanalytic Model

Principal Constructs

The psychoanalytic theory of Sigmund Freud and its subsequent extensions by Hartmann (1958), Erikson (1950), and Rapaport (1959) under the name of "ego psychology" formed the basis for one of the earliest comprehensive frameworks for psychological assessment to be employed in this country. In his capacity as the Menninger Clinic's first full-time psychologist, David Rapaport, together with a student, Roy Schafer, and a psychoanalyst colleague, Merton Gill, provided a detailed statement of the manner in which psychoanalytic theory could serve as an integrative model for guiding the theory and practice of personality assessment (Rapaport, Gill, and Schafer, 1946; Schafer, 1948). The Rapaport-Gill-Schafer formulations, together with a body of clinical observations and theory relating psycho-analysis to psychopathology (e.g., Fenichel, 1945), guided the daily practice of many clinical psychologists in hospital and clinic settings during the late forties and early fifties.

The theory and practice of psychoanalysis are founded on the assumption that a complete understanding of any behavior or sequence of behaviors can be achieved only through a thorough assessment and reconstruction of the multiple causes of the behavior in question. In practice, such assessment requires the consideration of the same behavior simultaneously from multiple "points of view" (Rapaport and Gill, 1959). Theoretically, these points of view represent a set of assumptions underlying psychoanalytic theory which are considered both necessary to and sufficient for a complete explanation of human behavior. Alternatively, we might consider such points of view as conceptually distinct "sources of variance" which together determine be-havior. The points of view of psychoanalytic theory and the assumptions which underlie them have been designated as (1) dynamic, (2) economic, (3) structural, (4) genetic, and (5) adaptive.

1. The *dynamic* point of view relates to instinctual forces and the direc-tionality they impart to behavior. The major dynamic constructs of psycho-analysis are concerned with the nature of instinctual drives (sexual, aggressive, and effectance), the three components of instinct (source, aim, and object), and the manner in which behavior is determined by multiple instincts (conflict, ambivalence, and drive fusion).

2. The *economic* point of view relates to instinctual energies and the manner in which they are discharged, distributed, and transformed. The primary economic constructs relate to the manner in which instinctual energies are invested and distributed (cathexes and countercathexes) and the principles governing energy discharge (pleasure principle and reality principle).

3. The *structural* point of view relates to psychological processes charac-terized by a relatively slow rate of change and by a permanence of organization and function. The major structural constructs specify substructural organiza-tions within the domains of the ego (identifications, defenses, and means), the superego (conscience and ego-ideal), and the id (not clearly differentiated with respect to structure).

4. The *genetic* point of view relates to the history and development of mental life and the manner in which past experiences influence current structures and functions. The main genetic constructs have reference to stages of

psychosexual development (oral, anal, phallic, latency, puberty, and genital) and the psychosocial crises that must be resolved at each stage (trust versus mistrust, autonomy versus shame, initiative versus guilt, industry versus inferiority, identity versus diffusion, and intimacy versus isolation).

5.   The *adaptive* point of view relates to the manner in which the organism effects adaptive coordinations between instinctual drives and the demands of external reality.   The major adaptive constructs involve processes of adaptation that are initiated by ego apparatuses of primary and secondary autonomy.[1]

Assessment Procedures

The purpose of assessment within a psychoanalytic framework, whether it is implemented by a series of psychoanalytic interviews or a battery of psychological tests, is to "form an impression of the person" (Chapter 4) based on interpretations placed on behavior viewed from the multiple perspectives of psychoanalytic theory.   In this connection, it is important to note that the word "assessment" is not used synonomously with the applied activities of prediction, selection, or decision-making.   Prelinger and Zimet (1964) suggest a distinction between "assessment for" and "assessment of," the former denoting the "prediction" emphasis which has characterized the present text and the latter the "understanding" emphasis that characterizes psychoanalytic investigation.   This is not to deny that psychoanalytic interpretations may serve as "judgmental input" to either clinical or statistical data-combination systems whose aim is the forecasting of socially relevant criterion categories (Chapter 5).   However, psychoanalytic interpretations must be distinguished from predictions (diagnostic conclusions) to emphasize the fact that their validities are established by recourse to different sources of evidence (Schafer, 1948).   Whereas predictions are evaluated within the context of validity coefficients and number of correct decisions, psychoanalytic interpretations are evaluated within an extraordinarily complex context of internal consistency among multiple sources of evidence (Schafer, 1954).   These two contexts are, of course, the familiar ones of discovery and justification (Chapter 4).

Just as the practicing psychoanalyst relies on multiple sources of information (e.g., history, free associations, dreams, expressive behavior) to

---

1.   The reader who is unfamiliar with psychoanalytic theory is likely to be more baffled than enlightened by the listings above of the principal constructs within the five points of view of psychoanalysis.   The present summary is based on Rapaport's (1959) classic formulation of psychoanalytic theory.   An introductory-level treatment of this formulation (Wiggins, Renner, Clore, and Rose, 1971, pp. 469–494) may be helpful in preparing the interested reader for Rapaport's rather formidable exposition.

determine the significance of a given behavior sequence from the multiple perspectives of psychoanalytic theory, the psychodiagnostician relies on multiple sources of information (e.g., structured techniques, unstructured techniques, behavior in the testing situation) to arrive at integrative interpretations within the framework of psychoanalytic theory. Hence the procedures of psychoanalytic assessment require *a diverse battery of individually administered psychological tests, all of which may be interpreted from the multiple perspectives or points of view of psychoanalytic theory.*

Rapaport, Gill, and Schafer (1946) presented an elaborate theoretical analysis of the manner in which psychological functioning is expressed in a variety of psychological tests, together with a potpourri of clinical and empirical evidence which they felt supported their formulations. Shortly thereafter, Schafer (1948) summarized the diagnostic implications of these formulations in the form of an interpretive "cookbook" that related patterns of test response to membership in psychiatric diagnostic categories (e.g., obsessive-compulsive neurosis). The original test battery employed by Rapaport, Gill, and Schafer (1946) included several measures of intelligence, learning efficiency, and concept formation, a word association test, the Rorschach, and the Thematic Apperception Test (TAT). Several of the more time-consuming intellective measures were subsequently dropped from the battery (Schafer, 1948), and contemporary proponents of this approach (e.g., Allison, Blatt, and Zimet, 1968) now limit the battery to the Wechsler Adult Intelligence Scale (Wechsler, 1958), the TAT, and the Rorschach, the more or less standard trinity of psychodiagnostic testing.

The tests included in a diagnostic battery are thought to sample behavior along a continuum of psychological functioning that can be viewed from the multiple and interrelated perspectives of psychoanalytic theory. "This continuum ranges from functioning in situations which put a premium on highly logical, reality-oriented, secondary process modes of thought (WAIS) to those which allow for more personal, less conventionally constrained thinking (TAT) and finally those which allow for considerably novel, personalized, and regressive modes of thinking (Rorschach)" (Allison, Blatt, and Zimet, 1968, p. vii). Each test (as well as clinical observations made during testing) is viewed as measuring, in varying degrees, all levels of psychological functioning rather than one particular psychological function. Further, each test is thought to provide multiple sources of information based on: (a) formal test scores, (b) the content or themes of responses, (c) style of verbalization (attitudinal and affective reactions), and (d) the interpersonal relationship between the tester and the subject (Allison, Blatt, and Zimet, 1968). The manner in which such information can be used as a basis for interpretation has been described separately for the WAIS (Blatt and Allison, 1967), the TAT (Holt, 1951, 1961), the Rorschach (Schafer, 1954), and the interpersonal transactions that may occur between the tester and his subject (Sarason, 1954; Schafer, 1954).

Traditionally, both psychoanalytic theory and psychodiagnostic interpretations made within its context have deemphasized the external considerations of construct validity ("reality"). It is consequently difficult, if not impossible, to evaluate the contribution of psychodiagnostic interpretations to the decision-making processes that occur within a psychiatric hospital or clinic setting. The end product of assessment within a psychoanalytic model is typically a "psychological report," which presumably provides the therapist or administrator with information that is useful in planning for the treatment or disposition of a given patient. Although there is virtually no empirical evidence that would tend to substantiate the incremental validity of such assessment procedures, psychodiagnostic practices have been sustained over the years by an enduring faith in their "clinical validity": "The common pessimism surrounding the frequent failures in validation studies of clinical tests does not seem to be consistent with the reality in clinical settings when tests are skillfully used" (Allison *et al.*, 1968, p. vii).

To capitalize on the potential richness of psychoanalytic interpretations as "judgmental input," such interpretations must be stated in quantified form. The recent work of Prelinger and Zimet (1964) is noteworthy in this respect because it represents one of the few attempts to develop a psychoanalytic model that could be employed in "assessment for" (prediction) as well as "assessment of" (understanding). Within an "ego-psychological approach to character assessment," eight major categories were delineated in increasing order of complexity: (1) ideational styles, (2) prominent affects, (3) prominent defenses, (4) superego, (5) adaptive strengths, (6) sense of self, (7) psychosocial modalities, and (8) character elaborations. Finer "characterological dimensions" were identified within each of these categories and expressed in the form of 78 "five-point" rating scales. The "five-point" rating scales represented a remarkable combination of cumulative and dynamic measurement models. In addition to a sixth category of "cannot say," half-point ratings (e.g., 3.5) were permissible so that ten different single judgments could be recorded on a scale. In addition, it was recognized that more than one rating would sometimes be appropriate, so that a given scale could be rated 1.5 *and* 3, for example!

The material to be rated on the 78 scales consisted of *interpretations* made on the basis of a test battery (WAIS, TAT, Rorschach) or on the basis of a three-hour interview. In a pilot study of 19 normal Yale freshmen, test protocols were rated independently by two raters, and interview records were rated independently by three different raters. On the basis of a questionable measure of interjudge agreement, it was concluded that: "Thirty-nine scales, exactly half of the complete set, were judged reliably at least at the .05 level on the basis of both test and interview material" (Prelinger and Zimet, 1964, p. 198). Although the obvious issue of convergent validity was not faced as directly, it was reported that "very high agreement" between test and interview ratings occurred in seven of the 19 cases. Until additional psychoanalytic assessment models are forthcoming, it must be concluded that this theoretical orientation is not readily translatable into meaningful "assessment for" operations.

The Interpersonal Model

Principal Constructs

Whereas the psychoanalytic theory of Freud has been relatively unproductive as a source of useful assessment models, the interpersonal theory of Harry Stack Sullivan and others has inspired the development of an unprecedented number of promising assessment models. This state of affairs is somewhat ironic in view of the obscure and incomplete nature of Sullivan's writings in comparison with the voluminous and highly articulated works of Freud and the later ego psychologists. For whatever reasons, interpersonal conceptions of personality have appealed to psychologists whose research reflects both substantive and methodological sophistication in the realm of personality assessment (e.g., Becker and Krug, 1964; Foa, 1961; Leary, 1957; Lorr and McNair, 1963; Rinn, 1965; Schaefer, 1959; Schutz, 1958). Consequently, the relative fruitfulness of interpersonal theory as a source of assessment models must be attributed in part to the ingenuity with which such models have been developed. More important, perhaps, is the *empirical generalizability* of assessment variables conceived within an interpersonal framework. Despite substantial differences in universes of content, populations studied, media of observation, and strategies of test construction, the variables from different interpersonal assessment models have shown remarkable "convergences" of both substance and structure (Foa, 1961).

For Sullivan (1947, 1953, 1954, 1956), the basis unit for the observation and study of personality is an interpersonal situation involving the interaction of two or more persons. This is not the usual notion of a "personality" existing in the context of a "social situation." Instead, personality is treated as a hypothetical construct which is inferred from interpersonal situations and which cannot be said to exist independently of such situations. Virtually all situations are construed by Sullivan as interpersonal in nature. The behavior of a solitary individual can be understood only in the context of its relation to the significant others in his environment. Moreover, significant others need not be real to be influential, since much of our behavior can be understood in relation to fictionalized images that represent "personifications" based on earlier experiences with real persons. Likewise, psychological processes such as thinking, remembering, perceiving, and imagining are held to be interpersonal in nature since these processes are not "given" but develop in an interpersonal context.

A *dynamism* is a "relatively enduring configuration of energy which manifests itself in characterizable processes in interpersonal relations" (Sullivan, 1947, p. 128). Dynamisms are not properties of a single organism but are patterns which arise out of and are manifested in interpersonal situations. They may be thought of as the habitual reaction patterns of one individual toward another, which may occur as actions, attitudes, or feelings toward that other. The *self-dynamism* consists primarily of symbolic representations of the "reflected appraisals" of significant others which have arisen in the course of an individual's development. In infancy the organism is believed to respond "empathically" to the dynamisms of the mother, and through this empathic process, the natural anxiety or concern of the mother for her child is transmitted to the infant. Eventually a self-dynamism develops as a system that can avoid or minimize anxiety. With the recognition that his own behavior has much to do with the empathized dynamisms of adults, the infant learns to differentiate between behaviors which will win the approval of adults ("good-me") and those which will lead to disapproval and anxiety ("bad-me"). Most adult dynamisms, i.e., habitual interpersonal reaction patterns, may be thought of as motivated by the desire to avoid anxiety and maintain self-esteem.

To illustrate the manner in which interpersonal reaction patterns have been represented within assessment models, we shall now derive a general model which incorporates the ideas and suggestions of several investigators, most notably those of Foa (1961), Leary (1957), and Rinn (1965). We begin by noting that ordinary language characterizations of interpersonal transactions employ gross categories of description. Thus, when we describe an individual's behavior as "cooperative" with respect to another person, we refer not to a single act but to a set of components, all of which add up to our categorization of the interpersonal behavior as cooperative. Although such molar descriptive units as "cooperative," "responsible," and "competitive" are sufficient as explanatory principles in "understanding others" in the ordinary sense of that phrase, a scientific analysis of interpersonal behavior requires the reduction of such gross categories to more basis units of behavior.

Facet analysis (Guttman, 1954; Foa, 1965) provides a conceptual framework for the reduction of complex concepts into their underlying elements, or *facets*. Facets represent *conceptual dimensions* which are believed to be useful in distinguishing the basis elements involved in any complex behavior. There are always many possible dimensions or facets that might be distinguished in any behavioral situation. The choice of the particular facets to employ rests with the theorist. Although the end product of a facet analysis might be a rigorous deductive system, the initial choice of facets depends on the creativity and perceptiveness of the theorist.

Foa (1961) proposed that three facets underlie interpersonal behavior. These facets distinguish the content, the object, and the mode of interpersonal transactions. The *content* of interpersonal behavior refers to the directionality of interchange between two actors. In this facet, one may (a) give something to the actor or (b) take something away from him. In interpersonal terms, one may accept the actor or some aspect of his behavior, or one may reject him or some aspect of his behavior. Thus the content facet may take on two values which indicate the directionality of the interpersonal exchange: (a) accept and (b) reject. The second facet of interpersonal behavior identifies the *object* of that behavior, namely: (a) the self (actor) or (b) the other (nonactor). The third facet involves the *mode* in which the interpersonal behavior takes place. A distinction is made between (a) the social mode and (b) the emotional mode. The social mode refers to the norms and rules of society, which involve such distinctions as status and role within a social unit. The emotional mode refers to the affect or feelings of the participants, which may be positive or negative in nature.

On the basis of these three facets of interpersonal behavior, it is possible to specify eight units which represent combinations of the values of the facets, as illustrated in Figure 10.4. At the top is the first facet, *content*, which may take on the values of "accept" and "reject." The second row shows the *object* of interpersonal behavior, which may be "self" or "other." For each of the four possible combinations of the content and object facets there are two possible media of expression given by the *mode* facet: "social" or "emotional." At the bottom of Figure 10.4 appear the units of interpersonal behavior which may be formed from a combination of the three

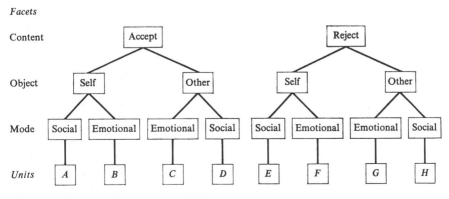

Fig. 10.4 Facets of interpersonal behavior.

facets. These units are labeled $A, B, \ldots, H$ and represent all possible combinations of the three basic facets. Unit A, for example, is one in which there is acceptance of self in the social mode. Unit F is one in which there is rejection of self in an emotional mode.

Although it is not formally necessary, we may attempt a preliminary substantive specification of the units in Figure 10.4. One such specification might be: (A) confidence, (B) emotional stability, (C) affection, (D) submission, (E) lack of confidence, (F) emotional instability, (G) hostility, and (H) ascendance. The reader is invited to assess for himself whether accepting one's self in the social mode connotes confidence, whether accepting one's self in the emotional mode involves emotional stability, etc. However, by labeling such units we do not wish to imply that they may be readily abstracted from the observation of ongoing, interpersonal behaviors. These units are themselves to be considered *abstractions* which require a further step before translation into observational terms. For example, when we describe a behavioral interaction as "competitive," we are doing so on the basis of a *combination* of the more basis units at the bottom of Figure 10.4.

At this point, we call attention to the fact that the units of interpersonal behavior, $A, B, \ldots, H$, are meant to be *ordered* as implied by their alphabetization. The units are in the order given because they are thought to combine in such a fashion as to obtain a circular ordering of interpersonal *variables*. A circular ordering of variables is called a *circumplex* (Guttman, 1954; Foa, 1965). Variables that are adjacent to each other on the circle are thought to be more similar than variables that are separated from each other. The variables become less similar as the distance between them increases on the circumference of the circle. The notion of variable similarity is meant to apply both geometrically and substantively. In facet analysis, under the *contiguity principle*, variables that are geometrically close to each other are those which have underlying units in common. Variables that are geometrically separated have fewer units in common.

An eight-variable circumplex based on combinations of underlying units is presented in Table 10.4. Variables comprising four units each may be arranged in several ways to achieve the circularity required by the circumplex model. Table 10.4 presents Rinn's (1965) adaptation of a system first proposed by Foa (1961). Ignoring for a moment the ordinary language descriptions provided at the right of the table, note that these eight variables will be ordered in a circumplicial fashion under the contiguity principle. Variable 1 and Variable 2 have three units in common (A, G, H) and differ by only one unit. Variables 1 and 3 differ by two units and thus are farther apart. Although each successive variable differs from its neighbor by only one unit, the two extreme variables (1 and 8) also differ by only one unit. These are the conditions which must be met for a perfect circumplex (Foa, 1965).

Table 10.4 An eight-variable system based on eight units of interpersonal behavior (after Rinn, 1965)

Variable number	Units								Ordinary language description
1	A	B					G	H	Managerial
2	A					F	G	H	Competitive
3					E	F	G	H	Aggressive
4				D	E	F	G		Skeptical
5			C	D	E	F			Modest
6		B	C	D	E				Docile
7	A	B	C	D					Cooperative
8	A	B	C					H	Responsible

Figure 10.5 presents the circumplicial ordering of interpersonal *variables* that would be generated both theoretically and mathematically by the arrangement of units shown in Table 10.4. The units are labeled inside the circle but for illustrative purposes only since these labels do not correspond to ordinary descriptive language. These units are simply theoretical building blocks that were derived from all combinations of values of the three basic facets of content, object, and mode. Having specified the substantive and structural considerations underlying the eight interpersonal variables, we should now make clear that the circumplicial arrangement among variables in Figure 10.5 is meant to hold *empirically* as well. That is, the pattern of intercorrelations among self-report or observational measures of the eight variables should form a circumplex. Adjacent variables should be more highly correlated than nonadjacent variables, and the degree of correlation between any two variables should be a direct function of their distance from each other on the circle.

Assessment Procedures

The Interpersonal System of Personality Diagnosis must be considered a milestone in the development of interpersonal assessment models. Developed by Leary and associates during the early fifties (Freedman *et al.*, 1951; LaForge *et al.*, 1954; LaForge and Suczek, 1955; Leary, 1957), the system is notable for its imaginative translations of Sullivanian theory into highly innovative methodological procedures. The circular arrangement of variables depicted in Figure 10.5 was postulated to be generated by two orthogonal axes representing *power* (dominance versus submission) and *affiliation* (love versus hate). The power dimension is marked at its positive pole by the managerial variable, or octant, as it is conceived in geometric terms. The negative pole of the power axis passes through the modest octant. The

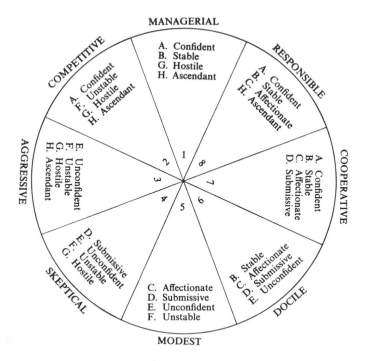

Fig. 10.5 Eight-variable circumplex of interpersonal behavior.

affiliation axis passes through the aggressive and cooperative octants at a 90° angle to the power axis. All other variables are held to be "blends" of these two orthogonal axes. Thus responsible behavior is a blend of dominance and love, docile behavior is a blend of love and submission, etc.

Within each of the eight octants, the distance from the center of the circle to the perimeter is interpreted as the degree of *intensity* with which the interpersonal dynamism is manifest in a given situation. Within the cooperative octant, for example, behaviors of mild intensity would fall near the center of the circle and be described by such terms as "cooperative" and "friendly." Behaviors farther from the center of the circle would be described as "always pleasant and agreeable" and "sociable and neighborly." At the perimeter of the circle, intense forms of the behavior would be described as "too easily influenced by friends" and "friendly all the time." Thus any interpersonal transaction may be classified with respect to both its *kind* (managerial, competitive, etc.) and its *intensity* (mild, moderate, intense).

The Interpersonal Check List (LaForge, 1963; LaForge and Suczek, 1955) consists of sets of descriptive statements, calibrated for different levels of intensity, for each of the eight variables or octants of the system. Careful wording of items and attention to empirical endorsement frequencies resulted in a final form of the ICL which is reasonably balanced with respect to the intensity of the eight variables. Under a cumulative scoring model, eight separate scores are obtained which are typically displayed as a circular profile of interpersonal dynamisms. If one considers the eight scores as vectors in two-dimensional space, it is possible to obtain a weighted sum of the vectors, which may be represented as a *single point* with reference to the two principal coordinates of power and affiliation. This single point may be employed in the diagnosis of an individual's characteristic interpersonal behaviors in terms of both kind and intensity. Single points that fall near the center of the circle, i.e., the origin of the two axes, are considered as falling within the normal range of interpersonal emphases (e.g., "managerial"). Those falling toward the perimeter of the circle are interpreted in pathological terms (e.g., "autocratic"). The ICL, a remarkably flexible instrument, can be employed for self-ratings, ratings of significant others (mother, spouse, ideal-self) or peer ratings.

A variety of other measures have been employed to assess interpersonal behavior within the two-dimensional circumplex of the Interpersonal System. They have included specially constructed devices, such as the Interpersonal Fantasy Test, as well as adaptations of more conventional instruments, such as the MMPI and TAT. In general, Leary (1956, 1957) construes these different *methods* of measurement as representing different "levels" of personality in the sense in which that term was employed in the early topographic viewpoint of psychoanalysis (Gill, 1963). Discrepancies between levels are given direct psychoanalytic interpretations, such as interpreting differences between ICL and TAT scores as indices of repression (Leary, 1957). Unfortunately, there appears to be little substantive, structural, or empirical justification for such interpretations (Wiggins, 1965). Nevertheless, there is no a priori reason why other measures of the variables in the Interpersonal System could not be derived under the same logic that guided the development of the ICL.

Schutz (1958) has presented an alternative conceptualization of interpersonal behavior based on what he calls the Fundamental Interpersonal Relations Orientations (FIRO). His presentation reflects his awareness of both the empirical work of the Leary group and the facet-analytic methods of Guttman. Schutz's work differs from that of the Leary group in that no explicit attention is given to the circumplex ordering of variables. Although facet considerations entered into the choice of initial descriptive parameters, the derivation of the structural relations among the final variables is less formal than that of Foa (1961). Nevertheless, there is considerable similarity between the interpersonal variables of FIRO and those of explicit circumplex models (Lorr and McNair, 1963, 1965).

The principal assessment device that has emerged from this system is FIRO-B (Schutz, 1967). That instrument was designed to measure three basic interpersonal needs (inclusion, control, and affection) with respect to the facets of expressed ("I try to . . .") and wanted ("I want others to . . .") behaviors. Items representing these interpersonal behaviors were selected under the rigorous cumulative measurement model of Guttman (1950), and the final six scales are extraordinarily homogeneous. A variety of other measures have been developed to measure the basic interpersonal needs of inclusion, control, and affection with respect to other facets, but their psychometric characteristics are less fully reported (Schutz, 1967).

A consolidation of almost two decades of extensive research and theoretical efforts may be found in the more recent work of Lorr and associates. On the basis of the previous empirical and theoretical work of others, Lorr and McNair (1963) hypothesized 13 interpersonal behavior categories whose order would be circular. Ten psychologists were provided with brief descriptions of the interpersonal categories and asked to write statements about *manifest behaviors* in each situation. After revisions and editing, a preliminary set of behavioral statements in "yes-no" format was selected to constitute the first version of the Interpersonal Behavior Inventory (IBI). Large and representative samples of psychotherapists rated large and representative samples of psychiatric outpatients on the manifest behaviors. Multivariate procedures were employed to extract group factors and construct nine scales which conformed to the hypothesized circular ordering. Additional investigations were conducted to clarify departures of some of the interpersonal categories from theoretical expectations and to identify additional variables that had failed to appear in earlier analyses (Lorr and McNair, 1965, 1966). The most recent form of the Interpersonal Behavior Inventory (Lorr and Suziedelis, 1969) involves 15 reliable dimensions of interpersonal behavior which conform to the circumplex model and which have been interpreted in light of the earlier work of Leary (1957), Schutz (1958) and others. Preliminary efforts to develop an interpersonal typology from configurations of IBI profiles have resulted in a promising and substantively sensible classification system for psychiatric outpatients (Lorr, Bishop, and McNair, 1965; McNair and Lorr, 1965).

The Transactional Model

Principal Constructs

The personality theory or "personology" of Henry Murray (1938, 1951, 1959) has been an extraordinarily rich source of both assessment variables and assessment models. A distinctive emphasis of Murray's theory is his insistence that behavior be analyzed with reference to the environmental context in which it occurs, a point of view held in common with Lewin (1935) and referred to by Dewey and Bentley (1949) as *transactional*. Murray's conception of, and particularly his taxonomy of, psychological *needs* has formed the basis for the construction of a variety of structured instruments (Chapter 9) as well as his own Thematic Apperception Test (Murray, 1943). "A need is a construct . . . which stands for . . . a force which organizes perception, apperception, intellection, conation and action in such a way as to transform in a certain direction an existing, unsatisfying situation" (Murray, 1938, pp. 123–124). Murray's formulation of the need construct is considerably more elaborate than is indicated by this brief quotation, but it is the *organizing* and *directional* quality of needs that has been emphasized in assessment models. In his original enumeration of the "variables of personality," Murray (1938) distinguished manifest needs (e.g., achievement), latent needs (e.g., repressed aggression), internal factors (e.g., ego ideal), and general traits or attributes (e.g., endurance). All these classes of personality variables have been investigated by means of a variety of personality tests, although the conceptual distinctions among the different classes have not always been sharply maintained.

We have selected the term press (*plural* press) *to designate a directional tendency in an object or situation. Like a need, each press has a qualitative aspect—the kind of effect which it has or might have upon the subject . . . —as well as a quantitative aspect, since its power for harming or benefitting varies widely. Everything that can supposedly harm or benefit the well-being of an organism may be considered* pressive. (Murray, 1938, pp. 118–119)

Aspects of an individual's physical or social environment which an objective observer would classify as capable of affecting the individual are designated *alpha press*. Aspects of the environment which are subjectively perceived by the individual as capable of affecting his own behavior are called *beta press*. This distinction is made to draw attention to the fact that an individual's *perception* of sources of environmental press will, for the most part, determine his reactions to his environment. Stern *et al.* (1956) make a further distinction: "When a particular way of perceiving the environment is *shared* by members of a functional group, it is called the *common beta press* and it usually reflects some of the means by which the group maintains its orientation to reality" (p. 37). The more distinctive, personal, and occasionally pathological manner in which a single individual interprets his environment is called *private beta press*. Although private beta press is of importance in the intensive clinical study of a single individual, large-scale assessment programs are most concerned with the identification of sources of alpha and common beta press.

One can profitably analyse an environment, a social group or an institution from the point of view of what press it applies or offers to the individuals that live within or belong to it. These would be its dynamically pertinent attributes. Furthermore, human beings, in general or in particular, can be studied from the standpoint of what beneficial press are available to them and what harmful press they customarily encounter. This is partly a matter of the potentialities of the environment and partly of the attributes of the subject. (Murray, 1938, p. 120)

The analysis of need-press *interactions* provides a powerful framework from which to predict behavioral outcomes. The character and quality of an individual's performance in a given criterion situation will be determined by the opportunities for, and obstacles to, the satisfaction of his primary needs. Such predictions do not follow automatically from a characterization of the environment, since alpha press may be ignored, misinterpreted, or not perceived by any individual. One can hope, however, that it is possible to identify subgroups of individuals with similar need configurations who will respond in similar ways to similar environmental press configurations (Stern, 1970).

Assessment Procedures

The transactional model of personality assessment requires both a comprehensive taxonomy of needs and a comprehensive and parallel taxonomy of environmental press. Several investigators have developed self-report instruments based on Murray's taxonomy of needs (e.g., Campbell, 1959; Edwards, 1959; Gough and Heilbrun, 1965; Jackson, 1967). There have also been several attempts to develop taxonomies and techniques for calibrating aspects of the environment (e.g., Astin and Holland, 1961; Barker, 1968; Sells, 1963), but none of these has done so in terms of environmental press concepts that parallel psychological needs. It is primarily in the work of Stern (1970) and his associates (e.g., Pace, 1962; Stern, Stein, and Bloom, 1956) that we find the full implementation of a transactional model within Murray's need-press framework. The major thrust of their extensive program of research has been directed toward: (a) the development of a comprehensive measure of needs, (b) the development of parallel measures of environmental press, and (c) the study of the manner in which needs and press interact in determining behavioral outcomes across a broad range of individuals and environments.

The Activities Index was developed and refined over a period of years to provide a self-report measure of the relative strength of 30 needs as expressed in preferences ("like-dislike") for "commonplace daily activities and feelings which appeared to represent unambiguous manifestations of need processes"

(Stern, 1970, p. 13). An initial pool of more than a thousand items was coded independently by eight psychologists in terms of Murray's need constructs. Items that were unanimously judged to be related to need categories were retained, and the resultant need scales were subsequently refined on the basis of a series of item-analytic investigations. In its present form, the Activities Index (AI) consists of 30 nonoverlapping, ten-item scales that are homogeneous and temporally stable and that discriminate among diverse samples of student populations.

When the intercorrelations among the 30 AI need scales were factored, twelve distinct underlying factors emerged. The intercorrelations among these twelve factors were themselves factored, and three second-order factors were identified as representing *achievement orientation, dependency needs,* and *emotional expression.* When the twelve first-order factors are viewed in relation to the three second-order factors, it is clear that the first-order factors form a *circumplex.* In an especially enlightening discussion of multivariate procedures for investigating circumplex orderings, Stern (1970, pp. 58–72) concludes that the need factors of the AI approximate Guttman's (1954) criteria for circumplexity more closely than do the Interpersonal Check List variables from Leary's (1957) system or than do the manifest behavior ratings from an early version of Lorr and McNair's (1963) Interpersonal Behavior Inventory. This conclusion is based on the observation that the variables in the Leary and Lorr-McNair systems do not exhibit a "closed" circular ordering and that they have noticeable gaps in representation in several sectors of the circle.

Stern's (1970) conception of the probable relationships among dimensions of the three instruments is presented in Figure 10.6. Although it is of some interest to speculate on the extent to which the interpersonal variables of the Leary and Lorr-McNair instruments are "subsumed" by the need variables of the Activities Index, the most striking features of this representation are the substantive convergences that occur when presumably diverse personality variables are examined with reference to a common circumplex model. In a sense, Guttman's *structural model* (Guttman, 1954; Foa, 1965) of the relationships among psychological variables provides a more powerful framework for identifying universes of content than do the substantive considerations provided by the theories of Sullivan and Murray.

Within a transactional framework, measures of environmental press should be developed which parallel the needs of individuals who operate within a given social or institutional setting. However, although basic human needs are readily identifiable in their manifestations in a variety of activities and feelings, press variables must be defined with reference to more circumscribed environmental situations:

What kind of item, for example, would encompass the diverse forms that a press for order might take in an academic, industrial, and military setting? Taking attendance, punching the clock, and bedcheck are part of the jargon of each group and not necessarily known well enough by an outsider for him to be able to equate them readily with the comparable activity from his own institutional setting. (Stern, 1970, p. 12)

Thus far, the work of Stern and his colleagues has been concerned, almost exclusively, with the identification of dimensions of press within educational institutions. Their major analyses are based on data collected from almost 10,000 college students in 100 institutions of higher learning. Investigations

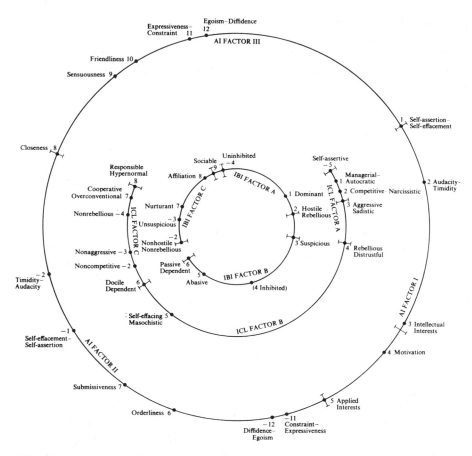

Fig. 10.6 Common elements in the circumplex fans from the Interpersonal Behavior Inventory, the Interpersonal Check List, and the Activities Index. (From Stern, 1970, p. 63)

of other environments are planned, however, and a preliminary form of a *general* instrument has been developed which is held to be applicable to the analysis of all formal administrative structures.

The College Characteristics Index (CCI) parallels the Activities Index as a measure of dimensions of environmental press within a college setting. The 30 need variables of the AI were translated into 30 press variables deemed appropriate for an academic setting. With respect to the *achievement* variable, for example, representative need items from the Activities Index are: "Setting difficult goals for myself" and "Taking examinations." Represent- ative press items for this variable from the College Characteristics Index are: "Students set high standards of achievement for themselves" and "Examina- tions here provide a genuine measure of a student's achievement and under- standing." As is true of the AI, the CCI consists of 30 nonoverlapping, ten-item scales that are homogeneous and temporally stable and that dis- criminate among diverse samples of student environments. Whereas the AI items are responded to as personal evaluations ("like-dislike"), the CCI items are judged for their relevance to a specific college setting ("true-false").

A fascinating issue arises with respect to the relative *independence* of the Activities Index and the College Characteristics Index. The AI presumably provides measures of individual differences in personal needs that will vary within, and to a lesser extent between, institutions. The CCI, on the other hand, should provide relatively veridical, or at least generally agreed upon, measures of common beta press that should vary between, but to a con- siderably lesser extent within, institutions. The results of multivariate analyses performed on a sample of 1,076 college students from 23 colleges, who had taken both the AI and the CCI, tended to confirm these expected relationships (Saunders, 1969). Analysis of variance of the principal dimensions measured by both instruments suggested that AI variance was mainly attributable to individual differences within colleges, whereas CCI variance was mainly attributable to differences between colleges. The fact that some dimensions of the AI were found to vary between colleges, however, suggests a tendency of students with particular needs to apply to colleges with particular environmental characteristics.

Factor analyses of the 30 press variables of the College Characteristics Index have suggested that there are 11 major dimensions of college environ- ment. These dimensions appear to be *independent* of the 12 major need dimensions of the Activities Index. In the analysis cited above of data from 1,076 college students, factor analyses of the intercorrelations among all variables from the AI and the CCI revealed two sets of relatively independent AI and CCI factors. Within the CCI, the 11 factorial dimensions do *not* form a circumplex array. This may reflect the fact that the universe of content sampled by the CCI is limited to a single type of institution—the American college (Stern, 1970).   However, the structure of variables from Stern's *general* index of organizational climates tends to replicate the structure suggested by the CCI.   It would be premature to speculate on the general structure of "environments" since that domain has received relatively little attention in comparison with the "personality" domain.   The work of Stern and his colleagues represents a commendable exception to this relative neglect of situational variables, and it illustrates the fruitfulness of employing transactional models in personality assessment.

The Cognitive Model

Principal Constructs

The personal construct theory of George A. Kelly (1955, 1963, 1970; Maher, 1969) has provided both a unique approach to the problems of personality assessment and a set of procedures for implementing this approach.   The basic point of departure for Kelly's theory is the observation that the subjects psychologists study are themselves engaging in the same methods, for the same ends, as are those who study them.   Thus the common aims of prediction, control, and understanding of the environment make all men "scientists," not just those who wear laboratory coats or hold specialized degrees.   All men experience events, perceive similarities and differences among them, and formulate constructs as a basis for anticipating future events.   But just as one scientist construes his subject matter somewhat differently than does a scientist of a different theoretical persuasion, so each man construes the world in terms of a unique set of personal constructs.   To the extent that we can obtain detailed knowledge of the organization and content of his construct system, we can understand and anticipate (predict) his future actions.

Kelly's fundamental postulate is that "a person's processes are psychologically channelized by the ways in which he anticipates events" (1955, p. 46). He elaborates this postulate in eleven corollaries which specify how persons evolve construct systems for discerning meaning in abstracted patternings or replications of events and are thus able to anticipate events and to select courses of action.   The most radical feature in Kelly's theory of personality is contained in his emphasis on man's capacity to *represent* rather than merely react to his environment.   Because man is able to make different kinds of representations, he is not bound by his environment, but only by his interpretations or representations of it.

Persons construe events by abstracting elements in terms of a similarity-contrast dichotomy.   Thus a *construct* is a way in which at least two elements of events are similar and in contrast with a third.   Consider the following: John, George, Mary, and an apple.   We may abstract an aspect of John, George, and Mary which we may call "sex" or gender.   In terms of this construct, John and George are similar and in contrast to Mary.   The apple is not encompassed by the construct of gender, however; in other words, apples fall outside the *range of convenience* of this construct. The *focus of convenience* of the construct of gender is on those characteristics which distinguish men from women.

But suppose we were to claim that our construct was "masculinity" rather than gender. Could we then argue that both Mary and the apple fall outside the range of convenience of that construct? According to Kelly, we decidedly could not. The notion of similarity always implies a contrast, and the construct of masculinity would be meaningless in the absence of femininity. The contrast pole of a construct is of critical importance in Kelly's theory, for it may frequently be *submerged*. Thus a hysteroid patient may see everyone as "good" or as "kind" without being aware of the submerged poles of "bad" and "cruel." The clinician's knowledge of the submerged or implicit pole of a person's construct is especially important, because it enables prediction of the direction that person will follow if he no longer sees himself as falling at the emergent end of a bipolar dimension. This result is possible because constructs are two-way streets which channelize an individual's psychological processes and determine the directions in which he may change.

A person's psychological processes are further channelized by the *hierarchical ordering* of his construct system. Superordinate constructs subsume the similarity-contrast dimensions of subordinate constructs. Thus the construct "intelligent versus stupid" may be subsumed by the higher-order construct of "good versus bad," which includes the intelligent-stupid distinction but extends its meaning to a broader range of convenience. Or the construct "intelligent versus stupid" may be subsumed by the higher-order construct of "evaluative versus descriptive," which is a more abstract superordinate distinction. Hence, by extension and abstraction, constructs evolve into a complex hierarchy of subordinate and superordinate relationships. In general, subordinate constructs are peripheral in nature and can be altered without serious modification of the person's total construct system. However, superordinate *core constructs* are the fundamental beliefs and values a person holds, and these are considerably less subject to modification.

Kelly explained the structure and dynamics of personal construct systems in terms of several distinctions that specify the formal nature of constructs, the manner in which they are interrelated, and the conditions under which they may change. For example, a construct is *preemptive* if it restricts its elements exclusively to its own domain. A construct is *constellatory* if it fixes the other possible realm membership of its elements, as in stereotyping. A construct is *propositional* if it carries no implications regarding the other possible realm membership of its elements. These and other aspects of constructs, such as permeability-impermeability, dilation-constriction, and tightness-looseness, serve to specify in detail the manner in which persons' processes are psychologically channelized by the ways they anticipate events.

Perhaps the most heuristic construct about constructs in Kelly's system is that of *cognitive complexity*. Both the range and focus of convenience of this construct have varied in its successive application to the realms of person perception (Crockett, 1965), human judgment (Bieri *et al.*, 1966), and information processing (Schroder, Driver, and Streufert, 1967). For Bieri and associates (1966), cognitive complexity involves both *differentiation* (number of different dimensions underlying a construct system) and *articulation* (extent of discriminations made within a dimension). These variables have been shown to influence the processing of social cues in human judgment. Harvey, Hunt, and Schroder (1961) have emphasized the *concrete-abstract* dimension of complexity and the manner in which this dimension interacts with the complexity of the stimulating environment (Schroder, Driver, and Streufert, 1967). Other investigators have adopted different definitions of complexity, and there appear to be few convergences among the many available measures of this construct (Vannoy, 1965). But Kelly's seminal construct of cognitive complexity clearly influenced most of these divergent lines of investigation.

Assessment Procedures

The most direct implementation of Kelly's personal construct theory is found in the Role Construct Repertory Test and its variants. Although the many forms this instrument has taken are referred to as the "Rep test," the term is used to denote a general set of procedures for eliciting and analyzing personal constructs, rather than any specific form these procedures might take (Bannister and Mair, 1968). The original focus of convenience of the test was that of a diagnostic aid in planning for individual psychotherapy (Kelly, 1955). Within this context, Kelly stressed that the importance of the test lay in furnishing clinical hypotheses which could subsequently be tested, rather than in providing the clinician with conclusive findings. This is not to imply that Rep test procedures cannot be standardized with respect to formal psychometric criteria; it is only to suggest that the original form of the test was somewhat informal and exploratory. Basically, Kelly wished to explore the pathways along which a client was free to move in terms of the client's own set of personal constructs. Such information, when properly "subsumed" (i.e., understood) by the clinician, was valuable in planning various treatment procedures, such as Kelly's (1955) *fixed-role therapy*.

In the original form of the Rep test, the client was provided with a list of 24 role titles, such as: "a teacher you like," "a teacher you dislike," "wife (or girl friend)," "the most successful person you know personally," etc.

The client was required to supply the name of a different person to fit each role, and the names were recorded on separate cards. The examiner then selected three of the cards and asked the client to suggest some important way in which two of the persons were alike and different from the third. In this manner, both the similarity and contrast poles of the construct were named by the client, e.g., "friendly versus cold." The examiner then continued to present successive triads of persons to the client until he judged that an adequate sample of the client's personal construct system had been elicited. Questions as to the similarity of two constructs or the meaning of a particular construct were approached by direct interrogation of the client. The data yielded by this procedure were subjected to both formal and clinical analyses designed to yield information about the structure and permeability of the client's construct system and about the manner in which he construed significant others in his environment.

The several *grid* forms of the Rep test represent more formal and more psychometrically sophisticated approaches to the assessment of personal constructs. One such grid form is illustrated in Figure 10.7. The subject is presented with the 15 role titles indicated in the column headings and asked to write the names of corresponding persons on 15 cards. The cards are then presented, three at a time, in the order indicated by the circles within the grid. For example, the first comparison is of mother, father, and sister. In this instance, the subject indicated that mother and father were similar with respect to "kind" and different from sister with respect to "cruel." The subject is next required to apply the "kind-cruel" construct to the remaining 12 persons in the first row, by indicating which of them are also perceived as "kind" (indicated by ×). By implication, those who are not perceived as "kind" are perceived as "cruel" (indicated by blank). The entire procedure is repeated for the next triadic comparison, in which the elicited construct of "unassuming versus pretentious" is applied to all significant others in the second row. The comparisons continue until 15 constructs have been elicited and applied to the 15 persons.

The matrix of constructs by persons illustrated in Figure 10.7 provides a considerable amount of information concerning the personal construct system of a given subject. The constructs were elicited from the subject rather than imposed on him by the examiner. The complexity and structure of his personal construct system may be determined by a comparison of each row (construct) with every other row. Two constructs are similar to each other to the extent that their row patterns are similar in terms of ×s and blanks. Kelly suggested that these patterns of row similarity be subjected to a "nonparametric factor analysis" in order to reveal both the structure and complexity of the subject's construct system, the assumption being that the more factors found, the more complex is the subject's system. It is also possible

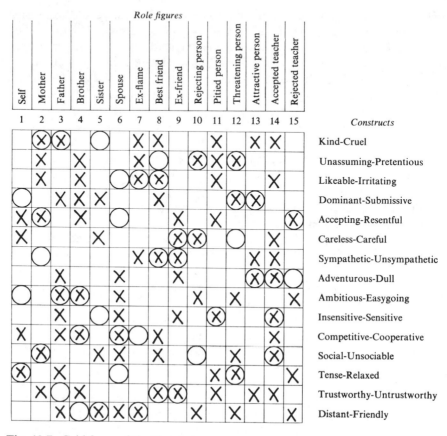

Fig. 10.7 Grid form of the Rep test.

to compare the patterns of column similarity to reveal the complexity and structure of the subject's perceptions of significant others, as well as their perceived similarity to himself.

Although less widely employed, the metric or *rating* form of the Rep test seems to be psychometrically superior to the form just described (Bannister and Mair, 1968). After the examiner has elicited the initial bipolar construct from a given triad of persons, the subject is required to rate all persons on a five- or seven-place scale ranging from, for example, "extremely kind" to "extremely cruel," with the middle rating category signifying the *non-applicability* of the construct to a person. In addition to providing a more differentiated metric for multivariate analyses, the rating procedure seems to provide a more accurate assessment of the range of convenience of individual constructs. Levy and Dugan (1956) were among the first to present assessment data from a rating form of the Rep test. They employed a standard form of the Rep test in which all significant others were rated on five-place scales for each of the elicited constructs. The correlations among the elicited constructs were factor-analyzed to reveal the superordinate constructs of each subject. The results for one of their subjects, a 31-year-old, single, male graduate student, are presented in Table 10.5. These results suggest that the 15 elicited constructs may be thought of as subsumed by only four higher-order dimensions. Although personal construct theorists would be reluctant to impose names on them, these dimensions appear to be potentially understandable (subsumable) by a clinician given the opportunity of discussing them further with the subject.

Table 10.5 Factorial structure of personal constructs of a 31-year-old male graduate student (from Levy and Dugan, 1956, p. 54)

Constructs		Factor loadings*			
Construct	Contrasting construct	I	II	III	IV
1. Unassuming	Pretentious		90		
2. Creative	Uncreative; static			90	
3. Rigid	Flexible		−55	−55	−53
4. Original; daring	Unoriginal; conventional			40	58
5. Sincere; unaffected	Insincere; affected		91	33	
6. Aggressive	Submissive		−58	−59	
7. Sexual	Asexual	84			
8. Intelligent	Stupid			92	
9. Refined	Crude		87		
10. Intellectual	Nonintellectual			89	
11. Nonproductive	Productive			−62	
12. Liberal	Conservative	40		62	51
13. Ascetic	Sensual	−75			−52
14. Introjected values	Experienced-derived values			−54	−33
15. Socially inept	Socially skilled			48	

* Factor loadings less than .33 have been omitted.

Because Rep test procedures represent a general approach to the elicitation and analysis of personal constructs, it is difficult to evaluate the usefulness of either the procedures or the personality model which underlies them for specific assessment problems. There exists a broad base of empirical support for the theory itself (Bonarius, 1965), and the recent literature of personality suggests an increasing recognition of the importance of Kelly's deceptively simple but, in fact, extraordinarily sophisticated view of man. Extensions of Kelly's ideas concerning cognitive complexity have opened up new areas of psychological investigation (Bieri *et al.*, 1966; Harvey, Hunt, and Schroder, 1961; Schroder, Driver, and Streufert, 1967). Similarly, empirical studies of Rep test methodology have attested to both the fruitfulness and the generality of this measurement approach (Bannister and Mair, 1968). But the fruitfulness of employing this cognitive model in personality assessment has not been so clearly documented.

The nature of personal construct theory and the procedures of the Rep test make it clear that Kelly considered this assessment approach to be of value in the assessment of individuals, considered one at a time. Although it is difficult to evaluate the clinical literature of Rep test procedures, the method shows potential in its original focus of convenience, i.e., the initial assessment of individuals who will undergo cognitively oriented psychotherapy. In fact, the Rep test approach advocated by Kelly appears to be the most sophisticated and convincing example of "idiographic measurement" in the sense in which Allport (1961) employed that term. Personal construct theory is, by assumption, idiographic in *content* since each individual is held to construe the world in a unique fashion. But the procedures for eliciting, analyzing, and especially "subsuming" such content seem to represent an advance over earlier idiographic methods.

Although idiographic in content, personal construct theory may be applied nomothetically to the analysis of structural parameters of construct systems. This is especially evident with respect to cognitive complexity, which has been construed as an individual-difference variable for some time (e.g., Bieri and Blacker, 1956). It is equally true of such parameters as constellatory-propositional (Levy, 1954), permeable-impermeable (Gottesman, 1962) and tightness-looseness (Bannister and Fransella, 1966). In fact, with the exception of content, all the parameters of personal constructs are capable of expression as quantitative individual differences among persons. Hence, to the extent that cognitive attributes, such as complexity, are considered to be essential features underlying successful criterion performance, these attributes may be assessed with reference to the personal construct model of Kelly. Although the evidence for the effectiveness of this model in traditional assessment programs is indirect, the model, nevertheless, seems to be worth serious consideration.

The Multivariate Model

Principal Constructs

Of the many available personality models which might be employed in the practice of personality assessment, the multivariate-trait model of Raymond B. Cattell (1946, 1950, 1957, 1964a, 1965a) appears, on the surface at least, to be the one most ideally suited to the aims of assessment. A personality theorist who defines personality as "that which permits a prediction of what a person will do in a given situation" (Cattell, 1950, p. 2) is clearly sympathetic to the applied goals of the assessment psychologist. Perhaps an even more appealing feature of Cattell's approach is the extraordinarily close relationship that exists between the principal constructs of his theoretical model and the assessment procedures that are suggested by that model. Some personality models, such as that of psychoanalytic theory, represent subtle and complex constructs that are extremely difficult to translate into concrete psychometric operations. By contrast, in the multivariate-trait model of Cattell, the theoretical constructs and the psychological assessment procedures whereby they are measured are virtually one and the same. Whereas Cattell has been widely, and frequently glibly, praised for the diversity of his explorations in personality theory, measurement, and assessment, his greatest contribution may lie in his insistence that these "diverse" areas are all of the same cloth.

For Cattell, the fundamental unit of personality study is the trait. Traits are entities whose organization and dynamic interrelationships determine the behaviors we observe and the behaviors we wish to predict. *Surface traits* are clusters of observable attributes that tend to be encoded in the ordinary language of personality and are said to constitute the "language personality sphere" (Cattell, 1946). *Source traits*, on the other hand, are the underlying entities that literally cause the surface manifestations observable in behavior. Surface traits are easily identified by noting the correlations or clusterings among the terms ordinarily used to describe others. Source traits can be discovered only by an appropriate multivariate analysis of the dimensions which underlie surface clusterings. For many who study personality traits, factor analysis is a method of "data reduction" or a method of achieving a more parsimonious description of the relationships among a large set of variables. For Cattell, factor analysis is the method which both discovers and provides measurements of underlying source traits that are not detectable by other procedures.

In an initial taxonomy for organizing psychological phenomena, Cattell distinguishes among ability, temperament, and dynamic traits. *Ability traits* are reflected in the effectiveness with which an individual achieves a goal in complex situations. *Temperament traits* are reflected in primarily constitutional aspects of response, such as personal tempo, excitability, and dominance. *Dynamic traits* are reflected in the motivational aspects which give direction to behavior, as well as interests, attitudes, and sentiments. Other, somewhat less enduring aspects of personality organization include *states*, which reflect momentary conditions of the organism due to mood or fatigue, and *roles*, which reflect recurring patterns of response to social and institutional stimuli.

The nature and organization of traits may be discovered through empirical investigations conducted in three different data media. *Life-record data* (*L*-data) are obtained from naturalistic observations of subjects in everyday life situations. Such data may be obtained by intrusive techniques, such as direct behavioral observations, or by less reactive procedures, such as the analysis of biographies or life-history documents. Of particular value here are the retrospective naturalistic observations obtained from peer rating procedures (see Chapter 8). *Questionnaire data* (*Q*-data) are obtained from the self-reports of subjects. Cattell distinguishes the correspondence view of self-reports as introspections (*Q'*-data) from the instrumental view of self-reports as behavioral data (*Q*-data). *Objective test data* (*T*-data) are obtained from the behavioral responses of subjects to controlled stimulus situations. The stimuli may be verbal, pictorial, or physical, and the responses may be motoric, verbal, or physiological; but the defining characteristic of this data medium is that the subject's behavior is measured in such a way that he cannot perceive the relationship between his responses and the construct being assessed.

The most distinctive and perhaps least understood feature of Cattell's theory of personality is the central role which multivariate analysis—in particular, factor analysis—plays in his definition of trait constructs. In Cattell's view, factor analysis is the procedure that, when properly implemented, permits the direct identification and measurement of the fundamental source traits that account for the observed covariation among surface traits in *L*-, *Q*-, or *T*-data. Within the context of the distinctions developed in Chapter 9, Cattell's approach to test construction and theory development is *construct-oriented*. Further, within the construct point of view, Cattell's position is closer to the *substantive* or "realistic" position of Loevinger (1957) than it is to the positivistic position of Cronbach and Meehl (1955). For Cattell, surface traits are manifestations of *source traits* and not manifestations of constructs about source traits. Further, the factors that emerge from multivariate analyses of the covariation among surface traits are quantitative expressions of *traits* and not "operational definitions" of traits. Note, however, that mathematical factors are not considered identical to source traits, the latter being physical, physiological, psychological, or social in nature:

... *a fine but important conceptual difference can, in the last resort, be drawn between a factor (even a uniquely rotated factor) and a source trait. A factor is a* pattern among variables (*though not all patterns are factors*) *which will alter somewhat from study to study—though in general recognizably—owing to sampling or experimental errors. However, apart from these errors, it will show* real *alteration with change in age, level, etc. of the population. The source trait is some single influence which produces this pattern. It remains the same identical and identifiable influence, inferable from the pattern of effects despite the* real *changes in the latter. ... The source trait is to be understood, if we may borrow that genetic analogy for psychology once more, as the "genotype of which the factor is the phenotype," and it is only through the latter, initially, that we may identify the former.* (Cattell, 1957, p. 42)

Because factors are phenotypic representations of source traits, the procedures whereby they are obtained are of more than casual interest to the theory. In fact, because Cattell's theory of personality is an empirical one, the substantive implications of the theory may be said to stand or fall on the appropriateness of the factor-analytic procedures that have been employed in the identification of the principal constructs. And as is perhaps well known, factor analysts are in less than unanimous agreement on such technical issues as: (a) the basic data matrix to be analyzed (e.g., correlations versus covariances), (b) the method of estimating variable communality (e.g., squared multiple-correlation versus unity), (c) the method of factor extraction (e.g., principal component versus maximum likelihood), (d) the number of factors to be extracted (e.g., many versus few), (e) the method of factor rotation (e.g., analytic versus visual), and (f) the relationships among rotated factors (orthogonal versus oblique).

In the course of his empirical investigations, Cattell has attempted to provide both conceptual and mathematical justifications for his preferred factor-analytic techniques (e.g., Cattell, 1952, 1966b) and has thereby made substantial methodological contributions to this area. Although no attempt will be made here to summarize these contributions, several principles will be noted which have guided Cattell's factor-analytic work and which distinguish his approach from that of other multivariate personality theorists, such as Eysenck (1953b). In the design of a factor-analytic study, Cattell advocates the inclusion of as large a number of variables as possible within the constraints of subject time and computer capacity. These variables should include: (a) a representative sample of variables from the substantive domain under investigation, (b) a set of "marker variables" which will serve to relate the present findings to those of earlier studies in similar or related domains, and (c) a set of variables which are known or thought to be unrelated to the substantive domain under investigation and which will provide a reference background of "hyperplane stuff" that is independent of the specific domain under study.

Although he followed certain statistical guidelines for extracting the "proper" number of factors, Cattell tended to err, if at all, in the direction of overextraction rather than underextraction. Whereas an unnecessary factor may be identified as such on rotation, an unextracted factor is lost forever. The fine point of factor analysis about which Cattell (1966b) is most adamant concerns the rotation of the obtained factors to "general scientific meaningfulness." In the first place, the final relationship among factors should be allowed to become oblique (correlated) rather than forced to orthogonality (independence) as a means of "recognizing the right of the data to its own inherent structure" (Cattell, 1957, p. 309). Second, Cattell's interpretation of the concept of "simple structure" emphasizes high loadings of a very small number of variables on each factor and near-zero loadings of all other variables on each factor, the latter being assessed by a "hyperplane count." The actual procedures employed by Cattell for factor rotation are extraordinarily complex and time-consuming, and they have not been widely employed by others outside his laboratory. The amount of care and artistry Cattell invested in factor rotation was motivated by his expressed intention to *measure traits*, rather than simply to reduce a number of variables to a more simplified mathematical form.

Once the structures of ability, temperament, and dynamic source traits have been identified in a series of properly conducted multivariate studies, it is possible to develop multiscale test batteries which provide measurements of those traits. The conceptual and psychometric criteria for evaluating multifactor personality scales are held to be different from those which have been traditionally applied to personality scales not developed by multivariate procedures (Cattell, 1964b, Cattell and Tsujioka, 1964). Conceptually, Cattell's notion of "concept validity" is similar to Loevinger's (1957) interpretation of construct validity. Both Loevinger and Cattell conceive of the construct (concept) validity of a personality scale as being expressed by the correlation between the scale and the underlying trait construct. For Loevinger, this correlation is hypothetical and can be estimated only with reference to relationships within the total nomological network of constructs (Cronbach and Meehl, 1955). For Cattell, this correlation is less hypothetical because of the near isomorphism between "trait" and "factor" in his system. Consequently, it is possible to evaluate the concept validity of a personality scale with reference to such psychometric criteria as "factor trueness" and "factor homogeneity" (Cattell and Warburton, 1967). This is not to imply that structural considerations alone are employed to evaluate concept validity, since the substantive considerations involved in the initial definition of the universe of content (the language personality sphere) were equally important. The theoretical importance assigned to external considerations in Cattell's system should be evident from his definition of personality as "that which permits a prediction of what a person will do in a given situation."

Once multifactor batteries of ability, temperament, and dynamic source traits become available, it is possible to predict behavior in any criterion situation by means of a *specification equation*, which is stated in the following generalized form:

$$P_{ji} = s_{j1}T_{1i} + s_{j2}T_{2i} + \cdots + s_{jn}T_{ni} + s_{j}T_{ji} + s_{jei}.$$

On the left of the equation, the P_{ji} represents the performance of individual i in situation j. The right-hand side of the equation indicates that such performance is predictable from a knowledge of the individual's endowments in abilities, temperament, and dynamic source traits. The traits are symbolized as T_1, T_2, ..., T_n, and they are measured by appropriate factor scales. The coefficients, s_{j1}, s_{j2}, ..., s_{jn}, represent factor loadings which are called "situational indices." Such indices state, for each individual, the degree to which each source trait is stimulated or brought into action by criterion situation j. The expression $s_j T_{ji}$ indicates a factor trait specific to situation j and not encountered elsewhere. The expression s_{jei} represents error of measurement in P_{ji} which is specific to situation j and individual i.

The generalized specification equation given above represents a theoretical statement of the determinants of behavior as conceived within Cattell's multivariate model of personality. Note, however, that once psychometric measures of trait factors become available and the appropriate situational coefficients have been determined empirically, the equation becomes a prediction model. In its generalized form the specification equation is stated in terms of prediction for *individuals* and could be implemented by, for example, obtaining observations of a single individual over repeated occasions. The model does not imply a theoretical preference for idiographic prediction, however, and its most frequent application is likely to be nomothetic. In its nomothetic form, the model becomes the "basic prediction model" (Chapter 1) for personality assessment.

Assessment Procedures

The goal of Cattell's basic research strategy was the identification of virtually all significant source traits in the ability, temperament, and dynamic realms. This extraordinarily broad-band design has been vigorously implemented by Cattell and his collaborators over a period of more than 30 years, and the sheer volume of empirical results defies any attempt at a comprehensive summary. The characteristic assessment procedures employed by Cattell are perhaps best illustrated with reference to temperament traits. Within this realm, the initial universe of content was taken to be the language personality sphere as defined by Allport and Odbert's (1936) list of approximately 4,500 trait terms culled from the Webster unabridged dictionary. Cattell (1946) reduced this list to 171 terms representing "synonym groups" and, on the basis of cluster-analytic procedures, identified approximately 35 surface-trait variables. The surface-trait variables were expressed as bipolar rating scales that were employed as peer-rating variables in the medium of *L*-data.

Within the realm of *L*-data, Cattell identified approximately 15 distinct factors which he felt accounted for the intercorrelations among surface traits in the language personality sphere. The source traits identified in *L*-data are listed as the first 15 bipolar factors in Table 10.6. The descriptive labels in that table are "popular" rather than the "professional" ones Cattell used (e.g., parmia versus threctia, premsia versus harria, comention versus abcultion), which are not self-explanatory. Cattell felt it necessary to invent neologistic terms to describe source traits to distinguish them clearly from the surface traits of ordinary language. For the most part, these neologisms are shorthand symbols for more complex expressions (e.g., comention = conformity or cultural amenability through good parent self-identification; abcultion = abhorring and rejecting cultural identification). Although intended as convenient mnemonic devices, these neologisms appear to have reduced rather than increased effective communication between Cattell's workers and those in other laboratories. In any event, a thorough mastery of this specialized terminology is a requisite for understanding Cattell's system.

Table 10.6   Primary source traits in life-record and questionnaire realms

Letter symbols	Popular labels
A	outgoing *versus* reserved
B	more intelligent *versus* less intelligent
C	emotionally stable *versus* affected by feelings
(L_1)	excitable *versus* undemonstrative
E	assertive *versus* humble, obedient
F	happy-go-lucky *versus* sober
G	conscientious *versus* expedient
H	venturesome *versus* shy
I	tender-minded *versus* tough-minded
(L_2)	doubting *versus* vigorous
(L_3)	analytical *versus* unreflective
L	suspicious *versus* trusting
M	imaginative *versus* practical
N	shrewd *versus* forthright
O	apprehensive *versus* placid
(Q_1)	experimenting *versus* conservative
(Q_2)	self-sufficient *versus* group-dependent
(Q_3)	controlled *versus* undisciplined self-conflict
(Q_4)	tense *versus* relaxed

The stability and generalizability of Cattell's L-data source-trait measures were discussed in Chapter 8 with reference to the studies of Tupes and Christal (1961) and Norman (1963). As the reader may recall, those investigators maintained that five orthogonal factors, rather than fifteen oblique factors, were sufficient to represent the language personality sphere. This difference of opinion reflects a more fundamental disagreement as to whether factor analysis is primarily a "data reduction" technique or a method for measuring source traits. In the studies of Tupes and Christal (1961), it was apparent that predictive validity could be most consistently and most parsimoniously achieved by a reduction of L-data variables to five orthogonal factors. In Cattell's system, however, it is essential that L-data source traits be "properly" identified by factor analysis, that is, identified by the method of oblique simple structure which Cattell maintains is the method of choice for trait discovery. Once a source trait is properly *measured*, its predictive significance in a given assessment problem may be evaluated with reference to the size of its factor coefficient, s_j, in a specification equation. But a conceptual distinction must be maintained between a factorial trait model of personality (Cattell's theory) and a multivariate prediction model (which can assume the many forms described in earlier chapters).

Cattell's second major series of factor-analytic investigations was conducted in the questionnaire or Q-data realm. Items were constructed to represent the 171 surface-trait variables identified in the L-data studies. In addition, items were written to cover several areas of interests and values that were thought to represent general dimensions of personality. A survey of all previously reported factorial dimensions of temperament suggested that there were 22 distinguishable and replicable patterns (Cattell, 1946). Two marker variables from each of these putative factors were also included in the initial item pool. Thus the universe of content for the Q-data studies was exceptionally broad and well defined.

Selection and construction of items on the basis of the personality sphere and on the grounds of previous research resulted in an initial pool of 1,800 items. Because it was not possible to intercorrelate and factor-analyze an item pool of this size, the method employed was that of "parcelled factor analysis," in which individual items were clustered initially into groups of variables (Cattell, 1957). The results of a series of systematic factor-analytic investigations suggested that there were at least 16 source traits in the questionnaire realm for adults. The "popular" names for these factors are given in Table 10.6. The factors labeled L_1, L_2, and L_3 were found in life-record data but not in the questionnaire realm. Those labeled Q_1, Q_2, Q_3, and Q_4 were found in Q-data but not in L-data.

The principal assessment device for measuring source traits in the questionnaire realm has been the Sixteen Personality Factor Questionnaire (Cattell, Eber, and Tatsuoka, 1970). Over a period of years, this instrument has undergone successive refinements, most of which have been directed toward obtaining more precise and reliable estimates of the sixteen primary source traits that are thought to underlie surface traits of temperament.

The most recent version of the 16 PF is available in three forms: Form A (187 items), Form B (187 items), and Form C (106 items). In addition to providing parallel forms for the assessment of change, the three versions of the 16 PF enable the practitioner to select the degree of reliability of factor estimation that is appropriate to the conditions of assessment. In routine screening situations, Form A or Form B may be employed and 16 factor estimates obtained on the basis of approximately ten items per factor scale. For precise estimation, however, the use of all three forms is recommended, with each factor being estimated on the basis of 30 items per scale.

The evidence for the construct (concept) validity of the 16 PF rests, at least in part, on the empirical demonstration that the source traits identified in the questionnaire realm represent the *same* factors originally identified in the personality sphere of L-data. Cattell has clearly indicated that three of the original L-data source traits (L_1, L_2, L_3) do not have counterparts in the questionnaire realm and that four Q-data factors (Q_1, Q_2, Q_3, Q_4) were not found in life-record data. However, it is equally clear that Cattell (1957) considers the remaining 12 factors in the questionnaire realm to have been convincingly "matched" to corresponding factors in the life-record realm.

Becker (1960) has challenged the evidence for "cross-media matching" of factors between L-data and Q-data on the basis of a reexamination of the data which Cattell originally presented as confirmatory. Becker called attention to the fact that factor estimates of presumably the "same" source trait from L-data and Q-data tended to be uncorrelated and that presumably matching variables from the two media did not have substantial and unique patterns of loadings on common factors. In response to Becker, Cattell (1961) enumerated the many sources of variance which militate against the direct alignment of factors from the two data media, especially the intrusion of "instrument factors" that represent method variance peculiar to a single data medium. Despite the complexity of the problem, the available empirical evidence for cross-media matching between L-data and Q-data factors is less than compelling.

The principal assessment applications of the 16 PF have been designated "profile matching" and "criterion estimation" (Cattell and Eber, 1957). It should be noted that these are prediction models which are not peculiar to the 16 PF or to the personality model which underlies the 16 PF. In *profile-matching* procedures, the similarity of an applicant's profile of 16 factor scales to the mean profile of a given occupational group is assessed by means of a pattern-similarity coefficient (Cattell, 1949). Strong's (1943) assumption concerning the relation between interests and occupational satisfaction is here extended to the temperament realm. Mean 16 PF profiles are available for more than 50 different occupations (Cattell, Eber, and Tatsuoka, 1970). The procedures of *criterion estimation* involve the use of specification equations, which may be thought of as multivariate variations on the basic prediction model in personality assessment. In its multivariate application, criterion estimation requires the factoring of a matrix that includes both the 16 personality variables and measures of performance in the criterion situation. The end product of such an analysis enables the specification of the weighted contribution of each personality factor to one or more dimensions of criterion performance. In its less elaborate and more typical application, criterion estimation reduces to the determination of weights for each of 16 factor scales in the multiple-regression prediction of a continuous criterion score.

The third and, in a sense, ultimate series of factor-analytic investigations was conducted in the objective test or *T*-data realm. An objective test is defined as "a portable, exactly reproducible, stimulus situation, with an exactly prescribed mode of scoring the response, *of which the subject is not informed*" (Cattell, 1957, p. 225). For Cattell, the measurement of source traits by objective tests represents the ultimate form of error-free measurement in personality. Cattell is more aware than most psychologists of the sources of distortion and "perturbations" of measurement that are present in observer ratings (*L*-data) and self-reports (*Q*-data) (see Cattell and Digman, 1964). As a consequence, the final stage of his master plan of investigations called for the identification of ability, dynamic, and temperament source traits in the *T*-data realm.

The universe of content for objective tests was extremely difficult to define because, as Cattell (1957) notes, "it is easier to define what is the objective test among personality measures than to define what is a personality measure among objective tests" (p. 227). A survey of previously available objective tests of personality showed that the vast majority were restricted to the perceptual area (e.g., the Rorschach). As a consequence, Cattell and his collaborators attempted to expand the realm of measurement to include ability tests, esthetic tests, games, performance tests, physical tests, physiological tests, preference tests, and situational tests. In a recently published compendium of objective tests, Cattell and Warburton (1967) describe 412 testing procedures which together yield 2,366 possible test scores. Because of the relatively narrow sampling of the realm of objective tests by previous investigators, most of the 412 testing procedures were developed by Cattell and his associates.

The identification of source traits in the *T*-data realm was achieved through a series of interlocking studies that were conducted in strict accordance with Cattell's psychometric criteria for the determination of oblique simple structure among factors. The most comprehensive report available on the structure of *T*-data (Hundleby, Pawlik, and Cattell, 1965) maintains that no fewer than 21 distinct and replicable source traits have been identified.

However, although several cross-media studies have been conducted, Cattell has avoided the implication that the 21 *T*-data source traits have been clearly "matched" or aligned with either the 16 factors from *Q*-data or the 15 factors from *L*-data. Consequently, the *T*-data factors have been given separate labels based on the nature of the objective tests that load them and on their correlations with other variables.

Although few claims have been made for a one-to-one correspondence of *T*-data factors with those found in *L*-data and *Q*-data, there is considerable evidence suggesting a correspondence between *T*-data factors and higher-order relationships among the factors of the two other data modes. Recall that the factors in *L*-data and *Q*-data are oblique, or correlated, some of them substantially so. Because the factors are correlated, it is possible to "factor the factors" and thereby obtain *second-order factors* that, presumably, represent a higher level of abstraction. When the first-order, or primary, factors in *L*-data or *Q*-data are factored, from five to six second-order factors emerge, the largest and most consistent of which are "extraversion versus introversion" and "anxiety versus adjustment." Extraversion and anxiety are the two most generalizable factors that have yet been identified in the realm of structured personality testing (Wiggins, 1968). The significance of these factors for objective tests lies in the fact that they appear to emerge as *first-order factors* within the realm of *T*-data. This relationship is illustrated in Figure 10.8.

At the bottom of the figure are represented the pool of 374 items that might be included if both Form A and Form B of the 16 PF were administered.

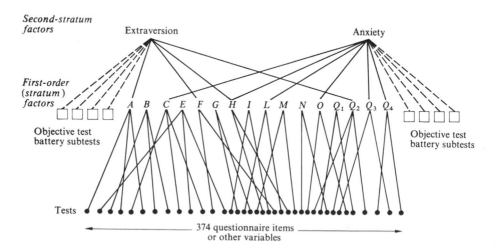

Fig. 10.8 Second-order factor structures and the relation of questionnaire and objective test factors. (From Cattell, 1965a, p. 118)

A factor analysis of these items would reduce them to 16 variables or factor scales $(A, B, \ldots, Q_4)$, which represent the first-order factors of the 16 PF. A factor analysis of these 16 factor scales, in turn, would reduce them to the second-order factors of extraversion and anxiety. Note, for example, that the first-order factors labeled A, F, H, and Q_2 are primary source traits, which are subsumed by the superordinate secondary source trait of extraversion. The figure is also meant to convey the fact that a battery of subtests from the realm of T-data will define a primary factor that is directly related to extraversion. Cattell (1965b) makes a further distinction between *factor order* and *factor stratum* that avoids a possible confusion regarding terminology. Order may be thought of in the strictly operational sense, that is, which variables are factored first, second, etc. Stratum, on the other hand, refers to the level on which a variable is conceptualized. Thus extraversion and anxiety are construed as second-stratum source traits even though they are identified by second-order factoring of L- and Q-data and first-order factoring of T-data. The practical significance of the identification of second-stratum source traits in T-data lies in the possibilities for measuring personality variables of broad theoretical significance by completely objective procedures. Thus the Objective-Analytic Anxiety Battery (Cattell and Scheier, 1960) provides a standard set of procedures for the measurement of anxiety that is presumably free of the sources of distortion typically encountered in life-record and questionnaire measures of the same trait.

In summary, the multivariate personality model of Cattell provides an extraordinarily comprehensive framework within which it is possible to conduct programs of personality assessment employing a wide variety of standardized tests of ability, temperament, and motivation that have been constructed in accord with the theoretical assumptions of the model (Institute for Personality and Ability Testing, 1971). Within this framework, individual tests, such as the 16 PF, have frequently been criticized on the grounds that too little attention has been paid to practical matters of external validation within specific assessment contexts (e.g., Rorer, 1972). It is certainly true that the major expenditures of energy of Cattell and his associates have been directed toward substantive and structural considerations in the measurement of source traits, rather than toward the demonstration of the practical value of such trait measurements in applied assessment contexts. Cattell (1957) seems to assume, and properly so, that his own contributions as a theoretician and psychometrician should be directed toward test development and that the application of such tests should fall within the province of the practitioners of educational, industrial, and clinical assessment.

The issue under consideration at the moment is not whether one of Cattell's many commercially available tests should be employed for a specific purpose, but whether the multivariate-trait *model* is an appropriate frame of reference for personality assessment. If one accepts the model, one almost inevitably employs the tests; although better instruments may be constructed, it seems unlikely that any one person or group of persons will replicate the 30 years of research that have culminated in the current instruments. On the other hand, if one challenges the appropriateness of factor analysis as a method for the identification of the principal dimensions of personality (e.g., Lykken, 1971), then one may reject both the model and the instruments which stemmed from it. Metatheoretical issues of such scope are unlikely to be resolved within the next few decades. Nonetheless, the utility of the multivariate-trait model in personality assessment would soon become apparent if this ready-made system were applied more widely than it has been in the past.

The Social Learning Model

Principal Constructs

The manner in which the social learning model of personality differs from the multivariate-trait model has already been considered in some detail in Chapter 8. The reader may recall that social behaviorists have rejected the trait construct as the basic unit for personality study because such units (a) are held to be lacking in consistency or generalizability, (b) are employed as dispositional concepts on the basis of circular reasoning, and (c) are conceptualized without regard for the situational factors which determine their manifestations. As an alternative to trait conceptualizations, social behaviorists have advocated: (a) a view of behavioral assessments as samples rather than as signs of criterion measures, (b) an emphasis on specificity and objectivity in criterion classification, and (c) the employment of strategies for the functional analysis of behavior that permit predictions to be qualified by the situations in which criterion behaviors occur.

The roots of contemporary social behaviorism can be traced back to the early formulations of Pavlov, Thorndike, and Watson, which inspired the classical theories of learning formulated by Tolman, Guthrie, Skinner, and Hull in the 1930's (see Hilgard and Bower, 1966). Social learning theory emerged as a distinctive orientation from the interdisciplinary seminars, held at the Institute of Human Relations at Yale from 1935 to 1939, in which an extraordinarily talented group of scientists attempted to integrate knowledge from the areas of psychology, sociology, anthropology, and psychiatry. One of the many important by-products of these seminars was an attempt by Neal E. Miller (an experimental psychologist) and John Dollard (a sociologist) to incorporate the findings of psychoanalysis and cultural anthropology within the stimulus-response learning theory of Clark Hull.

Dollard and Miller (1950) defined *drives* as stimuli that have reached sufficient intensity to motivate behavior. Although primary drives (e.g., hunger, sex) are important for survival, secondary drives (e.g., fear, dependency), acquired through repeated association with primary drives, are responsible for most complex social behaviors. Habits are acquired on the basis of *reinforcement*, which is defined as the reduction of drive-stimulus intensity. The distinctiveness of a drive stimulus serves as a *cue*, which becomes linked, through reinforcement, with specific responses and thus determines what pattern of behavior will occur. Whereas *instrumental responses* have direct effects on the environment, *cue-producing responses* serve as mediators for other responses. The so-called higher mental processes may be thought of as cue-producing responses. Reinforcement of a response to a given cue increases the tendency of similar cues to elicit the same response by the process of *stimulus generalization*. Reinforcement of a response to one cue and the nonreward or punishment of the response to somewhat different cues establishes a *discrimination* that tends to correct for faulty generalization. On the basis of these and other principles of learning, Miller and Dollard (1941) have provided analyses of imitation and crowd behavior, as well as alternative explanations of psychoanalytic constructs such as conflict and displacement (Dollard and Miller, 1950).

The social learning theory of Julian B. Rotter (1954) is also a reinforcement theory. Unlike Miller and Dollard, however, Rotter rejects the drive reduction interpretation of reinforcement in favor of a cognitive approach that reflects the influence of both Lewin and Tolman. Rotter focuses attention on life situations as perceived by the individual, rather than as defined by external characteristics. An *expectancy* is an individual's subjective probability that reinforcement will occur in a given situation. Such an expectancy is determined by the individual's past history of reinforcement in such situations and his generalized expectancies gained from experience in other, similar situations. In familiar situations, the individual's behavior is guided mainly by his previous reinforcement history in those situations, whereas in novel settings he must rely on generalized expectations gained from situations perceived as similar to the one at hand. A *reinforcement value* is the degree of preference an individual has for the occurrence of one reinforcing event over another. Such values may be obtained from self-reports or inferred from typical behaviors which bring about specific reinforcing events. The probability that a given behavior will occur (behavior potential) is thus held to be a function of an individual's expectations that reinforcement will occur (expectancies) and his personal preference for that class of reinforcing events (reinforcement values). In addition to providing a new framework for clinical psychology, Rotter's concepts have provided unique explanations of such phenomena as preference for delayed (as opposed to immediate) reward (Mischel, 1966) and the tendency to attribute the causes of one's behavior to internal (as opposed to external) forces (Rotter, 1966).

The social learning theory of Albert Bandura and Richard H. Walters is currently among the most influential of all contemporary viewpoints in personality, child, and clinical psychology.   Bandura and Walters (1963) were critical of earlier social learning theories, which were, in their view, based on a limited range of principles established by research on animals or on humans in one-person situations. They called for an extension and modification of such principles, as well as the introduction of new principles, in the light of research studies conducted on humans in social situations. By far the most distinctive principle stressed by Bandura and Walters is that of *observational learning*, in which novel responses are acquired without their being either emitted by the subject or reinforced. In a series of ingenious experiments with nursery school children, Bandura and his students have clearly demonstrated that a variety of responses can be acquired vicariously by exposure to a *model* who displays such responses (Bandura, 1965). Whether or not such acquired responses will be performed subsequently by the child is a function of a number of variables, including the motivational set given to the child and the reward or punishment of the model's behavior. That children learn by observation can hardly be considered a major discovery. However, the fact that traditional *S-R* reinforcement theories have neither emphasized nor adequately accounted for such an obvious area of human learning seems to substantiate Bandura and Walters' claim that revisions and extensions are in order.

Bandura and Walters rejected the formal theoretical structures of both Hull and Freud, and they developed instead an eclectic framework which emphasizes principles that have been verified in laboratory and field studies of social learning. Within this framework, heavy emphasis is placed on the manner in which behavior is acquired and maintained on the basis of different patterns or *schedules* of social reinforcement (Ferster and Skinner, 1957). Other emphasized principles include *generalization* and *discrimination*, and symbolic mechanisms of *self-regulation*. This eclectic framework is employed in an attempt "to explain the development of all forms of social behavior in terms of antecedent social stimulus events, such as the behavioral characteristics of the social models to which a child has been exposed, the reinforcement contingencies of his learning history, and the methods of training that have been used to develop and modify his social behavior" (Bandura and Walters, 1963, p. 44). The same set of principles are also used to explain the development of deviant behavior and the procedures whereby it may be modified (Bandura, 1969).

It is not entirely clear how "social learning theory" differs from other accounts of the learning process or on what grounds Bandura and Walters dismiss the formulations of Miller and Dollard and of Rotter as being less "social" than their own (Levy, 1970). Therefore it may be best to consider social learning theory as an "ideological umbrella under which have gathered theorists whose major concern is the learning of socially relevant behaviors in social contexts" (Levy, 1970, p. 410). The principal constructs employed by these theorists were originally developed by Hull, Tolman, Guthrie, and Skinner, but it is the insistence that these constructs be employed within a realistic social context that gives the distinctive emphasis to social learning theories.

Assessment Procedures

Those social behaviorists who have addressed themselves to issues of personality assessment have devoted more time and energy to the criticism of "traditional" models of assessment (e.g., psychoanalytic, multivariate) than to the development of assessment procedures which stem directly and uniquely from a social learning model. Thus most suggestions for assessment have been either broadly programmatic (e.g., Mischel, 1968; Peterson, 1968; Wallace, 1966) or of questionable practical relevance (e.g., Weiss, 1968). A notable exception to this generalization may be found in the work of Goldfried and D'Zurilla (1969). Although developed with reference to a local assessment problem, the work of Goldfried and D'Zurilla is of broad import because it illustrates the fact that psychometrically sophisticated assessment procedures may be employed within a social learning framework without compromising either the principles of personality assessment or the tenets of social learning theory.

In employing a social learning model within the context of an assessment program, Goldfried and D'Zurilla adopted a variant of Stern, Stein, and Bloom's (1956) analytic approach, which they called a "behavioral-analytic" approach. The principal differences between the analytic approach described earlier in this chapter (see Figure 10.1) and the behavioral-analytic approach may be considered with reference to Figure 10.9. Within a behavioral-analytic approach to assessment, the criterion analysis is carried out separately for (a) the environmental situations of interest and (b) the potential responses that may be elicited by these environmental situations.

Hence, instead of focusing on the individual and arriving at hypothetical personality characteristics that emphasize internal forces and dynamics, our goal is to give emphasis to both individuals and situations, and to assess the various possible specific behavior-environment interactions. (Goldfried and D'Zurilla, 1969, p. 163)

Once the potential responses to the situations of interest have been enumerated, their appropriateness is evaluated by significant others, whose opinions are likely to enter into eventual criterion judgments. The chief advantage of this three-stage criterion analysis is that, prior to the stage of

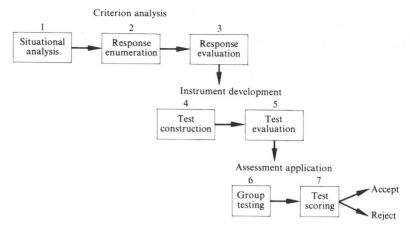

Fig. 10.9 The behavioral-analytic approach.

instrument development, both the content of the items and their empirically determined criterion significance have already been established. When these items are assembled into an appropriate testing format, the procedures for evaluating the resultant instrument are the same as those employed in the evaluation of any standardized psychological test. Should the instrument be judged to have acceptable psychometric properties, it may then be applied in group testing situations.

Goldfried and D'Zurilla (1969) were interested in the identification, measurement, and facilitation of effective behavior among college freshmen at the State University of New York at Stony Brook. Competence was defined as the "*effectiveness or adequacy with which an individual is capable of responding to the various problematic situations which confront him*" (p. 161). The social behavioral model which guided this definition of competence is illustrated in Figure 10.10. For any specific problematic situation, S_p, there is a range of possible responses, R_a, R_b, . . . , R_z, which may be ordered with respect to their effectiveness in resolving the problematic nature of the situation. Note that under a social behavioral model, attention is focused on what an individual *does* (resolves problematic situations) rather than on what he *has* (the trait of competence).

College freshmen were asked to observe their own behavior for seven consecutive days and to record the nature and background of typical problem situations, their responses to them, and the outcomes of such responses. Additional descriptions of problematic situations were obtained from resident assistants, faculty and staff members, and clinical folders supplied by the student counseling service. The list of more than 600 problematic

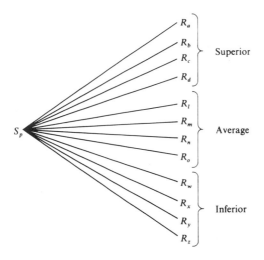

Fig. 10.10 A social behavioral model of competence. (From Goldfried and D'Zurilla, 1969, p. 161)

situations was reduced to 491 by eliminating redundant, trivial, or improbable situations. A new sample of college freshmen was requested to indicate whether or not they had encountered situations similar to those in the list of 491. Situations that occurred less than once for half of this sample were eliminated, and the list was thereby reduced to 181 problematic situations.

After a sample of high school seniors listed all their possible reactions to the 181 problematic situations, 48 situations were eliminated on the grounds that they elicited only a few different reactions and were thus not appropriate for measuring individual differences. Still another sample of college freshmen gave detailed reactions to each of the remaining 133 separate problematic situations. Those responses were rated for effectiveness on a seven-point scale by two independent judges. Again, problematic situations that failed to elicit a full range of effective responses were eliminated, and the list was thereby reduced to 88 situations, which were about equally distributed across the three judged categories of "academic," "interpersonal," and some combination of the two. Responses to these 88 situations that were then obtained from a new sample of freshmen were considered "typical" responses for purposes of instrument development.

Significant others (e.g., faculty, dormitory counselors) were provided with a detailed description of "competence" and asked to evaluate the typical responses to each of the problematic situations on that characteristic. Consensus was found among judges by combining the seven-place ratings into the categories of inferior (ratings of 1 or 2), average (ratings of 3, 4, or 5), and superior (ratings of 6 or 7), in accord with the model illustrated in Figure 10.10. In the final test version, the Survey of Problematic Situations consists of a list of problematic situations and the background in which they occur. The respondent is asked to provide a detailed description of his own most likely reactions. His responses are then evaluated against the previously established standards for inferior, average, or superior effectiveness.

Although preliminary evidence on the usefulness of the Survey of Problematic Situations appears promising (Goldfried and D'Zurilla, 1971), it would be premature to attempt to evaluate its construct validity at this time. The fate of this particular instrument at Stony Brook will be of considerable import, however, because the *general approach* advocated by the authors has widespread implications for assessment in a variety of industrial, educational, and clinical settings (Goldfried and D'Zurilla, 1969). Moreover, the work of Goldfried and D'Zurilla may provide the most direct evidence available on the utility of employing a social learning model in personality assessment. The theoretical assumptions of social behaviorism guided the behavioral-analytic approach to assessment at *every step* of the procedures illustrated in Figure 10.9. This fact seems to suggest that, far from discouraging attempts to forecast individual differences by psychological assessment procedures, social learning theory provides a specific and novel rationale for guiding such procedures.

SUMMARY

Theories of personality arose in the context of medical practice, in which physicians (e.g., Janet, Charcot, Freud, and McDougall) felt the need for rationales and procedures that would guide their attempts to cope with the psychological problems presented by their patients. As a consequence, such theories differed from experimentally based theories of behavior in their concern with (a) practical problems, (b) causes of behavior, (c) the total organism, and (d) the integration of diverse findings. Both personality theory and general behavior theory underwent rapid development in the first two decades of the present century, and in the following three decades, there were indications of convergences between the two types of formulations. Academic personologists (Murray, Allport, and Murphy) attempted to integrate experimental findings within the framework of personality theories, and experimental psychologists (Miller and Dollard) attempted to extend the scope of general behavior theory to include the clinical phenomena emphasized by psychoanalytic theory. In recent years, however, there has been a trend away from grand-scale theorizing and, instead, an emphasis on experimentation in limited behavioral domains within both personality theory and general behavior theory.

By the *formal* criteria that are employed to evaluate scientific theories, most personality theories are very poor theories. They are generally lacking in clarity and explicitness and have not been sufficiently formalized to allow for the generation of hypotheses by formal axiomatic deduction. It is therefore difficult to make meaningful comparisons among personality theories on the basis of formal criteria. On the other hand, it is quite meaningful to compare personality theories with respect to such *substantive* issues as the relative emphasis they place on cultural determinants of behavior, on heredity, etc. It is also possible to compare personality theories with respect to the basic *metaphor* or analogy the theorist had in mind when he first constructed his theory. Thus, for example, psychoanalytic theory may be said to be based on a spatial-hydraulic metaphor, whereas self theory is based on a metaphor stressing the incongruence created when alien elements from an environment intrude on the internal system of an organism. Although the metaphorical basis of a theory of personality is often implicit, making it explicit may lead to an increased understanding of the nature of the theory.

An important but as yet unanswered question concerns the extent to which personality theories may facilitate the prediction of human behavior in applied settings. We noted earlier that human judgment may enter into any or all of the steps in the basic prediction paradigm, such as criterion analysis, selection of instruments, development of the prediction battery, and application of the battery. The question considered was the extent to which such human judgment should be guided by explicit theoretical considerations. In order for a personality theory to facilitate prediction, it must be relevant to the particular criterion situation, must be explicit enough to suggest the selection of specific testing instruments, must have definite implications for criterion performance, and must be capable of being evaluated. Because the implementation of a theoretical model involves costly personnel, it can be justified only if it can be shown to produce incremental validity and a greater generality of application than does the use of procedures not guided by theoretical considerations.

Personality assessment programs can be ordered on a continuum expressing the extent to which an explicit personality model is relied on in generating predictions about human behavior. At one end of this continuum is the *analytic approach*, which places the heaviest reliance on personality theory in defining the criterion, selecting instruments, and assessing candidates. In the analytic approach an intensive situational analysis is conducted to identify the psychological role requirements underlying successful criterion performance. Once the role requirements have been identified, a target model of personality is formulated which is explicit enough to suggest the use of particular psychological testing procedures. On the basis of the results of diagnostic testing, a diagnostic council evaluates the congruence of the candidate's personality characteristics with those of the target model. Success is predicted for those who resemble the model and failure for those who do not.

The *synthetic approach* to personality assessment attempts to bypass the elaborate situational analysis of the analytic approach. On the basis of personal knowledge of the criterion situations or the writings of others, an attempt is made to intuit the psychological role requirements underlying successful performance. Such requirements might suggest an already-known personality type or syndrome that has implications for performance in the criterion situation. Frequently the synthetic model suggested has been studied previously by means of questionnaires or other structured techniques. When this is so, the elaborate diagnostic testing and diagnostic council procedures of the analytic approach may also be bypassed by the use of group testing via structured techniques.

The *empirical approach* to personality assessment places the least emphasis on explicit theoretical considerations. Attention is focused on a concrete standard of performance (e.g., grade-point average) which may be used to designate criterion groups of currently employed subjects as success-ful or unsuccessful. Under the strategy of contrasted groups, batteries of tests are administered to both successful and unsuccessful candidates, and an item analysis is performed to identify those tests or items which discriminate between them. Tests or items which survive cross-validation on another sample are assembled into a testing battery that is administered to future job applicants. Applicants who score high on this selection battery are considered to be most like the original criterion group of successful subjects, and they are selected for the position or treatment.

The decision to rely on explicit theoretical considerations at various stages of the basic prediction paradigm does not commit the assessment psychologist to any particular theoretical model of personality. Nevertheless, despite predilections of any one psychologist for one type of theorizing over others, the personality models that are likely to be of greatest value to him are those whose principal constructs are most directly translatable into concrete testing procedures. With this in mind, we reviewed the principal constructs and associated assessment procedures for (a) the psychoanalytic model, (b) the interpersonal model, (c) the transactional model, (d) the cognitive model, (e) the multivariate model, and (f) the social learning model. Although some of these models appear more promising than others as theoretical frameworks for guiding assessment procedures, there are too few instances in which a given personality model has been fully implemented in a practical assessment situation to permit any general conclusions about the role of theory in facilitating prediction.

CHAPTER 11

SOME REPRESENTATIVE
ASSESSMENT PROGRAMS

EARLY METHODS OF SELECTION AND APPRAISAL

Because of the widespread emphasis on psychological assessment and selection in this country, it is tempting to think of such practices as uniquely American phenomena. Nothing could be further from the truth, however. Although the competitive and pragmatic values of our culture provided an atmosphere that was (originally) congenial to the practice of psychological assessment, the techniques employed were primarily of foreign and even of ancient origin. A relatively sophisticated program of civil service testing and selection appears to have been employed in China more than four thousand years ago.[1] At that time, civil service officials were administered oral examinations every third year to assess their fitness for continuing in their jobs or being promoted. During the period of the Han Dynasty (206 B.C.–220 A.D.), a battery of written civil service examinations was employed to assess competence in such areas as civil law, military affairs, agriculture, revenue, and geography.

By the time of the Ming Dynasty (1368–1644 A.D.), an objective, multiple-stage selection program was practiced on a nationwide basis. Local testing centers administered essay examinations in testing booths constructed for that purpose. Candidates who survived the first stage (approximately 4%) were then tested at provincial capitals, where they were subjected to nine days (and nights) of essay examinations stressing written expression and knowledge of the classics. To ensure objectivity, "examination copyists" transcribed all written materials before they were read independently by two raters. Those who survived the second stage (approximately 5%) were admitted to

---

1.   The reader who is interested in a history of psychological testing should consult DuBois (1970), which is the principal source of the material in this section. An entertaining account of the origins of selection may be found in Parkinson's (1957) essay, which also appears in Jackson and Messick (1967).

examinations conducted in the nation's capital, and the 3% or so who passed this third stage became eligible for public office.

The Chinese system of civil service testing was well known to British diplomats and missionaries who traveled in China during the early part of the nineteenth century. A modification of the Chinese system of competitive examinations was introduced in 1832 by the English East India Company for the purpose of selecting trainees for overseas duty. In 1855, a system of competitive examinations was introduced into the British Civil Service. Following the lead of the British (which the French and Germans had also meanwhile followed), the American Civil Service Commission was established in 1883 as a centralized agency for the administration of competitive examinations in certain departments of the government. Eventually, the individual-differences movement in America (Chapter 1) expanded the domain of psychological assessment to include educational, clinical, industrial, and military settings. But the basic idea of selection on the basis of testing was neither new nor of American origin.

Germany

The crushing defeat of the German army in World War I provided an occasion for a reappraisal of the way in which that army was utilized. Simoneit (1940) attributed the disappointing performance of German soldiers to (a) poor emotional adjustment to life at the battle front, (b) lack of proper indoctrination concerning the purpose of the war, and (c) inefficient utilization of manpower. He suggested that such a situation could have been averted by the use of more comprehensive psychological assessment procedures, followed by ideological indoctrination concerning the nature and purpose of the war. As a result of Simoneit's efforts and those of other influential psychologists, the German High Command established a program for the assessment and selection of officers and specialists that was of unprecedented proportions. In 1936, there were 15 German army psychological laboratories, in which 84 military psychologists processed more than 40,000 candidates a year (Harrell and Churchill, 1941).

The unique emphasis of German military psychology was on the assessment of the "total person" within the context in which he was expected to perform. This goal was accomplished by the implementation of a precursor of the analytic approach (Chapter 10), in which small groups of four or five candidates were assessed intensively for a period of two to two and a half days by an assessment team that placed heavy emphasis on behavior observations in interviews, performance tasks, and a variety of realistic situational tests (Farago and Gittler, 1941). Although such traditional measures as biographical data, intelligence tests, and a modified form of the Strong Vocational Interest Blank (Wohlfahrt, 1938) were employed, a greater emphasis was placed on the assessment of expressive behaviors, such as speech, handwriting, and facial expressions.

Within a holistic framework, "atomistic" distinctions between abilities and character traits disappeared (Simoneit, 1932). Thus the global concept of "practical disposition" (Mierke, 1938) replaced the earlier German concept of "pure intellect" and the American concept of multiple abilities measured by standardized tests. Practical disposition was assessed by observing the reactions of candidates to a variety of performance tasks and realistic situational tests that demanded resourcefulness, imagination, persistence, leadership, and the capacity to function under stress. Performance tasks were employed both as a source of objective test data and as an occasion for observing the expressive behavior of the candidate. In one of the more dramatic tasks, the candidate was required to pull an expanding-spring exerciser that emitted increasing amounts of electrical current as it was pulled. The candidate's facial reactions were recorded by a hidden camera, and his general behavior was observed by a team of assessors. A typical situational test required the candidate to plan and supervise the construction of a bridge. He was provided with a small group of men and the necessary ladders, ropes, etc., and his direction of the project was observed by a team of officers and psychologists.

The wealth of biographical, observational, and psychological test data gathered during the two-day "living-in" assessment was evaluated by a diagnostic council. An assessment board, consisting of an army officer (usually a colonel), a medical officer, and three psychologists, made recommendations to the commanding officer, who was invested with the authority to make final decisions concerning the suitability of candidates. In retrospect, it is clear that the strategies and methods of German military assessment introduced a new dimension to the ancient Chinese concept of selection on the basis of psychological testing. The candidate was no longer viewed as the sum of his isolated abilities (e.g., knowledge of the classics), but rather as a "total personality" whose potentialities must be globally assessed in realistic situations that simulate the press of the criterion environments in which he is expected to perform.

England

Prior to World War II, officer selection in the British army was based almost exclusively on the opinions of interview boards, which were often heavily influenced by considerations of social class (Eysenck, 1953a). Parkinson (1957) has provided a somewhat fanciful description of this process.

The Selection Committee would ask briskly, "What school were you at?" and would be told Harrow, Haileybury, or, Rugby, as the case might be. "What games do you play?" would be the next and invariable question. A promising candidate would reply, "I have played tennis for England, cricket for Yorkshire, rugby for the Harlequins, and fives for Winchester." The next question would then be "Do you play polo"—just to prevent the candidate's thinking too highly of himself. Even without playing polo, however, he was evidently worth serious consideration. Little time, by contrast, was wasted on the man who admitted to having been educated at Wiggleworth. "Where?" the chairman would ask in astonishment, and "Where's that?" after the name had been repeated. "Oh, in Lancashire*!" he would say at last. Just for a matter of form, some member might ask, "What games do you play?" But the reply, "Table tennis for Wigan, cycling for Blackpool, and snooker for Wiggleworth" would finally delete his name from the list. There might even be some muttered comment upon people who deliberately wasted the committee's time.* (pp. 48–49)

By 1941, it became evident that the traditional procedures for officer selection in England had broken down. The wartime demand for officers far exceeded the supply of candidates with the traditional social background, and it became increasingly apparent that the older system was both inequitable and inefficient (Eysenck, 1953a).

In the summer of 1942, War Officer Selection Boards (WOSBs) were established to meet the crisis situation created by the failure of traditional methods of selection. The procedures of these boards were patterned directly on those of the German military psychologists. Groups of eight to ten candidates were studied intensively over a two- to three-day period by an assessment staff consisting of military testing officers, a psychiatrist, several psychologists, and the board president, who had the rank of full colonel. Candidates were administered a battery of tests which included objective tests of abilities, self-report questionnaires, and projective tests. As in the German program, there was heavy emphasis on interviews and on the observation of expressive behaviors in realistic situational tests (Morris, 1949; Vernon and Parry, 1949).

Though not so dramatic as the tasks devised by the Germans, the situational tests employed by the WOBSs nevertheless attempted to simulate common social situations of army life. A heavy emphasis was placed on behavior observations made in "leaderless-group" situations, in which a group of candidates, assigned such a task as moving a heavy object over a set of obstacles, was left to work out its own solution. Under these unstructured circumstances, considerable individual differences were observed in the character and quality of candidates' contributions to the solution of the problem at hand. Some candidates attempted to dominate the group, often losing sight of the goal to be accomplished; others assumed the role of "followers"; still others emerged as natural, task-oriented leaders. Ratings based on such behavioral observations were collated with the interview and psychological test data in a diagnostic council presided over by the ranking military officer.

Even the more severe critics of the global procedures employed by the WOSBs (e.g., Eysenck, 1953a; Vernon and Parry, 1949) agreed that the selection program represented a considerable improvement over earlier methods. For a brief period of time, the WOSBs and the older interview boards were both in operation, and it was thus possible to compare the relative effectiveness of the two procedures with respect to subsequent ratings of officer performance. The WOSB procedures were clearly superior to those of the older boards, both in increasing the proportion of valid positives and in reducing the proportion of false positives (Eysenck, 1953a). Although the reliabilities of decisions made by WOSBs were demonstrated to be less than optimal, they were nevertheless higher than those of the older boards (Vernon and Parry, 1949).

Despite a lack of conclusive evidence for the success of the German procedures, as adapted to British officer selection, the holistic approach to personality assessment was later adopted enthusiastically by the British Civil Service (Vernon, 1950; Wilson, 1948). The Civil Service Selection Board (CISSB) was patterned after the WOSB as an organization for selecting candidates for senior civil service positions both in England and abroad. An extensive multiple-stage selection strategy culminated in the familiar "living-in" assessment conducted by administrative civil servants and psychologists in a country house outside London. Although these procedures did not enjoy unanimous approval (e.g., Herbert, 1952), they appear to have been implemented with an unexpected degree of success (Eysenck, 1953a).

AMERICAN MILESTONE STUDIES

Office of Strategic Services

Prediction Problem

When the United States entered World War II in December of 1941, there were many areas of war activity for which this country was ill prepared. Chief among the problems involved was the lack of a centralized agency to coordinate espionage, sabotage, and subversive activities on a worldwide basis. The Office of Strategic Services (OSS) was created by Congress in 1942, and under the charismatic leadership of General William J. Donovan, the organization moved with unprecedented speed to close the gap in national preparedness. The overall objectives of the OSS were:

(1) to set up research units in the United States and overseas as well as an elaborate network of agents to gather strategic information concerning the activities and vulnerabilities of the nation's enemies, to analyze and evaluate this information, and to report it to those concerned.

(2) to conduct a multiplicity of destructive operations behind enemy lines, to aid and train resistance groups, and by radio, pamphlets, and other means, to disintegrate the morale of enemy troops and encourage the forces of the underground. (OSS, 1948, p. 10)[2]

During the first year of its operation, the OSS recruited and trained thousands of men and women for a variety of assignments in many parts of the world. Personnel selection took place, of course, but without any uniform screening plan and without benefit of professional consultation.

In October of 1943, an OSS official who had recently visited a War Officer Selection Board unit in England proposed that the WOSB procedures be adopted for the selection of OSS personnel in the United States. This suggestion was well received by General Donovan and his staff. Robert C. Tryon, a member of that staff, recognized the role that psychologists might play in such an enterprise. Thus it was that the "German approach," as modified by the British, was adopted by Americans as the framework for the first of a series of assessment studies that have come to be referred to as "milestones" in the history of personality assessment (Taft, 1959).

The original plan for adapting the WOSB procedures to the OSS prediction problem called for a three-day "living-in" assessment, to be conducted at a secluded country estate outside Washington, D.C. Candidates who had been recruited by various branches of the OSS were processed in groups of 18 and, on the basis of the deliberations of a diagnostic council, were either accepted or rejected for specialized training at OSS schools. When the flow of candidates became too heavy for a single assessment site, an additional selection center was established, also in Washington, where abridged one-day assessments were conducted. Shortly thereafter, a station was established in California, and before the war was over, assessments had been conducted in India, China, and Korea. However, most of the assessments took place at the country estate in Virginia called Station S (for secret) and at Station W (for Washington), where a combined total of 5,391 candidates were assessed during the last 20 months of the war.

The prediction problem faced by the OSS staff was embedded in an exceptionally complex context of decision-theoretic considerations. For many assignments, the success or failure of a mission depended on the individual or individuals selected. Of greater concern, however, was the amount of damage to the war effort that might accrue from security leaks, impaired relationships with resistance forces, or decreased morale among OSS units. To this possible damage resulting from the selection of false positives was added the consideration that an unsuccessful candidate, by virtue of filling

---

2. The major source of information about the OSS assessment program is the report prepared by the OSS staff entitled *Assessment of Men* (Rinehart, 1948). Unless specified otherwise, page references in this section are to that book.

an assignment, deprived the organization of the services of a candidate who might have completed an important mission successfully. Therefore the overall decision policy adopted by the OSS was a minimax strategy aimed at avoiding large losses by keeping the proportion of false positive decisions to a minimum. However, that strategy was tempered in many instances by the need for "bodies" to fill especially critical assignments.

Whereas the War Officer Selection Boards were each designed to select men for one type of job, the OSS stations faced the problem of multiple selection for an extremely heterogeneous set of assignments. For a group of 18 candidates, simultaneous selection took place for as many as seven types of assignments, which might have included jobs as diverse as language expert, saboteur, nurse, undercover agent, script writer, paratrooper, and linotype operator. The variety of assignments to be considered precluded the possibility of developing tests of special skills for each assignment and made it necessary to assess a set of "general" dispositions, skills, and traits, at least some of which were irrelevant for most assignments. This situation, coupled with a lack of specific criterion information, forced the assessors to adopt a "global" (Taft, 1959) or "naive clinical" (Holt, 1958) approach to prediction, despite their preference for more analytic procedures.

The final OSS assessment report was prepared by Donald W. Fiske, Eugenia Hanfmann, Donald W. MacKinnon, James G. Miller, and Henry A. Murray. Although both the report and the assessment program itself were highly collaborative enterprises, they bear the unmistakable imprint of Murray's approach to personality assessment. The "multiform organismic system of assessment" described in detail in the OSS volume was the approach advocated earlier by Murray (1938) and described later by Stern, Stein, and Bloom (1956) as the analytic approach. But the particular form the analytic approach took in the OSS program assumed that "holistic" procedures would always be more effective than "atomistic" procedures. As a consequence, little consideration was given to the possibility that statistical combination of the predictor variables might have led to effective prediction. In fact, human judgment was relied on at every stage of the prediction paradigm, even when mere averaging of assessment ratings might have been a sensible procedure. Despite the self-critical attitude maintained by the assessment staff, the virtues of holism were never questioned. Because of the influential nature of the OSS report, many years passed before the role of human judgment in personality assessment was seriously questioned (Meehl, 1954).

Criterion Analysis

It is unlikely that any single large-scale assessment program has been confronted with a "criterion problem" of the magnitude of that encountered by the OSS assessment staff. Many OSS missions were conceived in remote parts of the world, communicated to administrative officers in Washington who were largely unfamiliar with field operations, and then described to an assessment staff who had little or no familiarity with either the job classifications (e.g., resistance group leader, liaison pilot) or with the situational context in which the job functions would be performed (e.g., Burmese jungles).

Many of the operations were still in the planning phase; others were being carried out behind enemy lines outside the range of witnesses, and even at the most advanced bases the officer in charge was often for long periods of time uncertain as to what his men were doing out there in the unknown. It was sometimes months before enough knowledge was accumulated to form the basis of a report that could be hurried back through channels to the United States. Rarely were the details in any series of reports sufficient to give the officers in Washington vivid concrete pictures of the real circumstances in this or that OSS installation overseas. (p. 12)

In only a few instances was the OSS assessment staff provided with material that would minimally qualify as a "job description."

Despite the ambiguity surrounding both job descriptions and situational contexts, the *initial* assessment procedures were directed toward the selection of men for more or less specific assignments overseas. In the absence of specific information, the criterion situations were often visualized in terms of somewhat fanciful images.

In the beginning, the judgments of many of us were confused by the influence of an enduring lodger in our minds, the figure of the Sleuth, acquired from Somerset Maugham's The British Agent, *from Helen MacInnes'* Assignment in Brittany, *from the thrillers of E. Phillips Oppenheim, and from who-can-say-what motion pictures and detective stories. Even the legendary cloak-and-dagger hero may have come into it.* (p. 14)

Such stereotyped impressions were corrected to some extent when more specific job specifications were received, when returned OSS personnel were interviewed, and when some members of the OSS staff had opportunities for first-hand observations of OSS schools and overseas assignments. But even though the assessors in the course of time formed increasingly sophisticated conceptions of the nature of the criterion situations, they soon discovered that many men, on arriving overseas, were assigned to duties that were significantly different from those for which they had been assessed (Murray and MacKinnon, 1946). Upon recognition of this disconcerting fact, the focus of criterion analysis shifted from attempts to assess candidates for specific assignments to an attempt to assess candidates with reference to a set of *general qualifications* considered essential to the effective performance of most OSS overseas assignments. Interviews were conducted with branch chiefs and their administrative officers in Washington for the purpose of eliciting dispositions, abilities, and traits which these officers considered necessary for their particular projects. An initial set of approximately twenty variables was eventually reduced to the ten presented in Table 11.1. The first seven variables listed in the table was considered necessary for most OSS activities, the remaining three only for certain kinds of assignments.

Table 11.1 General and special qualifications for OSS overseas service (from OSS, 1948, pp. 30–31)

General Qualifications

1. *Motivation for assignment:* war morale, interest in proposed job.
2. *Energy and initiative:* activity level, zest, effort, initiative.
3. *Effective intelligence:* ability to select strategic goals and the most efficient means of attaining them; quick practical thought—resourcefulness, originality, good judgment—in dealing with things, people, or ideas.
4. *Emotional stability:* ability to govern disturbing emotions, steadiness and endurance under pressure, snafu tolerance, freedom from neurotic tendencies.
5. *Social relations:* ability to get along well with other people, good will, team play, tact, freedom from disturbing prejudices, freedom from annoying traits.
6. *Leadership:* social initiative, ability to evoke cooperation, organizing and administering ability, acceptance of responsibility.
7. *Security:* ability to keep secrets; caution, discretion, ability to bluff and to mislead.

Special Qualifications

8. *Physical ability:* agility, daring, ruggedness, stamina.
9. *Observing and reporting:* ability to observe and to remember accurately significant facts and their relations, to evaluate information, to report succinctly.
10. *Propaganda skills:* ability to apperceive the psychological vulnerabilities of the enemy; to devise subversive techniques of one sort or another; to speak, write, or draw persuasively.

Thus the essentially insurmountable criterion problem faced by the OSS assessment staff was resolved, in part, by accepting a list of psychological characteristics underlying effective performance provided by a group of significant others as "the next best thing to job descriptions" (p. 30). This rather novel strategy illustrates the extent to which the somewhat idealized methods of personality assessment described in the preceding chapter must be compromised, on occasion, in the light of practical realities. Note, first of all, that the significant others employed in "criterion analysis" (branch officers in Washington) were considerably less informed of actual conditions in the field than were OSS officers serving overseas. Second, significant others were employed, not as sources of information for defining the criterion, but as "psychologists," who estimated the psychological characteristics underlying the successful enactment of a role in a criterion situation. Finally, having committed themselves to the assessment of general traits and dispositions, the OSS staff frequently relied on administrative officers for judgments concerning special aptitudes, an assessment that is typically made by psychologists. Under conditions of national emergency, men do what they have to do, not necessarily what they have been trained to do.

Models and Strategies

OSS procedures were guided by the holistic philosophy of assessment, first formulated by Simoneit and later adopted by British military psychologists. This approach emphasizes the assessment of the "total person" within the environmental context in which he is expected to perform. Consequently some consideration must be given to the issue of representative sampling. Under what Taft (1959) called "the assumption of safety in numbers," holistic approaches typically employ both a large number of data collection procedures and a large number of assessors. In the assessment program conducted at Station S, 35 different assessment procedures were employed, and each procedure permitted the measurement of from one to four variables. Thus it was possible to assess each major variable by a variety of techniques. For example, the single variable of social relations (see Table 11.1) was assessed by: interviews, informal observations, individual task situations, group task situations, projective tests, and sociometric questionnaires.

The assumption of safety in numbers was also met with respect to the number of assessors employed. The assessment personnel at Station S consisted of a senior staff of seven psychologists, psychiatrists, and sociologists and a junior staff of eight graduate students in psychology. Entering classes of eighteen candidates were divided into three groups, each of six men, to which a team of two senior and one junior staff members was assigned. Each three-man assessment team was responsible for interviewing, observing, and rating its group of candidates, so that ratings of all personality variables for each candidate were obtained from at least three independent raters. After a series of team conferences in which these ratings were discussed, the material was presented to the full diagnostic council, whose members also took into account the observations and impressions of other staff members in arriving at a final formulation for each candidate.

According to the authors of the final report on OSS assessment activities, the procedures at Station S were not designed with reference to any explicitly stated strategy of assessment (such as analytic, synthetic, or empirical) or with reference to any explicit model of personality (such as psychoanalytic, interpersonal, or transactional). The assessment staff consisted of behavioral scientists and physicians who represented a broad range of viewpoints concerning assessment and personality theory. The time pressure of the war precluded the possibility of their agreeing on a comprehensive or integrative framework prior to the conduct of the assessment program. In addition,

. . . there was a half-conscious tacit realization—shared, it seems, by the majority—that frank discussions on the conceptual level would reveal radical disagreements which might, by disturbing interpersonal relations, interfere with the smooth functioning of the unit. (p. 26)

Thus a group of psychologists, sociologists, anthropologists, and psychiatrists were able to put aside, temporarily, their conceptual differences and concentrate instead on the common assessment task at hand. Such cooperation was no doubt facilitated by the fact that assessment was conducted with reference to theoretically neutral variables (see Table 11.1) and that final reports were written in nontechnical language that was comprehensible to military officers.

Data Collection

Perhaps the most unusual feature of the OSS assessment program was the high level of secrecy that was maintained in all phases of the program. Once a mission had been planned, recruitment procedures were initiated by the Personnel Procurement Branch, the Civilian Personnel Branch, or any one of the many individual OSS branches. Although there was considerable variability in the amount of information imparted by recruiters about assignments, security considerations were such that many of the men being recruited did not have the faintest idea of the nature of the organization they were being asked to join or of the type of assignment for which they were being asked to volunteer. As a consequence, it is likely that a substantial proportion of those who volunteered were attracted by the idea of mysterious and unusually hazardous duties, even though many OSS assignments were of a relatively mundane nature.

A candidate judged suitable by a recruiting officer was ordered to report to an address in Washington. Here he was typically interviewed by a representative of the branch for which he had been recruited and, if still considered suitable, informed that he was to attend an "assessment school" for three days. He also learned that he would attend that school under complete anonymity and therefore was not to reveal his true name, vocation, rank, place of residence, or family background to anyone at the school. To ensure this anonymity, the candidate next turned in all personal belongings and donned Army fatigues and boots. Thus clad and under an assumed name, he traveled to Station S in a canvas-covered Army truck along with his anonymous "fellow students."

Upon arrival, the candidates were greeted by the assessment staff and given an orientation to the assessment program by the Director. During the orientation, the staff stressed that each candidate should develop a cover story to go with his assumed name and that he should be prepared to defend this deception. The candidates were also told that under certain circumstances ("X condition"), they were to answer biographical questions honestly and not in terms of their assumed identity. The variety and extensivenses of data collection procedures at Station S is apparent from the typical three-day schedule presented in Table 11.2. During their first evening, candidates were administered a battery of paper-and-pencil tests of intelligence and personality. They were then taken to a room containing articles of clothing, ticket receipts, etc., and allowed to examine the belongings of a hypothetical occupant for four minutes. Next came a series of questions about the man whose belongings they had just examined. By midnight, most of the candidates had finished, and they retired on the eve of the first full day of assessment.

After breakfast on the first day of assessment, the candidates were informed that they would be tested at a later time on their abilities to observe the terrain of Station S and its buildings and to reconstruct the probable history of the estate (terrain test). They were then assigned to one of three situational tests or to a personal interview. The Brook and the Wall were leaderless-group problem-solving tasks designed to provide a realistic situation in which the variables of energy and initiative, effective intelligence, social relations, leadership, and physical ability could be rated by the three-man assessment team. In the construction task, a candidate was provided with two "helpers" (junior staff members) whom he was to direct in the construction of a wooden frame structure. One helper (Kippy) was passive and sluggish, did nothing unless ordered to, and generally stood around and got in the way. The other helper (Buster) was aggressive, offered impractical suggestions, and was very adept at criticizing what he suspected were the candidate's weakest points. Although ostensibly a test of leadership, the construction task was designed primarily to assess the candidate's emotional maturity and frustration tolerance. A postconstruction interview was held to assess the candidate's reactions to the situation and to provide an opportunity for desensitization to what, for many men, was an emotionally traumatic situation. Although therapeutic in intent, the interview provided the first occasion on which a candidate might be tricked into breaking cover, since it was not conducted under "X conditions."

After lunch, all candidates were administered tests of propaganda skills, observation and memory, and mechanical comprehension. A leaderless group discussion was then held on the topic "What are the major postwar problems facing the United States?" and at its conclusion, candidates were asked to nominate, by secret ballot, the most persuasive speakers and the best leaders in their group. Of the several assessment procedures administered during the evening, the stress interview was the most demanding. Candidates were told to assume that they had been apprehended in the act of searching secret files in a government office building late at night. They were given twelve minutes to invent plausible cover stories prior to interrogation. Each candidate was taken to a darkened room and seated in a hard chair facing a spotlight and a panel that consisted of an interrogator and several other staff members. The interrogator began in a quiet and sympathetic manner but soon changed to a style of rapid and merciless cross-questioning designed to break the cover story. Upon completion of the stress interview, each candidate was told that he had failed the test and that he should report to the office of a senior staff member for an interview. The post stress interview was ostensibly therapeutic, and the interviewer did everything he could to make the candidate feel reassured and at ease. The main purpose of this pleasant interview, however, was to attempt to get the candidate to break his cover under "non-X conditions."

As Table 11.2 indicates, the schedule for the second day of assessment was no less rigorous than for the first. Again, the emphasis was on situational tests and performance tasks designed to elicit samples of behavior considered relevant to eventual criterion performance in OSS assignments. The improvisation task was a unique adaptation of the principles of psychodrama (Moreno, 1946) to the purposes of personality assessment (Bronfenbrenner and Newcomb, 1948). A pair of candidates were presented with a description of a hypothetical situation that preceded an encounter between two individuals. They were then required, in front of an audience consisting of assessors and fellow candidates, to improvise the interaction that might take place. One such situation was as follows:

A. moved to a small city about three months ago and opened a business there. He has been doing quite well and one month ago sent in an application for membership in a club in the town. He has heard nothing in response to this application and goes to the home of B., a prominent member of the club, with whom he is pleasantly acquainted. (A. is then sent out of the room and B. is told that A. has received several blackballs.) A. is then called back into the room. (p. 170)

Table 11.2 Schedule of assessment procedures at Station S

ORIENTATION PERIOD

Briefing in Washington, D.C.
Arrival and orientation at Station S

Dinner

Otis Test of Mental Ability, sentence completion test, health questionnaire, work conditions survey, vocabulary test, personal history form
Belongings test

FIRST DAY

Breakfast

Instructions for terrain test
The Brook
The Wall
Construction; postconstruction interview
Personal history interview (X condition)

Lunch

Propaganda skills, map memory test, Bennett Mechanical Comprehension
Test, Instructions for Manchuria Propaganda Assignment
Leaderless group discussion; sociometric assessment

Dinner

Instructions for interrogation test
Stress interview
Poststress interview
Test of ability to evaluate and to abstract intelligence information
Preparation for teaching test

On the basis of their impressions of the candidates, the staff created
tailor-made situations for each candidate in order to reveal specific faults he
was thought to have. In the example just cited, the role of A. was given to a
candidate thought to be unduly sensitive to rejection, and the role of B. was
assigned to a candidate thought to be lacking in tact and diplomacy. The
candidates were told that their performances were to be evaluated in terms
of (a) their effectiveness in handling the situation and (b) the extent to which
their performances corresponded to how they would actually handle such a
situation in real life. Alcoholic beverages were made available to the candidates during the last half hour of the improvisation session, and drinking
was permitted following the session and later during the debate task, which
ended the activities of the second day. The introduction of alcohol permitted
the candidates to relax and allowed the assessors to evaluate its effects on
each candidate's comportment.

During the morning of the third day of assessment, the candidates made

SECOND DAY

Breakfast

Assigned leadership tasks: Mined Road, Sentry, Agent's Room, Blown Bridge, Killing the Mayor

Teaching test

Terrain test

Lunch

Names and identifications test, movie observation test, code aptitude test

Interrogation test

Obstacle course

Dinner

Improvisations

Cocktails

Debate

THIRD DAY

Breakfast

Sociometric questionnaire

Personality sketches

Instructions for murder mystery test

Lunch

Athletic events

Baseball game

Murder mystery court

Dinner

sociometric ratings of one another, and each one wrote brief personality sketches of the five other members of his assessment group. Meanwhile the staff members finished scoring tests and met in team conferences to decide on the contents of their assessment reports. The events scheduled for the candidates during the afternoon were designed primarily to keep them occupied and to provide them with relaxation while the staff members wrote their reports and attended the diagnostic council meetings, which were held from 3:30 until 10:00 in the evening. Because the candidates were scheduled to return to Washington the next morning, it was necessary to make a final decision regarding each candidate's suitability by the evening of the third day of assessment.

Data Combination

The staff conference was the vehicle for integrating the mass of data collected over a three-day period into a set of final ratings and recommendations for each candidate. Since no information was available concerning the empirical validities of the many different assessment procedures, individually or collectively, it was not possible to consider statistical techniques for data combination. Even if such information had been available, it seems likely that the holistic philosophy to which the OSS staff subscribed would have predisposed them toward clinical rather than statistical data combination. From the holistic point of view, the significance of any single assessment datum must be evaluated in relationship to all available data, as well as in relationship to the anticipated criterion situation. Presumably, such global evaluations cannot be achieved through mechanical averaging or weighting; rather, they require human judgment.

The staff conference attended by all staff members, was presided over by the Director of Station S. The cardinal rules of the conference were "informality and dispatch." That is, an attempt was made to maintain an atmosphere in which full and uninhibited discussion could take place within the realistic constraints of time that existed at Station S. The senior staff members who had interviewed a candidate began the proceedings by reading a description of that candidate's proposed assignment. He next read his part of the personality description, which, because of the importance attached to the interview as an assessment technique, was weighted heavily in the deliberations. The remainder of the personality description was presented by the senior staff member in charge of the situational ratings.

Following the presentation of the personality description, the floor was opened for detailed discussion and criticism of the report prepared by the assessment team. At this point the assessment team might be asked to produce the evidential basis for their interpretations, or other staff members might contribute their own impressions which contradicted or corroborated those of the assessment team. Discussions focused on the adequacy of the personality description and on the manner in which the person described would fit into his particular assignment. These deliberations continued until a final selection decision could be made. An attempt was made to achieve consensus through discussion rather than by resorting to formal voting procedures. Although the final decisions were "accept" or "reject," these categories were sometimes qualified. For example, a candidate could be rejected for his particular assignment but recommended for a different type of assignment. A "red flag" indicated that the candidate should be accepted only on the condition that he complete his OSS training with a favorable report from his instructors.

Once the selection decision had been made, the staff proceeded to make final ratings on the ten qualifications considered necessary for OSS service (see Table 11.1). A large chart displayed all the ratings, based on 35 different data collection procedures, in such a way that both the central tendency and variability of each rating was apparent from inspection. The staff avoided statistical averaging of ratings because they felt that the data collection procedures varied in their relevance to different variables and because they were convinced that each rating must be considered in the light of the total information available for a candidate. For the most part, the final ratings given to a candidate were similar to those that would have been obtained from a weighted averaging procedure. In some instances, however, the opinions of the interviewer or the impressions of one or more staff members led to a group decision to adjust one or more ratings for a candidate. Ratings on suitability for assignment and on overall suitability were made independently by board members and then averaged, but, even those averaged ratings were subject to group discussion and possible change.

The final task of the council members was to make detailed ratings of the candidate's fitness for different conditions of assignment (e.g., behind enemy lines), different levels of responsibility (e.g., high level of authority), and different types of assignment (e.g., operational agent). Because those final ratings had been preceded by extensive discussion, there were seldom disagreements among the staff at this point. The selection decision, the personality description, and the detailed ratings on qualifications and suitability for assignment constituted the final report, which was delivered to OSS headquarters in Washington early the next morning.

Outcomes of Prediction

As indicated in Chapter 6, the utility of any personnel decision strategy can be evaluated fully only in comparison with the success of the procedure that was employed previously. In the case of the OSS, there was virtually no information available on the percentage of failures among the thousands of unassessed candidates who had been recruited prior to the introduction of formal selection at Station S, and thus, "at the outset we had to face the fact that we would never know certainly whether we had been an asset or a liability to the OSS" (p. 9). But the lack of a base line against which to evaluate incremental validity was almost a trivial problem in comparison with other circumstances which militated against overall evaluations of the outcomes of prediction. When formal assessment began, the demands of war required that all efforts be directed toward selection; no time or manpower was available for consideration of the accuracy of such selection. By the time resources became available for adequate appraisal of overseas performance, the war was over. Consequently, to a large extent, "the final verdict is a question mark" (p. 392).

During the relatively short period in which the OSS assessment program was in operation, four different methods of obtaining evaluations of overseas performance were employed, but none was considered entirely satisfactory.

1. *An overseas staff appraisal* was conducted by four members of the assessment staff in Europe, the Mediterranean area, and China. An attempt was made to interview the immediate chief of each man appraised and several of his associates. On the basis of these interviews, the staff members made overall ratings of performance and indicated the probable reliability of such ratings, considering the amount of information on which they were based.

2. *A theater commander appraisal* was obtained from immediate superiors, who used a number of the same variables that had been rated by the original assessment staff. Other remarks in this report were later read by members of the assessment staff, who then made an overall rating of proficiency.

3. *A reassignment area appraisal* took place at a relocation center for personnel who had completed one tour of duty and were being considered for another. The appraisal consisted mainly of a clinical interview and a self-report questionnaire. The assessment staff member who conducted the interview had access to the theater commander's report and on the basis of this, plus the interview and questionnaire, prepared a short report and rated the man on the same personality variables rated during assessment.

4. *A returnee appraisal* was conducted by the assessment staff in Washington and at a relocation center. Each returnee received a list of names of individuals who had been on duty in his theater of operations, and he was asked to check those with whom he was personally acquainted. He was then interviewed about the performance of those men whom he appeared to know reasonably well. This procedure sometimes yielded independent appraisals from peers, superiors, and subordinates.

Although these four methods of appraisal of overseas performance appear sound in principle, they proved less than satisfactory in practice. Because of time pressures and lack of resources, it was not possible to conduct appraisals on all assessed candidates who subsequently went overseas. Of the assessed candidates for whom some form of minimally acceptable appraisal data were available, almost half had been assessed at Station W in Washington under a quite different set of conditions. Further, of those appraised candidates who had been assessed at Station S, the majority had been processed during the first six months of the program when the selection procedures were still incomplete. As a consequence, the percentage of appraised men who had been assessed at Station S during the later and more representative period of its operation ranged from 4 percent to 7 percent for the four different appraisal techniques.

Because of these small numbers and because of a variety of shortcomings that were known or suspected to have existed in the four appraisal techniques, the authors of the final OSS assessment report were reluctant to accept these criterion measures as a standard against which to evaluate their selection program: "The complete detailed analysis of these appraisal data is not of sufficient interest to justify publication" (p. 418). Consequently, only a few selected findings were reported as illustrative of relationships which the OSS staff felt were far from conclusive.

Some indication of the comparability of the four different appraisal techniques is given by the correlations among ratings of overall effectiveness in carrying out overseas assignment for men on whom two or more such appraisal ratings were available. These intercorrelations are presented in the lower left of Table 11.3, and the numbers of cases on which they are based are given in the upper right. As is evident from the table, the correspondence between different methods of appraisal is less than striking.

Table 11.3 Intercorrelations among appraisal ratings (after OSS, 1948, p. 421)

Type of appraisal	Theater com-manders	Overseas staff	Reassign-ment area	Returnee
Theater commanders	—	(113)	(237)	(117)
Overseas staff	.59	—	(96)	(136)
Reassignment area	.58	.46	—	(109)
Returnee	.49	.50	.49	—

Note: Correlation coefficients are in the lower left of the table and the numbers of cases on which they are based appear in parentheses in the upper right.

The most direct published evidence concerning the effectiveness of the OSS assessment program is presented in Table 11.4. The correlations in this table are between job effectiveness ratings made by assessment staffs and job effectiveness ratings obtained from the four overseas appraisal methods. All correlations have been corrected for restriction in the range of assessment ratings. Next to these correlations are the percentages of men who had been assessed as "medium" or "high," but who were appraised as "low" in terms of satisfactory job performance, i.e., the percentages of false positives sent overseas. Thus, for those 88 men who were assessed at Station S and appraised by the overseas staff, the correlation between predicted and appraised performance was .37, and the percentage of false positives was 15 percent.

Several trends are immediately apparent from an inspection of the table: (a) the validity coefficients are positive and relatively low, (b) the assessment ratings are most highly correlated with appraisals by overseas staff, and (c) the ratings made at Station W appear to be more valid than those made

Table 11.4 Correlations between assessment job ratings and appraisal ratings with percentage of candidates appraised as unsatisfactory (after OSS, 1948, pp. 423, 425)

Type of appraisal	Station S job rating			Station W job rating		
	r	Unsatis-factory, %	N	r	Unsatis-factory, %	N
Overseas staff	.37	15	88	.53	6	83
Returnee	.19	16	93	.21	3	173
Theater commanders	.23	13	64	.15	15	158
Reassignment area	.08	11	53	.30	4	178

at Station S. On the basis of these and other findings, the authors of the OSS final report concluded that "none of our statistical computations demonstrates that our system of assessment was of great value" (p. 423). However, this pessimistic conclusion was based primarily on an examination of the magnitude of the validity coefficients and not on a consideration of the outcomes of prediction. As we repeatedly emphasized in Chapter 6, validity coefficients do not tell the whole story of prediction, and the OSS assessment study may serve as an illustration of this principle.

Table 11.4 contains information that may be employed to estimate the outcomes of prediction in the OSS assessment program. First, as already noted, the reported validity coefficients have been *corrected* for restriction in the range of the predictor variables, and they may therefore be viewed as estimates of the validity coefficients that would have been obtained in the total sample of candidates assessed (Gulliksen, 1950, p. 137). Second, the percentage of unsatisfactory candidates may be employed as an estimate of the percentage of false positives among men sent overseas. Third, the table provides the number of cases on which the statistics were computed. An additional source of information comes from the OSS final report, which indicates that the selection ratio employed in assessment was approximately .75. As will become apparent in the material that follows, these four numbers may be employed to estimate the outcomes of prediction.

The authors of the OSS assessment report indicated that the procedure for appraisal by overseas staff was considered the most valid from the beginning, and that they were "all too humanly disposed to be still more convinced" on the basis of the post hoc evidence shown in Table 11.4. For this reason, the results obtained with that appraisal procedure will be considered in some detail. In considering these results, we will illustrate a novel application of some of the principles for estimating outcomes of prediction that were discussed in Chapter 6. For reasons already indicated, the available data on the validity of OSS selection procedures are highly fallible. Consequently, our estimates of the outcomes of prediction must be considered equally fallible. But the method to be described is a *general* one that may be applied with greater confidence to other studies for which firmer data are available.

Table 11.4 shows that a total of 88 men were both selected at Station S and appraised by the overseas staff. Since the selection ratio was stated to be 75 percent, we will use a hypothetical sample of size 88/.75, or 117 men, as the population to be considered in our calculations. Table 11.4 also indicates that, of the 88 men selected, 15 percent, or 13 men, were appraised as unsatisfactory. These figures permit us to construct the following frequency table.

	Reject	Accept
	FN	VP
Satisfactory		75
	VN	FP
Unsatisfactory		13
	29	88	117

The frequencies may be expressed as probabilities by dividing each of them by the estimated population size of 117.

	Reject	Accept
	$P(FN)$	$P(VP)$
Satisfactory		.64
	$P(VN)$	$P(FP)$
Unsatisfactory		.11
	$1 - SR = .25$	$SR = .75$

In Chapter 6, we derived the following formula, which states the relationship between a validity coefficient and the outcomes of prediction:

$$\phi_{yy'} = \frac{P(VP) - BR \cdot SR}{\sqrt{BR(1 - BR)SR(1 - SR)}}.$$

Because the validity coefficient ($r = .37$) reported in Table 11.4 was corrected for restriction in range of the predictor variable, it may be employed as an estimate (admittedly tenuous) of the phi coefficient that would have been obtained in the total sample. The formula just given may be solved for the unknown quantity of base rate.[3] The results of these calculations are given in Table 11.5.

One must bear in mind that the outcomes of prediction given in Table 11.5 are *estimates* based on a number of plausible but not necessarily veridical assumptions. To the extent that these estimates are correct, they suggest a quite different conclusion from that drawn by the OSS staff on the basis of validity coefficients alone. Perhaps the most striking feature of these estimates is the high base rate of probable success. Obviously, such base rates would not obtain in a completely unselected population. Candidates sent to Station S had been carefully chosen by recruiting officers and were further screened by branch chiefs prior to assessment. Candidates sent to Station W tended to be either high-level executives who were already well known to the OSS administration or secretaries, office workers, and research workers whose technical qualifications had already been demonstrated. Thus the high base rate of success at S and the even higher base rate at W created a situation in which selection procedures of modest validities could result in relatively favorable outcomes of prediction.

As Table 11.5 indicates, it is estimated that 77 percent of the decisions made at Station S were correct. Under a strategy of random selection, $P(VP) = BR \cdot SR = .57$, and $P(VN) = (1 - BR)(1 - SR) = .06$. By random selection, therefore, the proportion of correct decisions would have been 63 percent. In view of the critical nature of the assignments, an increment of 14 percent over random selection is important. In evaluating the expected utility of the selection program at Station S, one would have to conclude that the costs of testing, though considerable in absolute terms, were slight in relative terms, given the economics of a world war. Yet the negative utility of false positive decisions was high, and in this respect, the false positive rate of .11 must be considered disappointing. Note, however, that selection procedures reduced the false positive rate by seven percent

---

3. Squaring both sides of the equation and rearranging terms permits the expression of the formula in quadratic form, and it may be solved by finding the roots of a quadratic equation.

Table 11.5 Estimated outcomes of prediction from Station S and Station W

Selection at Station S versus overseas staff ratings

	Reject	Accept	
	P(FN)	P(VP)	
Satisfactory	.12	.64	$BR = .76$
	P(VN)	P(FP)	
Unsatisfactory	.13	.11	$1 - BR = .24$

$1 - SR = .25$ $SR = .75$
Estimated $\phi_{yy'} = .37$
Overall correct $= .77$

Selection at Station W versus overseas staff ratings

	Reject	Accept	
	P(FN)	P(VP)	
Satisfactory	.12	.71	$BR = .83$
	P(VN)	P(FP)	
Unsatisfactory	.13	.04	$1 - BR = .17$

$1 - SR = .25$ $SR = .75$
Estimated $\phi_{yy'} = .53$
Overall correct $= .84$

under that which would have obtained under random selection. Given the need for manpower to fill critical assignments, the false negative rate is also somewhat disappointing.

The superiority of the abridged one-day assessment procedures at Station W is even more evident from a consideration of the outcomes of prediction in Table 11.5. The overall proportion of correct decisions of 84 percent represents a considerable improvement over the proportion of 66 percent that would have obtained under random selection. Most important, the false positive rate of four percent is within tolerable limits and represents a reduction of nine percent under random selection. The reasons for the superiority of selection at Station W, as compared with selection at Station S, have been a source of considerable controversy. The authors of the OSS assessment report speculated that the expected base rate of success in the two assessment populations differed, and our own estimates tend to support that speculation. The authors also speculated that the assessors at S might have been in possession of too much information about their candidates in relation to the amount of information they had regarding the probable job assignments. Thus, although assessors at Station S had a greater opportunity to discover the personality dynamics of their candidates, they were uncertain as to how such information could be applied to the practical selection problem at hand.

Some critics of the OSS assessment program have been less generous. Eysenck (1953a), for example, interpreted the superiority of selection at Station W as relatively conclusive evidence of the inappropriateness of holistic approaches to selection. There is little doubt that the brief and relatively nonglobal assessment conducted at Station W fell at the low end of a continuum of "holistic assessment," as compared with the elaborate clinical and situational procedures employed at Station S. Yet the principal conclusion drawn by the OSS staff was that the holistic approach to assessment is always the method of choice in complex selection programs. Unfortunately, these divergent interpretations of the implications of the results of the OSS assessment program cannot be resolved on the basis of available data. Both the populations and the circumstances of assessment at the two stations were too different from one another to justify viewing the data as stemming from a rigorously controlled experiment. On the other hand, the abiding faith of the OSS staff in the holistic approach seems to have prevented them from even considering the possibility that the strategy itself could be lacking in merit.

Critique

In some respects, the authors of the final OSS assessment report were their own most severe critics. A large proportion of their lengthy report is devoted to detailed criticisms of every phase of the OSS program, together with specific recommendations concerning the manner in which future assessment programs might be conducted to avoid their mistakes. Consequently, this remarkable volume must be considered as ranking among the most significant treatises on personality assessment ever written. The authors were painfully aware of the difficulties of conducting an assessment program in the absence of a satisfactory criterion analysis, with assessment procedures of unknown validity, in a situation in which adequate appraisals of the outcomes of prediction were not possible. Rather than congratulating themselves for making the best of an impossible situation, the authors focused on the procedural errors they committed within that situation. The result was a set of recommendations for future assessment programs that provides a concise summary of the state of the art as it existed in 1948.

Institute of Personality Assessment and Research

Prediction Problem

The challenging and exciting experience of participating in the OSS assessment procedures had a lasting influence on many prominent American psychologists. Several of them applied their OSS experience to subsequent large-scale assessment programs; for example, Donald W. Fiske participated in the Veterans Administration study of clinical psychologists, and Morris I. Stein participated in the Chicago studies of educational assessment, as well as some later studies conducted for the Peace Corps. Another group of OSS psychologists returned to the University of California after the war: Robert C. Tryon, who had served as Deputy Chief of the Planning Staff, and R. Nevitt Sanford and Edward C. Tolman, both of whom had served as staff members at Station S. These men were impressed with the potentials of the OSS methods for basic research on human effectiveness and the contributions such methods might make to the understanding of the development, structure, and functioning of human personality (Institute of Personality Assessment and Research, 1970).

Immediately after the Second World War, Tryon, Sanford, and Tolman began exploring possibilities with the University of California for the establishment of a center on the Berkeley campus for basic research in personality assessment. The Institute of Personality Assessment and Research (IPAR) was formally established in the summer of 1949. Funding was obtained from the Rockefeller Foundation, and the University provided a reconditioned fraternity house to serve as an assessment and research site. Donald W. MacKinnon, former Director of Station S, was brought in as the Institute's first director, and he continued in that capacity until his retirement 21 years later. We can obtain an indication of the variety and quality of research that has emanated from IPAR over the years from a partial listing of present and former staff members: Frank Barron, Jack Block, Richard S. Crutchfield, Erik H. Erikson, Harrison G. Gough, Robert E. Harris, and R. Nevitt Sanford.

IPAR was established, in part, to fill a gap in existing knowledge concerning the personality and background characteristics of highly effective personnel, such as the OSS candidates studied during the war. It was the belief of the IPAR staff that the methods employed during the war, i.e., the living-in assessment of candidates by multiple observers using a wide variety of assessment techniques, should be extended to the systematic study of high-level personnel generally, in the arts and sciences and in the world of commerce. In so doing, the staff placed the criterion focus on such attributes as creativity, personal soundness, effectiveness, and social maturity—in contrast to the more negative attributes which were traditionally the focus of clinical assessment. Since its inception, the Institute has assessed approximately 2,000 highly effective and creative professional persons, as well as students in training for the professions (IPAR, 1970). Although many basic contributions to knowledge have been made in the course of these studies, perhaps the most widely known work of the Institute is that relating to creativity (e.g., Barron, 1965, 1968, 1969; MacKinnon, 1962, 1965, 1967).

No attempt will be made here to summarize the results of the many assessment studies of mathematicians, architects, writers, research scientists, managers, and other personnel conducted by the Institute. Instead, we will describe a single assessment study of Air Force officers as illustrative of the general approach the IPAR staff followed in most of their assessment studies. It was generally true of all these studies that the major emphasis was on assessment rather than on prediction per se. Thus, in the study of Air Force officers to be described, the primary research emphasis was on criterion analysis and the development of methods to assess potential effectiveness, rather than on selection in an actual field setting (MacKinnon et al., 1958).

The two principal research questions were: (1) "*What patterns of ability, motivation and interest are associated with outstanding effectiveness of Air Force officers in their military assignments?*" and (2) "*By what psychological tests and procedures or by what combinations of such techniques can the distinguishing characteristics and the potential promise of the effective officer be identified and measured?*" (MacKinnon, 1958, p. 1). The research sample consisted of 343 Air Force captains who were eligible for promotion to major in the next promotion cycle. These officers were administered a battery of paper-and-pencil tests in a three-day field-testing program conducted at the seven different Air Force bases where they were on active duty. A random, stratified sample consisted of 100 officers from the total group who were invited to participate in a three-day, living-in assessment at Berkeley in ten groups of ten each. The living-in sample was considered representative of the field-tested sample, which was considered representative with some qualifications, of Air Force captains in general (Gough and Krauss, 1958).

Criterion Analysis

The criterion measures available for the 343 Air Force officers tested in the field were viewed as "reference variables for the development and evaluation of the prediction devices" (Barron *et al.*, 1958, p. 1). The four major sources of criterion measures available are listed in Table 11.6. The first two (promotion board ratings and officer effectiveness reports) had been obtained routinely in the course of Air Force personnel administration. The third and fourth measures had been obtained in the course of two different research projects concerned with criterion development.

The personnel folder of each officer was reviewed periodically by three independent promotion boards consisting of superior officers at the Wing, Command, and Air Force levels. Each board rated the officer on a three-place scale of overall suitability, and the mean of the three different boards

Table 11.6 Sources of criterion measures for Air Force captains

Criteria	Significant others	Variables	Dimensions
Promotion board ratings	Boards of superior officers at Wing, Command, and AF level	Overall suitability	Mean of 3 boards
Officer effectiveness reports	Commanding officer or representative	Job knowledge, cooperation, judgment, responsibility, leadership, growth potential, overall	I. General effectiveness (sum of 7 ratings)
Superior officers' ratings	Immediate superiors in interviews by research scientists	Administration, supervision, planning, responsibility, bearing, specialty, job responsibility, personal effectiveness, work effectiveness, level of responsibility, rank, staff position, command position, overall	I. General effectiveness II. Interpersonal relations III. Conscientiousness
Job concept interview ratings	Psychologists in interviews of candidates	39 variables (e.g., responsibility)	I. Work effectiveness and responsibility II. Human relations skills III. Conformance to military standards

was employed as an overall index of *promotion board ratings*. Officer
effectiveness reports were filled out periodically by the officer's commanding
officer or his delegated representative. Each officer was rated on the seven
variables listed in Table 11.6, which included an overall evaluation. A factor
analysis of the generally high correlations among the seven variables yielded
a large single factor of "general effectiveness" which accounted for 97 percent
of the common variance. The sum of the ratings of these seven variables
was employed as an overall index of *officer effectiveness reports.*

The immediate superior of each captain had been interviewed by a
research scientist as a basis for rating the 14 variables indicated in Table 11.6.
Factor analysis of the correlations among the variables yielded the three
factors indicated in the table. The now familiar factor of "general effectiveness" accounted for 88 percent of the common variance, whereas the other
two factors accounted for only 8 percent and 5 percent, respectively. Nevertheless, factor scores on each of these three dimensions were included as three
indices of *superior officers' ratings.* As part of another research project, each
captain was interviewed in the field by a research psychologist in accordance
with a 57-page interview schedule. The psychologist made summary ratings
on 39 different variables related to present effectiveness on the job. A cluster
analysis of these variables suggested the three dimensions indicated in the
table. Scores on these three clusters served as indices of *job concept interview
ratings.*

As Table 11.6 indicates, 61 different criterion ratings were reduced to
eight on the basis of factor- and cluster-analytic procedures. In an attempt
at further clarification of the dimensions underlying criterion ratings, the
eight summary variables were themselves intercorrelated and factor-analyzed.
Given the nature of the summary variables, one might anticipate that a large
single factor of "general effectiveness" would emerge from a factor analysis.
Instead, three relatively distinct factors emerged, each of which tended to be
associated with a different group of significant others. These factors were
named: I. General effectiveness as evaluated by commanding officers;
II. General effectiveness as rated by trained psychologists; and III. Task
accomplishment at the expense of interpersonal acceptance (as evaluated by
immediate superiors). Although these three factors may reflect different
components of overall effectiveness, it is also likely that they reflect method
variance peculiar to different procedures for evaluating effectiveness. The
first factor was defined primarily by ratings based on personnel folders in
the absence of much personal contact with the captains. The second factor
was defined exclusively by ratings made by psychologists on the basis of
structured interviews. The third factor was defined exclusively by ratings
made by immediate superiors, and the personality dimension of "lack of

interpersonal acceptance" (interpreted as dominance or harshness) may have reflected close personal involvement with the captains being rated.

The first factor (general effectiveness as evaluated by commanding officers) became a pivotal reference variable in the IPAR study, and it therefore warrants closer examination. In terms of the factor analysis, this factor was loaded significantly by *general effectiveness evaluations* from officer effectiveness reports (.73), superior officers' ratings (.66), and promotion board ratings (.53). As already indicated, this factor is distinct from those based on evaluations by trained psychologists and from the more personological dimensions of immediate supervisors' ratings. A *criterion index* was defined as the algebraic sum of scores on these three dimensions (the first three in Table 11.6), and this index served as a major reference point in analyzing the assessment data (Gough, 1958, p. 3; MacKinnon, 1958, p. 9). On an a priori basis, this index may be thought of as the most general, the most "objective," and the closest to significant criterion outcomes (e.g., promotion).

Models and Strategies

The IPAR study of effectiveness in Air Force officers comes closer to being representative of a solely *empirical strategy* (Chapter 10) than any other assessment program considered in this chapter. Nevertheless, even this study was guided, in part, by a conceptual model of the "ideal Air Force officer," which served as a basis for both instrument selection and data combination. During the planning stage of the study, an attempt was made to conduct a "personological job analysis" of a military officer's position that was partly based on a consideration of previous assessment research programs. The model was conceived as having ten functional components, each considered essential for superior performance. These ten components and their definitions are listed in Table 11.7.

In addition to guiding the selection of variables for both the field-testing and living-in assessments, the conceptual components were each represented directly by combinations of test variables that served as additional predictors. Some of these were simply composites of a number of test scores. Others were clinical ratings, based on analyses of biographical data. These ten summary variables were referred to as "field testing composites," and during the course of the study the relative validity of such rational composites was compared with the validity of traditional measures in forecasting criteria of officer effectiveness.

Traditionally, the empirical strategy requires the independent specification of a group of subjects known to possess the criterion quality of interest (e.g., "highly effective") and the specification of a group of subjects known,

Table 11.7 Components of the model of a successful Air Force officer (from MacKinnon, 1958, pp. 1–2)

1. *Soundness as a person.* Maturity in personal relations; self-insight and self-acceptance, as well as acceptance and understanding of others. Absence of serious emotional problems. Stability of mood and manner. Good balance of social conformity and spontaneity.

2. *Intellectual competence.* Effective intelligence. The ability to perceive and to solve problems, with particular emphasis on implications for action. This involves, first of all, clarity and intellectual power, but a factor of practicality and translation of cognition into action is also important.

3. *Good judgment.* Soundness and good judgment in evaluating self and others. Wisdom, the ability to see group situations and individuals in broad perspective and to draw dependable and practical inferences; capacity for independent thinking, and a willingness to make decisions on one's own.

4. *Health and vitality.* Consistent good health and stability of physiological functioning. Absence of minor as well as major illnesses. Resistance to disease. Ability to withstand stress and endure hardship, privation, and insalubrity. Vigor, robustness, stamina, sense of physical well-being.

5. *Military and social presence.* Poise and self-assurance in dealing with others. Impressive, able to command both attention and respect from observers. Executive manner—a matter-of-fact attitude of expecting one's orders to be obeyed and carried out. Decisiveness, absence of confusion, self-acceptance without egotism and self-confidence without arrogance.

on independent grounds, not to possess the criterion quality (e.g., "less effective"). Differences in psychological test scores and assessment ratings between these two groups of subjects are then interpreted as reflecting the critical personality attributes underlying effective role performance, and instruments are combined or developed in an attempt to reproduce the original criterion standard in future selection studies. This strategy of contrasted groups has characterized the majority of assessment studies conducted at IPAR over the last two decades. For example, in a study of creative writers (Barron, 1958), faculty nominations were employed to identify a group of writers of a conspicuously high degree of originality and creativeness, who were then brought in for a living-in assessment. This group was contrasted with a living-in group of successful and productive writers who had not been so nominated. Although both groups were to some extent creative, one was conspicuously so, and it was on this basis that a contrasted-groups analysis was conducted.

In the IPAR study of Air Force officers, there was no preselection of

6. *Personal courage*. Ability to meet danger without undue fear. Resourcefulness under stress. Absence of any tendency to side-step troublesome situations or to make concessions merely to avoid conflict. An appetite for hazard and risk-taking, but without foolhardiness or rashness. Willingness to commit oneself in a possibly dangerous situation.

7. *Originality*. Originality and creativity of thinking and in approaches to practical problems; constructive ingenuity; ability to set aside established conventions and procedures when appropriate; a flair for devising effective and economical solutions for perplexing problems; the knack of capitalizing on the odds instead of being dominated by them.

8. *Fair-mindedness*. Candor, forthrightness, honesty, impartiality, objectivity and sympathy. Ability to judge issues without bias, enmity, or spite, and to avoid dogmatism and prejudgments.

9. *Integrity and responsibility as a commander*. A linear relationship between inner ethicality and outer manner. Absence of subterfuge and deceitfulness. Effortless acceptance of superego values, and ability to project them as sensible and worthwhile. True respect for others; unembarrassed acceptance of personal dignity in self and others.

10. *Positive valuation of the military identity*. Capacity for loyalty and for devotion to military and patriotic ideals. Conviction about the worth of military activity and function; ability to tolerate frustration and discouragement and to maintain perspective and goal orientation under stress.

extreme groups by nomination or other procedures, and in this respect, the study is not entirely representative of the IPAR approach. In the first stage of assessment, 343 captains were tested in the field by a variety of paper-and-pencil procedures, and their scores were then correlated with the criterion measures described earlier. This procedure may be thought of as the "continuous" form of the contrasted-groups strategy. In the second stage of assessment, 100 captains were selected to participate in a living-in assessment on a more or less random basis. The major consideration in the selection of the smaller subgroup of subjects was economy, rather than extremity of criterion performance. The extensive data gathered during the living-in assessment have been employed in a variety of contrasted-groups analyses (e.g., Gough, McKee, and Yandell, 1955). The basic strategy has been that of selecting the 25 highest-scoring and 25 lowest-scoring captains on one variable and comparing their scores on another variable. Although these analyses took the form of a more traditional contrasted-groups comparison, the range of scores involved was rather limited.

Data Collection

Field testing was conducted at the seven Air Force bases which were geographically closest to Berkeley. Of those captains who were eligible for promotion in the next cycle, all who were not sick, on leave, or in highly essential work were administered a three-day battery of paper-and-pencil tests. These 27 different tests were primarily measures of (a) biographical variables, (b) personality and interests, (c) cognitive and intellectual functions, and (d) social insight and judgment. The measures of personality and interests were primarily of the empirical variety (SVIB, CPI, and MMPI); the intelligence and creativity tests were representative of standardized group tests widely employed in personnel selection; the tests of social insight and judgment were drawn from less familiar sources. The 27 tests yielded a total of 233 separate scores for each officer tested.

For the 100 officers in the living-in assessment, each of the three assessment days ran from 8:00 a.m. to 6:00 p.m., with lunch served at the Institute. On the first day of assessment, a social hour of relaxation was scheduled. When the officers were not participating in specific assessment procedures, they were interacting more informally with staff members. During the living-in assessment period, the subjects were administered additional paper-and-pencil tests as well as individual projective measures, such as the Rorschach and the Thematic Apperception Test. Detailed life-history interviews were conducted with each subject (Woodworth, Barron, and MacKinnon, 1957), as were physical examinations, and medical histories were obtained. A heavy emphasis was placed on the assessment of perceptual performance as manifested in scores on such tests as the rod-and-frame, embedded figures, and kinesthetic aftereffects (Crutchfield, Woodworth, and Albrecht, 1958).

The conditions of living-in assessment permitted the employment of a number of group and situational tests that provided observational material under a variety of social circumstances. The principal tests were those of decision-making behavior, charades, improvisations, and group pressure for conformity of judgment. From six to eight psychologists, who had observed the subjects under a variety of conditions, made ratings on 30 personality variables (Woodworth and MacKinnon, 1958) and performed *Q*-sorts on 76 items that tapped both phenotypic and genotypic aspects of personality (Block and Bailey, 1955). Ten staff psychologists also filled out the 300-item Adjective Check List (Gough and Heilbrun, 1965) for each subject. Although the latter pooled ratings were not used as direct predictors, they served to clarify substantive aspects of both predictor and criterion measures.

Data Combination

To reduce computational labor in the calculation of the intercorrelations among measures, all variables were transformed to single-digit *stanine* (a contraction of "standard nine") scores. Stanine scores range from one to nine, with a mean of five and a standard deviation of two, and are assigned in accord with expectations for the percentage of subjects falling into each category, based on a normal distribution (Anastasi, 1961). Although stanine scores were reported to be in general highly correlated with the raw scores on which they were based, it is possible that this reduction of metric may have served to attenuate many of the correlations reported (MacKinnon, 1958).

As indicated earlier, the 61 different criterion ratings available were reduced to eight on the basis of cluster- and factor-analytic procedures. Although some attempts were made to reduce the 631 different prediction variables by cluster-analytic procedures (Gough, 1958), the basic method of data analysis consisted of the computation of more than 5,000 Pearson product-moment correlation coefficients between predictor and criterion variables. Considering the sheer number of correlations computed, a large number of correlations would be expected to be significant by chance alone. As an internal check on the validity coefficients, the field-tested sample was divided into three subsamples of 100 subjects each, and the living-in sample was divided into two subsamples of 50 each. For most of the results reported, a relationship was not considered significant unless it occurred in all three of the field-tested subsamples or in both of the living-in subsamples (e.g., Barron *et al.*, 1958). However, in the final report, correlations that achieved the .05 level of significance in the total field or living-in samples were reported (MacKinnon, 1958).

Outcomes of Prediction

Because the primary emphasis of the IPAR study was on criterion analysis and the development of assessment variables, the "outcomes of prediction" cannot be evaluated in quite the same manner as the results of an actual selection study. At best, the correlations between assessment variables and criterion indices may be thought of as measures of "concurrent validity" (APA, 1954) since no attempt was made to forecast performance subsequent to assessment. Strictly speaking, the predictor-criterion relationships were *postdictions*, because most of the criterion indices were obtained well before the time of assessment, in some instances as much as five years earlier. Such a design raises questions of generalizability (Chapter 7), since it is not entirely clear to which future group of candidates the results of the IPAR study are meant to apply.

The major applied objective of the research was the development of a set of testing and assessment devices for the identification, early in their careers, of those officers with unusual potential for responsible and effective leadership in the higher echelons of the Air Force. (MacKinnon, 1958, p. 3)

However, since most of the subjects had been in the service more than ten years, some more than twenty years (Gough and Krauss, 1958), "early in their careers" could mean only sometime prior to consideration for promotion to the rank of major. Note, moreover, that the critical criterion measure of subsequent promotion to the rank of major was not included in the study. It therefore appears that "outstanding effectiveness" was assumed to be a criterion attribute which had considerable generalizability over time in service.

To what extent were the several criterion measures of officer effectiveness predictable from the extensive batteries of field and living-in assessment tests? Although some criteria were more predictable than others and some assessment variables appeared more promising than others, the overall results of the IPAR investigation were extraordinarily disappointing. In fact, if one were to adopt a rigorous criterion of statistical inference, it could be argued that the pattern of relationships between predictor and criterion variables did not depart significantly from that which would have been obtained by random generation of the data. The IPAR study was not designed as an exercise in statistical inference, however, but rather as a broad-band exploratory investigation of potential dimensions for instrument development. Under these circumstances, considerable experience and skill are required in the task of separating hopeful leads from chance relationships.

In relating the field-testing variables to the seven separate components of officer effectiveness reports (see Table 11.6), the investigators correlated 194 test scores with the seven components in three samples of 100 subjects each. Of the more than 4,000 correlations computed, six percent were significant at the .05 level, but none of the significant correlations were obtained in all three samples. These results were properly interpreted as chance relationships (Barron et al., 1958). Similarly, when the correlations of the field-testing variables with the three dimensions of superior officers' ratings were examined, no relationship obtained in one subsample was replicated in another, and the overall pattern was judged to have been due to chance.

The job concept interview ratings were obtained somewhat late in the study, and as a consequence, the correlations between field-testing variables and the three dimensions of these ratings were computed only for the sample of 100 captains who participated in the living-in assessment. Of the 233 field-testing variables, 52 were significantly correlated with the first dimension of job concept interview ratings ("work effectiveness and responsibility"), and this dimension was judged to be reasonably predictable from field-testing procedures. Unfortunately, it was not possible to examine the replicability of these correlations in other samples. The number of significant correlations between field-testing variables and the other two dimensions of job concept interview ratings did not exceed the number that would have been expected by chance. The criterion index, which was the sum of scores on three criterion dimensions, was also judged to be reasonably predictable from approximately

23 percent of the field-testing variables (MacKinnon, 1958). However, none of these variables were significantly correlated in all three subsamples of captains (Gough, 1958, p. 4). The intercorrelations among the 21 most promising predictors of the criterion index were cluster-analyzed and thereby reduced to four dimensions. The multiple correlation of these four cluster dimensions with the criterion index was .32 in a sample of 100 officers (Gough, 1958). This correlation was neither corrected for shrinkage nor cross-validated (Chapter 1).

From this pattern of admittedly disappointing relationships, the IPAR staff attempted to draw conclusions about the most promising variables for the prediction of officer effectiveness from field-testing procedures. In general, scales from empirical personality and interest inventories, such as the Strong Vocational Interest Blank, the California Psychological Inventory, and the MMPI, tended to have the largest number of significant correlations with the various global criterion measures (MacKinnon, 1958). This result is compatible with Goldberg's (1972) later finding that empirical scales tend to be predictive across a broad band of criterion measures. Of equal interest, however, is the finding that the field-testing composites, which were primarily rational combinations of variables based on a conceptual model (see Table 11.7), had the highest "survival rate" of any single source of data (Gough, 1958). Thus the use of a personality model, however informal, appeared to be a promising strategy, even within an empirical design. In order to include the most promising predictors, among them the field-testing composites, it would be necessary to administer a battery of 15 tests which take approximately 10 hours to complete. Although it was concluded that this battery held "considerable promise" (MacKinnon, 1958), the data reported hardly seem to justify the routine administration of such a time-consuming set of procedures.

From a strictly statistical standpoint, the tests administered individually to the 100 officers who participated in the three-day living-in assessment did not fare much better in predicting criteria of effectiveness. None of the living-in variables produced significant correlations with the composite officer-effectiveness measure in both subsamples of 50 officers (Barron et al., 1958). Among the 299 variables which were correlated with the first factor of superior officers' ratings, five attained a *combined* significance level of .05 in both samples: (1) percentage of whole responses on the Rorschach, (2) guessing effectiveness in a charades task, (3) age of subject, (4) pathogenicity of childhood, and (5) staff Q-sort on "undercontrolled." Although these five variables did not suggest a meaningful personality picture when considered alone, it was maintained that they made psychological sense when considered in conjunction with additional data from the Adjective Check List and California Psychological Inventory. Similarly, seven staff Q-sort ratings and four improvisations ratings were considered to be sensible correlates of the second factor of superior officers' ratings, when other data were taken into account.   However, the single significant correlate of the third factor of superior officers' ratings ("age at first intercourse") was not given a substantive interpretation.

The fact that 99 of the 398 living-in assessment variables were significantly related to the first dimension of the job concept interview ratings suggests that this dimension was equally predictable from living-in and field-testing measures.   Again, however, it was not possible to examine the replicability of these correlations in samples other than that of 100 subjects for which the correlations were computed.   The number of significant correlations between living-in assessment variables and the other two dimensions of the job concept interview ratings was approximately what would have been expected by chance.   The criterion index was significantly correlated with 51 of the 398 living-in assessment variables.   By a lenient criterion of statistical significance, eight of the 51 were judged to be significantly related in both subsamples of assessed officers (Gough, 1958).   Five of these variables were staff Q-sort ratings, one was an interview rating, one was a staff rating, and one a score from the Adjective Check List.   The intercorrelations among the 20 most promising predictors of the criterion index were cluster-analyzed and thereby reduced to four clusters.   The multiple correlation of these four cluster dimensions with the criterion index was .47 in a sample of 100 officers (Gough, 1958).   Again, this correlation was neither corrected for shrinkage nor cross-validated.

The most promising living-in assessment variables were the pooled staff ratings on 30 dimensions and 76 Q-sort items.   Thirteen of the rated dimensions and eighteen of the Q-sort items were correlated significantly with more than one criterion measure (MacKinnon, 1958).   This result suggests that reliable (i.e., pooled) judgments of clearly specified personality dimensions by assessors who have had considerable direct exposure to subjects are more promising predictors than any single living-in assessment procedure. Since the criteria with which staff ratings were correlated were themselves judgments of superior officers, one might expect such a result on the basis of generalizability considerations (Clark, 1960).   The situational tests involving improvisations, charades, and group pressure were considered promising, as was the life-history interview.   Several perceptual tests were also considered promising, especially the rod-and-frame test.   In general, it was concluded that a living-in assessment of at least one day and preferably two to three days would yield valuable data for the forecasting of officer effectiveness (MacKinnon, 1958).   Such a conclusion should be tempered by the considerable costs of a living-in assessment procedure that involves, among other things, the salaries of ten staff psychologists.

Critique

Basically, the IPAR study of officer effectiveness was a large-scale "search and employ" mission implemented under a strategy that has elsewhere been called a "statistical dragnet" (Kelly, 1955). Yet despite the thousands of correlations that were computed, and despite the lack of emphasis given to theoretical considerations, this particular study does not serve as an example of the empirical strategy in its purest form. As we have already indicated, a more traditional empirical strategy would have contrasted individuals with extreme scores on some composite of the criterion measures. A living-in assessment of, perhaps, the 75 highest- and 75 lowest-scoring officers on the criterion composite not only would have permitted a more precise evaluation of the potential of the testing instruments employed, but also would have facilitated the development of new instruments and different combinations of predictor variables. Such evaluation and instrument development would have been applicable to both field-testing and living-in assessment variables. The employment of a single standard of performance would have required a decision regarding the "best" criterion composite prior to the living-in assessment, but such a decision could have been based on the factorial structure of the criterion measures.

In evaluating assessment studies that yielded disappointing results, critics traditionally fault the predictor variables, the criterion measures, or both. However, one can hardly fault the predictor variables on the grounds that promising variables were excluded when 631 were employed. Despite a predilection for empirical self-report inventories, the investigators made a commendable effort to include almost every type of personality assessment procedure that had been found or had been claimed to be related to socially relevant criteria. In addition to using some admittedly experimental procedures (e.g., graphological analysis), the investigators included a large number of variables that had proved useful in previous studies of highly effective personnel (e.g., CPI-MMPI fighter factor scale, IPAR general effectiveness scale). The comprehensive battery of assessment procedures, assembled by this team of highly experienced and sophisticated investigators, cannot be held responsible for the generally disappointing findings of the study.

The criterion measures supplied to the investigators appear to have been both reliable and representative of the kinds of personnel evaluations made by superior officers in the Air Force. For the most part, the several criterion measures tended to converge on a dimension of overall or *general effectiveness*. To some extent this convergence may have reflected the prevailing military notion that "all officers are equally capable in all areas" of criterion performance (Clark, 1960, p. 73). Although not necessarily agreeing with such a philosophy, the assessment team accepted "general effectiveness" as a criterion concept simply because that was the only criterion information provided. But predictor-criterion relationships are almost certain to be attenuated when individual differences in patterns of personal, social, and intellectual competence are related to a single, global dimension of overall effectiveness.

Whether a given constellation of personality traits will be an asset or a liability depends heavily on the nature of the criterion situation in which duties are performed, and this situational specificity is masked by a compensatory model of "general effectiveness." A specification of the different role requirements of different kinds of criterion performance would, of course, have required a criterion analysis such as that employed under an analytic strategy. Obviously, such detailed criterion information was not available. But the disappointing performance of the predictor variables in forecasting overall effectiveness does not preclude the possibility that the same predictors might be relatively promising forecasters of differentiated patterns of performance. In fact, in the single instance in which more differentiated criterion information was available (flying versus nonflying officers), prediction appeared to have been enhanced (Woodworth and MacKinnon, 1958).

Since the nature of the criterion information available to the IPAR staff was such that it was not possible to design either a traditional selection study (prediction of future performance) or a study in which concurrent status on differentiated criteria could be examined, the most appropriate research questions seem to be primarily of a *methodological* nature. In view of the computer hardware and software available in the fifties, the data analyses performed by the IPAR staff were, understandably, of limited scope. Consequently, a lingering doubt remains as to whether or not significant patterns of predictor-criterion relationships could be unearthed by a fuller exploitation of the analytic potential of modern techniques of multivariate analysis. The large numbers of predictor and criterion variables now seem to demand dimensional reduction by such techniques as canonical correlation, discriminant analysis (Tatsuoka, 1971), and the method of principal predictors (Tucker, 1957), to name but a few. In the absence of a thoroughgoing multivariate analysis of these data, it seems premature to pass judgment on the predictive potential of the assessment variables employed in the IPAR study.

There were other lines of methodological investigation that could have been explored by the IPAR staff but that apparently fell outside the purview of their empirical strategy. Although a *diagnostic council* played a prominent role in the OSS and subsequent large-scale assessment studies, no consideration was given to this method of data combination in the IPAR study. This omission seems notable for an organization that was dedicated to the idea of continuing and extending the procedures employed by the OSS.

Moreover, certain aspects of the results of the IPAR study suggest that a diagnostic council might have been a fruitful method of data combination. The most promising living-in assessment variables were the pooled judgments of highly skilled staff members. The field-testing variables which had the highest survival rate were those based on rational combinations of variables in relation to a conceptual model of the ideal Air Force officer. It is tempting to speculate on the possible validity of the judgments of a highly skilled diagnostic council, made with reference to this target model. A direct comparison between analytic and empirical strategies in the identification of promising assessment procedures would have represented a major methodological contribution to the field of personality assessment.

From the convenient hindsight of almost 20 years, it is easy—and grossly unfair—to make pronouncements on what *might* have been done with the IPAR data in light of subsequent developments in the field of personality assessment. Nonetheless, in evaluating the net contribution to knowledge of the thousands of zero-order correlations computed, one finds considerable truth in Clark's (1960) view that the laboring mountain scarce brought forth a mouse.

Veterans Administration Selection Research Project

Prediction Problem

At the end of the Second World War, the Veterans Administration was faced with the task of rehabilitating thousands of returning servicemen, many of whom would require psychiatric services. To meet the critical need for manpower in the mental health professions, the Veterans Administration instituted a series of training programs, one of which was concerned with the training of clinical psychologists in the graduate departments of psychology of a number of cooperating universities. At the same time, the Veterans Administration sponsored an extensive program of research directed at an evaluation of the procedures used to select clinical psychologists. This research project was directed by E. Lowell Kelly and Donald W. Fiske in collaboration with a distinguished board of consultants, which included former participants in the OSS and IPAR assessment programs, as well as participants in the concurrent Menninger study to be described in the next section.

At the time the selection research project was initiated, various methods were being employed to select graduate students for VA traineeships in clinical psychology by the 22 different universities which offered such training. It was agreed at the outset that all assessment procedures employed by the project staff were to be considered experimental, in the sense that results for individual candidates were confidential and were not considered in the actual selection deliberations of the cooperating universities. Hence the VA assessment project was not a selection program but a research program designed to identify the most promising procedures for the selection of graduate students in clinical psychology. In addition, the project staff was charged with the responsibility of developing meaningful criterion measures for evaluating success in training and in the subsequent performance of professional duties. This aspect of the study represented the first large-scale job analysis ever conducted on the then fledgling profession of clinical psychology.

The VA assessment project was also designed to yield information on several basic issues which confronted the science of personality assessment at that time. Chief among them was the question of the relative merits of two quite divergent approaches to assessment: (a) the multiform, organismic, living-in assessment procedures exemplified by the OSS program and (b) the empirical, test-battery approach that theretofore had characterized personnel selection in industrial settings. Specific comparisons between these two approaches were designed to shed light on several issues we have already considered with reference to the topics of clinical prediction (Chapter 4) and clinical versus statistical prediction (Chapter 5).

For an initial overview of the VA assessment project, see the timetable of assessment projects provided in Table 11.8. In 1946, experimental living-in assessments were conducted with currently enrolled trainees from five universities at Ann Arbor, Michigan, at Farmingdale, Long Island, and at Asilomar, California. These assessments served as pilot studies in which decisions were made regarding the most practical and promising methods for

Table 11.8 Timetable of assessment projects in the VA selection research program

Project	Assessees	Sites	Assessors
1946 pilot assessment	Current trainees from 5 universities ($N = 42$)	7-day assessments at Ann Arbor, Farmingdale, and Asilomar	20 staff judges
1947 assessment	Incoming, accepted trainees from 30 universities ($N = 128$)	5-day assessments at Ann Arbor	30 staff judges
1948 assessment	Applicants to training programs in 30 universities ($N = 120$)	32 testing centers in United States (545 applicants tested)	24 staff judges at Wellesley
1949 reassessment	1947 sample ($N = 100$)	Ann Arbor	20 VA trainees

conducting the later large-scale assessments. The first major assessment was conducted in 1947 at Ann Arbor. Incoming graduate students, who had already been admitted to training programs at 30 different universities, participated in a five-day living-in assessment. This group of candidates will be referred to as the "1947 sample."

Because the candidates in the 1947 sample were aware that they had already been accepted to graduate school and that the results of assessment would not affect their status as students, it is possible that their behavior during assessment was not representative of the behavior of candidates assessed under "applicant conditions." Consequently, data were also obtained from a sample of applicants who believed the assessment procedures to be part of an actual selection program (the "1948 sample"). Unfortunately a number of practical and logistic considerations militated against the conduct of a living-in assessment program for applicants who were under consideration for admission to graduate school (Kelly and Fiske, 1951). As a consequence, it was decided to forgo a living-in assessment program in favor of a nationwide testing program, conducted in 32 testing centers across the United States. The test results of the 1948 sample were later assessed by a group of staff judges who met at Wellesley College and who had no face-to-face contacts with the candidates.

In 1949, part of the 1947 sample was reassessed by a group of advanced VA trainees from the University of Michigan. One purpose of this reassessment was to compare the accuracy of predictions made by relatively inexperienced clinicians with the accuracy of predictions made by the more senior staff judges who had originally assessed the 1947 sample. The reassessment was also designed to provide information on the validity of pooled judgments and on the validity of judgments based on projective techniques.

Criterion Analysis

As should be evident by now, most large-scale assessment programs have been plagued with a severe "criterion problem." In the OSS program, assessments were made with reference to a complex and vaguely defined set of criterion circumstances. The IPAR investigators were forced to work with criterion ratings provided by the Air Force, rather than with measures they developed themselves. In contrast to their counterparts in those earlier programs, the investigators in the VA assessment project had bestowed on them the mixed blessing of being free to develop their own criterion measures of proficiency for a relatively new and not yet clearly defined profession. The project was unique in that "approximately half of our research efforts were devoted to the evaluation of the profesisonal competences of clinical psychologists" (Kelly and Fiske, 1951, p. v). Unfortunately, the *order* that criterion analysis occupied in the program was the reverse of that required by an analytic approach to assessment. That is, most of the efforts at criterion development took place some time after predictions had been made at the assessment sites.

Ideally, the first stage of an assessment program is devoted to a situational analysis of dimensions of criterion performance. Once the psychological role requirements underlying successful performance have been identified, tests and assessment procedures are chosen with reference to these requirements. In the VA project, the assessments preceded the criterion analysis, and as a consequence, the programs were designed on the basis of an a priori definition of the duties assumed to be performed by clinical psychologists. Thus the assessment staff were asked to make a prediction (on an eight-place scale) of the extent to which candidates would eventually be effective in such duties as: clinical diagnosis, individual psychotherapy, group psychotherapy, research, administration, supervision, professional relations, integrity, and overall suitability for clinical psychology. Since criterion measures of performance of these duties had not been developed, the predictions were necessarily global in nature. With respect to individual psychotherapy, for example, the staff judges were asked to predict: "How effectively will he conduct various types of individual psychotherapy?"

The project directors assumed that adequate criterion measures of the categories of job performance noted above would eventually become available, and once available, they would be used in the appraisal of the effectiveness of various psychological assessment procedures in forecasting job performance. Few would quarrel with the a priori categories of job performance selected by the investigators, since job descriptions of the duties of a clinical psychologist were relatively uniform at that time; clinicians were expected to be competent in diagnosis, treatment, supervision, etc. However, in the absence of knowledge of the psychological role requirements of criterion performance, it is unclear on what basis one should select specific tests and assessment procedures for use in prediction. McNemar (1952) said it less diplomatically: "it is sheer nonsense to have proceeded with an extensive testing and assessment prediction program without having first devised satisfactory measures of that which was to be predicted" (p. 859).

Although their development was belated, the criterion analysis procedures of the VA assessment project were among the most extensive ever employed in the study of a profession. As a consequence, the detailed descriptions of the criterion measures employed (Kelly and Fiske, 1951, pp. 71–122) and of those considered but not employed (pp. 285–286) constitute a major contribution to the literature of personnel selection. Some appreciation of the number and kinds of criterion studies undertaken may be gained from the timetable of projects listed in Table 11.9. The primary criterion measures developed and employed were: (a) academic performance ratings, (b) supervisors' ratings, (c) content examinations, (d) work sample measures, (e) a

Table 11.9 Timetable of criterion projects in the VA selection research program

Project	Description
1948–1949	Performance ratings from university departments. Construction of content examinations in clinical and general psychology.
1949	Administration of content examinations. General consideration of measures of clinical competence. Criterion ratings collected from university and VA supervisors and from trainees themselves.
1949–1950	Item analyses of content examinations. Analyses of criterion ratings (reliabilities, intercorrelations, factor analyses). Additional consideration of measures of clinical competence.
1950	Determination of academic status of trainees (e.g., completed Ph.D., dismissed from program).
1950–1951	Field tests of work sample measures. Development of improved criterion rating scales. Administration of content examinations. Criterion ratings collected from university and VA supervisors and colleagues. Collection of work sample measures. Administration of trainee experience inventory. Analyses of new criterion measures.
1957	Mailing of nationwide follow-up questionnaire.

trainee experience inventory, and (f) a follow-up questionnaire mailed to the subjects who had participated in the original assessment programs.

The results of the several analyses, listed in Table 11.9, were summarized succinctly by Kelly and Fiske (1951, p. 194):

1. There is no satisfactory single criterion of success in training or practicing clinical psychology. University staff members and supervising clinical psychologists show wide individual differences in their conceptions of successful academic performance and of professional skills.

2. There are three general components of success in clinical psychology: (a) intellectual accomplishments (e.g., academic achievement and research productivity), (b) the clinical skills of diagnosis and therapy, and (c) skills in social relations. In general, judges agree much better on the first than on the latter two components.

3. Supervisors' ratings do not adequately differentiate the various job functions of the clinical psychologists.

4. Ratings of clinical competences appear to be as much a function of the role of the rater (e.g., teacher, supervisor, colleague) as of the person being rated.

5. No completely acceptable objective measures of competence in the purported functions of the clinical psychologist are available, but certain promising techniques for evaluating clinical skills were developed within this project. However, further developmental work on these measures is necessary before they can be used in the routine evaluation of clinical competence.

Models and Strategies

One of the main purposes of the VA assessment project was a comparison of the relative effectiveness of "clinical" and "statistical" strategies of selection. Although these designations were meant to correspond to the selection strategies we have characterized as *analytic* and *empirical*, it must be recognized that neither approach was employed in a manner that would be judged acceptable by advocates of the two opposing selection philosophies. Although it is true that the multiform, organismic, living-in assessment procedures advocated by the OSS staff were faithfully represented, the initial *situational analysis* recommended by that staff (OSS, 1948) and by subsequent exponents of the analytic strategy (e.g., Stern, Stein, and Bloom, 1956) was conspicuously absent from the VA project. Nevertheless, the design of the VA project permitted the examination of certain assumptions of the analytic approach that previously had not been subjected to empirical test. Chief among the assumptions were that: (a) ratings by assessment staff members are better predictors than are test scores, and (b) staff ratings, when pooled either arithmetically or clinically as in staff conferences, are better predictors than are ratings of individual judges.

The success of the empirical approach to personnel selection rests heavily on the appropriateness of the standard of performance employed to differentiate successful criterion subjects from unsuccessful control subjects. But the *method of contrasted groups*, the distinguishing feature of the empirical approach, was not employed in the VA assessment project. Instead, hundreds of zero-order correlations were computed between an "eclectic" selection of objective test scores and a set of criterion measures that were primarily judgmental. Even under these circumstances, the advantages of empiricism may be evident in the validities of cross-validated multiple-regression equations which have been appropriately weighted for optimal prediction. However, the investigators felt that "the inadequacies of currently available criterion measures of professional success impose realistic limitations on the increment in validity which might be achieved by refining either statistical or clinical procedures" (Kelly and Fiske, 1951, p. 199). Consequently, no attempt was made to exploit the full possibilities of either the empirical or analytic approach by cross-validational procedures.

The staff judges who participated in the assessments "were urged to use such personality theory or theories as they found most acceptable and were permitted to formulate the dynamics of their cases in any manner they wished" (Kelly and Fiske, 1951, p. 3). One can only speculate on the theoretical orientations which the judges actually employed. However, the list of distinguished staff judges includes the names of individuals who were later to become associated with the personality models considered in the last chapter: psychoanalytic (David Rapaport), interpersonal (Hubert S. Coffey), transactional (Morris Stein), cognitive (George A. Kelly), multivariate (Donald W. Fiske), and social learning (Julian Rotter). Hence it seems likely that various theoretical orientations were represented. The extent to which any staff judge relied on a specific model of personality was limited, of course, by the lack of a clearly formulated target model, as well as by a lack of testing instruments associated with specific personality models. Consequently, any predictions that were theoretically generated were necessarily "global."

Data Collection

The principal assessment program was conducted in the summer of 1947 at Ann Arbor, Michigan. During the course of the summer, 128 entering VA trainees from 30 universities participated in a living-in assessment that extended over five days. Trainees were assessed in six successive classes of approximately 24 each. They stayed in a sorority house that, together with a smaller residence building, served as the site for assessment. Although less dramatic and mysterious, the design of the assessment program was almost a carbon copy of that employed at Station S during the OSS program. Each class of 24 students was divided into six groups of four each, to which were assigned three staff members. The assessment staff consisted of 30 professionals, among whom were two VA psychiatrists and several VA psychologists.

The tests and assessment procedures employed at Ann Arbor are listed in Table 11.10. As was true of the OSS program, the implementation of these procedures required a complex scheduling of each team of three staff members in relation to their group of four candidates. The principal vehicle for the transformation of assessment procedures into clinical ratings was an eight-place rating scale employed by the staff members in evaluating the candidates' test results and their behavior in interviews and situational tests.

There were three general classes of variables to which the eight-place rating scales were applied. A set of 22 *phenotypic* variables was assembled, in consultation with Raymond B. Cattell, on the basis of his multivariate-trait

Table 11.10 Tests and assessment procedures employed at Ann Arbor

Credentials file	*Interviews*
College transcript	Initial interview (one hour)
Civil Service Form 57	Intensive interview (two hours)
Correspondence	Final interview
Letters of recommendation	*Biographical*
Intelligence and achievement	Biographical inventory
Cooperative General Culture Test	Autobiography
Miller Analogies Test	*Situational*
Primary Mental Abilities Tests	Leaderless group discussion
Interests	Improvisations
Allport-Vernon Study of Values	Block situation test
Kuder Preference Record	Expressive movement test
Strong Vocational Interest Blank	Party
Personality	*Sociometric*
Guilford-Martin Battery	Ratings of three teammates
Minnesota Multiphasic	Character sketches of teammates
Personality Inventory	
Projectives	
Thematic Apperception Test	
Sentence Completion	
Rorschach	
Bender-Gestalt	

model of personality (see Chapter 10). These variables represented temperamental aspects of behavior that were descriptive of the candidate as seen by the staff at the time of assessment (e.g., "assertive versus submissive"). A set of 10 *genotypic* variables included broader dimensions of behavior that required considerably more inference on the part of the rater (e.g., "appropriateness of emotional expression"). Finally, a set of 11 *criterion skills* variables served as predictors of future performance (e.g., "effectiveness in individual psychotherapy"). Before rating a candidate on these 43 variables, each judge made a rating on an eight-place scale of "degree of liking."

During the spring of 1948, 545 applicants to 30 universities were tested at 32 different testing centers. These candidates had been led to believe that their applications to graduate school would not be acted upon until the results of the testing were made available to the universities. Under these "applicant conditions," candidates were administered a highly abridged version of the test battery previously employed at Ann Arbor. Selection of instruments was influenced by considerations of economy and by preliminary findings from the 1947 sample. There were credentials files and biographical material for all candidates (see Table 11.10). In addition, all candidates were administered the Miller Analogies, Strong VIB, Guilford-Martin, Allport-Vernon, Sentence Completion, and Rorschach. The test protocols and scores were sent to Wellesley College, where a simulated assessment program was conducted in August of 1948.

Data Combination

The data combination procedures at Ann Arbor differed from those at Station S in a way that reflects skepticism about the value of holistically pooled clinical judgments (Kelly and Fiske, 1951)—a skepticism that was not apparent in the report of the OSS staff (1948). First, there was heavy emphasis on quantitative ratings of individual variables rather than on holistic integration of clinical judgments. Second, considerable efforts were directed toward the determination of the relative worth of differing amounts of input information in clinical prediction and the relative value of pooled, as opposed to individual, staff predictions. These and other research questions required a complex design for data combination.

Before seeing a candidate, an interviewer would rate him on the genotypic and criterion skills variables on the basis of the material in his credentials file. Following the interview, the candidate was rated on all variables. Next, the interviewer considered four sets of materials and rated the candidate on the genotypic and criterion skills variables after each set. The order in which the materials were considered was: (1) credentials file, (2) objective tests, (3) biographical data, and (4) projective tests. A projective tester would typically rate the candidate on all variables after the administration of each projective test. A "projective integrator" rated the candidate on all variables on the basis of a consideration of four projective tests. At this point, the three-man assessment team held a staff conference to make clinically pooled ratings of all variables for each of that team's four candidates.

The candidates' behavior in the situational tests was rated by the principal assessment team ("contaminated raters") and by another group of three staff members that did not have access to other assessment data ("uncontaminated raters"). Following the situational tests, the three members of the principal assessment team made independent ratings of the candidates, based on their total impressions at that point. After the final interviews and the sociometrics, a final team conference was held in which ratings on all variables were pooled clinically.

Since the assessment program at Wellesley was conducted without access to the candidates, it is perhaps best viewed as a systematic study of clinical judgment, rather than as a simulated assessment program. The 30 staff judges rated 120 subjects who had been accepted by graduate schools on 21 of the variables (the 10 genotypic and 11 criterion skills) employed at Ann Arbor. Of the 120 cases assessed, 99 were subsequently accepted into the VA training program in clinical psychology. An additional 24 cases from the 1947 sample were reassessed to provide a basis for comparison of the two assessment strategies.

Judges rated the protocols of candidates assigned to them at four successive levels of information. First, a judge rated a candidate on the basis of the candidate's credentials file and one other source of information (e.g., Rorschach). Second, the candidate was rated on the basis of his credentials file plus all other sources in a given category (e.g., Rorschach and Sentence Completion). Third, he was rated by each member of the staff team on all materials. Finally, a conference was held in which the final ratings were decided. Although all cases were rated independently by three judges, half were pooled by a team of three staff members and the remainder by a team of two.

Outcomes of Prediction

The overall design of the VA assessment project did not lend itself to a practical evaluation of the outcomes of prediction. The 1947 sample of candidates had already been accepted by graduate schools, and no data are reported on the magnitude of the selection ratios under which they were admitted. On the other hand, 545 applicants were *tested* in 1948, of whom 120 were subsequently accepted into graduate psychology programs and 99 were subsequently accepted into the VA training program. Consequently, one could conclude that the overall selection ratio in 1948 was approximately 20 percent. However, since the base rate of successful clinical psychologists is unknown, it is not possible to evaluate the outcomes of prediction by various assessment procedures with respect to such parameters as the proportions of correct and incorrect selection decisions. Nor is it possible to estimate the extent to which the use of predictions based on assessment procedures would improve on random selection.

The principal purpose of the VA assessment program was to identify promising predictor variables among the many test scores and staff ratings that were available. To this end, zero-order correlations were computed between criterion measures and the test scores and staff ratings. In general, the results obtained with the psychological test and assessment procedures were disappointing. The objective tests of intelligence, interests, and personality (see Table 11.10) yielded a total of 101 separate scores. Table 11.11 lists the correlations obtained with the *best predictor* for each of 13 criterion measures. The objective test scores corresponding to the raised letter symbols in that table are as follows: (a) Miller Analogies Test, (b) Strong Psychologist scale, (c) Strong Production Manager scale, (d) Guilford-Martin Cycloid Disposition scale, (e) Primary Mental Abilities Number scale, (f) Kuder Scientific Interests scale, (g) Guilford-Martin Thinking/Introversion scale, and (h) Gough's Social Status scale from the MMPI.

Table 11.11 Validity coefficients of best objective tests and pooled assessment ratings in 1947 and 1948 samples

	Best objective test		Pooled assessment ratings	
	1947	1948	1947	1948
Criterion ratings				
Academic performance	.47[a]	.16	.46	.42
Diagnostic competence	.31[e]	–	.16	.15
Individual psychotherapy	–.33[f]	–	.24	.15
Research competence	.43[b]	.09	.52	.27
Supervisory competence	.34[a]	–.09	.33	.14
Professional relations	–.30[c]	–.04	.26	.14
Integrity	.30[g]	.16	.30	.26
Clinical competence	.35[a]	–.11	.38	.12
Preference for hiring	.30[d]	.13	.37	.09
Liking	–.32[c]	–.07	.30	–
Content examination				
Clinical total	.58[a]	.43	.42	.40
General total	.58[a]	.52	.45	.37
Work sample				
Diagnostic cases	.39[h]	–	.35	–.01
Largest *N*	(93)	(81)	(92)	(81)

Note: See text for explanation of raised letter symbols.

From Table 11.11 it is evident that scores on the Miller Analogies Test were predictive of ratings of academic performance, scores on the objective, multiple-choice content examinations, and to some extent, ratings of supervisory and clinical competence. It is also evident that ratings of research competence were correlated with scores on the Strong Psychologist scale. The other correlations are less impressive when one bears in mind that they were selected as the highest among approximately 1,400 correlation coefficients. Although the Miller Analogies Test tended to remain predictive of scores on the content examination in the 1948 sample, all the other correlations washed out (see third column of Table 11.11). The general unpredictability of the 1948 sample in comparison with the 1947 sample may be attributed to such factors as the following. (a) The 1948 sample was tested under applicant conditions. (b) The 1948 sample was younger, intellectually more able, and more homogeneous in age and intellectual ability. (c) The 1948 group had been in training a shorter time when criterion measures were collected. (Kelly and Fiske, 1951). Even if we grant these explanations, the absence of a suitable replication group makes it difficult to place much faith in the findings for the 1947 sample.

Table 11.11 also presents the validities of the final pooled assessment ratings in predicting the several criterion measures. Kelly and Fiske considered the validities of these ratings to be "about equal in predictive efficiency" to those of the objective tests, and the correlations listed in the table might even suggest that objective tests had a slight edge. Note, however, that whereas the correlations in Table 11.11 for the objective test scores are the *best* from many possible predictors, the correlations for the assessment ratings are based on the *corresponding* predictors. That is, staff ratings of academic competence were correlated with criterion ratings of academic competence, staff ratings of integrity with criterion ratings of integrity, etc. However, when the *best* staff rating predictors were considered, they tended to have a slight edge over the best objective test predictors. The latter circumstance is due, in part, to the predictive generality of the staff rating variable of *individual psychotherapy*. In the 1947 sample, pooled final assessment ratings of effectiveness in individual psychotherapy outpredicted all other staff ratings for seven of the thirteen criteria listed in Table 11.11.

One might speculate, after the fact, that effectiveness in individual psychotherapy is the quintessential interpersonal skill of the clinical psychologist. The criterion variables best predicted by this staff rating do not contradict such a speculation (diagnostic competence, individual psychotherapy, supervisory competence, professional relations, integrity, preference for hiring, and liking). The validities of staff ratings of individual psychotherapy are not reported for the 1948 sample. However, given the general trend for all predictors to have severely attenuated validities in the 1948 sample, there is no reason to expect that staff ratings of individual psychotherapy would have fared any better.

Other outcomes of interest from the VA assessment project were summarized by Kelly and Fiske (1951, pp. 195–196) as follows:

(a) Predictive ratings show fair to high interjudge reliability when based on the same materials.

(b) The relationship between the accuracy of assessment prediction and the amount of materials on which the predictions are based is markedly non-linear. In general, assessment predictions based on the credential file plus the objective test profile tend to be almost as accurate as those based on more materials including an autobiography, projective tests, interviews, and situation tests.

(c) The findings do not reveal any clear-cut superiority in the validity of pooled ratings made in "staff conference" or of arithmetical ratings over those of the individual staff members.

(d) Self-ratings by the candidates have some predictive value for criteria of intellectual success but show no relationship to other criteria of professional success.

(e) Judgments made by assessment teammates and judgments by staff members on the basis of observing the candidates only in situation tests both have some predictive value; in general, they are about as valid as staff ratings based on the credential file alone.

(f) Predictions of success in clinical psychology made on the basis of single projective techniques tend to have very low correlations with any of the criterion measures. The same is true for predictions based on an integrative study of the protocols for the four projective techniques.

The outcomes of prediction we have been considering all have reference to *immediate* criteria of success that were collected quite early in the professional careers of the candidates. Although few variables appeared to be promising predictors of immediate criteria, it is possible that some of the variables would have been predictive of more intermediate criteria of professional accomplishment. This possibility was investigated by Kelly and Goldberg (1959) in a follow-up study initiated in 1957. The principal source of intermediate criterion measures was a follow-up questionnaire mailed to all candidates who had participated in the 1947 and 1948 assessments. Collection of these data required both ingenuity and perseverance on the part of the investigators. Addresses were located from such sources as college alumni associations and telephone directories of major cities; questionnaires were mailed repeatedly until they were completed. These efforts were repaid with a 93 percent return rate from the 245 living candidates.

On the basis of the follow-up questionnaire and archival sources, criterion indices were obtained for: (a) academic attainment, (b) scholarly productivity, (c) membership in the American Psychological Association, (d) reported identification with clinical psychology, (e) reported satisfaction with choice of clinical psychology, and (f) reported satisfaction with present specialization. Zero-order correlations were computed between approximately 200 predictor variables from the 1947 and 1948 assessments and these new criteria of accomplishment. The disappointing results of these analyses are easily summarized: "In general, predictor-criterion intercorrelations were low, in no case accounting for more than 10% of the criterion variance. Moreover, for each criterion a set of significant correlations for the 1947 sample disappeared upon replication with the 1948 sample." (Kelly and Goldberg, 1959, p. 25)

Critique

An interesting by-product of the Kelly-Goldberg follow-up study was a determination of the degree of satisfaction with clinical psychology as a career reported by alumni of the 1947 and 1948 assessment programs. Respondents were asked to indicate whether they would choose the field of clinical psychology "if I had my life to live over again (knowing what I now know)."

Only half of the sample indicated that they would again choose clinical psychology as a professional specialization. It would be interesting to conduct a similar poll of the professional staff of the VA selection research project with respect to whether they would choose to conduct this milestone assessment project again (knowing what they now know). It seems likely that those who would agree to do so would insist that satisfactory criterion measures of professional competence in clinical psychology be developed well in advance of any assessment of candidates.

It is difficult to improve on McNemar's (1952) final verdict on the Veterans Administration selection research project:

In summary, the major prediction project of our time fell far short of expectations. Its fall involved tripping over the criterion problem despite the recent experiences of wartime psychologists with this old stumbling block. With its feet enmeshed in a web of uncritically selected tests, and its head overburdened with clinical intuitions, it never attained equilibrium, but landed prostrate in a field already strewn with efforts, noble and otherwise. Its collapse might have been forestalled by the injection of fruitful new ideas, but such ideas are indeed hard to come by. (p. 860)

Menninger School of Psychiatry

Prediction Problem

At the end of World War II, an unprecedented number of physicians were interested in obtaining residency training in psychiatry. The critical importance of psychiatry and allied mental health professions had become evident during the course of the war. Despite the fact that approximately 24 percent of potential inductees had been rejected for psychiatric reasons, about one soldier in thirteen had at least one psychiatric admission to an army hospital, and 40 percent of all disability discharges were psychiatric in nature (Holt and Luborsky, 1958a). The sheer number of psychiatric breakdowns in the army meant that many physicians with little or no previous experience in coping with psychiatric disorders became aware of the scope and nature of such problems. Such experiences, combined with intensive in-service training in psychiatry, resulted in a greatly increased interest in psychiatry on the part of physicians who previously had considered other medical careers (Holt and Luborsky, 1958a).

The Menninger School of Psychiatry was founded in 1945 to manage the psychiatric training program in Winter General Hospital, which had just been taken over by the Veterans Administration. The prestigious Menninger Foundation was of course well known in medical circles as a center for psychoanalytically oriented treatment, education, and research. Consequently, when it became known that approximately 100 positions for residents in psychiatry were available, more than 600 physicians applied during the first year. The need for a systematic program for the selection of psychiatric residents was thus evident from the beginning. In keeping with the long-standing research tradition of the Menninger Foundation, a program of investigation was instituted to study the accuracy of the school's selection methods and to determine ways in which improvements could be introduced. The original research plans were devised by two of the foundation's senior psychiatrists, Karl A. Menninger and Robert P. Knight, and the psychologist in charge of the department of research David Rapaport.

One need hardly belabor the importance of selecting those physicians who will become the most effective psychiatric practitioners. Considerable social and economic costs (utilities) are involved at all levels of criteria. In terms of immediate criteria, false positive decisions are costly since enormous amounts of professional time may be wasted on applicants who fail to complete their three years of residency, not to mention the personal inconvenience to physicians who must change their medical specialty. At the level of intermediate criteria, such as certification by the American Board of Psychiatry and Neurology, false positive decisions may be very costly, although it is difficult to estimate this utility. Since it is legal for physicians to practice psychiatry without certification, there is the possibility that some of those who do not become certified may practice psychiatry poorly or even harmfully. In terms of ultimate criteria, the Menninger School aspires to produce *exceptional* psychiatrists who will become leaders in different aspects of their fields (Holt and Luborsky, 1958a). Under the circumstances, therefore, the value of valid positive decisions is enormous, both for psychiatry and for the patients whom psychiatrists treat.

Criterion Analysis

In their detailed report of the Menninger selection program, Holt and Luborsky (1958a, 1958b) devote considerable space to a consideration of the "criterion problem" in research on the selection of psychiatric residents. Within the period of the Menninger selection study, it was not possible even to attempt the development of measures of ultimate criteria. In place of such long-term measures, three objective indices of an intermediate sort were employed: (a) completing three years of residency at the Menninger School, (b) obtaining certification from the American Board of Psychiatry and Neurology, and (c) remaining in the practice of psychiatry.

The first index is the familiar "graduate versus nongraduate" criterion; though somewhat removed from ultimate criteria, it is nevertheless of critical interest to a training institution. The second index is ambiguous on several counts. Since certification requires two years' experience beyond residency, there are a variety of personal and fortuitous reasons why a psychiatrist might have delayed submitting himself for examination during the first three or four years following his residency. Further, although certification is considered desirable by the school, it is probably true that some highly competent psychiatrists never seek it. Finally, the judgmental procedures involved in the examination itself may not produce an infallible index of competence in psychiatry. The variable of remaining in the practice of psychiatry is, of course, a very indirect measure of competence, though, again, one that is of importance to a training institution.

The principal immediate criteria employed in the study were judgmental ratings by supervisors and peers during the last two years of residency. Both supervisors and peers rated candidates on the variables of (a) overall competence, (b) psychotherapeutic competence, (c) diagnostic competence, (d) management (of psychiatric patients) competence, and (e) administrative competence. Decisions leading to the selection of these five criterion variables and their definitions were made on the basis of interviews with psychiatric consultants and in the light of the experiences of the VA selection research project. In addition, an attempt was made to perform a small-scale situational analysis on the basis of interviews of supervising psychiatrists (significant others). Specific instances of both good and poor psychiatric work were identified and categorized into a final schedule of 14 "minor" criterion variables (e.g., "ability to show warmth," "capacity to tolerate stress"), which were rated by psychiatric supervisors but not by peers. An overall "qualitative" criterion rating (ranging from "superior" to "drop out") was also made on the basis of the preceding variables and all additional information available about the candidates.

Models and Strategies

A unique feature of the Menninger study is that an attempt was made to evaluate the relative effectiveness of two separate strategies for the selection of psychiatric residents. The first strategy was called the "rule-of-thumb" method because it relied on the "intuitive abilities of experienced clinicians, using their favorite instruments and knowledge of what a psychiatric resident does and should be like" (Holt and Luborsky, 1958a, p. 128). The second strategy was called the "systematic" method (Luborsky and Holt, 1957), and its rationale is described elsewhere by Holt (1958) as a "sophisticated clinical prediction" strategy (see Chapter 5). The rule-of-thumb strategy was the standard method of selecting residents actually practiced by the school during the entire period of study (1946–1950). The systematic strategy was an experimental procedure, which was evaluated on data gathered from the last two classes of residents (1949–1950). Although the two assessment strategies differed, both were implemented with reference to a *psychoanalytic model* of personality (Chapter 10) that, in this unique situation, stemmed from the common theoretical orientation held by assessors, assessees, and significant others.

Under the rule-of-thumb strategy, applicants were required to appear in Topeka for two days of interviews and psychological tests. A certain amount of self-selection took place at this stage, since not all invited applicants followed through on their initial application. The procedures followed under the rule-of-thumb strategy are presented in schematic form in Figure 11.1. Each candidate was interviewed for approximately one hour by three different psychiatrists, each of whom filled out an interview report form, made a prediction of success on a 10-place scale, and gave a recommendation to the Admissions Committee in the form of "accept," "doubtful," or "reject." A clinical psychologist administered a battery of psychological tests, wrote a psychological report, made a prediction of success, and gave a recommendation to the committee. The Admissions Committee (which included the clinical psychologist and at least one of the psychiatric interviewers) considered the interview and test data, as well as the other sources of information indicated in Figure 11.1. Attempts were made to reconcile conflicting opinions through group discussion, and a final decision (accept or reject) was then made.

The procedures employed under the systematic or "sophisticated clinical" strategy were highly complex, and as Holt (1958) has done elsewhere, we will have to "skip lightly over many complicated details, and make things look a little more orderly than they actually were" (p. 7). The first four stages of the systematic strategy were similar to those described earlier (Chapter 10) with reference to the *analytic approach*: (a) situational analysis, (b) analysis of role requirements, (c) development of a target model, and (d) development of assessment techniques appropriate to the target model.

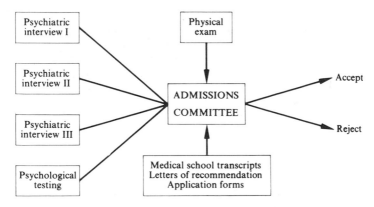

Fig. 11.1 Rule-of-thumb strategy for selection at the Menninger School.

As mentioned earlier, the situational analysis was based on interviews of psychiatric consultants, and it resulted in the development of five criterion measures of competence plus 14 "minor" criterion variables.   Further insights into the role requirements of being a psychiatrist were gained from an intensive study of 12 successful and 12 unsuccessful residents, as judged by their psychiatric supervisors.   These residents were retested by a variety of novel assessment procedures in an effort to identify the personality variables that differentiated successful from unsuccessful candidates.   The results of the retesting provided information for the construction of several detailed manuals to guide selection on the basis of those test and interview variables which appeared to discriminate success from failure.   The final stage of the systematic study involved a complex prediction study in which the validity of the test manuals and of four clinical judges was assessed within a design to be described below under "Data Combination."

Data Collection

Perhaps the best way to gain an overview of the complexities of the Menninger study is through an inspection of the distribution of research subjects by classes, as reported in Table 11.12.   Although in all 456 candidates were assessed during the four-year period indicated in the table, the assessment, selection, and criterion-analysis procedures were by no means uniform over the entire sample.   For example, under the rule-of-thumb procedure, two quite different interview report forms were employed by the psychiatric interviewers during the periods of 1946–1947 and 1947–1950 (Holt and Luborsky, 1958b).   As is true of any long-term selection program, the assessment and decision-making personnel, like the candidates themselves, changed over time.   That such changes occurred should not be surprising in a period

Table 11.12 Distribution of research subjects by classes in the Menninger School study (from Holt and Luborsky, 1958a, p. 36)

Class	Date of entry	Number of applicants	Accepted, entered	Accepted, did not enter	Rejected	Selection ratio
I	Jan., April 1946	85	49	6	27	.65
II	July, Oct. 1946	101	56	1	44	.56
III	July 1947	66	37	6	23	.65
IV	July 1948	79	32	11	36	.54
V	July 1949	93	46	20	27	.71
VI	July 1950	35	18	2	15	.57
	Totals	456	238	46	172	.62

that included the ending of one war (1945) and the beginning of still another (1949). Some of these changes are probably reflected in the selection statistics reported in Table 11.12, particularly the variation in selection ratios over different classes.

For the purposes of the systematic study, 12 successful and 12 unsuccessful residents were reinterviewed and retested approximately two years after their enrollment in the school. On the basis of a detailed analysis of the differences between these two groups, an attempt was made to compile a list of personality variables which appeared to differentiate them. Next, the investigators attempted to specify interview and test cues to these personality variables which could be expressed in the form of a scoring manual. Such preliminary manuals were prepared for a structured interview, the TAT, Rorschach, Picture Reaction Test, and background information. The manuals were then "cross-validated" on earlier classes of residents, and some were judged to have promise. The systematic study itself involved the 64 residents in classes V and VI. In order to obtain data judged to be promising from the scoring manual study—structured interview, supplementary background information, TAT, Self-Interpretation of the TAT (Self-TAT), Picture Reaction Test—it was necessary to subject candidates in classes V and VI to an additional day of testing. Candidates in those classes were also given the standard battery required by the rule-of-thumb procedure, which included three psychiatric interviews and a battery of psychological tests (Rorschach, Wechsler-Bellevue, Word Association, Szondi, and Strong VIB).

Data Combination

The methods a diagnostic council used to combine psychiatric interview and psychological test data have already been described for the rule-of-thumb strategy of selection practiced by the Menninger School. The purpose of the *systematic study* was fourfold: (a) to discover procedures which might improve on those of the rule-of-thumb method, (b) to compare the validity of predictions made on the basis of "objectified" scoring manuals with the validity of "free predictions" made from the same data sources, (c) to compare the validity of predictions based on varying amounts and types of input data, and (d) to establish the level of generalizability at which predictions of competence in psychiatric work are most effectively made (Holt and Luborsky, 1958a). The first goal was the principal one, to which the remaining three were expected to contribute.

These issues to which the systematic study was addressed are by now familiar to the reader. Appropriate experimental designs for comparing the relative effectiveness of two or more methods of data combination were discussed in Chapter 5, and several illustrations were provided (e.g., Goldberg, 1965a). The more complex experimental designs required for the comparison of predictions based on varying amounts and types of input data were discussed in Chapter 4 and illustrated with reference to the studies of Kostlan (1954), Sines (1959), and Golden (1964). Chapter 7 covered issues of generalizability and provided examples of the manner in which generalizability studies should be designed to furnish appropriate information for decision studies. Given this familiarity with the purposes and problems of the systematic study, one would expect that an exposition of its implementation would be a relatively straightforward task. Unfortunately, such is not the case because none of the several procedures of data combination employed in the Menninger study would remotely qualify as a "systematic study" within the ground rules we have adopted for discussing relative predictive efficiency, utilization of input data, or generalizability.

Unlike the experiments discussed in previous chapters, the Menninger "systematic study" was conducted within the broader context of an ongoing selection and training program for psychiatric residents, a program that could not be casually manipulated to suit the purposes of scientific research. The diagnostic, teaching, and therapeutic demands on professional time placed very real limitations on both the scope and rigor of any program of research that could have been designed within the constraints of a teaching and service-oriented setting. In many instances, the research psychologists were fully aware of the limitations of their design and procedures, and they resigned themselves to settling for the best that could be done. In other instances, they became aware of flaws in design during and, especially, after the data had been collected. Finally, one should bear in mind that these data were gathered in the late forties and early fifties, whereas the conceptual and methodological advances we have been discussing in this book were achieved mainly in the late fifties and early sixties.

The overall experimental design of the data combination study is presented in Table 11.13. Basically, four judges were required to perform the following tasks, among others: (a) collect the input data, (b) develop and cross-validate the scoring manuals, (c) make both "free" and specific predictions on the basis of varying amounts and kinds of input data, and (d) keep a running record of their impressions throughout the process.

Let us begin with a consideration of Judge I, in relation to the procedures outlined in Table 11.13. As fate would have it—and fate seemed to consistently conspire against this research project—Judge I was both the most accurate predictor from any or all kinds of data and the only judge to participate in all six stages of the prediction design. Although the procedures followed by Judge I varied considerably, we shall attempt a "typical" description of his activities. To a given member of class V, Judge I might administer the Picture Reaction Test (PRT) and record his initial impressions immediately afterward (Stage 0). Approximately one year later (Stage 1),

Table 11.13 Design for prediction study in the systematic strategy (from Holt and Luborsky, 1958a, p. 155)

Stage of analysis	Judge I	Judge II	Judge III	Judge IV
(Stage 0)	(Initial impressions)	(Initial impressions)	(Initial impressions)	
Stage 1	PRT	TAT	Interview	Rorschach
Stage 2	Rorschach	Self-TAT	TAT	Credentials
Stage 3	TAT	Interview	Self-TAT	PRT
Stage 4	Self-TAT			
Final stage	All data	All data		

he might be asked to begin making predictions for the same candidate, beginning with data from the PRT only. Or for a member of class VI, Judge I might begin his analysis with the credentials of the candidate, since this variation was later introduced into the procedure for 17 candidates in class VI (Holt and Luborsky, 1958a). By the time of Stage 1, the candidate (and his criterion performance) might be known to Judge I, so that if his data were recognized at this or any subsequent stage of prediction, he was discarded from further consideration.

Given the candidate's PRT results at State 1, Judge I was first required to score according to the cues specified in the PRT manual. Next, he made "free predictions" of as many personality variables as he wished from the PRT. Finally, he made specific predictions on both competence and minor criterion variables. The process began anew at Stage 2. The judge scored the Rorschach according to the manual, made free predictions, and made specific predictions of criterion variables on the basis of information gleaned from both the Rorschach and the PRT. He made similar successive predictions for the TAT and Self-TAT. Provided at the final stage with *all data* (Wechsler-Bellevue, Word Association, credentials, supplementary face sheet, and his own "initial impression"), Judge I was asked to predict the competence and minor criterion variables.

Unfortunately, the clinical acumen of Judge I was so great that he was able to recognize the identity of most of his cases by the final stage. Accordingly, he decided to stop making predictions entirely at that stage. Later, however, the project directors decided that such predictions might be worth the effort, even if a substantial number of cases had to be discarded on the grounds of "contamination." "Consequently, Judge I went back over his most recent cases, attempting in a quick review to recapture the frame of mind he had been in when making the personality ratings, and he added hasty ratings of the major variables for a good many of the non-contaminated cases" (Holt and Luborsky, 1958b, p. 230). Judge I did not have much faith in these hastily reconsidered ratings, but the authors report that they were about as good as the other ratings he made at the final stage. For one reason or another, Judge I made final stage ratings on slightly more than half of the available cases.

Both the *order* and *kind* of input variables provided Judge II differed from those of Judge I (see Table 11.13). In addition, Judge II was required to make final stage predictions *earlier* (after only three stages) than Judge I, although all data were made available for these final predictions. As already indicated, however, the principal difference between Judge I and Judge II was in their predictive accuracy at *all* stages. Judge III was provided the same input variables as Judge II but in a different order. Such a design would have permitted the examination of order effects in final stage predictions. Unfortunately, it became apparent that Judge III (who had been brought back for three months to make ratings) was taking too long on his initial cases, and he was therefore told to complete only three stages and asked to make a minimum of explanatory notes. "Judge IV" was, in reality, two female graduate students who did not participate in the original testing and therefore had no "initial impressions." It is not clear whether "Judge IV" was unable to make final stage ratings or whether this omission was part of the experimental design. "Judge IV" may have been included as a control for experience or sex of judge, or perhaps for both. The *number of cases* for which predictions were made, in the experimental design of Table 11.13, varied from 17 to 64 across judges. Some of the reasons for this variability have already been discussed; the reader who wishes more of the often painful details is referred to the original report (Holt and Luborsky, 1958b, pp. 229–231).

Outcomes of Prediction

How well did the Menninger School do in selecting residents by the rule-of-thumb method? In terms of the objective intermediate criterion indices, it appears that they did fairly well. The hit rates of the Admissions Committee for the three major objective indices are presented in Figure 11.2. These data must be considered *estimates* for a number of reasons, including the mysterious manner in which the number of subjects varies in different parts of the published reports on which Figure 11.2 is based.

Figure 11.2(a) indicates the outcomes of prediction regarding the completion of three years of residency. In this analysis, the fate of those rejected from the program was determined from a follow-up questionnaire, which in this instance had a return rate of only 62 percent. Because complete data are not available for rejects, the selection ratio is exaggerated, and the false negative and valid negative proportions may not be representative. One might speculate that rejected candidates who successfully completed a psychiatric residency elsewhere would have been more likely to reply than those who did not. If that is true, the estimated validity coefficient of .39 (see Chapter 6 for computational details) and the overall proportion of correct decisions of .75 are underestimates of the success of the Admissions Committee. Selecting 70 percent of the candidates at random (with a base rate of success of .73) would result in a proportion of correct decisions of .59. Perhaps at a minimum, then, the assessment and data-combination procedures of the rule-of-thumb method resulted in an increment of 16 percent over selection at random.

As is also true of selection in many industrial settings, the Menninger School would not assign very high utility values to the outcomes of rejected candidates. Surely the school would not view with alarm the fact that some of the candidates they had rejected were able to complete psychiatric residencies elsewhere. Given the shortage of trained psychiatrists, this would be welcome news. But the statistic of greatest interest to the school is the one indicating that 84 percent of those applicants admitted to the program completed three years of residency. Of all the information provided in Figure 11.2, that statistic $[P(\text{VP})/SR]$ is of the greatest practical interest.

The data on which Figure 11.2(b) is based are relatively complete, since the fact that a psychiatrist is or is not certified by the American Board of Psychiatry and Neurology is a matter of public record. The validity coefficient of .37 and the proportion of correct decisions of .69 may therefore be considered reasonable estimates of the success of the Admissions Committee. Selecting 59 percent of the candidates at random would result in a proportion of correct decisions of .51, a proportion that is 18 percent less than that attained by the Committee. Again, however, the school was most interested in the fact that 73 percent of accepted applicants had been certified at the time these data were collected. And quite possibly more were certified in later years.

The data on which Figure 11.2(c) is based are almost complete, so that the estimated validity coefficient of .37 and the proportion of correct decisions of .68 can be considered reasonably accurate. The impressive and important statistic here is the one indicating that 96 percent of Menninger alumni continued in the specialty of psychiatry (at least for the brief period during which the study was conducted). The base rate of continuation in psychiatry is high, however, and an estimated 87 percent of randomly selected applicants might be expected to continue.

We have stressed that the data in Figure 11.2 are *estimates*, and this point requires further elaboration. Clearly, not all candidates rejected by the Menninger School were accepted elsewhere, so that the valid and false negative information must be viewed with considerable skepticism. In fact, there is some evidence indicating that rejection by the Menninger School was a sufficient cause of the decisions of applicants not to pursue the field of psychiatry, a situation that, if true, would exaggerate the apparent hit rate of valid negatives. A related point, which is stressed by Holt and Luborsky (1959b) and for which there is some evidence, is that Menninger-trained psychiatrists tend to do well precisely *because* they are Menninger-trained

	Reject	Accept	
	$P(FN)$	$P(VP)$	
Completed residency	.14	.59	$BR = .73$
	$P(VN)$	$P(FP)$	
Did not complete	.16	.11	$1 - BR = .27$

(a)

$$1 - SR = .30 \qquad SR = .70$$
$$\text{Estimated } \phi_{yy'} = .39$$
$$\text{Overall correct} = .75$$
$$P(VP)/SR = .84$$

	Reject	Accept	
	$P(FN)$	$P(VP)$	
Certified	.15	.43	$BR = .58$
	$P(VN)$	$P(FP)$	
Not certified	.26	.16	$1 - BR = .42$

(b)

$$1 - SR = .41 \qquad SR = .59$$
$$\text{Estimated } \phi_{yy'} = .37$$
$$\text{Overall correct} = .69$$
$$P(VP)/SR = .73$$

	Reject	Accept	
	$P(FN)$	$P(VP)$	
Continued	.30	.57	$BR = .87$
	$P(VN)$	$P(FP)$	
Dropped out	.11	.02	$1 - BR = .13$

(c)

$$1 - SR = .49 \qquad SR = .59$$
$$\text{Estimated } \phi_{yy'} = .37$$
$$\text{Overall correct} = .68$$
$$P(VP)/SR = .96$$

Fig. 11.2 Outcomes of prediction under rule-of-thumb strategy.

psychiatrists. To some extent, this fact tends to exaggerate the valid positive hit rate, although it speaks well for the Menninger School as a training institution.[4]

The major purpose of the *systematic study* was to discover procedures which might improve on those of the rule-of-thumb method. To establish that one selection method is superior to another, one must compare their predictive outcomes with reference to a common set of criterion data. One such comparison might be of the outcomes of predictions of the intermediate criteria of Figure 11.2 under the rule-of-thumb and the systematic methods. Another might be a comparison of the two systems with respect to the prediction of the immediate criteria of competence as rated by supervisors and peers. Unfortunately, since neither these nor any other direct comparisons were made of the two selection methods, the major goal of the systematic study was never accomplished. Instead, a number of "related" analyses were performed which, because of limitations of design and execution, did not yield information of very great import for either assessment research in general or the Menninger selection program in particular.

---

4. An analogous situation exists in psychology, where certain high-quality graduate departments—operating under low selection ratios—produce outstanding alumni. Such success in selection should probably be attributed to the schools rather than to their admissions procedures.

Both the psychiatric interviewers and the psychologists who participated in the rule-of-thumb method were also asked to make overall ratings of suitability, which were later compared with supervisor and peer evaluations of competence. The interviewers' ratings did not show high inter-judge agreement ("about .4"), nor were they highly correlated with psychologists' ratings ($r = .31$). The validity of interviewers' ratings increased as they were pooled: .19 for one, .24 for two, and .27 for three. This "remarkable and comforting fact" (Holt and Luborsky, 1958a, p. 136) seems to follow from the general logic of reliability theory. The validities of the psychologists who participated in the rule-of-thumb procedure were higher than those of the interviewers, but they were not better than the validities of Judge I from the systematic study, and they were about the same as those of Judge II.

In general, the attempt to "objectify" the scoring of psychological tests by the development of manuals based on specific cues was not successful: "Of the six, two proved worthless; the other four all showed more or less promise, but there was none that yielded consistently significant validities regardless of who used it. Reliability, in terms of scorer agreement, was on the whole not very good, for a good deal of clinical judgment was still demanded." (Holt, 1958, p. 8) The rather chaotic manner in which these manuals were developed and "cross-validated" precluded a rigorous evaluation of their potential worth. Furthermore, the potential of actuarial prediction was not systematically investigated: "We never took such a possibility very seriously, but we did try out a few such objective predictors in our spare time, just out of curiosity" (Holt, 1958, p. 7).

The frequently cited results of the prediction study under the systematic strategy are presented in Table 11.14. To the many procedural variations already mentioned, we now add the information that the number of cases varies from 46 to 64 in the left half of the table, from 43 to 45 in the right

Table 11.14 Results of the prediction study in the systematic strategy (from Holt and Luborsky, 1958a, p. 206)

Basis of predictive rating	Supervisors' evaluations Predicted by Judge				Peers' evaluations Predicted by Judge			
	I	II	III	IV	I	II	III	IV
Stage 0 (Impression)	.12	−.05	.12		.27	.26	.18	
Stage 1	.26	−.10	.14	.11	.23	−.02	.17	.02
Stage 2	.26	−.08	.08	.12	.21	.09	.13	.04
Stage 3	.28	.03	.07	.15	.25	.22	.11	.17
Stage 4	.29				.27			
All data	.57	.22			.52	.48		

half, and that the validity coefficients for Judge I at the all-data stage are based on 38 cases for supervisors' evaluations and 31 cases for peer evaluations. It is difficult to know what conclusions to draw from these data. Judge I appears to be a rather skilled psychodiagnostician, although it is not clear to whom he should be compared in performance or to what population that performance should be generalized. Nor does the design permit an evaluation of the effects on predictive accuracy of varying amounts and kinds of input data: "We hoped to be able to study the contribution of each procedure (test or interview) by juggling the figures in Table 11.14, and indeed some attempts were made to do so, but the results were quite inconclusive" (Holt and Luborsky, 1958b, p. 221–223). More conclusive data on this topic were discussed in Chapter 4.

Critique

It seems likely that if the investigators of the Menninger study had had an opportunity to repeat their study, they would have either done it quite differently or not done it at all. The most obvious shortcoming of their research was the overall *design*, since the eventual yield of useful information was quite small in relation to the extraordinary expenditure of professional time and effort. The basic problem confronting the investigators was that of mapping a research program onto an ongoing selection process. The rule-of-thumb selection procedure followed by the school was the major issue, and the most relevant questions were: (a) How well does the rule-of-thumb procedure actually work? (b) How might it be improved upon? In retrospect, it appears that more attention should have been directed to the first question than to the second.

Even the fragmentary results of the outcomes of prediction by the rule-of-thumb method suggest that it is a procedure well worth investigating in careful detail. A much more thorough analysis of that method could have been conducted without interfering with the ongoing mechanisms of selection. The fact that the possibility of developing actuarial indices from available data was never taken "very seriously" connotes a prejudice that runs contrary to all available data on that issue. The rule-of-thumb method of selection is a prototype of global psychodiagnostic assessment, and one might legitimately raise the question whether it could be improved upon. But the alternative "systematic" strategy explored was also a global psychodiagnostic procedure that differed little, in detail, from the method with which it was to be compared.

The vicissitudes that befell the systematic study are likely to strike a sympathetic cord in the hearts of those who have conducted research in applied assessment settings. But most of the misfortunes that occurred appear to have been brought about by internal problems of the research team itself rather than by external problems that could be attributed to the applied setting. Given that the results of the major predictive study were not compared directly with the decisions of the Admissions Committee, one might raise the question whether the predictive study needed to be conducted within the framework of the ongoing selection program. Certainly the results of studies conducted under more controlled and less criterion-contaminated circumstances (e.g., Kostlan, 1954; Sines, 1959; Golden, 1964) have shed more light on the clinical judgment process than the study conducted at Menninger. Thus the principal shortcomings of the Menninger study can be attributed to the manner in which available resources were allocated within the framework of the many problems which could have been profitably studied (Thorndike, 1960).

Peace Corps

Prediction Problem

In March of 1961, President John F. Kennedy fulfilled a campaign promise of the previous year by establishing the Peace Corps as a government agency. The purpose of the Peace Corps Act of Congress (September 22, 1961) was:

To promote world peace and friendship through a Peace Corps, which shall make available to interested countries and areas men and women of the United States qualified for service abroad and willing to serve, under conditions of hardship if necessary, to help the peoples of such countries and areas in meeting their needs for trained manpower, and to help promote a better understanding of the American people on the part of the peoples served and a better understanding of other peoples on the part of the American people.

Under the dynamic leadership of Sargent Shriver, this newly created agency moved rapidly to comply with its congressional mandate. Within its first year of existence, the Peace Corps recruited, selected, and trained more than 900 volunteers for service in 12 different countries. By the summer of 1964, almost 2,000 volunteers had completed service in 40 different countries throughout the world (Peace Corps, 1964).

The Peace Corps was and is an extraordinary "experiment" on the part of the United States government. Although suggested and initiated by one political party, it was supported by the majority of the opposition party and later praised by the leaders of both parties. Thus the Peace Corps, from its inception, was a national enterprise rather than a partisan endeavor.[5] Nevertheless, although few openly opposed the idealistic purposes of the Peace

---

5.   Remarks by R. Sargent Shriver, Jr., at the 17th National Conference on Higher Education, Chicago, March 6, 1962.

Corps, many, if not most, citizens and political leaders were extremely skeptical of the extent to which such far-reaching goals could be realized in practice. Consequently, this innovative experiment in international relations was conducted under the scrutiny of a worldwide audience of potential critics.

During the first year of Peace Corps service, a mildly critical postcard from a single volunteer was discovered by someone in a developing nation, and its subsequent publication created a flurry of international publicity of an unfavorable sort. The negative utility attached to false positive selection decisions during the early years of the Peace Corps created a situation in which a conservative minimax selection strategy was demanded (Chapter 6). Whereas the hostile environment of the countries in which OSS undercover agents operated permitted that program to bury its false positives, the mistakes in Peace Corps selection were occasionally magnified out of all proportion in the eyes of the world.

The mandate from Congress to make available men and women "qualified for service abroad" created one of the most demanding and sensitive prediction problems in the history of personality assessment. The challenge was met by the creation of the Division of Selection within the agency, a division of greater scope and power than any previous assessment unit operating within the context of a large organization. Nicholas Hobbs was appointed as the first Director of the Division of Selection, and it was primarily during his period of leadership that the internal structure of the division and its strategies for assessment and selection were decided upon. Hobbs was succeeded by E. Lowell Kelly, whose many years of previous experience in assessment research enabled him to implement the policies of the division in a realistic and efficient fashion. During the ensuing years, hundreds of assessment psychologists served the Peace Corps, many in Washington and more at distant centers.

The manifold purposes of the Peace Corps Act created several distinct prediction problems at several levels of criteria. As is true of any social action program, the ultimate criteria involve measures of the program's impact on host countries (Gollin, 1963). The extent to which a given volunteer or a group of volunteers helped a host country "in meeting their needs for trained manpower" is less easily objectified than one might think. Perhaps the most striking feature of Peace Corps overseas service was the *diversity* of assignments in vastly different parts of the world. Projects varied considerably in their degree of "structure," ranging from formal classroom instruction in large urban centers to rural community development in remote and isolated villages. The "conditions of hardship" varied from the poverty and squalor of Indian villages to the "paradise" of tropical islands in the Pacific. Although such objective criterion measures as wheat yield were sometimes available, most criterion variables were considerably less tangible in nature. Evaluating the impact of a program of rural community development, for example, is a difficult task that involves subtle attitudinal variables.

The extent to which a volunteer was able to "help promote a better understanding of the American people" could, in principle, lend itself to attitude measurement, but the variety of settings in which volunteers served almost precluded the development of standardized procedures. The impact of the service experience on the volunteer's attitudes toward and understanding of other peoples is a more straightforward task that was evaluated, in part, by extensive end-of-service interviews and questionnaires. But an assessment of the more interesting long-range effects on the volunteer's career plans and on his social and political attitudes requires extensive longitudinal research and appropriate control groups. For the most part, ultimate criteria of Peace Corps "impact" must be inferred from the judgments and impressions of a variety of significant others, who might range in status from a poor child in an African village to a senator of the United States.

Criterion Analysis

Requests for the services of Peace Corps volunteers were initiated by host countries through diplomatic or other governmental channels. On the basis of a series of conferences between host country and Peace Corps officials, a contract for Peace Corps services was prepared and signed. In the drawing up of such contracts, an attempt was made to specify the extent and kinds of services involved, including the number of volunteers required, the services they would be expected to perform, the conditions under which they would live, and the kind of support the host country was to provide. Working with that information, a classification specialist prepared a job description (Form 104) that specified the duties to be performed, the kinds of skills required, and the general atmosphere of the working environment. This job description provided the initial definition of criterion performance, and it played an important role in the initial screening of Peace Corps applicants.

Since Peace Corps contracts were usually renewed, more extensive information concerning the psychological and skill requirements of specific projects became available as successive groups of Peace Corps volunteers completed their 21 to 22 months of assigned duty. Information from overseas staff, host nationals, and Peace Corps volunteers enabled the Division of Selection to compile a more comprehensive picture of the role requirements of specific assignments for use in the selection process. Thus criterion analysis procedures in the Peace Corps yielded at the outset a general, somewhat global job description that became successively more explicit over time.

Jones (1968a, 1969b) has proposed and implemented a model for investigating overseas activity of Peace Corps volunteers that distinguishes three important facets of such activity. *Kinds* of information may be classified as descriptive or evaluative in nature. *Sources* of information may be classified with respect to the groups which provide the information, such as volunteers, overseas staff, and host nationals. *Referents* of information may be individual volunteers or entire projects. The primarily descriptive information provided by the job description includes information concerning both the project and the expected performance of individual volunteers. Evaluative information, on the other hand, must be obtained from judgments of significant others (overseas staff, host nationals) regarding the performance of individual volunteers or the effectiveness of a specific project. Descriptive information is most useful in the process of selection, whereas evaluative information is required for the appraisal of the effectiveness of selection.

Efforts to obtain evaluative ratings of the overseas performance of individual volunteers were frequently thwarted, both by the pressures and demands on overseas staff and by the difficulty of maintaining contact with volunteers who were often widely separated geographically. The most widely used standard evaluation form was a "rating scale for overseas performance," which was typically filled out by the overseas representative or one of his officials. Ratings were made after three months, after twelve months, and at the completion of the overseas assignment. A five-place scale was employed to rate job competence, relationships with other volunteers, relationships with host national counterparts, relationships with other nationals, and emotional maturity, as well as to make an overall evaluation.

The selection, training, and service programs of the Peace Corps provided several useful indices of immediate and intermediate criteria. The efficiency of an initial suitability screening program was evaluated with reference to both attrition during training and ratings obtained during training. The effectiveness of selection during training was evaluated with reference to overseas performance ratings and the objective criterion of "return rate" during two years of service. The multiple-stage selection strategy employed lent itself to evaluations of the relationships among the various components of the system. Measures obtained at one point in time were compared with later measures in an effort to evaluate the possibility of eliminating one or more stages of the selection strategy.

Models and Strategies

As one might expect of an agency of change, the assessment and selection strategies employed by the Peace Corps have undergone almost continuous revision. The changes have largely reflected the changing nature of the agency itself. In the early days of the Peace Corps, selection involved, among other things, an attempt to place large numbers of "A.B. generalists" (i.e., recent college graduates in the humanities and social sciences) in broadly defined assignments (e.g., community development) within the constraints of a minimax strategy. More recently, the Peace Corps has changed from a somewhat frenetic experiment in social action to a mature and established government agency. There has been a shift of emphasis from the employment of A.B. generalists as community developers to the employment of skilled technicians and specialists in well-defined job categories. As a consequence, current selection and assessment strategies are less like those of the OSS and more like those of other civil service agencies. We shall not attempt a historical account of the many different selection and assessment strategies employed by the Peace Corps over the last decade but shall provide instead a general outline of procedures that is representative of those employed in the earlier years of Peace Corps selection. Though not representative of current practices, this outline is of special interest because it describes the most elaborate selection strategy employed in the history of large-scale personality assessment.

As indicated earlier, the job description prepared from the contract with a host country was the principal focus of Peace Corps selection. Like the OSS and many other large-scale assessment programs, Peace Corps selection and assessment were typically directed toward the determination of "overall suitability" for overseas performance. In addition, however, some candidates were recruited, trained, and selected to perform specific duties in a reasonably well-defined criterion environment. Once the final negotiations of a contract with a host country were completed, a number of interrelated and coordinated operations began. One set of operations involved the establishment of a training site appropriate for the particular program under consideration. Most training contracts were made with universities because of the availability in such settings of specialists who could be employed in teaching and consultative capacities. There were also some special training centers in such places as Puerto Rico and Hawaii, where it was possible to some extent to simulate the conditions of the eventual overseas placement. In some later programs, much of the training was conducted in the host country itself.

While training negotiations were being conducted, recruiting and screening operations were also under way. An individual interested in the Peace Corps in general, or in some specific project, was urged to fill out the Peace Corps questionnaire, which requested detailed information on his or her training, experience, and technical qualifications. After completing the questionaire, the candidate took the Peace Corps placement tests, which included measures of language and verbal aptitude, at one of the centers at which they were administered. The candidate was also required to provide the names of individuals who were familiar with his background and to furnish transcripts of formal academic training. All this information was then employed in the initial suitability screening strategy diagrammed in Figure 11.3.

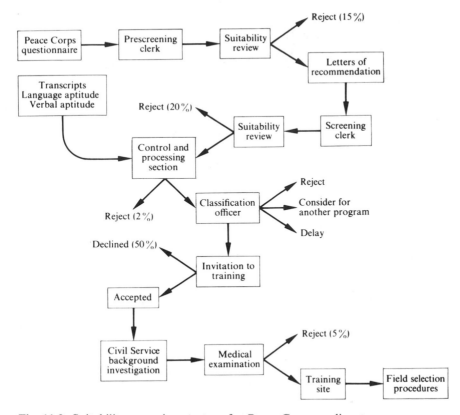

Fig. 11.3 Suitability screening strategy for Peace Corps applicants.

A prescreening clerk examined the Peace Corps questionnaires for the purpose of eliminating applicants who were obviously not suitable on legal or medical grounds or on the basis of lacking the appropriate education or skills. Some of these folders were referred to legal or medical specialists. Approximately 15 percent of the applicants were eliminated at this stage, and letters of recommendation (about 17 for each candidate) were solicited for the remainder. The respondents were asked to include in their letters of recommendation specific ratings for such categories as job competence, emotional maturity, and interpersonal relationships, as well as to make written comments in the same areas. The letter of solicitation promised confidentiality and stressed the fact that no candidate would be eliminated on the basis of a single negative rating.

A screening clerk scrutinized the letters of recommendation and referred to appropriate Peace Corps officials those folders in which legal or medical problems were encountered. At this point, approximately 20 percent of the applicants were rejected for reasons of gross unsuitability or on medical or legal grounds.   The folders of surviving applicants were referred to the Control and Processing Section, along with transcripts and the results of placement tests.   Next, an initial screening for minimal skills resulted in the rejection of a small number of candidates.   The remaining folders went to a classification officer familiar with existing or anticipated Peace Corps training programs for specific jobs.   The classification officer evaluated all available material and made detailed ratings on the suitability of a candidate for a specific project.   On the basis of these ratings, the candidate was rejected, referred to another program specialist, or issued an invitation to a specific training program.

The invitation to training, a letter from the Director of the Peace Corps, informed the candidate of the nature of the job for which he had been selected and of the time and place his training would begin.   For a variety of reasons, only about half of those invited to training accepted.   The typical Peace Corps applicant was a graduating college senior who was considering, in addition to the Peace Corps, such alternatives as employment, graduate school, military service, marriage, etc.   Prior commitments to any of these alternatives contributed to the high attrition rate at this stage, as did self-selection due to changes of interests or changes in applicants' views of the Peace Corps itself.   Every candidate who accepted the invitation to training was asked to fill out a Civil Service Commission background information questionnaire that served as the basis for an extensive field investigation of his prior history, conducted by Civil Service investigators.   He was also required to undergo a thorough medical examination, and approximately five percent of the applicants were eliminated on medical grounds.   Those who passed their medical examinations appeared at the training site as scheduled.

The elaborate prescreening strategy illustrated in Figure 11.3 was a complex set of operations that relied on computer data processing and the judgment of experts.   The extensiveness of screening prior to training is evident in the fact that only one of six who initially applied to the Peace Corps eventually reached the training site (Henry, 1965).   Note also that this extensive screening was accomplished without any personal contacts with the candidates.   When the screening program was instituted, there was considerable pressure to establish a nationwide network of individual interviewers.   This pressure was properly resisted on the grounds that the validity of such interviews would probably have been close to zero, despite the fact that interviews were traditional in industry and other government agencies (Hobbs, 1963).   In any event, the suitability screening strategy employed by the Peace Corps was probably more thorough and soundly based than the entire assessment programs of many other institutions.   But suitability screening was not the major assessment strategy employed by the

Peace Corps. In fact, such screening only set the stage for the more elaborate procedures of field selection.

The principal vehicle of selection at the training sites was the advisory selection board. Although that board was basically a diagnostic council operating under an analytic strategy (Chapter 10), the inputs to it and its composition were more complex than those of any previous programs employing that strategy. The general form of the field selection strategy is diagrammed in Figure 11.4. The advisory selection board held its first meeting about halfway through the training program, which typically was of two or three months' duration. At the time of this meeting, the diagnostic council members listed in Figure 11.4 integrated the input data for each candidate and arrived at a decision of "reject," "provide feedback," or "transfer."

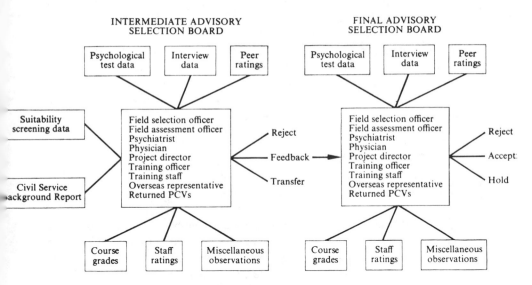

Fig. 11.4 Field selection strategy for Peace Corps trainees.

In the early years of Peace Corps selection, the decision to reject was employed rather frequently at this stage, since the overall strategy was a conservative minimax strategy. In later years, the investigatory decision (Chapter 6) to provide feedback became the most frequent one. When this decision was made, the trainee received extensive feedback relating to the manner in which the board viewed his potential for fulfilling the role requirements of the assignment for which he was being trained. The feedback was intended to serve several purposes. First, it was meant to foster an atmosphere of openness and honesty in which the trainee was fully informed of his status and the reasons for it. Second, it provided the trainee with sufficient information to adopt the strategy of "self-selection," should he so choose. Third, it pinpointed shortcomings seen by the board, areas in which the board expected evidence of improvement prior to final selection. The "transfer" decision was made on those relatively rare occasions when the board felt the candidate unsuited for the project under consideration but suited for another.

A "feedback" decision initiated a recycling of the data-gathering sources indicated in Figure 11.4, up to the time of the final advisory selection board meeting, which occurred at the end of the training period. Once again, the diagnostic council members evaluated all available information on each trainee. Note that the input information available to the board was cumulative in nature. Beginning with the data gathered during suitability screening and continuing with the extensive assessments made for both advisory boards, data were collected, rated, and collated in a systematic manner. It seems likely that the information on which the final board made its decision was more comprehensive than that available to any other project in the history of personality assessment. The final board made primarily clear-cut decisions to accept or reject, although certain administrative circumstances (e.g., medical clearance) occasionally necessitated a delay in final action.

It should be apparent from the sheer number of items in Figure 11.4 that the field selection strategy does not lend itself to a simple summary. Perhaps the best way to grasp the complex interrelationships among the components of this process is to understand the functions of the members of the advisory selection boards. The strategy is fundamentally one of making decisions based on assessments made with reference to both immediate and intermediate criteria. In this sense, the functions of different members of the board may be thought of as related to: (a) *decision making* (field selection officer), (b) *assessment* (field assessment officer, psychiatrist, physician), (c) *immediate criteria* (project director, training officer, training staff), and (d) *intermediate criteria* (overseas representative, returned Peace Corps volunteers).

Selection boards were "advisory" in the sense that final decisions regarding overseas placement were made by the field selection officer. The authority of that officer was not absolute since his decisions could be appealed to an internal Peace Corps Review Board, but it was quite clear to the staff and trainees that the field selection officer was the principal decision maker. Typically, he was an academic, industrial, or clinical psychologist who served the Peace Corps in a consulting capacity. His status in his own field would make him roughly equivalent to the full colonel who chaired the military assessment boards discussed earlier in this chapter. Typically, the field selection officer did not reside at the training site but appeared there only to provide an initial orientation for the staff and trainees and to chair the intermediate and final advisory selection boards. Consequently, he had no official face-to-face contact with the trainees prior to the meetings of the selection boards. His decisions were based on the data provided by the staff and on the results of the Civil Service background investigation, which were classified for use only by selection officers. Although selection officers were assumed to be competent decision makers, the soundness of their decisions was thought to stem in part from the objectivity of their vantage point. Presumably, their lack of personal or professional involvement in the training, assessment, and overseas operations of the Peace Corps enabled them to collate judiciously these diverse sources of input information about a given trainee and his anticipated assignment.

The field assessment officer was charged with the duties of collecting psychological assessment data and collating the many sources of observational data that came from the training staff. In addition to administering standard psychological tests (e.g., the MMPI), that officer supervised the collection of peer ratings prior to each board meeting, interviewed each trainee, and met regularly with the training staff to oversee the collection of systematic ratings from the staff members. Before each board meeting, he prepared a detailed summary of the many sources of information available for each trainee. After each meeting, he prepared an overseas placement report that alerted the overseas personnel to the strengths and weaknesses of each potential volunteer. The assessment officer also worked closely with the project psychiatrist, who usually interviewed each trainee, and the project physician, who was responsible for evaluating medical problems in relation to the physical demands of the overseas assignment. It should be clear that the comprehensiveness and quality of assessment for any training program were directly related to the energies and skills of the individual who exercised the considerable responsibilities of the field assessment officer.

The training situation itself provided an immediate criterion against which the performance of individual trainees could be evaluated. The project director was administratively in charge of training, and his broad perspective on current and past training programs could make him a valuable member of selection boards. The training officer was a representative of Peace Corps–Washington who was familiar with both training procedures and the circumstances of overseas placement. The training staff consisted of language instructors (frequently nationals of the host country), instructors in background topics related to the overseas assignment (e.g., geography, anthropology, history, political science), and instructors in special skills related to overseas duties (e.g., malaria control, community development). In addition to course grades, the training staff rated each trainee on the basis of observations made both inside and outside the classroom.

A unique feature of Peace Corps selection was the presence on the boards of individuals who had direct knowledge of the conditions of overseas assignment. In some instances, this source of input would be the director of the overseas project (the overseas representative) or one of his administrative assistants. In other instances, the overseas project was represented by an official from Washington who had direct knowledge of that project. Frequently, the criterion situation was described to the final selection board by the man under whom the volunteers would actually be working. This careful matching of the candidate to the criterion epitomizes the analytic selection strategy. Finally, many later training projects had returned Peace Corps volunteers (PCVs) as staff members. In addition to their valuable contributions to training, the returned PCVs brought a unique perspective to the selection boards, since many of them had served in assignments virtually identical to those under consideration.

Data Collection

The suitability screening strategy (Figure 11.3) employed at the first stage of selection resulted in the collection of an impressive array of data in the absence of any personal contacts with the candidates or those who served as references for them. Letters of recommendation were solicited from the list of references provided by the candidate on his Peace Corps questionnaire, as well as from other names listed therein. As many as 22 letters were received for a single candidate. Since these letters required the respondents to make five-place ratings on specific dimensions, an impressive sample of pooled, quantified ratings was available for screening and prediction. Later studies of the predictive effectiveness of indices based on these ratings have indicated promising correlations with overseas performance (Jones, 1969b). An equally promising set of screening and prediction indices was provided by the assessment summaries made by the classification officers. On the basis of all available data, five-place ratings were made of such characteristics as language, motivation for Peace Corps, emotional maturity, and overall project suitability. Candidates who received less than 3 on the last rating were not invited to training. Assessment summary ratings for invited candidates served as input to field selection procedures.

Data collection procedures during training were more costly in their use of professional time. Although the MMPI was the only personality test administered routinely, the assessment officer was free to administer other tests, either routinely or occasionally for special diagnostic purposes. The use of at least 34 different psychological tests has been reported, ranging from the Rorschach to the Wechsler Adult Intelligence Scale (Colmen, Kaplan, and Boulger, 1964). Despite a certain amount of ambivalence concerning the predictive validity of the interview, it was used extensively in field selection. Prior to each of the two board meetings, each trainee was typically interviewed

at least once by the assessment officer. The frequency of psychiatric interviewing ranged from routine interviewing of all trainees to interviewing on
referral from the assessment officer or selection officer. Peer ratings were
typically obtained shortly before the meetings of the intermediate and final
selection boards. Trainees were asked to predict the five most successful and
five least successful peers in their group. They were also asked to indicate
the names of the five trainees they would most prefer to be assigned with and
the five they would least prefer. Success nominations were employed as
predictive input to selection boards, and assignment preferences were used
for overseas placement and as a source of sociometric data. Training staff
ratings took the form of specific course grades and an indication of quartile
standings, as well as ratings of overall suitability for Peace Corps service.
Miscellaneous observations ranged from formal observations made during
situational tests to informal observations made by any staff member during
work or leisure time.

The Civil Service Commission background report, or "full field investigation," provided a novel source of assessment data for the Peace Corps.
Although collected routinely by the Civil Service Commission for a number
of government agencies, the full field report had previously been viewed as
a method for investigating the loyalty or security of an applicant, rather than
as a life-history document that could be used for purposes of personality
assessment. Trained Civil Service Commission investigators in various
regions of the country conducted interviews with former employers, neighbors,
peers, landlords, and others who had known the candidate at various phases
of his life. Routine checks were also conducted of police files, credit
bureau records, school records, and other sources of information that could
be used to verify statements made by the applicant. The end product of these
investigations was a narrative document of, on the average, 25 pages of
single-spaced typing that was made available to the selection officer under
conditions of strict confidentiality.

The use of the full field report as a source of assessment data by the Peace
Corps was somewhat controversial, both because of its cost (approximately
$450 per trainee) and because of its possible invasion of the privacy of the
trainees. Some form of background investigation was required by law, however, and the Division of Selection chose to employ the already-established
full field investigation procedure as a potentially valuable source of assessment data. Because the full field report was a nonquantified source of input
data that was integrated clinically with other sources of information by the
field selection officer, it is difficult to evaluate its contribution to selection.
Some indirect evidence is available from a study conducted by Jones (1969a)
in which the overseas performance of a group of volunteers selected without
the full field report (because of time pressures) was compared with the

overseas performance of a control group for whom full field reports were available at the time of selection. No significant differences were found between the two groups on three dimensions of staff ratings of overseas performance, and although the attrition rate for the control group was slightly *higher* than that of the no-full-field group, the difference was not statistically significant. Other studies by Jones (1969b) suggest that when the full field report is quantified by the use of objective rating scales (Jones, 1968b), the instrument has significant correlations with overseas performance, although the incremental validity of the full field report over letters of recommendation was slight.

It should be apparent from the preceding account of data collection procedures during field selection that an extraordinary amount of information was collected and collated within a relatively short period of time. Although the field assessment officer and his staff assumed the major burden of responsibility for data collection, the pressures of assessment were felt by all staff members and, of course, by the trainees themselves. Although it was clear that the field selection officer was entrusted with the final decision regarding overseas selection, it was equally apparent that all staff members (and peers) contributed data on which such decisions were based. The multiple and sometimes conflicting purposes of training and selection created an atmosphere that many trainees felt was oppressive. The dual roles of counselor and assessor were also difficult for the professional staff to maintain consistently, and this fact, together with the sheer work load of assessment, created a set of working conditions that placed severe demands on the professional and emotional resources of staff members. To quote from McNeil's (1969) perceptive and gracefully written account of life at a Peace Corps training center:

Working hours were exceptionally long, the labors of training were demanding, living quarters were cramped and primitive, all the staff members were some distance from home and loved ones, and all had to be on stage playing their role nearly 16 hours a day. Few human beings are designed to give continuously without adequate time to recharge their psychological batteries and when even the most dedicated persons try to give without ever taking, insight and maturity suffer invisible erosion and the psychic apparatus chooses regression as a means to restore emotional balance. (pp. 17–18).

Data Combination

The intermediate and final advisory selection boards were the principal vehicles of selection at training sites. Thus the Peace Corps continued the tradition of the diagnostic council, which had characterized most large-scale assessment programs since it was introduced by the Germans prior to the Second World War. A unique feature of Peace Corps selection boards was the sharp distinction maintained between the decision-making roles (field selection officer) and assessment roles (field assessment officer, psychiatrist, physician) of professional board members. An additional innovation was the practice of using board members who provided input regarding both immediate criteria (project director, training officer, training staff) and intermediate criteria (overseas respresentative, returned Peace Corps volunteers). Technically, the composition and size of a given board was determined by the selection officer, who invited those members of the staff who, in his judgment, would make the maximum contribution to the proceedings of the board. In practice, most board meetings were attended by at least the field assessment officer, a psychiatrist, the project director, the training officer, and an overseas representative.

Just prior to each board meeting, the assessment officer prepared an assessment summary for each trainee and distributed it to each board member. The detailed results of psychological testing or psychiatric interviewing were typically available only to the field selection officer and members of the assessment staff. The results of the full field investigation were available only to the selection officer. But in general, the members of the advisory board had common information available to them in summary form. Each trainee was considered individually in board deliberations that varied in length from ten minutes to two hours. Typically, the consideration of a given trainee began with a discussion of his assessment summary, which was supplemented by information provided by various board members. The assessment staff were the primary resource persons with respect to the psychological strengths and weaknesses of the trainee. The training staff were the primary resource persons regarding the significance of the candidate's performance during training. The overseas representative or others familiar with the conditions of overseas placement were the primary resource persons with respect to intermediate criteria. The order and manner in which information concerning a trainee was considered varied somewhat as a function of the composition of the board and the administrative style of the field selection officer. Eventually, however, the deliberations of the board culminated in a set of ratings and a specific administrative decision by the field selection officer.

Each candidate was rated on a five-place scale for the components of skills, motivation, interpersonal relations, language ability, and emotional maturity. In addition, each candidate was placed in one of the following administrative categories: *reject* (no reconsideration, reconsideration after one year, immediate reconsideration), *provisional accept* (special placement, high risk–high gain), or *accept* (bottom, second, third, or top quartile of expected performance overseas). The several categories of *reject* indicated varying degrees of prognosis for eventual suitability, since many trainees were separated from the Peace Corps primarily on the grounds that they had not yet matured sufficiently for overseas service. The *provisional accept* category included two kinds of placement problems. "Special placement" indicated that a trainee could be expected to perform satisfactorily only if certain special conditions of job placement could be guaranteed and that the trainee should not be considered "generally suitable" for any Peace Corps assignment. The rather controversial "high risk–high gain" category signified a candidate of exceptional potential who, for a variety of reasons, might be expected to be a disruptive force in a sensitive overseas assignment. The descriptive label for that category reflected the decision-theoretic orientation of Peace Corps selection. Each of the four categories of *accept* represented both an administrative decision and an attempted prediction of overseas performance.

It is difficult to evaluate either the validity or the efficiency of the complex group problem-solving process that eventuated in the decisions of the Peace Corps advisory selection boards. Nevertheless, there are certain character- istics of such problem solving that should distinguish rational from random or irrational decision processes. First of all, the board members came to advisory board meetings with different amounts and kinds of information, so that we would expect inter-judge agreement to be greater after discussion than before. Second, since board discussions presumably provided board members with more critical and differentiating information about individual candidates (as opposed to halos or stereotypes), we would expect ratings given after discussion to be generally lower (more critical) and more widely dispersed (more discriminating) than ratings given prior to discussion. Finally, the critically important ratings given by the selection officer should, in some sense, be "representative" of the consensus of the board. By choosing to entrust the final decision to the selection officer, the Peace Corps purchased the administrative convenience of separating decision making from assessment and training, at the possible cost of sacrificing the higher reliabilities that are known to obtain for pooled judgments. However, such a procedure could be justified if it was demonstrated that the judgments of the selection officer were highly correlated with the *composite judgments* of the group, since the latter are expected to be more reliable than individual judgments.

The results of a study of inter-judge agreement among members of Peace Corps selection boards tend to be reassuring with respect to the several considerations just raised. Goldberg (1966) studied selection boards from five different training projects at the Peace Corps Center of the University of Hawaii at Hilo. The composition of individual boards varied in terms of which assessment officers, psychiatrists, training coordinators, and overseas representatives were members, but the project director and field selection officer were the same for all boards. Each board member was asked to rate each trainee on an 11-place scale ranging from 0 (immediate separation) to

10 (ideal Peace Corps volunteer). These ratings were obtained at different times for different boards, but they included: (a) ratings made prior to receiving the assessment summaries provided to board members, (b) ratings made after receiving assessment summaries but prior to discussion by the board, and (c) ratings made after discussion by the board.

The general nature of the findings from Goldberg's study may be illustrated with reference to the data in Table 11.15. In this particular analysis, the board members were first asked to rate each trainee after receiving the assessment summaries but prior to any discussion, and they were asked to rate the trainees again after the deliberations of the intermediate advisory selection board. The correlations among board members *prior* to any discussion are presented in the upper right of the table. Correlations among the same board members *after* discussion are presented in the lower left. As would be anticipated from an examination of the table, the mean prediscussion correlation was .66 and the mean postdiscussion correlation was .82. It can also be seen that the mean ratings given to the trainees tended to decrease after discussion (more critical) and that the standard deviation of these ratings tended to increase (more discriminating).

The extent to which the selection officer's ratings tended to be representative of the consensus of the board can be evaluated with reference to the last row of Table 11.15. After board discussion, individual board members' ratings tended to be most highly correlated with the ratings of the selection officer ($\bar{r} = .86$). All ratings tended to be highly correlated after board discussions, however, and this average correlation is not significantly different from the correlations of board members' ratings with those of the training coordinator, for example. The important point is that a clear consensus appeared to exist following discussion and that the selection officer's ratings were highly correlated with this consensus. The circled entries of Table 11.15 represent the prediscussion versus postdiscussion correlations for each board member. In comparison with other board members, the selection officer tended to be relatively uninfluenced by the discussions, a finding that was replicated in the results of the other boards studied. Goldberg (1966) attributes this finding to the fact that the selection officer had the results of the full field report prior to discussion and that, to some extent, he conveyed the tenor of that report to other members of the board. Goldberg may very well have special insight into the manner in which the full field report was weighted by these boards since he was, in fact, the selection officer. Nevertheless, it would be inappropriate to generalize these findings to all selection officers (Jones, 1969a).

The results of an analysis of ratings made by another selection board revealed an orderly progression in judgmental covergence from ratings made prior to receiving assessment summaries ($\bar{r} = .41$) to ratings made after the summaries but prior to discussion by the board ($\bar{r} = .68$) to ratings made

Table 11.15 Agreement among seven selection board participants before and after board discussion: Board A, 57 Trainees (from Goldberg, 1966, p. 402)

	Selection officer	Assessment officer 1	Assessment officer 2	Psychiatrist 1	Project director	Training coordinator 1	Overseas representative 1	Prediscussion M	Prediscussion σ	Prediscussion r
Selection officer	(97)	.78	.69	.65	.78	.59	.63	5.0	2.6	.69
Assessment officer 1	.91	(89)	.83	.76	.78	.57	.59	5.3	1.9	.72
Assessment officer 2	.92	.89	(83)	.69	.71	.62	.62	6.0	1.6	.69
Psychiatrist 1	.80	.83	.72	(89)	.75	.70	.54	5.2	2.4	.68
Project director	.86	.86	.84	.87	(87)	.65	.63	5.2	1.6	.72
Training coordinator 1	.91	.90	.91	.81	.86	(76)	.39	6.3	1.5	.59
Overseas representative	.74	.68	.72	.69	.76	.71	(86)	4.8	1.4	.57
Postdiscussion M	4.8	5.0	5.7	5.0	5.0	5.8	4.6			
Postdiscussion σ	2.7	2.5	2.4	2.7	2.5	2.1	2.0			
Postdiscussion r	.86	.84	.83	.79	.84	.85	.72			

after discussion ($\bar{r} = .83$). As before, the mean ratings tended to decrease (from 5.6 to 5.1 to 4.9) and the standard deviation of ratings tended to increase (from 1.8 to 2.2 to 2.8). These and other data presented by Goldberg (1966) suggest that the group problem solving of advisory selection boards was rational in nature and that the ratings given trainees were both critical and discriminating. Although encouraging, such findings cannot be interpreted as being relevant to the *validity* of final board ratings.

Outcomes of Prediction

How well did the Division of Selection fare in complying with the Congressional mandate to provide men and women "qualified for service abroad?" There are, of course, many possible answers to this complex question. In the first place, the continued tenure of the Peace Corps agency seems to attest, at least in part, to the effectiveness of the organization in meeting public and Congressional expectations. However, more direct evidence on the role of the Division of Selection in this generally successful enterprise should be available from return rate data.

Published and reported estimates of the proportion of volunteers who failed to complete their full term of duty have varied considerably, as a function of different samples studied, but the figure appears to be somewhere between 11 and 15 percent. Data presented by Krug and Wertheim (1965), based on 7,652 volunteers, indicate that the return rate was approximately 12 percent. In a smaller sample of 1,178 volunteers, the return rate was reported to be 11 percent (Menninger and English, 1965). Somewhat higher figures have been reported by others (e.g., Cobb, Wrigley, and Kline, 1966; Henry, 1965), and there is considerable fluctuation from project to project, and especially from country to country. That approximately 13 percent of volunteers who were sent overseas failed to complete their full term of duty may be a cause of some concern for an agency that has a limited tolerance of false positives. But the more basic question, from the standpoint of selection, has to do with the proportion of these cases that may be considered *selection errors*.

The proportion of volunteers who returned for psychiatric reasons appears to be reasonably estimated at .7 percent, that is, less than one percent (Menninger and English, 1965). The proportion of volunteers who returned for medical reasons was .6 percent, or approximately the same. Given the stressful and physically demanding nature of many Peace Corps assignments, the psychiatric and medical screening procedures appear to have been extraordinarily successful. Henry (1965) stated that about half of the volunteers who returned home did so for "compassionate" reasons, such as a death in the family that required the volunteer to take on a family business. On the basis of this and other figures, Henry concluded that the rate of out-and-out selection errors was only 3 to 4 percent. Other published data suggest that this figure is probably an underestimate, but even a 95 percent valid positive hit rate is an extraordinary statistic for a large-scale selection program of this kind.

The principal predictor of overseas performance was the final board rating given by the field selection officer, since that rating represented the official selection decision. A number of studies have correlated measures obtained prior to and during training with this final board rating (Krug, 1963; Colmen, Kaplan, and Boulger, 1964). In general, final board ratings appear to be most highly correlated with assessment measures obtained during training, such as instructors' ratings in technical studies, peer ratings of success, field assessment officers' ratings of success, and psychiatrists' ratings of success. Of course, this finding is not surprising in light of the general agreement that appeared to obtain among board members (Goldberg, 1966). Among measures obtained prior to training, the assessment ratings provided by classification officers and letters of recommendation appear to be the most promising, although the magnitude of their correlations would not justify their being substituted for final board ratings.

The fact that predictions of success made by field assessment officers and psychiatrists were correlated with final board ratings might appear to suggest, at first consideration, that psychological assessment or psychiatric interviewing prior to training would be an inexpensive substitute for the elaborate field selection procedures. However, such an inference is not justified because the ratings of success made by assessment officers and psychiatrists were based on much of the same data that were available to the field selection officer. In a sense, the correlations between various component measures obtained during training and final board ratings provide a paramorphic model (Chapter 4) of the clinical judgment of field selection officers. It appears that field selection officers tended to "weight" relevant technical skills, peer ratings, and the judgments of their professional colleagues more heavily than the many other sources of information available to them.

Several summaries are available of the relationship between various predictor variables and overall ratings of success made by overseas staff (Colmen, Kaplan, and Boulger, 1964; Krug, 1963; Wrigley, Cobb, and Kline, 1966). As one might hope, the best predictor of overseas performance was the final board rating made by the field selection officer. Peer ratings of overall success ran a strong second, as one might expect from the nature of Peace Corps assignments and from other evidence on the validity of peer ratings (Chapter 8). Instructors' ratings and predictions by field assessment officers were also significantly correlated with overseas performance. However, the magnitude of all these correlations was quite modest.

It is heartening to note that the extraordinarily expensive final board rating was the best predictor of success, despite the small magnitude of the correlations themselves. However, the significance attached to this finding must be tempered by the realization that an unknown, but very likely considerable, amount of criterion contamination is involved in this relationship (Cotton, in preparation). As noted earlier, the overseas representative or one of his delegates was frequently present at the meeting of the final advisory selection board. Thus it was not unusual for the criterion rater to have been a member of the group that contributed to the final board rating. Recall also that the deliberations of the advisory selection board were communicated to the field by the field assessment officer in his overseas placement reports. Without denying the validity of the final board rating, one must consider the possibility that predictor-criterion relationships in Peace Corps selection appear to have contained an element of self-fulfilling prophecy.

Ideally, a large-scale assessment program should be evaluated with reference to its success in predicting individual differences in performance in the criterion situation. In this respect, the magnitude of the correlations between predictor and criterion variables in the Peace Corps selection program does not represent a significant departure from that reported for other large-scale assessment programs. However, in an evaluation of the overall success of predictions in Peace Corps selection, it is important to bear in mind the very real limitations that the selection strategy itself imposed on the possible magnitude of predictor-criterion relationships (Cotton, in preparation). On the predictor side, an extensive, multiple-stage screening strategy was implemented under a low selection ratio in such a manner that individuals who were sent overseas represented a severely attenuated sample on a variety of predictor measures. Even if we assume that the selection procedures had substantial validity in terms of immediate criteria, it must be noted that their generalizability was being assessed over a two-year period. On the criterion side were ratings by significant others that, for reasons already discussed, were not collected under optimal circumstances. Since the overseas performance ratings were typically made by a single individual, there is reason to question their generalizability. Finally, measurements on both the predictor and criterion variables tended to be expressed in relatively gross units that would tend not to permit fine distinctions among individuals. Thus restriction of range, coarseness of measurement, and unreliability of both predictors and criteria would all militate against the demonstration of statistically impressive relationships between predictor and criterion variables (Cotton, in preparation).

The effectiveness of Peace Corps selection and the impact of overseas programs cannot be evaluated properly by an impressionistic pooling of the scattered results of studies conducted in all parts of the world. Such summary statistics must be supplemented by in-depth, longitudinal evaluations of individual Peace Corps projects as they evolve from training into the field setting. Excellent examples of such evaluations may be found in the study by Holtzman *et al.* (1966) of community development volunteers in Brazil, Smith's (1969) study of volunteer teachers in Ghana, and Stein's (1966) study of community development volunteers in Colombia. These absorbing works constitute "miniature milestones" of assessment research and convey graphically the complexities of Peace Corps selection and evaluation.

Critique

Despite our specialized interest in the assessment and selection strategies employed by the Peace Corps, we must realize that the Division of Selection was created as a unit to serve the purposes of the Peace Corps, rather than the converse. Obviously, selection would have been improved by more systematic and extensive efforts to evaluate the empirical effectiveness of the many separate components of the overall strategies employed during the early years. But the cost of such evaluations must be considered in relation to the already extensive commitment of funds to the implementation of the selection program itself. And any suggestion that more research personnel should have been employed must be tempered by the realization that overseas projects were highly sensitive and understaffed operations and that a substantial proportion of prominent American assessment psychologists were already committed to service roles in the Peace Corps.

The principal problem faced by the Peace Corps was that of designing and executing a selection strategy, on the basis of available knowledge concerning principles of personality assessment, without a great deal of opportunity for evaluating the immediate effectiveness of such a strategy. Given this problem, as well as the complex web of sociopolitical considerations in which it was embedded, it seems only fair to conclude that the Peace Corps made the best of a very demanding assignment. Peace Corps selection procedures were not exemplary of every principle of personality assessment considered in this book, but the procedures were surely more sophisticated and more likely to be successful than those of any previous large-scale assessment project. Here it seems appropriate to give credit, not only to those assessment psychologists who served the Peace Corps so well, but to those far-sighted administrators, such as Sargent Shriver, who recognized that effective selection is a scientific problem, as well as an administrative one.

As a minimax *screening* strategy, without regard to testing costs, the procedures employed by the Division of Selection must be considered highly successful. Note, however, that with an empirical selection ratio of approximately .17 at the stage of suitability screening and with an $SR = .75$ at the site of field selection, the overall selection ratio might be estimated at .125. Although it is difficult to estimate the base rate of success among applicants to the Peace Corps, such a rigorous selection ratio is almost certain to result in a substantial proportion of false negative decisions at various stages of screening. Both the Peace Corps and the Division of Selection have paid the price of possible false negative decisions in terms of unfavorable publicity. In the early years of the Peace Corps, the Division of Selection was among the most powerful and most unpopular of all divisions within the agency. At almost all training sites, the field selection officer was, hands down, the least popular man on campus. In recent years, the participation of assessment psychologists in the selection procedures and policies of the Peace Corps has been severely curtailed. Whether this change represents a decreased need for extensive selection or a reaction to the cumulative effects of eight years of intensive screening is difficult to assess.

SUMMARY

The origins of psychological assessment and selection may be traced back to ancient China, where a relatively sophisticated program of civil service testing was employed more than four thousand years ago. The Chinese system of civil service testing became known to British diplomats and missionaries during the early part of the nineteenth century, and a modification of that system was introduced into the British Civil Service. Following the lead of the British (which the French and Germans had also meanwhile followed), the American Civil Service Commission was established in 1883 as a central-ized agency for the administration of competitive examinations in certain departments of the government. Hence the basic idea of selection on the basis of testing is neither new nor of American origin.

Prior to the Second World War, a new approach to psychological assess-ment and selection was introduced by German military psychologists. Under the leadership of Simoneit, the Germans developed a set of procedures for assessing the "total person" within the environmental context in which he was expected to perform. Using a variety of assessment procedures, the Germans emphasized the direct observation of candidates' reactions to realistic situational and performance tasks. The wealth of data gathered during these living-in assessments was evaluated by a diagnostic council which attempted a holistic integration of all that was known about a candidate in relation to his anticipated criterion assignment.

The procedures of the German military psychologists were adopted by the British in the conduct of War Officer Selection Boards during the Second World War. The results of selection from the British assessment programs were considered superior to those of earlier methods for selecting officers, and the WOSB method was later adopted by the British Civil Service as well. In 1943, an official from the Office of Strategic Services visited a War Officer

Selection Board unit in England and concluded that these methods could be adapted to the selection of American personnel for critical overseas assignments. The program of assessment and selection conducted by the OSS was the first of a series of American projects that have come to be referred to as "milestones" in the history of personality assessment.

Five American milestone studies were considered in this chapter: (a) the selection of personnel for intelligence operations overseas by the Office of Strategic Services, (b) the investigation of assessment procedures for the prediction of effectiveness among Air Force officers by the Institute of Personality Assessment and Research, (c) the investigation of assessment procedures for the prediction of professional competence among clinical psychologists by the Veterans Administration selection research project, (d) the evaluation of procedures employed for the selection of psychiatric residents by the Menninger School of Psychiatry, and (e) the selection of volunteers for overseas duty by the United States Peace Corps.

Each of the American milestone studies was described with reference to: (a) the nature of the prediction problem, (b) the methods of criterion analysis employed, (c) the assessment models and strategies utilized, (d) the manner in which data were collected, (e) the manner in which data were combined, and (f) the outcomes of prediction. A brief critique of each study was also presented. In our consideration of these diverse and extensive programs, it was apparent that somewhat idealized methods of personality assessment, described in Chapter 10, are almost inevitably compromised in the light of practical realities. Without exception, all these assessment studies fell short of an optimal level of *criterion analysis* that could have guided both the selection of appropriate assessment procedures and the manner in which data were combined. Until more adequate criterion measures are developed, it will not be possible to evaluate fully the effectiveness of contemporary methods of personality assessment and selection.

In some respects, the results of the American milestone studies do not appear to have been utilized in a cumulative manner; procedures of questionable validity from earlier studies were incorporated into later studies, on the basis of tradition more than appropriateness. To cite a single example, the Improvisations test was enthusiastically adopted by the OSS assessment staff as a situational test that provided a simulation of conditions that might be encountered by OSS agents. Although there was no direct evidence on the validity of this procedure, it was incorporated in the IPAR study for presumably similar reasons. The Improvisations test was considered "promising" by the IPAR staff, but it is not entirely clear why it was incorporated in the design of the VA selection research project. There seems to be little similarity between this "situation" and the job duties typically performed by a clinical psychologist. In fact, none of the situational tests employed by the VA assessment staff resembled situations in which clinical psychologists would be expected to perform. It appears that situational tests have achieved a functional autonomy that is unrelated to their original purpose of simulating criterion press.

In other respects, there are indications that the practice of personality assessment became increasingly sophisticated in the twenty-year time span of the American milestone studies. The uncritical acceptance of global procedures by the OSS staff gradually gave way to the more analytic procedures of the Peace Corps, in which decision making (selection officer) and assessment (assessment officer) operated separately in relation to immediate criteria (training staff) and intermediate criteria (overseas representative). Although the concepts of assessment and selection may be four thousand years old, contemporary personality assessment is less than thirty. It is perhaps more than a wishful thought to view this youthful science as showing some of the promise of our current generation of youth.

REFERENCES

Abelson, R. P., E. Aronson, W. J. McGuire, T. M. Newcomb, M. J. Rosenberg, and P. H. Tannenbaum (eds.), *Theories of Cognitive Consistency: A Sourcebook*, Rand McNally, Chicago (1968).

Abrahams, N. M., "Off-quadrant comment," *Journal of Applied Psychology* **53**, 66–68 (1969).

Adams, H. E., and J. R. Butler, "The deviation hypothesis: a review of the evidence." In I. A. Berg (ed.), *Response Set in Personality Assessment*, Aldine, Chicago (1967), pp. 191–208.

Adorno, T. W., E. Frenkel-Brunswick, D. J. Levinson, and R. N. Sanford, *The Authoritarian Personality*, Harper, New York (1950).

Alf, E. F., Jr., and D. D. Dorfman, "The classification of individuals into two criterion groups on the basis of a discontinuous payoff function," *Psychometrika* **32**, 115–123 (1967).

Allison, J., S. J. Blatt, and C. N. Zimet, *The Interpretation of Psychological Tests*, Harper and Row, New York (1968).

Allport, G. W., *Personality: A Psychological Interpretation*, Holt, New York (1937).

Allport, G. W., *The Use of Personal Documents in Psychological Science*, Social Science Research Council, New York (1942).

Allport, G. W., "What units shall we employ?" In G. Lindzey (ed.), *Assessment of Human Motives*, Rinehart, New York (1958), pp. 239–260.

Allport, G. W., *Pattern and Growth in Personality*, Holt, Rinehart and Winston, New York (1961).

Allport, G. W., "The general and the unique in psychological science," *Journal of Personality* **30**, 405–421 (1962).

Allport, G. W., and H. S. Odbert, "Trait-names: a psycholexical study," *Psychological Monographs* **47**, (1, Whole No. 211) (1936).

Alumbaugh, R. V., H. G. Davis, and A. B. Sweney, "A comparison of methods for constructing predictive instruments," *Educational and Psychological Measurement* **29**, 639–651 (1969).

American Psychological Association, "Technical recommendations for psychological tests and diagnostic techniques," *Psychological Bulletin* **51**, No. 2, Part 2 (1954).

American Psychological Association, "Ethical standards of psychologists, *American Psychologist* **18,** 16–60 (1963).

American Psychological Association, *American Psychologist* **20,** 857–1002 (1965). (Special Issue: Testing and Public Policy.)

American Psychological Association, *Standards for Educational and Psychological Tests and Manuals*, American Psychological Association, Washington, D.C. (1966).

American Psychological Association, *American Psychologist* **22,** No. 3, Cover 2 (1967).

Anastasi, A., *Psychological Testing*, second edition, Macmillan, New York (1961).

Anderson, N., "Application of an attitude model to impression formation," *Science* **138,** 817–818 (1962).

Aronson, E., and J. M. Carlsmith, "Experimentation in social psychology," In G. Lindzey and E. Aronson (eds.), *The Handbook of Social Psychology*, second edition, Vol. 2, Addison-Wesley, Reading, Mass. (1968), pp. 1–79.

Arrow, K. J., *Social Choice and Individual Values*, Wiley, New York (1963).

Arsenian, J., "Young children in an insecure situation," *Journal of Abnormal and Social Psychology* **38,** 225–249 (1943).

Arthur, A. Z., "A decision-making approach to psychological assessment in the clinic," *Journal of Consulting Psychology* **30,** 435–438 (1966).

Ash, P., "The reliability of psychiatric diagnoses," *Journal of Abnormal and Social Psychology* **44,** 272–276 (1949).

Ashby, W. R., *Design for a brain*, second edition, Chapman and Hall, London (1960).

Astin, A. W., and J. L. Holland, "The environmental assessment technique: a way to measure college environments," *Journal of Educational Psychology* **52,** 308–316 (1961).

Astington, E., "Personality assessment and academic performance in a boys' grammar school," *British Journal of Educational Psychology* **30,** 225–236 (1960).

Bandura, A., "Vicarious processes: a case of no-trial learning." In L. Berkowitz (ed.), *Advances in Experimental Social Psychology*, Vol. 2, Academic Press, New York (1965), pp. 1–55.

Bandura, A., "A social learning interpretation of psychological dysfunctions." In P. London and D. Rosenhan (eds.), *Foundations of Abnormal Psychology*, Holt, Rinehart and Winston, New York (1968), pp. 293–344.

Bandura, A., *Principles of Behavior Modification*, Holt, Rinehart and Winston, New York (1969).

Bandura, A., and R. H. Walters, *Social Learning and Personality Development*, Holt, Rinehart and Winston, New York (1963).

Bannister, D., and F. Fransella, "A grid test of schizophrenic thought disorder," *British Journal of Social and Clinical Psychology* **5,** 95–102 (1966).

Bannister, D., and J. M. M. Mair, *The Evaluation of Personal Constructs*, Academic Press, London and New York (1968).

Bannister, D., P. Salmon, and D. M. Leiberman, "Diagnosis-treatment relationships in psychiatry: a statistical analysis," *British Journal of Psychiatry* **110**, 726–732 (1964).

Barker, R. G., "Ecology and motivation." In M. R. Jones (ed.), *Nebraska Symposium on Motivation*, University of Nebraska Press, Lincoln (1960), pp. 1–49.

Barker, R. G. (ed.), *The Stream of Behavior*, Appleton-Century-Crofts, New York (1963).

Barker, R. G., "Explorations in ecological psychology," *American Psychologist* **20**, 1–14 (1965).

Barker, R. G., *Ecological Psychology: Concepts and Methods for Studying the Environment of Human Behavior*, Stanford University Press, Stanford, Calif. (1968).

Barker, R. G., T. Dembo, and K. Lewin, "Frustration and regression: a study of young children," *University of Iowa Studies in Child Welfare* **18**, No. 1 (1941).

Barker, R. G., and P. V. Gump, *Big School, Small School*, Stanford University Press, Stanford, Calif. (1964).

Barker, R. G., and H. F. Wright, "Psychological ecology and the problem of psychosocial development," *Child Development* **20**, 131–143 (1949).

Barker, R. G., and H. F. Wright, *One Boy's Day*, Harper, New York (1951).

Barker, R. G., and H. F. Wright, *Midwest and Its Children: The Psychological Ecology of an American Town*, Row, Peterson, New York (1955).

Barnes, E. H., "The relationship of biased test responses to psychopathology," *Journal of Abnormal and Social Psychology* **51**, 286–290 (1955).

Barron, F., "Some studies of creativity at the Institute of Personality Assessment and Research." In G. A. Steiner (ed.), *The Creative Organization*, University of Chicago Press, Chicago (1965), pp. 118–129.

Barron, F., *Creativity and Personal Freedom*, Van Nostrand, Princeton, N.J. (1968).

Barron, F., *Creative Person and Creative Process*, Holt, Rinehart and Winston, New York (1969).

Barron, F., J. Block, D. W. MacKinnon, and D. G. Woodworth, *An Assessment Study of Air Force Officers: Part III. Assessment Correlates of Criteria of Officer Effectiveness*, Wright Air Development Center Technical Report No. 91 (III). Personnel Laboratory, Lackland Air Force Base, Texas.

Bartlett, C. J., "The relationships between self-ratings and peer ratings on a leadership behavior scale," *Personnel Psychology* **12**, 237–246 (1959).

Bass, B. M., "Authoritarianism or acquiescence?" *Journal of Abnormal and Social Psychology* **51**, 616–623 (1955).

Bass, B. M., and I. A. Berg (eds.), *Objective Approaches to Personality Assessment*, Van Nostrand, Princeton (1959).

Baumrind, D., "An analysis of some aspects of the 'Interpersonal System'," *Psychiatry* **23,** 395–402 (1960).

Baumrind, D., "Some thoughts on ethics of research: after reading Milgrim's behavioral study of obedience," *American Psychologist* **19,** 421–423 (1964).

Bechtoldt, H. P., "Selection." In S. S. Stevens (ed.), *Handbook of Experimental Psychology*, Wiley, New York (1951), pp. 1237–1266.

Bechtoldt, H. P., "Construct validity: a critique," *American Psychologist* **14,** 619–628 (1959).

Beck, L. W., "Constructions and inferred entities." In H. Feigl and M. Brodbeck (eds.), *Readings in the Philosophy of Science*, Appleton-Century-Crofts, New York (1953), pp. 368–381.

Beck, S. J., *Rorschach's Test. I. Basic Processes*, second edition (revised), Grune and Stratton, New York (1950).

Beck, S. J., "The science of personality: nomothetic or idiographic?" *Psychological Review* **60,** 353–359 (1953).

Becker, H. S., *Outsiders: Studies in the Sociology of Deviance*, Free Press of Glencoe, New York (1963).

Becker, W. C., "The matching of behavior rating and questionnaire personality factors," *Psychological Bulletin* **57,** 201–212 (1960).

Becker, W. C., and R. S. Krug, "A circumplex model for social behavior in children," *Child Development* **35,** 371–396 (1964).

Bender, L., *A Visual Motor Gestalt Test and Its Clinical Use*, Research Monograph No. 3, American Orthopsychiatric Association, New York (1938).

Benney, M., D. Riesman, and S. A. Star, "Age and sex in the interview," *American Journal of Sociology* **62,** 143–152 (1956).

Bentler, P. M., D. N. Jackson, and S. Messick, "Identification of content and style: a two-dimensional interpretation of acquiescence," *Psychological Bulletin* **76,** 186–204 (1971).

Bentler, P. M., D. N. Jackson, and S. Messick, "A rose by any other name," *Psychological Bulletin* **77,** 109–113 (1972).

Berg, I. A., "Response bias and personality: the deviation hypothesis," *Journal of Psychology* **40,** 61–71 (1955).

Berg, I. A., "Deviant responses and deviant people: the formulation of the deviation hypothesis," *Journal of Counseling Psychology* **4,** 154–161 (1957).

Berg, I. A., "The unimportance of test item content." In B. M. Bass and I. A. Berg (eds.), *Objective Approaches to Personality Assessment*, Van Nostrand, New York (1959), pp. 83–99.

Berg, I. A., "Measuring deviant behavior by means of deviant response sets." In I. A. Berg and B. M. Bass (eds.), *Conformity and Deviation*, Harper, New York (1961), pp. 328–379.

Berg, I. A., "The deviation hypothesis: a broad statement of its assumptions and postulates." In I. A. Berg (ed.), *Response Set in Personality Assessment*, Adline, Chicago (1967), pp. 146–190.

Berg, I. A., W. A. Hunt, and E. H. Barnes, *The Perceptual Reaction Test*, Irwin A. Berg, Evanston, Ill. (1949).

Bergin, A. E., "An empirical analysis of therapeutic issues." In B. Arbuckle (ed.), *Counseling and Psychotherapy: An Overview*, McGraw-Hill, New York (1967), pp. 75–208.

Berne, E., "The nature of intuition," *Psychiatric Quarterly* **23**, 203–226 (1949).

Bernreuter, R. G., *The Personality Inventory*, Consulting Psychologists Press, Palo Alto, Calif. (1931).

Bieri, J., A. L. Atkins, S. Briar, R. L. Leaman, H. Miller, and T. Tripodi, *Clinical and Social Judgment: The Discrimination of Behavioral Information*, Wiley, New York (1966).

Bieri, J., and E. Blacker, "The generality of cognitive complexity in the perception of people and inkblots," *Journal of Abnormal and Social Psychology* **53**, 112–117 (1956).

Bijou, S. W., and R. F. Peterson, "The psychological assessment of children: a functional analysis." In P. McReynolds (ed.), *Advances in Psychological Assessment*, Vol. 2, Science and Behavior Books, Palo Alto, Calif. (1971), pp. 63–78.

Bijou, S. W., R. F. Peterson, F. R. Harris, K. E. Allen, and M. S. Johnston, "Methodology for experimental studies of young children in naturalistic settings," *Psychological Record* **19**, 177–210 (1969).

Blatt, S. J., and J. Allison, "The intelligence test in personality assessment." In A. I. Rabin (ed.), *Projective Techniques in Personality Assessment*, Springer, New York (1967).

Block, J., "The development of an MMPI-based scale to measure ego control," Berkeley: Institute of Personality Assessment and Research, University of California, 1953 (mimeographed).

Block, J., *The Q-sort Method in Personality Assessment and Psychiatric Research*, Charles C Thomas, Springfield, Ill. (1961).

Block, J., *The Challenge of Response Sets: Unconfounding Meaning, Acquiescence and Social Desirability in the MMPI*, Appleton-Century-Crofts, New York (1965).

Block, J., "Remarks on Jackson's 'review' of Block's *Challenge of Response Sets*," *Educational and Psychological Measurement* **27**, 499–502 (1967).

Block, J., "On further conjectures regarding acquiescence," *Psychological Bulletin* **76**, 205–210 (1971).

Block, J., and D. E. Bailey, *Q-sort Item Analyses of a Number of MMPI Scales*, Technical Memorandum No. 7, Officer Education Research Laboratory, Maxwell Air Force Base, Alabama, May 1955.

Boe, E. E., and W. S. Kogan, "Effect of social desirability instructions on several MMPI measures of social desirability," *Journal of Consulting Psychology* **28,** 248–251 (1964).

Bonarius, J. C. J., "Research in the personal construct theory of George A. Kelly: role construct repertory test and basic theory." In B. A. Maher (ed.), *Progress in Experimental Personality Research*, Vol. 2, Academic Press, New York (1965), pp. 1–46.

Bordin, E. S., "The personality of the therapist as an influence in psychotherapy." Paper presented at the State University of Buffalo, Symposium on Psychotherapy, October 1966.

Borko, H. (ed.), *Computer Applications in the Behavioral Sciences*, Prentice-Hall, Englewood Cliffs, N.J. (1962).

Boulger, J. R., and J. G. Colmen, "Research findings with peer ratings." Research Note No. 8, Division of Research, Peace Corps, August 1964.

Braithwaite, R. B., *Scientific Explanation*, Cambridge University Press, Cambridge (1953).

Broen, W. E., and R. D. Wirt, "Varieties of response sets," *Journal of Consulting Psychology* **22,** 237–240 (1958).

Brogden, H. E., and E. K. Taylor, "The dollar criterion—applying the cost accounting concept to criterion construction," *Personnel Psychology* **3,** 133–154 (1950).

Bronfenbrenner, U., J. Harding, and M. Gallwey, "The measurement of skill in social perception." In D. C. McClelland (ed.), *Talent and Society*, Van Nostrand, New York (1958), pp. 29–111.

Bronfenbrenner, U., and T. M. Newcomb, "Improvisations: an application of psychodrama in personality diagnosis," *Sociatry* **4,** 367–382 (1948).

Brown, F. G., and D. A. Scott, "The unpredictability of predictability," *Journal of Educational Measurement* **3,** 297–301 (1966).

Brown, F. G., and D. A. Scott, "Differential predictability in college admissions testing," *Journal of Educational Measurement* **4,** 163–166 (1967).

Brown, R., *Words and Things*, Free Press, Glencoe, Ill. (1958).

Brown, W., "Some experimental results in the correlation of mental abilities," *British Journal of Psychology* **3,** 269–322 (1910).

Bruner, J. S., J. J. Goodnow, and G. A. Austin, *A Study of Thinking*, Wiley, New York (1956).

Bruner, J. S., and R. Tagiuri, "The perception of people." In G. Lindzey (ed.), *Handbook of Social Psychology*, Vol. 2, Addison-Wesley, Reading, Mass. (1954), pp. 634–654.

Brunswick, E., *Systematic and Representative Design of Psychological Experiments*, University of California Press, Berkeley (1947).

Brunswick, E., "Representative design and probabilistic theory," *Psychological Review* **62,** 236–242 (1955).

Brunswick, E., *Perception and the Representative Design of Psychological Experiments*, University of California Press, Berkeley (1956).

Buchwald, A. M., "Verbal utterances as data." In H. Feigl and G. Maxwell (eds.), *Current Issues in the Philosophy of Science*, Holt, New York (1961), pp. 461–468.

Buchwald, A. M., "Values and the use of tests," *Journal of Consulting Psychology* **29,** 49–54 (1965).

Burke, R. C., and W. G. Bennis, "Changes in perception of self and others during human relations training," *Human Relations* **14,** 165–182 (1961).

Buss, A. H., *The Psychology of Aggression*, Wiley, New York (1961).

Butcher, J. N., and A. Tellegen, "Objections to MMPI items," *Journal of Consulting Psychology* **30,** 527–534 (1966).

Butt, S. D., and D. W. Fiske, "Comparison of strategies in developing scales for dominance," *Psychological Bulletin* **70,** 505–519 (1968).

Buzby, D. E., "The interpretation of facial expression," *American Journal of Psychology* **35,** 602–604 (1924).

Byrne, D., "Assessing personality variables and their alteration." In P. Worchel and D. Byrne (eds.), *Personality Change*, Wiley, New York (1964), pp. 38–68.

Cahlahan, D., V. Tamulonis, and H. W. Verner, "Interviewer bias involved in certain types of opinion survey questions," *International Journal of Opinion and Attitude Research* **1,** 63–77 (1947).

Campbell, D. P., "The Strong Vocational Interest Blank: 1927–1967." In P. McReynolds (ed.), *Advances in Psychological Assessment*, Vol. 1, Science and Behavior Books, Palo Alto, Calif. (1968), pp. 105–130.

Campbell, D. P., *Handbook for the Strong Vocational Interest Blank*, Stanford University Press, Stanford, Calif. (1971).

Campbell, D. T., "A typology of tests, projective and otherwise," *Journal of Consulting Psychology* **21,** 207–210 (1957).

Campbell, D. T., and D. W. Fiske, "Convergent and discriminant validation by the multitrait-multimethod matrix," *Psychological Bulletin* **56,** 81–105 (1959).

Campbell, J. P., "Cross validation revisited." Paper presented at the Midwestern Psychological Association, Chicago, 1967.

Campbell, M. M., *The Primary Dimensions of Item Ratings on Scales Designed to Measure 24 of Murray's Manifest Needs*, University of Washington, Seattle (1959) (mimeographed).

Cannell, C. F., and R. L. Kahn, "Interviewing." In G. Lindzey and E. Aronson (eds.), *The Handbook of Social Psychology*, second edition, Vol. 2, Addison-Wesley, Reading, Mass. (1968), pp. 526–595.

Cantor, J. M., "Syndromes found in a psychiatric population selected for certain MMPI code endings." Unpublished Ph.D. thesis, University of Minnesota, Minneapolis (1952).

Cantril, H., *Gauging Public Opinion*, University Press, Princeton, N.J. (1944).

Cantril, H., "Perception and interpersonal relations." In E. A. Hollander and R. G. Hunt (eds.), *Current Perspectives in Social Psychology*, Oxford University Press, New York (1963), pp. 290–297.

Carnap, R., "Empiricism, semantics, and ontology." In P. P. Wiener (ed.), *Readings in Philosophy of Science*, Scribner's, New York (1953), pp. 509–521.

Cartwright, D., "Factor analyzing theories of personality," *Counseling Center Discussion Papers* **3**, No. 24, University of Chicago, Chicago (1957).

Cartwright, D., "Lewinian theory as a contemporary systematic framework." In S. Koch (ed.), *Psychology: A Study of Science*, Vol. 2, McGraw-Hill, New York (1959), pp. 7–91.

Cassotta, L., J. Jaffe, S. Feldstein, and R. Moses, *Operating Manual: Automatic Vocal Transaction Analyzer*, William Alanson White Institute, New York (1964).

Cattell, R. B., "The principal trait clusters for describing personality," *Psychological Bulletin* **42**, 129–161 (1945).

Cattell, R. B., *The Description and Measurement of Personality*, World Book, Yonkers-on-Hudson, N.Y. (1946).

Cattell, R. B., "The primary personality factors in women compared with those in men," *British Journal of Psychology* **1**, 114–130 (1948).

Cattell, R. B., "r_p and other coefficients of pattern similarity," *Psychometrika* **14**, 279–298 (1949).

Cattell, R. B., *Personality: A Systematic, Theoretical, and Factual Study*, McGraw-Hill, New York (1950).

Cattell, R. B., *Factor Analysis*, Harper, New York (1952).

Cattell, R. B., *Personality and Motivation Structure and Measurement*, World Book, Yonkers-on-Hudson, N.Y. (1957).

Cattell, R. B., "Personality theory growing from multivariate quantitative research." In S. Koch (ed.), *Psychology: A Study of Science*, Vol. 3, McGraw-Hill, New York (1959), pp. 257–327.

Cattell, R. B., "Theory of situational, instrument, second order, and refraction factors in personality structure research," *Psychological Bulletin* **58**, 160–174 (1961).

Cattell, R. B., "Personality, role, mood, and situation perception: a unifying theory of modulators," *Psychological Review* **70**, 1–18 (1963).

Cattell, R. B., *Personality and Social Psychology: Collected Papers of Raymond B. Cattell*, Robert R. Knapp, San Diego (1964). (a)

Cattell, R. B., "Validity and reliability: a proposed more basic set of concepts," *Journal of Educational Psychology* **55**, 1–22 (1964). (b)

Cattell, R. B., "Higher order factor structures and reticular vs. hierarchical formulas for their interpretation." In C. Banks and P. L. Broadhurst (eds.), *Studies in Psychology Presented to Cyril Burt*, University of London Press, London (1965), pp. 223–266. (a)

Cattell, R. B., *The Scientific Analysis of Personality*, Penguin, Baltimore (1965). (b)

Cattell, R. B., Guest editorial: "Multivariate behavioral research and the integrative challenge," *Multivariate Behavioral Research* **1**, 4–23 (1966). (a)

Cattell, R. B., "The meaning and strategic use of factor analysis." In R. B. Cattell (ed.), *Handbook of Multivariate Experimental Psychology*, Rand McNally, Chicago (1966), pp. 174–243. (b)

Cattell, R. B., "Patterns of change: measurement in relation to state-dimension, trait change, lability, and process concepts." In R. B. Cattell (ed.), *Handbook of Multivariate Experimental Psychology*, Rand McNally, Chicago (1966), pp. 355–402. (c)

Cattell, R. B., M. A. Coulter, and B. Tsujioka, "The taxonometric recognition of types and functional emergents." In R. B. Cattell (ed.), *Handbook of Multivariate Experimental Psychology*, Rand McNally, Chicago (1966).

Cattell, R. B., and J. Digman, "A theory of the structure of perturbations in observer ratings and questionnaire data in personality research," *Behavioral Science* **9**, 341–358 (1964).

Cattell, R. B., and H. W. Eber, *Handbook for the Sixteen Personality Factor Questionnaire*, Institute for Personality and Ability Testing, Champaign, Ill. (1957).

Cattell, R. B., and H. W. Eber, *Manual for Forms A and B of the Sixteen Personality Factor Questionnaire*, Institute for Personality and Ability Testing, Champaign, Ill. (1962).

Cattell, R. B., H. W. Eber, and M. Tatsuoka, *Handbook for the Sixteen Personality Factor Questionnaire*, Institute for Personality and Ability Testing, Champaign, Ill. (1970).

Cattell, R. B., and I. H. Scheier, *Handbook for the Objective-Analytic (O-A) Anxiety Battery*, Institute for Personality and Ability Testing, Champaign, Ill. (1960).

Cattell, R. B., and I. H. Scheier, *The Meaning and Measurement of Neuroticism and Anxiety*, Ronald, New York (1961).

Cattell, R. B., and B. Tsujioka, "The importance of factor-trueness and validity, versus homogeneity and orthogonality in test scales," *Educational and Psychological Measurement* **24**, 3–30 (1964).

Cattell, R. B., and F. W. Warburton, *Objective Personality and Motivation Tests: A Theoretical Introduction and Practical Compendium*, University of Illinois Press, Urbana (1967).

Challman, R. C., "Factors influencing friendships among preschool children," *Child Development* **3**, 146–158 (1932).

Champney, H., "The measurement of parent behavior," *Child Development* **12**, 131–166 (1941).

Chandler, R. E., "Two additional formulae for use with suppressor variables," *Educational and Psychological Measurement* **21**, 947–950 (1961).

Chandler, R. E., "Validity, reliability, boloney, and a little mustard." Paper presented at the Midwestern Psychological Association, Chicago (1964).

Churchman, C. W., *Prediction and Optimal Decisions: Philosophical Issues in a Science of Values*, Prentice-Hall, Englewood Cliffs, N.J. (1961).

Churchman, C. W., and R. L. Ackoff, "An approximate measure of value," *Journal of the Operations Research Society of America* **2**, 172–187 (1954).

Clark, K. E., "The mountain's mouse," *Contemporary Psychology* **5**, 72–73 (1960).

Clarkson, G. P. E., *Portfolio Selection: A Simulation of Trust Investment*, Prentice-Hall, Englewood Cliffs, N.J. (1962).

Cliff, N., "Adverbs as multipliers," *Psychological Review* **66**, 27–44 (1959).

Cline, V. B., "Interpersonal perception." In B. A. Maher (ed.), *Progress in Experimental Personality Research*, Vol. 1, Academic Press, New York (1964), pp. 221–284.

Cline, V. B., and J. M. Richards, Jr., "Accuracy of interpersonal perception: a general trait?" *Journal of Abnormal and Social Psychology* **60**, 1–7 (1960).

Cline, V. B., and J. M. Richards, Jr., "The generality of accuracy of interpersonal perception," *Journal of Abnormal and Social Psychology* **62**, 446–449 (1961).

Cline, V. B., and J. M. Richards, Jr., "Components of accuracy of interpersonal perception scores and the clinical and statistical prediction controversy," *Psychological Record* **12**, 373–379 (1962).

Cobb, J. A., "The relationship of observable classroom behaviors to achievement of fourth-grade pupils." Unpublished doctoral thesis, University of Oregon, Eugene (1969).

Cobb, J., C. Wrigley, and D. Kline, "The prediction of early termination of Peace Corps Volunteers." Research Report No. 9, November 1966, Computer Institute for Social Science Research, Michigan State University.

Cohen, J., "Multiple regression as a general data-analytic system," *Psychological Bulletin* **70**, 426–443 (1968).

Colmen, J. G., S. J. Kaplan, and J. R. Boulger, "Selection and selection research in the Peace Corps." Research Note No. 7, August 1964, Research Division, Peace Corps.

Cottle, W. C., *The MMPI: A Review*, University of Kansas Press, Lawrence (1953).

Cotton, J. W., *Par for the Corps: A Review of Research on Selection, Training, and Performance of Peace Corps Volunteers.* In preparation.

Cowen, E. L., and A. Stiller, "The social desirability of trait descriptive terms: order and context effects," *Canadian Journal of Psychology* **13**, 193–199 (1959).

Crewe, N. M., "Comparison of factor analytic and empirical scales," *Proceedings of the 75th Annual Convention of the American Psychological Association*, pp. 367–368 (1967).

Crockett, W. H., "Cognitive complexity and impression formation," In B. A. Maher (ed.), *Progress in Experimental Personality Research*, Vol. 2, Academic Press, New York (1965) pp. 47–90.

Cronbach, L. J., "Response sets and test validity," *Educational and Psychological Measurement* **6**, 475–494 (1946).

Cronbach, L. J., "Further evidence on response sets and test design," *Educational and Psychological Measurement* **10**, 3–31 (1950).

Cronbach, L. J., "Coefficient alpha and the internal structure of tests," *Psychometrika* **16**, 297–334 (1951).

Cronbach, L. J., "Processes affecting scores on 'understanding of others' and 'assumed similarity'," *Psychological Bulletin* **52**, 177–193 (1955).

Cronbach, L. J., "Assessment of individual differences." In P. R. Farnsworth (ed.), *Annual Review of Psychology*, Vol. 7, Annual Reviews Inc., Stanford, Calif. (1956), pp. 173–196.

Cronbach, L. J., "The two disciplines of scientific psychology," *American Psychologist* **12**, 671–684 (1957).

Cronbach, L. J., "Proposals leading to analytic treatment of social perception scores." In R. Tagiuri and L. Petrullo (eds.), *Person Perception and Interpersonal Behavior*, Stanford University Press, Stanford, Calif. (1958), pp. 359–379.

Cronbach, L. J., and H. Azuma, "Internal-consistency reliability formulas applied to randomly sampled single-factor tests: an empirical comparison," *Educational and Psychological Measurement* **21**, 645–665 (1962).

Cronbach, L. J., and G. C. Gleser, "Assessing similarity between profiles," *Psychological Bulletin* **50**, 456–473 (1953).

Cronbach, L. J., and G. C. Gleser, *Psychological Tests and Personal Decisions*, University of Illinois Press, Urbana (1957).

Cronbach, L. J., and G. C. Gleser, "The signal noise ratio in the comparison of reliability coefficients," *Educational and Psychological Measurement* **24**, 467–480 (1964).

Cronbach, L. J., and G. C. Gleser, *Psychological Tests and Personnel Decisions*, second edition, University of Illinois Press, Urbana (1965).

Cronbach, L. J., G. C. Gleser, H. Nanda, and N. Rajaratnam, *The Dependability of Behavioral Measurements*, Wiley, New York, in press.

Cronbach, L. J., H. Ikeda, and R. A. Avner, "Intraclass correlation as approximation to the coefficient of generalizability," *Psychological Reports* **15**, 727–736 (1964).

Cronbach, L. J., and P. E. Meehl, "Construct validity in psychological tests," *Psychological Bulletin* **52**, 281–302 (1955).

Cronbach, L. J., N. Rajaratnam, and G. C. Gleser, "Theory of generalizability: a liberalization of reliability theory," *British Journal of Statistical Psychology* **16**, 137–163 (1963).

Cronbach, L. J., P. Schönemann, and D. McKie, "Alpha coefficients for stratified-parallel tests." *Educational and Psychological Measurement* **25**, 291–312 (1965).

Crow, W. J., "The effect of training upon accuracy and variability in interpersonal perception," *Journal of Abnormal and Social Psychology* **55,** 355–359 (1957).

Crow, W. J., and K. R. Hammond, "The generality of accuracy and response sets in interpersonal perception," *Journal of Abnormal and Social Psychology* **54,** 384–390 (1957).

Crowne, D. P., and D. Marlowe, *The Approval Motive: Studies in Evaluative Dependence*, Wiley, New York (1964).

Crutchfield, R. S., D. G. Woodworth, and R. E. Albrecht, *Perceptual Performance and the Effective Person*, Wright Air Development Center Technical Report No. 60, Personnel Laboratory, Lackland Air Force Base, Texas, April 1958.

Cureton, E. E., "Recipe for a cookbook," *Psychological Bulletin* **54,** 494–497 (1957).

Dahlstrom, W. G., and G. S. Welsh, *An MMPI Handbook: A Guide to Use in Clinical Practice and Research*, University of Minnesota Press, Minneapolis (1960).

Dailey, C. A., "The effects of premature conclusions upon the acquisition of understanding of a person," *Journal of Psychology* **33,** 133–152 (1952).

D'Andrade, R. G., "Trait psychology and componential analysis," *American Anthropologist* **67,** 215–228 (1965).

Danielson, J. R., and J. H. Clark, "A personality inventory for induction screening," *Journal of Clinical Psychology* **10,** 137–143 (1954).

Darlington, R. B., "Multiple-regression in psychological research and practice," *Psychological Bulletin* **69,** 161–182 (1968).

Darlington, R. B., and G. F. Stauffer, "A method for choosing a cutting point on a test," *Journal of Applied Psychology* **50,** 229–231 (1966).

Davidson, D., P. Suppes, and S. Siegel, *Decision Making: An Experimental Approach*, Stanford University Press, Stanford, Calif. (1957).

Dawe, H. C., "An analysis of two-hundred quarrels of pre-school children," *Child Development* **5,** 139–157 (1934).

Dawes, R. M., "A note on base rates and psychometric efficiency," *Journal of Consulting Psychology* **26,** 422–424 (1962).

de Groot, A. D., "Via clinical to statistical prediction," *Acta Psychologica* **18,** 274–284 (1961).

Dewey, J., and A. F. Bentley, *Knowing and the Known*, Beacon, Boston (1949).

Dicken, C., "Simulated patterns on the California Psychological Inventory," *Journal of Counseling Psychology* **7,** 24–31 (1960).

Dicken, C., "Good impression, social desirability and acquiescence as suppressor variables," *Educational and Psychological Measurement* **23,** 699–720 (1963).

Diggory, J. C., "Calculation of some costs of suicide prevention using certain predictors of suicidal behavior," *Psychological Bulletin* **71,** 373–386 (1969).

Doll, R. E., "Officer peer ratings as a predictor of failure to complete flight training," *Aerospace Medicine* **34,** 130–131 (1963).

Dollard, J., L. W. Doob, N. E. Miller, O. H. Mowrer, and R. R. Sears, *Frustration and Aggression*, Yale University Press, New Haven, Conn. (1939).

Dollard, J., and N. E. Miller, *Personality and Psychotherapy*, McGraw-Hill, New York (1950).

Drake, L. E., and E. R. Oetting, *An MMPI Cookbook for Counselors*, University of Minnesota Press, Minneapolis (1959).

DuBois, P. H., *A History of Psychological Testing*, Allyn and Bacon, Boston (1970).

Dudycha, A. L., and J. C. Naylor, "Characteristics of the human inference process in complex choice behavior situations," *Organizational Behavior and Human Performance* **1,** 110–128 (1966). (a)

Dudycha, A. L., and J. C. Naylor, "The effect of variations in the cue R matrix upon the obtained policy equation of judges," *Educational and Psychological Measurement* **26,** 583–603 (1966). (b)

Dustin, D. S., and P. M. Baldwin, "Redundancy in impression formation," *Journal of Personality and Social Psychology* **3,** 500–506 (1966).

Edwards, A. L., "The relationship between the judged desirability of a trait and the probability that the trait will be endorsed," *Journal of Applied Psychology* **37,** 90–93 (1953).

Edwards, A. L., *Manual for the Edwards Personal Preference Schedule,* Psychological Corporation, New York (1954).

Edwards, A. L., *The Social Desirability Variable in Personality Assessment and Research,* Dryden, New York, (1957).

Edwards, A. L., *Edwards Personal Preference Schedule*, Psychological Corporation, New York (1959).

Edwards, A. L., "A comparison of 57 MMPI scales and 57 experimental scales matched with the MMPI scales in terms of item social desirability scale values and probabilities of endorsement," *Educational and Psychological Measurement* **26,** 15–27 (1966). (a)

Edwards, A. L., "Relationship between probability of endorsement and social desirability scale value for a set of 2,824 personality statements," *Journal of Applied Psychology* **50,** 238–239 (1966). (b)

Edwards, A. L., "The social desirability variable: a review of the evidence." In I. A. Berg (ed.), *Response Set in Personality Assessment*, Aldine, Chicago (1967), pp. 48–70.

Edwards, A. L., *The Measurement of Personality Traits by Scales and Inventories*, Holt, Rinehart and Winston, New York (1970).

Edwards, A. L., and C. J. Diers, "Social desirability and the factorial interpretation of the MMPI," *Educational and Psychological Measurement* **22,** 501–509 (1962).

Edwards, A. L., C. J. Diers, and J. N. Walker, "Response sets and factor loadings on sixty-one personality scales," *Journal of Applied Psychology* **46,** 220–225 (1962).

Edwards, A. L., and L. B. Heathers, "The first factor of the MMPI: social desirability or ego strength?" *Journal of Consulting Psychology* **26,** 99–100 (1962).

Edwards, A. L., and J. N. Walsh, "The relationship between the intensity of the social desirability keying of a scale and the correlation of the scale with Edwards' *SD* scale and the first factor loading of the scale," *Journal of Clinical Psychology* **19,** 200–203 (1963).

Edwards, A. L., and J. N. Walsh, "Response sets in standard and experimental personality scales," *American Educational Research Journal* **1,** 52–61 (1964).

Edwards, W., "The theory of decision making," *Psychological Bulletin* **51,** 380–418 (1954).

Edwards, W., "Behavioral decision theory." In P. R. Farnsworth (ed.), *Annual Review of Psychology*, Vol. 12, Annual Reviews, Palo Alto, Calif. (1961), pp. 473–498.

Elliott, L. L., "Factor analysis of WAF peer nominations," *USAF WADD Technical Note*, No. 60-217 (1960).

Ellis, A., "The validity of personality questionnaires," *Psychological Bulletin* **43,** 385–440 (1946).

Ellson, D. G., and E. C. Ellson, "Historical note on the rating scale," *Psychological Bulletin* **50,** 383–384 (1953).

Endler, N. S., and J. McV. Hunt, "Sources of behavioral variance as measured by the S-R Inventory of Anxiousness," *Psychological Bulletin* **65,** 336–346 (1966).

Endler, N. S., and J. McV. Hunt, "S-R inventories of hostility and comparisons of the proportions of variance from persons, responses, and situations for hostility and anxiousness," *Journal of Personality and Social Psychology* **9,** 309–315 (1968).

Endler, N. S., and J. McV. Hunt, "Generalizability of contributions from sources of variance in the S-R inventories of anxiousness," *Journal of Personality* **37,** 1–24 (1969).

Endler, N. S., J. McV. Hunt, and A. J. Rosenstein, "An S-R inventory of anxiousness," *Psychological Monographs* **76** (17, Whole No. 536) (1962).

Erikson, E. H., *Childhood and Society*, Norton, New York (1950).

Erlich, J., and D. Riesman, "Age and authority in the interview," *Public Opinion Quarterly* **25,** 39–56 (1961).

Estes, S. G., "Judging personality from expressive behavior," *Journal of Abnormal and Social Psychology* **33,** 217–236 (1938).

Estes, W. K., S. Koch, K. MacCorquodale, P. E. Meehl, C. G. Mueller, Jr., W. N. Schoenfeld, and W. S. Verplanck, *Modern Learning Theory*, Appleton-Century-Crofts, New York (1954).

Ewart, E. S., "Factorial structure of airman peer nominations," *USAF WADD Technical Note*, No. 60-40 (1960).

Eysenck, H. J., "Assessment of men." In H. J. Eysenck, *Uses and Abuses of Psychology*, Penguin, Baltimore (1953), pp. 138–159. (a)

Eysenck, H. J., *The Structure of Human Personality*, Wiley, New York (1953). (b)

Eysenck, H. J., "The science of personality: nomothetic," *Psychological Review* **61**, 339–341 (1954).

Ezekiel, M., and K. A. Fox, *Methods of Correlation and Regression Analysis*, third edition, Wiley, New York (1959).

Falk, J., "Issues distinguishing idiographic from nomothetic approaches to personality theory," *Psychological Review* **63**, 53–62 (1956).

Farago, O., and L. F. Gittler (eds.), *German Psychological Warfare: Survey and Bibliography*, Committee for National Morale, New York (1941).

Fawl, C. L., "Disturbances experienced by children in their natural habitats." In R. G. Barker (ed.), *The Stream of Behavior*, Appleton-Century-Crofts, New York (1963), pp. 99–126.

Fechner, G. T., *Elemente der Psychophysik*, Breitkopf and Hartel, Leipzig, Germany (1860).

Feigl, H., "Logical empiricism." In H. Feigl and W. Sellars (eds.), *Readings in Philosophical Analysis*, Appleton-Century-Crofts, New York (1949), pp. 3–26.

Feigl, H., "Existential hypotheses," *Philosophy of Science* **17**, 35–62 (1950).

Fenichel, O., *The Psychoanalytic Theory of Neurosis*, Norton, New York (1945).

Ferguson, L. R., and E. E. Maccoby, "Interpersonal correlates of differential abilities," *Child Development* **37**, 549–571 (1966).

Ferster, C. B., "Classification of behavioral pathology." In L. Krasner and L. P. Ullmann (eds.), *Research in Behavior Modification*, Holt, Rinehart and Winston, New York (1965), pp. 9–26.

Ferster, C. B., and B. F. Skinner, *Schedules of Reinforcement*, Appleton-Century-Crofts, New York (1957).

Festinger, L., *A Theory of Cognitive Dissonance*, Stanford University Press, Stanford, Calif. (1957).

Festinger, L., H. W. Riecken, and S. Schacter, *When Prophecy Fails*, University of Minnesota Press, Minneapolis (1956).

Finney, J. C., "The MMPI as a measure of character structure as revealed by factor analysis," *Journal of Consulting Psychology* **25**, 327–336 (1961).

Finney, J. C., "Prolegomena to epidemiology in mental health," *Journal of Nervous and Mental Disease* **195**, 99–104 (1962),

Finney, J. C., "Development of a new set of MMPI scales," *Psychological Reports* **17**, 707–713 (1965). (a)

Finney, J. C., "Effects of response sets on new and old MMPI scales," *Psychological Reports* **17**, 907–915 (1965). ((b)

Finney, J. C., "Purposes and usefulness of the Kentucky Program," paper presented to the American Psychological Association, Chicago (1965). (c)

Finney, J. C., "Programmed interpretation of MMPI and CPI," *Archives of General Psychiatry* **15**, 75–81 (1966). (a)

Finney, J. C., "Relations and meaning of the new MMPI scales," *Psychological Reports* **18**, 459–470 (1966). (b)

Fisher, R. A., *The Design of Experiments*, Oliver and Boyd, Edinburgh and London (1937).

Fiske, D. W., "Consistency of the factorial structures of personality ratings from different sources," *Journal of Abnormal and Social Psychology* **44**, 329–344 (1949).

Fiske, D. W., "Variability among peer ratings in different situations," *Educational and Psychological Measurement* **20**, 283–290 (1960).

Fiske, D. W., and J. A. Cox, Jr., "The consistency of peer ratings," *Journal of Applied Psychology* **44**, 11–17 (1960).

Flanagan, J. C., "The aviation psychology program in the Army Air Forces," *Army Air Force Aviation Psychology Research Report No. 1*, Government Printing Office, Washington, D.C. (1948).

Flanagan, J. C., "The critical incident technique," *Psychological Bulletin* **51**, 327–358 (1954).

Flanagan, J. C., J. T. Dailey, M. F. Shaycroft, W. A. Gorham, D. B. Orr, and I. Goldberg, *Design for a Study of American Youth*, Houghton Mifflin, Boston (1962).

Flavell, J. H., "Meaning and meaning similarity: II. The semantic differential and co-occurrence as predictors of judged similarity in meaning," *Journal of General Psychology* **64**, 321–335 (1961).

Flyer, E. S., "Prediction of unsuitability among first-term airmen from aptitude indexes, high school reference data, and basic training evaluations," *USAF PRL Technical Report*, No. 63–17 (1963).

Flyer, E. S., and L. R. Bigbee, "The light plane as a pre-primary selection and training device: III. Analysis of selection data," *USAF PRL Technical Report* (December 1954).

Foa, U. G., "Convergences in the analysis of the structure of interpersonal behavior," *Psychological Review* **68**, 341–353 (1961).

Foa, U. G., "New developments in facet design and analysis," *Psychological Review* **72**, 262–274 (1965).

Ford, L. H., Jr., and M. Meisels, "Social desirability and the semantic differential," *Educational and Psychological Measurement* **25**, 465–475 (1965).

Fordhand, G. A., "Relationships among response sets and cognitive behaviors," *Educational and Psychological Measurement* **22,** 287–302 (1962).

Foulds, G. A., "The reliability of psychiatric, and the value of psychological, diagnoses," *Journal of Mental Science* **101,** 851–862 (1955).

Fowler, R. D., Jr., "Computer processing and reporting of personality test data." Paper presented to the American Psychological Association, Los Angeles (1964).

Fowler, R. D., Jr., "Purposes and usefulness of the Alabama Program for the automatic interpretation of the MMPI." Paper presented to the American Psychological Association, Chicago (1965).

Fowler, R. D., Jr., *The MMPI Notebook: A Guide to the Clinical Use of the Automated MMPI*, Roche Psychiatric Service Institute, Nutley, N.J. (1966).

Fowler, R. D., Jr., "Automated interpretation of personality test data." In J. N. Butcher (ed.), *MMPI: Research Developments and Clinical Applications*, McGraw-Hill, New York (1969), pp. 105–126.

Franks, C. M. (ed.), *Behavior Therapy: Appraisal and Status*, McGraw-Hill, New York (1969).

Frederiksen, N., and A. Gilbert, "Replication of a study of differential predictability," *Educational and Psychological Measurement* **20,** 759–767 (1960).

Frederiksen, N., and S. D. Melville, "Differential predictability in the use of test scores," *Educational and Psychological Measurement* **14,** 647–656 (1954).

Frederiksen, N., and S. Messick, "Response set as a measure of personality," *Educational and Psychological Measurement* **19,** 137–159 (1959).

Frederiksen, N., D. R. Saunders, and B. Wand, "The in-basket test," *Psychological Monographs* **71,** No. 9 (Whole No. 438) (1957).

Freeberg, N. R., "Relevance of rater-ratee acquaintance in the validity and reliability of ratings," *ETS Research Bulletin*, No. 55, Educational Testing Service, Princeton, N.J. (1967).

Freedman, M. B., T. Leary, A. G. Ossorio, and H. S. Coffey, "The interpersonal dimension of personality," *Journal of Personality* **20,** 143–161 (1951).

French, J. W., "A machine search for moderator variables in massive data," *Office of Naval Research Technical Report*, Educational Testing Service, Princeton, N.J. (1961).

Freud, S., *A General Introduction to Psychoanalysis*, Garden City Publishing, Garden City, N.Y. (1943).

Fricke, B. G., "Response set as a suppressor variable in the OAIS and MMPI," *Journal of Consulting Psychology* **20,** 161–169 (1956).

Fricke, B. G., *Opinion, Attitude, and Interest Survey Handbook*, University of Michigan, Ann Arber (1963)

Fulkerson, S. C., "An acquiescence key for the MMPI," *USAF School of Aviation Medicine, Report No. 58-71*, Randolph Air Force Base, Texas (July 1958).

Gage, N. L., and L. J. Cronbach, "Conceptual and methodological problems in interpersonal perception," *Psychological Review* **62,** 411–422 (1955).

Galton, F., "Co-relations and their measurement," *Proceedings of the Royal Society* **45,** 135–145 (1888).

Gardner, G., "The psychotherapeutic relationship," *Psychological Bulletin* **61,** 426–437 (1964).

Garner, W. R., H. W. Hake, and C. W. Eriksen, "Operationism and the concept of perception," *Psychological Review* **63,** 149–159 (1956).

Gergen, K. J., "Personal consistency and the presentation of self." In C. Gordon and K. Gergen (eds.), *The Self in Social Interaction*, Vol. 1, Wiley, New York (1968), pp. 299–308.

Ghiselli, E. E., "The forced-choice technique in self-description," *Personnel Psychology* **7,** 201–208 (1954).

Ghiselli, E. E., "Differentiation of individuals in terms of their predictability," *Journal of Applied Psychology* **40,** 374–377 (1956).

Ghiselli, E. E., "Differentiation of tests in terms of the accuracy with which they predict for a given individual," *Educational and Psychological Measurement* **20,** 675–684 (1960). (a)

Ghiselli, E. E., "The prediction of predictability," *Educational and Psychological Measurement* **20,** 3–8 (1960). (b)

Ghiselli, E. E., "Moderating effects and differential reliability and validity," *Journal of Applied Psychology* **47,** 81–86 (1963).

Ghiselli, E. E., *Theory of Psychological Measurement*, McGraw-Hill, New York (1964).

Ghiselli, E. E., "Interaction of traits and motivational factors in the determination of the success of managers," *Journal of Applied Psychology* **52,** 480–483 (1968).

Ghiselli, E. E., and E. P. Sanders, "Moderating heteroscedasticity," *Educational and Psychological Measurement* **27,** 581–590 (1967).

Gibb, C. A., "Leadership," In G. Lindzey and E. Aronson (eds.), *Handbook of Social Psychology*, second edition, Vol. 4, Addison-Wesley, Reading, Mass. (1969), pp. 205–282.

Gilberstadt, H., and J. Duker, *A Handbook for Clinical and Actuarial MMPI Interpretation*, Saunders, Philadelphia (1965).

Gill, M. M., "The present state of psychoanalytic theory," *Journal of Abnormal and Social Psychology* **58,** 1–8 (1959).

Gill, M. M., "Topography and systems in psychoanalytic theory," *Psychological Issues* **3,** Monograph No. 10 (1963).

Gleser, G. C., "Projective methodologies." In P. R. Farnsworth (ed.), *Annual Review of Psychology*, Vol. 14, Annual Reviews Inc., Stanford, Calif. (1963), pp. 391–422.

Gleser, G. C., L. J. Cronbach, and N. Rajaratnam, "Generalizability of scores influenced by multiple sources of variance," *Psychometrika* **30,** 395–418 (1965).

Goldberg, L. R., "The effectiveness of clinicians' judgments: the diagnosis of organic brain damage from the Bender-Gestalt Test," *Journal of Consulting Psychology* **23**, 25–33 (1959).

Goldberg, L. R., "A model of item ambiguity in personality assessment," *Educational and Psychological Measurement* **23**, 467–492 (1963).

Goldberg, L. R., "Diagnosticians versus diagnostic signs: the diagnosis of psychosis versus neurosis from the MMPI," *Psychological Monographs* **79** (9, Whole No. 602), (1965). (a)

Goldberg, L. R., "Still wanted—a good cookbook." Paper presented to the American Psychological Association, Chicago (1965). (b)

Goldberg, L. R., "Reliability of Peace Corps Selection Boards: a study of inter-judge agreement before and after board discussions," *Journal of Applied Psychology* **50**, 400–408 (1966).

Goldberg, L. R., "Seer over sign: the first 'good' example?" *Journal of Experimental Research in Personality* **3**, 168–171 (1968). (a)

Goldberg, L. R., "Simple models or simple processes? Some research on clinical judgments," *American Psychologist* **23**, 483–496 (1968). (b)

Goldberg, L. R., "Some ruminations on the search for configural relationships in personality assessment: the diagnosis of psychosis versus neurosis from the MMPI," *Multivariate Behavioral Research* **4**, 523–536 (1969).

Goldberg, L. R., "Man versus model of man: a rationale plus evidence for a method of improving on clinical inferences," *Psychological Bulletin* **73**, 422–432 (1970).

Goldberg, L. R., "Parameters of personality inventory construction and utilization: a comparison of prediction strategies and tactics," *Multivariate Behavioral Research Monographs* **7**, No. 2 (1972).

Goldberg, L. R., and W. Chaplin, "A computer program for evaluating the expected utilities of personnel decision strategies." Unpublished manuscript, Oregon Research Institute, Eugene (1970).

Goldberg, L. R., and L. G. Rorer, "Learning clinical inference: the results of intensive training on clinicians' ability to diagnose psychosis versus neurosis from the MMPI." Paper presented to the Western Psychological Association, Honolulu (June 1965).

Goldberg, L. R., L. G. Rorer, and M. M. Greene, "The usefulness of 'stylistic' scales as potential suppressor or moderator variables in predictions from the CPI," *Oregon Research Institute Research Bulletin* **10**, No. 3 (1970).

Goldberg, L. R., and P. Slovic, "Importance of test item content: an analysis of a corollary of the deviation hypothesis," *Journal of Counseling Psychology* **14**, 462–472 (1967).

Golden, M., "Some effects of combining psychological tests on clinical inferences," *Journal of Consulting Psychology* **28**, 440–446 (1964).

Goldfried, M. R., and T. J. D'Zurilla, "A behavioral-analytic model for assessing competence." In C. D. Spielberger (ed.), *Current Topics in Clinical and Community Psychology*, Vol. 1, Academic Press, New York (1969), pp. 151–196.

Goldfried, M. R., and T. J. D'Zurilla, "Assessment of competence among male college freshmen: an application of the behavioral-analytic model." Paper presented at the 79th Annual Convention of the American Psychological Association, Washington, D.C. (September 1971).

Goldfried, M. R., and D. M. Pomerantz, "Role of assessment in behavior modification," *Psychological Reports* **23**, 75–87 (1968).

Gollin, A. E., *Evaluating Programs and Personnel Overseas: A Review of Methods and Practices*, Columbia University, Bureau of Applied Social Research, New York (February 1963).

Gollob, H. F., "Cross-validation using samples of size one." Paper presented at the American Psychological Association, Washington, D.C. (1967).

Goodenough, F. L., "Inter-relationships in the behavior of young children," *Child Development* **1**, 29–47 (1930).

Goodenough, F. L., *Mental Testing*, Rinehart, New York (1949).

Goodfellow, L. D., "The human element in probability," *Journal of General Psychology* **33**, 201–205 (1940).

Gordon, J. E., "Interpersonal predictions of repressors and sensitizers," *Journal of Personality* **6**, 686–698 (1957).

Gottesman, L. E., "The relationship of cognitive variables to therapeutic ability and training of client-centered therapists," *Journal of Consulting Psychology* **26**, 119–125 (1962).

Gough, H. G., "Diagnostic patterns on the MMPI," *Journal of Clinical Psychology* **2**, 23–37 (1946).

Gough, H. G., "On making a good impression," *Journal of Educational Research* **46**, 33–42 (1952).

Gough, H. G., "Tests of personality: questionnaires," In A. Weider (ed.), *Contributions toward Medical Psychology*, Ronald Press, New York (1953).

Gough, H. G., "Some common misconceptions about neuroticism," *Journal of Consulting Psychology* **18**, 287–292 (1954).

Gough, H. G., *California Psychological Inventory Manual*, Consulting Psychologists Press, Palo Alto, Calif. (1957).

Gough, H. G., *An Assessment Study of Air Force Officers: Part IV. Predictability of a Composite Criterion of Officer Effectiveness*, Wright Air Development Center Technical Report No. 91 (IV), Personnel Laboratory, Lackland Air Force Base, Texas (December 1958).

Gough, H. G., "Clinical versus statistical prediction in psychology." In L. Postman (ed.), *Psychology in the Making*, Knopf, New York (1962), pp. 526–584.

Gough, H. G., "Misplaced emphasis in admissions," *Journal of College Student Personnel* **6**, 130–135 (1965).

Gough, H. G., W. B. Hall, and R. E. Harris, "Admissions procedures as forecasters of performance in medical training," *Journal of Medical Education* **38**, 983–998 (1963).

Gough, H. G., and A. B. Heilbrun, *The Adjective Check List Manual*, Consulting Psychologists Press, Palo Alto, Calif. (1965).

Gough, H. G., and I. Krauss, *An Assessment Study of Air Force Officers: Part II. Description of the Assessed Sample*, Wright Air Development Center Technical Report No. 91 (II), Personnel Laboratory, Lackland Air Force Base, Texas (September 1958).

Gough, H. G., M. G. McKee, and R. J. Yandell, *Adjective Check List Analyses of a Number of Selected Psychometric and Assessment Variables*, Technical Memorandum No. 10, Officer Education Research Laboratory, Maxwell Air Force Base, Alabama (May 1955).

Grant, D. A., "The Latin-square principle in the design and analysis of psychological experiments," *Psychological Bulletin* **45**, 427–442 (1948).

Grebstein, L., "Relative accuracy of actuarial prediction, experienced clinicians, and graduate students in a clinical judgment task," *Journal of Consulting Psychology* **37**, 127–132 (1963).

Green, B. F., Jr., "Descriptions and explanations: a comment on papers by Hoffman and Edwards." In B. Kleinmuntz (ed.), *Formal Representation of Human Judgment*, Wiley, New York (1968), pp. 91–98.

Greenspoon, J., and C. D. Gersten, "A new look at psychological testing: psychological testing from the standpoint of a behaviorist," *American Psychologist* **22**, 848–853 (1967).

Guilford, J. P., *Psychometric Methods*, second edition, McGraw-Hill, New York (1954).

Gulliksen, H., *Theory of Mental Tests*, Wiley, New York (1950).

Guthrie, G. M., "Six MMPI diagnostic profile patterns," *Journal of Psychology* **30**, 317–323 (1950).

Guttman, L., "A basis for scaling qualitative data," *American Sociological Review* **9**, 139–150 (1944).

Guttman, L., "The basis for scalogram analysis." In S. A. Stouffer *et al.*, *Measurement and Prediction*, Princeton University Press, Princeton, N.J. (1950), pp. 60–90.

Guttman, L., "A special review of Harold Gulliksen, *Theory of Mental Tests*," *Psychometrika* **18**, 123–130 (1953).

Guttman, L., "A new approach to factor analysis: the radex." In P. R. Lazarsfeld (ed.), *Mathematical Thinking in the Social Sciences*, Free Press, Glencoe, Ill. (1954). (a)

Guttman, L., "An outline of some new methodology for social research," *Public Opinion Quarterly* **18**, 395–404 (1954). (b)

Haggard, E. A., J. P. Chapman, K. S. Isaacs, and K. W. Dickman, "Intraclass correlation versus factor analytic techniques for determining groups of profiles," *Psychological Bulletin* **56**, 48–57 (1959).

Haggerty, H. R., "Personnel research for the U.S. Military Academy, 1942–1953," *PRB Technical Research Report 1077*, Department of the Army (1953).

Hakel, M. D., "Significance of implicit personality theories for personality research and theory," *Proceedings of the 77th Convention of the American Psychological Association* (1969), pp. 403–404.

Halbower, C. C., "A comparison of actuarial versus clinical prediction to classes discriminated by MMPI." Unpublished Ph.D. thesis, University of Minnesota, Minneapolis (1955).

Hall, C. S., and G. Lindzey, *Theories of Personality*, Wiley, New York (1957).

Hallworth, H. J., "Teachers' personality ratings of high school pupils," *Journal of Educational Psychology* **52**, 297–302 (1961).

Hallworth, H. J., "Dimensions of personality and meaning," *British Journal of Social and Clinical Psychology* **4**, 161–168 (1965).

Hamilton, D. L., "Personality attributes associated with extreme response style," *Psychological Bulletin* **69**, 192–203, (1968).

Hammond, K. R., "Probabilistic functioning in the clinical method," *Psychological Review* **62**, 255–262 (1955).

Hammond, K. R. (ed.), *The Psychology of Egon Brunswik*, Holt, Rinehart and Winston, New York (1966).

Hammond, K. R., C. J. Hursch, and F. J. Todd, "Analyzing the components of clinical inference," *Psychological Review* **71**, 438–456 (1964).

Hammond, K. R., and D. A. Summers, "Cognitive dependence on linear and nonlinear cues," *Psychological Review* **72**, 215–224 (1965).

Hanks, L. M., Jr., "Prediction from case material to personality data," *New York Archives of Psychology* **29**, No. 207 (1936).

Hanley, C., "Deriving a measure of test-taking defensiveness," *Journal of Consulting Psychology* **21**, 391–397 (1957).

Hanley, C., "The 'difficulty' of a personality inventory item," *Educational and Psychological Measurement* **22**, 577–584 (1962).

Hare, A. P., "Factors associated with Peace Corps Volunteer success in the Philippines." Unpublished paper, Haverford College, Haverford, Pa. (1962).

Harrell, T. W., and R. D. Churchill, "The classification of military personnel," *Psychological Bulletin* **38**, 331–353 (1941).

Harris, J. G., Jr., "Judgmental versus mathematical prediction: an investigation by analogy of the clinical versus statistical controversy," *Behavioral Science* **8**, 324–335 (1963).

Harris, J. G., Jr., and J. C. Baxter, "Ambiguity in the MMPI," *Journal of Consulting Psychology* **29**, 112–118 (1965).

Hartmann, H., *Ego Psychology and the Problem of Adaptation*, International Universities Press, New York (1958).

Harvey, O. J., D. E. Hunt, and H. M. Schroder, *Conceptual Systems and Personality Organization*, Wiley, New York (1961).

Hase, H. D., and L. R. Goldberg, "The comparative validity of different strategies of deriving personality inventory scales," *Psychological Bulletin* **67**, 231–248 (1967).

Hatch, R. S., *An Evaluation of a Forced Choice Differential Accuracy Approach to the Measurement of Supervisory Empathy*, Prentice-Hall, Englewood Cliffs, N.J. (1962).

Hathaway, S. R., and J. C. McKinley, *The Minnesota Multiphasic Personality Inventory*, revised, Psychological Corporation, New York (1951).

Hathaway, S. R., and P. E. Meehl, *An Atlas for the Clinical Use of the MMPI*, University of Minnesota Press, Minneapolis (1951). (a)

Hathaway, S. R., and P. E. Meehl, "The MMPI." In *Military Clinical Psychology*, Department of the Army, Technical Manual, TM8-242, Government Printing Office, Washington (1951). (b)

Hays, W. L., "An approach to the study of trait implication and trait similarity." In R. Tagiuri and L. Petrullo (eds.), *Person Perception and Interpersonal Behavior*, Stanford University Press, Stanford, Calif. (1958), pp. 289–299.

Heider, F., *The Psychology of Interpersonal Relations*, Wiley, New York (1958).

Hempel, C. G., *Fundamentals of Concept Formation in Empirical Science*, University of Chicago Press, Chicago (1952).

Henry, E. R., "What business can learn from Peace Corps selection and training," *Personnel* **42**, 17–25 (1965).

Herbert, A. P., *Number Nine, or the Mind Sweepers*, Doubleday, Garden City, N.Y. (1952).

Hermans, H. J. M., "The validity of different strategies of scale construction in predicting academic achievement," *Educational and Psychological Measurement* **29**, 877–883 (1969).

Herzberg, P. A., "The parameters of cross-validation," *Psychometrika Monograph Supplement* **34**, No. 16 (1969).

Hess, E. H., and J. N. Polt, "Pupil size as related to interest value of visual stimuli," *Science* **132**, 349–350 (1960).

Hesterly, S. O., and I. A. Berg, "Deviant responses as indicators of immaturity and schizophrenia," *Journal of Consulting Psychology* **22**, 389–393 (1958).

Heusler, A., G. Ulett, and J. Blasques, "Noise-level index: an objective measurement of the effect of drugs on the psycho-motor activity of patients," *Journal of Neuropsychiatry* **1**, 23–25 (1959).

Hiler, E. W., and D. Nesvig, "An evaluation of criteria used by clinicians to infer pathology from figure drawings," *Journal of Consulting Psychology* **29**, 520–529 (1965).

Hilgard, E. R., *Theories of Learning*, Appleton-Century-Crofts, New York (1948).

Hilgard, E. R., and G. H. Bower, *Theories of Learning*, third edition, Appleton-Century-Crofts, New York (1966).

Hobbs, N., "A psychologist in the Peace Corps," *American Psychologist* **18**, 47–55 (1963).

Hobert, R., and M. D. Dunnette, "Development of moderator variables to enhance the prediction of managerial effectiveness," *Journal of Applied Psychology* **51**, 50–64 (1967).

Hoffman, E. L., and J. H. Rohrer, "An objective peer evaluation scale: construction and validation," *Educational and Psychological Measurement* **14**, 332–341 (1954).

Hoffman, P. J., "The paramorphic representation of clinical judgment," *Psychological Bulletin* **57**, 116–131 (1960).

Hoffman, P. J., "Assessment of the independent contributions of predictors," *Psychological Bulletin* **59**, 77–80 (1962).

Hoffman, P. J., "Cue-consistency and configurality in human judgment." In B. Kleinmuntz (ed.), *Formal Representation of Human Judgment*, Wiley, New York (1968), pp. 53–90.

Holdrege, F. E., "Factorial structure of basic training performance variables," *USAF AFD Technical Note*, No. 61-50 (1961).

Holland, J. L., A. H. Krause, M. E. Nixon, and M. F. Tremblath, "The classification of occupations by means of Kuder interest profiles: I. The development of interest groups," *Journal of Applied Psychology* **37**, 263–369 (1953).

Hollander, E. P., "Buddy ratings: military research and industrial implications," *Personnel Psychology* **7**, 385–393 (1954). (a)

Hollander, E. P., "Peer nominations on leadership as a predictor of the pass-fail criterion in naval air training," *Journal of Applied Psychology* **38**, 150–153 (1954). (b)

Hollander, E. P., "The reliability of peer nominations under various conditions of administration," *Journal of Applied Psychology* **41**, 85–90 (1957).

Holt, R. R., "The Thematic Apperception Test." In H. H. Anderson and G. L. Anderson (eds.), *An Introduction to Projective Techniques*, Prentice-Hall, Englewood Cliffs, N.J. (1951), pp. 181–229.

Holt, R. R., "Clinical *and* statistical prediction: a reformulation and some new data," *Journal of Abnormal and Social Psychology* **56**, 1–12 (1958).

Holt, R. R., "The nature of TAT stories as cognitive products: a psychoanalytic approach." In J. Kagan and G. Lesser (eds.), *Contemporary Issues in Thematic Apperceptive Methods*, Charles C. Thomas, Springfield, Ill. (1961), pp. 3–40.

Holt, R. R., "Individuality and generalization in the psychology of personality: an evaluation," *Journal of Personality* **30**, 377–402 (1962).

Holt, R. R., and L. Luborsky, *Personality Patterns of Psychiatrists, Vol. 1: A Study of Methods for Selecting Residents*, Basic Books, New York (1958). (a)

Holt, R. R., and L. Luborsky, *Personality Patterns of Psychiatrists, Vol. 2: Supplementary and Supporting Data*, Menninger Foundation, Topeka, Kansas (1958). (b)

Holtzman, W. H., J. F. Santos, S. Bouquet, and P. Barth, *The Peace Corps in Brazil: An Evaluation of the Sao Francisco Valley Project*, International Office, University of Texas, Austin (1966).

Holzberg, J. D., "The clinical and scientific methods: synthesis or antithesis?" *Journal of Projective Techniques* **21**, 227–242 (1957).

Horst, P., *The Prediction of Personal Adjustment*, Social Science Research Council, New York (1941).

Huff, F. W., "Use of actuarial description of personality in a mental hospital," *Psychological Reports* **17**, 224 (1965).

Hull, C. L., *Principles of Behavior*, Appleton-Century-Crofts, New York (1943).

Humphreys, L. G., "Clinical versus actuarial prediction," *Proceedings of the 1955 Invitational Conference on Testing Problems*, Educational Testing Service, Princeton, N.J. (1956), pp. 129–135.

Humphreys, L. G., "Note on the multitrait-multimethod matrix," *Psychological Bulletin* **57**, 86–88 (1960).

Hundleby, J. D., K. Pawlik, and R. B. Cattell, *Personality Factors in Objective Test Devices*, Robert R. Knapp, San Diego (1965).

Hursch, C. J., K. R. Hammond, and J. L. Hursch, "Some methodological considerations in multiple-cue probability studies," *Psychological Review* **71**, 42–60 (1964).

Hutt, M. L., "Actuarial and clinical approaches to psychodiagnosis," *Psychological Reports* **2**, 413–419 (1956).

Institute for Personality and Ability Testing, *Psychological Tests and Services*, Champaign, Ill. (1971).

Institute of Personality Assessment and Research, *Annual Report: 1969–1970*, University of California, Berkeley (1970).

Isaacson, R. L., W. J. McKeachie, and J. E. Milholland, "Correlation of teacher personality variables and student ratings," *Journal of Educational Psychology* **54**, 110–117 (1963).

Jackson, D. N., "Balanced scales, item overlap, and the Stables of Augeas," *Educational and Psychological Measurement* **27**, 502–507 (1967). (a)

Jackson, D. N., *Personality Research Form Manual*, Research Psychologists Press, Goshen, N.Y. (1967). (b)

Jackson, D. N., "A review of J. Block, *The Challenge of Response Sets*," *Educational and Psychological Measurement* **27**, 207–219 (1967). (c)

Jackson, D. N., "Multimethod factor analysis in the evaluation of convergent and discriminant validity," *Psychological Bulletin* **72**, 30–49 (1969).

Jackson, D. N., "A sequential system for personality scale development." In C. D. Spielberger (ed.), *Current Topics in Clinical and Community Psychology*, Vol. 2, Academic Press, New York (1970), pp. 61–96.

Jackson, D. N., "The dynamics of structured personality tests: 1971," *Psychological Review* **78**, 229–248 (1971).

Jackson, D. N., and G. M. Guthrie, "Multitrait-multimethod evaluation of the Personality Research Form," *Proceedings of the 76th Annual Convention of the American Psychological Association* (1968), pp. 177–178.

Jackson, D. N., and C. Lay, "Homogeneous dimensions of personality scale content," *Multivariate Behavioral Research* **3**, 321–338 (1968).

Jackson, D. N., and S. Messick, "Content and style in personality assessment," *Psychological Bulletin* **55**, 243–252 (1958).

Jackson, D. N., and S. Messick, "Acquiescence and desirability as response determinants on the MMPI," *Educational and Psychological Measurement* **21**, 771–790 (1961).

Jackson, D. N., and S. Messick, "Response styles on the MMPI: comparison of clinical and normal samples," *Journal of Abnormal and Social Psychology* **65**, 285–299 (1962). (a)

Jackson, D. N., and S. Messick, "Response styles and the assessment of psychopathology." In S. Messick and J. Ross (eds.), *Measurement in Personality and Cognition*, Wiley, New York (1962), pp. 129–155. (b)

Jackson, D. N., and S. Messick (eds.), *Problems in Human Assessment*, McGraw-Hill, New York (1967).

Jellinek, E. M., *The Disease Concept of Alcohol*, Millhouse Press, New Haven, Conn. (1962).

Jessor, R., and K. R. Hammond, "Construct validity and the Taylor anxiety scale," *Psychological Bulletin* **54**, 161–170 (1957).

Johnston, R., and B. F. McNeal, "Statistical versus clinical prediction: length of neuropsychiatric hospital stay," *Journal of Abnormal Psychology* **72**, 335–340 (1967).

Jones, R. R., "The Peace Corps overseas: some first steps toward description and evaluation," *Oregon Research Institute Technical Report* **8**, No. 3 (1968). (a)

Jones, R. R., "The validity of the Full Field Background Report in Peace Corps selection," *Oregon Research Institute Research Monograph* **8**, No. 1 (1968). (b)

Jones, R. R., "Peace Corps selection without the Full Field," *Research Report No. 7*, January 1969, Division of Research, Peace Corps. (a)

Jones, R. R., "Selection and overseas experiences of Peace Corps Volunteers," Final Report, August 1969, Peace Corps Contract No. 80-1539, Oregon Research Institute. (b)

Jones, R. R., and L. R. Goldberg, "Interrelationships among personality scale parameters: item response stability and scale reliability," *Educational and Psychological Measurement* **27**, 323–333 (1967).

Kamfer, L., "The predictor value of two situational tests," *Journal of the National Institute of Personnel Research* **8**, 15–18 (1959).

Kanfer, F. H., and J. S. Phillips, *Learning Foundations of Behavior Therapy*, Wiley, New York (1970).

Kanfer, F. H., and G. Saslow, "Behavioral analysis: an alternative to diagnostic classification," *Archives of General Psychiatry* **12**, 529–538 (1965).

Kanfer, F. H., and G. Saslow, "Behavioral diagnosis." In C. M. Franks (ed.), *Behavior Therapy: Appraisal and Status*, McGraw-Hill, New York (1969), pp. 417–444.

Kantor, J. R., *The Logic of Modern Science*, Principia Press, Bloomington, Ind. (1953).

Katz, D., "Do interviewers bias poll results?" *Public Opinion Quarterly* **6**, 248–268 (1942).

Kelley, T. L., "Principles underlying the classification of men," *Journal of Applied Psychology* **3**, 50–67 (1919).

Kellogg, R. L., "The Strong Vocational Interest Blank as a differential predictor of engineering grades," *Educational and Psychological Measurement* **28**, 1213–1217 (1968).

Kelly, E. L., "An evaluation of the interview as a selective technique," *Proceedings of the 1953 Invitational Conference on Testing Problems*, Educational Testing Service, Princeton, N.J. (1954).

Kelly, E. L., "Multiple criteria of medical education and their implications for selection." In H. H. Gee and J. T. Cowles (eds.), *The Appraisal of Applicants to Medical Schools*, Association of American Medical Colleges, Evanston, Ill. (1957), pp. 185–196.

Kelly, E. L., and D. W. Fiske, *The Prediction of Performance in Clinical Psychology*, University of Michigan Press, Ann Arbor (1951).

Kelly, E. L., and L. R. Goldberg, "Correlates of later performance and specialization in psychology: a follow-up study of the trainees assessed in the VA Selection Research Project," *Psychological Monographs* **73**, (12, Whole No. 482) (1959).

Kelly, G. A., *The Psychology of Personal Constructs,* Vols. 1 and 2, Norton, New York (1955).

Kelly, G. A., "The theory and technique of assessment." In P. R. Farnsworth (ed.), *Annual Review of Psychology*, Annual Reviews, Palo Alto, Calif. (1958), pp. 323–352.

Kelly, G. A., *A Theory of Personality*, Norton, New York (1963).

Kelly, G. A., "A summary statement of a cognitively-oriented comprehensive theory of behavior." In J. C. Mancuso (ed.), *Readings for a Cognitive Theory of Personality*, Holt, Rinehart and Winston, New York (1970), pp. 27–58.

Kelman, H. C., "Human use of human subjects: the problem of deception in social psychological experiments," *Psychological Bulletin* **67**, 1–11 (1967).

Kleinmuntz, B., "MMPI decision rules for the identification of college maladjustment: a digital computer approach," *Psychological Monographs* **77** (14, Whole No. 477) (1963).

Kleinmuntz, B., *Personality Measurement*, Dorsey, Homewood, Ill. (1967). (a)

Kleinmuntz, B., "Sign and seer: another example," *Journal of Abnormal Psychology* **72,** 163–165 (1967). (b).

Kleinmuntz, B., "Personality test interpretation by computer and clinician." In J. N. Butcher (ed.), *MMPI: Research Developments and Clinical Applications,* McGraw-Hill, New York (1969), pp. 97–104.

Klett, W. G., and N. D. Vestre, "Demographic and prognostic characteristics of psychiatric patients classified by gross MMPI measures," *Journal of Consulting and Clinical Psychology* **32,** 271–275 (1968).

Kliger, W. A., J. E. deJung, and A. U. Dubuisson, *Peer Ratings as Predictors of Disciplinary Problems*, U.S. Army Personnel Research Office, Washington, D.C. (1962).

Klopfer, B., M. D. Ainsworth, W. G. Klopfer, and R. R. Holt, *Developments in the Rorschach Technique. Vol. I. Technique and Theory*, World, New York (1954).

Kneale, W., *Probability and Induction*, Clarendon Press ,Oxford (1949).

Koch, S. (ed.), *Psychology: A Study of Science*, Vol. 2, McGraw-Hill, New York (1959).

Kogan, L. S., "Review of Meehl's *Clinical versus Statistical Prediction,*" *Psychological Bulletin* **52,** 539–540 (1955).

Kostlan, A., "A method for the empirical study of psychodiagnosis," *Journal of Consulting Psychology* **18,** 83–88 (1954).

Krasner, L., and L. P. Ullmann (eds.), *Research in Behavior Modification: New Developments and Implications*, Holt, Rinehart and Winston, New York (1965).

Kremers, J., *Scientific Psychology and Naive Psychology*, Drukkerij Gebr. Janssen N.V., Nijmegen, Netherlands (1960).

Krug, R. E., "An analysis of the selection process in eighteen Peace Corps projects." Paper presented at the Peace Corps–National Institute of Mental Health Conference on the "Peace Corps and the Behavioral Sciences," Washington, D.C. (March 1963).

Krug, R. E., and M. M. Wertheim, "On overseas attrition." Research Note No. 11, October 1965, Division of Research, Peace Corps.

Krumboltz, J. D., R. E. Christal, and J. H. Ward, Jr., "Predicting leadership ratings from high school activities," *Journal of Educational Psychology* **50,** 105–110 (1959).

Kuder, G. F., and M. W. Richardson, "The theory of the estimation of test reliability," *Psychometrika* **2,** 151–160 (1937).

Kuusinen, J., "Affective and denotative structures of personality ratings," *Journal of Personality and Social Psychology* **12,** 181–188 (1969).

Laabs, G. J., and R. M. Dawes, "Probability estimates of selected personality-trait pairs and trait triplets," *Oregon Research Institute Research Bulletin*, Vol. 9, No. 1, Eugene, Oregon (1969).

Lachman, R., "The model in theory construction," *Psychological Review* **67**, 113–129 (1960).

LaForge, R., "Research use of the ICL," *Oregon Research Institute Technical Report* **3**, No. 4, Eugene, Oregon (1963).

LaForge, R., M. B. Freedman, T. Leary, H. Naboisek, and H. S. Coffey, "The interpersonal dimension of personality. II. An objective study of repression," *Journal of Personality* **23**, 129–154 (1954).

LaForge, R., and R. F. Suczek, "The interpersonal dimension of personality. III. An interpersonal check list," *Journal of Personality* **25**, 94–112 (1955).

Lay, C. H., and D. N. Jackson, "An analysis of the generality of trait inferential networks," *Journal of Personality and Social Psychology* **12**, 12–21 (1969).

Lazarsfeld, P. F., "A conceptual introduction to latent structure analysis." In P. F. Lazarsfeld (ed.), *Mathematical Thinking in the Social Sciences*, Free Press, Glencoe, Ill. (1954), pp. 349–387.

Lazarsfeld, P. F., "The logical and mathematical foundation of latent structure analysis." In S. A. Stouffer *et al.*, *Measurement and Prediction*, Princeton University Press, Princeton, N.J. (1959), pp. 263–412.

Leary, T., *Multilevel Measurement of Interpersonal Behavior*, Psychological Consultation Service, Berkeley, Calif. (1956).

Leary, T., *Interpersonal Diagnosis of Personality*, Ronald Press, New York (1957).

Lecky, P., *Self-consistency: A Theory of Personality*, Island Press, New York (1945).

Lee, E. B., and L. P. Thorpe, *Occupational Interest Inventory*, California Test Bureau, Monterey (1956).

Lee, J. C., and R. Tucker, "An investigation of clinical judgment: a study in method," *Journal of Abnormal and Social Psychology* **64**, 272–280 (1962).

Lee, M. C., "Interactions, configurations, and nonadditive models," *Educational and Psychological Measurement* **21**, 797–805 (1961).

Levine, A. S., "A technique for developing suppression tests," *Educational and Psychological Measurement* **12**, 313–315 (1952).

Levy, B. I., and E. Ulman, "Judging psychopathology from painting," *Journal of Abnormal Psychology* **72**, 182–187 (1967).

Levy, L. H., *Psychological Interpretation*, Holt, Rinehart and Winston, New York (1963).

Levy, L. H., "A study of the relative information value of constructs in personal construct theory." Unpublished doctoral thesis, Ohio State University, Columbus (1954).

Levy, L. H., *Conceptions of Personality: Theories and Research*, Random House, New York (1970).

Levy, L. H., and R. D. Dugan, "A factorial study of personal constructs," *Journal of Consulting Psychology* **20**, 53–57 (1956).

Lewin, K., *A Dynamic Theory of Personality*, McGraw-Hill, New York (1935).

Lewin, K., *Principles of Topological Psychology*, McGraw-Hill, New York (1936).

Lindquist, E. F., *Design and Analysis of Experiments in Education and Psychology*, Houghton Mifflin, Boston (1953).

Lindsley, O. R., "Direct measurement and prosthesis of retarded behavior," *Journal of Education* **147**, 62–81 (1964).

Lindzey, G., "Thematic Apperception Test: interpretive assumptions and related empirical evidence," *Psychological Bulletin* **49**, 1–25 (1952).

Lindzey, G., "Seer versus sign," *Journal of Experimental Research in Personality* **1**, 17–26 (1965).

Little, K. B., and E. S. Shneidman, "Congruencies among interpretations of psychological test and anamnestic data," *Psychological Monographs* **73**, (6, Whole No. 476) (1959).

Loehlin, J. C., *Computer Models of Personality*, Random House, New York (1968).

Loevinger, J., "Objective tests as instruments of psychological theory," *Psychological Reports* **3**, 635–694 (Monograph No. 9) (1957).

Loevinger, J., "Measuring personality patterns of women," *Genetic Psychology Monographs* **65**, 53–136 (1962).

Loevinger, J., "Person and population as psychometric concepts," *Psychological Review* **72**, 143–155 (1965).

Loevinger, J., G. C. Gleser, and P. H. DuBois, "Maximizing the discriminating power of a multiple-score test," *Psychometrika* **18**, 309–317 (1953).

Lord, F. M., "Efficiency of prediction when a regression equation from one sample is used in a new sample," *Research Bulletin*, 50-40, Educational Testing Service, Princeton, N.J. (1950).

Lord, F. M., and M. R. Novick, *Statistical Theories of Mental Test Scores*, Addison-Wesley, Reading, Mass. (1968).

Lorge, I., "Personality traits by fiat," *Journal of Educational Psychology* **26**, 273–278 (1935).

Lorr, M., P. F. Bishop, and D. M. McNair, "Interpersonal types among psyciatric patients," *Journal of Abnormal Psychology* **70**, 468–472 (1965).

Lorr, M., and D. M. McNair, "An interpersonal behavior circle," *Journal of Abnormal and Social Psychology* **67**, 68–75 (1963).

Lorr, M., and D. M. McNair, "Expansion of the interpersonal behavior circle," *Journal of Personality and Social Psychology* **2**, 823–830 (1965).

Lorr, M., and D. M. McNair, "Methods relating to evaluation of therapeutic outcome." In L. A. Gottschalk and A. H. Auerbach (eds.), *Methods of Research in Psychotherapy*, Appleton-Century-Crofts, New York (1966), pp. 573–594.

Lorr, M., and A. Suziedelis, "Modes of interpersonal behavior," *British Journal of Social and Clinical Psychology* **8**, 124–132 (1969).

Lovell, V. R., "Components of variance in two personality inventories." Unpublished doctoral thesis, Stanford University (1964).

Lovell, V. R., "The human use of personality tests: a dissenting view," *American Psychologist* **22**, 383–393 (1967).

Lubin, A., "Some formulae for use with suppressor variables," *Educational and Psychological Measurement* **17**, 286–296 (1957).

Luborsky, L., and R. R. Holt, "The selection of candidates for psychoanalytic training: implications from research on the selection of psychiatric residents," *Journal of Clinical and Experimental Psychopathology* **18**, 166–176 (1957).

Luft, J., "Implicit hypotheses and clinical predictions," *Journal of Abnormal and Social Psychology* **45**, 756–760 (1950).

Lundberg, G. A., "Case-studies versus statistical methods: an issue based on misunderstanding," *Sociometry* **4**, 379–383 (1941).

Lykken, D. T., "Multiple factor analysis and personality research," *Journal of Experimental Research in Personality* **5**, 161–170 (1971).

McArthur, C. C., "Clinical versus actuarial prediction," *Proceedings of the 1955 Invitational Conference on Testing Problems*, Educational Testing Service, Princeton, N.J. (1956), pp. 99–106. (a)

McArthur, C. C., "The dynamic model," *Journal of Counseling Psychology* **3**, 168–171 (1956). (b)

McArthur, C. C., "Comment on studies of clinical versus statistical prediction," *Journal of Counseling Psychology* **15**, 172–173 (1968).

McClelland, D. C., J. W. Atkinson, R. A. Clark, and E. L. Lowell, *The Achievement Motive*, Appleton, New York (1953).

McCord, W., and J. McCord, *The Psychopath: An Essay on the Criminal Mind*, Van Nostrand, Princeton, N.J. (1964).

MacCorquodale, K., and P. E. Meehl, "On a distinction between hypothetical constructs and intervening variables," *Psychological Review* **55**, 95–107 (1948).

McGee, R. K., "The relationship between response style and personality variables. I. The measurement of response acquiescence," *Journal of Abnormal and Social Psychology* **64**, 229–233 (1962). (a)

McGee, R. K., "The relationship between response style and personality variables. II. The prediction of independent conformity behavior," *Journal of Abnormal and Social Psychology* **65**, 347–351 (1962). (b)

McGee, R. K., "Response style as a personality variable: by what criterion?" *Psychological Bulletin* **59**, 284–295 (1962). (c)

McGee, R. K., "Response set in relation to personality: an orientation." In I. A. Berg (ed.), *Response Set in Personality Assessment*, Aldine, Chicago (1967), pp. 1–31.

McHugh, R. D., and P. C. Apostolakos, "Methodology for the comparison of clinical with actuarial predictions," *Psychological Bulletin* **56**, 301–308 (1959).

MacKinnon, D. W., *An Assessment Study of Air Force Officers: Part V. Summary and Applications*, Wright Air Development Center Technical Report No. 91 (V). Personnel Laboratory, Lackland Air Force Base, Texas (December 1958).

MacKinnon, D. W., "The nature and nurture of creative talent," *American Psychologist* **17**, 484–495 (1962).

MacKinnon, D. W., "Personality and the realization of creative potential," *American Psychologist* **20**, 273–281 (1965).

MacKinnon, D. W., "The study of creative persons: a method and some results." In J. Kagan (ed.), *Creativity and Learning*, Houghton Mifflin, Boston (1967), pp. 20–35.

MacKinnon, D. W., R. S. Crutchfield, F. Barron, J. Block, H. G. Gough, and R. E. Harris, *An Assessment Study of Air Force Officers: Part I. Design of the Study and Description of the Variables*, Wright Air Development Center Technical Report No. 91 (I), Personnel Laboratory, Lackland Air Force Base, Texas (April 1958).

McNair, D. M., and M. Lorr, "Differential typing of psychiatric outpatients," *Psychological Record* **15**, 33–41 (1965).

McNeil, E. B., "The measure of man," *Trends* **2**, No. 2, University of Hawaii Peace Corps Training Program, Hilo (1969).

McNemar, Q., "The mode of operation of suppressant variables," *American Journal of Psychology* **58**, 554–555 (1945).

McNemar, Q., "Review of E. L. Kelly and D. W. Fiske, *The Prediction of Performance in Clinical Psychology*," *Journal of Abnormal and Social Psychology* **47**, 857–860 (1952).

McNemar, Q., "Review of *Clinical versus Statistical Prediction*, by P. E. Meehl," *American Journal of Psychology* **68**, 510 (1955).

McNemar, Q., "Moderation of a moderator technique," *Journal of Applied Psychology* **53**, 69–72 (1969). (a)

McNemar, Q., *Psychological Statistics*, fourth edition, Wiley, New York (1969). (b)

Maccoby, E. E., and L. Rau, *Differential Cognitive Abilities*. Final report on U.S. Office of Education Cooperative Research Project No. 1040, Stanford University, Stanford, Calif. (1962).

Maccoby, N., J. Jecker, H. Breitrose, and E. Rose, "Sound film recordings in improving classroom communications: experimental studies in nonverbal communication," Institute for Communication Research, Stanford University (1964).

Madden, J. M., and R. D. Bourdon, "Effects on judgment of variations in rating scale format," Technical Documentary Report PRL-TDR-63-2, Personnel Research Laboratory, Lackland Air Force Base, Texas (January 1963).

Mahalanobis, P. A., "On the generalized distance in statistics," *Proceedings of the National Institute of Science and Industry* **12**, 49–55 (1936).

Maher, B. (ed.), *Clinical Psychology and Personality: The Selected Papers of George Kelly*, Wiley, New York (1969).

Mann, R. D., "A critique of P. E. Meehl's *Clinical versus Statistical Prediction*," *Behavioral Science* **1**, 224–230 (1956).

Marks, M. R., R. E. Christal, and R. A. Bottenberg, "Simple formula aids for understanding the joint action of two predictors," *Journal of Applied Psychology* **45**, 285–288 (1961).

Marks, P. A., and W. Seeman, *The Actuarial Description of Abnormal Personality*, Williams and Wilkins, Baltimore (1963).

Martin, B., "The assessment of anxiety by physiological behavioral measures," *Psychological Bulletin* **58**, 234–255 (1961).

Martin, H. P., Jr., "The nature of clinical judgment." Unpublished doctoral thesis, Washington State College, Pullman (1957).

Maslow, A. H., *Motivation and Personality*, Harper, New York (1954).

Mead, M., *Anthropology, a Human Science: Selected Papers, 1939–1960*, Van Nostrand, Princeton, N.J. (1964).

Medley, D. N., and H. E. Mitzel, "Some behavioral correlates of teacher effectiveness," *Journal of Educational Psychology* **50**, 239–246 (1959).

Medley, D. N., and H. E. Mitzel, "Measuring classroom behavior by systematic observation." In N. L. Gage (ed.), *Handbook of Research on Teaching*, Rand McNally, Chicago (1963), pp. 247–328.

Meehl, P. E., "The dynamics of 'structured' personality tests," *Journal of Clinical Psychology* **1**, 296–303 (1945). (a)

Meehl, P. E., "A simple algebraic development of Horst's suppressor variables," *American Journal of Psychology* **58**, 550–554 (1945). (b)

Meehl, P. E., *Clinical versus Statistical Prediction: A Theoretical Analysis and a Review of the Evidence*, University of Minnesota Press, Minneapolis (1954).

Meehl, P. E., "Wanted—a good cookbook," *American Psychologist* **11**, 263–272 (1956).

Meehl, P. E., "When shall we use our heads instead of the formula?" *Journal of Counseling Psychology* **4**, 268–273 (1957).

Meehl, P. E., "A comparison of clinicians with five statistical methods of identifying psychotic MMPI profiles," *Journal of Counseling Psychology* **6**, 102–109 (1959).

Meehl, P. E., "The cognitive activity of the clinician," *American Psychologist* **15**, 19–27 (1960).

Meehl, P. E., "Seer over sign: the first good example," *Journal of Experimental Research in Personality* **1**, 27–32 (1965).

Meehl, P. E., and W. G. Dahlstrom, "Objective configural rules for discriminating psychotic from neurotic MMPI profiles," *Journal of Consulting Psychology* **24**, 375–387 (1960).

Meehl, P. E., and S. R. Hathaway, "The *K* factor as a suppressor variable in the MMPI," *Journal of Applied Psychology* **30**, 525–564 (1946).

Meehl, P. E., and A. Rosen, "Antecedent probability and the efficiency of psychometric signs, patterns, or cutting scores," *Psychological Bulletin*, **52**, 194–216 (1955).

Mehlman, B., "The reliability of psychiatric diagnoses," *Journal of Abnormal and Social Psychology* **47**, 577–578 (1952).

Mehrabian, A., *An Analysis of Personality Theories*, Prentice-Hall, Englewood Cliffs, N.J. (1968).

Menninger, W. W., and J. T. English, "Psychiatric casualties from overseas Peace Corps service," *Bulletin of the Menninger Clinic* **29**, 148–158 (1965).

Messick, S., "The psychology of acquiescence: an interpretation of research evidence." In I. A. Berg (ed.), *Response Set in Personality Assessment*, Aldine, Chicago (1967), pp. 115–145.

Messick, S., and D. N. Jackson, "The measurement of authoritarian attitudes," *Educational and Psychological Measurement* **18**, 241–253 (1958).

Messick, S., and D. N. Jackson, "Desirability scale values and dispersions for MMPI items," *Psychological Reports* **8**, 409–414 (1961).

Messick, S., and J. Ross (eds.), *Measurement in Personality and Cognition*, Wiley, New York (1962).

Michaelis, A. R., *Research Films in Biology, Anthropology, Psychology, and Medicine,* Academic Press, New York (1955).

Mierke, K., "Uber die praktische Veranlagung," *Zeitschriftfuer angewandte Psychologie* **55**, 154–192 (1938).

Miller, N. E., and J. Dollard, *Social Learning and Imitation*, Yale University Press, New Haven (1941).

Miron, M. S., "What is it that is being differentiated by the semantic differential?" *Journal of Personality and Social Psychology* **12**, 189–193 (1969).

Miron, M. S., and C. E. Osgood, "Language behavior: the multivariate structure of qualification." In R. B. Cattell (ed.), *Handbook of Multivariate Experimental Psychology*, Rand McNally, Chicago (1966), pp. 790–819.

Mischel, W., "Theory and research on the antecedents of self-imposed delay of reward." In B. A. Maher (ed.), *Progress in Experimental Personality Research*, Vol. 3, Academic Press, New York (1966), pp. 85–132.

Mischel, W., *Personality and Assessment*, Wiley, New York (1968).

Mitzel, H. E., and W. Rabinowitz, "Assessing social-emotional climate in a class-room by Withall's technique," *Psychological Monographs* **67,** (18, Whole No. 368) (1953).

Moreno, J. L., *Psychodrama*, Vol. 1, Beacon House, New York (1946).

Morris, B. S., "Officer selection in the British Army, 1942–1945," *Occupational Psychology* **23,** 219–234 (1949).

Morris, C. W., *Signs, Language and Behavior*, Prentice-Hall, New York (1946).

Mosier, C. I., "Problems and designs of cross-validation," *Educational and Psychological Measurement* **11,** 5–11 (1951).

Mulaik, S. A., "Are personality factors raters' conceptual factors?" *Journal of Consulting Psychology* **28,** 506–511 (1964).

Murphy, G., *Historical Introduction to Modern Psychology*, Harcourt, Brace and World, New York (1929).

Murphy, L. B., *Social Behavior and Child Personality*, Columbia University Press, New York (1937).

Murray, H. A., *Explorations in Personality*, Oxford University Press, New York (1938).

Murray, H. A., *Thematic Apperception Test Manual*, Harvard University Press, Cambridge, Mass. (1943).

Murray, H. A., "Toward a classification of interaction." In T. Parsons and E. A. Shils (eds.), *Toward a General Theory of Action*, Harvard University Press, Cambridge, Mass. (1951), pp. 434–464.

Murray, H. A., "Preparations for the scaffold of a comprehensive system." In S. Koch (ed.), *Psychology: A Study of Science*, Vol. 3, McGraw-Hill, New York (1959), pp. 7–54.

Murray, H. A., and D. W. MacKinnon, "Assessment of OSS personnel," *Journal of Consulting Psychology* **10,** 76–80 (1946).

Murstein, B. I., *Theory and Research in Projective Techniques*, Wiley, New York (1963).

Naylor, J. C., A. L. Dudycha, and E. A. Schenck, "An empirical comparison of ρ_a and ρ_m as indices of rater policy agreement," *Educational and Psychological Measurement* **27,** 7–20 (1967).

Naylor, J. C., and E. A. Schenck, "ρ_m as an 'error free' index of rater agreement," *Educational and Psychological Measurement* **26,** 815–824 (1966).

Naylor, J. C., and R. J. Wherry, "The use of simulated stimuli, multiple regression, and the JAN technique to capture and cluster the policies of raters," *Educational and Psychological Measurement* **25,** 969–986 (1965).

Neill, J. A., and D. N. Jackson, "An evaluation of item selection strategies in personality scale construction," *Educational and Psychological Measurement* **30,** 647–661 (1970).

Newell, A., and H. A. Simon, "Computer simulation of human thinking," *Science* **134,** 2011–2017 (1961).

Newton, J. R., "Judgment and feedback in a quasi-clinical situation," *Journal of Personality and Social Psychology* **1,** 336–342 (1965).

Norman, W. T., "Development of self-report tests to measure personality factors identified from peer nominations," *USAF Technical Note*, No. 61-44 (1961).

Norman, W. T., "Relative importance of test item content," *Journal of Consulting Psychology* **27,** 166–174 (1963). (a)

Norman, W. T., "Toward an adequate taxonomy of personality attributes: replicated factor structure in peer nomination personality ratings," *Journal of Abnormal and Social Psychology* **66,** 574–583 (1963). (b)

Norman, W. T., "Double-split cross-validation: an extension of Mosier's design, two undesirable alternatives, and some enigmatic results," *Journal of Applied Psychology* **49,** 348–357 (1965).

Norman, W. T., 2800 *Personality Trait Descriptors: Normative Operating Characteristics for a University Population*, Department of Psychology, University of Michigan, Ann Arbor (April 1967).

Norman, W. T., and L. R. Goldberg, "Raters, ratees, and randomness in personality structure," *Journal of Personality and Social Psychology* **4,** 681–691 (1966).

Notcutt, B., and A. L. M. Silva, "Knowledge of other people," *Journal of Abnormal and Social Psychology* **46,** 30–37 (1951).

Nunnally, J., "The analysis of profile data," *Psychological Bulletin* **59,** 311–319 (1962).

Office of Strategic Services Assessment Staff, *Assessment of Men*, Rinehart, New York (1948).

Ogden, D. T., *Psychodiagnostics and Personality Assessment: A Handbook*, Western Psychological Services, Beverly Hills, Calif. (1967).

Osgood, C. E., "Studies on the generality of affective meaning systems," *American Psychologist* **17,** 10–28 (1962).

Osgood, C. E., "Semantic differential technique in the comparative study of cultures," *American Anthropologist* **66,** 171–200 (1964).

Osgood, C. E., "On the whys and wherefores of E, P, and A," *Journal of Personality and Social Psychology* **12,** 194–199 (1969).

Osgood, C. E., and G. J. Suci, "A measure of relation determined by both mean differences and profile information," *Psychological Bulletin* **49,** 251–262 (1952).

Osgood, C. E., G. J. Suci, and P. H. Tannenbaum, *The Measurement of Meaning*, University of Illinois Press, Urbana (1957).

Oskamp, S., "The relationship of clinical experience and training methods to several criteria of clinical prediction," *Psychological Monographs* **76** (28, Whole No. 547) (1962).

Owens, W. A., and D. O. Jewell, "Personnel selection." In P. H. Mussen and M. R. Rosenzweig (eds.), *Annual Review of Psychology*, Vol. 20, Annual Reviews, Palo Alto, Calif. (1969), pp. 419–446.

Pace, C. R., "Methods of describing college cultures," *Teachers College Record* **63**, 267–277 (1962).

Pap, A., "Reduction-sentences and open concepts," *Methodos* **5**, 3–30 (1953).

Parker, C. A., "As a clinician thinks . . . ," *Journal of Counseling Psychology* **5**, 253–262 (1958).

Parkinson, C. N., "The short list, or principles of selection." In C. N. Parkinson, *Parkinson's Law*, Houghton Mifflin, New York (1957), pp. 45–58.

Passini, F. T., and W. T. Norman, "A universal conception of personality structure?" *Journal of Personality and Social Psychology* **4**, 44–49 (1966).

Patterson, G. R., "Intervention in the homes of predelinquent boys," Summary Progress Report, USPHS Grant MH 15985-02, Oregon Research Institute, Eugene (1969).

Patterson, G. R., and G. G. Bechtel, "Formulating the situational environment in relation to states and traits," *Oregon Research Institute Research Bulletin* **11**, No. 18 (1971).

Patterson, G. R., and A. Harris, "Some methodological considerations for observation procedures." Paper presented at the meetings of the American Psychological Association, San Francisco (September 1968).

Patterson, G. R., R. S. Ray, and D. A. Shaw, *Manual for Coding of Family Interactions*, fifth revision, Oregon Research Institute, Eugene (1968).

Pauker, J. D., "Identification of MMPI profile types in a female, inpatient, psychiatric setting using the Marks and Seeman Rules," *Journal of Consulting Psychology* **30**, 90 (1966).

Paul, G. L., "Extraversion, emotionality, and physiological response to relaxation training and hypnotic suggestion," *International Journal of Clinical and Experimental Hypnosis* **17**, 89–98 (1969). (a)

Paul, G. L., "Outcome of systematic desensitization. I. Background procedures, and uncontrolled reports of individual treatment." In C. M. Franks (ed.), *Behavior Therapy: Appraisal and Status*, McGraw-Hill, New York (1969), pp. 63–104. (b)

Paul, G. L., "Outcome of systematic desensitization. II. Controlled investigations of individual treatment, technique variations, and current status." In C. M. Franks (ed.), *Behavior Therapy: Appraisal and Status*, McGraw-Hill, New York (1969), pp. 105–159. (c)

Payne, F. D., and J. S. Wiggins, "The effects of rule relaxation and system combination on classification rates in two MMPI 'cookbook' systems," *Journal of Consulting and Clinical Psychology* **32**, 734–736 (1968).

Peabody, D., "Trait inferences: evaluative and descriptive aspects," *Journal of Personality and Social Psychology Monograph* **7** (4, Whole No. 644) (1967).

Peabody, D., "Evaluative and descriptive aspects in personality perception: a reappraisal," *Journal of Personality and Social Psychology* **16,** 639–646 (1970).

Peace Corps, *Third Annual Report*, U.S. Government Printing Office, Washington (1964).

Pearson, J. S., W. M. Swenson, and H. P. Rome, "Age and sex differences related to MMPI response frequency in 25,000 medical patients," *American Journal of Psychiatry* **121,** 998 (1965).

Pearson, J. S., W. M. Swenson, H. P. Rome, P. Mataya, and T. L. Brannick, "Further experience with the automated MMPI," *Proceedings of the Mayo Clinic* **39,** 823–829 (1964).

Pearson, K., "Mathematical contributions to the theory of evolution: regression, heredity, and panmixia," *Philosophical Transactions* **187a,** 253–318 (1896).

Peterson, C. R., K. R. Hammond, and D. A. Summers, "Multiple probability-learning with shifting weights of cues," *American Journal of Psychology* **4,** 660–663 (1965).

Peterson, C. R., Z. J. Ulehla, A. J. Miller, L. E. Bourne, and D. W. Stilson, "Internal consistency of subjective probabilities," *Journal of Experimental Psychology* **70,** 526–533 (1965).

Peterson, D. R., "Scope and generality of verbally defined personality factors," *Psychological Review* **72,** 48–59 (1965).

Peterson, D. R., *The Clinical Study of Social Behavior*, Appleton-Century-Crofts, New York (1968).

Phillips, L., and J. G. Smith, *Rorschach Interpretation: Advanced Technique*, Grune and Stratton, New York (1953).

Piotrowski, Z. A., *Perceptanalysis*, Macmillan, New York (1957).

Podell, J. E., "A comparison of generalization and adaptation-level as theories of connotations," *Journal of Abnormal and Social Psychology* **62,** 594–597 (1961).

Polansky, N. A., "How shall a life history be written?" *Character and Personality* **9,** 188–207 (1941).

Polansky, N., W. Freeman, M. Horowitz, L. Irwin, N. Papanis, D. Rapaport, and E. Whaley, "Problems of interpersonal relations in research on groups," *Human Relations* **2,** 281–291 (1949).

Prelinger, E., and C. N. Zimet, *An Ego-Psychological Approach to Character Assessment*, Free Press, New York (1964).

Purcell, K., and K. Brady, *Assessment of interpersonal behavior in natural settings: a research technique manual*, Children's Asthma Research Institute, Denver (1965).

Quinn, R. P., and E. Lichtenstein, "Convergent and discriminant validities of acquiescence measures," *Journal of General Psychology* **73,** 93–104 (1965).

Rajaratnam, N., "Reliability formulas for independent decision data when reliability data are matched," *Psychometrika* **25**, 261–271 (1960).

Rajaratnam, N., L. J. Cronbach, and G. C. Gleser, "Generalizability of stratified-parallel tests," *Psychometrika* **30**, 39–56 (1965).

Rapaport, D., "The structure of psychoanalytic theory." In S. Koch (ed.), *Psychology: A Study of Science*, Vol. 3, McGraw-Hill, New York (1959), pp. 55–183.

Rapaport, D., "The structure of psychoanalytic theory," *Psychological Issues* **2**, Monograph No. 6 (1960).

Rapaport, D., and M. M. Gill, "The points of view and assumptions of metapsychology," *International Journal of Psychoanalysis* **40**, 153–162 (1959).

Rapaport, D., M. Gill, and R. Schafer, *Diagnostic Psychological Testing*, 2 vols., Year Book, Chicago (1946).

Rappoport, L., "Interpersonal conflict in a probabilistic situation." Unpublished doctoral thesis, University of Colorado, Boulder (1963).

Reichenbach, H., *Experience and Prediction*, University of Chicago Press, Chicago (1938)

Reik, T., *Listening with the Third Ear*, Farrar, Straus, New York (1948).

Rhees, R., "Can there be a private language?" *Proceedings of the Aristotelian Society* **28**, 77–94 (1954).

Richards, J. M., Jr., "Reconceptualization of the clinical and statistical prediction controversy in terms of components of accuracy of interpersonal perception scores," *Psychological Reports* **12**, 443–448 (1963).

Richards, J. M., Jr., and V. B. Cline, "Accuracy components in person perception scores and the scoring system as an artifact in investigations of the generality of judging ability," *Psychological Reports* **12**, 363–373 (1963).

Rimm, D., "Cost efficiency and test prediction," *Journal of Consulting Psychology* **27**, 89–91 (1963).

Rinn, J. L., "Structure of phenomenal domains," *Psychological Review* **72**, 445–466 (1965).

Roberts, R. R., and G. A. Renzaglia, "The influence of tape recording on counseling," *Journal of Counseling Psychology* **12**, 10–16 (1965).

Robins, A. R., H. L. Roy, and J. E. deJung, "Assessment of NCO leadership: test criterion development," *USA TAGO Personnel Research Branch Technical Research Report*, No. 1111 (1958).

Robinson, E. S., "The psychology of public education," *American Journal of Public Health* **23**, 1–125 (1933).

Rogers, C. R., "A theory of therapy, personality and interpersonal relationships, as developed in the client-centered framework." In S. Koch (ed.), *Psychology: A Study of Science*, Vol. 3, McGraw-Hill, New York (1959), pp. 184–256.

Roitzsch, J. C., and I. A. Berg, "Deviant responses as indicators of immaturity and schizophrenia," *Journal of Consulting Psychology* **22**, 389–393 (1958).

Rome, H. P., P. Mataya, J. S. Pearson, W. M. Swenson, and T. L. Brannick, "Automatic personality assessment." In R. W. Stacy and B. Waxman (eds.), *Computers in Biomedical Research*, Academic Press, New York (1965), pp. 505–524.

Rome, H. P., W. M. Swenson, P. Mataya, C. E. McCarthy, J. S. Pearson, R. F. Keating, and S. R. Hathaway, "Symposium on automation technics in personality assessment," *Proceedings of the Mayo Clinic* **37,** 81–82 (1962).

Rommetveit, R., *Selectivity, Intuition, and Halo Effects in Social Perception*, Oslo University Press, Oslo, Norway (1960).

Ronan, W. W., and E. P. Prien, *Toward a Criterion Theory: A Review and Analysis of Research and Opinion*, Richardson Foundation, Greensboro, N.C. (1966).

Rorer, L. G., "The great response style myth," *Psychological Bulletin* **63,** 129–156 (1965).

Rorer, L. G., "Sixteen Personality Factor Questionnaire." In O. K. Buros (ed.), *Seventh Mental Measurements Yearbook*, Vol. 1, Gryphon Press, Highland Park, N.J. (1972), pp. 332–333.

Rorer, L. G., and L. R. Goldberg, "Acquiescence in the MMPI?" *Educational and Psychological Measurement* **25,** 801–817 (1965).

Rorer, L. G., P. J. Hoffman, and K-C. Hsieh, "Utilities as base-rate multipliers in the determination of optimum cutting scores for the discrimination of groups of unequal size and variance," *Journal of Applied Psychology* **50,** 364–368 (1966). (a)

Rorer, L. G., P. J. Hoffman, G. E. LaForge, and K-C. Hsieh, "Optimum cutting scores to discriminate groups of unequal size and variance," *Journal of Applied Psychology* **50,** 153–164 (1966). (b)

Rorschach, H., *Psychodiagnostik*, Huber, Bern, Switzerland (1921).

Rosen, A., "Development of some new MMPI scales for differentiation of psychiatric syndromes within an abnormal population." Unpublished Ph.D. thesis, University of Minnesota, Minneapolis, (1952).

Rosen, A., "Detection of suicidal patients: an example of some limitations in the prediction of infrequent events," *Journal of Consulting Psychology* **18,** 397–403 (1954).

Rosen, A., "Differentiation of diagnostic groups by individual MMPI scales," *Journal of Consulting Psychology* **22,** 453–457 (1958).

Rosenberg, S., and K. Olshan, "Evaluative and descriptive aspects in personality perception," *Journal of Personality and Social Psychology* **16,** 619–626 (1970).

Rosenthal, R., "The effect of the experimenter on the results of psychological research." In B. A. Maher (ed.), *Progress in Experimental Personality Research*, Vol. 1, Academic Press, New York (1964), pp. 79–114.

Rosenzweig, S., "Levels of behavior in psychodiagnosis with special reference to the Picture-Frustration Study," *American Journal of Orthopsychiatry* **20,** 63–72 (1950).

Ross, A. O., H. M. Lacey, and D. A. Parton, "The development of a behavior checklist for boys," *Child Development* **36,** 1013–1027 (1965).

Rotter, J. B., *Social Learning and Clinical Psychology*, Prentice-Hall, New York (1954).

Rotter, J. B., "Generalized expectancies for internal versus external control of reinforcement," *Psychological Monographs* **80,** (1, Whole No. 609) (1966).

Rowan, T. C., "Some developments in multidimensional scaling applied to semantic relationships." Unpublished Ph.D. thesis, University of Illinois, Urbana (1954).

Sanford, R. N., "Clinical and actuarial prediction in a setting of action research," *Proceedings of the 1955 Invitational Conference on Testing Problems*, Educational Testing Service, Princeton, N.J. (1956), pp. 93–98.

Sanner, K., "Measurement of aggression in preadolescent boys." Unpublished Ph.D. thesis, Stanford University, Stanford, Calif. (1964).

Sarason, S. B., *The Clinical Interaction: With Special Reference to the Rorschach*, Harper, New York (1954).

Sarbin, T. R., "The logic of prediction in psychology," *Psychological Review* **51,** 210–228 (1944).

Saunders, D. R., "The moderator variable as a useful tool in prediction," *Proceedings of the 1954 Invitational Conference on Testing Problems*, Educational Testing Service, Princeton, N.J. (1955), pp. 54–58.

Saunders, D. R., "Moderator variables in prediction," *Educational and Psychological Measurement* **16,** 209–222 (1956).

Saunders, D. R., "A factor analytic study of the AI and the CCI," *Multivariate Behavioral Research* **4,** 329–346 (1969).

Sawrey, W. L., L. Keller, and J. J. Conger, "An objective method of grouping profiles by distance functions and its relation to factor analysis," *Educational and Psychological Measurement* **20,** 651–673 (1960).

Sawyer, J., "Measurement *and* prediction, clinical *and* statistical," *Psychological Bulletin* **66,** 178–200 (1966).

Schachter, S., *The Psychology of Affiliation*, Stanford University Press, Stanford, Calif. (1959).

Schaefer, E. S., "A circumplex model for maternal behavior," *Journal of Abnormal and Social Psychology* **59,** 226–235 (1959).

Schaeffer, R. W., "Clinical psychologists' ability to use the Draw-A-Person Test as an indicator of personality adjustment," *Journal of Consulting Psychology* **28,** 383 (1964).

Schafer, R., *The Clinical Application of Psychological Tests*, International Universities Press, New York (1948).

Schafer, R., *Psychoanalytic Interpretation in Rorschach Testing*, Grune and Stratton, New York (1954).

Scheffé, H. A., *The Analysis of Variance*, Wiley, New York (1960).

Schoggen, P., "A study in psychological ecology: structural properties of children's behavior based on sixteen day-long specimen records." Unpublished doctoral dissertation, University of Kansas, Lawrence (1954).

Schoggen, P., "Environmental forces in the everyday lives of children." In R. G. Barker (ed.), *The Stream of Behavior*, Appleton-Century-Crofts, New York (1963), pp. 42–69.

Schroder, H. M., M. J. Driver, and S. Streufert, *Human Information Processing: Individuals and Groups in Complex Social Situations*, Holt, Rinehart and Winston, New York (1967).

Schuh, A. J., "A synthesis of personality theories by cluster analysis," *Journal of Psychology* **64,** 69–71 (1966).

Schultz, T. D., P. J. Gibeau, and S. M. Barry, "Utility of MMPI 'cookbooks'," *Journal of Clinical Psychology* **24,** 430–433 (1968).

Schutz, W. C., *FIRO: A Three-dimensional Theory of Interpersonal Behavior*, Rinehart, New York (1958).

Schutz, W. C., *FIRO-B*, Consulting Psychologists Press, Palo Alto, Calif. (1967).

Scott, W. A., "Reliability of content analysis: the case of nominal scale coding," *Public Opinion Quarterly* **19,** 321–325 (1955).

Sechrest, L., "Incremental validity: a recommendation," *Educational and Psychological Measurement* **23,** 153–158 (1963).

Sechrest, L., and D. N. Jackson, "The generality of deviant response tendencies," *Journal of Consulting Psychology* **26,** 395–401 (1962).

Sechrest, L., and D. N. Jackson, "Deviant response tendencies: their measurement and interpretation," *Educational and Psychological Measurement* **23,** 33–53 (1963).

Seeman, W., "Psychiatric diagnosis: an investigation of interperson reliability after didactic instruction," *Journal of Nervous and Mental Disease* **118,** 541–544 (1953). (a)

Seeman, W., "Concept of 'subtlety' in structured psychiatric and personality tests: an experimental approach," *Journal of Abnormal and Social Psychology* **48,** 239–247 (1953). (b)

Seeman, W., "Some persistent misconceptions about actuarial (statistical) descriptions of personality." Paper presented to the Midwestern Psychological Association, St. Louis (1964).

Sellars, W. S., "Concepts as involving laws and inconceivable without them," *Philosophy of Science* **15,** 287–315 (1948).

Sells, S. B. (ed.), *Stimulus Determinants of Behavior*, Ronald, New York (1963).

Selltiz, C., M. Jahoda, M. Deutsch, and S. Cook, *Research Methods in Social Relations*, Holt, Rinehart and Winston, New York (1964).

Shils, E. A., "Social inquiry and the autonomy of the individual." In D. Lerner (ed.), *The Human Meaning of the Social Sciences*, Meridian, New York (1959), pp. 114–157.

Shneidman, E. S., *Thematic Test Analysis*, Grune and Stratton, New York (1951).

Siddiqui, M. M., "Tests for regression coefficients when errors are correlated," *Annals of Mathematical Statistics* **31**, 929–938 (1960).

Siegelman, M., "Loving and punishing parental behavior and introversion tendencies in sons," *Child Development* **37**, 985–992 (1966). (a)

Siegelman, M., "Psychometric properties of the Wiggins and Winder Peer Nomination Inventory," *Journal of Psychology* **64**, 143–149 (1966). (b)

Siller, J., and A. Chipman, "Response set paralysis: implications for measurement and control," *Journal of Consulting Psychology* **27**, 432–438 (1963).

Simon, H. A., and A. Newell, "The uses and limitations of models." In L. D. White (ed.), *The State of the Social Sciences*, University of Chicago Press, Chicago (1956).

Simoneit, M., "Zur charakterologischen Auswertung von Reaktionspruefungen," *Anchiv fuer die gesamte Psychologie* **83**, 357–384 (1932).

Simoneit, M., *Deutsches Soldatentum, 1914 und 1939*, Junker und Duennhaupt, Berlin (1940).

Sines, J. O., "Actuarial methods as appropriate strategy for the validation of diagnostic tests," *Psychological Review* **71**, 517–523 (1964).

Sines, J. O., "Actuarial methods in personality assessment." In B. A. Maher (ed.), *Progress in Experimental Personality Research*, Vol. 3, Academic Press, New York (1966), pp. 133–193.

Sines, L. K., "The relative contribution of four kinds of data to accuracy in personality assessment," *Journal of Consulting Psychology* **23**, 483–492 (1959).

Skinner, B. F., *The Behavior of Organisms*, Appleton-Century-Crofts, New York (1938).

Skinner, B. F., "Are theories of learning necessary?" *Psychological Review* **57**, 193–216 (1950).

Skinner, B. F., *Science and Human Behavior*, Macmillan, New York (1953).

Skinner, B. F., *Cumulative Record*, Appleton-Century-Crofts, New York (1959).

Slovic, P., "Cue-consistency and cue-utilization in judgment," *American Journal of Psychology* **79**, 427–434 (1966).

Smedslund, J., *Multiple Probability Learning*, Oslo University Press, Oslo, Norway (1955).

Smith, G. M., "Usefulness of peer ratings of personality in educational research," *Educational and Psychological Measurement* **27**, 967–984 (1967).

Smith, M. B., *Explorations in Competence*, Wiley, New York (1969).

Snider, J. G., and C. E. Osgood (eds.), *Semantic Differential Technique: A Sourcebook*, Aldine, Chicago (1969).

Soskin, W. F., "Bias in postdiction from projective tests," *Journal of Abnormal and Social Psychology* **49,** 69–74 (1954).

Soskin, W. F., and V. P. John, "The study of spontaneous talk." In R. G. Barker (ed.), *The Stream of Behavior,* Appleton-Century-Crofts, New York (1963), pp. 228–281.

Spearman, C., "Correlation calculated from faulty data," *British Journal of Psychology* **3,** 271–295 (1910).

Spielberger, C. D., "Theory and research on anxiety." In C. D. Spielberger (ed.), *Anxiety and Behavior,* Academic Press, New York (1966), pp. 3–20.

Stanley, J. C., and M. D. Wang, "Weighting test items and test-item options, an overview of the analytical and empirical literature," *Educational and Psychological Measurement* **30,** 21–35 (1970).

Stein, M. I., *The Thematic Apperception Test,* Addison-Wesley, Reading, Mass. (1955).

Stein, M. I., "The criterion, prediction and changes in the Colombia I Peace Corps Volunteers upon completion of their two year assignment," Final Technical Report, Peace Corps, Washington, D.C. (1963).

Stein, M. I., *Volunteers for Peace: The First Group of Peace Corps Volunteers in a Rural Community Development Program in Colombia, South America,* Wiley, New York (1966).

Steinemann, J. H., "Use of a logically related predictor in determining intragroup differential predictability," *Journal of Applied Psychology* **48,** 336–338 (1964).

Stephenson, W., "Some observations on Q-methodology," *Psychological Bulletin* **49,** 483–498 (1952).

Stephenson, W., *The Study of Behavior: Q-technique and Its Methodology,* University of Chicago Press, Chicago (1953).

Stern, G. G., *Preliminary Manual: Activities Index—College Characteristics Index,* Syracuse University Psychological Research Center, Syracuse, N.Y. (1958).

Stern, G. G., *People in Context: Measuring Person-Environment Congruence in Education and Industry,* Wiley, New York (1970).

Stern, G. G., M. I. Stein, and B. S. Bloom, *Methods in Personality Assessment,* Free Press, Glencoe, Ill. (1956).

Stevens, S. S., "Measurement, psychophysics, and utility." In C. W. Churchman and P. Ratoosh (eds.), *Measurement: Definitions and Theories,* Wiley, New York (1959), pp. 18–63.

Stevens, S. S., "Operationism and logical positivism." In M. H. Marx (ed.), *Theories in Contemporary Psychology,* Macmillan, New York (1963), pp. 47–76.

Stricker, G., "Actuarial, naive clinical, and sophisticated clinical prediction of pathology from figure drawings," *Journal of Consulting Psychology* **31,** 492–494 (1967).

Stricker, L. J., "Acquiescence and social desirability response styles, item characteristics and conformity," *Psychological Reports* **12,** 319–341 (1963).

Stricker, L. J., "Compulsivity as a moderator variable: a replication and extension," *Journal of Applied Psychology* **50,** 331–335 (1966).

Strong, E. K., Jr., *Vocational Interests of Men and Women*, Stanford University Press, Stanford, Calif. (1943).

Strong, E. K., Jr., *Strong Vocational Interest Blank*, Consulting Psychologists Press, Palo Alto, Calif. (1959).

Strupp, H. H., "Patient-doctor relationships: the psychotherapist in the therapeutic process." In A. J. Bachrach (ed.), *Experimental Foundations of Clinical Psychology*, Basic Books, New York (1962), pp. 576–615.

Suci, G. J., T. R. Vallance, and A. S. Glickman, "An analysis of peer ratings: the assessment of reliability of several question forms and techniques used at the Naval Officers Candidate School," *U.S. Bureau of Naval Personnel Technical Bulletin*, No. 54-9 (1954).

Sullivan, H. S., *Conceptions of Modern Psychiatry*, William Alanson White Foundation, Washington, D.C. (1947).

Sullivan, H. S., *The Interpersonal Theory of Psychiatry*, Norton, New York (1953).

Sullivan, H. S., *The Psychiatric Interview*, Norton, New York (1954).

Sullivan, H. S., *Clinical Studies in Psychiatry*, Norton, New York (1956).

Summers, D. A., and K. R. Hammond, "Inference under varying levels of linear and non-linear task variance," *Behavior Research Laboratory Report*, No. 56, University of Colorado (1964).

Summers, D. A., and G. R. Oncken, "The logical consistency of person perception," *Psychonomic Science* **10,** 63–64 (1968).

Summers, S., "The learning of responses to multiple weighted cues," *Journal of Experimental Psychology* **64,** 29–34 (1962).

Swenson, W. M., "Purposes and usefulness of the Mayo Clinic Program for automatic interpretation of the MMPI." Paper presented to the American Psychological Association, Chicago (1965).

Swenson, W. M., and J. S. Pearson, "Automation techniques in personality assessment: a frontier in behavioral science and medicine," *Methods of Information in Medicine* **3,** 34–36 (1964). (a)

Swenson, W. M., and J. S. Pearson, "Experience with large-scale psychologic testing in a medical center." Paper presented to the 6th IBM Medical Symposium, Poughkeepsie and Brookhaven National Laboratory (1964). (b)

Swenson, W. M., J. S. Pearson, and H. P. Rome, "Automation techniques in personality assessment: a fusion of three professions," *Proceedings of the Conference on Data Acquisition and Processing in Biology and Medicine*, Pergamon Press, New York (1962), pp. 149–156.

Swenson, W. M., H. P. Rome, J. S. Pearson, and T. L. Brannick, "A totally automated psychological test: experience in a medical center," *Journal of the American Medical Association* **191,** 925 (1965).

Swets, J. A., W. P. Tanner, and T. G. Birdsall, "Decision processes in perception," *Psychological Review* **68,** 301–340 (1961).

Sydiaha, D., "On the equivalence of clinical and statistical methods," *Journal of Applied Psychology* **43,** 395–401 (1959).

Symonds, P. M., *Diagnosing Personality and Conduct*, Century, New York (1931).

Taft, R., "The ability to judge people," *Psychological Bulletin* **52,** 1–23 (1955).

Taft, R., "Multiple methods of personality assessment," *Psychological Bulletin* **56,** 333–352 (1959).

Taft, R., "A statistical analysis of personality theories," *Acta Psychologia* **17,** 80–88 (1960).

Tatsuoka, M. M., *Multivariate Analysis: Techniques for Educational and Psychological Research*, Wiley, New York (1971).

Taylor, H. C., and J. T. Russell, "The relationship of validity coefficients to the practical effectiveness of tests in selection," *Journal of Applied Psychology* **23,** 565–578 (1939).

Taylor, J. A., "A personality scale of manifest anxiety," *Journal of Abnormal and Social Psychology* **48,** 285–290 (1953).

Thorndike, R. L., *Personnel Selection: Test and Measurement Techniques*, Wiley, New York (1949).

Thorndike, R. L., "Predicting psychiatrists' psyches," *Contemporary Psychology* **5,** 116–118 (1960).

Thorndike, R. L., *The concepts of over- and under-achievement*, Bureau of Publications, Teachers College, Columbia University, New York (1963).

Thorndike, R. L., "Reliability." In *Proceedings of the 1963 Invitational Conference on Testing Problems*, Educational Testing Service, Princeton, N.J. (1964), pp. 23–32.

Tiedeman, D., "The trait model," *Journal of Counseling Psychology* **3,** 164–168 (1956).

Todd, F. J., "A methodological study of clinical judgment." Unpublished doctoral thesis, University of Colorado, Boulder (1954).

Todd, F. J., and K, R. Hammond, "Differential feedback in two multiple-cue probability learning tasks," *Behavioral Science* **4,** 429–435 (1965).

Tomkins, S. S., *The Thematic Apperception Test*, Grune and Stratton, New York (1947).

Tomkins, S. S., and S. Messick (eds.), *Computer Simulation of Personality*, Wiley, New York (1963).

Torgerson, W. S., *Theory and Methods of Scaling*, Wiley, New York (1958).

Travers, R. M. W., "Rational hypotheses in the construction of tests," *Educational and Psychological Measurement* **11,** 128–137 (1951).

Trott, D. M., and D. N. Jackson, "An experimental analysis of acquiescence," *Journal of Experimental Research in Personality* **2,** 278–288 (1967).

Truax, C. B., and R. R. Carkhuff, *Toward Effective Counseling and Psychotherapy: Training and Practice*, Aldine, Chicago (1967).

Tryon, R. C., "Reliability and behavior domain validity: reformulation and historical critique," *Psychological Bulletin* 54, 229–249 (1957).

Tryon, R. C., "Cumulative communality cluster analysis," *Educational and Psychological Measurement* 18, 3–35 (1958).

Tucker, L. R, "Some experiments in developing a behaviorally determined scale of vocabulary," Research Memorandum 55-10, Educational Testing Service, Princeton, N.J. (1955).

Tucker, L. R, "Transformation of predictor variables to a simplified regression structure," Unpublished report, Educational Testing Service, Princeton, N.J. (1957).

Tucker, L. R, "A suggested alternative formulation in the developments by Hursch, Hammond, and Hursch, and by Hammond, Hursch, and Todd," *Psychological Review* 71, 528–530 (1964).

Tupes, E. C., "Relationships between behavior trait ratings by peers and later officer performance of USAF Officer Candidate School graduates," *USAF Personnel Training Research Center Research Report*, No. 57-125 (1957).

Tupes, E. C., "Personality traits related to effectiveness of junior and senior Air Force Officers," *USAF WADC Technical Note*, No. 59-198 (1959).

Tupes, E. C., and R. E. Christal, "Stability of personality trait rating factors obtained under diverse conditions," *USAF WADC Technical Note*, No. 58-61 (1958).

Tupes, E. C., and R. E. Christal, *Recurrent Personality Factors Based on Trait Ratings*, USAF ASD Technical Report, No. 61-97 (1961).

Tupes, E. C., and M. N. Kaplan, "Relationships between personality traits, physical proficiency, and cadet effectiveness reports of Air Force Academy Cadets," *USAF AFD Technical Report*, No. 61-53 (1961).

Uhl, C. N., "Learning interval concepts. I. Effects of differences in stimulus weights," *Journal of Experimental Psychology* 66, 264–273 (1963).

Uhl, N., and T. Eisenberg, "Predicting shrinkage in the multiple correlation coefficient," *Educational and Psychological Measurement* 30, 487–489 (1970).

Ullmann, L. P., and L. Krasner, *A Psychological Approach to Abnormal Behavior*, Prentice-Hall, Englewood Cliffs, N.J. (1969).

Ullmann, L. P., and J. S. Wiggins, "Endorsement frequency and the number of differentiating MMPI items to be expected by chance," *Newsletter of Research in Psychology* 4, 29–35 (1962).

Vannoy, J. S., "Generality of cognitive complexity-simplicity as a personality construct," *Journal of Personality and Social Psychology* 2, 385–396 (1965).

Vernon, P. E., "The validation of Civil Service Selection Board procedures," *Occupational Psychology* 24, 75–95 (1950).

Vernon, P. E., *Personality Assessment: A Critical Survey*, Wiley, New York (1964).

Vernon, P. E., and J. B. Parry, *Personnel Selection in the British Forces*, University of London Press, London (1949).

von Neumann, J., and O. Morgenstern, *Theory of Games and Economic Behavior*, Princeton University Press, Princeton, N.J. (1947).

Wahler, H. J., "Item popularity and social desirability in the MMPI," *Journal of Applied Psychology* **49**, 439–445 (1965).

Wald, A., *Statistical Decision Functions*, Wiley, New York (1950).

Walker, H. M., *Studies in the History of Statistical Method*, Williams and Wilkins, Baltimore (1929).

Wallace, J., "An abilities conception of personality: some implications for personality measurement," *American Psychologist* **21**, 132–138 (1966).

Wallace, J., "What units shall we employ? Allport's question revisited," *Journal of Consulting Psychology* **31**, 56–64 (1967).

Walters, H. A., and D. N. Jackson, "Group and individual regularities in trait inference: a multidimensional scaling analysis," *Multivariate Behavioral Research* **1**, 145–163 (1966).

Walters, R. H., N. V. Bowen, and R. D. Parke, "Experimentally induced disinhibition of sexual responses." Unpublished manuscript, University of Waterloo (1963).

Ward, J. H., Jr., "An application of linear and curvilinear joint functional regression in psychological prediction," *Research Bulletin 54-86*, Air Force Personnel Training Research Center, Lackland Air Force Base, Texas (1954).

Ward, J. H., Jr., "Comments on 'The paramorphic representation of clinical judgment'," *Psychological Bulletin* **59**, 74–76 (1962).

Ware, E. E., "Relationships of intelligence and sex to diversity of individual semantic meaning spaces," Unpublished Ph.D. thesis, University of Illinois, Urbana (1958).

Warr, P. B., and C. Knapper, *The Perception of People and Events*, Wiley, New York (1968).

Waters, L. K., "Factor analysis of cadet peer ratings," *USN School of Medicine Research Report*, No. 5 (1960).

Watson, R. I., "Historical review of objective personality testing: the search for objectivity." In B. M. Bass and I. A. Berg (eds.), *Objective Approaches to Personality Assessment*, Van Nostrand, Princeton, N.J. (1959), pp. 1–23.

Webb, E. J., D. T. Campbell, R. D. Schwartz, and L. Sechrest, *Unobtrusive Measures: A Survey of Nonreactive Research in the Social Sciences*, Rand McNally, Chicago (1966).

Weber, E. H., "Der Tastsinn und das Gemeingefühl," In R. Wagner (ed.), *Handwörtebuch der Physiologie*, Vol. III (1846), pp. 481–588.

Wechsler, D., *The Measurement and Appraisal of Adult Intelligence*, fourth edition, Williams and Wilkins, Baltimore (1958).

Wedell, C., and K. U. Smith, "Consistency of interview methods in appraisal of attitudes," *Journal of Applied Psychology* **35**, 392–396 (1951).

Weick, K. E., "Systematic observational methods." In G. Lindzey and E. Aronson (eds.), *The Handbook of Social Psychology*, second edition, Vol. 2, Addison-Wesley, Reading, Mass. (1968), pp. 357–451.

Weinreich, U., "Travels through semantic space," *Word* **14**, 346–366 (1958).

Weiss, R. L., "Operant conditioning techniques in psychological assessment." In P. McReynolds (ed.), *Advances in Psychological Assessment*, Vol. 1, Science and Behavior Books, Palo Alto, Calif. (1968), pp. 169–190.

Weitz, J., "Selecting supervisors with peer ratings," *Personnel Psychology* **11**, 25–35 (1958).

Welsh, G. S., and W. G. Dahlstrom (eds.), *Basic Readings on the MMPI in Psychology and Medicine*, University of Minnesota Press, Minneapolis (1956).

Wernimont, P. F., and J. P. Campbell, "Signs, samples, and criteria," *Journal of Applied Psychology* **52**, 372–376 (1968).

Wherry, R. J., "A new formula for predicting shrinkage of the coefficient of multiple correlation," *Annuals of Mathematical Statistics* **2**, 440–457 (1931).

Wherry, R. J., "Test selection and suppressor variables," *Psychometrika* **11**, 239–247 (1946).

Wherry, R. J., "Comparison of cross-validation with statistical inference of betas and multiple R from a single sample," *Educational and Psychological Measurement* **11**, 23–28 (1951).

Wherry, R. J., and D. H. Fryer, "Buddy ratings: popularity contest or leadership criterion?" *Personnel Psychology* **2**, 147–159 (1949).

Whorf, B. L., *Language, Thought, and Reality*, Institute of Technology Press, Boston, Massachusetts (1956).

Wiener, D. N., "Subtle and obvious keys for the MMPI," *Journal of Consulting Psychology* **12**, 164–170 (1948).

Wiggins, J. S., "Self-statements in personality assessment," *Contemporary Psychology* **3**, 326–328 (1958).

Wiggins, J. S., "Interrelationships among MMPI measures of dissimulation under standard and social desirability instructions," *Journal of Consulting Psychology* **23**, 419–427 (1959).

Wiggins, J. S., "Strategic, method and stylistic variance in the MMPI," *Psychological Bulletin* **59**, 224–242 (1962).

Wiggins, J. S., "Convergences among stylistic response measures from objective personality tests," *Educational and Psychological Measurement* **24**, 551–562 (1964). (a)

Wiggins, J. S., "An MMPI item characteristic deck," *Educational and Psychological Measurement* **24,** 137–141 (1964). (b)

Wiggins, J. S., "Interpersonal diagnosis of personality." In O. K. Buros (ed.), *Sixth Mental Measurements Yearbook*, Gryphon Press, Highland Park, N.J. (1965), pp. 451–453.

Wiggins, J. S., "Substantive dimensions of self-report in the MMPI item pool," *Psychological Monographs* **80,** No. 22 (Whole No. 630) (1966).

Wiggins, J. S., "Personality structure," In P. R. Farnsworth (ed.), *Annual Review of Psychology*, Vol. 19, Annual Reviews, Palo Alto, Calif. (1968), pp. 293–350.

Wiggins, J. S., "Personality Research Form." In O. K. Buros (ed.), *Seventh Mental Measurements Yearbook*, Vol. 1, Gryphon Press, Highland Park, N.J. (1972), pp. 301–303.

Wiggins, J. S., and L. R. Goldberg, "Interrelationships among MMPI item characteristics," *Educational and Psychological Measurement* **25,** 381–397 (1965).

Wiggins, J. S., and V. R. Lovell, "Communality and favorability as sources of method variance in the MMPI," *Educational and Psychological Measurement* **25,** 399–412 (1965).

Wiggins, J. S., K. E. Renner, G. L. Clore, and R. J. Rose, *The Psychology of Personality*, Addison-Wesley, Reading, Mass. (1971).

Wiggins, J. S., and C. L. Winder, "The Peer Nomination Inventory: an empirically derived sociometric measure of adjustment in preadolescent boys," *Psychological Reports* **9,** 643–677 (Monograph Supplement 5-V9) (1961). (a)

Wiggins, J. S., and C. L. Winder, *Peer Nomination Inventory: Technical Supplement*, Stanford University, Stanford, Calif. (1961). (b)

Wiggins, N., M. Blackburn, and J. R. Hackman, "Prediction of first-year graduate success in psychology: peer ratings," *Journal of Educational Research* **63,** 81–85 (1969).

Wiggins, N., and M. Fishbein, "Dimensions of semantic space: a problem of individual differences." In J. G. Snider and C. E. Osgood (eds.), *Semantic Differential Technique*, Aldine, Chicago (1969), pp. 183–193.

Wiggins, N., and P. J. Hoffman, "Three models of clinical judgment," *Journal of Abnormal Psychology* **73,** 70–77 (1968).

Williams, S. B., and H. J. Leavitt, "Group opinion as a predictor of military leadership," *Journal of Consulting Psychology* **11,** 283–291 (1947).

Willingham, W. W., "A note on peer nominations as a predictor of success in naval flight training," *USN School of Aviation Medicine Project Report*, No. 14 (1958).

Willingham, W. W., "Estimating the internal consistency of mutual peer nominations," *Psychological Reports* **5,** 163–167 (1959).

Willingham, W. W. (ed.), "Invasion of privacy in research and testing," *Journal of Educational Measurement* **4,** No. 1 (supplement) (1967).

Willmorth, N. E., E. L. Taylor, W. B. Lindelien, and S. L. Ruch, "A factor analysis of rating scale variables used as criteria of military leadership," *USAF Personnel Training Research Center Research Report*, No. 57-154 (1957).

Wilson, N. A. B., "The work of the Civil Service Selection Board," *Occupational Psychology* **22,** 204–212 (1948).

Winder, C. L., and L. Rau, "Parental attitudes associated with social deviance in preadolescent boys," *Journal of Abnormal and Social Psychology* **64,** 418–424 1962).

Winder, C. L., and J. S. Wiggins, "Social reputation and social behavior: a further validation of the Peer Nomination Inventory," *Journal of Abnormal and Social Psychology* **68,** 681–684 (1964).

Winer, B. J., *Statistical Principles in Experimental Design*, McGraw-Hill, New York (1962).

Withall, J., "Development of a technique for the measurement of socioemotional climate in classrooms," *Journal of Experimental Education* **17,** 347–361 (1949).

Wittenborn, J., J. Holzberg, and B. Simon, "Symptom correlates for descriptive diagnosis," *Genetic Psychology Monographs* **47,** 237–301 (1953).

Wohlfahrt, E., "Die Interessenforschung als Hilfsmittel der Persoenlichkeits-diagnose," *Beih Z. angew. Psychol.* **79,** 118–131 (1938).

Wonderlic, E. F., *Wonderlic Personnel Test*, E. F. Wonderlic and Associates, Northfield, Ill. (1939).

Woodworth, D. G., F. Barron, and D. W. MacKinnon, *An Analysis of Life-History Interviewer's Ratings for 100 Air Force Captains*, Air Force Personnel and Training Research Center Research Report No. 129, Lackland Air Force Base, Texas (November 1957).

Woodworth, D. G., and D. W. MacKinnon, *The Use of Trait Ratings in an Assessment of 100 Air Force Captains*, Wright Air Development Center Technical Report No. 64, Personnel Laboratory, Lackland Air Force Base, Texas (September 1958).

Woodworth, R. S., *Personal Data Sheet*, Stoelting, Chicago (1917).

Woodworth, R. S., *Contemporary Schools of Psychology*, Ronald, New York (1931).

Wright, H. F., "Observational child study." In P. H. Mussen (ed.), *Handbook of Research Methods in Child Development*, Wiley, New York (1960), pp. 71–139.

Wrigley, C., J. Cobb, and D. Kline, "Validities of the Peace Corps training measures," Research Report No. 5, Computer Institute for Social Science Research, Michigan State University (March 1966).

Yntema, D. B., and W. S. Torgerson, "Man-machine cooperation in decisions requiring common sense," *IRE Transactions on Human Factors in Electronics* **2,** 20–26 (1961).

Zubin, J., "The determination of response patterns in personality adjustment inventories," *Journal of Educational Psychology* **28,** 401–413 (1937).

Zubin, J., "Clinical versus actuarial prediction: a pseudo-problem," *Proceedings of the 1955 Invitational Conference on Testing Problems,* Educational Testing Service, Princeton, N.J. (1956), pp. 107–128.

AUTHOR INDEX

Abelson, R. P., 365
Abrahams, N. M., 72-73
Ackoff, R. L., 229
Adams, H. E., 419
Adler, A., 450-451
Adorno, T. W., 466
Albrecht, R. E., 546
Alf, E. F., 259
Allison, J., 473-474
Allport, G. W., 129, 144, 148, 305, 319, 338-339, 352, 355, 369, 445, 448, 450-451, 494, 499
Alumbaugh, R. V., 430
American Psychological Association, 43, 83, 228, 283-284, 300, 398, 547
Anastasi, A., 547
Ashby, W. R., 451
Anderson, N., 176
Angyal, A., 450-451
Apostolakos, P. C., 193
Aronson, E., 299
Arrow, K. J., 228
Arsenian, J., 301
Arthur, A. Z., 259
Arner, R. A., 284
Ash, P., 389
Astin, A. W., 484
Astington, E., 357
Austin, G. A., 328
Azuma, H., 284

Bailey, D. E., 546
Baldwin, D. L., 336

Bandura, A., 299, 363, 365-367, 372-374, 508,
Bannister, D., 389, 490, 492, 494
Barker, R. G., 296, 300, 306, 313, 315-319, 484
Barnes, E. H., 418-419
Barron, F., 540-541, 544, 546-549
Barry, S. M., 116
Bartlett, C. J., 357
Bass, B. M., 380, 436
Baumrind, D., 300, 429
Baxter, J. C., 436
Bechtel, G. G., 309
Bechtoldt, H. P., 39, 369, 400
Beck, L. W., 400
Beck, S. J., 148, 201
Becker, H. S., 88
Becker, W. C., 349, 475, 502
Bender, L., 133
Benney, M., 301
Bennis, W. G., 349
Bentler, P. M., 425
Bentley, A. F., 483
Berg, I. A., 88, 373, 380, 401, 416-420, 438
Bergin, A. E., 302
Berne, E., 152
Bernreuter, R. G., 42
Bieri, J., 490, 494
Bigbee, L. R., 357
Bijou, S. W., 370, 373-377
Birdsall, T. G., 383
Bishop, P. F., 482

I-1

SUBJECT INDEX